lonely planet

W9-AZY-892

Western Balkans

Slovenia
p373

Croatia
p133

Bosnia &
Hercegovina
p89

Serbia
p322

Montenegro
p233

Kosovo
p218

North
Macedonia
p284

Albania
p50

Peter Dragicevich, Mark Baker, Stuart Butler, Vesna Maric,
Brana Vladisavljevic, Anthony Ham, Jessica Lee, Kevin Raub

Contents

BUREK/BYREK

CESARZ/SHUTTERSTOCK ©

PEJA (PEĆ; P225), KOSOVO

O.JAY PHOTOGRAPHY/SHUTTERSTOCK ©

COLORMAKER/SHUTTERSTOCK ©

Contents

LAKE OHRID (P300),
NORTH MACEDONIA

ON THE ROAD

THETH (P81), THE ACCURSED
MOUNTAINS, ALBANIA

Contents

OSCARPORRAS/SHUTTERSTOCK ©

KOTOR (P240), MONTENEGRO

Welcome to the Western Balkans

Cramming in more history, culture and spectacular scenery than seems entirely reasonable for its size, the Western Balkans is one of Europe's most intriguing regions.

Great Outdoors

Rocky mountains and terracotta-roofed towns plunge spectacularly into crystal-clear waters all along the Adriatic coast. Among all the crowded beach resorts, Croatia's myriad islands provide nooks of quiet seclusion, while Albania's less-visited riviera still has donkeys wandering through olive groves abutting secluded bays. Craggy mountains stretch along the entire region, offering endless opportunities for hiking, biking, skiing, climbing and paragliding. In their shadows are rowable lakes, raftable rivers and scramble-able canyons.

Home to History

Though change is coming quickly to the Western Balkans, timeless traditions retain their currency. It's a region where you can barely keep up with the nightlife, but still get stuck behind a horse and cart. Urban landscapes are a pop-up book of European architectural history on a grand scale. Winding Ottoman streets are punctuated with Byzantine churches, Austro-Hungarian villas and angular communist-era blocks. Throw in Roman ruins and Venetian palaces, then wrap it all in a medieval wall and plonk it by the sea.

Culinary Adventures

Foreign invaders have plundered the Balkans for millennia and the region's cooks have plundered right back, incorporating Venetian, Austrian, Hungarian and Ottoman flavours into the mixing pot. You might tuck into crumbed schnitzel in Ljubljana, seafood risotto in Split, octopus carpaccio in Budva, goulash in Novi Sad, *burek* (savoury pastry) in Sarajevo, kebab in Kosovo, baklava in Tirana and stuffed peppers in Skopje. Locally produced olive oil, truffles and wine hold their own against the best in the world, as does the seafood and herb-grazed lamb.

Cultural Pursuits

Aside from the ever-present architectural legacy, the Balkans are liberally scattered with artistic treasures, from church frescoes to socialist modernist sculptures and an edgy contemporary art scene. You're likely to stumble on streetside *klapa* (unaccompanied vocal harmony) performances in Dalmatia, plaintive *sevdah* singers in Bosnia, bards wielding *gusle* (single-stringed instruments) in Montenegro and upbeat Roma *trubači* (trumpet bands) in Serbia. Religious feasts, film festivals and large-scale music festivals are all celebrated with gusto.

Why I Love the Western Balkans

By Peter Dragicevich, Writer

With two of my grandparents hailing from the region, I have always had the Western Balkans in my blood – but then it somehow got under my skin. As a travel destination it's got a bit of everything that I love: beaches; islands; mountains; lakes; waterfalls; forest; wildlife; ancient buildings; historic towns; fascinating museums and galleries; excellent wine; and delicious food. But most striking of all are its people. Despite their much vaunted differences, the more you travel in the Western Balkans, the more you're struck by the similarities between the hospitable, gregarious, larger-than-life characters that you meet.

For more about our writers, see p480

For more about our writers, see p480

Above: Kravica Waterfall (p116), Bosnia and Hercegovina

Western Balkans

Lake Bled, Slovenia
Surreally beautiful
blue depths (p389)

Mt Triglav, Slovenia
Majestic symbol of
a nation (p396)

**Sarajevo, Bosnia &
Hercegovina**
A fascinating cultural
collision (p92)

Island-Hopping in Croatia
Clear waters and walled
towns (p150)

Mostar, Bosnia & Hercegovina
Scenic showcase of Ottoman
architecture (p109)

**Durmitor National Park,
Montenegro**
Dramatic peaks and plunging
canyon (p272)

Dubrovnik, Croatia
Honey-coloured walls over
cerulean waters (p197)

Bay of Kotor, Montenegro
Fjord-like beauty on the
Adriatic (p235)

AUSTRIA

HUNGARY

Lake
Balaton

Maribor

Celje

Varaždin

Bled

Mt Triglav

LJUBLJANA

Brežice

Trieste

SLOVENIA

Sava

ZAGREB

Osijek

CROATIA

Slavonski
Brod

Rijeka

Karlovac

Sava

Krk

Krk

Bihac

Una

Banja
Luka

Doboj

Pula

Cres

BOSNIA &
HERCEGOVINA

Jajce

Zenica

Zadar

Kornat

CROATIA

SARAJEVO

SAN MARINO

Šibenik

Split

Mostar

Brac

ITALY

Hvar

Vis

Hvar

Korcula

Korcula
Town

Mijet

Dubrovnik

ROME

Adriatic
Sea

Tyrrhenian
Sea

45°N

44°N

43°N

42°N

40°N

16°E

17°E

13°E

$\hat{N}$ 0 —————— 200 km
0 —————— 100 miles

Vojvodina, Serbia
Tranquil and rustic
agricultural region (p345)

Belgrade, Serbia
Scintillating
capital city (p325)

Subotica

Sombor

Kikinda

Timisoara

ROMANIA

VOJVODINA

Tisa

Zrenjanin

Vukovar

Novi Sad   Vršac

BELGRADE

Sava

Smederevo Đerdap
National
Park

Craiova

Bijeljina

Arandelovac

Negotin

Tuzla

SERBIA

Danube

Zaječar

Tara
National
Park   Cacak
Užice   **Kragujevac**

Prizren, Kosovo
Historic churches, mosques
and fortress (p227)

Kraljevo   **Kruševac**

Niš   Pirot

Prijepolje

Novi
Pazar

Velika Morava

BULGARIA

Durmitor
National
Park

SOFIA

MONTENEGRO

PRISTINA

Kolašin   Peja
(Peć)   **KOSOVO**

Vranje

**Pelister National Park,
North Macedonia**
Wildlife and traditional
mountain villages (p310)

Trebinje   **Nikšić**
Herceg   **PODGORICA**
Novi
Kotor   Accursed
Mountains   Prizren

Drin

SKOPJE

Plav

Budva

Shkodra   Tetovo

Bar

Drim

**NORTH
MACEDONIA**

TIRANA

Prilep

19°E   Durrës   Elbasan   Pelister
National
Park

*Lake
Ohrid*

Lake Ohrid, North Macedonia
Beaches, churches and
archaeological sites (p300)

41°N   **ALBANIA**   Ohrid

Lushnja

*Prispansko
Ezero*

25°E

Fier   **Berat**   Korça

40°N

GREECE

40°N

24°E

*Aegean
Sea*

Vlore

Meteora

39°N

Accursed Mountains, Albania
Remote and foreboding
mountain wilderness (p78)

Berat, Albania
Step back into Ottoman
times (p62)

Western Balkans' Top 15

Bay of Kotor, Montenegro

1 There's a sense of secrecy and mystery to the Bay of Kotor. Grey mountain walls rise steeply from steely blue waters, getting higher and higher as you progress through their folds to the hidden reaches of the inner bay. Here, ancient stone settlements hug the shoreline, with the old alleyways of Kotor (p240) concealed in its innermost reaches behind hefty stone walls. Talk about drama! But you wouldn't expect anything else of coastal Montenegro, where life is lived in an exuberant Mediterranean style.

Dubrovnik, Croatia

2 Get up close and personal with breathtaking Dubrovnik (p197) with a walk around the spectacular old town walls (pictured), as history is unfurled from the battlements. No visit is complete without a leisurely stroll along these ramparts, the finest in the world and Dubrovnik's main claim to fame. Built between the 13th and 16th centuries, they are still remarkably intact and the views they afford over the terracotta rooftops and the brilliantly blue Adriatic are sublime. For a bird's-eye perspective, take the cable car up Srd, the city's craggy backdrop.

3

4

PAUL BIRIS / GETTY IMAGES ©

Lake Bled, Slovenia

3 There's a Disney-esque quality to the beauty of Lake Bled (p389) – it's almost too perfect to be believed. First there's the preposterously blue colour of the water itself. Add to that a precisely positioned island capped by a picture-postcard church, overlooked by a medieval castle clinging to a rocky cliff on the lake's edge. Then there's the spectacular backdrop of the Julian Alps... It's all just a bit much. All of that unsettling beauty comes at a price: Lake Bled is Slovenia's busiest tourist destination. Church of the Assumption (p389), Bled Island

Mostar, Bosnia & Hercegovina

4 If the 1993 destruction of the famous 16th-century bridge at the heart of Mostar (p109; pictured) underlined the heartbreaking pointlessness of Yugoslavia's brutal civil war, its painstaking reconstruction has proved symbolic of the post-conflict era. The charming Ottoman quarter has been convincingly restored and is once again an atmospheric patchwork of stone mosques, souvenir stalls and street cafes. Meanwhile, rows of bombed-out buildings hint at how far there is to go until full reconciliation is achieved in this still-divided town.

Mt Triglav, Slovenia

5 For such a small country, Slovenia packs a lot in: charming towns, great wines, a Venetian-inspired seashore and, most of all, mountains. The highest peak, Mt Triglav (2864m; p393), stands particularly tall in local lore. Indeed, the saying goes that you're not really Slovene until you've climbed to the top. If time is an issue and you're driving, head for the high-altitude Vršič Pass, which crosses the Julian Alps and leads down to the sunny coastal region in one hair-raising, spine-tingling hour.

5

Sarajevo, Bosnia & Hercegovina

6 There's something appealing about Bosnia's capital Sarajevo (p92). It's partly to do with the East-meets-West, Ottoman-meets-Austrian architecture, for sure. And it's definitely related to the heady scent of Bosnian coffee (pictured) and the nation's best *burek* (heavy pastry stuffed with meat or cheese) and *ćevapi* (lozenges of minced meat served with bread) permeating the fascinating Turkic-era alleyways of Baščaršija. It's also there in the city's long history as a unique ethno-religious melting pot. War history aside, Sarajevo is simply beguiling.

6

LIFEINVIEWFINDER/SHUTTERSTOCK ©

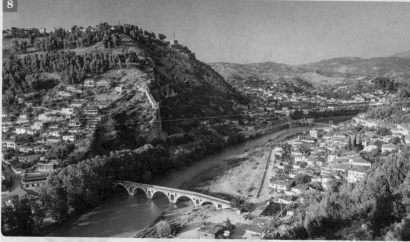

Lake Ohrid, North Macedonia

7 Whether you come to hilly Ohrid (p303) for its sturdy medieval castle, to wander the stone lanes of its old town or to gaze at the Plaošnik archaeological site, every visitor pauses for a few moments at the Church of Sveti Jovan at Kaneo (pictured), set high on a bluff overlooking Lake Ohrid and its beaches. It's the prime spot for absorbing the town's interesting architecture, idling sunbathers and distant fishing skiffs – all framed by the green of Mt Galičica and the endless expanse of lake.

Berat, Albania

8 Declared a 'museum town' under the communist regime and now a Unesco World Heritage Site, this gorgeous ensemble of Ottoman houses gazes down at the Osumi River from a hillside, earning Berat (p62) the epithet 'town of a thousand windows'. At the very top it's capped by a sturdy fortress scattered with tiny chapels and churches, and a 15th-century mosque. It's easily one of Albania's most charming towns and it can also boast some of the country's most atmospheric accommodation, including an excellent hostel and historic hotels.

Belgrade, Serbia

9 Belgrade (p325) is a fascinating living museum of its turbulent past; its measured rise from former Yugoslavian ashes is today its catalyst for cool. By day, a melange of communist-era blocks and art nouveau architecture corral a cocktail of old-world culture and cutting-edge cosmopolitanism. By night (and well past dawn), Belgrade throbs to the beat of its infamous *splavovi* (river-barge nightclubs), born of the city's live-for-the-moment ethos and sociable spirit. A capital in transition, the 'White City' now teeters between comfortably unhurried and overzealously progressive.

Island-Hopping in Croatia

10 Travelling by ferry is a great and inexpensive way to experience the Croatian side of the Adriatic. Take in the spectacular coastal scenery as you whiz past some of Croatia's 1244 islands and islets, and stop to explore hidden beaches and historic towns like those on glamorous Hvar (p189; pictured). And if you have cash to splash, take it up a couple of notches and charter a sailboat to see the islands in style, propelled by winds and sea currents to places that are otherwise inaccessible.

Durmitor National Park, Montenegro

11 This rugged expanse at the very north of Montenegro consists of the plunging depths of the Tara River canyon and the wild uplands of the Durmitor mountain range. Reflecting the beauty of the imposing grey peaks are 18 glacial lakes, known as *gorske oči* (mountain eyes). The largest and most beautiful is the Black Lake, its inky appearance caused by the surrounding pines and the peak rearing above it. In summer, Durmitor (p272) is a magnet for rafters and hikers; in winter, it's a well-priced and reliable ski resort.

Prizren, Kosovo

12 Kosovo's most charming town is pretty little Prizren (p227), nestled in the valley of the Bistrica River and dominated by the minarets and church towers of its old town (pictured). Despite the dark legacy of war, Prizren today is a forward-looking place, with one of Eastern Europe's best film festivals, Dokufest, bringing a splash of international sophistication every summer. The rest of the year you can explore the town's rich heritage in the form of its hilltop fortress, grand mosques and ancient churches.

DAN TAUTAN/SHUTTERSTOCK ©

MILOS65O/SHUTTERSTOCK ©

Accursed Mountains, Albania

13 Albania's natural landscape is its greatest drawcard, and it's best experienced in the country's north, where the Accursed Mountains (p78) offer superb hiking, traditional mountain villages, and the ferry ride across picturesque Lake Koman. The most popular hike is the gorgeous and only moderately challenging day trek from Valbona to Theth, which shouldn't be missed. But for keen walkers there are dozens of opportunities to walk in the wilds of high Albania.

Pelister National Park, North Macedonia

14 Encompassing North Macedonia's third-highest mountain range, Pelister National Park (p310) is home to big native mammals such as wolves, chamois, deer, wild boars and bears. There's excellent hiking to be had, not least the track to the summit and its two glacial lakes, known as 'Pelister's Eyes'. On the lower slopes, guesthouses in the villages of Brajčino and Dihovo offer authentic experiences of rural life, delivering traditional food and hospitality. For added buzz, you can even book a session with a local beekeeper.

Vojvodina, Serbia

15 The multicultural northern Serbian province of Vojvodina (p345) may be best known for its main city of Novi Sad, the 2021 European Capital of Culture and the home of the mega-popular EXIT Festival (pictured). But this rustic region is also distinguished by its tranquil nature, mellow villages, unhurried vibe, Hungarian-influenced gastronomy and a laid-back legacy of big-hearted hospitality. Compact and well linked by good roads, the quirky highlights of Vojvodina offer a slow-travel treat for those keen on kicking back.

Need to Know

For more information, see Survival Guide (p447)

Currency
Albania: lek (lekë);
Bosnia & Hercegovina:
convertible mark (KM);
Croatia: kuna (KN);
Kosovo, Montenegro and
Slovenia: euro (€); North
Macedonia: denar (MKD),
Serbia: dinar (RSD)

Languages
Albanian, Bosnian,
Croatian, Macedonian,
Montenegrin, Serbian,
Slovene

Visas
Generally not required for
stays of up to 90 days,
although some nationali-
ties do need them.

Money
ATMs are widely avail-
able in most towns. Ac-
ceptance of credit cards
is normally confined
to upper-end hotels,
restaurants and shops,
although it's becoming
more widespread.

Mobile Phones
Users with unlocked
phones can buy a local
SIM card. Otherwise,
you may be charged
roaming rates.

Time
Central European Time
(GMT plus one hour)

When to Go

Ljubljana
GO Apr–Oct

Belgrade
GO May–Nov

Sarajevo
GO May–Sep

Dubrovnik
GO May–Oct

Skopje
GO May–Oct

Tirana
GO Jun–Sep

Mild year round
Mild summers, very cold winters
Cold Climate

High Season
(Jun–Aug)

➡ High
temperatures and
balmy evenings.

➡ Hotels will be
about 30% more
expensive and you
may need to book in
advance, particularly
by the beach.

➡ Big draws like the
Croatian islands will
be crowded.

Shoulder
(Apr–May &
Sep–Oct)

➡ The weather is
mild and warm.

➡ Prices drop and
crowds dwindle.

➡ Various festivals
spark up; all up, it's
the best time to
travel in the region.

Low Season
(Nov–Mar)

➡ Days can be dark
and cold.

➡ Hotel prices drop
to their lowest.

➡ Many attractions
and coastal towns all
but close – time to
hit the ski slopes!

Useful Websites

Lonely Planet (www.lonely planet.com/balkans) Destination information, hotel bookings, traveller forum and more.

Hidden Europe (www.hidden europe.co.uk) Fascinating magazine and online dispatches from all the continent's corners.

Independent Balkan News Agency (www.balkaneu.com) Region-specific economics and politics.

Balkan Insight (www.balkanin sight.com) Find out what's going on before you get there.

Calvert Journal (www.calvert journal.com) Online magazine on contemporary culture in Eastern Europe, including the Balkans.

Important Numbers

To call from outside individual countries, dial your international access code, then the country code, the area code (without the initial 0) and the local number.

| International access code | ☏00 |
| General emergency | ☏112 |

Exchange Rates

Albania	100 lekë	€0.82
Australia	A$1	€0.62
Canada	C$1	€0.63
Bosnia & Hercegovina	1KM	€0.51
Croatia	1KN	€0.14
Japan	¥100	€0.79
New Zealand	NZ$1	€0.59
North Macedonia	100MKD	€1.63
Serbia	100RSD	€0.85
UK	UK£1	€1.11
USA	US$1	€0.88

For current exchange rates, see www.xe.com.

Daily Costs

Budget: Less than €50

➡ Dorm bed: €10–25

➡ Cheap meal or takeaway: €2–8

➡ Beer: €1.30–3

Midrange: €50–180

➡ Double room in a midrange hotel: €30–100

➡ Meal at a decent restaurant: €7–25

➡ Admission to museums: €1–4

Top end: More than €180

➡ Top-end, prime-view hotel: €100–300

➡ Dinner at a leading restaurant: €25–50

➡ Hire car per day: €40–80

Opening Hours

Business hours vary across the region, changing by season and arbitrarily at will. As a rough guide:

Banks & Offices 8am–5am Monday to Friday, with an hour or two off over lunch; some open on Saturday mornings

Cafes & Bars 8am–midnight

Restaurants noon–11pm or midnight; often closed Sundays outside peak season

Shops 8am–7pm; siesta can be any time between noon and 4pm

Arriving in the Western Balkans

Belgrade Nikola Tesla Airport A taxi to central Belgrade (18km) should cost around 1800RSD. Local bus 72 (89RSD to 150RSD) and A1 minibus (300RSD) connect the airport to town.

Zagreb Airport Croatia Airlines buses (30KN) leave from the airport every half-hour or hour from about 7am to 10.30pm. Taxis to the centre cost between 150KN and 200KN.

Split Airport Buses head to the main bus station at least 14 times a day (30KN, 30 minutes). Local buses 37 and 38 stop near the airport every 20 minutes, heading to Split (17KN) or Trogir (13KN). Taxis to Split cost between 250KN and 300KN.

Nënë Tereza International Airport (Tirana) Rinas Express buses operate an on-the-hour service to the city centre (250 lekë). The going taxi rate is 2000 to 2500 lekë.

Getting Around

Car Useful for travelling at your own pace, or for visiting regions with minimal public transport. Cars can be hired in every city or larger town. Drive on the right.

Bus Reasonably priced, with comprehensive coverage of the region and frequent departures.

Boat Croatia has a sizeable network of car ferries and faster catamarans all along the coast and the islands.

Air There's an extensive schedule of flights between the major cities of the region.

Train Less frequent and much slower than buses, with a limited network.

For much more on **getting around**, see p455

What's New

Dark History in Tirana

Two museums in the Albanian capital take a critical look at the communist past. The House of Leaves (p54) examines surveillance and interrogation under the old regime. Bunk'Art 2 (p54), housed in hidden bunkers, looks at the nefarious role of the secret police.

New Attractions for Sarajevo

The Sarajevo Cable Car (p96) has finally reopened for the first time since the 1990s siege, linking the centre with a viewpoint high up Mt Trebević. The Museum of Crimes Against Humanity & Genocide 1992–1995 (p95) covers the horrors of the Bosnian War in unflinching detail.

Belgrade Museum Reopenings

After being closed for 10 and 15 years respectively, due to reconstruction and a lack of funds, two of Belgrade's major museums have finally reopened – the Museum of Contemporary Art (p326) and the National Museum (p326).

Sveti Stefan Island Tours, Montenegro

The walled island village of Sveti Stefan has been off limits to nonguests since it was converted into an exclusive resort for the uber-rich. Limited but pricy tours are now available (p256).

European Capital of Culture, Rijeka

Croatia's cultural cred hasn't been lost on the EU, with the gritty coastal city of Rijeka (p159) set to receive the rotating honour in 2020. Expect concerts, exhibitions and other activities.

Via Ferrata Berim, Kosovo

A new *via ferrata* (iron path) climbing route has been laid on Mokra Gora (p229) in northern Kosovo, climbing 520m over the course of 3km.

Archaeological Museum of Macedonia

This recently opened museum (p287) is the culmination of Skopje's splurge on edifices to bolster national pride. Its three floors extol the riches of North Macedonia's weighty history better than anywhere else in the country.

Golubac Fortress, Serbia

The remains of this 14th-century fortress (p361) on the Danube stand sentinel at the entrance to the Iron Gates gorge and Đerdap National Park. A massive EU-funded reconstruction was completed in 2019.

Bear Watching, Slovenia

The number of operators offering bear-watching tours (p408) has expanded, and the Lož Valley (Loška Dolina) area has emerged as one of Europe's best wildlife-watching opportunities.

Next Wave Cafes, Croatia

Following international trends, specialist roastery cafes have started to sprout in Croatia. Zagreb's Cogito (p144) has expanded to Zadar and Dubrovnik, while D16 (p184) has set up shop in Split's Roman palace.

For more recommendations and reviews, see lonelyplanet.com/western-balkans

If You Like...

Outdoors Action

Extreme sports in Bovec, Slovenia The region's unrivalled location for extreme sports, offering everything from canyoning to hydrospeeding. (p401)

Great-value skiing, Bosnia & Hercegovina Sarajevo's two Olympic ski resorts, Bjelašnica and Jahorina, offer reliable and affordable skiing. (p105)

Rafting the Tara Canyon, Montenegro Hit the rapids of the Tara River hidden within Europe's deepest canyon. (p275)

Windsurfing in Bol, Croatia The famous Zlatni Rat beach attracts crowds of swimmers and windsurfers in summer. (p187)

Hiking in the Accursed Mountains, Albania Snow-capped peaks and traditional mountain villages in one of Europe's most remote corners. (p78)

Danube Cycling Path, Serbia Cycle along the Danube through the mighty Iron Gates gorge in Serbia's Đerdap National Park. (p360)

Kayaking in Canyon Matka, North Macedonia Paddle your way through this gorgeous river canyon, only 15km from the Macedonian capital. (p296)

Rock climbing on Mokra Gora, Kosovo Experienced climbers can tackle the challenging 3km-long Via Ferrata Berim route to 1731m-high Berim peak. (p229)

Swimming beneath Kravica Waterfall, Bosnia & Hercegovina Swim in the emerald waters at the base of this broad, beautiful arc. (p116)

Outdoor Pursuits in Rugova Valley, Kosovo Gorgeous mountain and river vistas in a serpentine valley, with access to active pursuits aplenty. (p226)

Old Towns

Dubrovnik, Croatia Marble-paved streets and glorious sea views can be admired from Dubrovnik's resplendent city walls. (p197)

Kotor, Montenegro Walled Kotor is dramatically wedged between the sea and the steeply rising grey mountainside. (p240)

Sarajevo, Bosnia & Hercegovina Enjoy a Bosnian coffee in Baščaršija, the bustling old Turkish quarter. (p92)

Berat, Albania A meandering Unesco-listed town filled with black-and-white Ottoman-style houses. (p62)

Ohrid, North Macedonia Picturesque churches and ancient ruins perched above one of Europe's deepest and oldest lakes. (p303)

Prizren, Kosovo An atmospheric town overlooked by a hilltop fortress and crammed with mosques and churches. (p227)

Piran, Slovenia Venetian-Gothic architecture fills the historic core, set on a narrow peninsula jutting into the Adriatic. (p412)

Korčula Town, Croatia A mini Dubrovnik, with hefty walls encircling a thumb-shaped promontory gazing over the Adriatic. (p193)

Ancient Remnants

Diocletian's Palace, Croatia Imposing and remarkably intact Roman architecture in the beating heart of Split. (p177)

Butrint, Albania Enchanting 2500-year-old ruins scattered throughout a forest on the Ionian coast. (p71)

Belgrade Fortress, Serbia Destroyed over 40 times, this promontory on the Danube has been fortified since Celtic times. (p325)

Kokino Observatory, North Macedonia Take in the atmosphere of this archaeo-astronomical site, where ancients performed complex lunar calculations. (p297)

Pula, Croatia Along with its magnificent 1st-century amphitheatre, Pula has a complete Roman temple and triumphal arch. (p147)

Apollonia, Albania The future Emperor Augustus studied at this once-important town, where only ruins remain. (p69)

Lepenski Vir, Serbia This Mesolithic-era settlement is famous for its stone fish-like idols with human faces. (p361)

Museum on Water – Bay of Bones, North Macedonia A prehistoric settlement of pile dwellers on Lake Ohrid, excavated by an underwater team. (p301)

Wining & Dining

Istrian treats, Croatia Restaurants serve up truffles, wild asparagus and fresh seafood, while wineries produce top drops. (p146)

Slow food, North Macedonia Homespun cooking, from paprika-tinged sausages to foraged mushrooms, is putting North Macedonia firmly on the menu. (p285)

Fast food, Bosnia & Hercegovina There's no better place for *burek* (savoury pastries) or *ćevapi* (skinless sausages) than Sarajevo. (p92)

Vojvodinian cuisine, Serbia Serbian and Hungarian flavours combine in the rustic food of this border region. (p345)

Mountain produce, Montenegro Njeguši village in Lovćen National Park is famous for its *pršut* (prosciutto), cheese and honey. (p261)

Wine tours, Slovenia Enjoy gourmet treats and tour the wine cellars of Vipava Valley by car or bike. (p409)

Dalmatian delights, Croatia If you like wine, olive oil, garlic and fresh seafood, you're in the right place. (p193)

Nightlife

Belgrade, Serbia Belgrade's eclectic party scene is limited only by imagination and hours in the day. (p325)

CREATIVE FAMILY/SHUTTERSTOCK ©

CHRISTIAN WITTMANN/SHUTTERSTOCK ©

Top: Canyon Matka (p296), North Macedonia

Bottom: Baptistry (p72), Butrint, Albania

Zrće Beach, Croatia It's incredible that Pag Island hasn't sunk with all the jumping up and down. (p171)

Tirana, Albania The Albanian capital has a particularly lively scene in and around its famous Blloku neighbourhood. (p53)

Ljubljana, Slovenia Pubs, cafes, cocktail bars and a set of scruffy clubs in an old army barracks. (p375)

Sarajevo, Bosnia & Hercegovina Smoke *nargile* (hookah) in former *caravanserai (inn)* courtyards, or slink into back-alley bars. (p92)

Budva, Montenegro Scores of beachside bars and clubs have earned Budva the nickname 'the Montenegrin Miami'. (p249)

Hvar Town, Croatia Post-beach sundowners inevitably lead on to cocktails, then crowded little dance bars. (p189)

Contemporary Art

Belgrade Museum of Contemporary Art, Serbia Art from the former Yugoslavia is showcased in this renovated museum on the Sava River. (p326)

Bunk'Art, Tirana, Albania Contemporary art and history displays now fill this huge communist-era bunker on Tirana's fringes. (p53)

Zagreb Museum of Contemporary Art, Croatia Striking architecture combines with edgy art in this huge Novi Zagreb museum. (p138)

Skopje Museum of Contemporary Art, North Macedonia The permanent collection includes works from the likes of Picasso and Hockney, alongside local luminaries. (p288)

Zepter Museum, Belgrade, Serbia One of the region's best private collections, housed in an impressive 1920s building. (p326)

Ars Aevi, Sarajevo, Bosnia & Hercegovina Leading lights of the international scene donated works to this collection during the 1990s war. (p97)

Relics of Communism

Museum of Yugoslavia, Belgrade, Serbia A vast collection of Yugoslav-era artefacts, capped off by Marshal Tito's final resting place. (p325)

House of Leaves, Tirana, Albania The dark side of the Albanian regime is covered in this former torture house. (p54)

D-0 ARK, Konjic, Bosnia & Hercegovina A huge, secret bunker designed to protect the Yugoslav high command from a nuclear attack. (p108)

Sazan Island, Albania This once-secret military base has only recently been opened to the public. (p77)

Partisan Memorial, Sutjeska National Park, Bosnia & Hercegovina A striking example of the hundreds of Partisan

memorials erected in Yugoslavia following WWII. (p108)

Brijuni Islands National Park, Croatia Tito's summertime playground, where he entertained heads of state and founded the nonaligned movement. (p150)

Wildlife

Lošinj Dolphin Reserve, Croatia This reserve off Lošinj Island protects the Adriatic's only known resident pod of dolphins. (p156)

Lož Valley, Slovenia A good place to see bears in the wild, and you may even spot lynx or wolves. (p408)

Lake Skadar National Park, Montenegro An important reserve for wetland birds, including the Dalmatian pelican, pygmy cormorant and whiskered tern. (p265)

Uvac Canyon, Serbia Keep an eye out for griffon vultures swooping about, along with 130 other bird species. (p360)

Mavrovo National Park, North Macedonia Home to a small population of the threatened Balkan lynx and Balkan snow vole. (p297)

Bear Sanctuary, Kosovo Bears rescued from confined cages are given room to roam in semi-wooded enclosures. (p224)

Sokolarski Centre, Croatia A rehabilitation service for injured birds of prey is offered along with public education. (p453)

Month by Month

January

As everyone recovers from New Year celebrations, the Orthodox community prepares for Christmas. If you can't beat the cold, it's better to embrace it by hitting the snow-covered mountains for white days and cosy nights.

★★ Vevčani Carnival, North Macedonia

This traditional pagan carnival is thought to have existed for 1400 years, and is still celebrated in Vevčani with elaborate costumes, music and general revelry. (p302)

February

The cold continues and towns can still be quiet, unless Carnival is being celebrated. Carnival can happen anywhere between late January and early March, depending on when Easter falls.

★★ Carnival, Croatia

Carnival is a big deal in parts of Croatia, with the Rijeka Carnival the most salubrious of them all. Over two weeks, pageants, street dances, concerts, masked balls, exhibitions and parades take place. (p160)

★★ Kurentovanje, Slovenia

A procession of hairy masks, bell-ringing and the occasional wry slap form the dramatic rites of spring in Ptuj for Kurentovanje, Slovenia's most distinctive Mardi Gras festival. (p420)

★★ Strumica Carnival, North Macedonia

Drawing several thousand visitors from North Macedonia and elsewhere, the Carnival involves three days of drinking, music, parades and costumed merrymaking.

March

Spring brings flowers and warmer weather to the Balkans, but still some unpredictable rainfall. Further north in Slovenia, the ski season sees thrilling competitions on the slopes.

☆ Festival 84, Bosnia & Hercegovina

An offshoot of Serbia's EXIT Festival, showcasing electronic music in the Jahorina ski resort near Sarajevo – one of the main venues of the 1984 Winter Olympic Games (www.festival84.com).

April

In Catholic areas, Holy Week brings with it elaborate ceremonies and processions. On the coast, tourist infrastructure starts to wake from its winter slumber around Easter. Expect milder temperatures and increasing sunshine.

☆ Music Biennale Zagreb, Croatia

Held over 10 days every odd-numbered year, Zagreb's Music Biennale is Croatia's headline music festival which attracts world-class performers from the field of modern-day classical music. (p138)

May

Beautiful sunny weather makes this a wonderful time to visit the region. Life on the coast is starting to heat up and the festival calendar shifts into gear.

⭐ Druga Godba, Slovenia

Ljubljana's flamboyant festival of alternative and world music features everything from new jazz to contemporary folk music. There are also film screenings, workshops, debates and seminars to attend. (p381)

⭐ Sea Star Festival, Croatia

One of a growing number of offshoot events sprung from Novi Sad's EXIT Festival, Sea Star (www.seastar festival.com) brings four days of electronic music to the Istrian town of Umag right at the beginning of the tourist season.

June

Summer has arrived and with it comes hot, sunny weather and a full festival schedule. This is a great time for sunning yourself on the beach before the school-holiday hordes descend and prices peak.

⭐ Kala Festival, Albania

Held on the beach in Dhërmi, this week-long festival (www.kala.al) features mainly DJs and a few high-profile dance acts. Get in early for a ticket; they go on sale the October prior.

July

Stake your claim early to get in on the action during July. Temperatures and crowds peak particularly in coastal resorts as school breaks up for the long summer vacation.

⭐ Ohrid Summer Festival, North Macedonia

The month-long Ohrid Summer Festival comprises a wealth of performances ranging from classical, opera and rock acts to theatre and literature. The best events are held in the open-air Roman amphitheatre. (p306)

⭐ EXIT Festival, Serbia

Thousands of revellers enter the state of EXIT each July within the walls of the Petrovaradin Fortress in Novi Sad. International headlining acts draw music lovers from all over the continent. (p347)

⭐ Ultra Europe, Croatia

Held over three days in Split's Poljud Stadium, this electronic-music fest then heads to the islands for the rest of Destination Ultra Croatia Music Week. (p182)

⭐ Dubrovnik Summer Festival, Croatia

From 10 July to 25 August, Croatia's most prestigious summer festival presents a roster of theatre, opera, concerts and dance on open-air stages throughout the city. (p199)

⭐ Motovun Film Festival, Croatia

This film festival, Croatia's most fun and glamorous, presents a roster of independent and avant-garde films in late July. Nonstop outdoor and indoor screenings, concerts and parties take over the medieval streets of this Istrian hilltop town. (p157)

August

This is the hot height of summer, with the region's coastal resorts packed out with holidaymakers and roads jammed with traffic. Inland cities are quieter.

⭐ Dokufest, Kosovo

This superb annual documentary festival has gained a loyal following from documentary lovers from around the world. Outdoor cinemas are set up around Prizren, including one stage over the river and another inside the castle. (p228)

⭐ Sarajevo Film Festival, Bosnia & Hercegovina

Since it grew out of the ruins of the 1990s civil war, the Sarajevo Film Festival (www.sff.ba) has become one of the largest film festivals in Europe. Commercial and art-house flicks are showcased, mostly with English subtitles.

⭐ Guča Festival, Serbia

In one of the most exciting and bizarre events in all of the Balkans, hundreds of thousands of revellers descend on the tiny town of Guča to test their eardrums, livers and sanity over four cacophonous days of trumpet-fuelled revelry (www.gucafestival.rs).

☆ Nišville International Jazz Festival, Serbia

The sprawling Niš Fortress hosts this jazz festival each August with acts from around the world taking to the stage. (p365)

✵ Boka Night, Montenegro

Kotor goes crazy on its night of nights – celebrated since the 19th century (and possibly before) – with a parade of lavishly decorated boats, Old Town parties and seemingly never-ending fireworks. (p243)

☆ Sea Dance Festival, Montenegro

This fantastic, frenetic three-day electronic and alternative music festival (www.seadancefestival.me) on the sunny sands of Buljarica Beach (near Petrovac) attracts tens of thousands of revellers.

September

September is a lovely month to be beside the seaside. The summer crowds have gone and taken peak prices with them, but it's still hot enough for swimming and hiking.

🍷 Kavadarci Wine Carnival, North Macedonia

The wine harvest in North Macedonia's Tikveš Wine Region is celebrated with a costumed parade, public wine tasting and merry-

making in early September each year.

✵ Cow's Ball, Slovenia

This mid-September weekend (www.bohinj-info.com) of folk dancing, music, eating and drinking in Bohinj marks the return of the cows from their high pastures to the valleys in typically ebullient Balkan style.

🏊 Red Bull Cliff Diving, Bosnia & Hercegovina

Crowds throng the rocky banks of the Neretva River to watch daredevil divers leap off Mostar's old bridge and plunge into the green waters 21m below (http://cliffdiving.redbull.com).

October

October is still warm in the south of the region but already getting cold in the north. Prices remain low and crowds lessen with each passing day, making it a good time to visit.

◉ October Salon, Serbia

Held in Belgrade, this prestigious exhibition of contemporary visual arts features dozens of local and international artists; it actually starts in mid-September. (p332)

November

November is a quiet time with not a whole lot going on. On the plus side, accommodation is cheap and readily available. Head south for a chance

of sunshine or settle for indoor attractions.

☆ Jazz Fest Sarajevo, Bosnia & Hercegovina

This well-known and well-organised festival packs out venues around Sarajevo in early November, showcasing the best of local and international jazz talent. (p130)

☆ Tirana International Film Festival, Albania

Tirana's annual film festival is the only one of its kind in Albania. It brings together everything from feature films to short films, animated films and documentaries. (p55)

🍷 Martinje, Slovenia & Croatia

St Martin's Day is celebrated in all the wine-producing regions across Slovenia and Croatia on 11 November. There are wine celebrations and lots of feasting and sampling of new wines.

December

The build-up to Christmas is a jolly time in Catholic areas, often marked by gift-giving, family get-togethers and midnight Mass on 24 December. In the mountains, the ski season kicks off mid-month.

☆ Christmas Concerts, Slovenia

Held in early to mid-December throughout Slovenia, but the most famous are in Postojna Cave, where you can also attend the Live Christmas Crib, a re-enactment of the Nativity.

Itineraries

2 WEEKS Breezing through the Balkans

Consider this a 'greatest hits' of the Western Balkans, taking in a slice of each of the eight countries featured. It can easily be tackled on public transport, although a car will give you more flexibility for exploring the extraordinary countryside along the way.

Start by city-hopping through four of the capitals: **Ljubljana** in Slovenia, **Zagreb** in Croatia, **Belgrade** in Serbia and **Sarajevo** in Bosnia. While the first two are cute, mid-sized, Central European cities, Sarajevo's fascinating cultural fusion lets you know that you're on the east side, while Belgrade is a hub of history, culture and late-night hedonism.

Stop to take a look at the famous bridge in **Mostar** on your way to the ancient walled city of **Dubrovnik**, then hop across the Croatia–Montenegro border to its 'mini me' **Kotor**. From here you can take an extraordinary drive via Budva, Podgorica, the breathtaking Morača Canyon and through the mountains to historic **Prizren** in Kosovo.

Continue on to North Macedonia, and spend a night amid the old-world architecture of **Ohrid** on the shores of the eponymous lake. Cross into Albania to experience the wild colours of the vibrant capital, **Tirana**.

3 WEEKS **Cruising the Coast**

This itinerary traces a leisurely path along arguably the Mediterranean's most spectacular coastline, from the Adriatic Sea all the way to the Ionian. An extensive network of ferries and buses makes car-free travel a breeze.

Spend your first week exploring the Istrian peninsula, starting in pretty **Piran**, the main attraction of Slovenia's tiny slice of coast. Cross the border into Croatia and head to **Poreč**, where an extraordinary Byzantine basilica awaits. Continue on to the gorgeous old town of **Rovinj** and the ancient city of **Pula**, replete with Roman ruins. Be sure to take day trips into the interior to visit Istria's historic hill towns and to experience its exemplary cuisine. The best beach is in **Rabac**, on Istria's east coast; stop for a swim before heading up to the shabby but interesting city of **Rijeka**.

Set aside your second week for exploring Dalmatia but, before you do, detour to **Plitvice Lakes National Park** to witness its famed waterfalls. Plunge down to **Zadar** and wander through the slippery marble streets of the old town. Keep cruising the coast to the sun-kissed city of **Split**, home to Diocletian's Palace and gateway to the Dalmatian islands. After a couple of days on party- and beach-loving **Hvar Island**, hop over to **Korčula Town** on the island of the same name. This picturesque little fortified town is a taster for the main course, the famous walled city of **Dubrovnik**.

Start your third week by crossing into Montenegro and driving around the extraordinarily beautiful Bay of Kotor. Take a look at palazzo-packed **Perast** and then press on to the fortified old town of **Kotor** for a couple of days. As you continue down the coast, stop for a quick look at the still-charming walled town of otherwise-overdeveloped **Budva** and pause along the highway for the obligatory photo of the fortified island village of **Sveti Stefan**. Stop for the night in buzzy **Ulcinj** before crossing the border into Albania and following the coast as the sea switches from the Adriatic to the Ionian. Spend your last two nights on the **Albanian Riviera**, making sure to visit Gjipe Beach and the ancient ruins of **Butrint**.

DREAMER4787/SHUTTERSTOCK ©

ZVONIMIR ATLETIC/SHUTTERSTOCK ©

Top: Old Town city walls (p197), Dubrovnik, Croatia. **Bottom:** Mosaic, National History Muesum (p53), Tirana, Albania

 Remote Ramblings

4 WEEKS

If you've got a few months to spare, excellent fitness and a local crew handling the logistics, you could tackle the extraordinary 1261km cross-border Via Dinarica hiking trail. If not, this car-based itinerary roughly traces the route. Start in the the Slovenian capital, **Ljubljana**. Stop for a look around **Postojna Cave** before heading to **Cerknica** to check out the disappearing lake and Notranjska Regional Park. Book in a bear-spotting tour in the **Lož Valley** the following day, then continue across the Croatian border to **Risnjak National Park**. Look out for the park's elusive namesake, lynx (*ris*), as you hike through the forested mountains, then continue on to busy but beautiful **Plitvice Lakes National Park**. Cut through the Velebit range to the coast and base yourself in Starigrad-Paklenica for a day hike in rugged **Paklenica National Park**. The next day, briefly leave the mountains to explore the waterfalls and lakes of **Krka National Park**.

Cross the border into the Hercegovina region of Bosnia and drive through **Konjic** to the ski resort of **Bjelašnica**. Spend the next day hiking to the lost-in-time villages of Umoljani and Lukomir and sampling traditional Bosnian cuisine. Continue on to **Sarajevo** for a taste of the Bosnian capital and then take a detour up to **Tara National Park**, the most scenic part of western Serbia. Back in Bosnia, pause to view the famous bridge on the Drina River in **Višegrad** before pushing on to **Sutjeska National Park**, where excellent mountain hiking awaits.

Enter Montenegro and allow a couple of days to explore the mountains and famous river canyon in **Durmitor National Park** and then another day for lakeside **Biogradska Gora National Park**. Cross into Kosovo and base yourself in **Peja (Peć)** to visit its famous Orthodox monastery and to tackle the walking tracks in the nearby Rugova Valley. Continue down into Albania and head to **Valbona** in the Accursed Mountains, the official end of the Via Dinarica. From here you can take day hikes into the mountains or organise a cross-border trek through a local agency, venturing into Montenegro's Prokletije National Park. Press on to North Macedonia and spend a couple of days in **Mavrovo National Park** before finishing up in the capital, **Skopje**.

3 WEEKS The Middle Road

A trio of capital cities, five national parks and a medley of historic towns punctuate this route through the heart of the Balkans, traversing Serbia, Bosnia and Montenegro.

Start your journey with a few days in Serbia's rambunctious capital, **Belgrade**. Once you've explored its museums, fortress, cafes and bars, take a detour northwest to **Novi Sad**, the principal city of the nation's multi-ethnic Vojvodina region. From here it's only a half-hour drive to **Fruška Gora National Park**; set aside a day for hiking, wine tasting and expeditions to historic Serbian Orthodox monasteries. Head south to **Tara National Park** and linger to explore the forested mountains and dramatic Drina River canyon.

Cross the border into Bosnia and visit **Višegrad**, the town immortalised in Ivo Andrić's acclaimed novel *The Bridge on the Drina*. From here, **Sarajevo** is due west and worthy of a multiday stay. Soak up the sights, sounds and tastes of its historic Baščaršija quarter, feasting on *burek* (filled pastry twists), baklava and Bosnian coffee in the shadow of historic mosques, churches and synagogues.

Continue on to sun-scorched Hercegovina, where the highway hugs the emerald-hued Neretva River. Stop in **Konjic** to see the old stone bridge and secret nuclear bunker, before continuing on to gaze upon the exquisite architectural ensemble that is the Ottoman-era core of **Mostar**. Pause in **Blagaj** to visit the peaceful *tekke* (dervish house) before continuing east to **Sutjeska National Park**, distinguished by its mountain scenery and extraordinary Partisan memorial.

Hop across the Montenegrin border and spend a couple of days hiking and rafting in mountainous **Durmitor National Park**. One night is enough to get the gist of the modern capital, **Podgorica**, and allow another to explore the museums and galleries of Old Montenegro's historic capital, **Cetinje**. From here take the spectacular route through **Lovćen National Park** and down the precipitous, serpentine road to **Kotor** – a walled gem positioned within the innermost fold of the fjord-like Bay of Kotor. With Kotor as a base, it's easy to explore the entire bay by boat, bus or car and then pop over to neighbouring Budva on the Adriatic coast.

Top: Trg Republike, Belgrade (p325), Serbia

Bottom: Partisan Memorial (by sculptors Miodrag Živković and Ranko Radović; p108), Sutjeska National Park, Bosnia & Hercegovina

West Side Glory
2 WEEKS

Wend your way around the western edge of the Balkans through Slovenia, Croatia and Bosnia and Hercegovina. Along the way you'll take in spectacular mountains, coast, rivers and waterfalls, plus ancient Roman, Venetian, Austrian and Ottoman towns.

Start at glorious **Lake Bled** before delving into the art nouveau delights of **Ljubljana**. Visit the **Škocjan Caves** and then hit the coast at picturesque **Piran**. Journey across the Croatian border to the glamorous seaside town of **Rovinj**. On the next leg you'll edge past interesting Pazin, Opatija and Rijeka en route to the extraordinary **Plitvice Lakes National Park**. From here, it's a breeze to duck across the Bosnian border to Bihać, gateway to the waterfalls of **Una National Park**.

Cross back into Croatia and continue on to **Zadar**, a walled coastal city with a profusion of Roman remains. There's more of ancient Rome to be spotted in **Split**. From here, venture back into the heart of Bosnia to visit the charming Ottoman town of **Jajce**. More Ottoman architecture can be seen in **Mostar**, including its signature bridge. Press on to **Trebinje**, a pleasant little place with a walled riverside old town.

An Eastern Circuit
2 WEEKS

This itinerary traces a ring through Albania, Kosovo and North Macedonia and can be commenced from any of the three capital cities and tackled in either direction.

Allocate a couple of days to **Tirana**, the kooky Albanian capital. Take the picturesque journey north to remote **Theth National Park**. Double back to the historic city of **Shkodra** and then cut east to Kosovo. Just across the border, **Prizren** has a historic core and is a good base for hikes in the nearby **Shar National Park**. The capital, **Pristina**, is not as pretty but it has an enticing atmosphere all of its own.

Continue south and cross into North Macedonia. The capital **Skopje** contrasts wonderful socialist modernist architecture with a recent, much-derided, neoclassical makeover. From here, beat a path to mountainous **Mavrovo National Park**. Continue on to **Ohrid**, a highlight not just of North Macedonia, but of this eastern edge of the region. Follow the eastern shore of Lake Ohrid to the Albanian border, pausing to visit the imposing **Sveti Naum Monastery** along the way. Back in Albania, head to the Ottoman-era town of **Berat** and the coastal resort of **Durrës**.

Western Balkans: Off the Beaten Track

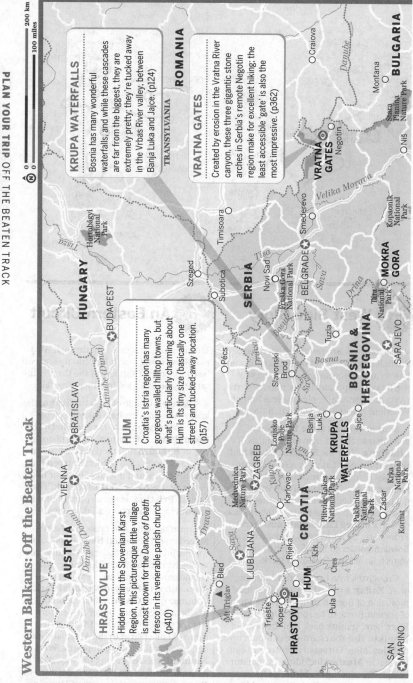

KRUPA WATERFALLS

Bosnia has many wonderful waterfalls, and while these cascades are far from the biggest, they are extremely pretty; they're tucked away in the Vrbas River valley, between Banja Luka and Jajce. (p124)

VRATNA GATES

Created by erosion in the Vratna River canyon, these three gigantic stone arches in Serbia's remote Negotin region make for excellent hiking; the least accessible 'gate' is also the most impressive. (p362)

HUM

Croatia's Istria region has many gorgeous walled hilltop towns, but what's particularly charming about Hum is its tiny size (basically one street) and tucked-away location. (p157)

HRASTOVLJE

Hidden within the Slovenian Karst Region, this picturesque little village is most known for the *Dance of Death* fresco in its venerable parish church. (p410)

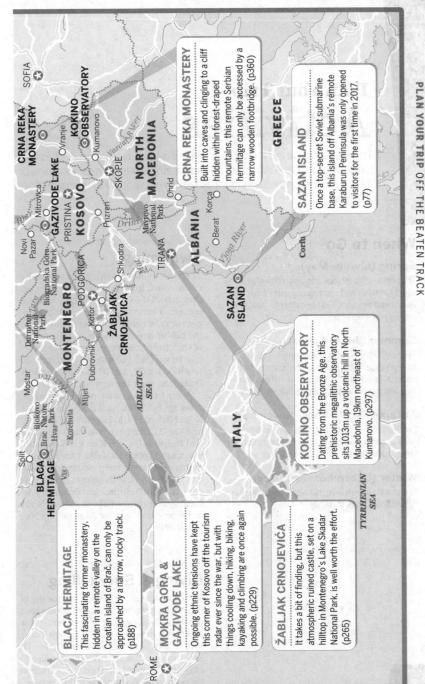

CRNA REKA MONASTERY

Built into caves and clinging to a cliff hidden within forest-draped mountains, this remote Serbian hermitage can only be accessed by a narrow wooden footbridge. (p360)

SAZAN ISLAND

Once a top-secret Soviet submarine base, this island off Albania's remote Karaburun Peninsula was only opened to visitors for the first time in 2017. (p77)

KOKINO OBSERVATORY

Dating from the Bronze Age, this prehistoric megalithic observatory sits 1013m up a volcanic hill in North Macedonia, 19km northeast of Kumanovo. (p297)

BLACA HERMITAGE

This fascinating former monastery, hidden in a remote valley on the Croatian island of Brač, can only be approached by a narrow, rocky track. (p188)

MOKRA GORA & GAZIVODE LAKE

Ongoing ethnic tensions have kept this corner of Kosovo off the tourism radar ever since the war, but with things cooling down, hiking, biking, kayaking and climbing are once again possible. (p229)

ŽABLJAK CRNOJEVIĆA

It takes a bit of finding, but this atmospheric ruined castle, set on a hilltop in Montenegro's Lake Skadar National Park, is well worth the effort. (p265)

Plan Your Trip
Activities

The Balkans' varied landscape makes it ideal terrain for endless outdoor pursuits – whether on mountains, lakes, rivers, canyons or the sea – and enthusiast local crews have stepped in to make them possible.

When to Go

Spring (March–May)
The best season for rock climbing, rafting, white-water kayaking, and spotting migratory birds in the various wetlands. Great weather for hiking, cycling and windsurfing.

Summer (June–August)
The best time for swimming, diving, kayaking, sailing, horse riding, bear-spotting tours in Tara National Park (Serbia) and the Lož Valley (Slovenia), and more sedate rafting and kayaking.

Autumn (September–November)
Excellent for hiking, cycling, horse riding, windsurfing, and birdwatching at various wetlands, and still good for rafting, diving and kayaking.

Winter (December–February)
Skiing and snowshoeing, but also birdwatching in Krka National Park (Croatia).

Swimming

There are good swimming spots along the entire coast, from Slovenia to Albania, and throughout the Croatian islands. Beaches come in a variety of textures: sandy, shingly, rocky or pebbly. Locals tend to favour the pebbly beaches, partly because many of the sandy beaches are extremely shallow. In summer the water temperature can reach over 25°C, and it's usually over 20°C from June right through to October.

Away from the coast, popular swimming spots in Croatia include the lakes at Krka National Park, Zagreb's Jarun Lake, and the Danube near Vukovar. In Bosnia and Hercegovina, the Kravica Waterfall is a magical place for a dip. Landlocked Serbia offers some good swimming, from city beaches on the Danube and Sava Rivers – Novi Sad's Štrand and Belgrade's Ada Ciganlija – to Silver Lake in eastern Serbia or Perućac and Zaovine lakes in Tara National Park.

Diving & Snorkelling

The clear waters and varied marine life of the Adriatic support a vibrant diving industry, and snorkelling is worthwhile just about everywhere. Visibility ranges from 10m to 25m but is usually around 15m. The best times to dive are from the middle of May until September, when the surface water is up to 25°C, dropping to 16°C under 30m (you'll need a 7mm neoprene wetsuit).

The area's turbulent history has also bequeathed it with numerous interesting underwater sights, from wrecks dating to antiquity through to a downed WWII plane. On top of that there are plenty of reefs, drop-offs, springs and caves to investigate. The main fauna you're likely to spot are swarms of young dentex, gilt-head bream and the occasional lobster or sea turtle. Look out for scorpionfish, conger eels, sea snails, sea slugs, octopuses, the rare giant mussel, red coral, red gorgonian fans and colourful sponges.

There are diving centres all along the Croatian coast and throughout the islands. In Montenegro, you'll find operators in Budva, Pržno and Ulcinj. In Slovenia, there are dive centres in Ankaran, Portorož and Piran, but diving is also possible in the Kolpa River. Cave diving takes place at Postojna, Škocjan and in the tunnel at Wild Lake (Divje Jezero) near Idrija – but only under the supervision of a professional guide. Another unusual diving tour delves into North Macedonia's Lake Ohrid to check out the remains of a Neolithic settlement at the Bay of Bones. 'Speed river diving' is an activity invented in Una National Park (Bosnia) involving scuba diving in fast-flowing waters.

Sailing

Sailing was once the exclusive preserve of the rich, but Croatia and Montenegro now offer plenty of more affordable opportunities for both day sails and organised multiday tours. Operators such as **Sail Croatia** (www.sail-croatia.com) even target multiday cruises to young backpacker types. As for the super-rich, you'll find them at Porto Montenegro (p246) in Tivat – rated one of the best superyacht marinas in the world. If you'd prefer to go it alone and you've got cash to splash, it's an easy matter to charter a boat, either with a skipper or, if you're suitably experienced, on a 'bareboat' basis.

Windsurfing & Kitesurfing

Bol on Brač Island and Viganj on Pelješac Peninsula in Croatia offer ideal conditions for windsurfing, while kitesurfers head to Montenegro's Velika Plaža.

PRACTICAL TIPS

➡ It's often easier to arrange active holidays through a specialist adventure tourism agency; there are reputable operators in each country.

➡ Mountain clubs – such as the **Alpine Association of Slovenia** (www.pzs.si), the **Mountaineering Association of Montenegro** (www.pscg.me) and the **Mountaineering Association of Croatia** (www.hps.hr) – operate chalets and mountain huts, offering dormitory accommodation and, sometimes, basic meals. They can also hook you up with local guides.

➡ Sadly, there are plenty of cowboy operators in the Balkans seeking to make a quick buck at the expense of safety. It's unlikely that the cheapest option will be the best. If you're rafting or canyoning, insist on a helmet and life jacket that fit and fasten – and make sure you wear them.

PLAN YOUR TRIP ACTIVITIES

Rafting & Kayaking

White-water rafting is offered from around April to October. The biggest thrills are in spring, when the melting snow speeds up the flows.

Commercial rafting is well established on the Tara River in Bosnia and Montenegro. The Montenegrin section includes the spectacular 1300m-deep Tara Canyon – best viewed on a two-day wilderness rafting trip. Elsewhere in Bosnia there's wonderful rafting through the Vrbas Canyon and on the Una and Neretva Rivers.

Slovenia's centre for kayaking and rafting is the Soča River at Bovec, famed as one of the best and least spoiled white-water routes in the European Alps. Other options include the Krka, Kolpa, Sava, Savinja and Drava rivers. Southern Serbia's fast-flowing Drina, Ibar and Lim Rivers offer good white-water rafting opportunities. Croatia's prime rafting locale is the Cetina River, which spills through a steep gorge and into the Adriatic at Omiš. In Albania, the key spots are the Vjosa and Osumi Canyons.

Inland kayaking destinations include Lake Skadar (Montenegro and Albania),

Gazivode Lake (Kosovo), Canyon Matka (North Macedonia), Uvac Canyon (Serbia) and Zagreb's Jarun Lake (Croatia).

As for sea kayaking, there's nowhere more dramatic to paddle than at the foot of the mighty walls of Dubrovnik at sunset – although Montenegro's fjord-like Bay of Kotor comes close. Kayaks can be hired from numerous locations in both countries, and there are many specialist operators offering both short paddles and multiday expeditions.

Hiking

Every country in the region offers excellent hiking, with marked trails through forests, mountains and national parks. But be aware: they're not all well maintained or well marked (Slovenia is the exception). Local tourist and national park offices are well equipped to recommend a walk to suit your time constraints and level of ability. The best months for hiking are from May to September, especially late August and early September, when the summer crowds will have largely disappeared. Whether you're armed with a tent or just planning a day walk, be well prepared for sudden changes in temperature and storms, and note that water supplies can be limited.

An exciting development in recent years has been the creation of long-distance, cross-border hiking tracks – although the infrastructure in place to support hikers (especially when it comes to organising the correct border permits) is yet to match the marketing drive. The 192km Peaks of

PEAKS OF THE BALKANS HIKING TRAIL

Winding 192km through the Accursed Mountains range, the border-hopping **Peaks of the Balkans** (PoB; www.peaksofthebalkans.com) hiking trail is the epitome of epic. The waymarked circuit, which runs through eastern Montenegro, northern Albania and western Kosovo, follows shepherds' paths and alpine trails along verdant valleys, remote villages and up (literally) breathtaking mountains; the highest point of the trail is 2300m. While there are other transnational hiking paths in Europe, this one is extra impressive, not only for its otherwise inaccessible, utterly astonishing scenery, but also the fact that it exists at all, given the centuries of bad blood between the countries and previously rigorously guarded borders.

Being a circular route, the trail has multiple entry points. Though the full hike takes between 10 and 13 days to complete, you can tailor your own trek; there are almost limitless shorter or alternative hikes to choose from, and it's possible to hop on and off to visit nearby historical sites, clamber up off-trail peaks or simply take a breather in relative civilisation.

Apart from wild camping, the only accommodation options along the trail are village guesthouses and homestays; the cultural immersion and traditional hospitality you'll receive are as magical as the mountains themselves. It's best to arrange your digs ahead of time; if you're not on an organised trek, local tourist offices can help.

Don't be lulled by its marketable name, the flash website and the fact that it's (mostly) signposted; the Peaks of the Balkans is not a journey to be undertaken lightly. Hikers should be fit and come equipped with proper equipment, including sturdy hiking boots, torches, GPS, phone (though don't count on reception), first-aid kit, sleeping bag, tent and waterproof clothing. June to October is the best time to make the trek, though inclement weather can strike at any time.

The trail meanders through some incredibly isolated areas: tackling it on your own is not recommended. Cross-border permits are required from each country you plan to cross in and out of, but these can be hard to arrange, especially from the Montenegrin side. We highly recommend engaging the services of a local adventure-travel agency to plan your trip. At present, Albania seems to have the best infrastructure for this, and there's also a good agency operating out of Kosovo.

If you don't want to join an agency-organised group trek, at the very least go with two or more friends. Better yet, hire a local guide; those listed on the PoB website have been trained by the DAV (Deutscher Alpen Verein; German Alpine Club).

the Balkans (p38) offers access to extraordinary wilderness in the remote corner between Montenegro, Albania and Kosovo. The new 495km **High Scardus Trail** crosses the border triangle between Albania, Kosovo and North Macedonia; it takes around 20 days to hike.

The **Via Dinarica** (www.viadinarica.com) is even more ambitious, with plans for three themed paths following the Dinaric Alps on their journey across the Western Balkans. Only one is complete: the 1261km **White Trail** from Postojna in Slovenia to Valbona in Albania, via Croatia, Bosnia and Montenegro, taking in each country's highest peaks along the way. The supporting infrastructure is still being developed, so you're wise to seek advice before setting out; refer to the official website or to that of the **Via Dinarica Alliance** (www.via-dinarica.org), which arranges tours and promotes tourist activity along the way. The lower-altitude, forest-delving **Green Trail** and the Adriatic-hugging **Blue Trail** are still being finalised.

Cycling

There are some confronting hills and mountains to conquer in the Western Balkans, but the effort is offset by the scenery. Bicycle touring is increasingly popular, both independently or with organised groups. Bike hire is easy to arrange and there are plenty of relatively quiet roads to explore. March, April, May, September and October are the best cycling months, with mild, mostly dry weather. The traffic is much busier from June to August, and it can get extremely hot.

Mountain bikers should consider Bike Park Kranjska Gora (Slovenia), Biokovo Nature Park (Croatia), and the Lovćen (Montenegro), Tara (Serbia) and Pelister (North Macedonia) National Parks.

Cross-border tracks include:

➡ the 80km **Pannonian Peace Route** between Osijek (Croatia) and Sombor (Serbia)

➡ the Parenzana Bike Trail (p155), which follows a former railway line between Trieste (Italy) and Poreč (Croatia) via Slovenia

➡ the **Ćiro Trail** (www.ciro.herzegovinabike.ba), following another historic rail route between Mostar (Bosnia and Hercegovina) and Dubrovnik (Croatia)

➡ the **TransDinarica** (www.transdinarica.com), a 2000km mountain-biking route through all of the Western Balkans countries; at present, only the Slovenia, Croatia and Bosnia sections are complete.

Skiing

Most ski areas in the Western Balkans are small and relatively unchallenging compared with the Alpine resorts of France, Switzerland and Italy, but they do have the attraction of lower prices and easy access. The season roughly runs from early December to late March. The peak time tends to be around the New Year, but February usually offers the most reliable snow. Many of the bigger resorts offer night skiing.

Cross-border, cross-country skiing between North Macedonia, Kosovo and Albania is now possible with specialist guides.

Downhill ski spots in the Balkans include:

➡ Kranjska Gora and Vogel in the Julian Alps, and Krvavec and Maribor Pohorje in Eastern Slovenia

➡ the Winter Olympic resorts of Bjelašnica and Jahorina in Bosnia and Hercegovina

➡ Durmitor and Kolašin in Montenegro

➡ Kopaonik, Zlatibor and Stara Planina in Serbia

➡ Mavrovo, Pelister and Šar Mountain in North Macedonia

➡ Brezovica in Kosovo

➡ Sljeme on Mt Medvednica in Croatia.

Rock Climbing

March, April and May are the best months for climbing, before the summer heat kicks in; the wind tends to pick up in autumn and winter.

The principal Alpine climbing areas in Slovenia include Mt Triglav's north face as well as the northern buttresses of Prisank overlooking the Vršič Pass. Another promising place for climbers is located in the coastal region, near the village of Osp, northeast of Koper.

Croatia's best rock climbing is in Paklenica National Park, and there are climbing crags on Split's Marjan Hill, Krk Island

and in the Žumberak Samoborsko Gorje range, west of Zagreb. The best climbing in Istria is in a defunct Venetian stone quarry near Rovinj; free climbing is also possible near Buzet and Pazin.

Kosovo has a challenging 3km *via ferrata* (iron path) on the Mokra Gora mountain and another in the Rugova Valley; other locations include Serbia's Ovčar-Kablar gorge and Montenegro's Durmitor National Park.

Extreme Sports

Bovec in Slovenia is a hotspot for hydrospeeding, canyoning and paragliding. Paragliders also leap from above Crikvenica or Motovun in Croatia and Mt Galičica in North Macedonia.

For a quick adrenalin fix you can jump off the famous bridge in Mostar (Bosnia and Hercegovina), and then double down with a zipline on the mountain above town. Ziplines also soar above the Tara Canyon (Montenegro), Cetina Canyon (Croatia), Pazin Chasm (Croatia) and Sava Dolinka (Slovenia). Planica Zipline (Slovenia) claims to be the world's steepest, while Europe's longest zipline (1700m) is the intriguingly named Beware of the Bear (Croatia). The ziplines at Zlatna Greda in Kopački Rit Nature Park (Croatia), the Black Lake in Durmitor National Park (Montenegro) and in Lovćen National Park (Montenegro) are suitable for the whole family.

Canyoning involves descending through gorges, sliding down waterfalls, swimming in rock pools and abseiling/rappelling. Montenegro is run through with countless canyons, the best of which is Nevidio (p276), while the most accessible is Škurda (p241). Canyoning is also possible in Tara National Park (Serbia), Vrbas Canyon (Bosnia) and near Lake Bled (Slovenia). If you're an experienced canyoner, the **Extreme Canyoning** (www.extremecanyon

ing.com) website also has a full list of canyons in Montenegro and Serbia.

Birdwatching & Wildlife-Watching

Some unusual bird species can be spotted in the region, including the endangered Dalmatian pelican around Lake Skadar (Albania and Montenegro), and the griffon vulture in Serbia's Uvac Canyon and Croatia's Kvarner islands.

Good locations for bear watching include Mavrovo and Pelister National Parks in North Macedonia, Tara National Park in Serbia and the Lož Valley in Slovenia.

Horse Riding

Slovenia is a nation of horse riders. You can join them at the **Lipica Stud Farm** (☑05-739 1696; www.lipica.org; Lipica 5; 1½hr trail ride €61) – birthplace of the famous Lipizzaner breed – and the Mrcina Ranč (p397) in Studor. Serbia also has several options, from Vojvodina's *salaši* (homesteads) and horse farms to gentle mountain regions like Zlatibor. In North Macedonia, saddle up in Mavrovo National Park.

Spas

Slovenia has around 20 thermal-spa resorts. Some specialise in old-world atmosphere, others in modern luxury, and still others in water slides and family fun. Serbia's countryside is dotted with thermal spas; however, most are in need of better infrastructure. Vrnjačka Banja (p358) is the most popular. Croatia, too, has a few scattered about – notably in Istria and Zagorje – but nothing exceptional.

Plan Your Trip

Eat & Drink Like a Local

The cuisines of the Western Balkans reflect the mishmash of cultures that have influenced the region over time, but wherever you are, you'll find tasty food made from top-notch, seasonal ingredients.

Local Specialities

The variation of cuisines across the Western Balkans reflects geography and history more than it respects national borders, so we've divided the region into four rough bands.

Coastal Cuisine

The food of the coast is typically Mediterranean, using a lot of olive oil, garlic, flat-leaf parsley, bay leaves and all manner of seafood. For hundreds of years Venice dominated the coast as far as Montenegro – leaving a legacy of excellent risotto, gnocchi and pasta.

Black risotto (*crni rižot*) gets its colour and flavour from squid ink and includes pieces of squid meat. Seafood risotto can also be red or white (with or without a tomato base). Hearty, flavoursome fish soup (*riblja čorba*) is a must-try, as are octopus (*hobotnica;* either carpaccio, in a salad or cooked under a *peka* – a domed baking lid), grilled squid (*lignje na žaru),* and stuffed squid (*punjene lignje)* filled with *pršut* (prosciutto) and cheese.

While all of these dishes make filling mains, at a formal dinner they're just a precursor to the whole grilled or baked fish. In most fish restaurants, whole fish (*ribe*) are presented to the table for you to choose from and sold by the kilogram according to a quality-based category. A

The Year in Food & Drink

Spring (March–May)

Wild asparagus comes into season in Istria (Croatia) and gets its own festival. In April, restaurants in Korčula (Croatia) show off signature dishes, and chocolate makers in Radovljica (Slovenia) get creative. Istrian winemakers throw open their cellar doors in late May.

Summer (June–August)

Berries and stone fruits are in season. Dine al fresco on freshly caught seafood along the coast, especially during the Isola (Slovenia) fishing festival. Muslim areas feast during Ramadan Bajram (June) and Kurban Bajram (August/September). Beat the heat with beer festivals in Belgrade and Skopje.

Autumn (September–November)

Mushroom-hunting shifts into high gear. Festivals showcase truffles (Istria), chestnuts (Kvarner, Croatia), cheese (Pljevlja, Montenegro) and the olive and wine harvests (almost everywhere). Dubrovnik holds its Good Food Festival.

Winter (December–February)

Start the season with the wine and fish festival at Lake Skadar (Montenegro), then prepare for hearty Christmas and Carnival treats.

standard portion is around 200g to 250g; ask for a rough price before you choose a fish if you're unsure. Local varieties tend to be small but tasty; the bigger ones are probably imported.

In Dalmatia and coastal Montenegro, the traditional accompaniment to most meals is a mixture of Swiss chard *(blitva),* mushy boiled potato, olive oil and garlic, often referred to on English menus as a 'Dalmatian garnish'. Lamb from the islands of Cres and Pag is deemed Croatia's best; they feed on fresh herbs, which gives the meat a distinct flavour. Try it spit-roasted or cooked under a *peka.* For a unique appetiser, try *paški sir,* a pungent hard sheep cheese from Pag. Other Dalmatian favourites include *brodet/brodetto/ brudet/brujet* (spiced seafood stew served with polenta), *gregada* (fish stew made with potatoes, white wine, garlic and spices) and *pašticada* (beef stewed in wine, prunes and spices and served with gnocchi).

Istrian cuisine has been attracting international foodies in recent years for its quality ingredients and unique specialities. Typical dishes include *maneštra* (thick vegetable-and-bean soup similar to minestrone), *fuži* (hand-rolled pasta often served with *tartufi* (truffles) or game meat) and *fritaja* (frittata, made with seasonal vegetables). Look for dishes featuring *boškarin,* an indigenous species of ox. Truffles are an Istrian obsession, as is wild asparagus when it's harvested in spring.

Highland Cuisine

In the mountains, food was traditionally more stodgy and meaty, providing comfort and sustenance on those long winter nights. Cooking *ispod sača* at a hearth set in the middle of the room also provided warmth. Lamb may also be slowly poached in milk with spices and potato *(brav u mljeku)* in a dish that's particularly popular in Albanian areas. Beef is cooked with cabbage-like *raštan,* rice and red peppers to make a rich stew called *japraci.* You might eat it with *cicvara* (a cheesy, creamy polenta or buckwheat dish) or *kačamak* (similar but with potato). The best honey *(med)* is also produced in the mountains. The higher up you go, the better the *kajmak,* somewhat similar to a salty clotted cream; slather it on bread, meat or potatoes.

Ottoman- and Greek-Influenced Areas

As well as the ubiquitous *burek/byrek* (heavy pastry stuffed with meat or cheese), you'll find excellent baklava, *lokum/ratluk* (Turkish delight) and Turkish-style coffee throughout the region. Unsurprisingly, the countries where the Ottoman influence is most pronounced are North Macedonia, Albania, Kosovo, Serbia and Bosnia.

Grilled meat is king here, usually served with bread and raw onions. *Dolma* (vegetables such as eggplant, tomato or capsicum stuffed with meat and rice) are also popular; a similar filling wrapped in a cabbage or vine leaf is called *sarma.*

Tomatoes grow abundantly and feature prominently in salads such as North Macedonia's and Serbia's *šopska salata* (with peppers, onion, cucumbers and tangy white cheese). These two countries are also the home of *ajvar* (pronounced *'eye-*var"), a condiment made from red peppers and oil; once barely known outside the Balkans, it's fast becoming a global food trend.

Austrian- and Hungarian-Influenced Areas

The Austrian influence is strongest in Slovenia and the Zagreb and Zagorje regions of Croatia. However, strudel and Wiener schnitzel have made their way across the Western Balkans. Zagreb has its own signature schnitzel (*zagrebački odrezak;* veal stuffed with ham and cheese, then crumbed and fried), as does Serbia (*Karađorđeva šnicla;* rolled veal or pork stuffed with *kajmak,* crumbed and fried). Dumplings are also popular, particularly *štruklji/štrukli* (stuffed with a savoury or sweet filling), *ajdovi krapi* (made from buckwheat, stuffed with cottage cheese) and *gomboce* (potato dough stuffed with plums).

The spicier tastes of Hungary dominate in the Slavonia (Croatia) and Vojvodina (Serbia) regions. Signature dishes include *gulaš/golaž* (goulash) and *paprikaš* (paprika-laced fish, chicken, venison, wild boar or beef stew). The regions' sausages are particularly renowned, especially *kulen,* a paprika-flavoured sausage cured over a period of nine months and usually served with *kajmak,* peppers, tomatoes and often *turšija* (pickled vegetables).

Top: Miro Tartufi (p157), Motovun, Croatia

Bottom: Rakija/raki (p45)

Food & Drink Experiences

Truffle hunting Truffle is the signature taste of Istria. It makes its way into most things, including, at more adventurous establishments, ice cream and chocolate cake. For the ultimate foodie outing, join a local family and their well-trained pooch in the Motovun Forest for a truffle hunt – then sample the booty at the end.

Wine tasting For a wine lover, the best thing about a tasting trip in the Western Balkans is the array of localised indigenous grape varieties on offer – most of which you're unlikely to have experienced anywhere else. Most wineries are small, family-run affairs which welcome visitors but usually require a little notice. Slovenia has three main regions: Podravje, Posavje and Primorska. Croatia produces some of the Balkans' best wine; the top regions to tour are Istria, Dalmatia (particularly the Pelješac Peninsula and the islands) and Slavonia (especially around Baranja). In Bosnia, head to Hercegovina to sample *žilavka* (white) and *blatina* (red). Most of Montenegro's grapes are grown around Lake Skadar and the plains leading to Podgorica; try *vranac*, their signature red. In North Macedonia, the Tikveš Wine Region is worth a visit for its scenery as much

as its top-notch wines. In Serbia, head to Fruška Gora, Negotin and Župa; try *prokupac* (red) and *tamjanika* (white).

Meat roasted 'ispod sača/peka' In this traditional cooking method, meat (usually lamb, veal, octopus or whole fish) is slow-cooked with potatoes in a metal pan under a dome-shaped metal lid called a *sač* (*peka* in Dalmatia), covered with charcoal. The end result is tender, slightly smoky and delicious. It's a long process, so most restaurants require you to order it in advance.

Spit-roasted meat The tantalising scent of the spit-roast wafts throughout the Balkans. Most commonly it's lamb, but you might also strike suckling pig or other meats. Specialist restaurants cater to locals craving the traditional fatty, smoky experience but without the space, time or inclination to do it themselves.

Pršut This dry-cured ham is every bit the equal of Italian prosciutto. The very best comes from the village of Njeguši in Montenegro, where it's lightly smoked – as it is in Dalmatia, Hercegovina and Serbia. Of the unsmoked (Italian-style) varieties, the Karst Region of Slovenia produces a beautiful version, as does Istria and the Croatian island of Krk.

Olive-oil tasting Istrian olive oil regularly wins international awards, and the region has plenty of boutique producers offering tastings and tours. The Dalmatian islands are also worth a visit, especially Brač and Pag. Montenegro and Albania are prime olive-growing territory too, although their producers are not as well set up for visitors.

Cheap Treats

Burek/byrek This savoury filo-pastry pie is the consummate Balkan snack, available from bakeries or speciality *burekdžinica/byrektorë* throughout the region. Usually they're flat pies except in Bosnia, where they're traditionally rolled into a spiral. The Bosnians also use slightly different terminology, as *'burek'* refers only to those stuffed with minced meat; other varieties include *sirnica* (stuffed with cheese), *zeljanica* (spinach and cheese) and *krompiruša* (potatoes), collectively known in Bosnia as *pita*. The traditional accompaniment is a glass of runny yoghurt.

Pljeskavica Common throughout Serbia, Bosnia and Croatia, *pljeskavica* is usually translated on menus as 'hamburger', leaving many travellers extremely confused. The word actually refers to just the meat patty, commonly served with the same accompaniments as *ćevapi*.

Ćevapi/ćevapčići Small skinless sausages of minced beef, lamb or pork – hugely popular throughout the Western Balkans but particularly in Bosnia and Serbia, where they're considered national dishes. They're usually served with flat bread, raw onion and *kajmak* (dairy product akin to a salty clotted cream) or *ajvar* (spread made from roasted peppers, aubergines and garlic).

Ražnjići Chunks of grilled meat (often pork) on a skewer.

Pizza You're never far from Neapolitan-style pizza anywhere in the Balkans. Pizza slices are a popular street snack.

Palačinke Thin pancakes are the default sweet offering; locals love to smother them in nutella.

Dare to Try

Fërgesë Tiranë Traditional Tirana dish of offal, eggs and tomatoes cooked in an earthenware pot.

Horseburger Slovenians aren't squeamish about horsemeat; Ljubljana even has a dedicated burger joint called **Hot Horse** (☏01-521 14 27; www.facebook.com/HotHorse; Park Tivoli, Celovška cesta 25; small/large burger €3/6; ☺9am-midnight Sun-Thu, to 2am Fri & Sat).

Kostelski želodec Stuffed pig's stomach, an Easter treat from Kostel (Slovenia).

Kukurec Sheep intestines stuffed with chopped liver – big in Albania and North Macedonia.

Lešo drobovi Boiled beef bowels, a dish that's failed to catch on outside Cetinje (Montenegro).

Neretvanski brudet Frog and eel stew, much loved by people living along the Neretva River in Dalmatia and Hercegovina.

Paçë koke Sheep's head soup, an Albanian dish that's usually served for breakfast.

Vitalac Lamb intestines grilled on a spit over hot coals – a speciality of the Croatian island of Brač.

Slane palačinke Pancakes stuffed with cheese and ham, crumbed and then deep fried – a popular heart-attack fuel in Croatia, Montenegro and Serbia.

Rakija/raki Pan-Balkan firewater distilled from a huge variety of fruits, berries, nuts and herbs, with an alcohol content upwards of 40%.

How to Eat & Drink
When to Eat

➡ The standard Balkan breakfast is coffee and a cigarette, perhaps accompanied by a *burek* grabbed from a bakery.

➡ Lunch is traditionally the main cooked meal of the day, preferably followed up with a siesta.

➡ Dinner is typically a light affair (often just cheese, sliced prosciutto and bread), but restaurants have adapted their schedules to the needs of tourists, who tend to load up at night.

Where to Eat

➡ If your accommodation doesn't provide breakfast, bakeries are your best bet. Cafes don't usually serve food, so they normally won't mind if you bring along a pastry to devour along with your morning coffee.

➡ Restaurants and taverns open for lunch around noon and usually serve continuously until midnight, which can be a major convenience if you're arriving in town at an odd hour or just feel like spending more time at the beach.

Vegetarians & Vegans

Although the locals still tend to be a bit bewildered when faced with the prospect of people not eating meat (or, heaven forbid, dairy products), things are slowly changing. Some of the bigger towns and cities (particularly in Croatia) now have dedicated vegetarian restaurants.

There are some delicious Turkish-style vegetable dishes to be had, such as grilled red peppers and aubergines (eggplants), cauliflower moussaka and vegetarian *burek,* which can be filled with cheese, potato or spinach. The local olives and cheeses are also excellent.

Otherwise, pasta, pizza and salad are the best fall-back options. It pays to learn some key food phrases in each country, so you can be clear about your requirements ('vegetarian' soup is often flavoured with ham, for instance). Be cautious when ordering 'stuffed vegetables' as they're usually stuffed with meat.

Countries at a Glance

Broadly speaking, the attractions of this region are split into three geological bands which run loosely from the northwest to the southeast and don't respect national boundaries. The spectacular coastline is the most popular part, with the best tourist infrastructure and highest visitor numbers; Croatia, Montenegro and Albania hog most of it. Next up is the band of rugged limestone mountains; each country has its share, suited to hiking, skiing and wildlife spotting. Finally, there are the languid plains and broad rivers of the north, running from eastern Slovenia through northern Croatia and Serbia. Each zone has its own attractions, punctuated by historic towns and cities. Another key division is a hangover of the Age of Empires: the Ottoman-dominated east and centre, the Venetian-influenced coast and the Austro-Hungarian north.

Top: Bear Sanctuary (p224), Kosovo
Centre: Street in Rovinj (p152), Croatia
Bottom: Women in traditional dress, Berat, Albania

Albania

Beaches
Mountains
Culture

Uncrowded Beaches

Unlike much of Europe's Mediterranean shoreline, there's still room to spread out along the more isolated parts of the gorgeous Ionian coast.

Remote Wilderness

Albania's mountains are some of Europe's most spectacular; the Koman ferry is possibly its most beautiful boat ride. Tucked away in far-flung landscapes, village life is still governed by traditions that have long been forgotten elsewhere.

Towns & Cities

In Tirana, cafe culture rules the day before club culture takes hold of the night. This is but one part of the Albanian urban experience, which includes the gorgeous Ottoman-era museum towns Berat and Gjirokastra.

p50

Bosnia & Hercegovina

Scenery
Adventure
History

Waterfalls

Jajce has a waterfall directly beneath its walls, while central Bihać has a series of cascades. Kravica Waterfall is Hercegovina's top swimming spot, but the most dramatic drops are on the Una River.

Outdoor Activities

The accessibility and affordability of outdoor adventures mean Bosnia is fast becoming a hub for kayaking, rafting, skiing, hiking and mountain biking.

The Edge of Empires

Bosnia's mixed religious heritage is reflected in its food, culture and architecture. Rebuilt historical centres showcase its history: the scars of recent horrors are still visible, Ottoman and Austro-Hungarian buildings loom in urban centres, and medieval castles are dotted around.

p89

Croatia

Architecture
Coastline
Food

Walled Towns

Croatia's most memorable sights are its fantastical walled towns, ranging from tiny hilltop Hum to the coastal drama of Dubrovnik. The core of the city of Split sits behind ancient Roman palace walls, and even Zagreb has a medieval walled town at its heart.

Islands

Off the Croatian coast, 1244 islands and islets cater for almost anyone's idea of idyllic, from Euro-chic yacht life to backpacker beach parties.

Istrian & Dalmatian Cuisine

The influence of Venice differentiates Croatia's coastal cuisine from the rest of the region, with its focus on pasta, risotto and seafood. In Dalmatia, the classic flavours of olive oil, garlic and parsley dominate. Istria is known for its truffles.

p133

Kosovo

History
Monasteries
Outdoors

Eclectic Architecture

Cosmopolitan Pristina has a mix of modern shops and Turkish-style bazaars. Prizren's old town is a showcase of Ottoman-era architecture juxtaposed with Orthodox churches and a medieval fortress.

Medieval Monasteries

Kosovo's medieval monasteries have outstanding frescoes, an age-old atmosphere and forbidding walls that have withstood turbulent times. They include some of the most significant sites in the Serbian Orthodox world.

Adventure Activities

The hills around Peja (Peć) are ideal for scenic hiking along with skiing, caving, rock climbing and ziplining. If wildlife spotting is more your thing, there's a bear sanctuary near Pristina.

p218

Montenegro

Scenery
Coastline
Adventure

Coastline & Mountains

Tiny Montenegro crams an awful lot into a small space, including sandy beaches, jagged mountain peaks and dramatic gorges. The cherry on top is the Bay of Kotor, where rugged mountains rise dramatically from the sea.

Historic Towns

Seaside Kotor is one of the country's most extraordinary sights. Nearby Perast is a vision from distant Venice, while Cetinje – high up in the mountains – is the heart of Old Montenegro. Ulcinj's Old Town gazes out to sea from ancient walls.

Outdoor Activities

Hikers gravitate to Montenegro's impressive national parks while rafters paddle their way through the Tara Canyon and kayakers traverse the Bay of Kotor.

p233

North Macedonia

Churches
Wine
Outdoors

Churches & Monasteries

North Macedonia's churches house important medieval art, while its monasteries are all about location, perched on ridges or even built into cliff faces. The most impressive is Sveti Jovan Bigorski Monastery in the mountains of Mavrovo.

Wine Tastings

Wine connoisseurs can enjoy a drop of vino with laid-back locals among the seemingly endless vineyards, especially in the country's premier wine region, Tikveš.

Outdoor Activities

Lake Ohrid is ringed by swimming spots, while at Lake Prespa you there's an island populated by tortoises and pelicans. Hikers and mountain bikers can enjoy panoramas over untouched mountain landscapes.

p284

Serbia

Culture
Festivals
Nature

Architectural Diversity

With art nouveau architecture up north, fine examples of Socialist Modernism in Belgrade, Turkish-toned Novi Pazar down south and Orthodox churches throughout, Serbia is more diverse than you might think.

Music & Festivals

The sounds emanating from the clubs of Belgrade, the all-out edgy EXIT Festival, and the Dragačevo Trumpet Assembly in Guča are putting Serbia firmly on the music map.

River-Based Activities

Some of Serbia's most memorable back-to-nature experiences are around rivers, whether it's rafting on the Drina through Tara National Park, cycling along the Danube in Đerdap National Park or searching for griffon vultures in the Uvac Canyon.

p322

Slovenia

Scenery
Adventure
Wine

Mountains, Caves & Lakes

Nearly all visitors are mesmerised by the sheer beauty of this tiny country – from the soaring peaks of the Julian Alps to the subterranean magic of Postojna Cave.

Outdoor Pursuits

The list of activities on offer is endless, with the most popular being skiing, hiking, cycling and rafting. An assault on Mt Triglav is challenging but a consummate Slovenian experience. The Soča and Krka Rivers are prime rafting routes, with the latter being the gentler option.

Wining & Dining

Slovenia's wines pair well with local gastronomic specialities, especially fresh Piran seafood. The Vipava Valley is the best of the three main wine regions, producing top-notch Merlot.

p373

On the Road

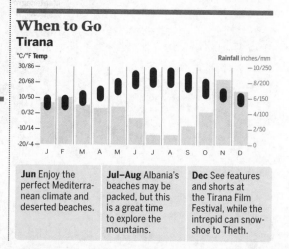

Albania

POP 2.93 MILLION

Best Places to Eat

➡ Onufri (p66)
➡ Pasta e Vino (p78)
➡ Met Kodra (p58)
➡ Otium (p59)
➡ Mrizi i Zanave (p59)

Best Places to Stay

➡ Stone City Hostel (p68)
➡ Rose Garden Hotel (p77)
➡ Trip'n'Hostel (p55)
➡ Hotel Mangalemi (p65)
➡ Hotel Rilindja (p79)
➡ B&B Tirana Smile (p57)

Why Go?

Closed to outsiders for much of the 20th century, Albania has long been Mediterranean Europe's enigma. Until fairly recently its rumpled mountains, fortress towns and sparkling beaches were merely a rumour on most travel maps. But, with the end of a particularly brutal strain of communism in 1991, Albania tentatively swung open its gates. The first curious tourists to arrive discovered a land where ancient codes of conduct still held sway and where the wind whistled through the shattered remnants of half-forgotten ancient Greek and Roman sites. A quarter of a century after throwing off the shackles of communism, Albania's stunning mountain scenery, crumbling castles, boisterous capital and dreamy beaches rivalling any in the Mediterranean continue to enchant. But hurry here, because as word gets out about what Albania is hiding, the still-tiny trickle of tourists threatens to become a flood.

When to Go
Tirana

Jun Enjoy the perfect Mediterranean climate and deserted beaches.

Jul–Aug Albania's beaches may be packed, but this is a great time to explore the mountains.

Dec See features and shorts at the Tirana Film Festival, while the intrepid can snowshoe to Theth.

Entering the Country

Albania has good connections in all directions: daily buses go to Kosovo, Montenegro, North Macedonia and Greece. There are no international train routes to/from Albania. The southern seaport of Saranda is a short boat trip from Greece's Corfu; in summer, ferries also connect Himara and Vlora to Corfu. Durrës has regular ferries to Italy.

ITINERARIES

One Week

Spend a day in busy Tirana (p53), checking out the various excellent museums as well as the Blloku bars and cafes. On day two, make the three-hour trip to the Ottoman-era town of Berat (p62). Overnight there before continuing down the coast, for a couple of days on the beach in Himara (p75) or Ksamil (p74). Make sure you leave time for Butrint (p71) before spending your last night in charming Gjirokastra (p67) and returning to Tirana.

Two Weeks

Follow the one-week itinerary and then head north into Albania's incredible Accursed Mountains (p78). Start in Italian-flavoured Shkodra (p76), from where you can get transport to Koman (p80) for the stunning morning ferry ride to Fierzë. Continue that day to the charming mountain village of Valbona (p79) for the night, then trek to Theth (p81) and spend your last couple of nights in the beautiful Theth National Park, before heading back to Tirana.

Essential Food & Drink

Byrek Pastry with cheese or meat.

Fergesë Baked peppers, egg and cheese, and occasionally meat.

Midhje Wild or farmed mussels, often served fried.

Paçë koke Sheep's head soup, usually served for breakfast.

Qofta Flat or cylindrical minced-meat rissoles.

Sufllaqë Doner kebab.

Tavë Meat baked with cheese and egg.

Konjak Local brandy.

Raki Popular spirit made from grapes.

Raki mani Spirit made from mulberries.

ALBANIA

AT A GLANCE

Area 28,748 sq km

Capital Tirana

Country Code ☑ 355

Currency Lek (plural lekë); the euro (€) is widely accepted.

Emergency ☑ 127 (Ambulance); ☑ 128 (Fire); ☑ 129 (Police)

Language Albanian

Population 2.77 million

Time Central European Time (GMT/UTC plus one hour)

Visas Nearly all visitors can travel visa-free to Albania for a period of up to 90 days.

Sleeping Price Ranges

The following price categories are based on the cost of a double room in high season.

€ less than €40

€€ €40–€80

€€€ more than €80

Eating Price Ranges

The following price categories are based on the cost of a main course.

€ less than 500 lekë

€€ 500 lekë to 1200 lekë

€€€ more than 1200 lekë

Resources

Visit Albania (www.albania. al) The official portal of Albania's nascent tourist board.

Tirana Times (www.tirana times.com) Comprehensive Albanian news in English.

Albania Highlights

1 Accursed Mountains (p78) Experiencing some of Albania's best scenery on the wonderful day-trek between the isolated mountain villages of Valbona and Theth.

2 Berat (p62) Exploring this Unesco World Heritage–listed museum town, known as the 'city of a thousand windows'.

3 Albanian Riviera (p70) Catching some sun at just one of the many gorgeous beaches on the Albanian Riviera.

4 Tirana (p53) Feasting your eyes on the wild colour schemes and experiencing Blloku cafe culture in the plucky Albanian capital.

5 Gjirokastra (p67) Taking a trip to this traditional Albanian mountain town, with its spectacular Ottoman-era mansions and impressive hilltop fortress.

6 Butrint (p71) Searching for the ghosts of ancient Greece and Rome among the forest-dappled ruins of one of Europe's finest archaeological sites.

TIRANA

04 / POP 557,000

Lively, colourful Tirana is where this tiny nation's hopes and dreams coalesce into a vibrant whirl of traffic, brash consumerism and unfettered fun. Having undergone a transformation of extraordinary proportions since awaking from its communist slumber in the early 1990s, Tirana's centre is now unrecognisable from those grey days, with buildings painted in primary colours, and public squares and pedestrianised streets that are a pleasure to wander.

Trendy Blloku buzzes with the well-heeled and flush hanging out in bars and cafes, while the city's grand boulevards are lined with fascinating relics of its Ottoman, Italian and communist past – from delicate minarets to loud socialist murals. Add to this some excellent museums and you have a compelling list of reasons to visit. With the traffic doing daily battle with both itself and pedestrians, the city is loud, crazy, colourful and dusty, but Tirana is never dull.

◉ Sights

The centre of Tirana is Sheshi Skënderbej (Skanderbeg Sq), a large traffic island with an equestrian statue of the eponymous Albanian national hero at its centre. Running through the square is Tirana's main avenue, Blvd Zogu I, which south of the square becomes Blvd Dëshmorët e Kombit (Martyrs of the Nation Blvd). Most of the city's sights are within walking distance of the square, though Tirana itself is now one huge urban sprawl.

★ Bunk'Art   MUSEUM
(067 207 2905; www.bunkart.al; Rr Fadil Deliu; 500 lekë; 9am-4pm Wed-Sun) This fantastic conversion – from a massive Cold War bunker on the outskirts of Tirana into a history and contemporary art museum – is Albania's most exciting new sight and easily a Tirana highlight. With almost 3000 sq metres of space underground spread over several floors, the bunker was built for Albania's political elite in the 1970s and remained a secret for much of its existence. Now it hosts exhibits that combine the modern history of Albania with pieces of contemporary art.

Just arriving at the bunker is quite an exciting experience, as you go through a long, dark tunnel in the hillside that leads you to the entrance on the side of a still-active Albanian military base. Once you're inside the bunker itself, you can wander through the furnished rooms intended for the communist elite as they faced the invasion that so terrified them. Elsewhere you'll find a very detailed history of modern Albania, beginning with the 1939 Italian invasion and ending with the overthrow of communism. The display arguably brushes over the true horrors of Hoxha's Stalinist regime, while at least recognising them, are some fascinating documents and photographs, including a video of Enver Hoxha's 1985 state funeral. Other highlights include the enormous Assembly Hall, the main social centre of the bunker, as well as the private chambers of other senior officials.

To get here from the centre of Tirana, take a bus bound for Linza from outside the **Palace of Culture** (Pallate Kulturës; Map p56; Sheshi Skënderbej) on Sheshi Skënderbej, and ask the driver to let you out at Bunk'Art. It's located very close to the **Dajti Express** (067 208 4471; www.dajtiekspres.com; Rr Dibrës; one-way/return 500/800 lekë; 9am-10pm Jul-Aug, to 9pm May-Jun & Sep-Oct, to 7pm Nov-Apr), so it makes sense to combine the two within one outing.

★ National History Museum   MUSEUM
(Muzeu Historik Kombëtar; Map p56; www.mhk.gov.al; Sheshi Skënderbej; 200 lekë; 9am-7pm) The largest museum in Albania holds many of the country's archaeological treasures and a replica of Skanderbeg's massive sword (how he held it, rode his horse and fought at the same time is a mystery). The lighting might be poor, but fortunately the excellent collection is almost entirely signed in English and takes you chronologically from ancient Illyria to the postcommunist era. The collection of statues, mosaics and columns from ancient Greek and Roman times is breathtaking.

A disturbing and very important gallery devoted to those who suffered persecution under the communist regime is the most recent addition to the collection, though frustratingly, almost none of this display is in English. Another highlight is a terrific exhibition of icons by Onufri, a renowned 16th-century Albanian master of colour. The modernist mosaic adorning the museum's facade is entitled *Albania* and shows Albanians victorious and proud from Illyrian times through to WWII, with some unsurprisingly communist overtones.

★ **National Gallery of Arts** GALLERY
(GaleriaKombëtareeArteve; Map p56; ☑ 042233975; www.galeriakombetare.gov.al/en/home/index. shtml; Blvd Dëshmorët e Kombit; adult/student 200/60 lekë; ☺9am-7pm) Tracing the relatively brief history of Albanian painting from the early 19th century to the present day, this beautiful space also holds temporary exhibitions. The interesting collection includes 19th-century paintings depicting scenes from daily Albanian life and others with a far more political dimension, including some truly fabulous examples of Albanian socialist realism.

The ground-floor part of the gallery is given over to temporary exhibitions of a far more modern and challenging kind.

Don't miss the small collection of communist statues in storage behind the building, including two rarely seen statues of Uncle Joe Stalin himself. Immediately in front of the gallery is a huge spider-web-like sculpture that local children have commandeered as a climbing frame.

Bunk'Art 2 MUSEUM
(Map p56; ☑ 067 207 2905; www.bunkart.al; Rr Sermedin Toptani; 500 lekë; ☺9am-9pm) The little cousin to the main Bunk'Art (p53), this museum, which is within a communist-era bunker and underground tunnel system below the Ministry of Internal Affairs, focuses on the role of the police and security services in Albania through the turbulent 20th century. While this might not sound especially interesting, the whole thing has been very well put together and makes for a fascinating journey behind police lines.

Be warned that some of the exhibits are dark and deeply disturbing and are not suitable for children (signs have been put up indicating which rooms are not suitable for children).

House of Leaves MUSEUM
(Map p56; ☑ 04 222 2612; www.muzeugjethi.gov. al; Rr Ibrahim Rugova; 700 lekë; ☺9am-7pm May–mid-Oct, 10am-5pm Tue-Sat, 9am-2pm Sun mid-Oct–Apr) This grand old 1930s building started life as Albania's first maternity hospital, but within a few years the focus turned from creating new life to ending lives, as the hospital was converted to an interrogation and surveillance centre (read: torture house). It remained as such until the fall of the communist regime. Today the House of Leaves is a museum dedicated to surveillance and interrogation in Albania.

There are numerous fascinating surveillance items and quite a few graphic displays about what happened to those considered enemies of the regime. Some exhibits are not suitable for children.

Mt Dajti National Park NATIONAL PARK
Just 25km east of Tirana is Mt Dajti National Park. It is the most accessible mountain in the country, and many locals go there to escape the city rush and have a spit-roast lamb lunch. A sky-high, Austrian-made cable car, Dajti Express (p53), takes 15 minutes to make the scenic trip (almost) to the top (1611m).

The area surrounding the upper cable-car station is a bit anticlimactic. There are some 'family-friendly' activities such as shooting things with toy machine guns and hitting things with swords, or you can ride about a patch of rubbish-strewn wasteland on a pony. Get past this lot and some abandoned buildings haunted by stray dogs, and things improve immeasurably. The mountainside is covered in lovely, shady beech and pine forests and a number of walking trails wend up and down the mountain. There are some very hit-and-miss trail markings, so it's wise to try and find a guide. Many of the hostels in town can arrange a day's hiking or mountainbiking up here.

If you just want to enjoy the view, there are grassy picnic spots just beyond the upper cable-car station, or try the lamb roast and spectacular views from the wide terrace of the cable-car station restaurant.

To get to the Dajti Express departure point, take the public bus from outside Tirana's **clock tower** (Kulla e Sahatit; Map p56; Rr Luigj Gurakuqi; 200 lekë; ☺9am-4pm Mon-Fri, to 2pm Sat) to Porcelan (40 lekë). From here, it's a 1.5km walk uphill, or you can wait for a free bus transfer (departures every 30 minutes, five minutes). Taxis seem to charge what they want to the Dajti Express drop-off point, but the trip from Tirana should only cost 600 lekë. It's also possible to drive or cycle to the top.

National Archaeological Museum MUSEUM
(Muzeu Arkeologjik Nacional; Map p56; Sheshi Nënë Tereza; 300 lekë; ☺10am-2.30pm Mon-Fri) The collection here is comprehensive and impressive in parts, but there's only minimal labelling in Albanian and none at all in English (nor are tours in English offered), so you may find yourself a little at a loss unless

this is your field. A total renovation is on the cards, but as one staff member pointed out to us, they've been waiting for that since 1985 – so don't hold your breath.

Sheshi Skënderbej
SQUARE

(Skanderbeg Sq; Map p56) Sheshi Skënderbej is the best place to start witnessing Tirana's daily goings-on. Until it was pulled down by an angry mob in 1991, a 10m-high bronze statue of Enver Hoxha stood here, watching over a mainly car-free square. Now only the equestrian statue of Skanderbeg remains, and the 'square' – once Tirana's most popular meeting point in the decades where 99% of people were forced to get around on foot – is now a huge traffic roundabout.

Early evening is a particularly nice time to come here. Buskers strum a few tunes and vendors sell popcorn and balloons as the locals stroll and chat.

Et'hem Bey Mosque
MOSQUE

(Map p56; Sheshi Skënderbej) To one side of Sheshi Skënderbej, the 1789–1823 Et'hem Bey Mosque was spared destruction during the atheism campaign of the late 1960s because of its status as a cultural monument. Small and elegant, it's one of the oldest buildings left in the city. At the time of research the mosque was closed to the public for major renovations.

☞ Tours

Tirana Free Tour
TOURS

(Map p56; ☐ 069 631 5858; www.tiranafreetour. com) This enterprising tour agency has made its name by offering a free daily tour of Tirana that leaves at 10am year-round. In July, August and September a second tour is offered at 3pm. Tours meet outside the Opera House on Sheshi Skënderbej (look on the website for a photo indicating the exact meeting spot). Tips are appreciated if you enjoy the two-hour tour, and further (paid) tours are available.

Outdoor Albania
TOURS

(Map p56; ☐ 04 222 7121; www.outdooralbania. com; Rr Gjin Bue Shpata 9/1; ⊙9am-5pm) This excellent, trailblazing adventure-tour agency offers hiking, rafting, snowshoeing, sea and white-water kayaking and, in summer, hikes through the Albanian Alps. It's been offering activity-based holidays for 25 years, and is definitely an expert in the field.

Albania Holidays
TOURS

(Map p56; ☐ 04 223 5688; www.albania-holidays. com; Rr Sami Frashëri 30, Blloku; ⊙8am-6pm Mon-Fri, to 4pm Sat) Experienced operator specialising in multiday tours around Albania, including tailor-made trips.

✻ Festivals & Events

Tirana International Film Festival
FILM

(www.tiranafilmfest.com; ⊙Nov) This festival is held early each November and features both short and feature films from its international competition winners, as well as new cinematic work from Albanian film-makers.

🛏 Sleeping

★ Trip'n'Hostel
HOSTEL €

(Map p56; ☐ 068 304 8905; www.tripnhostel.com; Rr Musa Maci 1; dm/d from €10/30; ☎) Tirana's coolest hostel is on a small side street, housed in a design-conscious self-contained house with a leafy garden out the back, a bar

---

BUNKER LOVE

On the hillsides, beaches and generally most surfaces in Albania, you will notice small concrete domes (often in groups of three) with rectangular slits. Meet the bunkers: Enver Hoxha's concrete legacy, built from 1950 to 1985. Weighing in at 5 tonnes of concrete and iron, these little mushrooms are almost impossible to destroy. They were built to repel an invasion and can resist full tank assault – a fact proved by their chief engineer, who vouched for his creation's strength by standing inside one while it was bombarded by a tank. The shell-shocked engineer emerged unscathed, and tens of thousands were built. Today some are creatively painted, one houses a tattoo artist, and some even accommodate makeshift hostels.

Two enormous bunkers, the scale of which do not compare to these tiny sniper installations, can be found in Tirana and Gjirokastra. In Tirana, Bunk'Art (p53) is the city's most fascinating site, a history museum housed inside a vast government bunker. In Gjirokastra the Cold War Tunnel (p68), in fact a similarly massive government bunker, can also be visited, though minus the history museum and art display.

Tirana

lined with old records, a kitchen and a cellar-like chill-out lounge downstairs. Dorms have handmade fixtures, curtains between beds for privacy and private lockable drawers, while there's also a roof terrace strewn with hammocks.

★ **Tirana Backpacker Hostel** HOSTEL €
(Map p56; ☑ 068 468 2353, 068 313 3451; www.tiranahostel.com; Rr Bogdani 3; dm from €8, d €27; ❄️@🛜) Albania's first-ever hostel continues to go from strength to strength. Housed in a charmingly decorated house, with a 1970s air of hazy hippy backpacker days, this superfriendly place has a funky design and an

excellent location. There's always a big crew of globally wandering backpackers staying.

You'll find a large kitchen downstairs, bathrooms on each floor and air-con in two dorms. Bike hire is available for €5 per day, and there's a great bar (and a paddling pool) in the garden. The kitchen also cooks up simple all-veg dinners (250 lekë) served communal-style.

Milingona Hostel HOSTEL €
(Map p56; ☑ 069 204 9836, 069 610 2875; www.milingonahostel.com; Rr Vehbi Agolli 5; dm €9-12, d €35; @🛜) This superchilled villa in a side street in the middle of Tirana's old town is

Tirana

◎ **Top Sights**
1 National Gallery of Arts C3
2 National History Museum B2

◎ **Sights**
3 Bunk'Art 2 ....C3
4 Clock Tower C2
5 Equestrian Statue of Skanderbeg........B2
6 Et'hem Bey Mosque...............................C2
7 House of Leaves.....................................B3
8 National Archaeological Museum........C5
9 Palace of Culture...................................C2
10 Sheshi Skënderbej.................................B2

◎ **Activities, Courses & Tours**
11 Albania Holidays.....................................A4
12 Outdoor Albania.....................................A4
13 Tirana Free Tour.....................................C2

◎ **Sleeping**
14 B&B Tirana Smile....................................A2
15 Green House..C4
16 Hotel Gloria..C2
17 Milingona Hostel....................................D2
18 Rogner Hotel Tirana...............................C4
19 Sar'Otel...C2
20 Tirana Backpacker Hostel.....................A2

21 Trip'n'Hostel...D1

◎ **Eating**
22 Boutique de l'Artiste..............................C4
23 Era..B4
Green House..(see 15)
24 Juvenilja...A4
25 King House...B5
26 Met Kodra..D2
27 Otium...A4
Sambal..(see 26)

◎ **Drinking & Nightlife**
28 BUFE..B3
29 Bunker 1944..A4
30 Komiteti Kafe Muzeum...........................C4
31 Radio..B4
32 The Tea Room...B3

◎ **Entertainment**
33 Kinema Millennium 2..............................C3
34 Metropol Theatre....................................B2

◎ **Shopping**
35 Adrion International Bookshop.............C2
36 New Market D2

a friendly place with five- and six-person dorms, though the basement's 12-bed dorm is the coolest spot in summer. There's a communal kitchen, plus an outside bar with hammocks slung between citrus trees and lots of space for socialising.

Extras include free yoga in summer and lockable individual boxes under each bed. It can be a little hard to find but is quite well-known in the neighbourhood, if you need someone to point it out.

★ **B&B Tirana Smile** HOTEL €€
(Map p56; ☑068 406 1507, 068 406 1561; www.bbtiranasmile.com; Rr Bogdani; d incl breakfast €42; ❀☞) The owners could not have picked a better name for this inspirational hotel. The eight rooms are bright, modern, colourful and all have light summery touches. Each has a big workspace and good beds (though bathrooms are small). The best part is the communal lounge with sofas, books and a large table where a breakfast of homemade products is served. There's an in-house travel agency that can help with visits to other parts of Albania.

Hotel Gloria BOUTIQUE HOTEL €€
(Map p56; ☑04 222 0036; www.hotelboutique gloria.al; Rr Qemal Stafa 5; s/d/ste €50/70/90; ❀☞) A snug six-room hotel rich with royal flushes and an old-fashioned sense of style.

The beds have plumped-up pillows and the bathrooms are decent. Downstairs there's a twee dining room with an open fireplace for those frigid winter nights. There's also a rooftop restaurant with all-glass walls giving memorable city views. Advance bookings are essential.

Sar'Otel BOUTIQUE HOTEL €€
(Map p56; ☑04 453 3000; www.sarotel.com; Rr Kostandin Kristoforidhi 89; d incl breakfast from €60; ❁❀☞) Bordering on being a boutique offering, this central 19-room hotel has comfortable rooms with polished wood floors and bunches of flowers adding an injection of colour. There's a convivial covered patio cafe (open to all), a small indoor pool and a full range of spa facilities.

Green House BOUTIQUE HOTEL €€
(Map p56; ☑069 205 7599; www.greenhouse.al; Rr Jul Variboba 6; d incl breakfast €60; ❁❀☞) You've got a fantastic location at this 10-room hotel with downlit, stylish rooms that might be some of the city's coolest. Some have balconies, all have low-slung beds, shagpile carpets, minibars and sleek furnishings. Downstairs is a large terrace restaurant where guests take breakfast each morning, and the whole place looks up at one of Tirana's more quirkily decorated buildings.

Rogner Hotel Tirana HOTEL €€€
(Map p56; ☑ 04 223 5035; www.hotel-europapark.com; Blvd Dëshmorët e Kombit; s/d/ste incl breakfast from €72/92/167; ❄️@🛜🏊) With an unbeatable location in the heart of the city, the Rogner feels more like a private club than a hotel. Its huge garden contains a great pool and tennis court, and it is home away from home for Tirana-posted diplomats. The rooms are spacious, extremely comfortable and come with flat-screen TVs.

✕ Eating

Most of Tirana's best eating is in and around Blloku, a square of some 10 blocks of shops, restaurants, cafes and hotels situated west of Blvd Dëshmorët e Kombit, but there are other options elsewhere. Particularly good kebabs can be found on Rr e Kavajës. The area known as the New Market (Pazari i ri), where Rr Luigj Gurakuqi runs into Sheshi Avni Rustemi, has a growing number of good traditional restaurants.

★**Met Kodra** ALBANIAN €
(Map p56; Sheshi Avni Rustemi; qofta 100 lekë; ⊙6am-9.30pm Sun-Thu, to midnight Fri & Sat) One of the great classics of Tirana dining. This tiny place which consists of nothing but a small smoky grill, does one thing and one thing only – qofta (rissoles) – and the same woman and her family have been making them to exactly the same recipe since 1957. Grab a hunk of bread, a handful of olives and some goats cheese from the market opposite and you have a perfect take-away meal.

Sambal ASIAN €
(Map p56; ☑ 068 205 6933; Sheshi Avni Rustemi; mains 300-400 lekë; ⊙8am-midnight) This beach-shack-like place on the edge of the New Market square looks decidedly out of place, but then the food it serves is also utterly different to anything else you might find in Tirana. Created by an Albanian chef who learnt his trade in Bali, Sambal serves classic Southeast Asian dishes such as nasi goreng and bakso (meatball soup). It's not exactly authentic, but it's a light and delicious change from the often-heavy Albanian food.

King House ALBANIAN €
(Map p56; ☑ 067 223 3335; www.king-house.net; Rr Ibrahim Rugova 12; mains 300-800 lekë; ⊙8am-11pm) Enough Albanian traditional artefacts to shame an ethnographic museum bedeck the walls of this charming Blloku place. There's an excellent selection of traditional Albanian cooking – try the delicious Korça meatballs – as well as Italian pasta and pizza, and prices are low. Try the terrace dining area if the interior is a little too much for you.

★**Era** ALBANIAN, ITALIAN €€
(Map p56; ☑ 04 224 3845; www.era.al; Rr Ismail Qemali; mains 400-900 lekë; ⊙11am-midnight; 🖥️) This local institution serves traditional Albanian and Italian fare in the heart of Blloku. The inventive menu includes oven-baked veal and eggs, stuffed aubergine, pizza, and pilau with chicken and pine nuts. Be warned: it's sometimes quite hard to get a seat, as it's fearsomely popular, so you may have to wait.

Mullixhiu ALBANIAN €€
(☑ 069 666 0444; www.mullixhiu.al; Lazgush Poradeci St; mains 800-1200 lekë; ⊙noon-4pm & 6-10.30pm; 🛜🖥️) Around the corner from the chic cafes of the Blloku neighbourhood, chef Bledar Kola's Albanian food metamorphosis is hidden behind a row of grain mills and a wall of corn husks. The restaurant is one of the pioneers of Albania's slow-food movement and it's also a place of culinary theatre, with dishes served in treasure chests or atop teapots.

Boutique de l'Artiste MEDITERRANEAN €€
(Map p56; Rr Ismail Qemali 12; mains 600-1000 lekë; ⊙noon-midnight Mon-Fri, from 9am Sat & Sun; 🛜) Despite its rather pretentious name, this place is all understatement, with a restrained decor and passionate staff who effortlessly translate the daily specials from a giant blackboard into English for guests. There's also a full à la carte menu, taking in various aspects of Mediterranean cooking, with a strong Italian flavour. Brunch is popular here, as is the in-house patisserie.

It's designed to look like a deli, with an open-plan, glass-fronted kitchen.

Green House ITALIAN €€
(Map p56; ☑ 069 205 7599; www.greenhouse.al; Rr Jul Variboba 6; mains 700-1200 lekë) Downstairs from the small eponymous hotel, the Green House boasts an enviable terrace and a classy atmosphere that hums with the buzz of the local Blloku crowds day and night. The menu is strongly Italian- and French-leaning, with homemade pastas and confit de canard, but there are Albanian and other international dishes, too.

Juvenilja ALBANIAN €€
(Map p56; ☑04 227 2222; www.juvenilja.com; Rr Sami Frashëri; mains 200-950 lekë; ⊙10am-11.30pm; 🛜) This fairly unassuming Blloku establishment actually has a range of excellent traditional Albanian dishes on the menu, including veal escalope with wine and lemon, and piglet ribs with broad beans. The seafood is also worthy of mention. There's an English menu and super-helpful, liveried staff.

★**Otium** FRENCH €€€
(Map p56; ☑04 222 3570; Rr Brigada e VIII; mains 1000-1500 lekë; ⊙noon-11pm Mon-Sat, to 6pm Sun) With its lace window-curtains and tubs of flowering plants, this might look like a simple French *bistrot* and indeed, the food leans heavily on Gallic cuisine. But a meal here reveals a refined operation, as attentive waiters talk you through the daily menu of artfully executed seasonal dishes, typically including seafood options and some fabulous starters.

There's also one of the best wine cellars in Tirana, with a wide selection of French, Italian and some good Albanian bottles. Limited tables: it's wise to book ahead.

★**Uka Farm** ALBANIAN €€€
(☑067 203 9909; Rr Adem Jashari, Laknas; mains 900-2500 lekë; ⊙9am-10pm Mon-Thu & Sun, to 11pm Fri & Sat) Uka Farm was founded in 1996 by former Minister of Agriculture Rexhep Uka, who started organic cultivation of agricultural products on a small plot of land. His son Flori, a trained winemaker and standout amateur chef, is now the driving force behind the restaurant. Guests can enjoy fresh, flavourful vegetables and locally sourced cheese, meat and quality homemade wine.

It's on the road out to the airport and a taxi will cost around 2000 lekë. It's essential to book ahead.

🍷 Drinking & Entertainment

Tirana runs on caffeine during the day then switches over to alcohol after nightfall. Popular places to get both are concentrated in the Blloku neighbourhood, and indeed several streets are almost nothing but bars and cafes, and become jam-packed at night. Nightlife in Tirana goes late, particularly in the summer months when the beautiful people are out until dawn.

DON'T MISS

SLOW FOOD

Albania has a growing 'slow food' scene where chefs use organic local produce to reinvent classic local dishes. Set on a sprawling farm in a remote village of the lush Lezhë District, 65km north of Tirana, the **Mrizi i Zanave** (☑069 210 8032; www.mrizizanave.com/mrizi; Rr Lezhë-Vau i Dejës, Fishtë; mains 600-2000 lekë; ⊙from 8pm by reservation; 🛜 🚗) restaurant is owned by Altin and Anton Prenga, the pioneers of Albania's slow-food movement. The restaurant is credited with taking Albanian food back to basics: fresh, organic farm-to-table produce and meat that celebrates the country's fertile terrain.

★**Komiteti Kafe Muzeum** BAR
(Map p56; ☑069 262 5514; Rr Fatmir Haxhiu; raki around 200 lekë; ⊙8am-midnight; 🛜) Styled as a cafe-museum, this little bohemian place looks like a flea market. Every spare centimetre is crammed with communist-era relics, farming implements (those pitchforks hanging from the bar are probably a warning), Japanese fans, old clocks and so on. It's certainly a memorable spot for a coffee or one of 25 varieties of *raki*, the local fruit-based spirit.

★**Radio** BAR
(Map p56; Rr Ismail Qemali 29/1; ⊙10am-midnight; 🛜) Named for the owner's collection of antique Albanian radios, Radio is an eclectic dream with decor that includes vintage Albanian film posters, deep-1950s lamp shades and even a collection of communist-era propaganda books to read at the bar over a cocktail. It attracts a young, intellectual and alternative crowd.

It's set back from the street, but is well worth finding in otherwise rather mainstream Blloku.

The Tea Room CAFE
(Map p56; Blvd Gjergj Fishta; teas from 120 lekë; ⊙7am-11pm) Styled like an old English-village teashop, this little place serves a dozen bio teas, although we're pretty certain that the mango and yoghurt tea isn't a standard of English-village teashops. More familiar to the tea-drinking establishment would be the range of black and green teas and the dainty homemade cakes and cheesecake.

BUFE
WINE BAR

(Map p56; ☑04 224 7353; Rr Reshit Çollaku; ⊙10am-midnight; 🛜) Tirana's best-loved wine bar is in a countrified red-brick building, its walls lined with dozens and dozens of bottles of wine (including some reasonable local bottles). The stereo is normally playing a bluesy soundtrack.

Bunker 1944
BAR

(Map p56; ☑067 600 6660; Rr Andon Zako Çajupi; ⊙6pm-1am Sun-Thu, to 2am Fri & Sat) This former bunker is now a bohemian bolthole amid a sea of fairly predictable Blloku bars. Inside it's stuffed full of communist-era furniture and antiques/junk including homemade paintings, old vinyl, clocks and radios. There's a great selection of beers available, including IPA, London Porter and London Pride, and a friendly international crowd.

Metropol Theatre
ARTS CENTRE

(Map p56; ☑067 227 0668; www.teatrimetropol. al; Rr Ded Gjo Luli; tickets from 500 lekë) Tirana's centre for alternative theatre and arts puts on a different theatrical performance each month. Some of these are reworked versions of Shakespeare classics, others are challenging modern tales, and some are tailored exclusively to children. Although performances are in Albanian, it's worth going to a show just for the atmosphere.

Kinema Millennium 2
CINEMA

(Map p56; ☑069 785 6678; www.kinemamillenni um.com; Rr Murat Toptani; tickets 300-600 lekë) Current-release movies, the earlier you go in the day, the cheaper your tickets.

🛍 Shopping

Adrion International
Bookshop
BOOKS

(Map p56; ☑04 225 7231; Palace of Culture, Sheshi Skënderbej; ⊙8am-9.30pm) Right in the heart of the city, this long-established bookshop has an excellent selection of books on Albania (including many in English) you're unlikely to find elsewhere, as well as good maps and guidebooks to the region. There's also a large selection of English-language novels and nonfiction titles, postcards and souvenirs.

New Market
MARKET

(Pazari i ri; Map p56; Sheshi Avni Rustemi; ⊙dawn-1am) Come here to witness Tirana's ebullient street life. Every day from dawn, traders come here to hawk fruit, vegetables, meat and fish, and whether you're actually looking to buy anything yourself or not, it's a wonderful place to stroll and soak up the atmosphere.

Recently given a massive facelift, the market is known as the New Market but is actually one of the oldest parts of the city. Some superb cheap restaurants ring the main market.

ℹ Information

MONEY
Tirana has plenty of ATMs, all of which can be used to withdraw money from foreign debit and credit cards.

POST
Post Office (Map p56; Rr Çameria; ⊙8am-8pm) A shiny and clean oasis in a street jutting west from Sheshi Skënderbej. Smaller offices operate around the city.

TOURIST INFORMATION
Tirana Tourist Information Centre (Map p56; ☑04 222 3313; www.tirana.gov.al; Rr Ded Gjo Luli; ⊙8am-4pm Mon-Fri) Friendly English-speaking staff make getting information easy at this government-run initiative just off Sheshi Skënderbej. Oddly, it's only open on weekdays.
Tourist Information Point (Map p56; www. tirana.gov.al; Sheshi Skënderbej; ⊙8am-4pm Mon-Fri) A sub-office of the main tourist information office and like that office, it's unhelpfully closed at weekends.

ℹ Getting There & Away

AIR
The modern **Nënë Tereza International Airport** (Mother Teresa Airport; ☑04 238 1800; www.tirana-airport.com; Rinas) is at Rinas, 17km northwest of Tirana. The Rinas Express airport bus operates an on-the-hour (6am to 6pm) service, with departures from the corner of Rr Mine Peza and Rr e Durrësit (a few blocks from the National History Museum) for 250 lekë one way. The going taxi rate is 2000 to 2500 lekë. The airport is about 20 minutes' drive away, but plan for possible traffic jams and give yourself plenty of time to get there if you're catching a flight.

BUS
There is no one official bus station in Tirana. Instead, there are a number of bus stations around the city from which buses to specific destinations leave. Do check locally for the latest departure points, as they have been known to change. You can almost guarantee that taxi drivers will be in the know; however,

you may have to dissuade them from taking you the whole way to your destination.

International services depart from the aptly named **International Bus Station** (off Rr Durresit). There are multiple services to Skopje (€13 to €20, eight hours) and Ohrid (€17.50, four hours) in North Macedonia and Pristina (via Prizren) in Kosovo (€10, four hours), and services to Budva, Kotor and Podgorica in Montenegro (€20 to €25, four hours). At the time of writing there was no direct bus to Ulcinj from Tirana, so your best bet is to change buses in Shkodra. Other international destinations include Istanbul, Dubrovnik, Sofia, Thessaloniki and Athens. It's best to double-check all international services locally, as routes and timings change with great frequency.

Furgon (shared minibus) to Bajram Curri (1000 lekë, 5½ hours, hourly 5am to 2pm), the jumping-off point for Valbona or the far side of Lake Koman, leave from **North Station** on Rr Dritan Hoxha, a short distance from the Zogu i Zi roundabout. Note that this service passes through Kosovo. Services to Shkodra (300 lekë, two hours, hourly until 5pm) also leave from here.

Departures to the south leave from – yes, you guessed it – **South Station** on Rr Muhedin Llagani. These include services to Berat (400 lekë, 2½ to three hours, every 30 minutes until 6pm), Himara (1000 lekë, five hours, 1pm and 6pm), Saranda (1300 lekë, seven hours, roughly hourly 5am to midday) and Gjirokastra (1000 lekë, five to six hours, regular departures until midday, also at 2.30pm and 6.30pm). Services to Himara and Saranda will drop you off at any of the coastal villages along the way. Services to Durrës (150 lekë, one hour, every 30 minutes) also leave from here.

For destinations to the southeast, head to, wait for it, **Southeast Station**. Several buses a day go to Pogradec (500 lekë; 3½ hours) and Korca (500 lekë; four hours).

DESTINATION	PRICE (LEKË)	DURATION (HR)	DISTANCE (KM)
Berat	400	2½-3	122
Durrës	150	1	38
Elbasan	150	1½	54
Fier	600	2	113
Gjirokastra	1000	5-6	232
Korça	500	4	181
Kruja	150	½	32
Pogradec	500	3½	150
Saranda	1300	7	284
Shkodra	300	2	116
Vlora	500	4	147

❶ Getting Around

There's now a good network of city buses running around Tirana costing 40 lekë per journey (payable to the conductor), although most of the sights can be covered easily on foot.

TAXI

Taxi stands dot the city, and taxis charge from 300 to 400 lekë for a ride within Tirana, and from 500 to 600 lekë at night and to destinations outside the city centre. Reach an agreement on the fare with the driver before setting off; while drivers are supposed to use meters, they almost never do. **Speed Taxi** (☑ 04 222 2555; www. speedtaxi.al), with 24-hour service, is reliable.

CENTRAL ALBANIA

Kruja

☑ 0511 / POP 20,400

Kruja is Skanderbeg's town. Yes, Albania's national hero was born here, and although it was over 500 years ago, there's still a great deal of pride in the fact that he and his forces defended Kruja from the Ottomans until his death. As soon as you get off the *furgon* (shared minibus), you're face to knee with a statue of Skanderbeg wielding his mighty sword with one hand, and the whole town just gets more Skanderdelic after that.

From the road below, Kruja's houses appear to sit in the lap of a mountain. An ancient castle juts out to one side, and the massive Skanderbeg Museum juts out of the castle itself. The local plaster industry is going strong so expect visibility-reducing plumes of smoke to cloud views of the Adriatic Sea. Kruja's sights can be covered in an hour or two, making this a great stop en route to elsewhere.

National Ethnographic Museum MUSEUM (☑ 0511 24 485; Kalaja; 300 lekë; ⊙ 9am-7pm daily May-Sep, to 4pm Tue-Sun Oct-Apr) This traditional home in the castle complex below the Skanderbeg Museum houses one of the best ethnographic museums in the country. Set in an original 19th-century Ottoman house that belonged to the affluent Toptani family, the museum shows the level of luxury and self-sufficiency the household maintained by producing its own food, drink, leather and weapons. They even had their very own mini *hammam* (Turkish bath) and watermill. The walls are lined with original frescoes from 1764.

Skanderbeg Museum
MUSEUM

(☑ 0511 22 225; Kalaja; 200 lekë; ⊙ 9am-2pm & 4-7pm Mon-Sat, 9am-7pm Sun May-Sep, 9am-1pm & 3-6pm Tue-Sun Oct-Apr) Designed by Enver Hoxha's daughter and son-in-law, this museum, inside the castle complex, opened in 1982. Its spacious seven-level interior displays replicas of armour and paintings depicting Skanderbeg's struggle against the Ottomans. The museum is something of a secular shrine, and takes itself very seriously indeed, with giant statues and dramatic battle murals.

Most of the information panels are displayed in Albanian, which can make it hard to follow for non-Albanian speakers.

Bazaar
MARKET

(⊙ 7am-7pm) This Ottoman-style bazaar was restored in 2015 and now looks better than ever. It's also one of the country's best places for souvenir shopping and has antique gems and quality traditional wares, including beautifully embroidered tablecloths, copper coffee pots and plates, although there is a growing amount of tourist tat as well.

The bazaar stretches through a tangle of streets, but a good place to start exploring is along Pazari Vjeter.

Restaurant Panorama
INTERNATIONAL €€

(☑ 0511 23 092; www.hotelpanoramakruje.com; Panorama Hotel, Rr Kala 1501; mains 500-700 lekë; ⊙ 7am-11pm) The town's best restaurant is well named. As you tuck into your meal, you can admire the stellar views over the city towards the castle. The food is a mix of modern Albanian and international favourites and it's all well presented and prepared. The steak, topped with local cheeses, is a work of culinary art.

The restaurant is within the Hotel Panorama: a building that's eye-catching for all the wrong reasons.

❶ Getting There & Away

Kruja is 30km from Tirana. Make sure your *furgon* from Tirana (100 lekë, one hour) is going to Kruja proper, not just Fushë Kruja, the modern town below. In Tirana, *furgon* depart throughout the day from near the Zogu i Zi Roundabout on Rr Mine Peza.

Berat

☑ 032 / POP 35,000

Berat weaves its own very special magic, and is easily a highlight of visiting Albania. Its most striking feature is the collection of white Ottoman houses climbing up the hill to its castle, earning it the title of 'town of a thousand windows' and helping it join Gjirokastra on the list of Unesco World Heritage sites, in 2008. Its rugged mountain setting is particularly evocative when the clouds swirl around the tops of the minarets, or break up to show the icy peak of Mt Tomorri. Despite now being a big centre for tourism in Albania, Berat has managed to retain its easygoing charm and friendly atmosphere.

◉ Sights & Activities

The old quarters are lovely ensembles of whitewashed walls, tiled roofs and cobblestone roads. Surrounding the town, olive and cherry trees decorate the gentler slopes, while pine woods stand on the steeper inclines. The modern town is dominated by the incongruously modern dome of Berat University, while elsewhere the bridges over the Osumi River to the charmingly unchanged Gorica quarter include a delightful 1780 seven-arched stone footbridge.

★ Kalaja
FORTRESS

(Map p63; Kalaja; 100 lekë; ⊙ 24hr, ticket booth 9am-6pm) Hidden behind the crumbling walls of the fortress that crowns the hill above Berat is the whitewashed, village-like neighbourhood of Kala; if you walk around the quiet cobbled streets of this ancient neighbourhood for long enough you'll invariably stumble into someone's courtyard, thinking it's a church or ruin (no one seems to mind, though).

In spring and summer the fragrance of chamomile is in the air (and underfoot), and wildflowers burst from every gap between the stones, giving the entire place a magical feel.

The highest point is occupied by the Inner Fortress, where ruined stairs lead to a Tolkienesque water reservoir. Views are spectacular in all directions. It's a steep 10 to 15-minute walk up the hill from the centre of town. For an even more impressive view, continue on right to the far southern end of the complex (the total opposite end from the main entrance) and you'll get to a viewpoint from where you can peer down onto the town far below. In summer, men sell fresh fruit from a stall here.

The Kala quarter's biggest church, **Church of the Dormition of St Mary** (Kisha Fjetja e Shën Mërisë), is the site of the Onufri Museum (p64). Ask at the Onufri

Berat

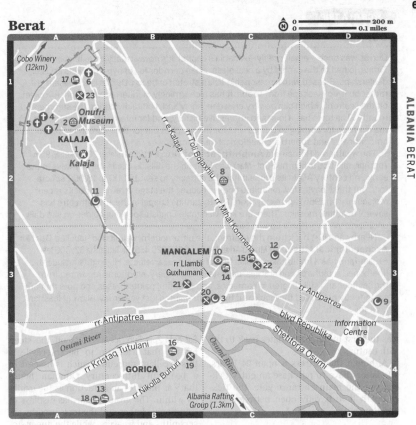

Berat

◎ Top Sights
1 Kalaja A2
2 Onufri Museum A1

◎ Sights
3 Bachelors' Mosque C3
4 Chapel of St Mary Blachernae........... A1
5 Chapel of St Nicholas A1
6 Church of St Theodore A1
7 Church of the Holy Trinity A1
8 Ethnographic Museum C2
9 Lead Mosque D3
10 Mangalem Quarter C3
11 Red Mosque A2
12 Sultan's Mosque C3

🛏 Sleeping
13 Berat Backpackers A4
14 Hotel Belgrad Mangalem C3
15 Hotel Mangalemi C3
16 Hotel Muzaka B4
17 Hotel Restaurant Klea A1
18 Lorenc Guesthouse & Hostel A4

🍴 Eating
19 Antigone... B4
20 Heaven's Kitchen C3
21 Lili Homemade Food B3
22 Mangalemi Restaurant...................... C3
23 Onufri... A1

Museum if you can see the other churches and tiny chapels in Kala (which are otherwise normally kept locked), including **St Theodore** (Shën Todher), close to the citadel gates; the substantial and picturesque **Church of the Holy Trinity** (Kisha Shën Triades), below the upper fortress; and the little chapels of **St Mary Blachernae** (Shën Mëri Vllaherna) and **St Nicholas** (Shënkolli). Some of the churches date back to the 13th century. Also keep an eye out for the **Red Mosque**, by the southern Kala walls, which

WORTH A TRIP

DURRËS

Durrës was once – albeit briefly – Albania's capital. It's now virtually an extension of Tirana, joined to the capital by a ceaseless urban corridor full of hypermarkets and car dealerships. Blessed with a reasonable 10km stretch of beach, Durrës is a pleasant – if rather built-up – escape from Tirana. It has a charmingly Mediterranean air once you get off the seafront, which can be very crowded, noisy and a bit tacky during the summer months. The town has a long and impressive history, and for international visitors, the main reason for coming to Durrës isn't for the beaches but for the interesting Roman amphitheatre and superb archaeological museum.

The weathered Roman-era **Amphitheatre of Durrës** (Rr e Kalasë; 200 lekë; ⊘ 9am-7pm Apr–mid-Oct, to 6pm mid-Oct–Mar) was built on the hillside inside the city walls in the early 2nd century AD. In its prime it had the capacity to seat 15,000 to 18,000 spectators, but these days a few inhabited houses occupy the stage, a reminder of its recent rediscovery (in 1966) and excavation. The Byzantine chapel in the amphitheatre has several beautiful mosaics. There are knowledgable English-speaking guides on site daily until 3pm; they work on a tipping basis.

Nearby and just back from the seafront, the ultramodern, well-lit and -labelled **Durrës Archaeological Museum** (Muzeu Arkeologjik; ☑ 052 220 455; Rr Taulantia 32; 300 lekë; ⊘ 9am-7pm) has a breathtaking collection of historical artefacts. Highlights include the fine-boned sculptures and statues, delicate gold jewellery, amphoras recovered from the seafloor and still covered in barnacles, and beautiful painted vases and pots that are so perfectly preserved they look as if they were painted just yesterday. Allow at least an hour for a visit.

was the first in Berat and dates back to the 15th century.

Although the fortress is open 24 hours, all visitors have to purchase an entry ticket from the main entrance gate, the ticket booth here is only open between 9am and 6pm.

★ Onufri Museum   GALLERY
(Map p63; Kalaja; 200 lekë; ⊘ 9am-6pm May–mid-Oct, to 4pm Tue-Sat, to 2pm Sun mid-Oct–Apr) The Onufri Museum is situated in the Kala quarter's biggest church, the **Church of the Dormition of St Mary** (Kisha Fjetja e Shën Mërisë). The church itself dates from 1797 and was built on the foundations of an earlier 10th-century chapel. Today Onufri's spectacular 16th-century religious paintings are displayed along with the church's beautifully gilded 19th-century iconostasis. Don't miss the chapel behind the iconostasis, or its painted cupola, whose frescoes are now faded almost to invisibility.

The church can get horribly busy with tour groups, but if you're lucky and get it to yourself, the play of shadow and light on the iconostasis, and the deep silence of the place, is utterly enchanting.

Ethnographic Museum   MUSEUM
(Map p63; ☑ 032 232 224; www.muzeumet-berat.al; 200 lekë; ⊘ 9am-7.30pm May-Sep, to 4pm Mon-Sat & to 2pm Sun Oct-Apr) Just off the steep hillside that leads up to Berat's castle is this excellent museum, which is housed in a beautiful 18th-century Ottoman house that's as much of an attraction as the exhibits within. The ground floor has displays of traditional clothes and the tools used by silversmiths and weavers, while the upper storey has kitchens, bedrooms and guest rooms decked out in traditional style.

Check out the *mafil,* a kind of mezzanine looking into the lounge where the women of the house could keep an eye on male guests (and see when their cups needed to be filled). There are information sheets in Italian, French and English.

Mangalem Quarter   AREA
(Map p63) Down in the traditionally Muslim Mangalem quarter, there are three grand mosques: the **Sultan's Mosque** (Xhamia e Mbretit; Map p63), the **Lead Mosque** (Xhamia e Plumbit; Map p63; Rr Antipatrea) and the **Bachelors' Mosque** (Xhamia e Beqarëvet; Map p63; Rr Antipatrea). All are worth a visit and each has its own idiosyncratic design and history.

The 16th-century Sultan's Mosque is one of the oldest in Albania. The Helveti *teqe* (a place of worship for those practising the Bektashi branch of Islam) behind the mosque has a beautiful carved ceiling and was specially designed with acoustic holes to improve the quality of sound during meetings. The Helveti, like the Bektashi, are a dervish order, or brotherhood, of Muslim mystics.

The big mosque on the town square is the 16th-century **Lead Mosque**, so named because of the lead coating its sphere-shaped dome. The 19th-century **Bachelors' Mosque** is down by the Osumi River. This mosque was built for unmarried shop assistants and junior craftsmen, and is perched between some fine Ottoman-era shopfronts along the river. At the time of research it was closed for renovations.

Çobo Winery WINE
(☑032 122 088; www.cobowineryonline.com; Ura Vajgurore; 🚗) The Çobo family winery is the best known in Albania, and it's worth checking out – tours of the vineyard and winery are possible with advance reservations. Unusually in-depth, each tour lasts two to four hours depending on the needs of the group.

The winery is 13km northwest of Berat just beyond the village of Ura Vajgurore. Any bus/*furgon* heading to Tirana can drop you off for 100 lekë.

Albania Rafting Group RAFTING
(☑067 200 6623; www.albrafting.com; Hotel Castle Park, Rr Berat–Përmet) 🛶 This pioneering group runs rafting tours for all levels to some stunning gorges around Berat and Përmet. Everyone from children to pensioners is welcome. Rafting starts at €50 per person and hiking tours start from €20 per person per day.

🛏 Sleeping

⭐**Berat Backpackers** HOSTEL €
(Map p63; ☑069 785 4219; www.beratbackpackers.com; 295 Gorica; tents/dm/r with shared bathroom €7/10/25; ⏰Apr–Oct; @🛜) This transformed traditional house in the Gorica quarter is home to one of Albania's friendliest hostels. The vine-clad establishment contains a basement bar and restaurant, an alfresco drinking area and a relaxed atmosphere that money can't buy. There are two airy dorms with original ceilings, and four gorgeous, excellent-value double rooms with antique furnishings. Shaded camping area and cheap laundry also available. All rooms share bathrooms.

⭐**Hotel Mangalemi** HISTORIC HOTEL €
(Map p63; ☑068 232 3238; www.mangalemihotel.com; Rr Mihail Komneno; s/d/tr from €25/35/50; 🅿❄@🛜) A true highlight of Berat is this gorgeous place inside two sprawling Ottoman houses where all the rooms are beautifully furnished in traditional Berati style, and balconies (superior rooms only) give memorable views. Its terrace **restaurant** (mains 300-800 lekë; ⏰noon-11pm; 🛜) is the best place to eat in town, with great Albanian food with bonus views of Mt Tomorri. It's on the left side of the cobblestone road leading to the castle.

Hotel Restaurant Klea GUESTHOUSE €
(Map p63; ☑032 234 970; Rr Shën Triadha, Kala; tw/d/tr incl breakfast €31/33/35) From the castle gates, go straight ahead and you'll find this gorgeous hilltop hideaway, run by a friendly English-speaking family. There are just five compact, wood-panelled rooms, each with its own clean and modern bathroom. The downstairs restaurant adjoins a wonderful garden and has a daily, changing specials menu featuring tasty Albanian fare (200 lekë to 450 lekë).

Lorenc Guesthouse & Hostel GUESTHOUSE €
(Map p63; ☑069 633 7254, 032 231 215; lorenc pushi@hotmail.com; Gorica; dm/d €12/26; 🛜) Push open the dark wooden door, clamber up the uneven whitewashed stone steps and enter the home of the loquacious Lorenc, a former opera singer who puts his talents on display with little urging. This 400-year-old Gorica house once belonged to King Zogu's Minister of Finance, and although hardly kingly today, the simple rooms have plenty of charm (some with gorgeous original ceilings).

The shaded garden is a perfect place to relax, and with Lorenc and his family living in the same building, you've a guaranteed homely atmosphere.

Hotel Belgrad Mangalem HISTORIC HOTEL €€
(Map p63; ☑069 784 3420; www.hotelbelgrad mangalem.yolasite.com; Rr Antipatrea; d from €35, ste from €60; ❄🛜) Filled with memories of yesteryear, this large and carefully restored Berat townhouse has a wide range of room types (including apartments suitable for a family of four in a newer neighbouring building), a pleasant garden where tortoises roam, a covered wooden outdoor dining

area with views over the town, and a fab breakfast spread.

Hotel Muzaka
HOTEL €€

(Map p63; ☎ 032 231 999; www.hotel-muzaka.com; Gorica; s/d/ste incl breakfast from €39/60/80; P❄🛜) This gorgeous Gorica hotel is a careful restoration of an old stone mansion on the riverfront, just over the footbridge from the centre of town. With wooden floorboards and window shutters, and hand-carved wooden ceilings, there's a real old-world ambience to it. In contrast to the historical feel are the modern bathrooms and super comfortable mattresses.

A pleasant restaurant is also here, open to the public for lunch and dinner (mains 400 lekë to 800 lekë). There are also cheaper rooms (doubles from €35) in another building further down the road, though these are much more basic.

✗ Eating

★ Onufri
ALBANIAN €

(Map p63; Rr Shën Triadha, Kalaja; mains 200-300 lekë, mixed plates from 1500 lekë; ☉noon-4pm) In the pretty village-like cobbled streets of the kalaja (fortress; p62), Onufri is the closest you'll get to a homestyle Albanian feast without actually gatecrashing a family lunch. Expect to be brought a heaving plate of stuffed peppers, byrek (stuffed savoury pastries), qofta (rissoles), stuffed aubergines and grilled chicken. Finish up with a slice of homemade honey cake and you've got a meal to remember.

Although there is an à la carte menu, the best option is to go for the mixed plates, which are for a minimum of two people.

Heaven's Kitchen
INTERNATIONAL €

(Map p63; ☎ 069 989 1303; Rr Antipatrea; mains 250-500 lekë; ☉8am-11pm) This wildly popular place serves typical Albanian fast food such as kebabs, pizzas and burgers, but with the quality is a step above normal. The real highlight though is the waiter who juggles bottles, spins trays on his finger and fast-talks any passerby into stopping and eating here.

Antigone
ALBANIAN €

(Map p63; ☎ 069 244 4522; Gorica; mains 400-600 lekë; ☉noon-10pm) This decent Gorica restaurant serves high-class versions of classic Albanian farmer dishes and is always crowded with locals. The food is really tasty, but even tastier are the views from the terrace, out

over the minty green river to the old town houses piled onto the hillside opposite. It's right at the end of the pedestrian bridge.

★ Lili Homemade Food
ALBANIAN €€

(Map p63; ☎ 069 234 9362; Mangalem; mains 500-700 lekë; ☉noon-3pm & 6.30-10pm) This charming family home deep in the Mangalem Quarter below the castle is the setting for one of Berat's best restaurants. Lili speaks English and will invite you to take a table in his backyard where you can order a meal of traditional Berati cooking. We heartily recommend the gjize ferges, a delicious mash of tomato, garlic and cheese.

To get here, keep going down the narrow flower-lined cobbled street around the top side of the Hotel Belgrad Mangalem (p65), and you'll find the house, signed on the right-hand side, about 200m further on. It's sensible to reserve a table in advance as space is limited.

ℹ Information

MONEY
There are plenty of banks with ATMs around the main square. There are no ATMs up in the kalaja and it can be a hot steep walk back to town if you need some more money.

TOURIST INFORMATION
Information Centre (Map p63; Rr Antipatrea; ☉9am-noon & 2-6pm Mon-Fri) This tourist information centre can be found on Berat's main square, and has lots of local information and English-speaking staff.

ℹ Getting There & Away

Berat now has a bus terminal, around 3km from the town centre on the main road to Tirana. Bus services run to Tirana (400 lekë, three hours, half-hourly until 3pm). There are also buses to Vlora (300 lekë, two hours, hourly until 2pm), Durrës (300 lekë, two hours, six per day) and Saranda (1600 lekë, six hours, two daily at 8am and 2pm). The earlier Saranda bus goes via Gjirokastra (1000 lekë, four hours, 8am). To get to the bus station from the centre, ask locals to put you on a bus to 'Terminali Autobusave'.

Korça

☎082 / POP 51,000

Korça is southern Albania's intellectual centre and a town with a proud cultural heritage. It's an exceptionally pleasant and well-cared-for place by Albanian standards; recent efforts at urban renewal have made this even more so, with a showcase pedestrian avenue linking the town's main square to its rebuilt Orthodox cathedral. The main reason to come here is to visit the town's excellent Museum of Medieval Art, but even though there's little to keep you here for much longer, many visitors are charmed by this characterful, green place, with a friendly population and some gorgeous countryside nearby.

★ **Museum of Medieval Art**   MUSEUM
(Muzeu Kombëtar i Artit Mesjetar; ☑ 067 513 8333; www.muzeumesjetar.gov.al; Bul Fan Noli & Rr Nenë Tereza; adult/student 700/200 lekë; ⊘ 9am-2pm & 5-7pm Tue-Fri, 9am-noon & 5-7pm Sat & Sun) Korça's best museum is housed within a new, purpose-built space that really allows the stellar collection of Orthodox icons to shine. Highlights of the spellbinding collection include pieces by the Albanian master Onufri and, the stunning centrepiece of the collection, a 19th-century iconostasis from the village of Rehova. Give yourself plenty of time to peruse the collection, and don't miss the icon of St Christopher with the face of a dog.

Archaeological Museum   MUSEUM
(Rr Mihal Grameno; 200 lekë; ⊘ 9am-2pm & 5-7pm Tue-Fri, 9am-noon & 5-7pm Sat & Sun) Housed in the guesthouse of a larger mansion dating from 1870, this interesting (though itself fairly antique) museum has an excellent collection. Highlights include numerous artefacts found at the prehistoric sites of Maliq, Podgorica, Dunaveci and Trajan, as well as two skeletons from the tumulus of Kamenica, an Illyrian burial site dating from the Bronze Age where some 440 skeletons have been recovered.

★ **Life Gallery Hotel**   BOUTIQUE HOTEL €€
(☑ 069 709 0222, 082 246 800; www.lifegallery.al; Bul Republika 55; r/ste incl breakfast from €65/125; ❋ ⊛ ⊠) This sleek design hotel would be a surprise almost anywhere in the Balkans, but in a charming backwater like Korça, it's almost unbelievable. Rooms are spacious, with contemporary fittings, minimalist design, high-thread-count sheets and exposed brickwork, while service hums along seamlessly. It's in a gorgeous old mansion that also houses a slew of bars and restaurants and a swimming pool.

Avenue 55   INTERNATIONAL €€
(Bul Republika 55; mains 500-1700 lekë; ⊘ 11am-11pm; ❋) Housed within the fancy Life Gallery Hotel, Avenue 55 is made up of a superpopular outdoor eating-and-drinking area, which is easily the most fashionable spot in town – favoured by a young crowd – and a smarter indoor dining room, where an international menu including steak, fish, pasta and pizza is served up.

Beer 55, the raucous bar to one side of the restaurant, is also Korça's best place to drink, and has a range of bottled beers from around the world.

❶ Information

Tourist Office (☑ 082 257 803; www.visit-korca.com; Sheshi Teatrit; ⊘ 9am-9pm Apr-Oct, to 7pm Nov-Mar) This small kiosk on the main square is run by English-speaking staff who can give you lots of suggestions for what to do in Korça.

❶ Getting There & Away

Buses go from the rather ad hoc bus station on Shëtitorja Fan Noli, in front of the bazaar, one block west of the main square, Sheshi Teatrit. Buses head to Tirana (500 lekë, 3½ hours, hourly) as well as to Gjirokastra, Berat and Saranda.

Gjirokastra
☑ 084 / POP 43,000

Defined by its castle, roads paved with chunky limestone and shale, imposing slate-roofed houses and views out to the Drina Valley, Gjirokastra is a magical hillside town described beautifully by Albania's most famous author, Ismail Kadare (b 1936), in *Chronicle in Stone*. There has been a settlement here for 2500 years, though these days it's the 600 'monumental' Ottoman-era houses in town that attract visitors. For Albanians, the town is also synonymous with former dictator Enver Hoxha, who was born here and ensured the town was relatively well preserved under his rule, though he is not memorialised in any way here today.

◉ Sights

★ **Gjirokastra Castle**   CASTLE
(200 lekë; ⊘ 9am-6pm mid-Apr–mid-Oct, 8am-4pm mid-Oct–mid-Apr) Gjirokastra's eerie hilltop castle is one of the biggest in the Balkans. There's been a fortress here since the 12th century, although much of what can be seen today dates to the early 19th century. The castle remains somewhat infamous due to its use as a prison under the communists. Inside there's a collection of armoury, two good museums, plenty of crumbling ruins

to scramble around, and superb views over the valley.

The castle grounds also house a recovered US Air Force jet with an interesting backstory as to how it got here. One is the official Albanian version, the other is the official American version. Both versions are what might today be termed as 'Fake News', but the US version is faker than the Albanian one...

★ Cold War Tunnel   TUNNEL
(Sheshi Çerçiz Topulli; 200 lekë; ⊘ 8am-4pm Mon-Fri, 10am-2pm Sat, 9am-3pm Sun) Gjirokastra's most interesting sight in no way relates to traditional architecture, but instead to a far more modern kind: this is a giant bunker built deep under the castle for use by the local authorities during the full-scale invasion that communist leader Enver Hoxha was so paranoid about. Built in secret during the 1960s, it has 80 rooms, its existence remained unknown to locals until the 1990s. Personal guided tours run from the tourist information booth on the main square all day.

It's an interesting contrast to Tirana's Bunk'Art (p53): unlike the capital's version, this bunker is virtually empty and feels even more creepy as a result. The rooms have their use displayed on the door and nothing else, though it's interesting to note that the bunker – which could hold up to 300 people – had everything from its own classroom to a law court.

★ Zekate House   HISTORIC BUILDING
(Rr Mazllëm Shazivari; 200 lekë; ⊘ 8am-8pm Apr-Oct) This incredible three-storey house dates from 1811 and has twin towers and a double-arched facade. It's fascinating to nose around the almost unchanged interiors of an Ottoman-era home, especially the upstairs galleries, which have carved wooden ceilings, stained-glass windows and detailed wall frescoes.

The owners live next door and although the opening hours are fairly standard through the summer months, in the winter it's simply a case of turning up and asking if they could show you around. To get here, follow the signs past the Hotel Kalemi and keep zigzagging up the hill.

Gjirokastra Museum   MUSEUM
(Gjirokastra Castle; entry 200 lekë incl Army Museum; ⊘ 9am-6pm mid-Apr–mid-Oct, 8am-4pm mid-Oct–mid-Apr) This interesting museum is a

beautifully lit and presented, fully English-signed display on the long and fascinating history of the town. Some highlights include a 6th-century grave containing the skeletons of two small children, as well as information on such luminaries connected with Gjirokastra as Ali Pasha, Lord Byron, Edward Lear and Enver Hoxha.

Skenduli House   HISTORIC BUILDING
(⌨ 069 577 0432; Rr Ismail Kadare; 200 lekë; ⊘ 9am-7pm Apr-Oct) The lovingly restored Ottoman-era Skenduli House has been in the hands of the same family for generations (apart from a few years during the communist period when the government took it over), and you'll most likely be shown around by a member of the family. Dating from the early 1700s, but partially rebuilt in 1827, the house has many fascinating features, including a room used only for wedding ceremonies and which has 15 windows, many with stained glass.

Note that opening hours can be a little flexible and in high summer it's frequently open later than the stated 7pm. Between November and March it's only open to pre-booked tours.

Ethnographic Museum   MUSEUM
(Rr Ismail Kadare; 200 lekë; ⊘ 9am-6pm mid-Apr–mid-Oct, 10am-4pm mid-Oct–mid-Apr) This museum houses local homewares and was built on the site of Enver Hoxha's former house, in the middle of the Old Town. Its collection is interesting if you're a fan of local arts and crafts, but don't come expecting anything about Hoxha himself.

🛏 Sleeping

★ Stone City Hostel   HOSTEL €
(⌨ 069 348 4271; www.stonecityhostel.com; Rr Alqi Kond; dm/d with shared bathroom incl breakfast €11/27; ⊘ Apr-Oct; ❈ 🛜) This hostel is a fantastic conversion of an Old Town house, created and run by Dutchman Walter. The attention to detail and respect for traditional craftswork is extremely heartening, with beautiful carved wooden panels in all the rooms. Choose between the dorm rooms with custom-made bunks or a double room, all of which share spotless communal facilities.

Walter is passionate about Gjirokastra and the surrounding region, and can offer all kinds of tours and excursions. There's an enticing terrace and garden, as well as some extraordinary views towards the town's iconic castle.

WORTH A TRIP

APOLLONIA

The evocative ruins of the ancient Illyiran city of **Apollonia** (Pojan; 400 lekë; ⊘8am-6pm Apr-Oct, to 5pm Nov-Mar) sit on a windswept hilltop some 12km west of the city of Fier. While a large part of the ruins remains buried under the ground, what has been excavated within the 4km of city walls is pure poetry. Highlights include the theatre and the elegant pillars of the restored facade of Apollonia's 2nd-century-AD administrative centre.

Few foreigners visit, but Apollonia is popular with locals for afternoon picnics.

Set on rolling hills among olive groves, with impressive views all around, Apollonia (named after the god Apollo) was founded by Greeks from Corinth and Corfu in 588 BC and quickly grew into an important city-state, which minted its own currency and benefited from a robust slave trade. Under the Romans (from 229 BC), the city became a great cultural centre with a famous school of philosophy.

Julius Caesar rewarded Apollonia with the title 'free city' for supporting him against Gnaeus Pompeius Magnus (Pompey the Great) during the civil war in the 1st century BC, and sent his nephew Octavius, the future Emperor Augustus, to complete his studies here. After a series of military and natural disasters (including an earthquake in the 3rd century AD that turned the river into a malarial swamp), the population moved southwards into present-day Vlora, and by the 5th century AD only a small village with its own bishop remained at Apollonia.

While definitely one of Albania's most important ancient sites, the ruins have fairly minimal descriptions and can be quite hard to piece together, though the on-site Apollonia Museum complex is excellent and does much to make up for the lack of context in the archaeological site itself. Inside the museum complex is the Byzantine monastery and Church of St Mary, which has gargoyles on the outside pillars and, inside, some faded wall frescoes and impressive Roman floor mosaics.

Few people bother to see much of the site beyond the museum, theatre and administrative centre, but archaeological buffs or those with a sense of romance for such places will enjoy poking around the rest of the site and trying to piece together the outline of the city from the few remaining walls. You may be able to see the 3rd-century-BC House of Mosaics as well, though they're often covered up with sand for protection from the elements.

Apollonia is best visited on a day trip from Tirana or Berat, or as a stop-off as you travel down the main road to Albania's south – you have to go through Fier to reach the coastal road, anyway. To get to Fier, *furgon* head from the Rr Myhedin Llegami stop in Tirana (300 lekë, 2½ hours) throughout the day. You can also catch a *furgon* from Berat (300 lekë, one hour). Once in Fier, *furgon* depart for the site (50 lekë) from Fier's '24th August Bar' (ask locals for directions). If you'd prefer not to wait for the *furgon*, a taxi will charge approximately 500 lekë one way from Fier.

★**Gjirokastra Hotel** HISTORIC HOTEL €
(☑084 265 982, 068 409 9669; hhotelgjirokastra@yahoo.com; Rr Sheazi Çomo; tw/d incl breakfast €35/40; ❄ 🛜) Combining modern facilities with traditional touches, this lovely family-run hotel inside a 300-year-old house has rooms with huge balconies and gorgeously carved wooden ceilings. If you can afford the extra, then taking the suite (which sleeps four), with its long Ottoman-style sofa, original wooden doors and ceiling, and magnificent stone walls, is like sleeping inside a museum.

Hotel Kalemi HOTEL €
(☑068 223 4373, 084 263 724; www.kalemihotels.com; Rr Bashkim Kokona; s/d/tr incl breakfast €30/35/55; P❄🛜) Claiming the crown for the hotel with the best view in town, the Kalemi has big, bright rooms with balconies and large windows from which to admire the vistas over the Drina Valley. When you finally bore of the view, chill out in the garden where tortoises plod and grapes dangle from vines.

Breakfast (juice, tea, a boiled egg and fresh bread with fig jam) is an all-local affair.

Hotel Old Bazaar 1790
BOUTIQUE HOTEL €€

(☑084 266 661; www.oldbazaar.al; Rr Astrit Karagjozi; incl breakfast d/tr/ste from 40/50/65; ❄🖳) Fabulous new 11-room boutique hotel housed inside an immaculately restored building that's older than some countries. Rooms mix just the right amount of old-world style with modern convenience. All have ornate handcrafted bedheads and some have multiple dollhouse-sized windows that reveal views of the town. The reception staff are unfailingly polite and helpful. A real treat.

Hotel Kalemi 2
HOTEL €€

(☑068 223 4373; www.kalemihotels.com; Rr Alqi Kondi; incl breakfast d from €50, ste from €90; @🖳) Very central, renovated stone mansion that has some beautiful fittings in its 16 individually decorated rooms. Modern bathrooms contrast with the elaborate traditional ceilings, and the huge suite is easily worth its price, and must rank among the most atmospheric sleeping options in Albania.

✖ Eating

Gjoça Restaurant
ALBANIAN €

(☑069 324 3544; Rr Gjin Zenebisi; mains 200-300 lekë; ⏱11am-10pm) Authentic Albanian home cooking is served at this tiny place on the main street of the Old Town. Everything is cooked at the counter on a small gas stove by an elderly lady who puts a lifetime of cooking know-how into every dish. There are only three interior tables plus one or two outside, so get there early to ensure a seat.

Grab a slice of her delicious honey-drenched baklava to finish off a memorable meal.

★ Odaja Restaurant
ALBANIAN €

(☑069 580 8687; Rr Gjin Bue Shpata; mains 250-600 lekë; ⏱10am-11pm) Cooking up a storm since 1937, Odaja is a small and cute 1st-floor restaurant serving good, honest home-cooked Albanian mountain dishes. Tuck into the oh-so-succulent meatballs with cheese, devour some stuffed peppers and relish the superb moussaka, and you'll quickly come to understand just how good Albanian food can be.

Kujtimi
ALBANIAN €

(☑068 353 7876; Rr Zejtareve; mains 350-650 lekë; ⏱11am-11pm) This laid-back outdoor restaurant, run by the Dumi family, is an excellent choice. Try the delicious *trofte* (fried trout; 400 lekë), the *midhje* (fried mussels; 350 lekë) and *qifqi* (rice balls fried in herbs and egg, a local speciality). The terrace is the perfect place to absorb the charms of the Old Town with a (rough!) glass of local wine.

Taverna Kuka
ALBANIAN €€

(☑069 340 5365; Rr Astrit Karagjozi; mains 300-750 lekë; ⏱9am-1am Mon-Sat, from 10am Sun; 🖳) Just beyond Gjirokastra's old mosque, this largely outdoor terrace restaurant has a wonderful location and a menu full of delicious Albanian cooking, including *qofta* (rissoles), Saranda mussels, pancetta and grilled lamb. There's a surprisingly cool decor given the rural Albanian setting, and its terrace is a firm local favourite on summer evenings.

❶ Information

Information Centre (☑084 269 044; www.gjirokastra.org; Sheshi Çerçiz Topulli; ⏱9am-5pm Mar-Nov, to 3pm Dec-Feb) In a kiosk on the main square at the entrance to the Old Town, the staff here are suitably clued-in on things to do and places to stay in and around the town. Tickets for the Cold War Tunnel (p68) are also on sale here. In low season it might be briefly closed when staff are conducting a tour.

❶ Getting There & Away

Buses stop at the ad hoc bus station just after the Eida petrol station on the new town's main road. Services include Tirana (1000 lekë, seven hours, every one to two hours until 5pm), Saranda (300 lekë, one hour, hourly) and Berat (1000 lekë, four hours, 9.15am). A taxi between the Old Town and the bus station is 300 lekë.

❶ Getting Around

The new town (no slate roofs here) is on the main Saranda–Tirana road, and a taxi up to or back from the Old Town is 300 lekë.

THE ALBANIAN RIVIERA & THE EAST

The Albanian Riviera was a revelation a decade or so ago, when backpackers discovered the last virgin stretch of the Mediterranean coast in Europe, flocking here in droves, setting up ad hoc campsites and exploring scores of little-known beaches. Since then, things have become significantly less pristine, with overdevelopment blighting many of the once-charming coastal villages. But worry not; while some beaches may be well-and-truly swarming in summer, with a little persistence there are still spots to kick back and enjoy the empty beaches the region was once so famous for.

The stretch of coastline dubbed the 'Albanian Riviera' stretches from the Roman theatre of Butrint in the south to the remote Karaburun Peninsula in the north. Along the way, the Riviera takes in easy-going beach towns, forested mountain passes, bird- and terrapin-filled marshes, noisy resort towns and brilliant snorkelling spots. Grab a beach towel and enjoy!

❶ Getting There & Away

The best way to explore this part of Albania is with your own wheels. Buses do connect the towns along the coast, but they're irregular and sometimes full – give yourself plenty of time and be patient when things don't go to plan. Also note that many beaches are not on the main road, but several kilometres downhill, which can feel like a huge distance in the summer sun. Most long-distance buses now take the new inland road between Saranda and Vlora, which means that there's even less traffic along the narrow – but stunningly beautiful – coastal road.

From Tirana, buses to Saranda (1300 lekë, five hours) leave at 6am, 9am and midday and take the coastal road via the Riviera villages. From Saranda, a daily bus travels up the Riviera to Vlora (1300 lekë, three hours, 7am) and can drop you anywhere along the way, while there are also Vlora buses (900 lekë; also three hours) at 7.30am and 1pm that go via the coast. An 11.30am bus from Saranda heads to Himara (500 lekë, two hours) via the coast.

Saranda

📋 0852 / POP 38,000

Saranda is the unofficial capital of the Albanian Riviera, and come the summer months it seems like half of Tirana relocates here to enjoy the busy beach and busier nightlife along its crowd-filled seaside promenade. What was once a sleepy fishing village is now a thriving city, and while Saranda has lost much of its quaintness in the past two decades, it has retained much of its charisma. The town's beaches are nothing special, but Saranda is a great base for exploring the beaches of the riviera if you have your own transport.

❍ Sights

★ **Butrint**　　　　　　　　　RUINS
(www.butrint.al; Butrint National Park; adult 700 lekë, children under 8yrs free, family ticket per person 300 lekë; ⏱8am-sunset, museum 8am-4pm)

Early in the morning, before the tourist crowds arrive and when the rocks are still tinged in the yellow dawn light, you might just imagine that the ancient walls of Butrint are whispering secrets to you of long-past lives. Easily the most romantic and beautiful – not to mention largest – of Albania's ancient sites, Butrint, 18km south of Saranda, is worth travelling a long way to see.

The ruins, which are in a fantastic natural setting and are part of a 29-sq-km national park, are from a variety of periods, spanning 2500 years. Set aside at least two hours to explore.

Although the site was inhabited long before, Greeks from Corfu settled on the hill in Butrint (Buthrotum) in the 6th century BC. Within a century Butrint had become a fortified trading city with an acropolis. The lower town began to develop in the 3rd century BC, and many large stone buildings had already been built by the time the Romans took over in 167 BC. Butrint's prosperity continued throughout the Roman period, and the Byzantines made it an ecclesiastical centre. The city then went into a long decline and was abandoned until 1927, when Italian archaeologists arrived. These days Lord Rothschild's UK-based Butrint Foundation helps maintain the site.

Buses from Saranda (100 lekë, 20 minutes, hourly from 8.30am to 5.30pm) leave from outside the ZIT Information Centre, returning from Butrint hourly, on the hour.

Blue Eye Spring　　　　　　　SPRING
(Syri i kaltë; Muzinë; per person/car 50/100 lekë; ⏱7am-7pm) The Blue Eye Spring is a magical place: a hypnotic pool of deep blue water surrounded by electric-blue edges like the iris of an eye. It's further enveloped in thick woods and is some 22km east of Saranda on the road to Gjirokastra. Swimming is forbidden, although some people seem to think this rule doesn't apply to them. If you don't mind a dusty 3km walk, buses between Saranda and Gjirokastra can drop you at the spring's turn-off.

A restaurant and cabins are nearby. In high summer it can get very busy (tour groups from as far afield as Corfu come here), but in early or late summer it's normally delightfully empty.

Ethnological Museum　　　　　　MUSEUM
(Muzeu i Tradites; Rr Flamurit; 100 lekë; ⏱9am-2pm & 6-8pm Mon-Wed & Fri, noon-8pm Thu, 6-8pm Sat & Sun) Housed in Saranda's old customs

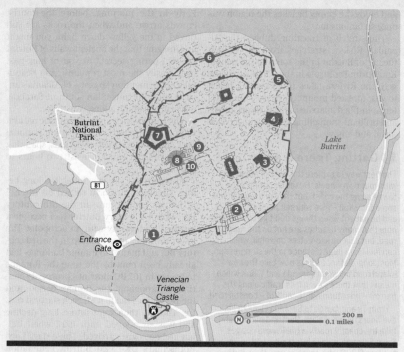

Butrint National Park

Lake Butrint

Venecian Triangle Castle

Entrance Gate

0   200 m
0   0.1 miles

Sight Tour
Butrint Ruins

LENGTH TWO TO THREE HOURS

Many people whizz straight to the theatre and other key Butrint sights, but you'll gain the most from a visit by taking your time and first visiting the more minor ruins, and slowly building up to the main event.

The moment you enter the site, the path forks. Left will take you towards the theatre and museum. Instead, go right to the comparatively modern ❶ **Venetian Tower**. Carry on along a narrow forest path busy with lizards to the atmospheric and often quiet ruins of the ❷ **Triconch Palace**. Starting life as a grand Roman villa, it was expanded in the early 5th century AD, though archaeologists believe it was abandoned before completion.

Along the same path and deeper in the forest is a wall covered with Greek inscriptions, and the 6th-century palaeo-Christian ❸ **baptistry**. It was once the largest such building between Rome and Constantinople; its floor is made up of one of the finest mosaics in Albania. Unfortunately, though, this is almost always covered with sand for its own protection. Beyond are the impressive arches of the 6th-century ❹ **basilica**.

Follow the massive ❺ **Cyclopean wall** (dating back to the 4th century BC) along the lake shore until you get to the imposing ❻ **Lion Gate**, which has a relief of a lion killing a bull and is symbolic of a protective force vanquishing assailants.

By slowly following the shady path to the top of the hill, you'll come to a Venetian castle that today houses an informative ❼ **museum**. The views from the museum's courtyard give you a good idea of the city's layout, and you can see the Vivari Channel connecting Lake Butrint to the Straits of Corfu.

Head back down the hill to marvel over Butrint's show-stoppers. First up is the 3rd-century-BC ❽ **Greek theatre**, secluded in the forest below the acropolis. Also in use during the Roman period, the theatre could seat about 2500 people. Close by is the ❾ **Forum** and the ❿ **public baths**, where geometric mosaics are buried under a layer of mesh and sand to protect them from the elements.

house overlooking the town wharf, this interesting museum contains many fascinating photographs from the communist era, alongside a rather motley collection of ethnographic relics. Particularly worth seeing are the early-20th-century photos, which illustrate how much the town has changed in a relatively short time.

Saranda Art Gallery GALLERY
(Rr Flamurit; ⊙9am-1pm & 6-10pm, closed Mon & Thu Oct-Apr) FREE This excellent gallery overlooking the seafront has high-quality temporary exhibits, with many works coming down from the National Gallery in Tirana.

🍴 Sleeping & Eating

SR Backpackers HOSTEL €
(⏰069 434 5426; www.backpackerssr.hostel. com; Rr Mitat Hoxha 10; dm from €11; @🛜) Your host at Saranda's most central hostel is the gregarious, English-speaking Tomi and he does much to give this place its party atmosphere. The 14 beds here are spread over three dorms, each with its own balcony, but sharing one bathroom and a communal kitchen. In Tomi's own words, 'It's not really suitable for couples after privacy'. You've been warned!

It's a little tricky to find as there's no obvious sign, but it's in an apartment block next door to a crêperie, and almost opposite the entrance to the port.

Hotel Titania HOTEL €€
(⏰0852 22 869; hoteltitania@yahoo.com; Rr Jonianët 25; r incl breakfast from €65; ❄🛜) Easy to miss amongst a rash of bigger, glitzier cousins, the sea-facing rooms at the Titania have huge wrap-around windows and terraces that overlook the Mediterranean and give the sense of sleeping inside a giant goldfish bowl. Breakfast is served on the roof terrace that looks over the bay. All up, it's a smashing deal.

★ Porto Eda Hotel HOTEL €€€
(⏰069 723 3180; www.portoeda.com; Rr Jonianët; r incl breakfast €80-100; P❄🛜) Referencing the name given to Saranda during the Italian occupation (Edda was Mussolini's daughter), this hotel is a charming place and about as central as you can get, overlooking the bay. The 24 rooms are comfortably and stylishly laid out with a contemporary style and all have balconies and sea views. From September to June, room prices drop by about 50%.

★ Mare Nostrum INTERNATIONAL €€
(⏰0852 24 342; Rr Jonianët; mains 700-1200 lekë; ⊙8am-2pm & 6.30pm-midnight Apr-Oct) This sleek restaurant immediately feels different to the others along the seafront: here there's elegant decor that wouldn't look out of place in a major European capital, the buzz of a smart, in-the-know crowd and an imaginative menu that combines the seafood and fish you'll find everywhere else with dishes such as Indonesian chicken curry and burgers.

Gërthëla SEAFOOD €€
(⏰069 621 5643; Rr Jonianët; mains 300-1000 lekë; ⊙11am-midnight; 🛜) One of Saranda's original restaurants, 'The Crab' is a long-standing taverna that only has fish and seafood on the menu, and locals will tell you with certainty that it offers the best-prepared versions of either available in town. The cosy glass-fronted dining room is full of traditional knick-knacks and there's a big wine selection to boot.

ℹ Information

ZIT Information Centre (⏰0852 24 124; Rr Skënderbeu; ⊙8am-midnight May-Sep, to 4pm Mar-Apr & Oct-Nov, 9am-5pm Dec-Feb) Saranda's tiny but excellent ZIT information centre provides information about transport and local sights and is staffed by friendly and helpful English-speaking staff. It's in a UFO-shaped building right on the waterfront.

ℹ Getting There & Away

BUS

The ZIT Information Centre (p73) has up-to-date bus timetables. Most buses leave just uphill from the ruins on Rr Vangjel Pando, right in the centre of town. Buses to Tirana (1300 lekë, eight hours) go inland via Gjirokastra (300 lekë, two hours) and leave regularly between 5am and 10.30am. There are later buses at 2pm and 10pm. The 7am Tirana bus takes the coastal route (1300 lekë, eight hours). There is also one bus a day to Himara at 11.30am (500 lekë, two hours), which can stop at any point along the way to let you off at riviera villages.

Buses to the Greek border near Konispoli leave Saranda at 8am and 11am (200 lekë); otherwise you can reach the Greek border via Gjirokastra.

Municipal buses go to Butrint (p71) via Ksamil, hourly on the half-hour, from 8.30am (100 lekë, 30 minutes), leaving opposite ZIT and returning from Butrint on the hour each hour.

ⓘ SARANDA–CORFU CONNECTIONS

Finikas Lines (☎ 0852 26 712, 0852 26 057; www.finikas-lines.com; Rr Mitat Hoxha; adult/child €24/13) at the port sells fast hydrofoil and slower ferry tickets for Corfu with a daily departure at 6.30am, 8.45am, 10.30am and 4pm in the summer months. The first two boats of the day are fast hydrofoils (30 minutes), while the two later sailings are slower ferries (1½ hours). Cars can be taken on the ferries for €42, while a motorbike is €10. Ferry boats are also operated by **Sarris Cruises** (☎ Greece 00 30 26610 25317; www.sarriscruises.gr; adult/child €24/13, 6pm, 70 minutes).

These boats are primarily aimed at tour groups on day trips to Butrint from Corfu, but anyone can sail with them. For all these crossings, see the relevant website for timings, which vary year-round. Prices are the same for all the boat types, no matter how fast (or slow!) they are. Note that timetables are not always accurate and a boat scheduled to leave at 10am can easily go at 9.30am or 10.30am. In addition to the official ferry company offices, the port area is full of travel agencies selling tickets for any of the boats. However, they sometimes push you onto the boat of their choice rather than the one you actually want to get. Keep in mind that Greek time is one hour ahead of Albanian time.

Ksamil

☑ 0852 / POP 3000

Delightful Ksamil, 17km south of Saranda, sits on a narrow arm of land between a sparkling lagoon famed for its mussels and a cobalt-coloured sea. The entire area surrounding the small town is a protected zone and the dusty tracks and pathways leading over olive-studded hills and along ancient water canals are a joy to explore. The coastline around Ksamil is also unusually attractive. Blessed with three small, dreamy islands (sadly, one of which is being quarried for construction material) within swimming distance of shore and dozens of pretty cove beaches, Ksamil is the kind of place where you can happily while away many sun-drenched days. However, do try and avoid high season when the place is overrun with other Nirvana seekers. Late September is idyllic. Ksamil is an ideal base exploring for the stunning ruins of nearby Butrint (p71).

Mussel Tour   FOOD
(☎ 067 200 0981; https://ksamil.al/mussel-tour; adult/child €25/12.50; ☺ May-Sep) The huge brackish Butrint lagoon is famed for its mussels, and fascinating 2½-hour tours by traditional boat will show you how the mussels are collected and cleaned. You then sail to the lagoon shore, where your haul is cooked up and served with local wine and homemade bread. Tours run in summer only; phone to reserve a place in advance.

In winter occasional orange-harvesting tours are available.

Hotel Luxury   HOTEL €€
(☎ 069 368 8205; www.hotel-luxury.al; Rr Jul Cezari; d incl breakfast from €70; ❇ 🔊) Perhaps not quite as luxurious as the name would imply, but nevertheless this fairly new and very good-value business-class hotel has slick rooms with toned-down colour schemes and thick mattresses on the bed. It's a couple of hundred metres back from one of the nicest beaches in town.

Hotel Joni   HOTEL €€
(☎ 069 209 1554, 069 543 1378; Sheshi Miqesia; d incl breakfast from €70; ❇ 🔊) This popular hotel in the middle of Ksamil is not on the beach, but its smart brick- and timber-lined rooms are some of the best value around. It's within easy walking distance of several nice places to swim, not to mention dozens of good eating and drinking spots.

Mussel House   SEAFOOD €€
(Km 10, Rr Sarande-Butrint; mains 500-1000 lekë; ☺ noon-midnight) With a winning view out over the vast Butrint lagoon and fronting the famed mussel beds, this laid-back, beach-shack-like restaurant a kilometre or so back along the road to Saranda dishes up mussels in any style you might care to think of. It also serves excellent grilled fish and other seafood.

ⓘ Getting There & Away

Any bus running between Saranda and Butrint will drop you off in Ksamil. The cost is 100 lekë.

Himara

📞 0393 / POP 5700

The busy resort of Himara is the biggest town on the riviera north of Saranda. Despite this, the beaches here – book-ended by forested cliffs – are fairly attractive, and the whole place has a more well-kept feel than some quieter beaches elsewhere on the coast. For those with their own wheels, there are heaps of other appealing beaches within a short drive.

Many hotels and restaurants in Himara remain open throughout the year, unlike elsewhere along the coast.

🔘 Sights

Himara Beach BEACH
There are two main beaches in Himara. The northern one is the main town beach and has a promenade lined with cafes and bars. Around the headland to the south is a much larger beach with less development but also less atmosphere. Both beaches are well maintained and kept clean.

Himara Castle RUINS
(100 lekë; ⏰ 7am-10pm May-Sep, 9am-6pm Oct-Apr) Himara is mainly known for its beaches, but its Old Town on the hills high above the seafront is an interesting place to stroll around. One highlight is the ruins of Himara Castle, which existed in various forms on this site since the Bronze Age. Despite it being a ruin, many people live in houses within its walls, and the sea views are superb.

Livadhi Beach BEACH
(Himara) Himara's longest stretch of beach is Livadhi, just north of the town. It's certainly very attractive but development hasn't been kind, with a slew of unsightly new buildings going up. Umbrellas and loungers line the beach, but there's also plenty of free space further down. There are several restaurants, hotels and two camping grounds directly on the beach.

🛏 Sleeping & Eating

Himara Downtown Hostel HOSTEL €
(📞 067 201 7574; https://himaradowntownhostel.business.site; dm/d €10/30) This small hostel has helpful staff and just three dorms, each with six beds, plus there's one double room for couples who want some privacy. The hostel walls are covered in squiggly bright wall art. When full it can feel a bit claustrophobic. It's just one block back from the town's main beach and is in the thick of the action.

Kamping Himare CAMPGROUND €
(📞 068 529 8940; www.himaracamping.com; Potami Beach, Himara; camping per person/car/electricity 700/420/240 lekë; ☀ May-Oct; 🅿) Set up a tent under the olive trees at this chilled-out camping ground across the main road from the beach. Facilities are basic, but nice touches include midnight movies in an open-air cinema and a lamplit bar-restaurant that serves as a natural social centre for guests. It's on the second (southern) beach in Himara if you're coming from Tirana.

Camping gear can be rented for just 300 lekë a night. Prices fall by around a third outside July and August.

ALBANIA HIMARA

WORTH A TRIP

RIVIERA BEACHES

Saranda, Ksamil and Himara are the main centres along the Riveria. All three have busy but attractive beaches and plenty of tourist facilities. If you want something a little more remote though, there are numerous other beaches. Some are near-empty rocky coves, others seasonally busy sweeps of sand. From south to north our favourites include the following.

Borsch Borsch is a huge, sweeping white-stone beach that is several kilometres long. While it's still far from over-run with development, it's hardly undiscovered either. There are plenty of summer-only bars and restaurants, plus a few places to stay.

Gjipe Beach A gorgeous stretch of isolated white sand and rock backed by big cliffs – and as yet almost entirely undeveloped. Turn off the main road for the Monastery of St Theodor and follow signs for the one-hour (3.5km) hike down to the beach. By car, carry on down the road until the paving ends then walk the last 20 minutes (1km).

Drymades One of the more attractive beaches on the Albanian Riviera is Drymades. It's a long, shingle white beach backed by olive groves and the first stirrings of development.

★Vila Kosteli   APARTMENT €€
(☑069 539 3262; vilakosteli@gmail.com; d/ste incl breakfast €70/130; ❄️🐾) Run by a family who learnt the tourist trade in Greece, Villa Kosteli has supersmart apartments decked out in driftwood- and rope- light fittings and there are painted, dried-tree-branch decorations and fishingnet mosquito nets over the beds. Some rooms have terraces with sunloungers overlooking the sea. It's on the cliffs between the town's two beaches.

Taverna Lefteri   SEAFOOD €€
(☑069 223 8499; mains 600-1200 lekë; ⊘noon-5pm & 7.30-midnight) In a town that's rich in delicious seafood, Lefteri stands out for the care put into the presentation and the quality of the fish and shellfish served. Enjoy it out on the foliage-shrouded terrace. For the seafood averse, there are also serve homemade pastas. It's one block back from the main town beach.

ℹ️ Getting There & Away

There are four buses a day (most in the morning) to Tirana (1000 lekë, five to six hours), and five a day to Saranda, with the last one leaving at 1pm (500 lekë, two hours).

Shkodra

☑022 / POP 135,000

Shkodra, the traditional centre of the Gheg cultural region, is one of the oldest cities in Europe and arguably the most attractive urban centre in Albania. The ancient Rozafa Fortress has stunning views over Lake Shkodra, while the pastel-painted buildings in the Old Town have a distinct Italian ambience. Many travellers rush through here while travelling between Tirana and Montenegro, or en route to the Lake Koman Ferry and the villages of Theth and Valbona, but it's worth spending a night or two to soak up this pleasant and welcoming place. Check out the interesting museums before moving on to the mountains, the coast or the capital.

The city is known in Albania as the 'City of Bicycles and Rain'. The bike bit is pretty obvious as the pancake-flat city is ideal for cycling (hotels rent bikes), but the rain part might confuse visitors from soggy northern Europe.

⊙ Sights & Tours

★Rozafa Fortress   CASTLE
(200 lekë; ⊘9am-8pm Apr-Oct, to 4pm Nov-Mar) With spectacular views over the city and Lake Shkodra, the Rozafa Fortress is the most impressive sight in town. Founded by the Illyrians in antiquity and rebuilt much later by the Venetians and then the Turks, the fortress takes its name from a woman who was allegedly walled into the ramparts as an offering to the gods so that the construction would stand.

The story goes that Rozafa, the unfortunate woman chosen to be walled-up in the castle for good luck, asked that two holes be left in the stonework so that she could continue to breastfeed her baby. There's a spectacular wall sculpture of her near the entrance to the castle's museum. There's little left to see inside the castle itself, save the ruins of various structures and the impressive walls. When exploring the quieter corners of the castle grounds, keep your eyes peeled for one of the many tortoises who have made the castle their home.

The castle is 3.5km south of the city centre. Grab a bicycle (many of the hotels rent them out) and enjoy the ride down here. Afterwards you could cross over the river and explore the fishing villages and big open countryside to the south of the castle. If cycling is too energetic, take one of the municipal buses (30 lekë) that stop near the turn-off to the castle. Or a taxi to the entrance costs 300 lekë from the city centre.

★Marubi National
Photography Museum   GALLERY
(Muzeu Kombëtari i Fotografise Marubi; ☑022 400 500; Rr Kolë Idromeno 32; adult/student 700/200 lekë; ⊘9am-7pm Apr-Oct, to 5pm Nov-Mar) The Marubi Museum is a one-of-a-kind Albanian photographic museum. The core of the collection is the impressive work of the Marubi 'dynasty', Albania's first and foremost family of photographers. The collection includes the first-ever photograph taken in Albania, by Pjetër Marubi in 1858, as well as fascinating portraits, street scenes and early photojournalism, all giving a fascinating glimpse into old Albania and the rise and fall of communism.

There are also changing temporary exhibitions and an interesting exhibit of camera equipment over the decades.

Site of Witness & Memory Museum
MUSEUM

(Vendi i Dëshmisë dhe Kujtesës; Blvd Skënderbeu; 150 lekë; ⊘9am-2.30pm Mon-Fri, 9.30am-12.30pm Sat) During the communist period this building, which started life as a Franciscan seminary, was officially used as the Shkodra headquarters of the Ministry of Internal Affairs. What that actually means is that it was an interrogation centre and prison for political detainees. Over the years, thousands of people spent time here – some never to re-emerge. The museum does a reasonable job of illustrating the horrors that took place here, although much of the signage is in Albanian.

There are walls of photos of some victims who died here, and testimonies from survivors, and you can still see the original cells and interrogation rooms.

Ebu Bekr Mosque
MOSQUE

(Xhamia Ebu Bekër; Rr Fushë Cele) Known more commonly to locals as the Great Mosque, this impressive centrepiece to the city actually dates from the 18th century, but was fully renovated and refaced in 1995 with donations from Saudi Arabia. Visitors are welcome to enter outside prayer time to see the beautiful interior and enjoy the contemplative atmosphere.

Kiri Adventures
TOURS

(☑069 225 1722; www.kiriadventures.al; ⊘10am mid-June-Sep) **FREE** Innovative local tour company Kiri Adventures offers free two-hour city tours daily at 10am between mid-June and the end of September, beginning from the City Hall (Bashkia). There's no need to book in advance; just turn up a few minutes before and look for someone holding a green folder. Although it's technically free, they suggest that you tip what you think the tour was worth.

The same crew also runs Rozafa Fortress tours (€9 including castle entry and transport from the town centre; 6pm mid-June to September), which do much to bring the bricks and breeze to life. In addition, Kiri takes hiking tours and cultural and community tours elsewhere in northern Albania.

🛏 Sleeping

★ Rose Garden Hotel
BOUTIQUE HOTEL €

(☑069 311 7127, 022 245 296; www.rosegarden hotel.al; Rr Justin Godard 18; d incl breakfast from €36; ❉ 🛜) A wonderfully restored old townhouse, the Rose Garden is all clean modern

SAZAN ISLAND

Floating off the coast of the remote Karaburun Peninsula, 5.7 sq km **Sazan Island** (⊘boat tours Jun-Sep) is little known, even to most Albanians. Once used as a submarine and chemical-weapons base by the Soviet Union during the Cold War, it's now home to an Albanian-Italian military base used to combat narcotics smuggling. In the summer of 2017, a small area of the island opened to visitors, making parts of its pristine coastline and historic relics accessible for the first time.

Boat tours to Sazan Island normally include stops at little coves with good snorkelling on the Karaburun Peninsula. Daily boats run from Vlora port to the island (€20 per person) but in general, a minimum of 20 people is required for the trip to run.

lines dusted with touches of old-fashioned class. Rooms are exceptionally inviting and include filigree door frames. The real highlight of a stay, though, is the hidden courtyard garden (which extends its botanical knowledge to more than just roses); sitting here with a good book is just perfect.

Wanderers Hostel
HOSTEL €

(☑069 212 1062; www.thewanderershostel.com; Rr Gjuhadol; dm/d incl breakfast €8/25; ❉ 🛜) Very popular with a young Anglophone crowd, this central and convivial hostel is a great place to hang out by the garden bar and make fast travel buddies. Dorms are frills-free and the bathrooms basic, but everyone seems to be having too much of a good time to care. Bikes are available for hire.

Mi Casa Es Tu Casa
HOSTEL €

(☑069 381 2054; www.micasaestucasa.it; Blvd Skënderbeu 22; dm €10-13, d €35, apt €40, camp-sites per person with/without own tent €5/7; @🛜) Shkodra's original hostel is a gorgeous arty space, and with a peaceful garden and open-air bar (selling local craft beers) you'd hardly guess that you were almost right in the heart of the city. There are attractive communal spaces littered with musical instruments and artwork and a bunch of friendly dogs. Dorms have between six and 10 beds. Bike hire is available for €5.

ALBANIA SHKODRA

Petit Hotel Elita — BOUTIQUE HOTEL €€
(📞067 664 9066, 022 801 228; www.petithotelelita.com; Rr Shtjefen Gjeçovi; d/tw incl breakfast from €35; 🅿🌐🛜) With bold statement art, dark tiled floors, subtle colour schemes, giant TVs and sharp, angular furnishings, this modern boutique hotel is easily one of the best-value deals in town. It has a very quiet side-street location but is just a moment from the city centre. Bicycles are available for rent.

Tradita G&T — BOUTIQUE HOTEL €€
(📞022 809 683; www.hoteltradita.com; Rr Edith Durham 4; s/d incl breakfast €43/64; 🅿🌐🛜) This innovative and hugely atmospheric hotel is as much a museum as a mere place to rest your head. Housed in a painstakingly restored 17th-century mansion that once belonged to a famous Shkodran writer, the Tradita heaves with Albanian arts and crafts and has traditional yet very comfortable rooms with terracotta-roofed bathrooms and locally woven bed linen.

A homemade, homegrown breakfast awaits guests in the garden each morning, while the restaurant serves excellent fish dishes. Try to avoid the small and charmless newer rooms in the back block, though – the older ones are much better.

Eating

Sofra — ALBANIAN €
(📞069 209 9022; Rr Kolë Idromeno; mains 200-500 lekë; ⏱noon-midnight; 🛜) Right in the middle of the busy *petonalja* (pedestrianised Rr Kolë Idromeno), with tables on the street as well as a cosy upstairs dining room, this traditional place presents an excellent opportunity to try a range of north Albanian dishes, with the set meals being particularly good value.

★Restaurant Elita — ALBANIAN €€
(📞069 206 2193; Rr Gjergj Fishta; mains 600-800 lekë; ⏱8am-4pm & 6.30-11pm) Respected and smart restaurant with an emphasis on imaginative recreations of classic Albanian and Italian dishes. The slow-cooked pork served in an inverted wine glass is just one such example. Very good value, considering the quality of the food. Earlier in the evening it seems to be mainly foreigners eating here, so for a more Albanian clientele, come later.

★Pasta e Vino — ITALIAN €€
(📞069 724 3751; www.facebook.com/pastaevinoshkoder; Rr Gjergj Fishta; mains 400-600 lekë; ⏱noon-11pm) Casually dressed waiters with tattoos, dried tree-branches dressed with herbs, and artworks made from wine corks all help to make this one of the more visually memorable places to eat in Shkodra. But what about the food? Well, it's classic Italian, it's authentic and it's very well prepared and presented. What's not to like?!

ℹ Information

MONEY
There are plenty of ATMs and banks throughout the city centre.

TOURIST INFORMATION
Tourist Information (Rr Teuta; ⏱9am-7pm Mon-Sat) The small tourist information office has a few token leaflets to hand out, but not much else of use. There was no telephone number available at the time of research, as the office was newly built.

ℹ Getting There & Away

BUS
There is no bus station in Shkodra, but most services leave from around Sheshi Demokracia in the centre of town. There are hourly *furgon* (shared minibus; 400 lekë) and buses (300 lekë) to Tirana (two hours, 6am to 5pm), which depart from outside Radio Shkodra near Hotel Rozafa. There are also several daily buses to Kotor, Ulcinj and Podgorica in Montenegro (€5 to €8, two to three hours) from outside the Ebu Bekr Mosque.

To get up into the mountains, catch the 6.30am bus to Lake Koman (600 lekë, two hours) in time for the wonderful Lake Koman Ferry to Fierzë. Several *furgon* also depart daily for Theth between 6am and 7am (1200 lekë, four hours). In both cases, hotels can call ahead to get the *furgon* to pick you up on its way out of town.

TAXI
It costs between €40 and €50 for the trip from Shkodra to Ulcinj in Montenegro, depending on your haggling skills. A private hire vehicle to Theth costs around €50. Ask at your hotel.

THE ACCURSED MOUNTAINS & THE NORTH

Names don't come much more evocative than the 'Accursed Mountains' (Bjeshkët e Namuna; also known as the Albanian Alps), but the dramatic peaks of northern Albania truly live up to the wonder in their name. Offering some of the country's most impressive scenery, and easily its finest hiking, the mountains spread over the bor-

DON'T MISS

HIKING IN THE ACCURSED MOUNTAINS

Most people come here to do the popular hike between Valbona and Theth, which takes between five and seven hours depending on your fitness and where in either village you start or end. It's not a particularly hard walk and is attempted by many first-time mountain walkers. Even so, it's quite long and steep and can get very hot, if you don't have much mountain walking experience you should allow extra time.

You can walk it either way, though the majority of people seem to go from Valbona to Theth as this allows for a neat circle, going from Shkodra via the Lake Koman ferry. The trail begins a couple of kilometres beyond Valbona, and many people get a lift to the trailhead – it's a tiring and monotonous walk over a dry – and often very hot – stone riverbed, otherwise. On the whole the trail itself is decently marked with red and white way markings and there are a number of tea houses where you can get refreshments (and even a bed), but there are a couple of problem spots. If you do choose to walk from your guesthouse in Valbona, then it's easy to get confused in the dry river bed. Stick to the right hand (true left) bank and you'll be OK. The other confusing part comes as you pass the last tea shop before the trail starts to climb sharply upwards. Another, wider and therefore more obvious trail continues straight ahead from this tea house. This leads to a pretty stream and wooden bridge. If you find yourself here, turn around and return to the tea house. The real, less distinct trail bends around the back of the tea house (north). After this last tea house, the trail climbs quickly upwards and in places is quite steep. Eventually you will arrive at the Valbona Pass (1800m), for memorable views over an ocean of jagged mountains. Heading down the other side of the pass is almost entirely in the delightful shade of old-growth forest. Conifer up high, and beech lower down (and in autumn this slope is ablaze in reds and oranges). It's a long but fairly gentle descent into the spread-out village of Theth.

If you are carrying significant weight, it's easy to hire a mule in Valbona to carry your bags. It's also possible (though not really necessary) to hire a guide for the route. The hike is spectacular and, for many visitors, the highlight of their visit to Albania.

There are many other trekking routes in these mountains, many of which are scenically more impressive than the Valbona–Theth trek. For the other treks you need to be fully self-sufficient with food and water (and camping gear for longer treks). Guesthouses in either village can advise, and there are information panels describing routes. For many of these routes a local guide is a wise idea.

ders of Albania, Kosovo and Montenegro, and in Albania they reach a respectable height of 2694m. But as we all know, size isn't everything and what these mountains lack in Himalayan greatness, they more than make up for with lyrical beauty. There are deep green valleys, thick forests where wolves prowl, icy-grey rock pinnacles and quaint stone villages where old traditions hold strong. Indeed, this is where shepherds still take their flocks to high summer pastures and where blood feuds continue to hold sway, and it feels as if you're far, far away from 21st-century Europe.

❶ Getting There & Away

Roads in this part of Albania are often little more than dirt tracks, so it's best to travel by bus with drivers who know their way around. As few locals drive cars in the mountains, public transport is well developed, cheap and relatively regular.

Valbona

📞 0213 / POP 200

Valbona has a gorgeous setting on a wide plain surrounded by towering mountain peaks, and its summer tourism industry is increasingly well organised. The village itself consists virtually only of guesthouses and camping grounds, nearly all of which have their own restaurants attached. Most travellers just spend a night here before trekking to Theth, which is a shame as there are a wealth of other excellent hikes to do in the area.

🛏 Sleeping

★ **Hotel Rilindja**   GUESTHOUSE €
(📞067 301 4637; www.journeytovalbona. com; Quku i Valbonës; tent/dm/d incl breakfast €4/12/35; 🛜) Pioneering tourism in Valbona

THE LAKE KOMAN FERRY

One of Albania's undisputed highlights is this superb three-hour **ferry ride** (www.komani lakeferry.com/en/ferry-lines-in-the-komani-lake) across vast Lake Koman, connecting the towns of Koman and Fierzë. Lake Koman was created in 1978 when the Drin River was dammed, with the result that you can cruise through spectacular mountain scenery where many incredibly hardy people still live as they have for centuries, tucked away in tiny mountain villages. Unfortunately, the scenic beauty is rather marred by the thousands of plastic bottles and other rubbish floating in the lake. In places this rubbish forms 'islands' so big they're virtually a shipping hazard.

Until recently the ferry was not set up for tourism, which made the entire trip feel like a great adventure. But recent developments, as well as word getting out among travellers, have made the trip both more accessible (with better-timed ferries) and, inevitably, rather more touristy.

The best way to experience the journey is to make a three-day, two-night loop beginning and ending in Shkodra, and taking in Koman, Fierzë, Valbona and Theth. Every hotel in Shkodra, and Valbona organises packages for the route for 2000 lekë. This includes a 6.30am *furgon* (shared minibus) pick-up from your hotel in Shkodra which will get you to the ferry departure point at Koman by 8.30am. There are normally two ferries daily and both leave from Koman at 9am. (One of the two, the *Berisha,* carries up to ten cars, which cost 700 lekë per square metre of space they occupy. There's also a big car ferry that leaves at 1pm, but it only runs when demand is high enough – call ahead to make a reservation.) On arrival in Fierzë, the boats are met by *furgon* that will take you to either Bajram Curri or to Valbon. There's no real reason to stop in Bajram Curri unless you plan to head to Kosovo. Hikers will want to head straight for Valbona, where you can stay for a night or two before doing the stunning day hike to Theth. After the hike you can stay for another night or two in glorious Theth before taking a *furgon* back to Shkodra (not included in the standard packages). It's also possible to do the whole thing independently, though you won't save any money or time by doing so.

since 2005, the Albanian-American–run Rilindja is a fairy-tale wooden house in the forest 3km downhill from Valbona village centre. It's hugely popular with travellers, who love the comfortable accommodation, easy attitude and excellent food. The simple rooms in the atmospheric farmhouse share a bathroom, except for one with private facilities.

The helpful owners speak fluent English and, having helped establish most of the hikes in the area, they are definitely the best people to see about exciting walking opportunities around Valbona.

Hotel Rilindja's management also runs a new property, Rezidenca, up the road; it offers a far more upmarket experience with en-suite singles, doubles and triples.

Jezerca   GUESTHOUSE **€**
(✆ 067 309 3202; r from €30; 🛜) Named after one of the soaring mountain peaks nearby, this guesthouse on Valbona's main (well, only) street has freestanding pine huts in a pleasant field, which sleep two, three or five people. The best huts have attached

bathrooms and little terraces with hanging flower baskets. There's a small restaurant that tries hard to use only locally sourced products. It's a good bet for travelling families.

Hotel Margjeka   HOTEL **€€**
(✆ 067 379 2003, 067 338 2162; www.hotelmargje ka.al; r per person incl breakfast €28; 🛜) Buried among dense pine forest a couple of kilometres beyond the village, this inviting and surprisingly plush hotel has modern rooms, smart service and a restaurant serving traditional meals (don't miss the juicy barbecued goat) that attracts families from far and wide.

❶ Getting There & Away

Valbona can be reached from Shkodra via the Lake Koman Ferry and a connecting *furgon* from Fierzë (400 lekë, one hour). Alternatively, it can be reached by *furgon* from Bajram Curri (200 lekë, 45 minutes). In general most people just organise the entire trip as one package from Shkodra (2000 lekë).

Theth

📷 022 / POP 400

This unique mountain village easily has the most dramatic setting in Albania. Just the journey here is quite incredible, whether you approach over the mountains on foot from Valbona or by vehicle over the high passes from Shkodra. Both a sprawling village along the valley floor amid an amphitheatre of slate-grey mountains, and a national park containing stunning landscapes and excellent hiking routes, Theth is now well on its way to being Albania's next big thing. An improved – though still incomplete – asphalt road from Shkodra has made access to this once virtually unknown village far easier in recent years, bringing with it the familiar problem of overdevelopment. Come quickly while Theth retains its incomparable romance and unique charm.

⊙ Sights

Blue Eye   NATURAL POOL

A superb half-day hike from Theth is to the Blue Eye, a natural pool of turquoise waters fed by a small waterfall, up in the mountains to the southwest of Theth. The walk will take you through forests and steeply up into the mountains; in summer it can get very hot, so you'll probably be keen for a swim when you get to the pool. But, be warned: the water is glacier cold. Are you brave enough?

It's a popular walk, so a guide isn't really needed, but do get detailed instructions from your guesthouse. Drinks and snacks are available from near the pool but it's sensible to take a packed lunch with you.

Theth Church   CHURCH

(Kisha e Thethit) This late-19th-century stone-and-shingle church looks incredible in silhouette against the mountains that surround it, topped as it is with a rustic wooden cross. The church was used as the village hospital during the communist era, meaning that most locals over 25 were born in the quaint structure. It is open only when the priest is in town – normally on Sundays.

Kulla   HISTORIC BUILDING

(Kulla e Ngujimit; 200 lekë) A visit to this fascinating 400-year-old 'lock-in tower' gives you an idea of the life those condemned by their family ties would lead as they waited, protected, during a blood feud (p85). You can visit two floors and imagine the spartan weeks or even months spent by those poor

souls who found themselves next in line to be killed. There are no set opening hours. If it's closed, ask in nearby houses and someone will come and open up.

🛏 Sleeping

Vila Zorgji   GUESTHOUSE €

(📲068 231 9610, 068 361 7309; pellumbkola@gmail.com; r per person incl full board €35; ⊙ Apr-Oct; 🛜) Zorgji is a gorgeous stone farmhouse with big, bright en-suite rooms and a dining room full of drying corn and old farming implements. The garden is equally attractive and is lined with grape vines and tomato plants. It's a little to the north of the village centre and up on the hillside near the turquoise-painted school.

Shpella Guesthouse   GUESTHOUSE €

(📲069 455 8825; d incl breakfast €34; ⊙ Apr-Oct; 🛜) The friendly Shpella family run their 110-year-old house as a traditional hotel and it's located in an atmospheric environment near to the Kulla. The 12 rooms each have two to four beds and all share small bathrooms. The owners are a great source of information on the region and hiking routes in the nearby mountains.

★Vila Pisha   GUESTHOUSE €€

(📲069 325 6415, 068 278 5057; r per person incl breakfast €34; 🛜) Next to the church, right in the centre of the village, this place has been totally rebuilt from the ground upwards. It is one of the best guesthouses in the village, with friendly, English-speaking owners, smart en-suite rooms with radiators for those cold mountain nights, large beds and wooden floors.

ℹ Information

Tourist Information (⊙9am-7pm Apr-Oct) This new tourist office is at the northern end of the village on the route in from Valbona. It has a few leaflets and some suggestions of things to see and do, but information on hiking trails is scant. At the time of research, there was no phone.

ℹ Getting There & Away

An asphalt road from Shkodra snakes through the deep mountain valleys and up towards the mountain pass at Belvedere Majet e Shales before suddenly becoming a lugubrious slog through rocks and mud the rest of the way to Theth. Even though the unsurfaced section of the road is no more than 15km, expect it to take at least an hour. Despite what many people might tell you, a 4WD is not normally required in the summer, though the going is certainly very rough in a normal saloon car, so a 4WD is recommended (and certainly needed in bad weather).

A daily *furgon* (1200 lekë, two hours) leaves from Shkodra at 7am and will pick you up from your hotel, if your hotel owner calls ahead for you. The return trip leaves between 1pm and 2pm, arriving late afternoon in Shkodra. During the summer months it's also easy to arrange a shared *furgon* (around €50) transfer to Shkodra with other hikers from Valbona.

UNDERSTAND ALBANIA

Albania Today

Albania has taken giant steps forward in the past two decades, but also faces enormous challenges ahead. The perennial problem of corruption continues to pervade almost every aspect of daily life. Having joined NATO in 2009, the country sees EU membership as its next big goal. Albania was given official EU membership candidate status in 2014, but for talks to continue, it had to combat corruption and organised crime, reorganise the judicial system and improve human rights. It's made moves in all these directions, particularly in regard to the judicial system, with massive reforms agreed in 2016. In acknowledgement of this, the EU has announced that Albania will begin accession talks, pending unanimous approval by the EU's 28 member states.

Former artist Edi Rama was first elected Prime Minister in 2013, replacing long-serving leader Sali Berisha and marking a comeback for Albania's socialists. Rama, who came to national prominence as the innovative and populist mayor of Tirana, has built on his reputation as a pragmatist and has deftly guided Albania through a series of potential crises. Although scandals have dogged his premiership, he has managed to survive the fallout and in the 2017 elections he was rewarded for his tenacity by retaining his position.

With some 80% of Albanians supportive of the country eventually becoming a part of the EU club, it's likely that Rama (and any future leaders) will be at least partially judged on how far down the EU path they can take Albania. Unfortunately for the aspirations of most Albanians, the EU has made it quite clear that although they are open to Albania joining, this is not something likely to happen soon.

History

Illyrian Origins

Albanians call their country Shqipëria ('Land of the Eagles'), and trace their roots to the ancient Illyrian tribes. Their language is descended from Illyrian, making it a rare survivor of the Roman and Slavic influxes and a European linguistic oddity on a par with Basque. The Illyrians occupied the western Balkans during the 2nd millennium BC. They built substantial fortified cities, mastered silver and copper mining, and became adept at sailing the Mediterranean. The Greeks arrived in the 7th century BC to establish self-governing colonies at Epidamnos (now Durrës), Apollonia and Butrint. They traded peacefully with the Illyrians, who formed tribal states in the 4th century BC.

Roman, Byzantine & Ottoman Rule

Inevitably, the expanding Illyrian kingdom of the Ardiaei, based at Shkodra, came into conflict with Rome, which sent a fleet of 200 vessels against Queen Teuta in 229 BC. A long war resulted in the extension of Roman control over the entire Balkan area by 167 BC.

Under the Romans, Illyria enjoyed peace and prosperity, and the Illyrians preserved their own language and traditions despite Roman rule. Over time the populace slowly replaced their old gods with the new Christian faith championed by Emperor Constantine. The main trade route between Rome and Constantinople, the Via Egnatia, ran from the port at Durrës.

When the Roman Empire was divided in AD 395, Illyria fell within the Eastern Empire, later known as the Byzantine Empire. Three early Byzantine emperors (Anastasius I, Justin I and Justinian I) were of Illyrian origin. Invasions by migrating peoples (Visigoths, Huns, Ostrogoths and Slavs) continued through the 5th and 6th centuries.

In 1344 Albania was annexed by Serbia, but after the defeat of Serbia by the Turks in 1389 the whole region was open to Ottoman attack. The Venetians occupied some coastal towns, and from 1443 to 1468 the national hero Skanderbeg (Gjergj Kastrioti) led Albanian resistance to the Turks from his castle at Kruja. Skanderbeg won all 25 battles he fought against the Turks, and even Sultan Mehmet-Fatih, the conqueror of Constantinople, could not take Kruja.

After Skanderbeg's death the Ottomans overwhelmed Albanian resistance, taking control of the country in 1479, 26 years after Constantinople fell.

Ottoman rule lasted 400 years. Muslim citizens were favoured and were exempted from the janissary system, whereby Christian households had to give up one of their sons to convert to Islam and serve in the army. Consequently, many Albanians embraced the new faith.

Independent Albania

In 1878 the Albanian League at Prizren (in present-day Kosovo) began a struggle for autonomy that the Turkish army put down in 1881. Further uprisings between 1910 and 1912 culminated in a proclamation of independence and the formation of a provisional government led by Ismail Qemali at Vlora in 1912. The Great Powers tried to install a young German prince, Wilhelm of Wied, as ruler, but he wasn't accepted and returned home after six months. With the outbreak of WWI, Albanian areas were controlled in succession by Greece, Serbia, France, Italy and Austria-Hungary.

In 1920 the capital city was moved from Durrës to less vulnerable Tirana. A republican government under the Orthodox priest Fan Noli helped to stabilise the country, but in 1924 it was overthrown by the interior minister, Ahmed Bey Zogu. A northern warlord, he declared himself King Zogu I in 1928, but his close collaboration with Italy backfired in April 1939 when Mussolini ordered an invasion of Albania. Zogu fled to Britain with his young wife, Geraldine, and newborn son, Leka, and used gold looted from the Albanian treasury to rent a floor at London's Ritz Hotel.

On 8 November 1941 the Albanian Communist Party was founded with the virtually unknown Enver Hoxha as first secretary. The communists led the resistance against the Italians and, after 1943, against the Germans.

Communist Albania

In January 1946 the People's Republic of Albania was proclaimed, with Hoxha as president and 'Supreme Comrade'. Hoxha quickly moved against his enemies both inside and outside the communist movement, launching purge after purge and imprisoning and executing thousands.

In September 1948 Albania broke off relations with Yugoslavia, which had hoped to incorporate the country into the Yugoslav Federation. Instead, it allied itself with Stalin's USSR and put into effect a series of Soviet-style economic plans – raising the ire of the USA and Britain, which made an ill-fated attempt to overthrow the government.

Albania collaborated closely with the USSR until 1960, despite Krushchev's denunciation of Stalin in his 1954 'secret speech'. However, when a heavy-handed Khrushchev demanded that a submarine base be set up at Vlora in 1961, Albania broke off diplomatic relations with the USSR and reoriented itself towards Maoist China.

From 1966 to 1967 Albania experienced a Chinese-style cultural revolution. Administrative workers were suddenly transferred to remote areas and younger party functionaries were placed in leading positions. The collectivisation of agriculture was completed and organised religion was completely banned.

Following the Soviet invasion of Czechoslovakia in 1968, Albania left the Warsaw Pact and embarked on a self-reliant defence policy. Some 60,000 igloo-shaped concrete bunkers were built at this time, the crumbling remains of which can still be seen in some parts of the country today. While the Hoxha era was a brutal and terrifying time to live, malarial swamps were drained, hydroelectric schemes and railway lines were built, and the literacy level was raised. Albania's people, however, lived in fear of the Sigurimi (secret police) and were not permitted to leave the country. Many were tortured, jailed or murdered for misdemeanours such as listening to foreign radio stations.

With the death of Mao Zedong in 1976 and the changes that followed in China after 1978, Albania's unique relationship with China also came to an end, and the country was left totally isolated and without allies. The economy was devastated and food shortages became more common.

Post-Hoxha

Hoxha died in April 1985 and his associate Ramiz Alia took over the leadership. Restrictions loosened (Albania was opened up to tourists in organised groups) but people no longer bothered to work on the collective farms, leading to food shortages in the cities. Industries began to fail and Tirana's population tripled as people took advantage of being able to freely move to the city.

In June 1990, inspired by the changes that were occurring elsewhere in Eastern Europe, around 4500 Albanians took refuge in Western embassies in Tirana. After a brief confrontation with the police and the Sigurimi, these people were allowed to board ships for Brindisi in Italy, where they were granted political asylum.

Following student demonstrations in December 1990, the government agreed to allow opposition parties, and the Democratic Party, led by heart surgeon Sali Berisha, was formed.

The March 1992 elections ended 47 years of communist rule, with parliament electing Sali Berisha president. Former president Alia was later placed under house arrest for writing articles critical of the Democratic government, and the leader of the Socialist Party, Fatos Nano, was also arrested on corruption charges.

During this time Albania switched from a tightly controlled communist regime to a free-market free-for-all. A huge smuggling racket sprang up, in which stolen Mercedes-Benz cars were brought into the country, and the port of Vlora became a major crossing point for illegal immigrants from Asia and the Middle East into Italy.

In 1996, 70% of Albanians lost their savings when private pyramid-investment schemes, believed to have been supported by the government, collapsed. Riots ensued, elections were called, and the victorious Socialist Party under Nano – who had been freed from prison by a rampaging mob – was able to restore some degree of security and investor confidence.

In 1999 a different type of crisis struck when 465,000 Kosovars fled to Albania during the war in Kosovo. The influx ultimately had a positive effect on Albania's economy, and strengthened the relationship between Albania and Kosovo.

Since the drama of the 1990s, life has improved immensely for the average Albanian. The Kosovar refugees largely returned to their homeland, the economy stabilised and unheard of prosperity (admittedly not for all), gradually became commonplace.

People

Albania's population is made up of approximately 95% Albanians, 3% Greeks and 2% 'other' – comprising Vlachs, Roma, Serbs, Macedonians and Bulgarians. The majority of young people speak some English, but your ability to speak a few words of Albanian (or Italian and, on the south coast, Greek) will be useful. Like most Balkan people, Albanians shake their heads sideways to say yes *(po)* and usually nod and 'tsk' to say no *(jo* – pronounced 'yo'*)*. The Ghegs in the north and the Tosks in the south have different dialects, music, dress and the usual jokes about each other's weaknesses.

Albanians are nominally 70% Muslim, 20% Christian Orthodox and 10% Catholic, but more realistic statistics estimate that up to 75% of Albanians are nonreligious. Religion was ruthlessly stamped out by the 1967 cultural revolution, when all mosques and churches were taken over by the state. By 1990 only about 5% of Albania's religious buildings were left intact. The rest had been turned into cinemas or army stores, or were destroyed, though many are slowly being taken back over by their original owners. While Albania remains a very secular society, Ramadan is widely observed by Muslims, and Islam does seem to be enjoying a significant comeback among younger people.

The Muslim faith has a branch called Bektashism, similar to Sufism, and its world headquarters are in Albania. Bektashi followers go to *teqe* (temple-like buildings without a minaret), which are found on hilltops in towns where those of the faith fled persecution. Most Bektashis live in the southern half of the country.

Arts
Literature

One Albanian writer who is widely read outside Albania is Ismail Kadare (b 1936). In 2005 he won the inaugural Man Booker International Prize for his body of work. His books are a great source of information on Albanian traditions, history and social events, and exquisitely capture the atmosphere of the country's towns, as in the lyrical descriptions of Kadare's birthplace, Gjirokastra, in *Chronicle in Stone* (1971). *Broken April* (1978), set in the northern highlands before the 1939 Italian invasion, describes the life of a village boy who is next in line in a desperate cycle of blood vendettas.

Cinema

During Albania's isolationist years the only Western actor approved by Hoxha was UK actor Sir Norman Wisdom (who became quite a cult hero). However, with so few international movies to choose from, the local film industry had a captive audience. While much of its output was propagandist, by the

THE KANUN

The *Kanun* (Code) was formalised in the 15th century by powerful northern chieftain Lekë Dukagjin. It consists of 1262 articles covering every aspect of daily life: work, marriage, family, property, hospitality, economy and so on. Though the *Kanun* was suppressed by the communists, there has been a revival of its strict precepts in the mountains (p78) of northern Albania.

According to the *Kanun*, the most important things in life are honour and hospitality. If a member of a family (or one of their guests) is murdered, it becomes the duty of the male members of that clan to claim their blood debt by murdering a male member of the murderer's clan. This sparks an endless cycle of killing that doesn't end until either all the male members of one of the families are dead, or reconciliation is brokered through respected village elders.

Hospitality is so important in these parts of Albania that the guest takes on a godlike status. There are 38 articles giving instructions on how to treat a guest – an abundance of food, drink and comfort is at his or her disposal, and it is also the host's duty to avenge the murder of his guest, should this happen during their visit. It's worth reading *Broken April,* by Ismail Kadare, a brilliant exploration of people living under the *Kanun* in modern times.

ALBANIA UNDERSTAND ALBANIA

1980s this little country was turning out an extraordinary 14 films a year. Despite a general lack of funds in the post-communist era, two movies have gone on to win awards at international film festivals. Gjergj Xhuvani's comedy *Slogans* (2001) is a warm and touching account of life during communist times. This was followed in 2002 by *Tirana Year Zero,* Fatmir Koçi's bleak look at the pressures on the young to emigrate. *Lorna's Silence* (2008), a film about Albanians living in Belgium, was awarded in the 2008 Cannes Film Festival, while *Amnesty* (2011), a drama about two spouses making conjugal visits to a prison together, was Albania's most commercially successful film of all time.

Music

Blaring from cars, bars, restaurants and mobile phones – music is something you get plenty of in Albania. Most modern Albanian music has clarinet threaded through it and a goatskin drum beat behind it. Polyphony, the blending of several independent vocal or instrumental parts, dates from ancient Illyrian times, and can still be heard, particularly in the south.

Visual Arts

One of the most delicious Albanian art treats is to be found in Berat's Onufri Museum. Onufri was the most outstanding Albanian icon painter of the 16th and 17th centuries, and his work is noted for its unique intensity of colour, derived from natural dyes that are as fresh now as the day he painted with them. Other superb collections of his work

can be found in Korça and at the National History Museum (p53) in Tirana.

More contemporary art with a political twist can be seen in Tirana's excellent Bunk'Art (p53).

Environment

Albania consists of 30% vast interior plains, 362km of coast and a mountainous spine that runs its length. Mt Korab, at 2764m, is Albania's highest peak.

The country's large and beautiful lakes include the Balkans' biggest, Lake Shkodra, which borders Montenegro in the north, and the ancient Lake Ohrid in the east (one-third Albanian, two-thirds Macedonian). Albania's longest river is the Drin (280km), which originates in Kosovo and is fed by melting snow from mountains in Albania's north and east. Hydroelectricity has changed Albania's landscape: Lake Koman was once a river, and the water from the Blue Eye Spring near Saranda travels to the coast in open concrete channels via a hydroelectricity plant. Agriculture makes up a small percentage of land use, and citrus and olive trees spice up the coastal plains. Most rural householders grow their own food.

National parks in Albania include Dajti, Llogara, Tomorri, Butrint, Valbona and Theth. Most are protected only by their remoteness, and tree-felling and hunting still take place. Hiking maps of the national parks are available, though they can be hard to find.

Albania's Alps have become a 'must-do' for hikers, and they're home to brown bear, wolf, otter, marten, wild cat, wild boar and deer. Falcons and grouse are also Alpine favourites, and birdwatchers can also flock to wetlands at Lake Butrint and Lake Shkodra (though the wetlands aren't pristine).

Lake Ohrid's unique trout species is endangered (but still eaten), and endangered loggerhead turtles nest on the Ionian coast and on the Karaburun Peninsula, where there have also been sightings of critically endangered Mediterranean monk seals.

Food & Drink

In coastal areas the calamari, mussels and fish will knock your socks off, while high-altitude areas like Llogara have roast lamb worth climbing a mountain for. Offal is popular; *fërgesë Tiranë* is a traditional Tirana dish of offal, eggs and tomatoes cooked in an earthenware pot.

Vegetarians will have a hard time of it outside large towns, but many restaurants serve pizza, pasta or grilled and stuffed vegetables.

Raki is a very popular drink in Albania. The two main types are grape *raki* (the most common) and *mani* (mulberry) *raki*. Ask for homemade if possible *(raki ë bërë në shtëpi)*. If wine is more your cup of tea, seek out the Çobo winery near Berat and its Shesh i Bardhe white. Albanian red wine is generally awful and don't be at all surprised if a waiter asks you if you want a sweet or a dry red. Local beers include Tirana and Korça – the latter gets our vote. Coffee remains the standard national drink of choice at any time of day: normally tiny, superstrong espresso combined with a cigarette.

SURVIVAL GUIDE

ℹ Directory A-Z

ACCESSIBLE TRAVEL
High footpaths and unannounced potholes make life difficult for mobility-impaired travellers. Tirana's top hotels do cater to people with disabilities, and some smaller hotels are making an effort to be more accessible. The roads and castle entrances in Gjirokastra, Shkodra, Berat and Kruja are cobblestone, although taxis can get reasonably close.

ACCOMMODATION
Hotels and guesthouses, including an expanding number of boutique and heritage properties, are easily found throughout Albania as tourism continues to grow. You will rarely have trouble finding a room for the night, though seaside towns are often booked out in late July and August.

Homestays abound in Theth and Valbona, while the number of camping grounds is increasing; you'll find them at Himara, Livadhi, Dhërmi and Drymades. Most have hot showers and on-site restaurants.

LGBTIQ+ TRAVELLERS
Extensive antidiscrimination legislation became law in 2010, but did not extend to legalising same-sex marriage. Gay and lesbian life in Albania is alive and well but is not yet shaped into clubs or organisations. The alternative music and party scene in Tirana is queer-friendly, but most contacts are made on the internet. As with elsewhere in the Balkans, discretion is generally the way to go for LGBTIQ+ travellers.

MONEY
ATMs are widely available in most towns. Acceptance of credit cards is normally confined to upper-end hotels, restaurants and shops, although every year their usage becomes more widespread.

OPENING HOURS
Banks 9am to 3.30pm Monday to Friday
Cafes & Bars 8am to midnight
Offices 8am to 5pm Monday to Friday
Restaurants 8am to midnight
Shops 8am to 7pm; siesta time can be any time between noon and 4pm

PUBLIC HOLIDAYS
New Year's Day 1 January
Summer Day 16 March
Nevruz 23 March
Catholic Easter March or April
Orthodox Easter March or April
May Day 1 May
Mother Teresa Day 19 October
Independence Day 28 November
Liberation Day 29 November
Christmas Day 25 December

TELEPHONE
Albania's country phone code is 355. Mobile coverage is excellent, but limited in very remote areas (though most places have some form of connection, including Theth).

TOURIST INFORMATION
The country's main tourist board website is www.albaniantourist.com. The tourist

information offices with some English-speaking staff operate in Tirana (p60), Saranda (p73), Korça (p67), Gjirokastra (p70) and Berat (p66), though they're rarely particularly proficient; the staff at the ZIT in Saranda are a pleasant exception. In general the best advice can be obtained from staff at hostels and travel agencies.

WOMEN TRAVELLERS

Albania is a safe country for women travellers, but outside Tirana it is mainly men who go out and sit in bars and cafes in the evenings. You may tire of being asked why you're travelling alone, but you'll rarely feel the target of more than curiosity.

ℹ️ Getting There & Away

Daily buses go from Albania to Kosovo, Montenegro, North Macedonia and Greece (note that there are no international train routes to/from Albania). Saranda is a short boat trip from Greece's Corfu, while in summer, ferries also connect Himara and Vlora to Corfu. There are regular ferries to Italy from Durrës.

ENTERING THE COUNTRY

All citizens of European and North American countries may enter Albania visa-free for up to 90 days. This is also true for Australians, New Zealanders, Japanese and South Korean citizens. Citizens of most other countries must apply for a visa.

AIR

Nënë Tereza International Airport (p60) is a modern, well-run terminal 17km northwest of Tirana. There are no domestic flights within Albania. Airlines flying to and from Tirana include **Adria Airways** (www.adria.si), **Alitalia** (www.alitalia.com), **Austrian Airlines** (www.austrian.com), **Lufthansa** (www.lufthansa.com), **Olympic Air** (www.olympicair.com), **Pegasus Airlines** (www.flypgs.com) and **Turkish Airlines** (www.turkishairlines.com).

LAND

Border Crossings

There are no passenger trains into Albania, so your border-crossing options are buses, *furgon* (shared minibus), taxis or walking to a border and picking up transport on the other side.

Montenegro The main crossings link Shkodra to Ulcinj (via Muriqan, Albania, and Sukobin, Montenegro) and to Podgorica (via Hani i Hotit).

Kosovo The closest border crossing to the Lake Koman Ferry terminal is Morina, and further south is Qafë Prush. Near Kukës, use Morinë for the highway to Tirana.

North Macedonia Use Blato to get to Debar, and Qafë e Thanës or Tushemisht, each to one side of Pogradec, for accessing Ohrid.

Greece The main border crossing to and from Greece is Kakavija on the road from Athens to Tirana. It's about half an hour from Gjirokastra and 250km southeast of Tirana, and can take up to three hours to pass through in summer. Kapshtica (near Korça) to Krystallopigi also gets long lines in summer. Konispoli (near Butrint in Albania's south) and Leskovik (between Gjirokastra and Korça) are both far less busy.

Bus

From Tirana, regular buses head to Pristina, Kosovo; to Skopje in North Macedonia; to Ulcinj in Montenegro; and to Athens and Thessaloniki in Greece. *Furgon* and buses leave Shkodra for Montenegro, and buses head to Kosovo from Durrës. Buses travel to Greece from Albanian towns on the southern coast as well as from Tirana.

Car & Motorcycle

Travellers heading south from Croatia can pass through Montenegro to Shkodra (via Ulcinj), and loop through Albania before heading into North Macedonia via Pogradec or into Kosovo via the Lake Koman Ferry, or the excellent Albania–Kosovo highway.

To enter Albania with your own vehicle you'll need a Green Card (proof of third-party insurance, issued by your insurer); check that your insurance covers Albania.

Taxi

Heading to North Macedonia, taxis from Pogradec will drop you off just before the border at Tushemisht/Sveti Naum. Alternatively, it's an easy 4km walk to the border from Pogradec. It's possible to organise a taxi (or, more usually, a person with a car) from where the Lake Koman Ferry stops in Fierzë to Gjakova in Kosovo. Taxis commonly charge €50 from Shkodra to Ulcinj in Montenegro.

SEA

Two or three boats per day ply the route between Saranda and Corfu, in Greece, and there are plenty of ferry companies making the journey to Italy from Vlora and Durrës. There are additional ferries from Vlora and Himara to Corfu in the summer.

ℹ️ Getting Around

BICYCLE

Cycling in Albania is tough but certainly feasible. Expect lousy road conditions including open drains, some abysmal driving from fellow road users, and roads that barely qualify for the title. Organised groups head north for mountain biking, and cyclists are even spotted cycling the long and tough Korça–Gjirokastra road.

Shkodra, Durrës and Tirana are towns where you'll see locals embracing the bike, and Tirana even has bike lanes and a bike-sharing scheme!

BUS

Bus and *furgon* are the main forms of public transport in Albania. Fares are low, and you either pay the conductor on board or when you hop off, which can be anywhere along the route.

Municipal buses operate in Tirana, Durrës, Shkodra, Berat, Korça and Vlora, and trips usually cost 40 lekë.

CAR & MOTORCYCLE

Despite severe neglect under the communists, nowadays the road infrastructure is improving; there's an excellent highway from Tirana to Kosovo, and the coastal route from the Montenegro border to Butrint, near Saranda, is in good condition.

Tourists are driving cars, motorbikes and mobile homes into the country in greater numbers, and, apart from heavy traffic and bad drivers, it's generally hassle free. One issue is the huge number of traffic cops running speed traps. If they stop you for speeding, you'll have to pay a 'fine' in cash (around €20).

Off the main routes a 4WD isn't a bad idea. Driving at night is particularly hazardous; following another car on the road is a good idea as there are rarely any road markings or street lighting. A valid foreign driving licence is all that's required to drive a car in Albania.

Car Hire

There are lots of car-hire companies operating out of Tirana and Saranda, including all the major international agencies in the capital. Rates are low and quality generally good: hiring a small car costs as little as €20 per day. Rates include third-party insurance, with extra charged for full cover.

Fuel & Spare Parts

There are petrol stations on almost every road in Albania, but fill up before driving into the mountainous regions. As the range of cars being driven around Albania increases, so does the availability of spare parts, but it almost goes without saying that if you're driving an old Mercedes-Benz there will be parts galore.

Road Rules

Drinking and driving is forbidden, and there is zero tolerance for blood-alcohol readings. Both motorcyclists and passengers must wear helmets. Speed limits are as low as 30km/h in built-up areas and 35km/h on the edges, and there are plenty of traffic police monitoring the roads. Keep your car's papers with you, as police are active checkers.

HITCHING

Hitchhiking is quite a common way for travellers to get around – though it's rare to see locals doing it. Hitching is never entirely safe, and we don't recommend it. Travellers who hitch should understand that they are taking a small but potentially serious risk.

TRAIN

Albanians prefer bus and *furgon* travel, and when you see the speed and the state of the (barely) existing trains, you'll know why. However, the trains are dirt cheap and travelling on them is an adventure. Daily passenger trains leave suburban Tirana (the main train station in the city has been demolished and a new one was under construction in Laprakë in the northwest of the city, at the time of writing) for Durrës. Check timetables at the station in person, and buy your ticket 10 minutes before departure.

Bosnia & Hercegovina
Босна и Херцеговина

POP 3.51 MILLION

Best Places to Eat

➜ Tima-Irma (p115)

➜ Avlija (p102)

➜ Rajska Vrata (p107)

➜ Želja (p102)

➜ Park Prinčeva (p102)

Best Places to Stay

➜ Isa-begov Hamam Hotel (p100)

➜ Pansion Čardak (p114)

➜ Halvat Guest House (p100)

➜ Hostel Nihad (p105)

➜ Hotel Aziza (p100)

Why Go?

Craggily beautiful Bosnia and Hercegovina is most intriguing for its East-meets-West atmosphere born of blended Ottoman and Austro-Hungarian histories filtered through a Southern Slavic lens. Many still associate the country with the heartbreaking civil war of the 1990s, and the scars from that time are all too visible. But today's visitors are likely to remember the country for its deep, unassuming human warmth, its beautiful mountains, numerous medieval castle ruins, raftable rivers, impressive waterfalls and bargain-value skiing.

Major drawcards include the reincarnated historical centres of Sarajevo and Mostar, counterpointing splendid Turkish-era stone architecture with quirky bars, inviting street-terrace cafes, traditional barbecue restaurants and vibrant arts scenes. There's plenty of interest to discover in the largely rural hinterland too, all at prices that make the country one of Europe's best-value destinations.

When to Go
Sarajevo

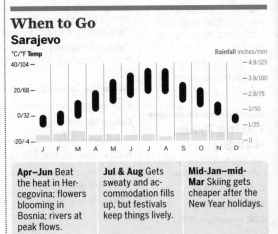

Apr–Jun Beat the heat in Hercegovina; flowers blooming in Bosnia; rivers at peak flows.

Jul & Aug Gets sweaty and accommodation fills up, but festivals keep things lively.

Mid-Jan–mid-Mar Skiing gets cheaper after the New Year holidays.

AT A GLANCE

Area 51,129 sq km

Capital Sarajevo

Country code ☑387

Currency Convertible mark (KM, BAM)

Emergency ambulance ☑124, fire ☑123, police ☑122

Languages Bosnian, Serbian and Croatian (all variants of the same language)

Money ATMs accepting Visa and MasterCard are ubiquitous

Population 3.51 million

Time Central European Time (GMT/UTC plus one hour)

Useful phrases *zdravo* (hello); *hvala* (thanks); *molim* (please), *koliko to košta?* (how much does it cost?)

Visas Not required for most visitors (see www.mvp.gov.ba)

Sleeping Price Ranges

The following price ranges refer to a double room with bathroom during high season.

€ less than 80KM

€€ 80KM–190KM

€€€ more than 190KM

Eating Price Ranges

The following price ranges refer to a main course.

€ less than 10KM

€€ 10KM–20KM

€€€ more than 20KM

Entering the Country

Bosnia has four main international airports, although only Sarajevo has an extensive range of flights. Depending where in the country you're heading to, it's often worth comparing prices on flights to Dubrovnik, Split or Zagreb in Croatia, then connecting to Bosnia by land. Belgrade (Serbia) and Podgorica (Montenegro) are also options.

Bosnia has multiple border crossings with Croatia, Serbia and Montenegro.

ITINERARIES

Four Days

Devote your first two days to exploring Sarajevo (p92). On day three, stop to admire the rebuilt Ottoman bridge (p108) in Konjic (p108) on your way to the even more famous rebuilt Ottoman bridge (p109) in Mostar (p109). The next day, stop in Blagaj (p116), the Kravica Waterfall (p116), Počitelj (p118) and the Radimlja Necropolis (p119) en route to Trebinje (p118).

Seven Days

Spend your first day soaking up the sights of the Una River Valley (p125) and your second exploring the lakes (p121), waterfall (p121) and historical old centre of Jajce (p121). Split day three between Travnik (p120) and Visoko (p105), pushing on to Sarajevo (p92) in time for bed. Then continue with the four-day itinerary above.

Essential Food & Drink

Bosanska kafa Traditional Bosnian coffee, made and served in a *džezva* (small, long-handled brass pot).

Burek Bosnian *burek* are cylindrical or spiral lengths of filo pastry usually filled with minced meat. *Sirnica* is filled with cheese, *krompiruša* with potato, and *zeljanica* with spinach. Collectively these pies are called *pita*.

Ćevapi (ćevapčići) Minced meat formed into cylindrical pellets and served in fresh bread with melting *kajmak* (see below).

Hurmašice Syrup-soaked sponge fingers.

Kajmak Thick semisoured cream.

Lokum Turkish delight.

Pljeskavica Patty-shaped *ćevapi*.

Rakija Grappa or fruit brandy.

Sarma Steamed dolma-parcels of rice and minced meat wrapped in cabbage or other green leaves.

Tufahije Whole stewed apple with walnut filling.

Bosnia & Hercegovina Highlights

1 **Sarajevo** (p92) Padding around Baščaršija's fascinating alleyways and downing Bosnian coffee, *burek* and *ćevapi*.

2 **Mostar** (p109) Gawping as men throw themselves off the rebuilt stone bridge.

3 **Jajce** (p121) Watching the waterfall tumble past Jajce's castle-crowned Old Town.

4 **Trebinje** (p118) Enjoying the low-key pace, walled riverside Old Town and leafy squares and parks.

5 **Kravica Waterfall** (p116) Cooling off in the turquoise waters beneath the fantastical falls.

6 **Počitelj** (p118) Soaking up the atmosphere of a tiny, picture-perfect hillside town.

7 **Rafting** (p124) Splashing down one of Bosnia and Hercegovina's fast-flowing rivers.

8 **Bjelašnica** (p105) Skiing the Olympic pistes in winter or exploring upland villages in summer.

SARAJEVO CAPAJEBO

🎵 033 / POP 395,000

Ringed by mountains, Sarajevo is a singular city with an enticing East-meets-West vibe all of its own. It was once renowned as a religious melting pot, earning it the epithet 'the Jerusalem of Europe'. Within a few blocks you can still find large Catholic and Orthodox cathedrals, Ashkenazi and Sephardic synagogues, and numerous mosques. However, the Jewish population was decimated during WWII and Sarajevo is now a divided city, with most of the Orthodox Christians living in Istočno Sarajevo (East Sarajevo) on the Republika Srpska side.

During the 20th century, two violent events thrust Sarajevo into the world's consciousness: the assassination which sparked WWI, and the brutal almost-four-year siege of the city in the 1990s. The scars of the longest siege in modern European history are still painfully visible, yet Sarajevo is once again a wonderful place to visit – for its intriguing architectural medley, vibrant street life and irrepressible spirit.

History

Romans had bathed at Ilidža's sulphur springs a millennium earlier, but Sarajevo was officially founded in 1462 by the Ottoman Turks. The name is thought to derive from the Turkish word for a court or palace (*saray*) surrounded by a plain (*ova*).

It rapidly grew wealthy as a silk-trading entrepôt and developed considerably during the 1530s when Ottoman governor Gazi Husrev-beg lavished the city with mosques and covered bazaars. In 1697 the city was burnt by Eugene of Savoy's Austrian army. When rebuilt, Sarajevo cautiously enclosed its upper flank in a large, fortified citadel, the remnants of which still dominate the Vratnik area. In 1850 the Ottomans shifted their Bosnian headquarters from Travnik to Sarajevo.

The Austro-Hungarians were back more permanently in 1878 and erected many imposing Central European–style buildings. However, their rule was put on notice by Gavrilo Princip's fateful 1914 pistol shot (near the Latin Bridge), which killed Austria-Hungary's Archduke Franz Ferdinand, plunging Europe into WWI.

Postwar, under the first Yugoslavia, Sarajevo lost its capital status. In 1941 it fell to the Germans and was incorporated into the fascist Independent State of Croatia, heralding a time of persecution for the city's Serbian and Jewish communities in which 85% of the latter were killed. After WWII Sarajevo once again became the Bosnian capital, within the Federal Republic of Yugoslavia.

Less than a decade after hosting the 1984 Winter Olympics, Sarajevo endured a nearly four-year siege that horrified the world. Between 1992 and 1995, the city was pounded by Bosnian Serb shelling from the surrounding mountains; its only access to the outside world was via a secret tunnel under the airport runway. Shelling and sniper fire killed more than 10,500 Sarajevans and wounded 50,000 more.

At the time of the Dayton Peace Accord in late 1995, the southern and eastern fringes of the city were under the control of the Bosnian Serbs. These areas are now a separate city known as Istočno Sarajevo (East Sarajevo) within the Republika Srpska, with a population that's 94% Serbian. The percentage of Serbs in Sarajevo proper has dropped from around 30% before the war, to under 4%.

◉ Sights

◎ Baščaršija

Centred on what foreigners call Pigeon Square, Baščaršija (pronounced barsh-*char*-shi-ya) is the very heart of old Sarajevo. The name is derived from the Turkish for 'main market' and it's still lined with stalls, a lively (if tourist-centric) coppersmiths alley, grand Ottoman mosques, *caravanserai* (inn) restaurants and lots of inviting little cafes. The east–west lane, Sarači, broadens out into the wide pedestrian boulevard Ferhadija, where Austro-Hungarian–era buildings take over. Some very grand examples line the waterfront.

★ Sarajevo City Hall ARCHITECTURE
(Gradska vijećnica Sarajeva; Map p94; Obala Kulina bana bb; adult/child 10/5KM; ⊙9am-6pm) A storybook neo-Moorish striped facade makes the triangular Vijećnica (1896) Sarajevo's most beautiful Austro-Hungarian–era building. Seriously damaged during the 1990s siege, it finally reopened in 2014 after laborious reconstruction. Its colourfully restored interior and stained-glass ceiling are superb. Your ticket also allows you to peruse the excellent *Sarajevo 1914–2014* exhibition in the octagonal basement. This gives well-explained potted histories of the city's various 20th-century periods, insights into

fashion and music subcultures, and revelations about Franz Ferdinand's love life.

In 1914 Franz Ferdinand and his much frowned-upon wife Sophie (his mother's former lady-in-waiting) had been on their way back from this very building when they were shot by Gavrilo Princip. From 1949 the building became the National Library but in August 1992 it was deliberately hit by a Serbian incendiary shell. Around two million irreplaceable manuscripts, books and documents were destroyed. Those that survived might one day return, but for now the building is used as the council chamber, for weddings and occasionally for concerts.

Various exhibitions are staged in the upper level and, in 2018, an ICTY (International Criminal Tribunal for the former Yugoslavia) information centre opened on the ground floor, including the contents of the original courtroom, which was shifted here from the Hague.

★ Galerija 11/07/95 　　　　　　　MUSEUM
(Map p94; ☑ 033-953 170; www.galerija110795.ba; 3rd fl, Trg Fra Grge Martića 2; admission/audioguide/tour 12/3/4KM; ⊙ 9am-10pm, guided tours 10.15am & 7.15pm) This gallery uses stirring photography, video footage and audio testimonies of survivors and family members to create a powerful memorial to the 8372 victims of the Srebrenica massacre, one of the most infamous events of the Bosnian civil war. You'll need well over an hour to make the most of a visit, and it's worth paying the extra for the audioguide to gain more insight.

BOSNIA & HERCEGOVINA SARAJEVO

THE SREBRENICA GENOCIDE

The Bosniak Muslim–majority town and municipality of Srebrenica had already been under constant attack by Bosnian Serb forces for a year before the town was declared a 'safe area' by the UN in April 1993, with the support of UNPROFOR troops. As the siege tightened around the town, Srebrenica drew thousands of refugees fleeing from Bosnian Serb assaults on nearby Bosniak villages.

There were an estimated 45,000 desperate people crammed into Srebrenica when, on 11 July 1995, Bosnian Serb forces entered the town following a week-long major offensive. Roughly 400 Dutch peacekeepers proved powerless to influence events, as the victorious forces of Bosnian Serb commander General Ratko Mladić marched another 7km north to the Potočari battery factory, then used as the local UN base. Some 5000 Bosniaks had taken temporary refuge within the base, with many thousands more gathering outside hoping in vain for protection. Instead, the Bosniak women and girls were separated from their menfolk and were eventually bussed out in convoys; many were raped. Over the following days, more than 8000 men and boys were summarily executed at various sites and buried in mass graves.

In 2007 the International Court of Justice upheld earlier rulings by the International Criminal Tribunal for the former Yugoslavia (ICTY) that the massacre, along with mass deportations of more than 20,000 women and elderly, constituted genocide, though a UN vote accepting that definition was vetoed by Russia in 2015. In 2004 the government of the Republika Srpska issued an official apology for the crimes that took place in Srebrenica, based on its own report into what had happened. However, in 2018, the Republika Srpska government annulled the 2004 report and called for a new probe.

The old UN base in Potočari now houses the **Srebrenica-Potočari Memorial Centre** (Memorijalni centar Srebrenica-Potočari; ☑ 056-440 082; www.potocarimc.org; Potočari bb, Srebrenica; ⊙ 8am-4pm Mon-Fri, by arrangement Sat & Sun), incorporating a major display entitled *Srebrenica Genocide – The Failure of the International Community*. You could easily spend hours here, starting by watching a 30-minute film and then examining the photographs, in-depth displays, graffiti left by Dutch peacekeepers and video testimonies of survivors. The deeply moving experience is made all the more intense when accompanied by a guide – likely a survivor whose own family was decimated in the events.

The main focus of the complex is the extensive **cemetery** directly across the road, with row after sentinel row of pointed white Islamic-style gravestones, each commemorating a reburied victim. More are added each year as the painstaking examination of bone fragments, rotted clothing and DNA samples slowly reveals the identities of more individuals. Within the cemetery, a one-room subterranean photographic gallery powerfully evokes the trauma of this heartbreaking identification process.

Central Sarajevo

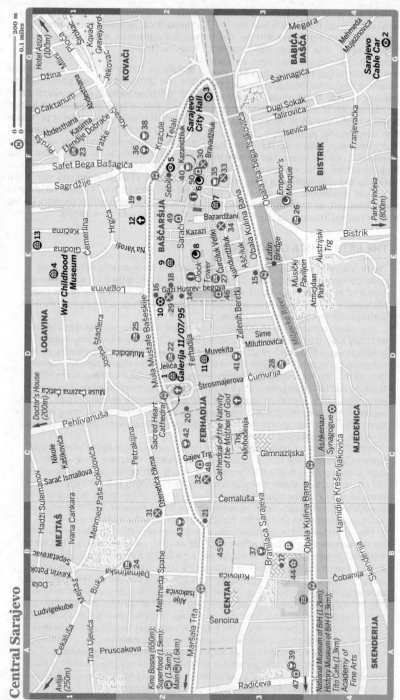

Central Sarajevo

BOSNIA & HERCEGOVINA SARAJEVO

Museum of Crimes Against Humanity & Genocide 1992–1995 MUSEUM

(Muzej zločina protiv čovječnosti i genocida; Map p94; ☑ 062 467 764; Muvekita 11; adult/child 10/8KM; ⊙ 9am-10pm Apr-Oct, to 6pm Nov-Mar) Nothing is sugar-coated in this confronting museum covering the many atrocities that took place throughout Bosnia during the 1990s war. Video footage combined with photographs, artefacts and personal testimonies illustrates the horror and brutality of the times. We wouldn't recommend bringing younger children.

Gazi Husrev-beg Mosque MOSQUE

(Gazi Husrev-begova džamija; Map p94; ☑ 033-573 151; www.begovadzamija.ba; Sarači 18; mosque 3KM, incl museum 5KM; ⊙ 9am-noon, 2.30-4pm & 5.30-7pm May-Sep, 9am-11am Oct-Apr) Bosnia's second Ottoman governor, Gazi Husrev-beg, funded a series of splendid 16th-century buildings, of which this 1531 mosque, with its 45m minaret, is the greatest. The domed

interior is beautifully proportioned and even if you can't look inside, it's worth walking through the courtyard with its lovely fountain, chestnut trees and the *turbe* (tomb) of its founder.

Gazi Husrev-beg Museum MUSEUM

(Map p94; www.vakuf-gazi.ba; Sarači 33-49; museum 3KM, incl mosque 5KM; ⊙ 9am-8pm) The 1537 Kuršumlija Madrasa building is distinctive for its pointed chimneys and the lead roof from which it takes its name. Although built as a religious school, it now hosts a small exhibition about the colourful life and philanthropic legacy of Ottoman governor Husrev-beg, who received the honorific 'Gazi' (meaning hero) for his role in the conquest of Belgrade. There's little in the way of artefacts but the video is well worth watching.

Brusa Bezistan MUSEUM

(Map p94; ☑ 033-239 590; www.muzejsarajeva. ba; Abadžiluk 10; adult/child 3/1KM; ⊙ 10am-6pm Mon-Fri, to 3pm Sat mid-Apr–mid-Sep, 10am-4pm Mon-Sat mid-Sep–mid-Apr) Built in 1551 as a silk-trading bazaar, this elegant two-storey building is topped with six green-metal domes and encircled by shops. It's now a branch of the Museum of Sarajevo, providing an overview of the city from prehistoric times up until 1914. At its centre is a scale model of Sarajevo as it looked in 1878. The only concession to recent history is a series of grisly large-scale photographs of the mass-grave excavations from the 1990s genocide.

Jewish Museum SYNAGOGUE
(Muzej Jevreja BiH; Map p94; ☑033-535 688; www.muzejsarajeva.ba; Mula Mustafe Bašeskije 40, Baščaršija; adult/child 3/1KM; ☉10am-6pm Mon-Fri, to 1pm Sun mid-Apr–mid-Sep, 10am-4pm Mon-Fri, to 1pm Sun mid-Sep–mid-Apr) More religiously open-minded than most of Western Europe in its day, the Ottoman Empire offered refuge to the Sephardic Jews who had been evicted en masse from Spain in 1492. While conditions varied, Bosnian Jews mostly prospered until WWII, when most of the 14,000-strong community fled or were murdered. The community's story is well told in this 1581 Sephardic synagogue that still sees active worship during Jewish New Year.

Old Orthodox Church CHURCH
(Stara pravoslavna crkva; Map p94; Mula Mustafe Bašeskije 59; museum 3KM; ☉8am-6pm Mon-Sat, to 4pm Sun, museum to 3pm Tue-Sun) While the final form of this outwardly austere stone church dedicated to the archangels Michael and Gabriel dates to 1730, it was founded considerably earlier – possibly as long ago as the 5th century. Inside, under a star-spangled night-blue ceiling, is a superb gilded iconostasis from 1674 fronted by a pair of 3m-high candlesticks. The cloister museum displays manuscripts, vestments and icons, the oldest of which were painted in the 15th century.

◉ Other Areas

During the 1992–95 siege, the city's wide east–west artery road (Zmaja od Bosne) was dubbed 'Sniper Alley' because Bosnian Serb gunmen in surrounding hills could pick off civilians as they tried to cross it. Most of the embattled journalists who covered that conflict sought refuge in what's now the Hotel Holiday, built in 1984 as the Holiday Inn; it looks like a cubist still life of pudding and custard. While there are still shell scars to be seen, a scattering of high-rise office blocks marks this out as the business end of town.

★**Sarajevo Cable Car** CABLE CAR
(Sarajevska žičara; Map p94; ☑033-292 800; www.zicara.ba; off Franjevačka, Babića bašča; single/return 15/20KM; ☉10am-8pm) Reopened in 2018 after being destroyed during the war, Sarajevo's cable car once again shuttles people on a nine-minute ride, climbing 500m to a viewpoint 1164m up on Mt Trebević. From here it's a short walk to the wreck of the Olympic bobsled track, seemingly held together by layers of graffiti.

★**War Childhood Museum** MUSEUM
(Muzej ratnog djetinjstva; Map p94; ☑033-535 558; www.warchildhood.org; Logavina 32, Logavina; adult/child 10/5KM; ☉11am-7pm) This affecting museum had its genesis in a 2013 book edited by Jasminko Halilović, in which he asked a simple question of survivors of the Sarajevo siege: 'What was a war childhood for you?' Of the hundreds of replies received, 50 short written testimonies are presented here, each illustrated by personal effects donated by the writer, such as diaries, drawings, toys and ballet slippers. It's a lighter, less gore-filled approach to the conflict than you'll find elsewhere, but equally devastating.

Svrzo House MUSEUM
(Svrzina kuća; Map p94; ☑033-535 264; www.muzejsarajeva.ba; Glođina 8, Logavina; adult/child 3/1KM; ☉10am-6pm Mon-Fri, to 3pm Sat mid-Apr–mid-Sep, 10am-4pm Mon-Sat mid-Sep–mid-Apr) An oasis of whitewashed walls, cobbled courtyards and partly vine-draped dark timbers, this 18th-century house-museum has been brilliantly restored and appropriately furnished, helping visitors to imagine Sarajevo life in Ottoman times.

Yellow Fortress FORTRESS
(Žuta Tabija; Map p98; Jekovac bb, Vratnik) FREE One of the most appealing yet accessible viewpoints gazing over Sarajevo's red-roofed cityscape is from this bastion, built in the 18th century as part of the walls encircling Vratnik. Now sprouting mature trees and a cafe, it's a popular place for picnickers and canoodling lovers. By tradition, the end of the Ramadan fast is formally announced by a canon shot from here.

National Museum of BiH MUSEUM
(Zemaljski muzej BiH; Map p98; www.zemaljskimuzej.ba; Zmaja od Bosne 3, Marijin dvor; adult/child 6/3KM; ☉10am-7pm Tue-Fri, to 2pm Sat & Sun) Bosnia's biggest and best-endowed museum of ancient and natural history is housed in an impressive, purpose-built quadrangle of

THE SARAJEVO HAGGADAH

Arguably the greatest treasure of the National Museum of BiH is the world-famous Sarajevo Haggadah, a priceless 14th-century illuminated codex (used during Passover) filled with beautiful hand-painted illustrations – a rarity in Jewish texts. Even more extraordinary is the story of its survival. It's thought to have been created in Barcelona and taken from Spain during the expulsion of the Sephardic Jews. At some point it turned up in Venice and was saved from destruction in 1609 by a Catholic priest who vouched for its contents. It was sold to Sarajevo's museum in 1894 and, during WWII, was hidden from the Nazis by a Muslim librarian and an Islamic cleric, who hid it in his mosque. During the 1990s siege, it survived a break-in at the National Museum (the thieves didn't realise its value) and was saved from the bombardment, again by a Muslim curator, by being interred in the vaults of the National Bank. Today it's once again on display, now in its own secure, air-conditioned showcase.

Geraldine Brooks' 2008 novel *People of the Book* is a fictionalised account of the Haggadah's extraordinary history.

neoclassical 1913 buildings. It's best known for housing the priceless Sarajevo Haggadah illuminated manuscript, but there's much more to see. Along with the Haggadah, the main building houses extraordinary Greek pottery and Roman mosaics. Behind this, the central courtyard has a pretty little botanical garden and an exceptional collection of medieval *stećci* (grave-carvings).

History Museum of BiH　　MUSEUM
(Map p98; ☑ 033-226 098; www.muzej.ba; Zmaja od Bosne 5, Novo Sarajevo; adult/child 5/2KM; ☺ 9am-7pm) Somewhat misleadingly named, this small yet engrossing museum occupies a striking, still partly war-damaged 1960s socialist-modernist building originally dubbed the Museum of the Revolution. It regularly hosts high-profile international exhibitions but the main attraction is the permanent *Surrounded Sarajevo* display, which charts local people's life-and-death battles for survival between 1992 and 1995. Alongside some heartbreaking photographs are personal effects such as self-made lamps, examples of food aid, stacks of Monopoly-style 1990s dinars and a makeshift siege-time 'home'.

Also interesting is the collection of 1996–2011 before-and-after Sarajevo images in the hallway. Directly behind the building, the tongue-in-cheek Tito (☺ 7am-11pm) bar is a museum in its own right.

Tunnel of Hope　　MUSEUM
(Tunel Spasa; ☑ 033-778 672; www.tunelspasa.ba; Tuneli 1, Ilidža; adult/child 10/5KM; ☺ 9am-4pm) During the 1992–95 siege, when Sarajevo was surrounded by Bosnian Serb forces, the only link to the outside world was an 800m-long, 1m-wide, 1.6m-high tunnel between two houses on opposite sides of the airport runway. Walking through a 25m section is the moving culmination of a visit to the shell-pounded house which hid the western tunnel entrance. The story of the siege and the tunnel's construction is told via video, information boards and an audioguide accessible via free wi-fi.

Although the airport was supposedly neutral and under tenuous UN control during the conflict, crossing it would have been suicidal. The solution was to secretly build the tunnel, which was eventually equipped with rails to transport food and arms. That proved just enough to keep Sarajevo supplied during nearly four years of siege.

Getting here by public transport is complicated; you're better off catching a taxi.

Vrelo Bosne　　PARK
(www.zppks.ba; Ilidža; adult/child 2/1KM) Ever popular with local families, this extensive park is home to a patchwork of lush mini-islands at the cliffed mouth of the Bosna River. The classic way to get there is to stroll or take a horse-drawn carriage ride (20KM) for 3km along elegantly tree-lined Velika Aleja, starting near Ilidža's Hotel Aleja.

Ars Aevi　　GALLERY
(Map p98; ☑ 033-216 927; www.arsaevi.org; Terezija bb, Skenderija; adult/child 4/2KM; ☺ 10am-6pm Tue-Sun) Many of the works in this thought-provoking contemporary art gallery were collected as donations for Bosnia during the 1990s conflict. The collection includes works by the likes of Anish Kapoor, Nan Goldin and Marina Abramović; a rotating selection of them is displayed in a factory-esque interior of metal ducts and polished chipboard within the lumpy Skenderija Centar.

Sarajevo

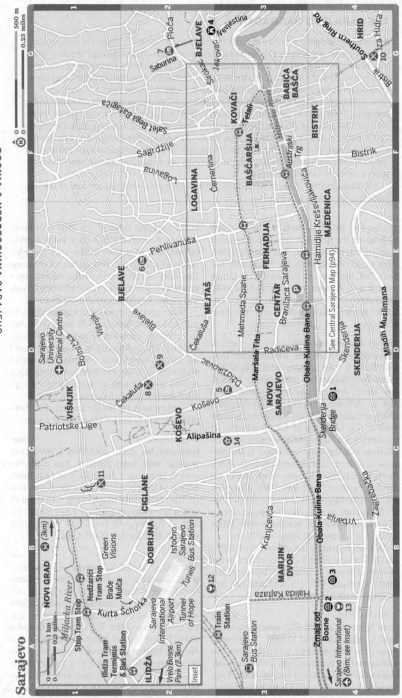

500 m
0.25 miles

HRID

Iza Hidra

Bistrik

Southern Ring Rd

BJELAVE

Pločča

Nevjestina

Jekovac

Saburina

Širokac

KOVAČI

Telali

BABIĆA
BAŠĆA

Safet Bega Bašagića

Sagrdžije

Logavina

Ćemerlina

BAŠČARŠIJA

Austrijski
Trg

BISTRIK

Bistrik

LOGAVINA

Pehlivanuša

FERHADIJA

Hamdije Kreševljakovića

See Central Sarajevo Map (p94)

MJEDENICA

BJELAVE

Bjelave

MEJTAŠ

Čekaluša

Mehmeda Spahe

CENTAR

Branilaca Sarajeva

Mladih Muslimana

Sarajevo
University
Clinical Centre

Višnjik

Bolnička

Maršala Tita

Radićeva

SKENDERIJA

Skenderija

VIŠNJIK

Čekaluša

Džidžikovac

NOVO
SARAJEVO

Obala Kulina Bana

Patriotske Lige

Koševo

KOŠEVO

Alipašina

Skenderija
Bridge

Zagrebačka

CIGLANE

Kranjčevića

MARIJIN
DVOR

Obala Kulina Bana

Vrbanja

Vrbanja

Halida Kajtaza

Zmaja od
Bosne

Train
Station

Sarajevo
Bus Station

Sarajevo International
(8km; see Inset)

Inset

1 km
0.5 miles

NOVI GRAD

Stup Tram Stop

Miljacka River

Nedžarići
Tram Stop

Brače
Mulića

Green
Visions

DOBRINJA

Istočno
Sarajevo
Bus Station

Kurta Schorka

Sarajevo
International
Airport

Tunel;
Tunelj: Bus Station

ILIDŽA

Ilidža Tram
Terminus
& Bus Station

Vrelo Bosne
Park (2.3km)

Sarajevo
Tunnel
of Hope

(3km)

Sarajevo

◎ Sights
1 Ars Aevi...D4
2 History Museum of BiH......................A4
3 National Museum of BiH....................B4
4 Yellow Fortress....................................G2

🛏 Sleeping
5 Colors Inn...D3
6 Doctor's House.....................................E2
7 Hotel Aziza...G2

🍴 Eating
8 4 Sobe Gospođe Safije.......................D2
9 Avlija..D2
10 Park Prinčeva......................................G4
11 Superfood..C1

🍷 Drinking & Nightlife
12 Caffe 35..B2
13 Tito..A4

🎭 Entertainment
14 Kino Bosna...C3

👣 Tours

Toorico Tours TOURS
(Map p94; ☑ 060 3026 994; www.tooricotours.
com) Free (pay tips) two- to three-hour walking tours depart from in front of the Eternal
Flame on Maršala Tita. There is also a five-
hour 'Complete Sarajevo War' tour (66KM),
day trips to Srebrenica (120KM) or Mostar/
Počitelj (120KM), and – most intriguingly –
dinners with a Bosnian family in their home
(70KM). Five per cent of your tips is donated to local charities.

Spirit TOURS
(Map p94; ☑ 033-219 159; www.bhspirit.com;
Ferhadija 19, Ferhadija; ⊙9am-5pm) Free (ie for
tips) 90-minute walking tours depart from
this office at 10am daily. The outfit also offers a two-hour full city walking tour (€15),
a driving tour to the Tunnel of Hope (€15),
and day trips including Srebrenica (€60)
and Mostar/Počitelj/Kravica (€75).

Meet Bosnia TOURS
(Map p94; ☑ 061 240 286; www.meetbosnia.com;
Gazi Husrev-begova 75, Baščaršija; ⊙9am-7pm)
As well as the obligatory free walking tour
(paid for by tips, departing from the office
at 10.30am daily), this well-regarded crew
offers a 3½-hour 'Fall of Yugoslavia' tour
(€25), along with excursions to Mostar,
Međugorje, Travnik, Jajce, Srebrenica and
Višegrad.

Neno's Free Walking Tour WALKING
(Map p94; www.sarajevowalkingtours.com; Pozorište trg, Centar; ⊙10.30am daily Apr-Oct, set
dates Nov-Mar) Neno's free walking tours sum
up the country's history and include fascinating personal reflections; 'free' means you
pay through tips. Walks start in front of the
National Theatre (p104) and take roughly
two hours; book ahead via email. Private
tours can also be arranged.

InfoBosnia TOURS
(Map p94; ☑ 061 076 756; www.infobosniatours.
com; Velika avlija Laure Papo Bohorete 2, Baščaršija;
⊙9am-8pm) Along with the usual free walking tour, broader city tours and excursions,
this agency offers interesting themed itineraries such as hour-long 'Get to Know Islam'
walks (€10) and three-hour 'Judaism, Christianity and Islam' walks (€20).

Sarajevo Funky Tours TOURS
(Map p94; ☑ 062 612 612; www.sarajevofunkytours.
com; Besarina Čikma 5, Baščaršija; ⊙8am-6pm
Mon-Fri, to 3pm Sat & Sun) This popular tour
outfit has a wide range of offerings in and
around Sarajevo, plus longer multiday tours
covering much of Bosnia.

Insider TOURS
(Map p94; ☑ 033-534 353; www.sarajevoinsider.
com; Zelenih Beretki 30, Baščaršija; ⊙9am-5pm
Mon-Sat, to 2pm Sun) Offers a wide range
of tours in and beyond Sarajevo. Popular
daily tours include the two-hour 'Tunnel
Tour' (€15) and excellent three-hour 'Times
of Misfortune' (€27) tour to sites related
to the 1990s conflict. There are also free
90-minute walking tours, departing from
the office at 9.30am and 4.30pm (run for
tips; book ahead).

Green Visions OUTDOORS
(☑ 033-717 290; www.greenvisions.ba; Trg Bar-
celone 5, Novi Grad; ⊙9am-5pm Mon-Fri) This
long-established ecotourism specialist offers a wide range of hiking, cycling and rafting trips. In winter it also runs snowshoeing
expeditions into the mountains surrounding the city (from €40, including pick-up
from anywhere in Sarajevo, snowshoe hire
and lunch).

Sarajevo Discovery TOURS
(Map p94; ☑ 061 818 250; www.sarajevodiscovery.
com; Gazi Husrev-begova 46a, Baščaršija; ⊙10am-
7pm) An experienced operator offering a
variety of themed Sarajevo walking and
driving tours.

🛏 Sleeping

Doctor's House
HOSTEL €

(Map p98; ☏061 222 914; www.thedoctors househostel.com; Pehlivanuša 67, Bjelave; dm/d from 24/70KM; 🛜) The Doctor's House is a healthy choice, if only for the workout you'll get walking up the hill from the centre of town. It's a nice neighbourhood; the French ambassador lives next door. The dorms all have privacy curtains, reading lights, power points and lockers, and there are also a couple of tidy private rooms.

Hostel Balkan Han
HOSTEL €

(Map p94; ☏061 538 331; www.balkanhan.com; Dalmatinska 6, Centar; dm/apt from €10/41; 🖭🛜🐕) Within seconds of arrival at this party hostel you're likely to find yourself in its bar with a shot of herb *rakija* chatting with gregarious owner Unkas, or lounging in the little triangle of garden at the rear. Newly enlarged, brightly coloured upper dorm rooms have one-plus-two bunks; the lower bed sleeps a couple.

Travellers' Home
HOSTEL €

(Map p94; ☏070-242 400; www.myhostel.ba; 1st fl, Ćumurija 4, Baščaršija; dm/r from 20/51KM; 🕙24hr; 🛜) Upstairs in a high-ceilinged old house, this friendly little hostel has helpful, informative staff, a tiny courtyard balcony, and a kitchen table at which travellers can converse. There are good lockers, bunk-accessible power points and a little library of books.

★Halvat Guest House
GUESTHOUSE €€

(Map p94; ☏033-237 715; www.halvat.com. ba; Kasima Efendije Dobrače 13, Kovači; s/d/tr 80/113/132KM; 🅿🖭🛜) The six rooms at this friendly, family-run guesthouse are clean and spacious, and surprisingly quiet for such a central location. Breakfast is available at an additional charge – but with Baščaršija just down the road, you might choose to skip it. Only the narrowest of vehicles should brave the secure garage (charged separately).

★Hotel VIP
HOTEL €€

(Map p94; ☏033-535 533; www.hotelvip.info; Jaroslava Černija 3, Baščaršija; s/d 138/177KM; 🅿🖭🛜) Tucked away on a quiet lane in the centre of town, this smart modern block only has a dozen rooms but the ambience, professional service, valet parking and well-provisioned breakfast buffet might have you think you're staying somewhere far ritzier. The bathrooms are excellent, and some rooms have balconies.

Franz Ferdinand Hostel
HOSTEL €€

(Map p94; ☏033-238 099; www.franzferdinand hostel.com; Jelića 4, Baščaršija; r with/without bathroom 90/82KM; 🖭@🛜) One of Sarajevo's most popular hostels, Franz Ferdinand uses giant sepia photos and a timeline floor to recall characters and scenes from Sarajevo's WWI history. The foyer walls are a-scribble with guest graffiti. Bunks have private power points and ample headroom, and the comfortably stylish kitchen-lounge is well designed for conversation between travellers. It also rents bikes.

Ovo Malo Duše
BOUTIQUE HOTEL €€

(Map p94; ☏033-972 800; www.ovo-malo-duse. com; Mudželiti mali 2, Baščaršija; s/d from €52/62; 🕙7am-10pm; 🖭🛜) The six-room former Villa Wien has been rebranded and given a minor makeover but it retains an appealing mixture of comfort and old-world elegance. Each room has its own idiosyncratic charm. There's no reception so you will need to check in at the Wiener Café downstairs before it closes at 10pm.

★Isa-begov Hamam Hotel
HERITAGE HOTEL €€€

(Map p94; ☏033-570 050; www.isabegovhotel. com; Bistrik 1, Bistrik; s/d from €80/100; 🖭) After many years of restoration, this ornate 19th-century *hammam* (Turkish bath), founded in 1462, reopened with a hotel attached in 2015. The 15 rooms are designed to evoke the spirit of the age, with lashings of handcrafted dark-wood furniture, ornately carved bedsteads and tube-glass chandeliers. Guests get free use of the *hammam*, which is also open to the general public.

★Hotel Aziza
HOTEL €€€

(Map p98; ☏033-257 940; www.hotelaziza.ba; Saburina 2, Vratnik; r/ste 196/235KM; 🅿🖭🛜) Not just an extremely comfortable and friendly family-run hotel, this place invites you to enter into the love story of its owners, Mehmed and Aziza Poričanin. The 17 spacious, light-filled rooms are numbered according to significant years in the couple's life, such as the births of children and grandchildren. A daily sauna is included in the rates.

Colors Inn
HOTEL €€€

(Map p98; ☏033-276 600; www.hotelcolorsinn sarajevo.com; Koševo 8, Koševo; s/d from €89/103; 🅿🖭🛜) Modernist decor is given a dramatic twist with wall-sized black-and-white photos of 20th-century Sarajevo and starlight-style twinkles in the corridors. The 37

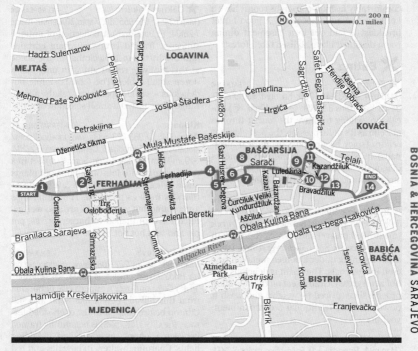

🏃 City Walk
A Sarajevo Stroll

START ETERNAL FLAME
END SARAJEVO CITY HALL
LENGTH 1.2KM; ONE HOUR

Start at the ❶ **Eternal Flame**, a Yugoslav-era symbol of togetherness, emphasising the joint role that Serbs, Bosniak Muslims, Croats and Montenegrins played in the WWII liberation of the city. It's named after postwar leader Marshal Tito.

Stroll past the cafes and shops of Ferhadija, pausing to admire the ostentatious Austro-Hungarian–era market hall, ❷ **Gradska Trznica** (Ferhadija 7, Centar). After another block you'll reach a square dominated by the Catholic ❸ **Sacred Heart Cathedral**, built in 1889 in the neo-Gothic style. Continuing east, a line set into the street proclaims the ❹ **'Sarajevo Meeting of Cultures'** at the point where the Austrian-style buildings suddenly give way to the low-slung terracotta roofs of Baščaršija.

Immediately to your right is the first significant Ottoman building, the ❺ **Bezistan** (www.vakuf-gazi.ba; Gazi Husrev-begova bb;

⊘8am-9pm Mon-Sat, 10am-3pm Sun), a narrow 16th-century bazaar. Walk past the stalls selling tourist tat as far as the first exit on your left. As you step outside you'll see ahead of you the 1529 ❻ **Clock Tower** – topped with an Islamic prayer clock – and the elegant minarets of the ❼ **Gazi Husrev-beg Mosque** (p95). Cut through the mosque courtyard and exit by the gate nearest the fountain. Across the lane is the 1537 Islamic school which houses the ❽ **Gazi Husrev-beg Museum** (p95).

Continue east along Sarači until you reach the square at the heart of ❾ **Baščaršija**. Straight ahead is the ❿ **Baščaršija Mosque** (Baščaršija džamija; Baščaršija 37), while to the left is the gazebo-like 1891 ⓫ **Sebilj** drinking fountain. Take the tiny lane, Luledžina, to the right by the fountain, and cut past the water-pipe bars. The first lane on your right brings you out onto ⓬ **Kazandžiluk**, the atmospheric coppersmiths alley. Turn right and follow it around until you hit ⓭ **Bravadžiluk**, Baščaršija's main eating strip. At its eastern end is the exuberant red-and-yellow striped ⓮ **Sarajevo City Hall** (p92).

comfortably fashion-conscious rooms have a kettle, coffee and chocolates. A good buffet breakfast is laid out in a basement dining room designed like a stylised birch forest.

✕ Eating

★ Željo
BALKAN €

(Map p94; ☑ 033-447 000; Kundurdžiluk 19 & 20, Baščaršija; mains 3.5-7KM; ⊙ 8am-10pm; 🐾) Locals are willing to brave the tourist throngs at Željo as it's quite possibly the best place for *ćevapi* (spicy beef or pork cylindrical meatballs) in Sarajevo. There are two branches diagonally across from each other. Both have street seating; neither serves alcohol.

Sač
BALKAN €

(Map p94; Bravadžiluk mali 2, Baščaršija; mains 3-4KM) Our pick for Sarajevo's best *burek* (meat-filled pastry) and *sirnica* (burek with cottage cheese), Sač bakes everything *ispod sača*, meaning under a domed metal lid covered in charcoals. The result is delicious and not at all greasy. Grab a seat on the side alley, order a slice (priced by weight) and wash it down with the traditional accompaniment, yoghurt.

Buregdžinica Bosna
BALKAN €

(Map p94; Bravadžiluk 9, Baščaršija; mains 3-7KM; ⊙ 7am-11pm) A classic spot for *burek* and other freshly cooked savoury pastries, sold by weight.

★ Avlija
EUROPEAN €€

(Map p98; ☑ 033-444 483; www.avlija.ba; Sumbula Avde 2, Višnjik; mains 7-15KM; ⊙ 8am-11pm Mon-Sat; 🐾) Locals and a few in-the-know expats cosy up at painted wooden benches in this colourful, buzzing covered yard, dangling with trailing pot plants, strings of peppers and the odd birdcage. Local specialities are served, along with pasta, risotto and schnitzel. Wash them down with inexpensive local draught beers and wines.

★ Superfood
INTERNATIONAL €€

(Map p94; www.facebook.com/SuperfoodStrEat Art; Husrefa Redžića 14, Ciglane; mains 5-27KM; ⊙ 11am-11pm Tue-Sat, noon-8pm Sun; 🐾) Tucked away among a set of much-graffitied apartment blocks, this hip cafe/restaurant wouldn't be out of place on the back streets of Auckland or Melbourne. It's a great place for brunch or a lunchtime sandwich, and they're particularly proud of their gourmet hamburgers here. Most of the ingredients are local, organic and free range.

★ Cakum Pakum
EUROPEAN €€

(Map p94; ☑ 061 955 310; Kaptol 10, Centar; mains 7-26KM; ⊙ 11am-11pm) A collection of antique suitcases, fringed lamps, gingham curtains and bright tartan tablecloths set the scene at this hip, wee restaurant with only half a dozen small tables. The food is simple but delicious – savoury pancakes, salads, a large range of pasta and a small selection of grills.

Klopa
INTERNATIONAL €€

(Map p94; ☑ 033-223 633; www.facebook.com/kloparestoran; Ferhadija 5, Centar; mains 6-28KM; ⊙ 9am-11pm Mon-Sat, 1-11pm Sun; 🐾☑) Set in a conservatory with lots of hanging pot plants and a living wall, this modern cafe has decor that's as fresh as its menu. The lamb chops are a staple, but vegetarians are also well catered for with their own burger, pizzas, pot pie and tofu hot pot. It also does breakfast.

Park Prinčeva
BALKAN €€€

(Map p98; ☑ 061 222 708; www.parkprinceva.ba; Iza Hrida 7, Hrid; mains 14-30KM; ⊙ 9am-11pm; 🅿 ✳) Gaze out over a superb city panorama from this hillside perch, like Bono and Bill Clinton before you. From the open-sided terrace, the City Hall (p92) is beautifully framed between rooftops, mosques and twinkling lights. Charming waiters in bow ties and red waistcoats deliver traditional dishes such as dumplings with cheese, veal *ispod sača* (roasted under a metal dome) and skewers.

Apetit
INTERNATIONAL €€€

(Map p94; ☑ 062 868 131; www.apetit.ba; Gazi Husrev-begova 61, Baščaršija; mains 14-35KM; ⊙ noon-11pm) Friendly, attentive staff and a central location make Apetit a popular choice. The menu includes pasta, risotto and wok-fried dishes, along with a good selection of meat- and fish-based mains. The spinach tagliatelle with seafood is particularly tasty.

4 Sobe Gospođe Safije
INTERNATIONAL €€€

(Map p98; ☑ 033-202 745; www.restoransarajevo.com; Čekaluša 61, Višnjik; mains 21-35KM; ⊙ 10am-midnight Tue-Sat, from noon Sun) With its hidden garden and backstory of forbidden love, the 'four rooms of Mrs Safija' is Sarajevo's most romantic and elegant restaurant. The menu shows a strong French and Mediterranean influence, tempered with the likes of sesame-crusted tuna, chicken with couscous and a soy-chicken salad. Ask for a table in the rear courtyard, by the gazebo and tinkling fountain.

🍷 Drinking & Nightlife

⭐ Zlatna Ribica
BAR

(Map p94; ☐ 033-836 348; Kaptol 5, Centar; ⊙ 8am-late) Sedate and outwardly grand, the tiny and eccentric 'Golden Fish' adds understated humour to a cosy treasure trove of antiques and kitsch, reflected in big art nouveau mirrors. Drink menus are hidden in old books that dangle by phone cords and the toilet is an experience in itself. Music swerves unpredictably between jazz, Parisian crooners, opera, reggae and the Muppets.

⭐ Art Kuća Sevdaha
CAFE

(Map p94; Halači 5, Baščaršija; ⊙ 10am-6pm Tue-Sun; 🛜) Sit in the intimate fountain courtyard of an Ottoman-era building sipping Bosnian coffee, juniper or rose sherbet, or herb-tea infusions while nibbling local sweets. The experience is accompanied by the lilting wails of *sevdah* (traditional Bosnian music) – usually recorded, but sometimes live. Within the building is a museum celebrating great 20th-century *sevdah* performers (5KM) along with a store selling CDs.

Čajdžinica Džirlo
TEAHOUSE

(Map p94; Kovači 16, Kovači; ⊙ 9am-10pm) Minuscule but brimming with character, Džirlo brews 29 types of tea, many of them made from distinctive Bosnian herbs. They are served in lovely little pots, each distinctive according to the blend. If you can't choose, let the flamboyant owner decide for you. Then unwind on low stools and watch the egg timer for the perfect time to start sipping.

Male Daire
CAFE

(Map p94; Luledžina 6, Baščaršija; ⊙ 9am-1am) This cute antique house is one of the most attractive *nargile* (water pipe) bars in the Old Town, with lots of outdoor tree-shaded seating. It is noticeably more relaxed than its noisy neighbour across the square. No alcohol is served.

Cafe Barometar
BAR

(Map p94; www.facebook.com/cafebarometar; Branilaca Sarajeva 23, Centar; ⊙ 7am-midnight; 🛜) Like something out of HG Wells' *Time Machine,* this steampunk cafe-bar is liberally strewn with dials, pipes and furniture crafted from axles, compressors and submarine parts. By day the vibe is mellow and jazzy, but DJs ramp things up on Friday and Saturday nights.

Birtija
BAR

(Map p94; Kovači 5, Kovači; ⊙ 8am-11pm) Popular with an artsy, bohemian crowd, this wonder-ful wee bar has an antiquey shabby-chic vibe. If it's packed downstairs (as it often is), head to the atmospheric slope-roofed upstairs room lined with dozens of tiny photos.

Caffe 35
BAR

(Map p98; 35th fl, Tešanjska 24a, Crni vrh; ⊙ 7am-11pm) If you're waiting for a train, what better place to do so than admiring a full city panorama from the 35th-floor cafe of the Avaz Twist Tower, just three minutes' walk from the station (p104). As the name suggests, the 2008 'Balkans' Tallest Tower' has a gently twisted look that brings a certain elegance to its sleek glass design.

Dekanter
WINE BAR

(Map p94; ☐ 033-263 815; www.facebook.com/vinoteka.dekanter; Radićeva 4, Centar; ⊙ 10am-midnight Mon-Sat, from 6pm Sun; 🛜) It's easy to sit for hours sampling from more than 100 local and world vintages in this glorious, low-lit wine bar decorated with bottles, chateau-boxes and swirling ceiling sculptures of intertwined wires. Stools and high tables spill onto a small square where a pub and two loungey bars vie for attention.

Tesla
PUB

(Map p94; Muvekita 1, Baščaršija; ⊙ 10am-1am) Contrasting with the pop-rock of the Anglo-Irish pubs nearby, Tesla's soundtrack is more contemporary and attracts a lively youthful crowd. The inventor's face is plastered all over the large vaulted brick space.

The Loft
GAY & LESBIAN

(Map p94; 6th fl, Mula Mustafe Bašeskije 6, Ferhadija; ⊙ 8pm-2.30am Fri & Sat) Discreetly tucked away on the 6th floor of a nondescript central-city building, Sarajevo's only gay club offers cheap drinks, surprisingly good wine, local pop hits and a friendly vibe.

☆ Entertainment

Kino Bosna
ARTS CENTRE

(Kinoteka BiH; Map p98; www.facebook.com/kinobosna; Alipašina 19, Koševo; ⊙ hours vary) This historical cinema overflows on Mondays during smoky singalongs to the house band playing Bosnian *sevdah* songs. Yugonostalgics pack in for New Wave nights and other themed parties. The building, originally industrial, was adapted into a workers club, then a theatre from the 1940s. It houses the national film archive.

Underground
LIVE MUSIC

(Map p94; www.facebook.com/undergroundclub sarajevo; Maršala Tita 56, Centar; ⊙ 8pm-late Fri

& Sat) On Friday and Saturday nights, local bands amp up in this medium-sized basement venue from around midnight. After the gig, music and drinking continues into the wee hours. It gets very smoky inside.

National Theatre Sarajevo
PERFORMING ARTS

(Narodno pozorište Sarajevo; Map p94; ☑ 033-221 682; www.nps.ba; Obala Kulina bana 9, Centar) Classically adorned with fiddly gilt mouldings, this proscenium-arch theatre hosts a ballet, opera, play or classical concert most nights from mid-September to mid-June. The grand, column-fronted, Renaissance-style building dates from 1921, adapted from its 1899 original form.

🛍 Shopping

Isfahan Gallery
HOMEWARES

(Map p94; ☑ 033-237 429; www.isfahans.com; Sarači 77, Baščaršija; ⊙ 9am-11pm) Specialising in high-quality Persian and Afghani rugs (with certificates of authenticity), along with glass lamps and richly glazed ceramic work, this entrancing shop brings a barrage of beautiful colours to the already enticing Morića Han *caravanserai* (inn).

BuyBook
BOOKS

(Map p94; ☑ 033-552 745; www.buybook.ba; Radićeva 4, Centar; ⊙ 9am-8pm Mon-Fri, 10am-6pm Sat) This excellent bookshop has a good selection of relevant works on the Balkans, including English-language fiction, nonfiction and guidebooks.

Kazandžijska Radnja Huseinović
ARTS & CRAFTS

(Map p94; ☑ 061 139 511; Kazandžiluk 18, Baščaršija; ⊙ 8am-9pm Mon-Sat, 10am-6pm Sun) Although coppersmiths shops fill the alleys of Baščaršija (especially Kazandžiluk), much is now imported or machine-made; only a handful are officially certified as producing genuinely handcrafted quality work. One of these is Ismet Huseinović, though not everything on display here is his work: the cute 'Aladdin' oil-lamps are Turkish. Look for the pens and sculptures fashioned from bullet casings.

ⓘ Information

Sarajevo University Clinical Centre (Klinički centar univerziteta u Sarajevu; Map p98; ☑ 033-445 522, 033-297 000; www.kcus.ba; Bolnička 25) Within the vast Koševo Hospital complex there's an English-speaking VIP outpatient clinic for people with foreign health insurance. The hospital also offers emergency care, including an emergency paediatrics department.

Tourist Information Centre (Turistički informativni centar; Map p94; ☑ 033-580 999; www.sarajevo-tourism.com; Sarači 58, Baščaršija; ⊙ 9am-9pm May-Oct, to 5pm Nov-Apr) Helpful official information centre. Beware of commercial imitations.

ⓘ Getting There & Away

AIR

The centrally located **Sarajevo International Airport** (SJJ; www.sarajevo-airport.ba; Kurta Schorka 36; ⊙ 5am-11pm) is less than 10km southwest of Baščaršija (p101). Airlines flying here year-round include Adria Airways, Air Serbia, Austrian Airlines, Croatia Airlines, Eurowings, flydubai, Lufthansa, Norwegian Air Shuttle, Pegasus Airlines, Qatar Airways, Turkish Airlines and Wizz Air. The terminal is modern but compact, with the usual array of car-hire and exchange offices, and a post office counter.

BUS

➡ Sarajevo's main **bus station** (Map p98; ☑ 033-213 100; Put života 8, Novo Sarajevo; ⊙ 24hr) has daily services to all neighbouring countries and to as far afield as Amsterdam and Istanbul.

➡ There are good links to Bosnian destinations including Mostar (20KM, 2½ hours, 10 daily), Međugorje (17KM, four hours, three daily), Visoko (5KM, 37 minutes, every half-hour), Banja Luka (32KM, five hours, six daily) and Bihać (42KM, 6½ hours, four daily).

➡ Further services to Republika Srpska (RS) and Serbia leave from the **Istočno Sarajevo Bus Station** (☑ 057-317 377; www.centrotrans-ad.com; Srpskih vladara 2, Lukavica; ⊙ 6am-11.15pm), although this isn't convenient for most travellers.

TRAIN

Trains departing Sarajevo's **railway station** (Željeznička stanica; ☑ 033-655 330; www.zfbh.ba; Trg žrtava genocida u Srebrenici, Novo Sarajevo; ⊙ ticket office 6.30am-8pm), adjacent to the bus station, head to destinations including Konjic (7.90KM, one hour, three daily), Mostar (18KM, two hours, two daily), Visoko (5.40KM, 45 minutes, six daily), Banja Luka (27KM, 4¾ hours, two daily) and Bihać (37KM, 6¼ hours, daily).

ⓘ Getting Around

TO/FROM THE AIRPORT

➡ On the meter, airport-bound taxis charge around 7KM from Ilidža or 16KM from Baščaršija, plus 2KM per bag for luggage in some cabs. However, at the terminal it's not always easy to find a taxi prepared to use the meter.

➡ A Centrotrans bus marked Aerodrom-Baščaršija (5KM, pay on-board) departs from outside the terminal and takes around 30 minutes to central Sarajevo. However, departures are (at most) once an hour. Buses follow the main tram route, heading east along the river via Obala Kulina bana and then looping back to the airport along Mula Mustafe Bašeskije, stopping on demand at all the main stops along the way.

PUBLIC TRANSPORT

Sarajevo has an extensive network of trams, buses, trolleybuses and minibuses, all operated by **GRAS** (☑ 033-293 333; www.gras.ba). Except for the airport bus (p104), all single-ride tickets cost 1.60KM if pre-purchased from kiosks, or 1.80KM if bought from the driver; they must be stamped once aboard. Two-ride (3KM), five-ride (7.10KM) and day tickets (*dnevna karta*, 5.30KM) are also available, but these are sold at official GRAS kiosks, which are few and far between.

These are the most useful routes.

Tram 3 (every four minutes during the day) From **Ilidža** it passes the National Museum (p96) then loops one-way (anticlockwise) around Baščaršija (p101).

Tram 1 (every 17 minutes during the day) Starts at the train station (p104) then does the same loop as Tram 3.

EASTERN BOSNIA

Aside from the extraordinary capital city, Sarajevo, Eastern Bosnia is largely off the radar for most travellers. The sad legacy of ethnic cleansing has cast a pall over much of the region, although many stop to pay their respects at Srebrenica (p93), the most notorious site of all. Other places of interest include magnificent Sutjeska National Park, the Olympic ski resorts Bjelašnica (p105) and Jahorina (p107), and Višegrad, with its Unesco-listed bridge (p107) and literary connections.

Bjelašnica Бјелашница

ELEV 2067M

The modest ski resort of **Bjelašnica** (www.bjelasnica.org; Babin Do bb; ski pass day/night 35/25KM, lift from 10KM in summer; ⊙ 8am-4pm & 6.30-9pm ski season, 10am-5pm May-Oct), around 25km south of Sarajevo, hosted the men's alpine events during the 1984 Winter Olympics. There's usually enough snow to ski from around Christmas, and New Year is the busiest time, though February is more reliable for good piste conditions. Floodlit night skiing is offered, and the main lift also operates May to October, allowing walkers easy access to high-altitude paths. In summer there are magical mountain villages to explore.

Hotel Han　　　　　　　　　　HOTEL €€
(☑ 033-584 150; www.hotelhan.ba; Babin Do bb; s/d from €64/80; ☎) With direct skiable access to the lift-base directly below, Han is a great choice. Stylishly appointed rooms are decorated like bleached Mondrian abstracts with added photo-panels of mountain and iceberg scenes. The restaurant echoes the relaxed yet elegant feel of the rooms. In summer, the hotel rents mountain bikes and offers guided quad tours.

❶ Getting There & Away

Bjelašnica is a 40-minute drive from central Sarajevo. In the ski season, a single bus service (44) runs from Sarajevo's National Museum (p96) at 9am, returning at 4.30pm.

Visoko Високо

☑ 032 / POP 39,900

Visoko was once the capital of medieval Bosnia and the spiritual centre of the long-suppressed Bosnian Church. By the 20th century little of this glory remained and it had become an unremarkable, largely forgotten leather-tanning town. Then came an audacious claim: that the partly wooded triangular hill that looms distinctively above Visoko is in fact the world's largest pyramid (see p106). Ever since, tourists and New Age mystics have poured in. The Pyramid of the Sun Foundation has since expanded the theory to incorporate a whole series of other hill-pyramids, a subterranean labyrinth and a web of energy fields focused with 21st-century stone circles.

🛏 Sleeping & Eating

Hostel Nihad　　　　　　　　　　B&B €
(☑ 062 721 011; www.hostelnihad.com; Mulići bb; s/d €22/37; ☞☎) Located right by the river on Visoko's rural fringes, 3km north of the bus station (p106), this superfriendly family-run place is much more of a B&B than a hostel. The five tasteful and well-kept en-suite rooms are positioned above a cafe, where excellent homemade breakfasts are served. There's also an auto camp attached.

Pyramid Lodge　　　　　　BOUTIQUE HOTEL €€
(☑ 032-941 123; www.pyramid-lodge.de; Grad bb; s/d from 88/144KM; ☞✳☎) This immaculate

hotel gives a sense of urban, artistic style that contrasts deliciously with the peaceful rural setting. It's high above Visoko, at the small parking area behind the 'pyramid' summit. The 12 rooms have very different prices according to size and view. There's a meditation room, cafe and large terrace, all with wonderful views.

Čevabdžinica
Ihtijarević
BALKAN €

(☑ 032-739 440; Čaršijska 25; 2.50-11KM; ⊘ 7am-10pm; ☎) It might look like a 1950s diner, but this fast-food restaurant has been churning out Bosnian-style grills since 1931. For a tasty, meaty, salty, fatty fix, try the house specialty, *pljeskavica u kajmaku* – a meat patty topped with cheesy sour cream.

Restaurant No. 1
EUROPEAN €€

(☑ 032-735 195; https://restaurantno1.business. site; Mule Hodžića 106; mains 8-16KM; ⊘ 9am-11pm; 🅿 🛜 🍴) On the main road at the foot of Visočica Hill, this local people-pleaser serves sandwiches, omelettes, pasta, grills and pizza, as well as a decent vegetarian and vegan selection catering to visiting pyramid chasers. Inside the fit-out is pure 1985 (when the restaurant opened), right down to the dark wood, mirrored ceiling and leather booths.

❶ Getting There & Away

There are services to **Visoko bus station** (☑ 032-735 830; Kadije Uvejsa bb; ⊘ 24hr) from Sarajevo (5KM, 37 minutes) every half-hour during the day. Trains from Sarajevo (5.40KM, 45 minutes) depart six times a day.

PYRAMID OF THE SUN?

On top of Visoko's 220m-high **Visočica Hill** are a few restored fragments of a fortress wall recalling Visoko's medieval role as Bosnian capital. It's well worth taking the steep walk to the top for the outstanding views that it affords. But is this really the summit of the world's greatest pyramid? That's the intriguing theory of Semir Osmanagić, an American-Bosnian businessman who claims it was built approximately 12,000 years ago (or perhaps 30,000, according to some 'pyramid' guides) by a long-disappeared superculture. This mainly forested 'Pyramid of the Sun' does indeed have a pyramidal shape when viewed from some angles (despite a long ridge at the back).

The Bosnian Pyramid theory has been widely discredited by archaeologists and geologists who deplore Bosnia's concentration of efforts on Visoko when so many more credible historical sites remain little investigated. But even so, the sheer audacity of the 'pyramid' claim is fascinating in its own right.

The theory is expounded at an **excavation site** (www.piramidasunca.ba; off Klisa; without/with guide 5/10KM; ⊘ 9am-7pm) on the side of the hill facing the town, situated at the end of a narrow lane with limited parking. Guides will direct you to slabs of exceedingly hard ancient 'concrete' cited as having once covered the hill, creating an artificially smoothed surface (credible geologists have described this as naturally occurring layers of conglomerate typical to the area). The presentation includes much talk about 'frequencies', culminating in a powerful beam of 'levitation frequency' said to emerge from the apex of the 'pyramid' (skeptics are free to smile and nod).

Visoko's most popular tourist draw is a guided tour through the **Tunnel Ravne** (www. piramidasunca.ba; guided tour per adult/child 20KM/free, day pass 40KM; ⊘ 9am-7pm, may close earlier in winter). At this highly commercialised site, a dozen or more kilometres of tunnels supposedly form a labyrinth that dates back many millennia. Guides postulate that the tunnels were originally excavated by the same superculture that built the 'pyramid'. Believers assert that monoliths found here give healthy vibrations, that the water inside is unusually pure (small bottles are sold for the princely sum of 10KM) and that 'negative radiation' probably made the site a place of healing. A half-hour hard-hat tour through the ever-growing network of accessible tunnels is a curious experience. The site is accessed from an unnamed road that's well signposted from Kakanjska at the northwestern approach to town. The ticket booth is part of a souvenir strip with stands hawking crystals and alternative 'healing' products, along with a juice and gelato bar.

In the meadow below the tunnel entrance is **Ravne 2 Park** (⊘ 9am-sunset), full of features designed to focus what Pyramid-ists believe to be powerful energy fields. These include a spiral herbarium, 'purification labyrinth', three concentric rock circles forming an 'aura-field amplifier' and 24 standing stones inscribed with circular 'cosmograms'.

JAHORINA ЈАХОРИНА

Of Sarajevo's two Olympic skiing resorts, multi-piste **Jahorina** (☑ 057-270 020; www. oc-jahorina.com; Olimpijska bb; ski pass per day 44-50KM, night 30-38KM, day & night 61-73KM; ⊙ Nov-Mar) (26km southeast of the city, on the Republika Srpska side) has the widest range of hotels, each within 300m of one of seven main ski lifts. There are still lots of bombed-out buildings to be seen, but reconstruction is continuing apace. The ski season usually starts in mid-November and continues through to late March. The best skiing is in mid-February, although the resort is at its busiest during the New Year holidays.

In summer the settlement becomes a semidormant cool-air retreat from the city, with some well-heeled locals escaping here for day-spa relaxation at the upmarket **Termag Hotel** (☑ 057-270 422; www.termaghotel.com; Poljice bb; r/ste from €54/67; P ⊛ 🕱 🖭).

Beside the longest slope, **Rajska Vrata** (☑ 057-272 020; www.jahorina-rajskavrata.com; Olimpijska 41; mains 8-20KM; ⊙ 9am-10pm Dec-Mar, to 5pm Apr-Nov; P 🕱) is a charming ski-in alpine chalet which sets diners beside a central fire with a giant metallic chimney or on the piste-side terrace. Specialties include double-cheese *uštipci* (Bosnian dough balls) and homemade juices (elderberry, rosehip, raspberry etc). Upstairs, six Goldilocks-esque pine-walled guest bedrooms have handmade beds fashioned from gnarled old branches.

Višegrad Вишеград

☑ 058 / POP 10,700

Famous for the Unesco-listed 'Bridge on the Drina' immortalised in Ivo Andrić's classic novel, Višegrad has parlayed this identity into a niche tourist industry by building Andrićgrad, a small but likeable mock-historical city nominally celebrating the author.

A majority Muslim town before the 1990s war, Višegrad suffered a brutal campaign of ethnic cleansing resulting in the death of at least a thousand Bosniaks in and around. The population is now 88% Serbian.

Mehmed Pasha Sokolović Bridge
BRIDGE

(Most Mehmed-paše Sokolovića; P) Built in 1571 and named after the grand vizier who commissioned it, this glorious 11-arch bridge is the only structure in Bosnia confirmed as being designed by Mimar Sinan, chief architect for the Ottoman Empire. The bridge rose to international fame after WWII when it played the starring role in Ivo Andrić's Nobel Prize–winning classic *Bridge on the Drina*. Declared a Unesco World Heritage site in 2007, it has been fully restored and is tastefully floodlit at night.

Andrićgrad
ARCHITECTURE

(☑ 066 703 722; www.andricgrad.com; Mlade Bosne bb; ⊙ 24hr) **FREE** Višegrad's faux-antique Old Town is a walled historical fantasy and custom-built tourist trap that is well worth a stroll. Although named after *Bridge on the Drina* author Ivo Andrić, it's a project of Sarajevo-born Serbian film director Emir Kusturica. Completed in 2014, it incorporates accommodation, cafe-bars, souvenir shops, a gallery, cinema and an Orthodox church. The architecture is a medley of Byzantine, Ottoman and Renaissance styles, and there are images of Serbian heroes (Andrić, Tesla, Njegoš, Princip) liberally scattered around.

Restoran Kruna
EUROPEAN €

(☑ 058-620 352; www.kruna.co.ba; Kralja Petra I 13; mains 7-12KM; ⊙ 7am-11pm) Lamps wear headscarves echoing the tablecloths, while exposed brickwork displays photos of Višegrad's bridge in various historical states of disrepair. Succulent veal, lamb or pork cooked *ispod sača* (roasted under a metal dome) is the speciality, albeit without a hint of green vegetables. The chicken-and-bacon skewers are very good. Squid, river fish and stuffed mushrooms supplement the extensive, meat-heavy menu.

ℹ Information

There's a helpful **tourist office** (☑ 058-620 950; www.visegradturizam.com; Trg palih boraca bb; ⊙ 8am-7pm Mon-Fri, to 4pm Sat & Sun May-Oct, 8am-4pm Mon-Sat Nov-Apr) at the back of the car park that faces the southern end of the old bridge.

ℹ Getting There & Away

Buses stop on the highway at the north side of the old bridge. Destinations include Foča (11KM, 1½ hours, five daily), Trebinje (26KM, five hours, three daily), Istočno Sarajevo (16KM, three hours, daily) and Banja Luka (45KM, nine hours, daily). There are also buses to Belgrade and Niš in Serbia.

WORTH A TRIP

KONJIC КОЊИЦ

Resting alongside the icy green Neretva River, the small town of Konjic was battered in both WWII and the 1990s war, but has revived its compact historical core centred on a beautiful six-span **Old Stone Bridge** (Stara kamena ćuprija; Konjic). Originally built in 1682, it was dynamited at the end of WWII by retreating Nazi forces but accurately reconstructed in 2009 on its original footings.

The area is also home to **D-0 ARK** (Tito's Bunker; ☑ 036-734 811; www.titosbunker.ba; per person 20KM; ⊙ tours 10am, noon & 2pm), one of the most extraordinary remnants of the Cold War, designed to keep Yugoslav president Tito and his high command safe from a 25-megaton blast. Built in secret between 1953 and 1979, this extensive subterranean command centre is reputed to have cost the equivalent of US$4 billion. It's located 4km southeast of Konjic; follow the signs.

There's also good hiking in the surrounding mountains, and rafting downstream on the Neretva. **RaftKor** (☑ 061 474 507; www.raft-kor.com; Varda 40/1; per person €35) is a reliable outfit that starts its tours with a visit to Boračko Lake. Rafting and canyoning trips can also be booked through **Visit Konjic** (☑ 061 072 027; www.visitkonjic.com; Donje polje bb; ⊙ 8am-8pm).

Numerous buses, including all Sarajevo–Mostar services, pass through Konjic. Three trains a day head north to Sarajevo (7.90KM, one hour) and south to Mostar (11KM, 50 minutes).

Sutjeska National Park
Национални Парк Сутјеска

Even from the road, it's easy to admire magnificent tree-dappled grey-rock crags that flank the Sutjeska canyon like scenes from a classical Chinese painting. But ideally, this splendid national park is a place to leave the asphalt behind, whether hiking or on a mountain bike. Tracks include a section of the multicountry **Via Dinarica** (☑ 062 393 393; www.viadinarica.com) megatrail.

You can organise guides and more in Tjentište, the park's only settlement and the site of a vast and oddly affecting concrete **Partisan memorial** commemorating a major WWII battle fought here.

🏃 Activities

The park has a network of mountain-bike and hiking trails. While these are waymarked, indications aren't as thorough or as frequent as you might hope, though you can arrange guides (preferably in advance) through the **National Park Information Office** (☑ 058-233 130; www.npsutjeska.info; Tjentište; ⊙ 7am-3pm mid-Mar–Oct) or a specialist adventure agency such as Encijan. Rafting is possible on the Tara River, just outside the national park.

Encijan   ADVENTURE SPORTS
(☑ 058-211 150; www.pkencijan.com; Krajiška bb, Foča; rafting from €60; ⊙ 9am-5pm Mon-Sat) This experienced Foča-based adventure-tourism outfit organises mountaineering and hiking within Sutjeska National Park. It also offers world-class rafting from its camp at Meštrevac on the Tara River, which cascades out of Europe's deepest canyon (across the Montenegrin border) then thunders over 21 rapids (class III to class IV in summer, class IV to class V in April).

🛏 Sleeping

Aside from mountain huts, there's a hotel, youth camp and holiday apartments in Tjentište. The town of Foča, 27km north, has further options. Perhaps the most memorable accommodation is outside the park at the Encijan rafting camp.

❶ Getting There & Away

Buses on the Trebinje–Foča route stop at Tjentište six times a day, including the three that continue on to Višegrad. Foča is 27km north of Tjentište.

❶ Getting Around

You can rent bicycles from the hotel in Tjentište. A sturdy rental car or jeep will prove useful to get to the start of some of the park's best trails from Tjentište, but be prepared for some seriously rough narrow lanes.

HERCEGOVINA
ХЕРЦЕГОВИНА

Hercegovina ('*hair*-tse-go-*vi*-na') is the sun-scorched southern part of the country, shadowing Croatia's Dalmatian coast. It takes its name from 15th-century duke (*herceg* in the local lingo) Stjepan Vukčić Kosača, under whose rule it became a semi-independent duchy of the Kingdom of Bosnia.

Its arid Mediterranean landscape has a distinctive beauty punctuated by barren mountain ridges and photogenic river valleys. Famed for its wines and sun-packed fruits, Hercegovina is sparsely populated but has intriguing historical towns and even has one little toehold on the Adriatic coast.

These days Western Hercegovina is dominated by Bosnian Croats, while Eastern Hercegovina is part of the Republika Srpska. Bosniak Muslims maintain an uneasy position between the two, especially in the divided but fascinating city of Mostar. Not counting the Catholic pilgrims who flood Međugorje, Mostar is far and away Hercegovina's biggest tourist drawcard. Trebinje is less known but has an appealing Old Town.

Mostar Мостар

⏺ 036 / POP 105,800

Mostar is the largest city in Hercegovina, with a small but thoroughly enchanting old town centre. At dusk the lights of numerous millhouse restaurants twinkle across gushing streams, narrow **Kujundžiluk** (Map p110) bustles joyously with trinket sellers and, in between, the Balkans' most celebrated bridge forms a majestic stone arc between medieval towers.

Stay into the evening to see it without the summer hordes of day trippers. Stay even longer to enjoy memorable attractions in the surrounding area and to ponder the city's darker side – beyond the cobbled lanes of the attractively restored Ottoman quarter are whole blocks of bombed-out buildings, a poignant legacy of the 1990s conflict.

Between November and April most tourist facilities go into hibernation, while summer here is scorchingly hot. Spring and autumn are ideal times to visit.

History

Mostar means 'bridge-keeper', a name that first entered the history books in 1474. In the 16th century the iconic stone Stari Most replaced the previous wooden suspension bridge, the wobbling of which had terrified traders as they gingerly crossed the fast-flowing Neretva River. The new 'old bridge' dates from a time when Mostar was booming as a key transport gateway within the powerful expanding Ottoman Empire. Some 30 *esnafi* (craft guilds) sprang up, including those for tanners (for whom the Tabhana was built) and goldsmiths (hence Kujundžiluk, 'gold alley').

Under Austro-Hungarian rule in the 19th century, the city's centre of gravity shifted north to Trg Musala where neo-Moorish buildings such as the City Baths and Hotel Neretva projected a grand new city image.

Before the 1990s conflict, Mostar was one of the most ethnically mixed cities in Yugoslavia, with one of the country's largest proportions of mixed marriages. Bosniak Muslims and Croats each comprised about 35% of the population, with Serbs at around 19%.

When Serb- and Montenegrin-controlled units of the Yugoslav army started bombarding Mostar in April 1992, the city's Bosniaks and Croats initially banded together. However, on 9 May 1993 a bitter conflict erupted between the former allies. A de facto front line emerged north–south along the Bulevar, with Croats to the west and Bosniaks to the east. For two years both sides swapped artillery fire and by 1995 Mostar resembled Dresden after WWII; all its bridges – including Stari Most – were destroyed, along with numerous historical buildings including all but one of its 27 Ottoman-era mosques. Around 2000 people lost their lives.

Vast international assistance efforts rebuilt almost all of the Unesco-listed old town core. However, more than two decades after the conflict, significant numbers of shattered buildings remain as ghostlike reminders. The psychological scars will take generations to heal and the city remains divided, with two bus stations and two postal systems – one Bosniak and the other Croatian. Serbs now number only 4% of the population, with Bosniaks at 44% and Croats at 48%.

◉ Sights

★ Stari Most   BRIDGE
(Map p110) The world-famous Stari Most (meaning simply 'Old Bridge') is Mostar's indisputable visual focus. Its pale stone magnificently reflects the golden glow of sunset or the tasteful night-time

Mostar

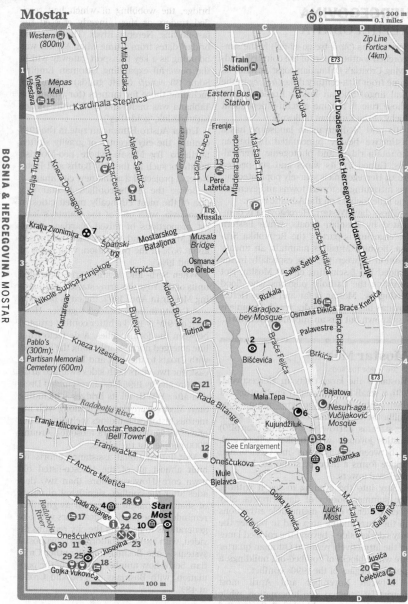

floodlighting. The bridge's swooping arch was originally built between 1557 and 1566 on the orders of Suleiman the Magnificent. The current structure is a very convincing 21st-century rebuild following the bridge's 1990s bombardment during the civil war.

Numerous well-positioned cafes and restaurants tempt you to sit and savour the splendidly restored scene.

An engineering marvel of its age, the bridge was nonetheless pounded into the river during a deliberate Croatian artil-

BOSNIA & HERCEGOVINA MOSTAR

Mostar

◉ Top Sights
1 Stari Most B6

◎ Sights
2 Biščevića Ćošak C4
3 Crooked Bridge A6
4 Hamam Museum A6
5 Kajtaz House D6
6 Koski Mehmed Pasha Mosque C5
7 Ljubljanska Banka Tower A3
8 MuM D5
9 Old Bridge Museum D5
10 War Photo Exhibition B6

◉ Activities, Courses & Tours
Bridge Divers' Club ....(see 10)
11 iHouse Travel A6
12 Mostar X Adventures B5

◎ Sleeping
13 Hostel David C2
14 Hostel Nina D6
15 Hotel Mepas A1

16 Muslibegović House D3
17 Old Town Hotel A6
18 Pansion Čardak A6
19 Shangri La D5
20 Taso's House D6
21 Villa Fortuna B4
22 Villa Mike B4

◎ Eating
23 Šadrvan B6
24 Tima-Irma B6

◎ Drinking & Nightlife
25 Black Dog Pub A6
26 Café de Alma B6
27 Club Calamus A2
28 Duradžik B5
29 Ima i Može Craft Beer Garden A6
30 Ljetna Bašta Oscar A6
31 OKC Abrašević B2

◎ Shopping
32 Kujundžiluk Bazaar D5

lery attack in November 1993. Depressing footage of this sad moment is shown on many a video screen in Mostar. After the war, Stari Most was painstakingly reconstructed using 16th-century building techniques and stone sourced from the original quarry. It reopened in 2004 and is now a Unesco World Heritage site famed for its bridge divers.

Partisan Memorial Cemetery MEMORIAL
(Partizansko spomen-groblje; Kralja Petra Krešimira IV bb) Although this cemetery is sadly neglected and badly vandalised, fans of 20th-century socialist architecture should seek out this magnificent memorial complex, designed by leading Yugoslav-era architect Bogdan Bogdanović and completed in 1965. Paths wind up past a broken bridge, a no-longer-functioning water feature and cosmological symbols to an almost Gaudi-esque upper section made of curved and fluted concrete, which contains the graves of 810 Mostar partisans who died fighting fascism during WWII.

Kajtaz House MUSEUM
(Kajtazova kuća; Map p110; ☑ 061 339 897; www.facebook.com/KajtazsHouse; Gaše Ilića 21; adult/child 4KM/free; ☉9am-6pm Apr-Oct) Hidden behind tall walls, Mostar's most interesting old house was once the harem (women's) section of a larger homestead built for a 16th-century Turkish judge. Full of original artefacts, it still belongs to descendants of

the original family but is now under Unesco protection. A visit includes a very extensive personal tour.

Hamam Museum MUSEUM
(Map p110; ☑036-580 200; www.facebook.com/thehamammuseum; Rade Bitange bb; adult/child 4/3KM; ☉10am-6pm) This late 16th-century bathhouse has been attractively restored with whitewashed interiors, bilingual panels explaining *hammam* (Turkish bath) culture and glass cabinets displaying associated traditional accoutrements. A wordless five-minute video gives a slickly sensual evocation of an imagined latter-day bathhouse experience.

War Photo Exhibition GALLERY
(Map p110; Stari Most; admission 6KM; ☉9am-9pm Jul-Sep, 10am-6pm Mar-Jun & Oct) This collection of around 50 powerful wartime photos by New Zealand photojournalist Wade Goddard is displayed in the western tower guarding Stari Most (p109), above the Bridge Divers' Club (p112).

Crooked Bridge BRIDGE
(Kriva ćuprija; Map p110) Built around 1558, this pint-sized bridge crosses the tiny Radobolja River amid a layered series of picturesque millhouse restaurants. The original bridge, weakened by wartime assaults, was washed away by floods on New Year's Eve 1999; it was rebuilt in 2002.

Old Bridge Museum   MUSEUM

(Muzej stari most; Map p110; ☑036-551 602; www.
muzejhercegovine.com; Kujundžiluk bb; adult/child
10KM/free; ☉10am-6pm Apr-Oct) This sparse
museum inhabits one of the defensive
towers that guard Stari Most (p109). Visits
start by climbing the five storeys for partial
views and interesting but limited displays
about the bridge's context and construction.
You then descend and walk through the
structure's archaeological bowels, where a
lengthy video (in Bosnian) gives a thorough
account of the bridge's reconstruction.

MuM   MUSEUM

(Museum of Mostar & Hercegovina; Map p110;
☑036-551 432; www.muzejhercegovine.com;
Maršala Tita 156; adult/student 5/3KM; ☉10am-
6pm Tue-Sun Apr-Oct, 9am-3pm Mon-Fri Nov-Mar)
Strong on poetry, far less so on content, the
slightly baffling 2014 annex of the Museum
of Hercegovina has a dozen showcases on
ethnographic lines and five silent big-screen
movies highlighting Hercegovina's scenic
and cultural highlights. These are complemented by an audioguide that offers a mix
of explanations, myths and flowery inspirational eulogies.

Bišćevića Ćošak   HOUSE

(Map p110; ☑036-550 677; Bišćevića 13; adult/
student 4/3KM; ☉8.30am-7pm Apr-Oct, winter
by tour only) Built in 1635, this is one of Mostar's very few traditional Ottoman houses
to retain its original appearance, albeit now
with trinkets for sale and a fountain made
of metal *ibrik* jugs. Afternoon light pours in
through the upstairs balcony room, which
juts out over the river and is colourfully furnished with rugs and carved wooden furniture. This is the only room you can enter, but
you can peer through the door of another
room and of the kitchen below.

Koski Mehmed
Pasha Mosque   MOSQUE

(Koski Mehmed-pašina džamija; Map p110; Mala
Tepa 16; mosque 6KM, incl minaret 12KM; ☉9am-
8.30pm Apr-Sep, 11am-5pm Oct-Mar) Entered
from a gated courtyard, this 1618 mosque
(substantially rebuilt after the war) has a
dome painted with botanical motifs and
punctuated by coloured-glass windows. You
can climb the claustrophobic minaret for
sweeping town views. Access to the charming courtyard doesn't require a ticket unless
you want to get close to the parapet for the
river view.

⚡ Activities

Bridge Divers' Club   ADVENTURE SPORTS

(Map p110; ☑061 388 552; Stari Most; training/
membership €10/25; ☉10am-dusk) In summer,
young men leap from the parapet of Stari
Most (p109) in a tradition dating back centuries, plummeting more than 20m into the
freezing cold Neretva. It's a hilarious spectacle, involving much stretching, preening and
posing in speedos and cajoling the crowd for
donations. Divers won't leap until 50KM has
been collected (in winter it's double).

If you want to experience one of Bosnia's
ultimate adrenaline rushes for yourself,
you'll first need to pay for training dives
from a much lower perch at the riverside
downstream. If you prove capable, you can
then join the club and test your mettle with
the real thing. You'll get a certificate to prove
your achievement. Don't underestimate the
dangers – diving badly can prove fatal. But if
you love it, your life membership means you
can subsequently dive as often as you like.

Zip Line Fortica   ADVENTURE SPORTS

(☑061 175 762; www.facebook.com/mtb.mostar.1;
25KM; ☉5-9pm Mon-Fri, 10am-9pm Sat & Sun)
Mostar's mountain-biking club now also operates Bosnia's longest zipline (570m), starting on a hill high above the city. The views
are sublime.

☞ Tours

Mostar X Adventures   OUTDOORS

(Map p110; ☑062 240 456; www.mostarxadven
tures.com; Onešćukova 44; bike hire per 2/5/12/24
hrs 6/12/17/22KM; ☉9am-4pm Mon-Sat) If it's
action or adventure you're after, this crew
can set you up with guided mountain biking
(from €30) and hiking (from €35), tandem
paragliding (€65), rafting (€45), and off-
road jeep (from €30) and quad expeditions
(€70). More gentle activities include themed
sightseeing, gastronomic and archaeological
tours. It also rents mountain bikes, if you'd
prefer to go it alone.

Mostar Travel   TOURS

(☑061 346 606; www.mostartravel.ba) Offers
city (€15, 1½ hours) and war-themed (€15,
two hours) walking tours around Mostar, a
themed 'Breakup of Yugoslavia' tour (€20,
two hours) and a trip to Blagaj and Počitelj
(€20, five hours). Full-day itineraries include
Sarajevo (€50, nine hours), Dubrovnik (€50,
nine hours), Kravica Falls (p116) (€20, seven
hours) and the 'Discover Hercegovina' tour
(€30, seven hours).

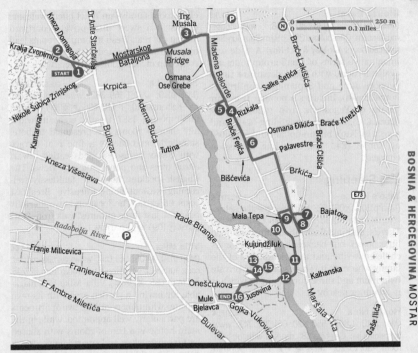

City Walk
Mostar's Scars

START ŠPANSKI TRG
END CROOKED BRIDGE
LENGTH 2KM; ONE HOUR

Start at ❶ **Španski trg**, where a monument honours Spanish peacekeepers killed during the Bosnian War. This square was on the front line between the Croatian and Bosniak sides of town. Several shell-pocked buildings remain in ruins, including the triangular ❷ **Ljubljanska Banka** (Snipers' Nest; Map p110; Kralja Zvonimira bb) block, once a notorious snipers' nest. Head towards the river and cross over to ❸ **Trg Musala**, once the heart of Austro-Hungarian Mostar. While the City Baths building (1914) has been restored, the once-splendid Hotel Neretva (1892) teeters on the verge of collapse. Turn right past the mosque onto the ❹ **Braće Fejića** shopping strip. Stop to admire the beautiful stonework of the ❺ **Roznamedži Ibrahimefendi Mosque**. Built before 1620, it was the only one of the city's old mosques to have survived the war. Further along is the substan-

tially rebuilt ❻ **Karadjoz-bey Mosque**. Take the next street to the left, passing various grand ruins, and then turn right onto Maršala Tita. Cut through the wartime cemetery and take the steps up to the 17th-century Ottoman ❼ **clock tower**, unusual in that it was commissioned by a woman. Walk back down towards the domed 1564 ❽ **Nesuh-aga Vučijaković Mosque**. Cross the road and take the cobbled lane nearly opposite and turn left past the two ❾ **tombs** onto Mala Tepa. The entrance to the ❿ **Koski Mehmed Pasha Mosque** (p112) is almost obscured behind the shops to your right. Continue through the ⓫ **Kujundžiluk Bazaar** (p109) to the ⓬ **Stari Most** (p109). After crossing it, take the first lane to your right and enter the ⓭ **Tabhana**, an old tannery complex where the central tanning pond is now a swimming pool. Head out onto the square, where you'll see the ⓮ **Hamam Museum** (p111) and the ⓯ **Tabačica Mosque**. Cut through to cobbled Onešćukova and look for the lane heading down to the ⓰ **Crooked Bridge** (p111).

iHouse Travel
TOURS

(Map p110; ☑036-580 048; www.ihouse-mostar.com; Oneščukova 25; ☉9am-9pm Jun-Sep, reduced hours Apr-May & Oct-Nov) A wide and imaginative series of small group tours are available here, with fixed departure times between June and September (confirm 24 hours ahead). Includes a popular two-hour 'Death of Yugoslavia' trip (€20), rafting (from €35), tandem paragliding (€49), and a visit to Tito's billion-dollar bunker (p108) at Konjic (€45 not including admission charges).

⌂ Sleeping

Taso's House
HOSTEL €

(Map p110; ☑061 523 149; www.guesthousetaso.com; Maršala Tita 187; dm/r from €8/20; ❉☎) There's nothing flash about this cramped little hostel, but backpackers love it for its chilled-out vibe and the friendliness of the family who runs it. There's only one private twin room and three dorms, one of which is in an annex nearby.

Hostel Nina
HOSTEL €

(Map p110; ☑036-550 820, 061 382 743; www.hostelnina.ba; Čelebica 18; dm/s/d without bathroom €10/15/20; ☐❉@☎) This popular homestay hostel is run by an obliging English-speaking woman whose husband is a former bridge-jumper who pioneered and still runs Hercegovina day tours (€30) and war tours sharing firsthand accounts of the siege (€15). There's a little patch of garden, a shared kitchen and free transfers from the bus and train stations.

Hostel David
HOSTEL €

(Map p110; ☑066 264 173; www.hosteldavid.com; Pere Lažetića 6; dm €11; ☉Feb-Sep; ❉☎) Hidden behind a high gate, this convivial place is given an unusual degree of charm by the palm tree and numerous flower boxes. It's on Mostar's hidden 'hostel street'.

★ Pansion Čardak
GUESTHOUSE €€

(Map p110; ☑036-578 249; www.pansion-cardak.com; Jusovina 3; r from €60; ☐❉☎) This old stone house on a central lane has been thoroughly modernised and now has seven spacious en-suite rooms with feature walls emblazoned with forest scenes. There's also a small guest kitchen.

Villa Fortuna
HOTEL €€

(Map p110; ☑036-580 625; www.villafortuna.ba; Rade Bitange 34; s/d 68/95KM; ☐❉☎) Set back from a street leading to the old bridge, this eight-room family-run hotel offers welcome drinks in a sweet little private courtyard area at the rear. Fresh if compact rooms lead off a hallway decorated with a museum-like collection of local tools and metalwork.

Shangri La
GUESTHOUSE €€

(Map p110; ☑061 169 362; www.shangrila.com.ba; Kalhanska 10; r €53-69; ☐❉☎) Behind an imposing 1887 facade, eight individually themed rooms are presented to hotel standards, and there's a fine roof terrace with comfy parasol-shaded seating, dwarf citrus trees and panoramic city views. The English-speaking hosts are faultlessly welcoming without being intrusive. Breakfast costs €6 extra. The location is wonderfully peaceful, just three minutes' walk from Stari Most (p109) up a narrow lane.

Villa Mike
GUESTHOUSE €€

(Map p110; ☑061 561 057; www.villamike-mostar.com; Tutina 15; s/d without bathroom from €27/45, apt from €55; ❉☎) Villa Mike is remarkable for having a garden area with its own private swimming pool. The two apartments are particularly well appointed, while in the main house is a trio of rooms with shared bathroom, kitchen and smart lounge-dining room. The obliging owner speaks Norwegian and good English.

Muslibegović House
HISTORIC HOTEL €€

(Map p110; ☑036-551 379; www.muslibegovichouse.com; Osmana Đikića 41; s/d from €60/75; ❉☎) In summer, tourists pay 4KM to visit this beautiful late-17th-century Ottoman courtyard house. But it's also an extremely charming boutique hotel. Room sizes and styles vary significantly, mixing excellent modern bathrooms with elements of traditional Bosnian, Turkish or even Moroccan design.

Hotel Mepas
HOTEL €€€

(Map p110; ☑036-382 000; www.mepas-hotel.ba; Kneza Višeslava bb; s/d from 167/203KM; ☐❉☎) Mostar's first five-star hotel inhabits a corner of the large Mepas Mall complex. The bright, glitzy reception is on the ground floor, but rooms, pool and spa centre are all on the 8th and 9th floors.

Old Town Hotel
BOUTIQUE HOTEL €€€

(Map p110; ☑036-558 877; www.oldtown.ba; Rade Bitange 9a; r/ste from €115/190; ☉Mar-Oct; ☐❉☎) ✎ Quiet yet supercentral, this art-decked 10-room hotel is designed to look like a classic Bosnian house, with kilim rugs and handmade, specially designed wooden furniture and fittings. Meanwhile its ecofriendly energy-saving systems include waste-burning furnaces for hot water and underfloor heating, with air-circulation systems to save on air-con. Standard rooms are tucked into sloping eaves.

✗ Eating

★ Tima-Irma
BALKAN €

(Map p110; ☑ 066 905 070; www.cevabdzinica-tima.com; Onešćukova bb; mains 5-11KM; ⊘ 8am-11pm; ☜) Despite the constant queues at this insanely popular little grill joint, the staff maintain an impressive equanimity while delivering groaning platters of *ćevapi* (cylindrical lozenges of minced meat), *pljeskavica* (burger meat) and shish kebabs. Unusually for this kind of place, most dishes are served with salad. Sandwiches and burgers are also on offer.

Šadrvan
BALKAN €€

(Map p110; ☑ 061 891 189; www.facebook.com/SadrvanMostar; Jusovina 11; mains 3.60-20KM; ⊘ 9am-midnight; ☜) On a vine- and tree-shaded corner where the pedestrian lane from Stari Most (p109) divides, this tourist favourite has tables set around a trickling fountain made of old Turkish-style metalwork. Obliging, costumed waiters can help explain a menu that covers many bases and takes a stab at some vegetarian options.

Pablo's
CROATIAN €€

(☑ 063 764 764; www.facebook.com/pablosrestaurant.mo; Kneza Branimira 11; 8-20KM; ⊘ 8am-midnight Sun-Thu, to 3am Fri & Sat; ✶ ☜) Incongruously named after Chilean poet Pablo Neruda, this contemporary-looking, conservatory-style restaurant serves a mixture of Croatian, Dalmatian and Italian dishes, including pasta, pizza, risotto, grilled fish, Zagreb-style schnitzel and rave-inducing steaks. Downstairs there's a clubby whisky and gin bar.

☷ Drinking & Nightlife

Black Dog Pub
PUB

(Map p110; www.facebook.com/Blackdogpubmostar; Jusovina 5; ⊘ 4pm-midnight) This Black Dog really starts to howl on summer nights, when musicians set up on the cobbles facing the Crooked Bridge (p111) and everyone lounges around on cushions. Inside, the historical millhouse is decked out with flags and car number-plates. Grab a seat on the riverside terrace and sip on some local craft beer.

Ima i Može Craft Beer Garden
CRAFT BEER

(Map p110; ☑ 061 799 398; www.facebook.com/oldbridz; Južni logor bb; ⊘ 9am-11pm) You're liable to hear old-school punk or Bowie blasting out of this open-sided wooden pavilion above the Radobolja River, given the predilections of the owner-manager, who's also behind the OldbridZ Brewery. Take a tasting flight of its excellent range, then start sampling the guest craft brews from elsewhere in Bosnia, Croatia and Serbia, accompanied by Mexican food or Bosnian cheese.

Café de Alma
CAFE

(Map p110; ☑ 063 315 572; www.facebook.com/cafedealma; Rade Bitange bb; ⊘ 9.30am-6pm Apr-Dec) Step back to Ottoman times at this excellent coffee roastery, with a shady front terrace and cool interior. The only things served are homemade juices and Bosnian-style coffee, and on your first visit you'll be taken through the whole traditional coffee-drinking ritual. Enquire about Alma's Tales personalised city tours (€30).

Ljetna Bašta Oscar
BAR

(Map p110; www.facebook.com/oscar.mostar; Onešćukova 33; ⊘ 10am-2am May-Sep; ☜) Layered through a large shady garden area, this cafe-bar and chill-out place creates an exotic feel with giant cushions, hammocks and colourful fabrics. It's popular for smoking *nargile* (water pipes; 10KM).

Club Calamus
ROOFTOP BAR

(Map p110; 5th fl, Integra Bldg, Dr Ante Starčevića bb; ⊘ 7am-2am; ☜) Perched on top of an inauspicious-looking office building in the bombed-out part of town, this urbane rooftop bar offers cocktails and engrossing city views. There's no sign: walk into the lobby and take the left-hand elevator to the 5th floor. It regularly hosts live music, usually of a jazzy persuasion.

Duradžik
BAR

(Map p110; ☑ 061 741 939; www.duradzik.com; Tabhana bb; ⊘ 6pm-3am Mon-Sat; ☜) This late-night rock-edged bar spills out into the central courtyard of the Tabhana (former tannery). There's live music most evenings around midnight.

OKC Abrašević
BAR

(Map p110; ☑ 036-561 107; www.okcabrasevic.org; Alekse Šantića 25; ⊘ 9am-midnight) Named after 19th-century proletarian poet Kosta Abrašević, this understatedly intellectual arts centre and associated Kosta cafe-bar make

BOSNIA & HERCEGOVINA BLAGAJ

DON'T MISS

KRAVICA WATERFALL

There's a slightly unreal, Disney-esque quality to this outstanding natural **waterfall** (Slap Kravica; www.kravica.ba; adult/child 10/5KM; ☺7am-10pm Jun-Sep, to 6pm Oct-Apr, to 8pm May), where the Trebižat River plummets in a broad 25m-high arc into an emerald pool. In spring this gorgeous mini-Niagara pounds itself into a dramatic, steamy fury. In summer it's a more gentle cascade, but the basin offers an idyllic respite from the sweltering heat for hundreds of locals and tourists.

Further downstream, kayaks can be hired (€8 per hour). Admission tickets include access to two nearby sights: a monastery museum in Humac and the Koćuša waterfall.

The falls are a 15-minute walk from a car park that's 4km down a dead-end road which is well signposted from the M6 (Čapljina–Ljubuški Rd). There's no public transport, but many Mostar group tours combine a stop at the falls with visits to Blagaj and Počitelj.

for Mostar's most vibrantly alternative venue for offbeat gigs. It's entered from an unlikely courtyard on a partly bombed-out street; look for the wall covered with street art.

ⓘ Information

Grad Mostar (www.turizam.mostar.ba)

Tourist Info Centre (Map p110; ☑036-580 275; www.hercegovina.ba; Rade Bitange 5; ☺9am-noon May-Oct)

Visit Mostar (www.visitmostar.org)

ⓘ Getting There & Away

AIR

Mostar Airport (OMO; ☑036-352 770; www. mostar-airport.ba) is 7km south of town off the Čapljina road. The only year-round flights are to Zagreb on Croatia Airlines, with additional airlines running seasonal services.

BUS

➡ Mostar has two bus stations, only 1.5km apart – one for each half of its ethnic divide. They even stress one of the few dialectal differences between Bosnian and Croatian by using different words for 'station': *stanica* on the east and *kolodvor* on the west. The main one is the **eastern bus station** (Autobusni stanica; Map p110; ☑036-552 025; Trg Ivana Krndelja), located right beside the train station; it's more convenient for travellers than the **western bus station** (Autobusni kolodvor; ☑036-348 680; Vukovarska bb; ☺5.30am-10pm).

➡ Domestic destinations include Međugorje (4KM, 50 minutes, eight daily), Trebinje (21KM, 3½ hours, four daily), Sarajevo (20KM, 2½ hours, 10 daily), Jajce (26KM, 4¼ hours, three daily) and Banja Luka (28KM, 5¼ hours, daily). There are also direct coaches to Croatia, Montenegro, Serbia, Slovenia, Austria, Switzerland and Germany.

➡ Most services stop at both stations, although Međugorje and some of the Croatian services

favour the western. Međugorje and Blagaj services also pick up near Španski trg.

TRAIN

Trains from Mostar's **railway station** (Željeznička stanica; ☑036-550 608; www.zfbh. ba; Trg Ivana Krndelja 1), adjacent to the eastern bus station (p116), depart every morning and evening for Konjic (11KM, 50 minutes) and Sarajevo (18KM, two hours).

ⓘ Getting Around

Local bus services, which extend as far as peripheral towns such as Blagaj, are operated by **Mostar Bus** (☑036-552 250; www.mostarbus.ba).

Blagaj Благај

☑036 / POP 2530

An easy day trip from Mostar, pretty Blagaj hugs the turquoise Buna River as it gushes out of a cave past a historical tekke (Sufi dervish spiritual house), several enticing restaurants and Ottoman-era homesteads.

In summer you can take a five-minute boat ride (adult/child 4/2KM), pulled along on a rope, into the Buna Cave from a landing directly opposite the tekke.

Blagaj Tekke　　　　ISLAMIC SITE
(Blagajska tekija; ☑061 371 005; www.tekijablagaj. ba/en; Blagaj bb; admission 5KM; ☺8am-10pm May-Oct, to 6pm Nov-Apr) Forming Blagaj's signature attraction, the centrepiece of this complex of traditional stone-roofed buildings is a very pretty half-timbered dervish house with wobbly rug-covered floors, carved doorways, curious niches and a bathroom with star-shaped coloured glass set into the ceiling. The dervishes follow a mystical strand of Islam in which the peaceful contemplation of nature plays a part, hence the *tekke*'s idyllic positioning above the cave

mouth from which the Buna River's surreally blue-green waters flow forth.

The *tekke*'s last sheikh died in 1923 and dervish spirituality was suppressed following WWII. The Blagaj Tekke is now once again a venue for Zikr praise-chanting three nights a week.

Hotel Blagaj HOTEL €€
(☑036-573 805; www.hotel-blagaj.com; Blagaj bb; s/d/apt €34/49/70; ☺reception 7am-midnight; 🅿✷🛜) Built in 2015, this professional 27-room hotel contrasts white and lavender-wash walls with sepia scenes of old Mostar. It's just beyond the main town car park en route to Blagaj Tekke.

Restoran Vrelo INTERNATIONAL €€
(☑036-572 556; www.restoranvrelo.com; Blagaj bb; mains 9-30KM; ☺10am-10.30pm; 🛜) Across the river from the tekke, this restaurant serves reliably good food on terraces overlooking a horseshoe of rapids. Local trout is served in a variety of styles, including *'probaj ova'* (literally 'try this') which comes in lemon sauce with pumpkin seeds. There are also schnitzels, steaks, seafood or meat platters, and delicious squid stuffed with three cheeses.

ℹ Information

The small **tourist information booth** (☺8am-8pm May-Sep) is in the main car park, 650m short of the tekke.

ℹ Getting There & Away

City bus routes 10 and 11 from Mostar run to Blagaj (2.10KM, 30 minutes), with a total of 10 services on weekdays (fewer on weekends).

Međugorje Međyropje

☑036 / POP 2300
Blending honest faith and cash-in tackiness, Međugorje is a Catholic pilgrimage town in the mould of Lourdes (France) or Fatima (Portugal) – although unlike these, it has never been officially approved by the Vatican. Apart from the affecting *Resurrected Saviour* statue and the piety of the faithful streaming around St James Church, there's little of beauty here and nonpilgrims generally find a one-hour visit enough to get the idea.

History

Before it was transformed into a bustling pilgrimage centre, Međugorje was a poor winemaking backwater populated almost entirely by Bosnian Croats. In 1941 it was the site of a major atrocity, when hundreds of Serbian women and children were thrown into deep pits at nearby Šurmanci by local Ustaše (Croatian fascists). Those who didn't die immediately were buried alive.

On 24 June 1981 six local teenagers claimed to have experienced a vision on what is now known as Apparition Hill, which they believe to have been a manifestation of St Mary, the mother of Jesus. Three of the six claim to still have daily apparitions, while the other three claim to receive them at least once a year.

The Catholic Church does not officially accept the veracity of the apparitions. A Franciscan priest, Fr Tomislav Vlašić, quickly became the children's main advocate and spiritual director, although he was subsequently defrocked after allegations of sexual misconduct with a nun. Matters are further complicated by tensions between the local Franciscans and the broader church. The Franciscan order has long been a significant force in Hercegovina, ministering to the Croat population throughout the Ottoman occupation. Their association with Croatian nationalism has been controversial, with some past members of the order directly implicated in Ustaše atrocities during WWII. In 1975 Pope Paul VI ordered the Franciscans to hand over control of most of their parishes to the Mostar-Duvno diocese, which they strongly resisted and have yet to fully comply with.

In recent years the Vatican has taken a pastoral approach, figuring that whether the apparitions are true or not, Međugorje can still be a force for good. And the core messages relayed by the visionaries are uncontroversial, calling for peace, prayer, penance and reconciliation.

◎ Sights

St James Church complex CHURCH
(Crkva svetog Jakova; ☑036-653 316; www.medjugorje.hr; Trg Gospin) Međugorje's central focus is this rather functional double-towered 1969 church and the parklike grounds behind it. The main daily service is a 6pm rosary followed by a 7pm Mass, which in summer is celebrated in the huge outdoor arc behind the church. From here an avenue, lined with mosaics representing the rosary's Luminous Mysteries, leads to a garden showcasing a mesmerising 5m-tall bronze statue – the *Resurrected Saviour* (1998) by Ajdo Ajdić – of Jesus standing crucified yet without a cross.

BOSNIA & HERCEGOVINA MEĐUGORJE

Apparition Hill
CHRISTIAN SITE

(Brdo ukazanja) A white statue of the Queen of Peace marks the site of the original 1981 visions on the hillside, 2km from central Međugorje. If you're fit you could nip up and back in 20 minutes from the car park, but pilgrims spend an hour or more, contemplating and praying the rosary. The trail is rough rock-studded red earth, but a few walk barefoot in deliberately painful acts of penitence.

Cross Mountain
CHRISTIAN SITE

(Križevac; Put Križevca) Erected in 1933 for the 1900th anniversary of Christ's crucifixion, the giant cross on the top of this 520m mountain has been a place of Catholic devotion since well before Međugorje became famous. Although it's marginally more shaded, the climb is tougher than Apparition Hill, taking about 30 minutes to the top; most pilgrims do both. It's lined by 14 bas-relief Stations of the Cross, with a 15th added at the top, representing the resurrection.

🛏 Sleeping & Eating

Medjugorje Hotel & Spa
HOTEL €€

(☑036-640 450; www.medjugorjehotelspa.com; Fra Slavka Barbarića 29; s/d/ste from €58/68/86; P ❈ @ 🛜) Positioned between the town centre and Apparition Hill, this snazzy modern hotel offers spacious rooms, a chapel and a fancy spa centre, should you have muscles that need soothing after climbing up to the pilgrimage sites.

Etno Kuća
BALKAN €€

(☑063 753 000; www.facebook.com/etno. kuca.14; Šurmanci bb; mains 6-26KM; ⊗8am-11pm Mon-Sat, noon-11pm Sun; 🛜) Wagon-wheel light fixtures and sheaves of tobacco hang from the ceiling of this rustic restaurant which sits surrounded by gardens and farmland, 3km east of central Međugorje. The charming staff can help you navigate the menu, which incorporates traditional Bosnian, Dalmatian and continental Croatian dishes, including Neretva Valley classics such as eel and frog. The homemade bread is delicious.

Gardens
DALMATIAN €€

(☑036-650 499; www.clubgardens.com; Pape Ivana Pavla II 62; mains 10-29KM; ⊗8am-11pm) Downstairs this buzzing cafe-bar is Međugorje's top post-prayer party spot, with an atmosphere somewhere between a Louisiana speakeasy and an Irish pub. Grab a

seat in the garden or in the suave upstairs dining room for a reliable meal of pasta, pizza, seafood or steaks. The Dalmatian-style fish soup is highly recommended.

ℹ Getting There & Away

Međugorje's remarkably well-connected **bus station** (☑036-651 393; www.globtour. com; Kardinala Alojzije Stepinac bb; ⊗6am-10.45pm Mon-Sat, 7.30am-10.45pm Sun) is operated by **Globtour** (☑063 321 206; www. globtour.com). Domestic destinations include Mostar (4KM, 50 minutes, eight daily) and Sarajevo (17KM, 3¾ hours, three daily). There are good connections to various Croatian cities, and almost-daily buses to Serbia, Slovenia and Austria.

Počitelj Почитељ
☑ 036 / POP 800

The stepped medieval fortress village of Počitelj is one of the most picture-perfect architectural ensembles in the country. Cupped in a steep rocky amphitheatre, it's a warren of stairways climbing between ramshackle stone-roofed houses and pomegranate bushes.

Bosnian Croat forces badly damaged the village in 1993, including the beautiful **Hajji Alijia Mosque** (Hadži Alijina džamija; adult/child 3KM/free; ⊗9am-6pm Apr-Oct), which was deliberately targeted. This 1563 structure has now been restored, although photos displayed within show how much of the decorative paintwork has been lost.

Nearby is a 16m Ottoman clock tower, while further up the hill is a partly ruined fortress, capped by the octagonal Gavrakapetan Tower. You can climb up the tower or save your energy for even better panoramas from the uppermost rampart bastions.

ℹ Getting There & Away

Počitelj is 28km south of Mostar. Buses from Mostar to Čapljina or Metković (Croatia) take this route.

Trebinje Требиње
☑ 059 / POP 31,500

By far the prettiest city in Republika Srpska, Trebinje has a compact centre with a tiny walled Old Town flanked by a leafy market square. The Trebišnjica River is slow and shallow as it passes through, its banks lined with swimming spots and replicas of

STOLAC СТОЛАЦ

Well worth a stop if you're driving from Mostar to Trebinje, Stolac is one of Hercegovina's prettiest castle towns, with a history going back to Roman times. Though it suffered serious conflict in 1993, the displaced population has long since returned and the town's greatest historical buildings have been painstakingly reconstructed, most notably Ottoman gems in the Čaršija area and mill races on the Bregava River.

In the vicinity of Stolac are two sets of classic *stećci* (grave-carvings), listed as World Heritage sites by Unesco since July 2016. Beside the Mostar road, 3km west of Stolac, is the famous **Radimlja Necropolis** (M6 Stolac-Čapljina Rd; adult/child 4KM/free; ⏰ 7am-7pm Mon-Fri, 9am-6pm Sat; P). At first glimpse it looks like a quarry yard, but on closer inspection you'll notice the group of around 110 white stone blocks are intricately carved.

While less celebrated than the *stećci* at Radimlja, the 270 **Boljuni Stećci** FREE – arranged in two groups under venerable oak trees – have a much more atmospheric setting and feature the cross-shaped tombstone of warrior-hero Vladko Vuković. Boljuni is 12km from Stolac, 4.2km off the Stolac–Neum road, itself a narrow, rural delight passing right beside the Hutovo fortress ruins and through several timeless villages.

BOSNIA & HERCEGOVINA TREBINJE

waterwheels, which were once used for irrigation. Mountains provide a sunbaked backdrop, while hills topped with Orthodox churches punctuate the suburbs.

It's barely 30km from Dubrovnik, but in tourist terms it's a world away – not to mention vastly cheaper. Some canny travellers base themselves here and 'commute'.

Trebinje's always been a Serb-majority town but more so since the war, with the proportion rising from 70% to 94%.

○ Sights

Trg Slobode SQUARE
(Трг слободе) Doze off at this pretty 'Freedom Square' and when you awake you might think yourself transported to southern France, with its chestnut trees and stone-flagged pavements, old stone buildings with wrought-iron overhangs, appealing street cafes. Directly to the southeast, shaded by mature plane trees, Dučić Trg looks like it's just waiting for a game of pétanque. It's also the site of a morning vegetable market.

Arslanagić Bridge BRIDGE
(Perovića most, Перовића мост) This unique double-backed structure was built in 1574 under the direction of Grand Vizier Mehmed Pasha Sokolović, who was also behind the Višegrad bridge (p107), though this one was named for the toll collector. It was originally 10km further upstream from its present location but in 1965 it disappeared beneath the rising waters of the Gorica reservoir. Rescued stone by stone, it took six years to be finally reassembled.

Hercegovačka Gračanica CHURCH
(Херцеговачка Грачаница; Miloša Šarabe bb) Offering phenomenal views, this hilltop complex comprises a bell tower, gallery, cafe-bar and bishop's palace, but most notably the compact but eye-catching Presvete Bogorodice (Annunciation) Church. The latter's design is based very symbolically on the 1321 Gračanica monastery in Kosovo, a historically significant building that's considered sacred by many Serbs. The Trebinje version was erected in 2000 to rehouse the bones of local poet-hero Jovan Dučić.

⊨ Sleeping

★ **Hostel Polako** HOSTEL €
(☎ 066 380 722; www.hostelpolakotrebinje.com; Vožda Karađorđa 7; dm/r from €11/28; ⏰ Jan-Nov; ⚎) Run by a friendly American/Polish couple, this much-loved hostel offers dorms and two private doubles; bathrooms are shared. It's a ten-minute walk from both the bus station (p120) and the Old Town. Rates include pancakes for breakfast.

Hotel Platani HOTEL €€
(☎ 059-274 050; www.hotel-platani-trebinje.com; Riste i Bete Vukanović 1; s/d/apt 72/105/164KM; P ❄ ⚎) Taking pride of place on Trebinje's pretty, central square, this landmark hotel evokes the elegance of the Austro-Hungarian era. Downstairs is one of Trebinje's best restaurants (mains 10KM to 34KM), while upstairs are spacious, well-presented rooms. One huge corner room is named after *Matrix* actress Monica Bellucci, who stayed here while filming locally. There's also an annex across the square.

Sesto Senso
HOTEL €€

(📞059-261 160; www.facebook.com/sestosenso trebinje; Obala Mića Ljubibratića 3; s/d from €42/52; P ❄️ 🛜) Wrapped up in an attractive white-stone-and-glass package, this modern four-storey block is big on 21st-century style. The cheapest rooms only have tiny, high windows; it's worth paying extra for a balcony and river view. Downstairs on the terrace is one of Trebinje's best international restaurants (7am to 11pm; mains 8KM to 29KM), serving everything from local grills to chicken curries.

🍷 Drinking & Nightlife

Underground
PUB

(Preobraženska bb; ⊙8am-2am Mon-Sat, 10am-2am Sun) Trebinje's late-night bar of choice has old green shutters, trees growing through its terrace roof and a sign designed like a Jack Daniels label. Bands regularly rock the beer garden in summer. It's just across the river from the Old Town via the new bridge.

Azzaro
BAR

(📞065 878 148; www.facebook.com/kafezazzaro; Stari Grad 14; ⊙8am-11pm Mon-Sat, 10am-11pm Sun; 🛜) The covered terrace of this popular Old Town cafe-bar is one of Trebinje's best see-and-be-seen spots.

ℹ️ Information

The extremely helpful **tourist office** (📞059-273 410; www.gotrebinje.com; Jovan Dučića bb; ⊙8am-4pm Mon-Fri, 9am-2pm Sat) is next to the Catholic cathedral, across the park from the Old Town's western gate.

ℹ️ Getting There & Away

Trebinje's **bus station** (Autobuska stanica; 📞059-220 466; Vojvode Stepe Stepanovića bb) is 600m southwest of the Old Town. Domestic destinations include Mostar (21KM, 3½ hours, four daily), Konjic (26KM, two daily), Istočno Sarajevo (27KM, 4¾ hours, three daily), Višegrad (26KM, five hours, three daily) and Banja Luka (48KM, 8¾ hours, two daily). There are also direct services to Croatia, Montenegro and Serbia.

If there's no traffic, the drive to Dubrovnik only takes about 30 minutes but be aware that queues at the Croatian border can take over an hour at peak times; buses (8KM, one hour, one or two daily) get priority. Taxis from Dubrovnik charge upwards of €60 to Trebinje, while taxis from Trebinje cost less than half that; you're best to book one through your Trebinje hotel or hostel.

WESTERN BOSNIA

Travelling through this region of green wooded hills, river canyons, rocky crags and mildly interesting historical towns, you'll find yourself constantly passing in and out of Bosniak-Croat Federation territory and the Republika Srpska. You'll always know when you're in the latter by the red-blue-and-white Serbian flags that sprout in profusion whenever you enter it. Prominent towns include the old Ottoman administrative capital Travnik, the gorgeous hilltop settlement of Jajce, and Republika Srpska's quasi capital Banja Luka. In the west, the Una River gushes flamboyantly over a series of waterfalls before joining the Sava on its rush to the Danube and, ultimately, the Black Sea.

Travnik Травник

📞030 / POP 53,500

Once the seat of Bosnia's viziers (Ottoman governors), the castle town of Travnik is now best known for its sheep's cheese and as the birthplace of Nobel Prize–winning author Ivo Andrić, who set his classic novel *Bosnian Chronicle (The Days of the Consuls)* here. It's a pleasant place to spend a couple of hours while travelling between Sarajevo and Jajce.

Old Town Fortress
FORTRESS

(Tvrđava Stari Grad; 📞030-518 140; www.muzej travnik.ba; Varoš 60; adult/child 3/1.50KM; ⊙8am-8pm Apr-Oct) Travnik's 15th-century fortress surveys the city from a shoulder of hillside above **Plava Voda**. The stone walls gleam so brightly in the sunshine that they appear to have been scrubbed. The restored multisided keep houses a modest museum of local history and folk costumes.

Many-Coloured Mosque
MOSQUE

(Šarena džamija; Bosanska 203) Although this mosque is officially called Sulejmanija, everyone in Travnik uses its longstanding nickname, a reference to its famous frescoed facade. The colours have since faded but the building remains notable for the *bezistan* (minibazaar) built into the stone arched arcade. There's been a mosque here, at Travnik's centre point, since the 16th century. Its current form dates from 1757, although it was largely reconstructed after a major fire in 1815.

ℹ️ Information

Tourist Information Centre (📞030-501 144; Bosanska 120; ⊙8am-4pm Mon-Fri, 9am-3pm Sat)

Getting There & Away

Travnik's **bus station** (☎030-511 889; Stanična bb) is centrally located, just off the main highway. The left-luggage room (1KM) theoretically works from 7am to 7pm. Destinations include Sarajevo (15KM, 1½ hours, three daily), Jajce (12KM, 1¼ hours, five daily) and Bihać (31KM, 6½ hours, daily).

Jajce Јајце

☎030 / POP 30,800

Jajce is a historical gem, with a highly evocative walled Old Town clinging to a steep rocky knoll with rivers on two sides. The Pliva River tumbles into the Vrbas River by way of an impressive urban waterfall right at the very foot of the town walls. Immediately to the west, the Pliva is dammed to form two pretty lakes which are popular with swimmers, strollers, bikers and boaters.

History

Founded in the 14th century (although a Roman-era Temple of Mithras points to earlier occupation), Jajce was the capital of the medieval Kingdom of Bosnia until it fell to the Ottomans briefly in 1459 and more permanently in 1527. The ruins of the church where the Bosnian kings were crowned can still be seen; it was converted into a mosque but fell into disrepair after a fire in the 1830s.

Before the 1990s, Jajce was ethnically mixed, with Bosniak Muslims comprising 39% of the population, Serbs 30%, Yugoslavs 16% and Croats 14%. The town fell to the Bosnian Serb army in 1992 and by the time it was retaken in 1995, all of its mosques and Catholic churches had been demolished. While many have subsequently been rebuilt, many war-damaged buildings can still be seen. The population is now fairly evenly split between Bosniaks and Croats, with Serbs numbering less than 2%. Large Bosniak and Croatian war memorials sit separately but side-by-side in the centre of the Old Town.

Sights

Jajce Waterfall WATERFALL

(Vodopad) Jajce's impressive 21m-high waterfall forms where the Pliva River tumbles abruptly into the Vrbas. A viewing platform (adult/child 4/2KM) has been built opposite the waterfall's base, accessed from stairs that start between the bus station (p122) and petrol station. If you don't want to get sprayed (nor pay), you can look down on it from either lip.

For the classic tourist-brochure photo, cross the big Vrbas bridge and turn left on the Banja Luka road. Walk 500m, then descend 150m through pinewoods from the roadside lay-by to a great but less-frequented alternative viewpoint.

In the first week in August, daredevils leap from the waterfall in an annual competition featuring around 30 professional divers.

Jajce Fortress FORTRESS

(Tvrđava u Jajcu; adult/child 2/1KM; ⏲8am-8pm May-Oct, to 4pm Nov-Apr) Jajce's fortress ruins have a powerful aspect when seen from afar, but inside is mostly bald grass. The ramparts offer sweeping views of the valleys and crags that surround Jajce's urban sprawl, though views of the fortress are generally more memorable than views from it. The castle's most photographed feature is the partially conserved Kotromanić stone crest beside the entrance portal, and you don't have to enter to see that.

Pliva Lakes LAKE

(Plivsko Jezero) These two idyllic lakes, west of Jajce, reflect the surrounding wooded mountains in their clear waters, and are popular for boating and simply strolling or cycling around. Between them lie the **Mlinčići**, a cute collection of 20 tiny wooden watermills. At the bottom of the lower, smaller lake, boardwalks cross a pretty set of rivulets spilling into a dam basin, which is a popular swimming spot.

Sleeping & Eating

Hotel Stari Grad HOTEL €€

(☎030-654 007; www.jajcetours.com; Sv Luke 3; s/d 57/84KM; P ❄ ☜) Although this hotel is not actually old, heavy beams, wood panelling and a heraldic fireplace give this comfortable little place a look of suavely modernised antiquity. Beneath the part-glass floor of the appealing lobby restaurant are the excavations of an Ottoman-era *hammam* (Turkish bath). The six standard rooms are somewhat cramped but decorated with monogrammed mirrors and framed pictures of old Jajce.

Kod Asima BALKAN €

(☎063 351 985; Sadije Softića bb; mains 4-11KM; ⏲8am-11pm) Central Jajce's most atmospheric eatery has tables within the historical

Travnik Gate and in the 17th-century Omer-bey House which adjoins it. The food choices includes soup, goulash, *lonac* (Bosnian hotpot) and the usual grills. Between meals, stop in for Bosnian coffee on the terrace.

Konoba Slapovi
BALKAN €€

(☑ 063 489 369; Plivskih jezera bb; mains 6-16KM; ⊙ 10am-8pm May-Sep) This magical tavern is perched above a horseshoe weir with a series of little footbridges allowing strolls between placid, tree-shaded shallows. The speciality here is fish although a range of Bosnian-style stews and delicious veal slow-roasted under a *sač* (domed metal hood) are served. It's 2.3km from the Old Town, along the riverside road towards the Pliva Lakes (p121).

Beer Pub
BAR

(☑ 063 374 617; www.facebook.com/BeerPubJajce; ZAVNOBiH-a bb; ⊙ 7am-11pm; 🐾) Jajce's liveliest drinking spot has a big range of beer, hosts live music and has a little outdoor seating area tucked up against the cliff that's topped by the eastern city wall. It's almost completely hidden behind a pharmacy.

❶ Information

Tourist Information Centre (☑ 030-659 888; www.agencija-jajce.ba; Hrvoja Vukčića Hrvatinića bb; ⊙ 9am-5pm Apr-Oct) This helpful English-speaking office is handily placed by the footbridge linking the **bus station** (☑ 030-658 047; II zasjedanja AVNOJ-a bb; ⊙ 6am-midnight) to the Old Town. It stocks Jajce maps, has a range of locally made souvenirs and can arrange homestays (about €10 per person).

❶ Getting There & Away

The centrally located bus station has services to Banja Luka (11KM, 1¼ hours, six daily), Bihać (25KM, 3½ hours, five daily), Travnik (12KM, 1¼ hours, five daily), Sarajevo (27KM, 3½ hours, five daily) and Mostar (26KM, 4¼ hours, three daily). It's also well connected to Zagreb (Croatia).

Banja Luka БАЊА ЛУКА

☑ 051 / POP 185,000

Banja Luka is the second-biggest city in Bosnia and the de facto capital of the Republika Srpska, but there's very little here to detain travellers for long. After Serbian nationalists systematically destroyed most of the city's historical and cultural heritage – including mosques, Catholic churches, a historical clock tower and various 16th-

century buildings – a rather bland, soulless place was left. The 'ethnic cleansing' wasn't limited to the built heritage either; the Serbian population, which sat at around 50% before the war, is now around the 90% mark.

Encouragingly, two rebuilt religious buildings from different traditions are now the city's biggest drawcards: a captivating reconstructed 16th-century mosque and a magnificent Orthodox cathedral. Banja Luka's lively nightlife is another redeeming feature, as is the close proximity to rafting on the emerald-green Vrbas River, which meanders through the city before disappearing into a lush canyon.

◉ Sights

Ferhadija Mosque
MOSQUE

(Ferhadija džamija; Map p123; Kralja Petra I Karađorđevića 42; ⊙ 10am-8pm) The standout sight in Banja Luka is this small but gorgeous mosque, built in 1579 at the behest of Ottoman district commander Ferhat-paša Sokolović. It was under Unesco protection when, in 1993, it was deliberately destroyed as part of a brutal campaign of ethnic cleansing which saw non-Serbs expelled from the city. A meticulous reconstruction commenced in 2001, using 16th-century techniques and incorporating around 60% of the original masonry rescued from various dumps. It was finally completed in 2016.

There's often someone on hand to show you around; headscarves are provided for women. It's worth calling in to see the vivid geometric frescoes that fill the dome.

Cathedral of Christ the Saviour
CHURCH

(Саборни храм Христа Спаситеља; Map p123; ☑ 051-233 370; www.hhsbl.org; Trg Srpskih vladara 3) Banja Luka's Serbian-Byzantine-style Orthodox cathedral is an impressive structure of layered gold-brown and crab-pink stones rising to golden domes and flanked by an unfeasibly tall free-standing bell tower. The interior has a splendid carved iconostasis and a giant central chandelier through which a dazzling image of Christ stares down from within the main dome.

Originally consecrated in 1939, the church was damaged by Nazi bombers before being demolished by the Ustaše (Croatian fascist) regime. The present structure is a faithful reconstruction, commenced in 1993 and completed in 2004.

Banja Luka

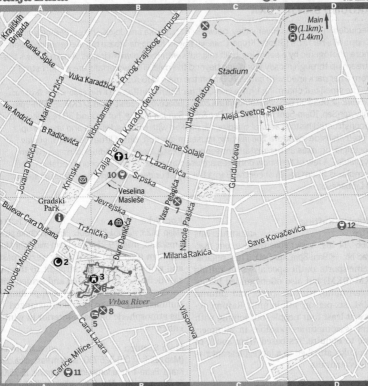

N 0 — 400 m
0 — 0.2 miles

Banja Luka

⊚ Sights
1 Cathedral of Christ the
  Saviour..B2
2 Ferhadija Mosque....................................A3
3 Kastel Fortress...B3
4 Museum of Republika
  Srpska...B3

🛏 Sleeping
5 Vila Vrbas...B4

🍴 Eating
6 Kazamat...B3
7 Kod Brke..B3
8 Kod Muje..B4
9 Mala Stanica...C1

🍷 Drinking & Nightlife
10 Mac Tire...B2
11 Maraton...A4
12 Monnet...D3

Kastel Fortress   FORTRESS
(Tvrđava Kastel, Тврђава Кастел; Teodora
Kolokotronisa bb) FREE The chunky walls
of this large, squat riverside fortress en-
close mainly unremarkable parkland.
It's thought there's been a fort here since
Neolithic and Roman times, but Kastel's
current look is largely 16th century. One
stone barracks has been converted into
an art gallery and there's an atmospheric
restaurant (www.restorankazamat.net; mains

12-26KM; ⏰ 9am-11pm; 🅿 ❄ 🛜) built into the
ramparts.

🏃 Activities

Banja Luka is known locally for its canoe-
sized punts *(dajak)* propelled by a standing
pilot with a long pole. Kayaking is also popular in the town centre, but the main activities require heading into the Vrbas Canyons
where there's fine rafting and an assortment
of other adventure sports.

WORTH A TRIP

AROUND BANJA LUKA

Secluded in the Vrbas River valley, between Banja Luka and Jajce, the exceedingly pretty **Krupa Waterfalls** (Slapovi Krupe, Слапови Крупе; Krupa-na-Vrbasu bb) are rendered even more photogenic by a set of log-built mill huts with their own millraces. A path follows the stream up through mossy woodland beyond the mills. The waterfalls are a short stroll from a car park lined with cafes, 700m off the main M16 road.

The small but charming **Ljubačke Dolina Ethno 'village'** (Етно село-музеј Љубачке Долине; ☑ 065 390 628; www.etno-muzej.com; Ljubačevo bb; adult/child 3/2KM; ⊕ 9am-9pm daily Apr-Sep, 10am-6pm Wed-Sun Oct-Dec & Sat-Sun Jan-Mar; P) of around 30 rescued and reconstructed historical rural buildings is packed with rustic artefacts and layered up a pretty hillside meadow. The inviting 'museum' section, with a little room of Yugoslav nostalgia, doubles as bar-restaurant serving forest juices and traditional meals (when available). A few of the show cottages are used as en-suite guest accommodation. The complex is 20km south of central Banja Luka, just under 1km from the industrial sawmill in Ljubačevo.

★**Kanjon Rafting Centre**   ADVENTURE SPORTS
(☑ 066 714 169; www.raftingnavrbasu.com; Karanovac bb; ⊕ 9am-8pm Apr-Oct) This reliable extreme-sports outfit specialises in rafting (35KM-70KM) but also offers guided hiking and canyoning trips in spring and autumn (40KM, six-person minimum). Rafting requires at least four people, but joining with others is sometimes possible in summer; phone to enquire. It's based 11km south of Banja Luka, attached to a large, pleasant riverside restaurant.

🍴 Sleeping & Eating

Vila Vrbas   HOTEL €€
(Map p123; ☑ 051-433 840; www.hotelvilavrbas.com; Braće Potkonjaka 1; s/d 92/130KM; P✳🗻) Twelve rooms with high ceilings, starched sheets, glossy woodwork and high-pressure showers are slightly marred by paintings of writhing or blurry nudes. Riverside rooms have glimpses of the Kastel (p123) fortress through the foliage of mature plane trees, as does the long-established terrace restaurant downstairs.

Kod Muje   BALKAN €
(Map p123; ☑ 051-926 530; Braće Potkonjaka bb; mains 3.25-12KM; ⊕ 7am-9pm; 🗻) Founded in 1923, Kod Muje produces square ćevapi (minced-meat lozenges) that many locals rate as Banja Luka's best. There are wonderful views across the river to the tree-framed castle (p123) site from the restaurant's wooden-beamed summer dining pavilion.

Kod Brke   PIZZA €€
(Map p123; ☑ 051-216 006; www.kodbrke.pizza; Srpska 36; mains 9-23KM; ⊕ 7am-midnight Mon-Sat, from noon Sun) Sure, they serve pasta and grills too, but skip straight to the pizza – delicious, thin-crusted and loaded with goodies. The front terrace is appealing in summer, but you're not short-changed by the atmospheric old-barn interior in winter, either.

Mala Stanica   INTERNATIONAL €€€
(Map p123; ☑ 051-326 730; www.malastanica.com; Kralja Petra I Karađorđevića bb; mains 15-35KM; ⊕ 7am-midnight Mon-Sat, 10am-midnight Sun; P🗻) Housed in an atmospheric former train-station building, this upmarket restaurant is quite possibly Republika Srpska's best. Service is slick and professional, and the menu includes the likes of pasta, Istrian lamb, delicious slow-cooked beef cheeks and Serbian specialties such as *Karađorđe* steak (rolled, breaded and fried schnitzel stuffed with creamy *kajmak* – thick semisoured cream). Save room for the chocolate fondant dessert.

🍷 Drinking & Nightlife

Mac Tire   PUB
(Map p123; ☑ 051-221 444; www.mactirepub.com; Srpska 2; ⊕ 8am-1am Mon-Fri, 10am-2am Sat, noon-1am Sun; 🗻) Banja Luka's large subterranean Irish-style pub offers 10 different draught beers and lots of live music. The kitchen serves Anglo-Irish breakfasts, grills, burgers and fish and chips.

Maraton
PUB
(Map p123; ☑065 300 967; www.facebook.com/
Maratoncaffe; Mirka Kovačevića 29; ⊘7am-
midnight; 🛜) Behind a tiled wooden porch,
this chilled-out pub is themed around a
cult Yugo-era movie (*The Marathon Family*), with scenes turned into cartoon strips
adorning the walls.

Monnet
BAR
(Map p123; ☑065 732 059; www.facebook.com/
monnetcaffe; Save Kovačevića 40; ⊘7am-midnight;
🛜) Raised above the river, this inviting
wooden bar is decorated with wicker-
work lampshades and backlit bottles of
herb hooch. The music ranges from Serbian
folkrock to Britpop, softened by the flowing
river if you sit on the rear balcony.

ⓘ Information

Tourist office (Map p123; ☑051-490 308;
www.banjaluka-tourism.com; Kralja Petra
I Karađorđevića 87; ⊘8am-6pm Mon-Fri,
9am-2pm Sat) Extremely helpful, with copious
brochures and free maps to grab or download.
Comprehensive website.

ⓘ Getting There & Away

AIR

Banja Luka International Airport (BNX,
Међународни аеродром Бања Лука; ☑051-
535 210; www.banjaluka-airport.com; Mahovljani
bb, Laktaši) is 22km north up the road towards
Gradiška, then 1km inland. The only services are
Air Serbia flights to Belgrade and Ryanair flights
to Charleroi (Belgium), Memmingen (Germany)
and Stockholm-Skavsta (Sweden).

BUS

➧ The **main bus station** (☑051-922 000;
Braće Podgornika bb) is in front of the train
station, 3km north of central Banja Luka. There
are no ATMs and barely any English is spoken.

➧ Even if you book your ticket through one of
the online booking sites, you'll still need to
buy another ticket (1.50KM) at the counter to
access the platform.

➧ Domestic destinations include Jajce (11KM,
1¼ hours, six daily), Sarajevo (32KM, five hours,
six daily), Višegrad (45KM, nine hours, daily),
Mostar (28KM, 5¼ hours, daily) and Trebinje
(48KM, 8¾ hours, two daily).

➧ Banja Luka is well connected to Zagreb, and
there are also direct buses to Serbia, Montenegro, Slovenia, Austria, Switzerland and Germany.

TRAIN

Trains head to Bihać (19KM, 3½ hours, daily) and
Sarajevo (27KM, 4¾ hours, two daily). The train
station is next to the main bus station.

ⓘ Getting Around

TO/FROM THE AIRPORT
A shuttle meets all services, charging 10KM to
central Banja Luka.

BUSES & TAXIS
➧ Local buses cost 1.60KM for short trips
around the city and up to 2.20KM to the outskirts; pay the driver on board.

➧ Taxis are cheap and efficient.

Una River Valley
Долина Ријеке Уне

The adorable Una River goes through widely
varying moods. In the lush green gorges to
the northeast, some sections are as calm as
mirrored opal, while others gush over widely fanned rafting rapids. The river broadens
and gurgles over a series of shallow falls
as it passes through the unassuming town
of Bihać (population 39,700). Occasionally it leaps over impressive falls, notably at
Štrbački Buk, which forms the centrepiece
of the 198-sq-km Una National Park (www.
nationalpark-una.ba).

◉ Sights

Ostrožac Fortress
FORTRESS
(☑061 236 641; www.ostrozac.com; Ostrožac; admission 2KM; ⊘9am-dusk) Ostrožac is one of
Bosnia's most photogenic castles, a spooky
Gothic place high above the Una Valley,
up 3km of hairpins towards Cazin. There's
plenty to explore from various epochs, ramparts to walk, towers to climb and a manor
house on the verge of collapse that all add
to the thrill (and danger) of poking about.
Off-season you might have to call the care-
taker to get in, but it's only officially closed
if it's snowing.

Štrbački Buk
WATERFALL
(Una National Park Entry Gate 3; adult/child 6/4KM;
⊘dawn-dusk) A strong contender for the
title of the nation's most impressive waterfall, Štrbački Buk is a seriously dramatic
40m-wide cascade, pounding 23.5m down
three travertine sections, including over a
superbly photogenic 18m drop-off, overlooked by a network of viewing platforms.
The easiest access is 8km along a graded
but potholed unpaved road from Orašac on
the Kulen Vakuf road. There are swimming
spots to stop at along the way.

Milančev Buk WATERFALL
(Una National Park Entry Gate 5, Martin Brod; adult/child 2/1.50KM; ☺ dawn–dusk) Collectively, this group of cascades tumbles down a vertical height of more than 50m, with a wide arc of rivulets pouring into a series of pools surrounded by lush, green foliage. The main viewpoint is a minute's walk from the ticket gate, 1.3km off the Bihać–Dravar Rd in Martin Brod village. Make sure you check out the view from the red footbridge near the car park, too.

Ostrovica FORTRESS
(Ostrovica) Crowning the forested mount behind Kulen Vakuf, this medieval fortress is much more ruinous than it might appear from below. The interior is almost impossibly overgrown with nettles and brambles, but the views down over the village and Una Valley are hard to beat. Climbing on foot takes around an hour, or you can drive up a convoluted 5.5km unpaved road; the last 500m gets pretty narrow.

🏃 Activities

Rafting is a draw here; in addition, there's kayaking, flyfishing (day's licence 40KM; two-fish maximum) and 'speed river diving', a sport invented here involving scuba diving in fast-flowing waters. Each activity centre has its own campsite and provides transfers from Bihać.

Various companies offer rafting, particularly on the 15km stretch from Štrbački Buk (p125) to Lohovo within the national park (p125). The best months for white water are April and May, after the spring melts, when it's graded level 3 to 5.

Una Aqua RAFTING
(☑ 061 604 313; www.una-aqua.com; Račić; rafting €31-43) This rafting centre is an attraction in itself, comprising five small islands interlinked with wooden bridges. There's a good swimming spot, a restaurant, a campsite and a tree house cabin raised on stilts above a supercomfy waterside hammock. Three different rafting routes are offered. It's located 4km off the main M5, turning west around 500m south of the mosque in Ripač.

🛏 Sleeping

Villa Una B&B €
(☑ 061 459 520; www.villa-una.com; Bihaćkih branilaca 20, Bihać; r from €39; P ❄ 🛜) Tucked behind a main-road jewellery shop, this friendly 12-room guesthouse is very handy for the bus station. Half the rooms have semicircular balconies with flower boxes, though no real views. Rooms are compact, with air-con and fridges.

Kostelski Buk HOTEL €€
(☑ 037-302 340; www.facebook.com/Kostelski.buk; M14, Kostela; s/d from €43/63; P ❄ 🛜) Set beside a triple-level set of rapids, this luxurious hotel offers stylish rooms with some of the most comfortable mattresses you could hope to sleep on. Some rooms have river views. The restaurant is excellent too – try the luscious trout fillet in cream sauce. It's located 9km north of Bihać, on the main road to Banja Luka.

Opal Exclusive HOTEL €€
(☑ 037-224 183; www.hotelopal.ba; Krupska bb, Bihać; s/d from 138/180KM; P ❄ 🛜) Hidden away but only 300m north of central Bihać, the Opal's spacious rooms have sturdy rosywood bedsteads and paintings in gilt frames. The best ones have lovely views over the river rapids.

🍴 Eating & Drinking

Čardaklije BALKAN €€
(☑ 066 810 000; www.cardaklije.com; M202, Vrtoče; mains 8-18KM; ☺ 8am-10pm; P 🛜) Though not quite in the Una Valley, this old-world-styled 'ethno village' is a brilliant place to stop for a meaty meal en route, sitting beneath oak trees in the extensive grounds. The specialities are huge schnitzels, metre-long smoked sausages and mixed-grill plates, savoured with delicious home-pressed juices. On-site accommodation includes antique-style cottages and a hostel.

Panache BALKAN €€
(Dr Irfana Ljubijankića bb, Bihać; 3-18KM; ☺ 6am-10pm; 🛜) Panache is not a word that you would normally associate with whole animals spit-roasting on a street-side grill. However, meat mavens will definitely like the style of this brightly lit place. Serves are substantial; the mixed grills are big enough for two.

Restoran River Una CAFE
(Džemala Bijedića 12, Bihać; ☺ 8am-10pm) The prize seats are on a terrace that forms an arc so close to the crystal-clear Una that you can watch fish as you sip. The interior is more pub than restaurant, with displays of angling trophies.

ℹ Information

Una National Park Information Centre
(☑ 037-221 528; www.nationalpark-una.ba;
Bosanska 1, Bihać; ☺ 8am-4.30pm Mon-Fri)

ℹ Getting There & Away

➤ Bihać's user-friendly **bus station** (Autobuska stanica Bihać; ☑ 037-311 939; www.unatransport.ba; Put Armije Republike BiH bb) is 1km west of the centre towards Sarajevo, partly obscured by what appears to be a downmarket casino. Destinations include Banja Luka (25KM, three hours, four daily), Jajce (25KM, 3½ hours, five daily), Travnik (31KM, 6½ hours, daily) and Sarajevo (42KM, 6½ hours, four daily).

➤ A daily train heads to **Bihać Railway Station** (☑ 037-312 282; www.zfbh.ba; Bihaćkih Branilaca 20) from Banja Luka (19KM, 3½ hours) and Sarajevo (37KM, 6¼ hours).

ℹ Getting Around

It's tricky to explore these parts without a car. From Bihać, there are six buses on weekdays (fewer on weekends) to Orašac and Kulen Vakuf (4.50KM, 70 minutes). A community centre in Kulen Vakuf hires out bikes (per half/full day 15/30KM), but you're best to arrange it in advance through the Una National Park Information Centre in Bihać. They can also help to arrange minibus transfers from Orašac to Štrbački Buk (p125).

UNDERSTAND BIH

Bosnia & Hercegovina Today

Although the war ended more than 23 years ago, Bosnia and Hercegovina is still divided on ethnic lines and tensions are rising once again. Much of the institutional complexity that ensured peace through the Dayton Agreement has come to be seen in recent years as causing economic and political paralysis. The country has a tripartite presidency (comprised of one Bosniak Muslim, one Serb and one Croat) and two semi-autonomous entities – the (mainly Bosniak and Croat) Federation of Bosnia and Hercegovina and the (mainly Serb) Republika Srpska – each with its own president and prime minister.

Following the October 2018 elections, one of its three national presidents – the Bosnian Serb representative Milorad Dodik – openly declared his desire to break up the country. A moderate was elected as the Bosnian Croat president, although this has

Entities of BiH

sparked fiery protests from Croatian nationalists who claim that he only came to power due to tactical voting by Bosniaks. The main Serbian opposition is also querying the outcome, given its disappointing results despite ongoing large-scale and long-running protests against institutional corruption within Republika Srpska, following claims of a high-ranking political cover-up in regard to the suspicious death of 21-year-old Banja Luka man David Dragićević.

The main beneficiaries of this escalation of tensions appear to be the nation's flag makers, with each ethnic enclave furiously aflutter with their side's colours.

History

Much of the history remains controversial and is seen differently according to one's ethno-religious viewpoint.

In AD 9, Illyrian Bosnia was conquered by the Romans. Slavs arrived from the late 6th century and were dominant by 1180, when Bosnia first emerged as an independent entity under former Byzantine governor Ban Kulina. Bosnia had a patchy golden age between 1180 and 1463, peaking in the late 1370s when Bosnia's King Tvrtko gained Hum (future Hercegovina) and controlled much of Dalmatia.

Blurring the borderline between Europe's Catholic west and Orthodox east, medieval Bosnia had its own independent church. This remains the source of many historical myths, but the long-popular idea that it was 'infected' by the Bulgarian Bogomil heresy is now largely discounted.

BOSNIA & HERCEGOVINA UNDERSTAND BOSNIA & HERCEGOVINA

Turkish Ascendancy

Turkish raids whittled away at the country throughout the 15th century, and by the 1460s most of Bosnia was under Ottoman control. Within a few generations, easy-going Sufi-inspired Islam became dominant among townspeople and landowners, with many Bosnians converting as much to gain civic privileges as for spiritual enlightenment. However, a sizeable proportion of the serfs *(rayah)* remained Christian. Bosnians also became particularly prized soldiers in the Ottoman army, many rising eventually to high ranks within the imperial court. The early Ottoman era also produced great advances in infrastructure, with fine mosques and bridges built by charitable bequests.

Later, however, the Ottomans failed to follow the West's industrial revolution. By the 19th century the empire's economy was archaic, and all attempts to modernise the feudal system were strenuously resisted by the entrenched Bosnian-Muslim elite. In 1873 İstanbul's banking system collapsed under the weight of the high-living sultan's debts. To pay these debts the sultan demanded added taxes. But in 1874 Bosnia and Hercegovina's harvests failed, so paying those taxes would have meant starving. With nothing left to lose the mostly Christian Bosnian peasants revolted, leading eventually to a messy tangle of pan-Balkan wars.

Austro-Hungarian Rule

The pan-Balkan wars ended with the farcical 1878 Congress of Berlin, at which the Western powers carved up the western Ottoman lands. Austria-Hungary was 'invited' to occupy Bosnia and Hercegovina, which was treated like a colony even though it theoretically remained under Ottoman sovereignty. An unprecedented period of development followed. Roads, railways and bridges were built. Coal mining and forestry became booming industries. Education encouraged a new generation of Bosnians to look towards Vienna. But new nationalist feelings were simmering: Bosnian Catholics increasingly identified with neighbouring Croatia (itself within Austria-Hungary), while Orthodox-Christian Bosnians sympathised with recently independent Serbia's dreams of a greater Serbian homeland. In between lay Bosnia's Muslims (around 40%), who belatedly started to develop a distinct Bosniak consciousness.

While Turkey was busy with the aftermath of the 1908 Young Turk revolution, Austria-Hungary annexed Bosnia and Hercegovina, undermining the aspirations of those who had dreamed of a pan-Slavic or greater Serbian future. The resultant scramble for the last remainders of Ottoman Europe kicked off the Balkan Wars of 1912 and 1913. No sooner had these been (unsatisfactorily) resolved than the heir to the Austrian throne, Archduke Franz Ferdinand was shot dead by Serbian nationalists while visiting Sarajevo. One month later Austria declared war on Serbia and WWI swiftly followed.

The Yugoslav Period

WWI killed an astonishing 15% of the Bosnian population. It also brought down both the Turkish and Austro-Hungarian empires, leaving Bosnia an invisible part of the Kingdom of Serbs, Croats and Slovenes, which changed its name in 1929 to Yugoslavia.

During WWII, after Yugoslavia fell to Nazi Germany, Bosnia was absorbed into the newly created fascist state of Croatia. Croatia's Ustaše decimated Bosnia's Jewish population and killed hundreds of thousands of Serbs. Meanwhile, a pro-fascist group of Bosniak Muslims committed its own atrocities against Bosnian Serbs, while pro-royalist Serbian Četniks did the same in reverse to Bosniaks.

Both the Četniks and the Communist partisans – led by future president of Yugoslavia Josip Broz Tito – put up some stalwart resistance to the Germans (as well as fighting each other). The Bosnian mountains proved ideal territory for Tito's flexible guerrilla army. Tito's antifascist council met at Bihać (1942) then at Jajce (1943), famously formulating a constitution for an inclusive postwar, socialist Yugoslavia.

Bosnia and Hercegovina was granted republic status within that Yugoslavia, but up until 1971 (when 'Muslim' became defined as a Yugoslav 'ethnic group'), Bosniaks were not considered a distinct community and in censuses had to register as Croat, Serb or 'Other/Yugoslav'. Despite considerable mining in the northeast and the boost of the 1984 Sarajevo Winter Olympics, the Bosnian economy remained relatively underdeveloped.

The 1990s Conflict

In the post-Tito era, religio-linguistic (often dubbed 'ethnic') tensions were ratcheted up by Serbia's president Slobodan Milošević, shoring up his position by appealing to ultranationalists within his own part of the Yugoslav federation. In June 1991 Slovenia and Croatia declared their independence from Yugoslavia, sparking the war in Croatia.

In early 1992 Bosnia and Hercegovina held its own independence referendum, which was largely boycotted by Bosnian Serbs. The referendum had a 63.4% turnout, with 99.7% voting in favour, and independence was declared on 3 March 1992.

By this stage, Bosnian Serb parliamentarians had set up their own rival government at Pale, 20km east of Sarajevo. Bosnia and Hercegovina was recognised internationally as an independent state on 6 April 1992 but Sarajevo was already under siege both by Serbian paramilitaries and the Yugoslav army (JNA).

Over the next three years a brutal and extraordinarily complex civil war raged. Best known is the campaign of ethnic cleansing in northern and eastern Bosnia, which aimed at creating a Serbian republic. By early 1993 fighting had broken out between Muslims and Croats in Hercegovina, creating another war front. Croats attacked Muslims in Stolac and Mostar, bombarding their historical monuments and blasting Mostar's famous medieval bridge into the river. Muslim troops, including a small foreign mujahideen force, desecrated churches and attacked Croat villages, notably around Travnik.

UN Involvement

With atrocities on all sides, the West's reaction was confused and erratic. In August 1992, pictures of concentration-camp and rape-camp victims (mostly Bosniaks) in northern Bosnia spurred the UN to create UNPROFOR, a protection force of 7500 peacekeeping troops. UNPROFOR secured the neutrality of Sarajevo's airport well enough to allow the delivery of humanitarian aid, but overall proved notoriously impotent.

'Ethnic cleansing' of Bosniaks (by Bosnian Serbs) from Foča and Višegrad led the UN to declare 'safe zones' around the Muslim-majority towns of Srebrenica, Župa and Goražde. But rarely has the term 'safe' been so misused. When NATO belatedly authorised air strikes to protect these areas, the Bosnian Serbs responded by capturing 300 UNPROFOR peacekeepers and chaining them to potential targets to keep the planes away.

In July 1995 Dutch peacekeepers monitoring the supposedly 'safe' area of Srebrenica proved unable to prevent a Bosnian Serb force led by the infamous Ratko Mladić from killing an estimated 8000 Bosniak men; it was Europe's worst mass killing since WWII. Miraculously, battered Goražde held out thanks to sporadically available UN food supplies. By this stage, Croatia had renewed its own internal offensive in the (majority Serb) Krajina region of Croatia in August 1995; at least 150,000 Croatian Serbs then fled to the Serb-held areas of northern Bosnia.

Finally, a second deadly Serbian mortar attack on Sarajevo's main market (Markale) kick-started a shift in UN and NATO politics. An ultimatum to end the Bosnian Serbs' siege of Sarajevo was made more persuasive through two weeks of NATO air strikes in September 1995. US president Bill Clinton's proposal for a peace conference in Dayton, Ohio, was accepted soon after.

The Dayton Agreement

While maintaining Bosnia and Hercegovina's prewar external boundaries, Dayton divided the country into today's pair of roughly equally sized 'entities', each with limited autonomy. Finalising the border required considerable political and cartographic creativity and was only completed in 1999 when the last sticking point, Brčko, was belatedly given a separate status all of its own. Meanwhile, the country's curious rotating tripartite presidency was kept in check by the EU's powerful High Representative.

For refugees (1.2 million abroad, and a million displaced within Bosnia and Hercegovina), the Dayton Agreement emphasised the right to return to (or to sell) their prewar homes. International agencies donated considerable funding to rebuild infrastructure, housing stock and historical monuments. The ancient cities of Mostar and Sarajevo were painstakingly restored using traditional building methods.

People

Bosniaks (Bosnian Muslims, 50% of the population), Bosnian Serbs (Orthodox Christians, 31%) and Bosnian Croats (Catholics, 15%) are all Southern Slavs and all but indistinguishable physically. The prewar population was mixed, with intermarriage common in the cities. Stronger divisions have inevitably appeared since the civil war which resulted in massive population shifts, changing the size and religious balance of many cities. Bosniaks now predominate in central Bosnia and the northwest corner; Bosnian Croats in western and central Hercegovina; and Bosnian Serbs in the north and east. Today social contact between members of the three groups remains somewhat limited. Religion is taken seriously as a badge of 'ethnicity', but spiritually most people remain fairly secular.

The Arts

Literature

Bosnia's best-known writer, Ivo Andrić (1892–1975), won the 1961 Nobel Prize for Literature. With extraordinary psychological agility, his epic novel, the classic *Bridge on the Drina* (1945), retells 350 years of Bosnian history as seen through the eyes of unsophisticated townsfolk in Višegrad. His *Travnik Chronicle* (aka *Bosnian Chronicle* or *The Days of the Consuls*; published 1945) is also rich with human insight, portraying local life through the eyes of jaded 19th-century foreign consuls in Travnik.

Another Yugoslav-era classic focussed on Ottoman times, which many consider the equal of Andrić's work, is Meša Selimović's *Death and the Dervish* (1966).

Many thought-provoking essays, short stories and poems explore the prickly subject of the 1990s conflict, often contrasting horrors against the victims' enduring humanity. Quality varies greatly, but recommended collections include Miljenko Jergović's *Sarajevo Marlboro* (1994) and Semezdin Mehmedinović's *Sarajevo Blues* (1992). Also worth seeking out is Ismet Prcic's wartime novel *Shards* (2011).

Film

Bosnia's most famous director is Sarajevo-born Emir Kusturica, who has won the Palme d'Or twice, for *When Father Was Away on Business* (1985) and *Underground* (1995). His last feature film was *On the Milky Road* (2016), which was partly filmed around Trebinje.

The relationship between two soldiers, one Muslim and one Serb, caught alone in the same trench during the Sarajevo siege, was the theme for Danis Tanović's Oscar-winning film *No Man's Land* (2001). The movie *Go West* (2005) takes on the deep taboo of homosexuality, as a wartime Serb-Bosniak gay couple become a latter-day Romeo and Juliet. *Fuse* (2003) is an irony-packed dark comedy set in the Bosnian castle town of Tešanj just after the war, parodying efforts to hide corruption and create a facade of ethnic reintegration for the sake of a proposed visit by US president Bill Clinton.

The Bridges of Sarajevo (2014) offered 13 influential directors the chance to contribute their own documentary take on the Bosnian capital in the 20th century.

Music

Sevdah (traditional Bosnian music) typically uses heart-wrenching vocals to recount tales of unhappy amours, though it was once used as a subtle courting technique. You can visit a *sevdah* museum-cafe (p103) in an antique Sarajevo *caravanserai* (inn). The capital also has an annual **Jazz Festival** (www.jazzfest.ba; ⊘ early Nov). In July, Banja Luka goes garage-band crazy with **Demofest** (📞051-220 750; www.demofest.org; ⊘ Jul).

Environment

Bosnia and Hercegovina is predominantly mountainous. The mostly arid south (Hercegovina) dips one tiny toe of land into the Adriatic Sea at Neum then rises swiftly into bare limestone uplands carved with deep grey canyons. The central mountain core has some 30 peaks topping out between 1700m and 2386m. Further north and east, the landscape becomes increasingly forested with more canyons and alpine valleys, most famously in the magnificent Sutjeska National Park. In the far northeast, the peaks subside into rolling bucolic hills, flattening out altogether in the far north.

Food & Drink

Rich, meaty stews dominate home cooking, while *ćevapi* (cylindrical spicy beef or pork meatballs) is the most common 'fast food'. Most villages have a *pekara* (bakery) for pastries, bread and *burek* (pastries stuffed with meat or cheese), also available from specialist outlets called *buregdžinica*. Vegetarian options are limited.

For dessert, try *tufahije*, baked apples stuffed with walnut paste and topped with whipped cream.

Cafe life is central to the experience here. Great espressos are almost ubiquitously available for as little as 1KM, or try a more traditional Bosnian coffee, made Turkish-style with the grounds and beautifully served. Hercegovinian wine is underrated – try Vranac or Blatina reds. Several local beers are excellent and there's a growing craft-beer scene. Don't miss sampling *rakija* (various types of strong fruit brandy/grappa).

SURVIVAL GUIDE

ℹ Directory A–Z

ACCOMMODATION

Accommodation is remarkably fair value by European standards. There's a good supply of guesthouses, rental apartments, motels and hostels (many homestay-style), plus some boutique and character hotels. Business and five-star hotels are rarer; ski areas have some upmarket resorts. Most hotels in Bosnia include some type of breakfast in the rates.

LGBTIQ+ TRAVELLERS

Although Bosnia decriminalised homosexuality in 1998 (2000 in the Republika Srpska), attitudes remain very conservative and attacks have occurred at queer festivals in the past. LGBTIQ+ advocacy organisation Sarajevo Open Centre (www.soc.ba) is active in fighting sexuality-based discrimination. In Sarajevo, the highlight of the queer year is the Merlinka Film Festival (www.merlinka.com) held in January or February. Sarajevo has a weekend-only gay bar, but you won't find any elsewhere.

MONEY

ATMs accepting Visa and MasterCard are ubiquitous.

OPENING HOURS

Closing times for many restaurants, cafes and bars depends on custom. In tourist areas such as Mostar, hotels and restaurants may close in the off-season.

Banks 8am to 6pm Monday to Friday, 8.30am to 1.30pm Saturday.

Bars and clubs Most bars are cafes by day, opening at 8am and closing at 11pm or later. Pubs and clubs open later and, at weekends, might close at 3am.

Office hours Typically 8am to 4pm, Monday to Friday.

Restaurants 7am to 10.30pm or until the last customer.

Shops 8am to 6pm daily, many stay open later.

POST

Bosnia and Hercegovina has three parallel postal organisations, each issuing their own stamps.

BH Pošta (www.posta.ba) The main provider.

Hrvatska pošta Mostar (www.post.ba) Operates in Croat areas such as western Mostar.

Pošte Srpske (www.postesrpske.com) Main operator in Republika Srpska.

PUBLIC HOLIDAYS

Nationwide holidays:

New Year's Day 1 and 2 January

May Day 1 and 2 May

Additional holidays in the Federation:

Independence Day 1 March

Catholic Easter Sunday March or April (in majority-Croat areas)

Catholic Easter Monday March or April (in majority-Croat areas)

Ramazan Bajram June (in majority-Bosniak areas)

Kurban Bajram August or September (in majority-Bosniak areas)

All Saints Day 1 November (in majority-Croat areas)

Statehood Day 25 November

Catholic Christmas 25 December (in majority-Croat areas)

Additional holidays in the Republika Srpska:

Orthodox Christmas 7 January

Republika Day 9 January

Orthodox New Year 14 January

Orthodox Good Friday March or April

Orthodox Easter Saturday March or April

Orthodox Easter Sunday March or April

Victory Day 9 May

Dayton Agreement Day 21 November

SAFE TRAVEL

Landmines and unexploded ordnance still affect 2% of Bosnia and Hercegovina's land area. **BHMAC** (www.bhmac.org) removes more every year, with the aim of full clearance by 2019. However, progress was slowed by floods in 2014 which added to the complexity of locating the last mines. For your safety, stick to asphalt/concrete surfaces or well-worn paths in affected areas, and avoid exploring war-damaged buildings.

TELEPHONE

Country code 387

International access code 00

Local directory information 1182 (Federation), 1185 (Republika Srpska), 1188 (Hrvatska pošta Mostar)

VISAS

It's wise to double-check the latest visa requirements by entering your nationality on the Ministry of Foreign Affairs website (www.mvp.gov.ba). Currently stays of less than 90 days require no visa for citizens of most European and American nations, plus Australia, New Zealand, Israel and several Arab and East Asian countries. If none of the visa-free conditions apply, then check carefully at which specified embassies you are expected to apply (eg that means London or Tripoli for South Africans). Visitors without access to 150KM per day could be refused entry.

Note that you do not need a Bosnia and Hercegovina visa to transit (without stopping) through Neum between Split and Dubrovnik, as long as you have the right to reenter Croatia.

ℹ Getting There & Away

ENTERING THE COUNTRY

Bosnia is encouraging of tourism and has kept red tape to a minimum for foreign visitors.

AIR

Bosnia doesn't have a national carrier.
➡ Sarajevo International Airport (p104) Bosnia's busiest, with flights all over Europe and the Middle East.

➡ Banja Luka International Airport (p125) Only used by Air Serbia (to Belgrade) and Ryanair (Charleroi, Memmingen and Stockholm-Skavsta).

➡ Mostar Airport (p116) (www.mostar-airport.ba) Year-round Croatia Airlines flights to Zagreb plus seasonal services.

➡ **Tuzla International Airport** (www.tuzla-airport.ba) Tiny but a hub for budget airline WizzAir, with flights to Austria, Switzerland, Germany, the Netherlands and Sweden.

LAND

Bus

Direct bus connections link Bosnia to all of its neighbours and to as far afield as Sweden. In most cases, passports are collected on the bus and handed over at the border; you usually won't leave the bus unless there's an issue that needs resolving. Useful websites include www.busticket4.me, www.eurolines.com, www.getbybus.com and www.vollo.net.

Croatia Direct buses go from most Croatian cities to Sarajevo, and from Zagreb to Banja Luka and Jajce. There are good connections between the Dalmatian coast and popular spots such as Trebinje, Mostar and Međugorje.

Montenegro Regular services run from Mostar and Trebinje to Podgorica, Cetinje, Budva, Tivat and Kotor, and from Banja Luka, Mostar and Trebinje to Herceg Novi.

Serbia Buses run from Belgrade to Banja Luka, Višegrad, Sarajevo, Mostar and Trebinje.

Slovenia Direct coaches depart from Ljubljana to Banja Luka and Sarajevo, and from Maribor to Sarajevo, Mostar and Međugorje.

Car & Motorcyle

Drivers need Green Card insurance and an EU or International Driving Permit. Transiting Neum in a Croatian hire car is usually not problematic.

Note that while most cars rented in Bosnia are covered for visits to neighbouring countries, Kosovo tends to be an exception, with insurance voided if you drive there. Since Croatia joined the EU in July 2013, many previously open minor border crossings with Bosnia and Hercegovina have been closed to international traffic, and border queues can be annoyingly long at busy times.

ℹ Getting Around

BICYCLE

Cyclists who can handle the hills will find Bosnia and Hercegovina's secondary routes helpfully calm. There are off-road trails for mountain bikers, notably around Bjelašnica, but beware of straying from them in areas where landmines remain a danger.

BUS

Bus services are excellent and relatively inexpensive. There are often different companies handling each route, so prices can vary substantially. Luggage stowed in the baggage compartment under the bus costs extra (around 2KM a piece).

Bus stations pre-sell tickets. Between towns it's normally easy enough to wave down any bus en route. Advance reservations are sometimes necessary for overnight routes or at peak holiday times. The biggest companies include Autoprevoz (www.autoprevoz.ba), Centrotrans (www.centrotrans.com) and Globtour (www.globtour.com). Useful websites offering schedules and bookings include www.busticket4.me, www.vollo.net and www.getbybus.com.

Frequency on some routes drops drastically at weekends. Some shorter routes stop on Sunday.

CAR & MOTORCYCLE

Bosnia and Hercegovina's winding roads are lightly trafficked and a delight for driving if you aren't in a hurry. Driving makes sense to reach the country's more remote areas. There are a few toll motorways in the centre of the country; collect your ticket from the machine at the set of booths where you enter, then pay at the booths where you leave the motorway.

TRAIN

Trains are slower and far less frequent than buses, but generally slightly cheaper. ŽFBH (www.zfbh.ba) has an online rail timetable search. The main routes are Sarajevo–Visoko–Banja Luka–Bihać and Sarajevo–Konjic–Mostar.

Croatia

POP 4.3 MILLION

Why Go?

If your Mediterranean fantasies feature balmy days by sapphire waters in the shade of ancient walled towns, Croatia is the place to turn them into reality.

The extraordinary Adriatic coastline, speckled with 1244 islands and strewn with historic towns, is Croatia's main attraction. The standout is Dubrovnik, its remarkable old oown ringed by mighty defensive walls. Split showcases Diocletian's Palace, one of the world's most impressive Roman monuments, where bars, restaurants and shops thrive amid the ancient walls. In the heart-shaped peninsula of Istria, Rovinj is a charm-packed fishing port with narrow cobbled streets.

Away from the coast, Zagreb, Croatia's lovely capital, has a booming cafe culture and art scene, while Plitvice Lakes National Park offers a verdant maze of turquoise lakes and cascading waterfalls.

Best Places to Eat

➡ Pelegrini (p175)

➡ Restaurant 360° (p203)

➡ Meneghetti (p152)

➡ Konoba Marjan (p183)

Best Places to Stay

➡ Art Hotel Kalelarga (p170)

➡ Meneghetti (p152)

➡ Design Hotel Navis (p162)

When to Go

Zagreb

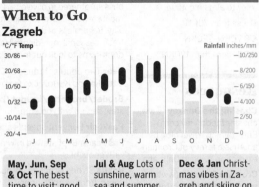

May, Jun, Sep & Oct The best time to visit: good weather, fewer people, lower prices.

Jul & Aug Lots of sunshine, warm sea and summer festivals; many tourists and highest prices.

Dec & Jan Christmas vibes in Zagreb and skiing on Mt Medvednica.

AT A GLANCE

Area 56,538 sq km

Capital Zagreb

Country Code ☑ 385

Currency Kuna (KN)

Emergency Ambulance ☑ 94, police ☑ 92

Language Croatian

Population 4.3 million

Time Central European Time (GMT/UTC plus one hour)

Visas Not required for most nationalities for stays of up to 90 days.

Sleeping Price Ranges

The following price ranges refer to a double room with a bathroom in July and August.

€ less than 450KN

€€ 450KN–900KN

€€€ more than 900KN

Eating Price Ranges

The following price ranges refer to a main course.

€ less than 70KN

€€ 70KN–120KN

€€€ more than 120KN

Resources

Chasing the Donkey (www.chasingthedonkey.com) Entertaining travel blog by an Aussie family of Croatian extraction living in Dalmatia.

Croatian Tourism (www.croatia.hr) Official tourism site; the best starting point for holiday planning.

Entering the Country

Getting to Croatia is becoming easier year-on-year, with both budget and full-service airlines flying to various airports in summer. On top of this, buses, trains and ferries also shepherd holidaymakers into the country. Flights, cars and tours can be booked online at lonelyplanet.com/bookings.

ITINERARIES

Three Days

Base yourself in Dubrovnik (p197) and explore the compact old town; start early and take a walk along the city walls before it gets too hot. Catch the cable car up Srd and explore the surrounding beaches. Once you've seen the sights and had a swim, consider boat trips to Cavtat (p207), Lokrum (p203) or the Elafiti Islands (p195).

One Week

Base yourself in Croatia's exuberant second city, Split (p177), for two days of sightseeing and nightlife, including a trip to the nearby postcard-perfect walled town of Trogir (p175). Spend the next few days island hopping by fast catamaran to Bol (p187) on the island of Brač; Hvar Town (p189), the vibrant capital of the island of the same name; and photogenic walled Korčula Town (p193). Continue by catamaran to magnificent Dubrovnik (p197) and spend the next two days taking in its sights.

Essential Food & Drink

Croatian food echoes the varied cultures that have influenced the country over its history. There's a sharp divide between the Italian-style cuisine along the coast and the flavours of Hungary, Austria and Turkey in the continental parts. From grilled sea bass smothered in olive oil in Dalmatia to robust, paprika-heavy meat stews in Slavonia, each region proudly touts its own speciality. Regardless of the region, you'll find tasty food made from fresh, seasonal ingredients. Here are a few essential food and drink items to look out for while in Croatia.

Beer Two popular brands of Croatian *pivo* (beer) are Zagreb's Ožujsko and Karlovačko from Karlovac.

Brodet/brodetto/brudet/brujet Slightly spicy seafood stew served with polenta.

Paški sir Pungent sheep's cheese from the island of Pag.

Pašticada Beef stewed in wine, prunes and spices and served with gnocchi.

Rakija Strong Croatian grappa that comes in different flavours, from plum to honey.

Ražnjići Small chunks of pork grilled on a skewer.

ZAGREB

⏱ 01 / POP 803,700

Zagreb is made for strolling. Wander through the Upper Town's red-roof and cobblestone glory, peppered with church spires. Crane your neck to see the domes and ornate upper-floor frippery of the Lower Town's mash-up of secessionist, neo-baroque and art deco buildings. Search out the grittier pockets of town where ugly-bland concrete walls have been transformed into colourful murals by local street artists. This city rewards those on foot.

Afterwards, do as the locals do and head to a cafe. The cafe culture here is just one facet of this city's vibrant street life, egged on by a year-round swag of events that bring music, pop-up markets and food stalls to the plazas and parks. Even when there's nothing on, the centre thrums with youthful energy, so it's no surprise that Croatia's capital is now bringing in the city-break crowd. Zagreb is the little city that could.

◎ Sights

As the oldest part of Zagreb, the Upper Town (Gornji Grad), which includes the neighbourhoods of Gradec and Kaptol, has landmark buildings and churches from the earlier centuries of Zagreb's history. The Lower Town (Donji Grad), which runs between the Upper Town and the train station, has the city's most interesting art museums and fine examples of 19th- and 20th-century architecture.

★Mirogoj   CEMETERY
(Aleja Hermanna Bollea 27; ⊘6am-8pm Apr-Oct, 7.30am-6pm Nov-Mar) A 10-minute ride north of the city centre (or a 30-minute walk through leafy streets) takes you to one of the most beautiful cemeteries in Europe, sited at the base of Mt Medvednica. It was designed in 1876 by Austrian-born architect Herman Bollé, who created numerous buildings around Zagreb. The majestic arcade, topped by a string of cupolas, looks like a fortress from the outside, but feels calm and graceful on the inside.

★Museum of Broken Relationships   MUSEUM
(Map p140; www.brokenships.com; Ćirilometodska 2; adult/child 40/30KN; ⊘9am-10.30pm Jun-Sep, to 9pm Oct-May) From romances that withered to broken family connections, this wonderfully quirky museum explores the mementos left over after a relationship ends.

Displayed amid a string of all-white rooms are donations from around the globe, each with a story attached. Exhibits range from the hilarious (the toaster someone nicked so their ex could never make toast again) to the heartbreaking (the suicide note from somebody's mother). In turns funny, poignant and moving, it's a perfect summing-up of the human condition.

★Croatian Museum of Naïve Art   MUSEUM
(Hrvatski Muzej Naivne Umjetnosti; Map p140; ⏱01-48 51 911; www.hmnu.hr; Ćirilometodska 3; adult/concession 25/15KN; ⊘10am-6pm Mon-Sat, to 1pm Sun) A feast for fans of Croatia's naive art (a form that was highly fashionable locally and worldwide during the 1960s and '70s and has declined somewhat since), this small museum displays 80 artworks (a smidgen of the museum's total 1900 holdings) that illustrate the full range of colourful, and often dreamlike, styles within the genre. The discipline's most important artists, such as Generalić, Mraz, Rabuzin and Smajić, are all displayed here.

Dolac Market   MARKET
(Map p140; off Trg Bana Jelačića; ⊘open-air market 6.30am-3pm Mon-Sat, to 1pm Sun, covered market 7am-2pm Mon-Fri, to 3pm Sat, to 1pm Sun) Right in the heart of the city, Zagreb's bustling fruit and vegetable market has been trader-central since the 1930s when the city authorities set up a market space on the 'border' between the Upper and Lower Towns. Sellers from all over Croatia descend here daily to hawk fresh produce.

Katarinin Trg   VIEWPOINT
(Map p140; Katarinin trg) One of the best views in town – across red-tile roofs towards the cathedral – is from this square behind the Jesuit Church of St Catherine (Crkva Svete Katarine; Map p140; Katarinin trg bb; ⊘Mass 6pm Mon-Fri, 11am Sun). It's the perfect spot to begin or end an Upper Town wander. The square is also home to Zagreb's most famous street art; the **Whale**, gracing the facade of the abandoned Galerija Gradec building, is a 3D work by French artist Etien.

Cathedral of the Assumption of the Blessed Virgin Mary   CHURCH
(Katedrala Marijina Uznešenja; Map p140; Kaptol 31; ⊘10am-5pm Mon-Sat, 1-5pm Sun) This cathedral's twin spires – seemingly permanently under repair – soar over the city. Formerly

CROATIA ZAGREB

Croatia Highlights

1 Dubrovnik (p197)
Circling the historic city's mighty walls and then catching the cable car up Mt Srđ for breathtaking views from above.

2 Plitvice Lakes National Park (p165) Marvelling at the otherworldly turquoise lakes and dramatic waterfalls of Croatia's top natural attraction.

3 Hvar Town (p189) Capping off endless beach days with sunset cocktails and back-lane boogie sessions.

4 Split (p177) Discovering the city's ancient heart in Diocletian's Palace, a quarter that buzzes day and night.

5 Zagreb (p135) Exploring the quirky museums and cafes of Croatia's cute little capital.

6 Rovinj (p152) Roam the steep cobbled streets and piazzas of Istria's showpiece coastal town.

7 Zadar (p167) Exploring Roman ruins, intriguing museums, local eateries and hip bars within the marbled streets of the old town.

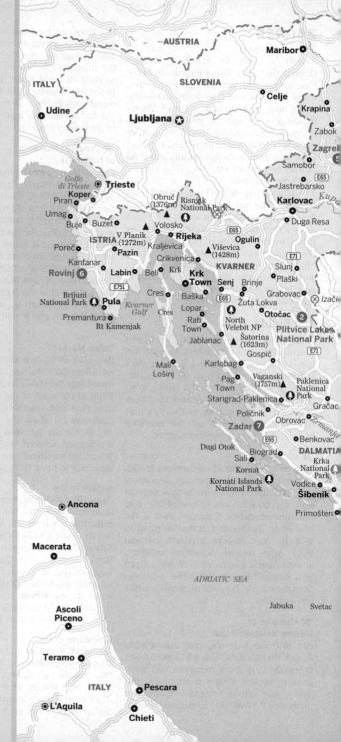

known as St Stephen's, the cathedral has an original Gothic structure that's been transformed many times over, but the sacristy still contains a cycle of frescos dating from the 13th century. An earthquake in 1880 badly damaged the building, and reconstruction in a neo-Gothic style began around the turn of the 20th century.

Archaeological Museum   MUSEUM

(Arheološki Muzej; Map p140; ☎01-48 73 101; www.amz.hr; Trg Nikole Šubića Zrinskog 19; adult/child/family 30/15/50KN; ⊘10am-6pm Tue, Wed, Fri & Sat, to 8pm Thu, to 1pm Sun) Spread over three floors, the artefacts housed here stretch from the prehistoric era to the medieval age. The 2nd floor holds the most interesting – and well-curated – exhibits. Here, displays of intricate Roman minor arts, such as decorative combs and oil lamps, and metal curse tablets, are given as much prominence as the more usual show-stopping marble statuary. An exhibit devoted to Croatia's early-medieval Bijelo Brdo culture displays a wealth of grave finds unearthed in the 1920s.

Zrinjevac   SQUARE

(Trg Nikole Šubića Zrinskog; Map p140) Officially called Trg Nikole Šubića Zrinskog but lovingly known as Zrinjevac, this verdant square is a major hang-out during sunny weekends and hosts pop-up cafe stalls during the summer months. It's also a venue for many festivals and events, most centred on the ornate music pavilion that dates from 1891.

Museum of
Contemporary Art   MUSEUM

(Muzej Suvremene Umjetnosti; ☎01-60 52 700; www.msu.hr; Avenija Dubrovnik 17; adult/child 30/15KN; ⊘11am-6pm Tue-Fri & Sun, to 8pm Sat) Housed in a city icon designed by local star architect Igor Franić, this museum displays both solo and thematic group shows by Croatian and international artists in its 17,000 sq metres. The permanent display, *Collection in Motion,* showcases 620 edgy works by 240 artists, roughly half of whom are Croatian. There's a packed year-round schedule of film, theatre, concerts and performance art.

Maksimir Park   PARK

(☎01-23 20 460; www.park-maksimir.hr; Maksimirski perivoj bb; ⊘information centre 10am-4pm Tue-Fri, to 6pm Sat & Sun) Maksimir Park is a peaceful wooded enclave covering 18 hectares,

easily accessible by trams 11 and 12 from Trg Bana Jelačića. Opened to the public in 1794, it was the first public promenade in southeastern Europe. It's landscaped like an English garden, with alleys, lawns and artificial lakes. The most photographed structure in the park is the exquisite Bellevue Pavilion, constructed in 1843. Also here is the Echo Pavilion, as well as a house built to resemble a rustic Swiss cottage.

⟟ Tours

Secret Zagreb   WALKING

(☎097 67 38 738; www.secret-zagreb.com; per person 75KN; ⊘7pm Tue & Fri Nov-Mar, 9pm Fri Apr, & Wed & Sun May-Oct) An ethnographer and inspiring storyteller, Iva Silla is the guide who reveals the Zagreb of curious myths and legends and peculiar historical personalities. Take her hit walking tour 'Zagreb Ghosts and Dragons' to peek into the city's hidden corners or forgotten graveyards, all set in the city centre.

Blue Bike Tours   CYCLING

(Map p140; ☎098 18 83 344; www.zagrebbybike.com; Trg Bana Jelačića 15; tour adult/child €29/14.50) The popular 'Zagreb Highlights' bike tour is a great introduction to the central city's sights. The 'Back to Socialism' tour explores the socialist architecture of Novi Zagreb. Tours last around 2½ hours and run year-round (at 10am or 2pm except for during the hot summer months, when start times move to 5pm).

⚜ Festivals & Events

Music Biennale Zagreb   MUSIC

(www.mbz.hr; ⊘Apr) Croatia's most important contemporary-music event. By 'contemporary', do not read 'pop' – this prestigious fest celebrates modern-day classical music. Held in odd-numbered years.

Subversive Festival   CULTURAL

(www.subversivefestival.com; ⊘May) Europe's activists and philosophers descend on Zagreb in droves for film screenings and lectures over two weeks in May.

Cest is d'Best   CULTURAL

(www.cestisdbest.com; ⊘May-Jun) This street festival delights Zagreb citizens for a few days in late May through early June each year, with six stages around the city centre, around 200 international performers, and acts that include music, dance, theatre, art and sports.

WORTH A TRIP

ZAGORJE

The bucolic Zagorje region provides rural escapades right on Zagreb's doorstep. The landscape of itsy villages squirrelled between verdantly forested hills, vineyards and cornfields, and medieval castles was made for easy-going road trips; it presents a relaxed foil to the bustling Mediterranean south. A trip here is blissfully crowd-free, although less so on summer weekends when day-tripping families from the capital debunk en masse to storm the area.

The Zagorje region begins north of **Mt Medvednica** (1035m) and extends west to the Slovenian border, and as far north as **Varaždin**, a showcase of baroque architecture. Castles are a hallmark of the region: Varaždin's now houses its **Town Museum** (Gradski Muzej; www.gmv.hr; Strossmayerovo Šetalište 3; adult/child 25/15KN; ⊙9am-5pm Tue-Fri, to 1pm Sat & Sun), but lakeside **Trakošćan Castle** (☑042-796 281; www.trakoscan.hr; Trakošćan 1; adult/child 40/20KN; ⊙9am-6pm Apr-Oct, to 4pm Nov-Mar) and hilltop **Veliki Tabor Castle** (www.veliki-tabor.hr; Košnički Hum 1, Desinić; adult/child/family 25/15/55KN; ⊙9am-5pm Mon-Fri, to 7pm Sat & Sun Apr-Sep, 9am-4pm Wed-Sun Nov-Mar, 9am-4pm Mon-Fri, to 5pm Sat & Sun Oct) are even more impressive.

Another highlight is the baroque **Church of the Virgin Mary of Jerusalem** (☑caretaker 095 52 86 213; M Krieže bb; ⊙8-10am Sun) in the neat-as-a-pin provincial centre of **Krapina**. If it's the rural idyll you're chasing, head to **Vuglec Breg** (☑049-345 015; www.vuglec-breg.hr; Škarićevo 151, Škarićevo; r from €80; P⛽) in the village of Škarićevo, 4km from spa town **Krapinske Toplice**. It has five traditional cottages for rent and a restaurant serving Zagorje specialities (mains 95KN to 120KN), such as *purica s mlincima* (slow-roasted turkey with baked noodles) and *štrukli* (baked cheese dumplings), on a terrace with panoramic vistas.

Ljeto na Štrosu   CULTURAL

(www.ljetonastrosu.com; ⊙late May–mid-Sep) This quirky annual event stages free outdoor film screenings, concerts, art workshops and best-in-show mongrel dog competitions, all along the leafy Strossmayerovo Šetalište.

INmusic Festival   MUSIC

(www.inmusicfestival.com; Jarun Lake; ⊙Jun) A three-day extravaganza every June, this is Zagreb's highest-profile music festival. Previous years have seen Alice in Chains, PJ Harvey, Nick Cave and the Bad Seeds, and St Vincent take to the Jarun Lake main stage.

Courtyards   CULTURAL

(Dvorišta; www.dvorista.in; ⊙Jul) For 10 days each July, Zagreb's historic Upper Town courtyards, many of which are normally off limits, open their doors for a string of concerts and performances, combined with food, booze and merrymaking.

Fuliranje   CHRISTMAS MARKET

(www.adventzagreb.com; ⊙Dec) Zagreb's award-winning Christmas market, which uses various locations around the city centre including Trg Bana Jelačića and Zrinjevac. It's held throughout December, as part of a bustling and packed Advent program in Zagreb, despite the subzero temperatures. The focus is on street food, mulled wine, craft stores, live music and plenty of activities to keep the wee ones busy.

🛏 Sleeping

★ Studio Kairos   B&B €

(☑01-46 40 690; Vlaška 92; s/d/tr/q from €36/50/65/70; ❄🛜) This adorable B&B in a street-level apartment has four well-appointed rooms decked out by theme – Writers, Crafts, Music and Granny's. The cosy common space, where a delicious breakfast is served, and the enthusiastic hosts, who are a fount of knowledge on all things Zagreb, add to this place's intimate and homely appeal. Bikes are also available for rent.

★ Swanky Mint Hostel   HOSTEL €

(Map p140; ☑01-40 04 248; www.swanky-hostel.com/mint; Ilica 50; dm 170-200KN, s/d 400/600KN; ❄@🛜♿) This backpacker vortex, converted from a 19th-century textile-dye factory, has a very happening bar at its heart. Dorms are small but thoughtfully kitted out with lockers, privacy curtains and reading lamps, while private rooms are bright and large. The hostel's popularity, however, lies in its super-social, friendly vibe, with welcome shots of *rakija* (grappa), organised pub crawls and an on-site travel agency.

Zagreb

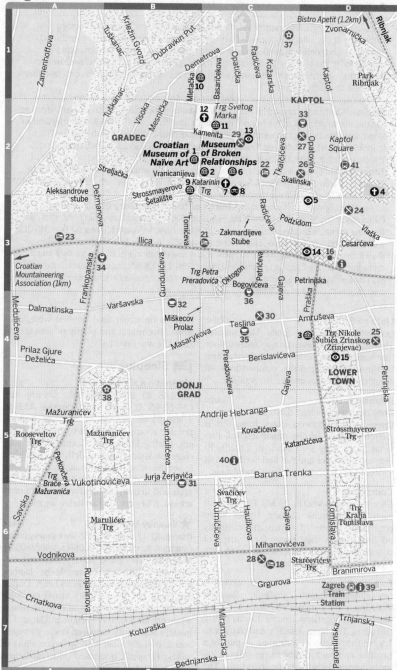

Hostel 63
HOSTEL €

(Map p140; ☎01-55 20 557; www.hostel63.eu; Vlaška 63/7; dm/d/apt €22/65/75; ☺❄🛜) Everything is kept shipshape and squeaky clean at this grey-yellow-and-white themed hostel, run by helpful staff. Four-bed dorms are thoughtfully equipped with lockers, privacy curtains and private bathrooms; there are even two dorms with two double-bed bunks for couples. Breakfast is €4. Its quiet location, in a courtyard off the main road, means you should get a good night's sleep.

Rooms Zagreb 17
BOUTIQUE HOTEL €€

(Map p140; ☎091 17 00 000; www.sobezagreb17. com; Radićeva 22; r €60-80, apt €120; ❄🛜) In the heart of the city, these spacious rooms overlooking the cafe-buzz of Tkalčićeva have swags of style thanks to owner Irena's eye for detail. Lashings of white are offset by fun, vibrant art, minifridges and perspex chairs, and all come well equipped with satellite TV (plentiful international channels) and kettles. Grab Room 2 for the nautical theme.

4 City Windows
B&B €€

(Map p140; ☎01-88 97 999; www.4citywindows. com; Palmotićeva 13; s/d €55/90; P❄🛜) Tanja and Ivo provide personalised service at this intimate B&B slap in the centre, making it feel more like staying with two cool Zagreb-insiders rather than in a hotel. Rooms have arty flair, and thanks to thick walls, you're guaranteed a good sleep. Breakfast is a feast, including *štrukli* (baked cheese dumplings), pancakes and homemade jams.

Hotel Astoria
BUSINESS HOTEL €€

(Map p140; ☎01-48 08 900; www.hotelastoria.hr; Petrinjska 71; s/d from €80/90; P☺❄🛜) Hotel Astoria is a solid choice just a stroll from the train station. Part of the Best Western Premier hotel family, the hotel has bright, business-brisk rooms all comfortably fitted out with kettles, TVs and good-sized bathrooms. Staff are superfriendly and keen to help.

★ Hotel Jägerhorn
HISTORIC HOTEL €€€

(Map p140; ☎01-48 33 877; www.hotel-jagerhorn. hr; Ilica 14; s/d/ste 950/1050/1500KN; P❄@🛜) The oldest hotel in Zagreb (around since 1827) is a peaceful oasis, brimming with character. The 18 rooms are elegantly outfitted, with soft neutral decor offset by blue accents, king-sized beds and swish, contemporary bathrooms. Top-floor rooms have views over leafy Gradec. Staff are charming and the downstairs terrace cafe is the perfect hang-out after your sightseeing is done.

Zagreb

Esplanade Zagreb Hotel
HISTORIC HOTEL €€€

(Map p140; ☑01-45 66 666; www.esplanade.hr; Mihanovićeva 1; r from €130; P🅿️❄️🌐@🛜) This art deco masterpiece was purpose-built to welcome the Orient Express crowd in 1925 and still holds on to many original features, from its grand marble staircase and intricate stained-glass windows to the glorious Emerald Ballroom. Rooms exude timeless elegance – as you'd expect for a place that has a roll call of kings and politicians on its past guest list.

✕ Eating

Heritage
CROATIAN €

(Map p140; Petrinjska 14; mains 18-39KN; ⊙11am-8pm Mon-Sat; ❄️) Tapas dishes, Croatian-style. This teensy place, with just one counter and a few bar stools, serves cheese and meat platters using all locally sourced ingredients. Try the flatbreads with prosciutto from Zagora, black-truffle spread and cheese from Ika, or the *kulen* (spicy

paprika-flavoured sausage) with grilled peppers and cream cheese. Service is warm and friendly.

La Štruk
CROATIAN €

(Map p140; www.facebook.com/La-Struk; Skalinska 5; mains 29-40KN; ⊙11am-10pm; ❄️🛜🚭) Serving one thing only, La Štruk devotes itself to *štrukli* (baked cheese dumplings). Keep traditional with a salty or sweet cheese *kuhani* (boiled) version or veer completely off-piste with the roasted-pepper or truffle *zapečeni* (baked) options – more like an ultracheesy lasagna. If inside is full, there's seating in the hidden garden accessed through an alley to the side.

Amelie
CAFE €

(Map p140; www.slasticeamelie.com; Vlaška 6; cakes 17-19KN; ⊙8am-11pm; ❄️🛜) Many locals regard this cafe as one of Zagreb's best cake-and-coffee stops. Seasonal specialities such as plum cake in summer are particularly good. On fine days, sit on the terrace, directly across the street.

★**Mali Bar** TAPAS €€
(Map p140; 📱01-55 31 014; www.facebook.com/
MaliBarZagreb; Vlaška 63; dishes 45-150KN;
🕧12.30pm-midnight Mon-Sat; 🍴) This earthy-
toned spot by star chef Ana Ugarković is
all about small plates, with influences cher-
ry-picked from across the Mediterranean,
the Middle East and Asia. Dig into labneh
balls on a bed of chard and roasted beetroot,
smoked tuna dressed in saffron, and Chinese pork dumplings all in the same sitting.

Lanterna na Dolcu CROATIAN €€
(Map p140; 📱01-48 19 009; www.lanterna-zagreb.
com; Opatovina 31; mains 55-95KN; 🕧11am-11pm
Tue-Sat, 4-11pm Sun & Mon; 🔊) Modern tweaks
on traditional Croatian classics and fabulous
service make Lanterna stand out amid the
central city's glut of restaurants. In the cosy
basement with brick-vaulted ceiling, dig
into mains of plum-stuffed pork loin doused
in a brandy and plum jus or steak in a pickled pepper sauce. There's an excellent wine
list here, too.

Trilogija MEDITERRANEAN €€
(Map p140; 📱01-48 51 394; www.trilogija.com;
Kamenita 5; mains 88-140KN; 🕧11am-midnight
Mon-Thu, to 10am Fri & Sat, to 4pm Sun; 🕳) Right
by the Stone Gate, in a location that has seen
many a restaurant open and close, Trilogija
seems to be here to stay. The secret lies in
its friendly staff and Mediterranean-fusion
menu with dishes like tuna steak with beetroot, and a risotto of shrimp and mango.

Vinodol CROATIAN €€
(Map p140; 📱01-48 11 427; www.vinodol-zg.hr;
Teslina 10; mains 85-160KN; 🕧11.30am-midnight;
🕳) Giving central European fare a modern
tweak, Vinodol is much loved by locals. On
warm days, eat on the covered patio (entered
through an ivy-clad passageway off Teslina).
Menu highlights include succulent lamb
or veal and potatoes cooked under *peka*
(a domed baking lid), and almond-crusted
trout.

★**Bistro Apetit** EUROPEAN €€€
(📱01-46 77 335; www.bistroapetit.com; Jurjevska
65a; mains 132-202KN; 🕧10am-midnight Tue-Sun;
🕳) High up on villa-lined Jurjevska steet,
this restaurant run by chef Marin Rendić,
who previously worked at Copenhagen's
Noma, serves up Zagreb's suavest contemporary dishes. Start with tuna tartare with
pear and sesame seeds then move on to
beef cheeks on bean spread, laced by carrot
and pistachio. Opt for a degustation menu

(five/seven courses 420/620KN) for flavour-
packed feasting.

Zinfandel's INTERNATIONAL €€€
(Map p140; 📱01-45 66 644; www.zinfandels.hr;
Mihanovićeva 1; mains 165-230KN; 🕧6am-11pm
Mon-Sat, 6.30am-11pm Sun; 🕳🍴) One of the
top tables in town, Zinfandel's is headed by
chef Ana Grgić, whose menu of creative flair
is also served in the grand dining room of
the Esplanade Zagreb Hotel (p142). Don't
miss the confit pigeon with beetroot and
cherries with a rhubarb sauce. After dinner move onto the Oleander Terrace for a
drink and prime people-watching across
Starčevićev trg.

Le Bistro FRENCH €€€
(Map p140; www.lebistro.hr; Mihanovićeva 1; mains
95-270KN; 🕧9am-11pm; 🕳🔊🍴) Executive
chef Ana Grgić leads the team at the casual-
chic restaurant of the Esplanade Zagreb
Hotel (p142), much favoured by local business folk for its lunchtime three-course daily menu (160KN). It's known for its *štrukli*
(cottage-cheese-filled dumplings), and its
classic French-style menu.

🍸 Drinking & Nightlife

In the Upper Town, Tkalčićeva is throbbing
with bars and cafes. With half a dozen bars
and sidewalk cafes between Trg Petra Preradovića (known locally as Cvjetni trg) and
Bogovićeva in the Lower Town, the scene
on summer nights resembles a vast outdoor party. Things wind down by midnight,
though, and get quieter from mid-July
through late August.

Pupitres WINE BAR
(Map p140; 📱098 16 58 073; http://pupitres.hr;
Frankopanska 1; 🕧9am-11pm Mon-Thu, to 1am Fri
& Sat; 🔊) When a wine bar is run by a top
sommelier, you know you're in good hands.
Jelene Šimić Valentić's casual-chic place
is the best spot in town to get acquainted
with Croatia's plethora of wines. Service is
charming and genuinely helpful and the
wine list is (unsurprisingly) a roll-call of the
country's best cellars plus some international names.

Craft Room CRAFT BEER
(Map p140; www.facebook.com/craftroombeer;
Opatovina 35; 🕧10am-2am; 🔊) In the city centre, this is the number-one stop for anyone
interested in Croatia's craft-beer scene. Plenty of local beers are on tap and there's a huge
menu of bottled international brands.

CROATIA ZAGREB

Garden Brewery
CRAFT BEER

(www.thegarden.hr/the-garden-brewery; Slavonska avenija 22f; ☺ noon-8pm Mon-Thu & Sun, to 2am Fri & Sat; 🛜) This boutique craft brewery and bar is worth the schlep out to the industrial east of Zagreb. Inside an old red-brick factory, it offers craft beer made on-site (try the Session Ale with floral overtones or the Kettle Sour full of fruity flavours), live music on Saturday and family-friendly Sunday sessions.

Vinyl
BAR

(Map p140; www.vinylzagreb.com; Bogovićeva 3; ☺ 8am-midnight Sun-Tue, to 2am Wed & Thu, to 4am Fri & Sat) Much beloved by the locals, this all-day lounge on a popular stretch is split into cafe and club areas. It delivers fun both day and night, including live-music events, readings and exhibitions of books and vinyl, such as Masters of Memories on Monday evening. Don't miss the vinyl-only DJ sets on weekends, and the superb range of whisky.

Quahwa
COFFEE

(Map p140; Teslina 9; ☺ 9am-9pm Mon-Thu, to 10pm Fri & Sat, 10am-5pm Sun; 🛜) Living up to its tagline ('for coffee lovers only'), Quahwa serves up some of the finest arabica in Zagreb, from superstrong lattes to traditional Turkish coffee. Caffeine heaven.

Cogito Coffee Shop
CAFE

(Map p140; www.cogitocoffee.com; Varšavska 11; ☺ 8am-8pm Mon-Fri, 9am-7pm Sat; 🛜) Down a passageway, this tiny ultracool cafe serves up coffee roasted by the local Cogito Coffee Roasters at Cafe u Dvorištu (Map p140; Jurja Žerjavića 7/2; ☺ 9am-midnight Mon-Sat, 11am-7pm Sun; 🛜). There's delicious Međenko ice cream on offer as well. Shorter hours in August.

☆ Entertainment

Booze & Blues
LIVE MUSIC

(Map p140; www.booze-and-blues.com; Tkalčićeva 84; ☺ 8am-midnight Sun-Tue, to 2am Wed-Sat; 🛜) It does what it says on the tin. Perched at the top of the buzzy Tkalča strip, this haven of jazz, blues and soul rhythms stands out with its weekend live-music line-up. The interior is designed in the tradition of American blues and jazz clubs, with music-history memorabilia, and Heineken on tap flowing from a functioning saxophone.

Tvornica
LIVE MUSIC

(www.tvornicakulture.com; Šubićeva 2; ☺ cafe 7am-11pm Mon-Fri, 4-11pm Sat & Sun, club 8pm-2am Sun-Thu, to 4am Fri & Sat) Excellent multimedia venue showcasing a variety of live-music

performances, from Bosnian *sevdah* (traditional music) to alternative punk rock. Check out the website to see what's on.

Strossmarte
LIVE MUSIC

(Map p140; www.ljetonastrosu.com; Strossmayerovo Šetalište; ☺ May-Sep) During the summer months, the Strossmayer promenade in the Upper Town hosts live music most nights, with makeshift bars. The mixed-bag crowd, great city views and leafy ambience make it a great spot to while away your evenings.

Croatian National Theatre
THEATRE

(Map p140; ☎ 01-48 88 415; www.hnk.hr; Trg Republika Hrvatska 15; ☺ box office 10am-7pm Mon-Fri, to 1pm Sat, plus 1hr before performances) This neobaroque theatre, established in 1895, stages a regular program of opera and ballet performances and plays. Check out Ivan Meštrović's sculpture *The Well of Life* (1905) standing out front.

ℹ Information

MEDICAL SERVICES

Emergency Health Clinic (☎ 01-63 02 911; Heinzelova 87; ☺ 24hr)

KBC Rebro Hospital (☎ 8am-4pm 01-23 88 029; www.kbc-zagreb.hr; Kišpatićeva 12; ☺ 24hr) Good public hospital with an emergency department. It's the teaching hospital of the University of Zagreb.

TOURIST INFORMATION

Main Tourist Office (Map p140; ☎ information 0800 53 53, office 01-48 14 051; www.info zagreb.hr; Trg Bana Jelačića 11; ☺ 8.30am-8pm Mon-Fri, 9am-6pm Sat, 10am-4pm Sun) Distributes free city maps and leaflets. Has several branches throughout the city.

Lotrščak Tower Tourist Office (Map p140; ☎ 01-48 51 510; Strossmayerovo Šetalište; ☺ 9am-9pm Mon-Fri, 10am-9pm Sat & Sun Jun-Sep, 9am-5pm Mon-Fri, 10am-5pm Sat & Sun Oct-May)

Main Bus Station Tourist Office (☎ 01-61 15 507; Avenija M Držića 4; ☺ 9am-9pm Mon-Fri, 10am-5pm Sat & Sun)

Main Railway Station Tourist Office (Map p140; Trg Kralja Tomislava 12; ☺ 9am-9pm Mon-Fri, 10am-5pm Sat & Sun)

Zagreb Airport Tourist Office (☎ 01-62 65 091; Zagreb Airport; ☺ 9am-9pm Mon-Fri, 10am-5pm Sat & Sun)

Zagreb County Tourist Association (Map p140; ☎ 01-48 73 665; www.tzzz.hr; Preradovićeva 42; ☺ 8am-4pm Mon-Fri) Has information and materials on attractions in Zagreb's surroundings, including wine roads and bike trails.

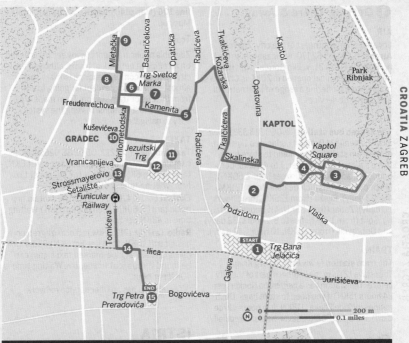

🏃 City Walk
Architecture, Art & Street Life

START TRG BANA JELAČIĆA
END TRG PETRA PRERADOVIĆA
LENGTH 1KM; 1½ HOURS

The natural starting point of any walk in Zagreb is buzzing **1 Trg Bana Jelačića**. Climb the steps up to **2 Dolac Market** (p135) before heading for the neo-Gothic **3 Cathedral of the Assumption of the Blessed Virgin Mary** (p135). Cross **4 Kaptol Square** (lined with 17th-century buildings), walk down Skalinska and come out at Tkalčićeva. Wander up the street, then climb the stairs that will take you up to **5 Stone Gate**, a fascinating shrine and the eastern gate to medieval Gradec Town. Next, go up Kamenita and you'll come out at Trg Svetog Marka, the site of the 13th-century **6 St Mark's Church**, one of Zagreb's most emblematic buildings, with a colourful tiled roof; the **7 Sabor**, the country's parliament; and **8 Banski Dvori**, the presidential palace.

Wander through the winding streets of the Upper Town to the **9 Meštrović Atelier** (www.mestrovic.hr; adult/child 30/15KN;

⏰10am-6pm Tue-Fri, to 2pm Sat & Sun). Walk back across Trg Svetog Marka and down Ćirilometodska, stepping into one of the country's most singular museums, the **10 Croatian Museum of Naïve Art** (p135). Cross Jezuitski trg and enter **11 Galerija Klovićevi Dvori** (www.gkd.hr; admission varies, up to 40KN; ⏰11am-7pm Tue-Sun), where art exhibitions await. When you're finished with art, gaze up at the gorgeous **12 Jesuit Church of St Catherine** (p135), before finally emerging at **13 Lotrščak Tower** (adult/child 20/10KN; ⏰9am-9pm Mon-Fri, 10am-5pm Sat & Sun), built in the middle of the 13th century and today offering dazzling 360-degree vistas of the city. Near the tower is a historic funicular railway, constructed in 1888, which connects the Lower and Upper Towns. Take in the cityscape then go down in the funicular, or take the verdant stairway – either will leave you on the side of **14 Ilica**, Zagreb's commercial artery.

Cross Ilica and walk to **15 Trg Petra Preradovića**, known to locals as Cvjetni trg, where you can take a break at one of the many cafes.

ℹ Getting There & Away

AIR

Located 17km southeast of the city, **Zagreb Airport** (☑ 01-45 62 170; www.zagreb-airport. hr; Rudolfa Fizira 21, Velika Gorica), with its supermodern terminal opened in 2018, is Croatia's major airport, offering a range of international and domestic services.

BUS

The **Zagreb bus station** (☑ 060 313 333; www. akz.hr; Avenija M Držića 4) is located 1km east of the train station. If you need to store bags, there's a *garderoba* (locker; 1 to 4 hours, per hour 5KN; additional hours per hour 2.50KN). Major destinations include Pula (from 121KM, 4½, 23 daily), Rijeka (from 126KN, three hours, 20 daily), Zadar (from 89KN, 4½ hours, 30 daily), Split (from 120KN, five to 8½ hours, 32 daily) and Dubrovnik (from 188KN, 10 hours, 12 daily).

TRAIN

The **train station** (www.hzpp.hr; Trg Kralja Tomislava 12) is in the southern part of the city centre. The station has a *garderoba* (locker; per 24 hours 15KN) if you need to store bags. Destinations include Rijeka (118KN, five hours, three daily) and Split (208KN, seven hours, three daily).

ℹ Getting Around

TO/FROM THE AIRPORT

The **Croatia Airlines bus** (www.plesoprijevoz. hr) runs from the airport to Zagreb bus station every half-hour or hour (depending on flight schedules) from 7am to 10.30pm (30KN, 40 minutes). Returning to the airport, bus services run from 4am to 8.30pm.

Bus line 290 (8KN, 1¼ hour) runs between Kvaternik trg, just east of the city centre, and the airport every 35 minutes between 4.20am and midnight.

Taxis cost between 150KN and 200KN from the airport to the city centre.

PUBLIC TRANSPORT

Buy single-use tickets at newspaper kiosks or from the driver for 4KN (for 30 minutes) or 10KN (90 minutes). You can use the same ticket when transferring trams or buses, but only in one direction. Night tram single-use tickets are 15KN.

Make sure you validate your ticket when you get on the tram or bus by getting it time-stamped in the yellow ticket-validation box at the front of the vehicle – the other boxes only work for multi-use transport cards.

Bus

Although Zagreb has an excellent bus network linking the centre with the city's suburbs, travellers will find little use for it. One exception is **bus line 106** (Map p140), which goes from Kaptol to Mirogoj.

Tram

Zagreb's public transport (www.zet.hr) is based on an efficient network of trams, although the city centre is compact enough to make them almost unnecessary except for going to and from the bus or train station. Tram maps are posted at most stations, making the system easy to navigate.

TAXI

Taxi Cammeo (☑ 1212, 01-62 88 926; https://cammeo.hr/en/cities/zagreb; basic tariff 6KN, then per km 6KN) Typically the cheapest taxi firm. Waiting time is 40KN per hour.

Ekotaxi (☑ 1414, 060 77 77; www.ekotaxi.hr; basic tariff 8.80KN, then per km 6KN) Waiting time is 43KN per hour.

Radio Taxi (☑ 1717; www.radiotaxizagreb.com; basic tariff 10KN, then per km 6KN) Radio Taxi ranks (usually at blue-marked taxi signs) can be found throughout the centre. Waiting time is 40KN per hour.

Zagreb also has an Uber service network.

ISTRIA

☑ 052

Continental Croatia meets the Adriatic in Istria (Istra to Croats), the heart-shaped, 3600-sq-km peninsula in the country's northwest. The bucolic interior of rolling hills and fertile plains attracts food- and culture-focused visitors to Istria's rural hotels and farmhouse restaurants, while the indented coastline is enormously popular with the sun-and-sea set. Though vast hotel complexes line much of the coast and the rocky beaches are not Croatia's best, facilities are wide-ranging, the sea is clean and secluded spots are still plentiful.

Istria's madly popular coast gets flooded with central European tourists in summer, but you can still feel alone and undisturbed in the peninsula's interior, even in mid-August. Add acclaimed gastronomy (starring fresh seafood, prime white truffles, wild asparagus, top-rated olive oils and award-winning wines), sprinkle it with historical charm and you have a little slice of heaven.

History

Towards the end of the 2nd millennium BC, the Illyrian Histrian tribe settled the region and built fortified villages on top of the coastal and interior hills. The Romans swept into

Istria in 177 BC and began building roads and more hill forts as strategic strongholds.

From AD 539 to 751, Istria was under Byzantine rule, the most impressive remnant of which is the Euphrasian Basilica in Poreč. In the period that followed, power switched between Slavic tribes, the Franks and German rulers until an increasingly powerful Venice wrestled control of the Istrian coast in the early 13th century.

With the fall of Venice in 1797, Istria came under Austrian rule, followed by the French (1809–13). During the 19th and early 20th centuries, most of Istria was little more than a neglected outpost of the Austro-Hungarian Empire.

When the empire disintegrated at the end of WWI, Italy moved quickly to secure Istria. Italian troops occupied Pula in November 1918 and, in the 1922 Treaty of Rapallo, the Kingdom of Serbs, Croats and Slovenes ceded Istria along with Zadar and several islands to Italy, as a reward for joining the Allied powers in WWI.

A massive population shift followed as 30,000 to 40,000 Italians arrived from Mussolini's Italy and many Croats left, fearing fascism. Their fears were not misplaced, as Istria's Italian masters attempted to consolidate their hold by banning Slavic speech, education and cultural activities. There was a ban on giving Slavic names to newborns, and adults were forced to use Italian forms of their first names.

Italy retained the region until its defeat in WWII when Istria became part of Yugoslavia, causing another mass exodus, as Italians and many Croats fled Tito's communists. Trieste and the peninsula's northwestern tip were points of contention between Italy and Yugoslavia until 1954, when the region was finally awarded to Italy. As a result of Tito's reorganisation of Yugoslavia, the northern part of the peninsula was incorporated into Slovenia, where it remains.

Pula

POP 57,500

A wealth of Roman architecture lifts otherwise-workaday Pula (ancient Polensium; Pola in Italian) from the humdrum. The star of the show is the remarkably well-preserved Roman amphitheatre, smack in the heart of the city, which dominates the streetscape and doubles as a venue for summer concerts and festivals.

Historical attractions aside, Pula is a busy commercial city on the sea that has managed to retain a friendly small-town appeal. Just a short bus ride away, a series of beaches awaits at the resorts that occupy the Verudela Peninsula to the south. Although marred with residential and holiday developments, the coast is dotted with fragrant pine groves, seaside cafes and a clutch of good restaurants.

Pula is also a good base for exploring the protected Cape Kamenjak nature park, to the south, and the Brijuni Islands National Park, to the north.

◉ Sights

The oldest part of the city follows the ancient Roman street plan circling the central citadel. The best beaches are to the south, on the Verudela Peninsula.

★**Roman Amphitheatre** HISTORIC BUILDING
(Flavijevska bb; adult/child 50/25KN, audio guide 40KN; ◷8am-midnight Jul & Aug, to 8pm Apr-Jun, Sep & Oct, 9am-5pm Nov-Mar) Pula's most famous and imposing sight is this 1st-century oval amphitheatre, overlooking the harbour northeast of the old town. It's a huge and truly magnificent structure, slotted together entirely from local limestone and known locally as the Arena. Designed to host gladiatorial contests and seating up to 20,000 spectators, it still serves the mass-entertainment needs of the local populace in the shape of concerts and film-festival screenings.

★**Temple of Augustus** TEMPLE
(Augustov hram; Forum; adult/child 10/5KN; ◷9am-7pm) Fronted by a high porch supported by six Corinthian columns, this small but perfectly proportioned temple was built sometime between 2 BC and AD 14. It survived the Christian era by being converted into a church, only for it to be destroyed by a bomb in 1944. The subsequent stone-by-stone reconstruction has brought it back to something closely approaching its former glory, and it now houses a small archaeological display.

Istria Historical & Maritime Museum MUSEUM
(Povijesni i pomorski muzej Istre; ☎052-211 566; www.ppmi.hr; Gradinski uspon 6; adult/child 20/5KN; ◷8am-9pm Apr-Sep, 9am-5pm Oct-Mar) Since ancient times the 34m hill at the centre of Pula's old town has been fortified. The current star-shaped fortress was built by the Venetians in

CROATIA PULA

CAPE KAMENJAK

Wild Cape Kamenjak on the **Premantura Peninsula**, 10km south of Pula, is Istria's southernmost point. This gorgeous, entirely uninhabited cape has lovely rolling hills, wild flowers (including 30 species of orchid), low Mediterranean shrubs, fruit trees and medicinal herbs, and around 30km of beaches and rugged swimming spots. It's criss-crossed with a maze of gravel roads and paths, making it easy to get around on foot or by bike.

Near the southern tip of the peninsula is a **viewpoint** providing an incredible vista out over the island of Cres and the peaks of Velebit. Nearby is a wonderfully ramshackle beach bar, half-hidden in the bushes, seemingly cobbled together out of flotsam. The adjacent cliffs are popular with daredevils who dive from them and swim through the shallow caves at the water's edge. Watch out for strong currents if swimming off the southern cape.

Getting to Cape Kamenjak by car is the easiest option, but drive slowly to avoid generating dust, which is detrimental to the environment. From May to September, you'll be charged 40KN for bringing a car onto the cape – this can be paid from 7am to 9pm at the entrance. Another option is taking city bus 28 from Pula to Premantura (15KN, 35 minutes, five to nine daily), at the entrance to the cape, then walking or renting a bike from **Windsurf Centar Premantura** (☑ 091 51 23 646; www.windsurfing.hr; Arena Stupice Campsite, Selo 250; windsurfing equipment/courses per hour from 80/200KN).

the 1630s. It's now a moody backdrop to exhibitions on an eclectic range of historic themes (the antifascist struggle and a local boxing club at the time of research), but it's worth visiting for the views alone. Hidden around the back of the castle are the ruins of a small ancient Roman theatre.

St Francis' Monastery
& Church   CHRISTIAN MONASTERY
(Samostan i crkva sv Franje; Uspon sv Franje Asiškog 9; adult/child 9KN/free; ⊘9am-6pm) Built in 1285, Pula's Franciscan monastery has an extraordinary 15th-century gilded altarpiece behind the altar of its cavernous church – but that's not its only, or even its oldest, treasure. Set into the floor of a Gothic chamber accessed via the Romanesque cloister is a Roman mosaic featuring a hippocampus (fish-tailed horse) and a swastika.

Arch of the Sergii   RUINS
(Slavoluk Sergijevaca; Sergijevaca) Also known as the Golden Gate (Zlatna vrata), this majestic arch was erected around 27 BC to commemorate three brothers from the Sergius family who fought in the naval battle of Actium (where the future emperor Augustus defeated Marc Antony and Cleopatra). It stood at the entrance to the Roman town, the walls of which can still be partly seen nearby on Trg Portarata and along Carrarina.

Tržnica   MARKET
(☑052-218-122; www.trznica-pula.hr; Narodni trg 9; ⊘7am-1pm Mon-Sat, to noon Sun) City life in Pula revolves around its gorgeous 1903 suc-cession-style market building, and the produce stalls and cafes that surround it.

Lighting Giants   PUBLIC ART
(Pula harbour; ⊘dusk-10pm) Don't miss Pula's star evening attraction, an amazing lighting display at the city's 19th-century Uljanik shipyard, one of the world's oldest working docks. Renowned lighting designer Dean Skira has lit up the shipyard's iconic cranes in 16,000 different colour schemes, which come alive on the hour for 15 minutes.

Pula Aquarium   AQUARIUM
(☑052-381 402; www.aquarium.hr; Verudella bb; adult/child 100/70KN; ⊘9am-9pm May-Oct, to 4pm Nov-Mar, to 6pm Apr) Not just any fish tank, this extraordinary aquarium occupies an entire 19th-century military fort – one of 55 built to defend the Austro-Hungarian Empire's main naval base. There are even sharks in an old artillery unit. The displays are well laid out and themed, with an emphasis on environmental issues. The aquarium does its bit, operating a sea-turtle rescue centre. Other attractions include rays, crabs, eels, starfish, anemones, seahorses, jellyfish, caimans, octopuses and a huge Indian python.

🏃 Activities

The Istria Bike (www.istria-bike.com) website outlines trails, bike shops and agencies that offer cycling trips. The tourist office stocks the Istria Bike map of Pula and its surrounds, outlining 29 trails, including a 60km route hugging the coast from Pula to Medulin.

Orca Diving Center
DIVING

(☑ 098 99 04 246; www.orcadiving.hr; Verudella 17) Arranges boat and wreck dives at this centre underneath the Hotel Plaza Histria on the Verudela Peninsula. It also rents kayaks and stand-up paddleboards.

Eat Istria
COOKING

(☑ 095 85 51 962; www.eatistria.com) Eat Istria offers cooking classes with food blogger Goran Zgrablić on a family farm between Medulin and the village of Ližnjan (transfers from Pula included), and wine tours around the peninsula.

🛏 Sleeping

Crazy House Hotel
HOSTEL €

(☑ 091 51 84 200; www.crazyhousehostel.com; Trščanska 1; dm/d from €20/58; ❊ ⟨⟩) Crazy? Hardly. Tucked into the bottom floor of an old apartment block, this bright hostel has six- to 10-bed dorms with privacy curtains and lots of lockers, as well as a handful of private doubles and twins. All bathrooms are shared, and there's a communal kitchen and large terrace.

★ Guest House
City Centre
GUESTHOUSE €€

(☑ 099 44 05 575; Sergijevaca 4; r from €84; P ❊ ⟨⟩) Feel like a local as you ascend the wonky stone stairs in this wonderful building right by the Forum. The rooms are spacious, stylish and surprisingly quiet at night, and the hostess couldn't be more helpful. It doesn't have its own website; reservations are handled through Booking.com.

Park Plaza Arena Pula
RESORT €€€

(☑ 052-375 000; www.parkplaza.com/arena; Verudella 31; s/d 1006/1320KN; ⟨⟩ May-Sep; P ❊ ⟨⟩ ⟨⟩) Hidden amid pines and manicured lawns facing a gorgeous pebbly cove, this upmarket hotel is the best of the Verudela resorts. As well as the low-slung main hotel block there's a set of two-bedroom suites in the garden.

✕ Eating

Corso
INTERNATIONAL €

(Giardini 2; mains 40-70KN; ⟨⟩ 7am-midnight Mon-Wed, to 2am Thu-Sat; ⟨⟩) The upstairs dining room of this popular cafe-bar serves tacos, pork ribs, stir fries and spring rolls – but it's included here on the strength of its mighty Corso burger, and the delicious hot chips (fries) that accompany it. Expect to get messy.

Fresh
SANDWICHES €

(☑ 052-418 888; Anticova 5; snacks 21-26KN; ⟨⟩ 8.30am-4.30pm Mon-Fri; ⟨⟩) Best for a quick and wholesome bite, this tiny sandwich-and-salad bar serves sandwiches, toasted panini, tortillas and extremely fresh-looking salads. If you're feeling shady, start the day with a juiced 'Imuno' smoothie.

★ Konoba Batelina
SEAFOOD €€

(☑ 052-573 767; Čimulje 25, Banjole; mains 75-125KN; ⟨⟩ 5-11pm Mon-Sat) This family-run tavern is well worth a trek to Banjole, 6km south of central Pula. It only serves seafood, and it's some of the best, most creative and lovingly prepared you'll find in Istria. There's no menu; instead the staff will rattle off the specials and present fresh fish for you to choose from. Book ahead; cash only.

Farabuto
MEDITERRANEAN €€

(☑ 052-386 074; www.farabuto.hr; Sisplac 15, Veruda; mains 75-160KN; ⟨⟩ noon-11pm Mon-Sat; ❊ ⟨⟩) It's worth a trek to this nondescript residential area, about 1.5km southwest of the centre, for stylish decor, but more importantly, finely executed Mediterranean fare with a creative touch. There are daily specials and a well-curated wine list; save room for the chocolate mousse with truffle ice cream.

Vodnjanka
ISTRIAN €€

(☑ 052-210 655; D Vitezića 4, Monte Zaro; mains 40-100KN; ⟨⟩ noon-5pm & 7-10pm Mon-Sat) Locals swear by the real-deal home cooking at this no-frills spot. It's cheap, casual and cash-only, and there's a reassuringly brief menu that focuses on simple, hearty Istrian cuisine. Nothing is frozen and even the pasta is made the night before. It's a bit of a trek out of town – to get here, walk south on Radićeva to Vitezića.

Milan
ISTRIAN €€€

(☑ 052-300 200; www.milanpula.com; Stoja 4, Stoja; mains 95-295KN; ⟨⟩ noon-11pm) An upmarket vibe, seasonal specialities, clued-up sommeliers and an olive-oil expert make this hotel restaurant, in an oddly dingy part of town, one of the city's best fine-dining options. Various set menus are offered (195KN to 385KN), including a four-course Istrian option loaded with prosciutto.

🍷 Drinking & Entertainment

★ Cabahia
BAR

(www.facebook.com/CabahiaPula; Širolina 4, Veruda; ⟨⟩ 7am-midnight Mon-Sat, 10am-midnight Sun; ⟨⟩) This artsy hideaway, 2km south of the centre in Veruda, has a cosy wood-beamed interior, eclectic objects and rock portraits on the walls, dim lighting, South American tiling and a great garden terrace out the back. It hosts live music and gets packed on weekends.

★**Bass**   BAR
(☑ 099 83 19 051; www.facebook.com/basscaffe; Širolina 3, Veruda; ⊘ 8am-midnight Mon-Sat, from 10am Sun; 🔊) Occupying the porch of a decaying Habsburg-era mansion, this hip, dishevelled bar is an oasis of boho cool with a long cocktail menu and a laid-back clientele.

Cvajner   CAFE
(Forum 2; ⊘ 8am-midnight) Housed in a former bank on the Forum (the huge safe is used as a storeroom), this is Pula's hippest cafe, scattered with random Tito-era furniture, the remnants of wall frescoes, painted ceiling beams, art by up-and-coming locals, and chilled staff. In the warmer months, most miss the joys of the interior by plumping for an alfresco seat out front.

Rojc   ARTS CENTRE
(http://rojcnet.pula.org; Gajeva 3) For an arty underground experience, check out the program at Rojc, a converted army barracks that houses a multimedia arts centre and studios with occasional concerts, exhibitions and other events.

❶ Information

Tourist Office (☑ 052-219 197; www.pulainfo. hr; Forum 3; ⊘ 8am-9pm Jul & Aug, 8am-6pm Mon-Fri, 10am-4pm Sat Apr-Jun & Sep, 9am-4pm Mon-Sat Oct-Mar) Knowledgeable and friendly staff provide maps, brochures and schedules of events. Pick up two useful booklets: *Domus Bonus,* which lists the best-quality private accommodation in Istria, and *Istra Gourmet,* with a list of restaurants. From mid-June to mid-September it also sells the Pula Card (adult/child 90/40KN), which allows free entry to key sights.

❶ Getting There & Away

AIR

Pula Airport (PUY; ☑ 052-550 926; www.air port-pula.hr) is located 6km northeast of town. Dozens of airlines fly here in summer but the only year-round operators are Croatia Airlines (to Zagreb and Zadar), Trade Air (to Split and Osijek) and Eurowings (to Düsseldorf).

BUS

Pula's **bus station** (☑ 052-544 537; Trg 1 istarske brigade 1) is 1km north of the town centre. Daily connections include Rovinj (37KN, 40 minutes, hourly), Rijeka (100KN, 2½ hours, at least 13 daily), Zagreb (164KN, 5½ hours, at least nine daily), Zadar (235KN, seven hours, at least two daily) and Split (345KN, 10½ hours, at least two daily).

❶ Getting Around

An airport bus (30KN) departs from the bus station, timed around flights. Taxis to the airport cost from 180KN to 200KN.

Local buses are operated by **Pulapromet** (☑ 052-222 677; www.pulapromet.com). Routes of use to visitors are 1, which runs to Camping Stoja, and 2A and 3A to Verudela. The frequency varies from every 15 minutes to every half-hour (from 5am to 11.30pm). Tickets are bought from the driver for 11KN to 15KN.

Brijuni Islands

The Brijuni archipelago (Brioni in Italian) consists of two main pine-covered islands and 12 islets off the coast of Istria, just northwest of Pula across the 3km-wide Fažana Channel. Covered by meadows, parks, and oak and laurel forests (including rare plants such as wild cucumber and marine poppy), the islands were pronounced a national park in 1983.

The largest island, **Veli Brijun**, can be visited on boats booked through the **National Park Office** (☑ 052-525 882; www. np-brijuni.hr; Brijunska 10, Fažana; boat & tour adult/child 210/105KN; ⊘ 8am-7pm) in Fažana; prices include a guided tour and entry to various sights. **Mali Brijun** can only be visited during the summertime **Ulysses Theatre** (☑ 052-525 829; www.ulysses.hr) season, when performances are staged in an abandoned fort (the boats are included in the ticket price).

Note that most boat tours, departing from Pula, dock at the islet of **Sveti Jerolim** for a picnic lunch but then only cruise around the main islands, as they're not permitted to land.

History

Even though traces of habitation go back to Roman times, the islands really owe their fame to Tito, the charismatic Yugoslav leader who turned them into his private retreat.

Each year from 1947 until just before his death in 1980, Tito spent six months in Brijuni at his hideaway. To create a lush comfort zone, he introduced subtropical plant species and created a safari park to house the exotic animals gifted to him by world

BIRDWATCHING IN BARANJA

Baranja is a small triangle in the far northeast of Croatia at the confluence of the Drava and Danube Rivers, north of Osijek. The Hungarian influence is strongly felt here: all the towns have bilingual names. Although flying well below the tourist radar, this largely agricultural area of wetlands, vineyards, orchards and wheat fields has been growing in popularity thanks to some good cycling routes, a clutch of wineries and the star attraction, the bird sanctuary of Kopački Rit. Anyone who fancies a slice of far-from-the-crowds appeal will enjoy a trip here.

Kopački Rit Nature Park (Park Prirode Kopački Rit; www.pp-kopacki-rit.hr; adult 10KN; child under 2yr free; ◷9am-5pm Apr-Oct, 8am-4pm Nov-Mar) is one of Europe's largest wetlands, home to more than 290 bird species and rich aquatic and grassland flora, showcasing water lilies, irises, duckweeds and ryegrass, as well as oak and poplar forests. Comprised of a series of ponds, backwaters and two main lakes, Sakadaško and Kopačevo, this massive floodplain was created by the meeting of the Drava and Danube Rivers. These two rivers, together with the Mura, make a Unesco biosphere reserve.

The park was heavily mined during the war and closed for many years as a result. Most mines have now been cleared and safe trails have been marked. The park **visitor centre** (✆031-445 445; https://pp-kopacki-rit.hr; ◷9am-5pm Apr-Oct, 8am-4pm Nov-Mar), located at the main entrance, along the Bilje–Kopačevo road, features a lovely interpretation centre in a string of straw-roofed wooden huts that house interactive exhibits and a cafe. You can walk the 2km series of wooden boardwalks and then take a boat tour on Sakadaško lake. Tours depart from an embarkation point on the lake about 1km from the visitor centre (at the end of the boardwalk area); book at the visitor centre when you arrive.

The quiet village of Kopačevo, on the edge of Kopački Rit, is home to the outstanding regional restaurant **Didin Konak** (✆031-752 100; www.didinkonak.hr; Petefi Šandora 93, Kopačevo; mains 55-150KN; ◷8am-10pm). Another good option is **Josić** (✆031-734 410; www.josic.hr; Planina 194, Zmajevac; mains 29-90KN; ◷1-10pm Tue-Thu & Sun, to midnight Fri & Sat), an upmarket winery restaurant in the village of Zmajevac in northern Baranja; wine tasting and tours are available by appointment.

While there are some bus connections between Osijek and the villages of Baranja, these are pretty limited so it's best to have your own wheels.

leaders. The Somali sheep you'll see roaming around came from Ethiopia, while a Zambian leader gave a gift of waterbuck.

At his summer playground, Tito received 90 heads of state and a bevy of movie stars in lavish style. Bijela Vila on Veli Brijun was Tito's 'White House': the place for issuing edicts and declarations as well as entertaining. The islands are still used for official state visits, but are increasingly a favourite on the international yachting circuit. They're also a holiday spot of choice for royalty from obscure kingdoms and random billionaires who love its aura of bygone glamour.

◉ Sights

As you arrive on Veli Brijun, after a 15-minute boat ride from Fažana, you'll dock in front of the conjoined Hotel Neptun (1912) and Hotel Istra (1962), where Tito's illustrious guests once stayed. A guide will take you on a four-hour island tour on a miniature Tourist Train, beginning with a visit to the 9-hectare Safari Park containing animals given to Tito by various famous individuals. Other stops on the tour include the ruins of a Roman Country House, dating from the 1st century BC, an Archaeological Museum inside a 16th-century Venetian summerhouse, and St Germain Church (1481), now a gallery displaying copies of medieval frescoes in Istrian churches.

Most interesting is the Tito on Brijuni Exhibition in a building behind Hotel Karmen. A collection of stuffed animals occupies the ground floor, all of which died naturally in the Safari Park. Upstairs are photos of Tito with stars such as Josephine Baker, Sophia Loren, Elizabeth Taylor and Richard Burton, and world leaders including Indira Gandhi and Fidel Castro. Outside is a 1953 Cadillac that Tito used to show the island to his eminent guests.

WORTH A TRIP

RURAL LUXURY

The focus is firmly on quality at rural retreat **Meneghetti** (☑052-528 800; www.meneghetti.hr; Stancija Meneghetti 1; r from €279, mains 190-290KN; ☺Apr-Dec; 🅿✴🛜🏊) – whether that be the estate's top-notch wine and olive oil, the architecture of the guest blocks, which sympathetically embrace the historic house at its core, or the exquisite modern Istrian cuisine served at the restaurant. Plus there's a private beach, accessed by a 25-minute walk through the vineyard. Sheer bliss.

It's located 8.5km southwest of Bale.

❶ Getting There & Away

From Pula, you can catch bus 21 to Fažana (15KN, 25 minutes, seven to 14 daily).

National-park boats head from Fažana to Veli Brijun 10 or 11 times a day from March to October, falling to three times a day from November to February. It's best to book in advance, especially in summer, and request an English-speaking tour guide.

Summer theatre performances on Mali Brijun have a boat trip included in the ticket.

Various travel and tour agencies offer day trips from Pula, Rovinj and Poreč.

❶ Getting Around

The only ways to get around Veli Brijun are by bike (35KN per hour or 110KN per day) and electric cart (300KN per hour).

Rovinj
POP 14,300

Rovinj (Rovigno in Italian) is coastal Istria's star attraction. While it can get overrun with tourists in summer and there aren't a lot of actual sights, it remains an intensely charming place. The old town is contained within an egg-shaped peninsula, webbed with steep cobbled streets and small squares, and punctuated by a tall church tower rising from the highest point. Originally an island, it was only connected to the mainland in 1763 when the narrow channel separating it was filled.

The main residential part of Rovinj spreads back from the old town and up the low hills that surround it, while resort-style hotels hug the coast to the north and south. When the crowds get too much, the 14 islands of the Rovinj archipelago make for a pleasant afternoon away.

⊙ Sights

★**St Euphemia's Church**   CHURCH
(Crkva Sv Eufemije; Trg Sv Eufemije bb; tower 20KN; ☺10am-6pm Jun-Sep, to 4pm May, to 2pm Apr) **FREE** Built from 1725 to 1736, this imposing structure – the largest baroque church in Istria – dominates Rovinj from its hilltop location in the middle of the old town. Its 61m-high bell tower is older than the present church; construction commenced in 1654 and lasted 26 years. It's modelled on the campanile of St Mark's in Venice, and is topped by a 4m copper statue of St Euphemia, who shows the direction of the wind by turning on a spindle.

Rovinj City Museum   MUSEUM
(Muzej grada Rovinj; ☑052-816 720; www.muzej rovinj.hr; Trg Maršala Tita 11; adult/child Jun-Aug 65/40KN, Sep-May 15/10KN; ☺10am-10pm Jun-Aug, to 1pm Tue-Sat Sep-May) Housed in a 17th-century baroque palace, this museum displays temporary exhibitions on the ground floor, 20th-century and contemporary art on the 1st floor, and 16th- to 19th-century works on the top floor. Croatian artists are well represented, alongside Venetian luminaries such as Jacopo Bassano.

🏃 Activities

In summer, boat trips to the islands, such as Crveni Otok and Sveta Katarina, and Limski Kanal are easily arranged through operators along the waterfront. The main diving attraction is the *Baron Gautsch* wreck, an Austrian passenger steamer sunk in 1914 by a mine in 40m of water. There's good cycling to be had in the surrounding area, along with rock climbing and birdwatching.

Rovinj Sub   DIVING
(☑052-821 202; www.rovinj-sub.hr; Braće Brajkovića bb) Professional diving outfit running boat dives down to the many wrecks that lie just offshore. Prices range from 75KN for a shore dive to 338KN for some of the trickier wrecks; equipment is an additional 188KN.

Stupica Excursions   CRUISE
(☑091 90 37 805; www.stupica-excursions.com; ☺half/full day €20/40) This family-run operation offers full-day 'fish picnic' tours taking in the Limski Kanal, a pirate's cave and the Rovinj archipelago on a small boat, including three swimming stops, breakfast, lunch

and unlimited drinks. There's also a half-day sunset-cruise option.

🛏 Sleeping

Roundabout Hostel
HOSTEL €

(📞 052-817 387; www.roundabouthostel.com; Trg na križu 6; dm 140-187KN; 🅿❄🛜) This simple budget option has bunks with individual reading lights, lockers and a small shared kitchen. It's located on the big roundabout as you come into Rovinj, about a kilometre from the old town.

Villa Dobravac
HOTEL €€

(📞 052-813 006; www.villa-dobravac.com; Karmelo 1; r €100-128; 🅿❄🛜) As well as making wine and olive oil, the Dobravac family rents a set of 10 spacious, modern rooms in this lovely old peach-coloured villa in the residential part of Rovinj. Most have a terrace and a sea view.

★Casa Alice
HOTEL €€€

(📞 052-821 104; www.casaalice.com; Paola Deperisa 1; r €200-220; 🅿❄🛜🏊) Escape the masses in this lovely 10-room hotel in Rovinj's suburban fringes, a 20-minute walk from the centre but only five minutes from the sea. If walking sounds too hard you can always laze around the blue-tiled pool and help yourself to coffee and cake. Some of the rooms have terraces and most have a spa bath.

Monte Mulini
HOTEL €€€

(📞 052-636 000; www.montemulinihotel.com; Antonija Smareglia 3; r from €550; 🅿❄🛜🏊🍽) This swanky and extremely pricey hotel slopes down towards Lone Bay, a 10-minute stroll from the old town along the Lungomare. Rooms all have balconies, sea views and upmarket trimmings. The spa and Wine Vault restaurant are tops, and there are three outdoor pools.

🍴 Eating & Drinking

Pizzeria Da Sergio
PIZZA €

(📞 052-816 949; www.facebook.com/DaSergioRv; Grisia 11; pizzas 35-82KN; ⏲11am-3pm & 6-11pm; 🛜📞) It's worth waiting in line to get a table at this old-fashioned, two-floor pizzeria. It dishes out Rovinj's best thin-crust pizza, with a huge range of toppings to choose from. It also serves decent house wine.

Bookeria
CAFE €

(📞 052-817 399; www.bookeria.net; Trg Pignaton 7; 40-80KN; ⏲9am-9pm May-Sep, to 6pm Oct-Apr) With little flower-adorned tables spilling onto the square, this sweet little cafe is a favourite Rovinj breakfast spot. Options include eggs, toast, muffins and croissants served with eggplant mousse. As the day progresses the menu expands to include burgers and pasta.

Barba Danilo
MEDITERRANEAN €€

(📞 052-830 002; www.barbadanilo.com; Polari 5; mains 110-125KN; ⏲6-11pm Mon-Sat) The last place you might expect to find one of Rovinj's best restaurants is on a campsite 3.5km from the centre. Only a handful of choices are offered on the ever-changing menu, with fresh seafood the main focus. With just 45 seats, booking ahead is essential in summer.

Monte
ISTRIAN €€€

(📞 052-830 203; www.monte.hr; Montalbano 75; 3-/4-/6-course menu 619/719/849KN; ⏲6.30-11pm May-Sep; 📞) The first restaurant in Croatia to be awarded a Michelin star, Monte offers a choice of three differently themed six-course Modern Istrian menus (one focused on local ingredients, one exclusively vegetarian and the last emphasising modern techniques). Or you can build your own three- or four-course meal, mixing and matching from all three.

Puntulina
ISTRIAN €€€

(📞 052-813 186; www.puntulina.eu; Sv Križa 38; mains 100-220KN; ⏲noon-10pm; 🐾) For an added burst of romance, book ahead at this family-run restaurant and request a table on one of the rocky terraces clinging to the cliffs circling the old town, mere steps from the water; it's especially pretty at sunset. The menu emphasises the Venetian influences on Istrian cuisine, with lots of pasta and seafood dishes.

Mediterraneo
COCKTAIL BAR

(www.facebook.com/mediterraneo.rovinj; Sv Križa 24; ⏲9am-2am Apr-Sep; 🛜) Clinging to the old-town sea cliffs, this gorgeous little bar feels like a secret. It's not, of course – Rovinj's fashionable set are already here, holding court on the pastel-coloured stools right by the water. It's a very relaxed Adriatic scene, with friendly waitstaff and good cocktails, too.

Circolo Aperitiv Bar
BAR

(www.facebook.com/aperitivbarcircolo; Trg Campitelli 1; ⏲8am-2pm & 5pm-2am Apr-Sep, 8am-2pm & 6pm-1am Mon-Sat Oct-Mar; 🛜) Rovinj's rowdiest live-music bar has the most rarified of settings, occupying a grand old building with a very pleasant front yard. In summer

CROATIA ROVINJ

there's a DJ, band, quiz or comedian on every night, but you can be guaranteed a Friday-night gig throughout the year.

ℹ️ Information

Medical Centre (☑ 052-840 702; Istarska bb; ☺ 24hr)

Tourist Office (☑ 052-811 566; www.rovinj-tourism.com; Pina Budicina 12; ☺ 8am-10pm Jul & Aug, to 8pm mid-May–Jun & Sep)

ℹ️ Getting There & Away

The **bus station** (☑ 060 333 111; Trg na lokvi 6) is just to the southeast of the old town. Destinations include Pula (37KN, 40 minutes, hourly), Poreč (43KN, 45 minutes, four daily), Rijeka (100KN, 2¼ hours, five daily), Zagreb (150KN, 4½ hours, 10 daily) and Varaždin (208KN, seven hours, two daily).

Poreč

POP 16,700

The ancient Roman town of Poreč (Parenzo in Italian) and the surrounding region are entirely devoted to summer tourism. Poreč is the centrepiece of a vast system of tourist resorts that stretches north and south along the west coast of Istria, attracting holiday-makers in their tens of thousands from June to September.

Mass tourism means this is definitely not the place for a quiet getaway (unless you come out of season). However, there's a World Heritage–listed basilica, a medley of Gothic, Romanesque and baroque buildings, and a well-developed tourist infrastructure, and the verdant Istrian interior is within easy reach. It's also become the party hub of Istria in the last couple of years, drawing in young partygoers from all corners of Europe.

◉ Sights & Activities

The compact old town is squeezed on to a small peninsula, packed with shops and restaurants. Three 15th-century, Venetian-built towers outline the position of the city's eastern wall: the **Round Tower** (Narodni trg), the Gothic **Pentagonal Tower** (Decumanus) and the **Northern Tower**. The ancient Roman street Decumanus, with its polished stones, is still the main street running through the peninsula's middle.

Nearly every activity you might want to enjoy is on offer in either Plava Laguna or Zelena Laguna, south of the town centre – including tennis, basketball, volleyball, windsurfing, rowing, bungee jumping, paintball, golf, waterskiing, parasailing, boat rentals, go-karting and canoeing. For details, pick up the annual booklet which lists all the recreational facilities in the area from the tourist office (p155).

★ Euphrasian Basilica   BASILICA

(Eufrazijeva 22; adult/child 40/20KN; ☺ 9am-4pm Mon-Fri, to 2pm Sat Nov-Mar, to 6pm Mon-Sat Apr-Jun, Sep & Oct, to 9pm Jul & Aug) Top billing in Poreč goes to the 6th-century Euphrasian Basilica, a World Heritage Site and one of Europe's finest intact examples of Byzantine art. Built on the site of a 4th-century oratory, the complex includes a church, an atrium and a baptistery. The glittering 6th-century mosaics in the apse of the church are the highlights. The belfry, accessed through the octagonal baptistery, affords an intimate view of the old town.

🛏️ Sleeping & Eating

Polidor   CAMPGROUND €

(☑ 052-219 495; www.campingpolidor.com; Bijela uvala 12, Funtana; per person/site/cabin from €9/20/45; 🅿 ✳ 🛜 ♨ 🐾) Tiny by Croatian standards and tightly packed, Polidor nevertheless crams a lot in. The ablutions block has underfloor heating and a slide to get kids down to the lower level. There's even a dedicated children's bathroom and pets' shower. Submerged bar stools mean you can order cocktails without having to leave the pool. It's 5km south of central Poreč.

Valamar Riviera   HOTEL €€€

(☑ 052-465 000; www.valamar.com; Obala Maršala Tita 15; s/d from €135/186; ☺ Apr-Oct; 🅿 ✳ 🛜) This rather swanky four-star pad right on the harbourside offers friendly service and some rooms with sea-gazing balconies. There's also a restaurant and bar, plus a long list of guest facilities. The hotel has a private beach on Sveti Nikola island that you can reach by a free boat, departing every 30 minutes.

Artha Bistro   VEGETARIAN €

(☑ 052-435 495; Jože Šurana 10; mains 40-80KN; ☺ 11am-3pm & 6-10pm Mon-Sat, 10am-3pm Sun May-Oct; 🖋) Vegetarians, vegans and broad-minded omnivores will be spoilt for choice at this meat-free restaurant, tucked away on a side street near the main square. Opt for something Istrian, like the classic pasta with truffles, or tuck into a tasty tofu, tempeh or seitan dish. It also serves cheap and filling sandwiches at lunchtime (from 22KN).

Burgerija BURGERS **€**
(☑ 095 51 49 703; www.facebook.com/burgerija; Nikole Tesle 8; mains 16-59KN; ☺ noon-11pm; 🖥) Loud rock music fills this bright little joint, where a dozen different meaty burgers are served, and one vegetarian one, with local craft beer to wash it all down. Meat lovers can choose between a 50g, 130g and a whopping 160g patty.

★**Konoba Daniela** ISTRIAN **€€**
(☑ 052-460 519; www.konobadaniela.com; Veleniki 15a; mains 65-150KN; ☺ noon-midnight) In the sweet little village of Veleniki, 5km east of Poreč, this rustic, family-run tavern is known for its steak tartare, huge beefsteaks, ravioli stuffed with mushrooms, and seasonal Istrian mainstays. Finish up with cinnamon dumplings with jam. It also rents two rooms (from 480KN).

Sv. Nikola MEDITERRANEAN **€€€**
(☑ 052-423 018; www.svnikola.com; Obala Maršala Tita 23; mains 77-179; ☺ 11am-1am; 👪) Gazing out towards the island of the same name, St Nick's is the swankiest restaurant on the waterfront strip but it's not remotely snooty – the service is charming and there's even a kids menu. The homemade tagliatelle with wild asparagus and truffle has a lot of fans, but the restaurant also serves steaks, duck and various seafood specialities.

🍸 **Drinking & Nightlife**

Le Mat Corner BAR
(☑ 095 87 82 366; www.facebook.com/TheCorner Caffe; Otokara Keršovanija 2; ☺ 7am-2am) Poreč's hippest bar is a dimly lit den with oddball art, mismatched chairs, little round tables, big metal-dome lamps, mezzanine seating, a fridge full of craft beer and PJ Harvey on the stereo. The slightly surly service somehow only adds to the bohemian atmosphere.

Fuego Wine & Bites WINE BAR
(Eufrazijeva 7; ☺ 10am-1am) Grab a seat on the lane and give in to its charms, and those of the wine and waitstaff at this bar. Snacks such as toasted sandwiches, bruschetta and truffle-filled meat-and-cheese platters are also served.

Vinoteka Bacchus WINE BAR
(☑ 052-433 539; Eufrazijeva 10; ☺ 10am-1am; 🖥) This sweet little wine shop has a clutch of tables on an atmospheric lane, where you can try local wine varietals such as *malvazija* and *refošk*, cure any ailments with *biska* (mistletoe grappa), and nibble on antipasti.

RIDING THE RAILS

The popular **Parenzana Bike Trail** (☑ 052-351 603; www.parenzana.net) runs along a defunct narrow-gauge railway that operated from 1902 to 1935 between Trieste and Poreč. Today, it traverses three countries: Italy, Slovenia and Croatia (the Croatian stretch is 78km), and has become quite a popular way to take in the highlights of Istria, especially in spring and autumn.

Torre Rotonda BAR
(☑ 098 255 731; www.torrerotonda.com; Narodni trg 3a; ☺ 10am-1am; 🖥) There's no more atmospheric place for a glass of wine in winter than the cosy, candlelit interior of this medieval tower. In summer take the steep stairs to the roof for action-packed views of the passing parade.

Byblos CLUB
(☑ 091 29 25 678; www.byblos.hr; Zelena Laguna 1; ☺ 11pm-6am event nights May-Aug) On summer weekends, celebrity guest DJs crank out electro-house tunes at this humongous open-air club, 3km south of town. Expect to pay up to €25 for admission on a big night.

ℹ **Information**

Poreč Medical Centre (☑ 052-451 611; Maura Gioseffija 2)

Tourist Office (☑ 052-451 293; www.myporec. com; Zagrebačka 9; ☺ 8am-9pm Jun-Sep, to 6pm Mon-Sat Oct-May)

ℹ **Getting There & Away**

The **bus station** (☑ 060 333 111; Karla Huguesa 2) is just outside the old town, and has a left-luggage facility at the station. Connections include Pula (60KN, 1½ hours, at least five daily), Rovinj (43KN, 45 minutes, at least four daily), Rijeka (100KN, 1½ hours, at least four daily) and Zagreb (160KN, four hours, at least six daily).

ℹ **Getting Around**

You can rent bikes for about 100KN per day. From April to October, tourist road trains run up and down the coastal promenades to the surrounding resorts, costing from 15KN to 25KN.

Motovun

POP 484

Motovun (Montona in Italian) is a captivating little walled town perched on a 277m hill in the Mirna River valley. The setting is

WORTH A TRIP

CRES & LOŠINJ ISLANDS

Separated only by an 11m-wide canal and joined by a bridge, these two sparsely popu-lated and scenic islands in the Kvarner archipelago are often treated as a single entity. Although their topography is different, the islands' identities are blurred by a shared history. Nature lovers will be in heaven here. Both islands are criss-crossed by hiking and biking trails, and the surrounding waters are home to the only known resident popula-tion of dolphins in the Adriatic. Much of the sea off the eastern coast is protected by the **Lošinj Dolphin Reserve**, the first of its kind in the Mediterranean.

Wilder, greener and more mountainous **Cres** (Cherso in Italian) has remote camp-grounds, pristine beaches, a handful of medieval villages and a real off-the-beaten-track feel. Strolling through the **Tramuntana** region in the north you might even begin to believe the old people's stories about elves lurking in the ancient forests. The lost-in-time hilltop villages of **Lubenice** and **Beli** have gorgeous beaches at their bases – but be prepared for a steep walk. Near the centre of the island is the pretty pastel-hued harbour of **Cres Town**, the island's capital. If you like lamb, seek out **Konoba Bukaleta** (☑ 051-571 606; Loznati 99; mains 42-120KN; ⊙ noon-11pm Apr-Sep) in nearby Loznati village. Guarding the inter-island canal, tiny **Osor** is a walled town as sleepy as you'll find on the entire coast.

The 31km-long island of **Lošinj** (Lussino in Italian) is more populated and touristy than its neighbour. Its largest town, **Mali Lošinj**, is set at the apex of a long natural har-bour and ringed by graceful, gently weathered Mediterranean town houses and green hills. A string of imposing 19th-century sea-captains' houses lines the seafront, and even with the summer tourist commotion, this historic quarter retains its charm and atmos-phere. Mali Lošinj has some excellent luxury hotels and restaurants, notably **Boutique Hotel Alhambra** (☑ 051-260 700; www.losinj-hotels.com; Čikat 16; r from 3900KN; P ✳ @ 🛜 ❄), **Mare Mare Suites** (☑ 051-232 010; www.mare-mare.com; Riva Lošinjskih Kapetana 36; s/d/apt 900/950/1400KN; P ✳ @ 🛜) and **Restaurant Rosemary** (☑ 051-231 837; www.facebook.com/restaurant.rosemary; Čikat 15; mains 110-220KN; ⊙ noon-11pm).

Veli Lošinj is much smaller, more languid and somewhat less crowded than Mali Lošinj. It's a scenic place with a huddle of pastel-coloured houses, cafes, hotels and stores gathered around a tiny harbour. It's home to the interesting **Lošinj Marine Edu-cation Centre** (☑ 051-604 666; www.blue-world.org; Kaštel 24, Lošinj; adult/child 20/15KN; ⊙ 10am-9pm Jul & Aug, to 8pm Jun, 10am-6pm Mon-Fri, to 2pm Sat May & Sep, 10am-2pm Mon-Fri Oct-Apr) ✎ and a top-notch Italian restaurant, **Bora Bar** (☑ 051-867 544; www.borabar. net; Rovenska Bay 3; mains 65-174KN; ⊙ noon-10pm Mar-Oct). If you only want to hit one beach, make it **Krivica**; it's a 5km drive from Veli Lošinj followed by a 30-minute descent from the parking area to an idyllic, sheltered bay, ringed by pine trees.

Buses head here from Rijeka (154KN, four hours, three daily) and Zagreb (from 175KN, seven hours, three daily). **Jadrolinija** (☑ 051-231 765; www.jadrolinija.hr; Riva Lošinjskih Kapetana 22, Mali Lošinj) runs the main car ferries between Brestova (on the mainland, 29km south of Opatija) and Porozina on Cres (adult/child/car 18/9/115KN, 20 minutes, seven to 13 daily), and between Valbiska on Krk and Merag on Cres (adult/child/car 18/9/115KN, 25 minutes, nine to 13 daily). A weekly (daily in July and August) car ferry runs between Mali Lošinj and Zadar (adult/child/car 59/30/271KN, seven hours). A daily passenger-only catamaran connects Mali Lošinj and Rijeka (60KN, four hours) via Cres Town (45KN, 2½ hours).

astonishingly gorgeous and a large part of its appeal is in the lost-in-time views over the verdant valley, with the town rising above it like something from a fairy tale. The damp, dark Motovun Forest at its base also has a mythical quality, especially as it con-tains hidden treasure in the form of Istria's famous truffles.

It was the Venetians who decided to for-tify the town in the 14th century, building two sets of thick walls. Within the walls, an atmospheric cluster of Romanesque and Gothic buildings houses a smattering of art-ist studios, restaurants and tourist-oriented shops. Newer houses and shops have sprung up on the slopes leading to the old town.

Motovun's main claim to fame is its popular film festival, which takes place every summer.

◉ Sights & Activities

Motovun: A History in Motion MUSEUM
(Motovun: Povijest u pokretu; Trg Andrea Antico 7; adult/child 25/15KN; ☉9am-5pm) Tucked away in a courtyard of the Hotel Kaštel, this small museum has interesting displays on the legendary giant of Motovun Forest, the grim lot of the local peasants forced to work as rowers on Venetian galleons, the truffle and olive-oil industries, the film festival, and Motovun-born motor-sport legend Mario Andretti.

Paragliding Tandem Istria PARAGLIDING
(☑098 92 28 081; www.istraparagliding.com; from 700KN) Jump off Motovun's hilltop on a tandem glide (with an instructor), and enjoy stunning vistas over Istria's hills. Book ahead.

Montona Tours CYCLING
(☑052-681 970; www.montonatours.com; Kanal 10; ☉hours vary) This local travel agency rents a fleet of bikes – and it's perfectly located (at the bottom of the hill, mercifully) for day rides on the Parenzana Bike Trail (p155), which passes right through here. Plus it takes bookings for truffle hunts, boats to Venice, accommodation and car rental.

⚑ Festivals & Events

Motovun Film Festival FILM
(www.motovunfilmfestival.com; ☉Jul) Around 40,000 people flock to this five-day festival, held in late July. Founded in 1999, it presents a roster of independent and avant-garde films, with nonstop outdoor and indoor screenings, concerts and parties.

🛏 Sleeping & Eating

★ **Villa Borgo** B&B €€
(☑052-681 708; www.villaborgo.com; Borgo 4; s/d/apt from 485/647/811KN; P❋🛜) Perched on the edge of the old town, this gorgeous place has 10 rooms of different styles and configurations – some with shared baths, some with panoramic views, others overlooking the street – plus a ground-floor apartment that sleeps four. There's a lovely shared terrace with sweeping valley views, perfect for sharing a bottle of wine and watching the sunset.

★ **Konoba Mondo** ISTRIAN €€€
(☑052-681 791; www.konoba-mondo.com; Barbacan 1; mains 75-195KN; ☉noon-3.30pm & 6-10pm; ☑) Just before the outer town gate, this little tavern with a small side terrace serves imaginatively conceived and poshly presented Istrian mainstays, many featuring truffles. And if you just can't get enough of truffles, you can order a top-up! Wash it all down with wines from local producers.

🔒 Shopping

Miro Tartufi FOOD & DRINKS
(☑052-681 724; www.miro-tartufi.com; Kanal 27) Truffles infuse olive oil, cheese and sausage in this cute wee shop. However, the main reason to visit is to arrange a truffle hunt (around €65 per person for a three-hour experience, including lunch). The family also rents four apartments upstairs.

ℹ Information

Tourist Office (☑052-681 726; www.tz-motovun.hr; Trg Andrea Antico 1; ☉9am-9pm Jun-Aug, to 7pm Apr, May & Sep, to 5pm Mar, Oct & Nov) Located on the main square.

ℹ Getting There & Away

It's not easy to visit Motovun without your own car or bike. Buses are limited to a daily service to Poreč (37KN, 42 minutes) and Rovinj (69KN, 1¾ hours).

ℹ Getting Around

There are three parking areas in town. The first is at the foot of the village, from where it's a steep 2km hike up to the city gates. Another is 300m below the old town. These both charge 20KN per day from April to October. The last one is within the cobbled streets of the old town itself, and is restricted to residents and hotel guests.

Hum

POP 28

The self-proclaimed 'world's smallest town' is a mere speck on the map, consisting of basically one street that loops around within its historic walls. Yet, in terms of atmosphere, it's huge. Legend has it that the giants who built Istria had only a few stones left over and they used them to build Hum.

It doesn't take many people for Hum to feel overrun; to experience it at its cosy best, visit in the off season or stay overnight.

It only takes around five minutes to circle the town – 30 minutes if you stop to read all of the informative multilingual plaques on the significant buildings.

St Jerome's Chapel   CHURCH

(Crkvica svetog Jeronima) Positioned in a cemetery just outside the town walls, this little 12th-century Romanesque chapel still has the remains of its original frescoes on the walls, along with graffiti in the archaic Glagolitic script dating from sometime before the 16th century. If it's locked, enquire at the tavern for the key.

Glagolitic Alley   LANDMARK

(Aleja Glagoljaša) The road from Roč to Hum has been dubbed Glagolitic Alley in reference to a series of 11 sculptures placed alongside it, commemorating the area's importance as a centre of the Glagolitic alphabet (an archaic Slavic script which survived in parts of Croatia until the 19th century).

★ Apartments & Rooms

Dores   GUESTHOUSE €

(☑ 091 56 66 661; www.facebook.com/app.rooms. doresHum; Hum 9; r/apt from €50/65; P ❄ ♠) As petite and gorgeous as Hum itself, this charming guesthouse has two fresh and modern en-suite rooms in a historic block, with a souvenir shop below and the young owners living above. The owners also rent three self-contained units in Hum (one's a darling free-standing cottage) and another in Roč with its own swimming pool.

Humska Konoba   ISTRIAN €

(☑ 052-660 005; www.hum.hr; Hum 2; mains 32-55KN; ☉ 11am-10pm Jun-Sep, Tue-Sun Apr, May & Oct, Mon-Fri Nov-Mar; ♠) The town's tavern serves first-rate Istrian mainstays on a lovely outdoor terrace offering panoramic views. Start with a shot of *biska* (white mistletoe grappa). Next try *maneštra s kukuruzom* (bean and corn soup); continue with truffle-topped *fuži* (homemade egg pasta twisted into unique shapes); and end with *kroštuli* (fried crispy pastry covered in sugar).

Raboš   WINE BAR

(☑ 091 26 60 003; www.facebook.com/wine.bar. and.shop.rabos; Hum 11; ☉ 10am-9pm Jun-Sep, Wed-Mon Apr, May, Oct & Nov, Sat & Sun Dec-Mar; ♠) The old loggia was the centre of Hum life in Venetian times and it remains so today, thanks to this friendly little bar. Drop by to sample local wine and *rakija* (grappa), and order a truffle-infused antipasto platter to go with it.

🛈 Getting There & Away

You'll need your own car to reach Hum, as no public transport passes this way.

Labin & Rabac

Perched on a hilltop near the coast, Labin is the heritage highlight of eastern Istria, as well as its administrative centre. The showcase here is the labyrinthine old town, a beguiling maze of steep streets, cobbled alleys and pastel houses festooned with stone ornamentation.

Below is Podlabin, a charmless new town that sprouted as a result of the coal-mining industry. Labin was the mining capital of Istria until the 1970s, its hill mined so extensively that the town began to collapse. Mining stopped in 1999, the necessary repairs were undertaken and the town surfaced with a new sense of itself as a tourist destination.

Labin's coastal resort is Rabac, a former fishing village 5km to the southeast hugging a shallow cove hemmed with beautiful pebble beaches. An ever-expanding array of ritzy resort-style hotels is a reflection of its increasing popularity.

★ Valamar Sanfior   RESORT €€€

(☑ 052-465 000; www.valamar.com; Lanterna 2; s/d from €147/195; P ❄ ♠ ⓦ ☼) Set on a beautiful stretch of pebbly and rocky shore, this large Rabac resort ticks all of the family-holiday boxes. The rooms are swish and modern, there's a choice of indoor and outdoor pools, and the prices include an extensive breakfast and dinner buffet. Added to this are playgrounds, a babysitting service and live music in the bar at night.

Restaurant Kvarner   ISTRIAN €€€

(☑ 052-852 336; www.kvarnerlabin.com; Šetalište San Marco bb; mains 75-195KN; ☉ 10am-11pm) This Labin old-town restaurant has a terrace overlooking the sea, a menu of authentic Istrian fare and a loyal local following. Handmade *fuži* (Istrian pasta) is the main speciality here but almost anything you order is guaranteed to be packed with local flavour, especially in the form of truffles. It also has rooms and apartments to rent.

🛈 Information

Tourist Office (☑ 052-852 399; www.rabac-labin.com; Titov trg 2/1; ☉ 8am-9pm Mon-Fri, 10am-2pm & 6-9pm Sat & Sun May-Sep, 9am-

3pm Mon-Sat Oct-Apr) At the entrance to the old town.

❶ Getting There & Away

Labin is well connected by bus with Pula (48KN, 55 minutes, 14 daily), Rijeka (54KN, 1½ hours, 15 daily), Zagreb (146KN, 4¼ hours, eight daily), Zadar (205KN, seven hours, five daily) and Split (280KN, 9½ hours, five daily).

❶ Getting Around

Buses stop at Trg 2 Marta in Podlabin, from where you can catch a local bus to the old town. This bus continues on to Rabac in the peak season.

KVARNER

☑ 051

Sheltered by soaring mountains, the Kvarner Gulf has long been loved by visitors attracted to the mild climate and cobalt waters, and those in search of more than just beach appeal. In the days of the Austro-Hungarian Empire, the wealthy built holiday homes here, bestowing places like Rijeka and Opatija with a rich legacy of stately Habsburg-era architecture. From both of these neighbouring towns you can easily connect to hiking trails inside the protected forests of Učka Nature Park and Risnjak National Park.

The islands of Cres, Lošinj, Krk and Rab all have highly atmospheric old port towns and stretches of unspoilt coastline dotted with remote coves for superb swimming. Wildlife puts in an appearance, too: Cres has an important griffon-vulture population, Lošinj has a marine centre devoted to preserving the Adriatic's dolphins and turtles, while bears (though elusive) may be sighted in both Učka and Risnjak.

Rijeka

POP 120,855

Named European Capital of Culture for 2020, Croatia's third-largest city Rijeka is a bustling blend of gritty 20th-century port and Italianate Habsburg grandeur. Most people speed through en route to the islands or Dalmatia, but those who pause will discover charm, culture, good nightlife, intriguing festivals and Croatia's most colourful carnival.

Despite some regrettable architectural ventures in the outskirts, much of the centre is replete with ornate Austro-Hungarian-style buildings. It's a surprisingly verdant city once you've left its concrete core, which contains Croatia's largest port, with ships, cargo and cranes lining the waterfront.

Rijeka is a vital transport hub, but as there's no real beach in the city, most people base themselves in nearby Opatija.

History

Following their successful conquest of the indigenous Illyrian Liburnians, the Romans established a port here called Tarsaticae. Slavic tribes migrated to the region in the 7th century and built a new settlement within the old Roman town.

The town changed feudal masters – from German nobility to the Frankopan dukes of Krk – before becoming part of the Austrian empire in the late 15th century. Rijeka was an important outlet to the sea for the Austrians and a new road was built in 1725 connecting Vienna with the Kvarner coast. This spurred economic development, especially shipbuilding, the industry that has remained the centrepiece of Rijeka's economy ever since.

In 1750 Rijeka was hit by a devastating earthquake that destroyed much of its medieval heart. Thirty years later the oldtown walls were removed to allow for the construction of a more modern commercial centre. Korzo, Rijeka's main pedestrian strip, was built as a grand avenue on the site of the demolished walls.

Between 1918, when Italian troops seized Rijeka and Istria, and 1945, when Rijeka became part of postwar Yugoslavia, it changed hands several times, with sporadic periods as a free city (known under its Italian name, Fiume). In 1991 Rijeka became part of independent Croatia, but it retains a sizeable Italian minority.

◉ Sights

★ **Trsat Castle** CASTLE
(Trsatska Gradina; Petra Zrinskoga bb; adult/child 15/5KN; ⊙9am-8pm Jun-Oct, to 5pm Nov-May) High on a hill above the city, this semi-ruined 13th-century fortress offers magnificent vistas from its bastions and ramparts, looking down the Rječina River valley to the docks, the Adriatic and the distant island of Krk. The present structure was built by the Frankopan dukes of Krk, but its latest facelift was in 1824, when Irish-born count Laval Nugent, a commander in the Austrian army, bought the castle and had it restored in a romantic neoclassical Biedermeier design.

Our Lady of Trsat Church   CHURCH

(Crkva Gospe Trsatske; Frankopanski trg; ⊙8am-5pm) According to legend, the angels carrying the house of Jesus' mother from Nazareth rested here in the late 13th century before moving it to Loreto across the Adriatic in Le Marche. Pilgrims started trickling into the chapel erected on the site, and then pouring in when the Pope donated an icon of St Mary in 1367 (it's located on the main altar, behind a magnificent wrought-iron gate). The church still attracts thousands of pilgrims each year.

St Vitus' Cathedral   CATHEDRAL

(Katedrala Sv Vida; Trg Grivica 11; ⊙6am-5pm Mon-Fri, to noon Sat, 9am-1pm Sun) FREE North of Rijeka's **Roman Arch** (Rimski Luk; Stara Vrata) is this unusual round cathedral, built by the Jesuit order in 1638 on the site of an older church and dedicated to Rijeka's patron saint. If it looks familiar, it's probably because it features on the reverse of the 100KN note. Massive marble pillars support the central dome, under which are housed baroque altars and a 13th-century Gothic crucifix.

Maritime & History Museum   MUSEUM

(Pomorski i Povijesni Muzej; ☑051-553 667; www.ppmhp.hr; Muzejski trg 1; adult/child 20/15KN; ⊙9am-4pm Mon, to 8pm Tue-Sat, 4-8pm Sun) The star of this museum is the building itself, the former palace of the Austro-Hungarian governor. It's a splendid showcase of Hungarian architecture, with grand staircases, glittering chandeliers and many sumptuously restored rooms. The maritime collection includes Roman amphorae, model ships, sea charts, navigation instruments and portraits of captains; little of it is captioned in English.

Natural History Museum   MUSEUM

(Prirodoslovni Muzej; www.prirodoslovni.com; Lorenzov Prolaz 1; adult/child 10/5KN; ⊙9am-7pm Mon-Sat, to 3pm Sun) 🍃 Located in a very grand 19th-century villa, this museum is devoted to the geology, botany and sea life of the Adriatic area. There's a small aquarium, exhibits on sharks, taxidermic animals and lots of insects. Don't miss the adjacent botanical garden, with more than 2000 native plant species.

🎊 Festivals & Events

★Rijeka Carnival   CARNIVAL

(Riječki Karneval; www.rijecki-karneval.hr; ⊙mid-Jan–early Mar) Rio it isn't, but the largest carnival in Croatia provides a good excuse to tarry in Rijeka between mid-January and Ash Wednesday. The festivities include pageants, street dances, concerts, masked balls, exhibitions and a parade. Check out the *zvončari*, masked men clad in animal skins who dance and ring loud bells to frighten off evil spirits.

Rijeka Summer Nights   THEATRE

(Riječke Ljetne Noći; ⊙Jun & Jul) Theatre performances and concerts are held at the Croatian National Theatre (p162) and on outdoor stages set up on the Korso and the beaches.

🛏 Sleeping

★Hostel Dharma   HOSTEL €

(☑051-562 108; www.dharmahostels.com; Spinčićeva 2; dm/s/tw 136/270/372KN; P❄🛜) A clever conversion of what was once an iron smelter on the eastern edge of town has produced this highly recommended hostel, with a yoga studio and vegetarian restaurant attached. Start your day with a free yoga class and tuck into a substantial vegetarian breakfast before chilling out in the large, verdant garden.

★Carnevale   HOSTEL €

(☑051-410 555; www.hostelcarnevale.com; Jadranski trg 1; dm/r 200/365KN; ❄🛜) With metallic paint on the walls, billowing fabric on the ceilings, animal-print bed linen and art scattered everywhere, this supercentral hostel should put you in a festive mood. Towels are provided (and changed regularly) and there are big suitcase-size lockers. The only downside is that there's no kitchen.

Grand Hotel Bonavia   HOTEL €€

(☑051-357 100; www.bonavia.hr; Dolac 4; r from 475KN; P❄🛜) Around for almost 140 years, this striking glass-fronted box of a hotel right in the heart of town offers well-equipped, comfortable, 21st-century rooms that are much more stylish than you might expect. There's also a restaurant, a spa and a small gym.

Hotel Jadran   HOTEL €€€

(☑051-216 600; www.jadran-hoteli.hr; Šetalište XIII Divizije 46; s/d from 625/780KN; P❄@🛜) Located 2km east of the centre, this immaculate four-star hotel clings to a cliff above the Adriatic: book a sea-view room and revel in the tremendous vistas from your balcony right above the water. There's a concrete-edged beach below, too.

RISNJAK NATIONAL PARK

Just 32km northeast of Rijeka, **Risnjak National Park** (Nacionalni Park Risnjak; ☑051-836 133; www.np-risnjak.hr; 2-day pass adult/child 45/25KN) occupies 63 sq km of thickly forested mountainscape, the highest peak being Veliki Risnjak (1528m). Linking the Alps and the Balkan mountains, these cool peaks provide respite from the sweltering heat, humidity and crowds of the coast. There are only a few villages within the park, which means limited accommodation and food. Those who do make it to these parts often visit on day trips from Rijeka.

Most visitors come here to hike, with the easy **Leska Path** of most appeal to day visitors – the trail can get busy on summer weekends in particular. To hike further in to scale the minor summits of Risnjak or Snježnik, contact the **Park Information Office** (☑051-836 133; www.np-risnjak.hr; Bijela Vodica 48, Crni Lug; ⏱9am-5pm; 🐾) for advice. Trekking to the aquamarine Kupa Spring is another highlight.

✖ Eating

★ **Mlinar** BAKERY €
(☑091 23 88 555; www.mlinar.hr; Frana Supila; snacks from 8KN; ⏱5.30am-8pm Mon-Fri, 6.30am-3pm Sat) The best bakery in town, with delicious filled baguettes, wholemeal bread, croissants and *burek* (pastry stuffed with meat, spinach or cheese). There are several branches around town and across Croatia.

Maslina Na Zelenom Trgu ITALIAN €
(☑051-563 563; www.pizzeria-maslina.hr; Koblerov trg bb; pizzas 32-65KN, mains 27-135KN; ⏱11am-midnight Mon-Sat) For the best pizza in the city centre head to this small Italian place with wobbly art nouveau decor and tiled tables. The wheels of pizza here are popular among Rijeka's Italian population. Grab an outdoor table in summer and enjoy the views of Rijeka's **City Tower** (Gradski Toranj; Korzo).

★ **Konoba Nebuloza** CROATIAN €€
(☑051-374 501; www.konobanebuloza.com; Titov trg 2b; mains 50-120KN; ⏱11am-midnight Mon-Fri, from noon Sat) Straddling the line between modern and traditional Croatian fare, this slightly upmarket riverside restaurant serves lots of seafood, along with selected beef and turkey dishes. Specialities include sous-vide swordfish and baby rump steak with prosciutto and cheese. The chef seems to have a thing about mangel-wurzel, a vegetable you may never have eaten (or heard of).

★ **Mornar** BISTRO €€
(☑051-312 222; www.facebook.com/bistromornar; Riva Boduli 5a; mains 40-115KN; ⏱noon-11pm) Amid the unappealing industrial surrounds of Rijeka's port, this lovely little white-wood bistro serves up excellent fish dishes, as well as a few grilled meats and pasta plates. The

service is friendly, the cooking assured. The fish soup is particularly enjoyable.

Na Kantunu CROATIAN, SEAFOOD €€
(☑051-313 271; Demetrova 2; mains 50-110KN; ⏱8am-11pm Mon-Sat) Fresh fish and seafood are the stars of the show at this bright and breezy restaurant in a somewhat grimy location by the port. It's a good place to try traditional fish or octopus stews, followed by crispy fruit pastries.

Placa 51 CROATIAN €€€
(☑051-546 454; Riva Boduli 3a; mains 59-190KN) Aged Dalmatian beef, brilliant tuna steaks, terrific octopus starters – the excellent cooking at Placa 51 spans a good range of northern Croatian cuisine and a few Italian dishes thrown in for good measure. Enjoy it in the welcoming, intimate interior.

🍷 Drinking & Entertainment

★ **Samovar Bar** CAFE
(☑051-215 521; www.samovar.hr; Trg Matije Vlačića Flaciusa; ⏱7am-10pm Mon-Sat) This warmly eclectic place has a wonderful range of teas, terrific coffees and other drinks such as a stellar rose lemonade. The decoration is delightfully retro, with everything from chandeliers to teddy bears.

★ **Tunel** BAR, CLUB
(Školjić 12; ⏱9am-midnight Tue & Wed, to 2am Thu, to 3am Fri, 7pm-3am Sat; 🐾) Tucked beneath the railway tracks in an actual tunnel, this popular place morphs from daytime cafe to comedy and live-music venue to late-night club. It gets rammed at weekends.

CukariKafe BAR
(☑099 58 38 276; Trg Jurja Klovica 2; ⏱7am-midnight Mon-Thu, to 2am Fri & Sat, 10am-10pm Sun)

CROATIA RIJEKA

WORTH A TRIP

VOLOSKO

Some 2km east of Opatija, Volosko is one of the prettiest places on this section of the Kvarner coastline, a fishing village that has also become something of a restaurant hot spot in recent decades. This is no tourist resort, though, and it's very scenic indeed: fishers repair nets in the tiny harbour, while stone houses with flower-laden balconies rise up from the coast via a warren of narrow alleyways. Whether you're passing through for a drink or having a gourmet meal, you're sure to enjoy the local ambience and wonderful setting.

Konoba Valle Losca The word *konoba* usually denotes a little **family-run eatery** (☑095 58 03 757; Andrije Štangera 2; mains 90-100KN; ☺11.30am-2pm & 5pm-midnight) – most of which have identikit menus. Here, French and Italian techniques combine with top-notch local ingredients to take things to another level entirely. But don't come here if you're in a hurry – it takes time to fully savour the deliciously rustic dishes, served by multilingual staff in the stone-walled dining room.

Skalinada An intimate, highly atmospheric, wholly unpretentious little **restaurant-bar** (☑051-701 109; www.skalinada.org; Uz Dol 17; snacks & mains from 25-110KN; ☺1pm-midnight Sun-Thurs, 3pm-2am Fri & Sat) with sensitive lighting, exposed stone walls and a creative menu of Croatian food (small dishes or mains) using seasonal and local ingredients. Many local wines available by the glass.

Plavi Podrum One of Kvarner's best restaurants, **Plavi Podrum** (☑051-701 223; www.plavipodrum.com; Obala Frana Supila 6; mains from 220KN; ☺noon-midnight) does wonderful, innovative cooking perfectly paired with great wines and olive oils. Its standout dishes include risotto with scampi and truffle (or wild asparagus); sea bass, foie gras and pumpkin-and-coriander purée; and scampi skewers with a dusting of coffee and black Istrian truffle accompanied by monkfish reduction and apple purée.

In terms of accommodation, the stunning **Design Hotel Navis** (☑051-444 600; www.hotel-navis.hr; Ivana Matetića Ronjgova 10; s/d 1400/1900KN; 🅿🕸@🛜) seems to cling to the cliff face, and has achingly stylish rooms with floor-to-ceiling windows looking out over the Adriatic. There's a spa and wellness centre, and a good restaurant.

Tucked into a tiny lane in the old part of town, this is Rijeka's coolest cafe-bar. Grab a seat on the oversized white wooden furniture on the covered deck or head inside to admire the oddball art nouveau–style knick-knacks. Enjoy great coffee and cakes along with a soothing soundtrack.

Filodrammatica Bookshop Cafe
CAFE, BAR

(☑051-211 696; Korzo 28; ☺7am-11pm) A cafe-bar with luxurious decor, comfy sofas and a **VBZ** (☑051-324 010; www.vbz.hr; Korzo 32; ☺7.30am-7.30pm Mon-Fri, to 5pm Sat) – Croatia's biggest publisher – bookshop at the back, Filodrammatica prides itself on specialist coffees and fresh, single-source coffee beans. It also serves sandwiches and snacks.

Croatian National Theatre Ivan Zajc
THEATRE

(Hrvatsko Narodnog Kažalište Ivana pl Zajca; ☑051-337 114; www.hnk-zajc.hr; Verdieva 5a) In 1885 the inaugural performance at this imposing theatre was lit by the city's first lightbulb. These days you can catch dramas in Croatian and Italian, as well as opera and ballet. Gustav Klimt painted some of the ceiling frescoes.

🛍 Shopping

★ Paška Sirana
CHEESE

(☑051-734 205; www.paskasirana.hr; Scarpina 3) Shopping for a picnic? This fine little shop sells all manner of Croatian cheeses and you can usually try some before you buy.

Šta Da?
GIFTS & SOUVENIRS

(Užarska 14; ☺10am-8pm Mon-Fri, to 1pm Sat) Literally translating as 'what yes?', '*šta da*' is an idiom peculiar to Rijeka meaning something like 'you what!?' or 'really, you don't say!'. This cool little store stocks T-shirts, jewellery and clocks, including many emblazoned with images of its logo and of the distinctive orange local buses.

ℹ️ Information

Clinical Hospital Center Rijeka (Klinički Bolnički Centar Rijeka; ☑ 051-658 111; www. kbc-rijeka.hr; Krešimirova 42)

Tourist Office (☑ 051-335 882; www.visitri jeka.hr; Korzo 14; ◉ 8am-8pm Mon-Sat, to 2pm Sun) Has good colour city maps, a few brochures and private accommodation lists.

ℹ️ Getting There & Away

AIR

Rijeka Airport (Zračna Luka Rijeka; ☑ 051-841 222; www.rijeka-airport.hr; Hamec 1, Omišalj), located 30km from town on the island of Krk, is only used for seasonal flights from April to October. There are international flights to London, Oslo, Warsaw and more. The only domestic routes are **Trade Air** (☑ 091 62 65 111; www.trade-air.com) services to Dubrovnik, Split and Osijek.

BOAT

Jadrolinija (☑ 051-211 444; www.jadrolinija. hr; Riječki Lukobran bb) A daily catamaran connects Rijeka to Novalja on Pag (80KN, 2¾ hours).

BUS

The **intercity bus station** (☑ 051-660 300; Trg Žabica 1) is in the town centre. Destinations include Dubrovnik (from 348KN, 12½ hours, two daily), Pula (89KN, 2½ hours, up to 18 daily), Split (from 236KN, eight hours, up to seven daily), Zadar (156KN, four hours, nine daily) and Zagreb (from 85KN, 2½ hours, at least hourly).

TRAIN

The **train station** (Željeznički Kolodvor; www. hzpp.hr; Trg Kralja Tomislava 1) is a 10-minute walk east of the city centre. Three trains a day head to Zagreb (119KN, 3¾ hours, three daily).

ℹ️ Getting Around

TO/FROM THE AIRPORT

➡ Rijeka Airport is on Krk Island, 30km from Rijeka.

➡ An airport bus meets all flights for the 30-minute ride to the intercity bus station; it leaves for the airport two hours and 20 minutes before flight times. You can buy a ticket (50KN) on the bus.

➡ Taxis from the airport charge 255KN for up to four people to the centre.

BUS

➡ Rijeka has an extensive network of orange city buses run by **Autotrolej** (☑ 051-311 400; www.autotrolej.hr), operating from the local **bus station** (Jelačićev trg). Buy two-trip tickets

for 15.50KN from any *tisak* (newsstand). A single ticket from the driver costs 10KN.

➡ The same company also operates a 24-hour, colourful, open-topped, double-decker, hop-on, hop-off sightseeing bus (adult/child 50/35KN) that runs between central Rijeka, Trsat and Opatija. The ticket is also valid for travel on all city buses.

Krk Island

Krk Island (Veglia in Italian) is connected to the mainland by a toll bridge. It is Croatia's largest island, and also one of the busiest – in summer, hundreds of thousands of central Europeans stream to its holiday houses, campsites and hotels. It's not the lushest or the most beautiful island, though its landscape is quite varied, ranging from forests in the west to sunburnt ridges in the east. The island's northwestern coast is rocky and steep, with few settlements, because of the fierce *bura* (cold northeasterly wind) that whips the coast in winter. The climate is milder in the southwest and can be scorching in the southeast. The main settlement is charming walled **Krk Town**, while **Malinksa** is the main transport hub.

Vrbnik

POP 975

Perched on a 48m cliff overlooking the sea, Vrbnik is a beguiling medieval village of steep, arched streets. It's not a real secret (tour groups pass through from time to time), but most of the year it's a peaceful, unhurried place.

Vrbnik was once the main centre where the Glagolitic script was used and was the repository for many Glagolitic manuscripts. The script was kept alive by priests, who were always plentiful in the town since many young men entered the priesthood to avoid serving on Venetian galleys.

Now the town is a terrific place to soak up the vistas and sample the *žlahtina* white wine produced in the surrounding region. After wandering the tightly packed cobbled alleyways, head down to the town beach for a swim.

⭐ **Hotel-Vinotel Gospoja**   HOTEL €€€
(☑ 051-669 350; www.gospoja.hr; Frankopanska 1; d from 1025KN) Beautifully designed rooms with lavishly painted walls and ceilings that follow a wine theme make this place a real contemporary standout; each room is

named after a Croatian wine. It's part of the growing Gospoja wine portfolio. It's all very classy, with a good restaurant, too.

Luce BOUTIQUE HOTEL €€€
(☑ 091 28 57 083; www.konoba-luce.hr; Braće Trinajstić 15; r 960KN) Four-star style has come late to Vrbnik, but this place is part of the new wave. Rooms are stunners, with exposed brickwork, splashes of bright colours, and stunning contemporary photographs. There's also a good tavern-restaurant. Minimum two-night stay in summer.

★**Gospoja – Konoba Žlahtina** CROATIAN €€
(☑ 051-857 142; www.gospoja.hr; Trg Pred Sparov zid 9; mains 50-110KN) Part of the Gospoja wine empire, this elegant place does the usual range of grilled fish and meat dishes, as well as an excellent seafood risotto. But it also serves local specialities, such as lamb or beef stew with *šurlice* (noodles), and rump steak stuffed with prosciutto and cheese, with fig sauce and gnocchi.

Restaurant Nada CROATIAN €€
(☑ 051-857 065; www.nada-vrbnik.hr; Glavača 22; mains 60-180KN; ⊗ 11am-midnight Apr-Oct) Nada is a great place to sample local favourites such as Krk lamb or *šurlice* (noodles) topped with meat goulash. There are two attractive dining terraces – one shaded and one overlooking the sea – plus a cellar where you can snack on deli treats surrounded by wine barrels.

★**AurA** FOOD & DRINKS
(Placa Vrbničkog Statuta 1; ⊗ 9am-6pm) This excellent little shop in the old town sells local wines, grappa, olive oils and truffles, as well as its homemade brandy and jams. Everything has an organic focus.

ℹ Information

Mare Tours (☑ 051-604 400; www.mare-vrbnik.com; Pojana 4; ⊗ 8am-8pm Mon-Sat, 9am-4pm Sun) Travel agency offering tourist information and renting private rooms.
Tourist Office (☑ 051-857 479; Placa Vrbničkog Statuta 4; ⊗ 10am-4pm) Small office; don't count on the official opening hours.

ℹ Getting There & Away

Two buses a day head to Vrbnik from Krk Town (32KN, 30 minutes) and Malinska (37KN, 40 minutes). If you're driving, you'll need to park at the base of the old town; it costs 5KN per hour.

Baška
POP 1674

The drive to the southern end of Krk Island is dramatic, passing through a fertile valley that's bordered by eroded mountains. Eventually the road peters out at Baška, where there's a fine crescent beach set below barren hills. With the peaks of the mainland directly opposite, you're effectively enveloped by soaring highlands, making the sea seem like an alpine lake.

However (and this is a considerable caveat), in summer tourists are spread towel-to-towel and what's otherwise a pretty, if slimline, pebble beach turns into a fight for your place in the sun.

Baška's small 16th-century core of Venetian town houses is pleasant enough, but what surrounds it is a bland tourist development of modern apartment blocks and generic restaurants. Facilities are plentiful and there are nice hiking trails into the surrounding mountains, and more secluded beaches to the east of town, reachable on foot or by water taxi.

★**Heritage Hotel Forza** HOTEL €€€
(☑ 051-864 036; www.hotelforza.hr; Zvonimira 98; r from 1400KN; 🅿 ❄ @ 🛜) The quality here is excellent. Rooms have wooden floors and/or exposed stone walls and larger-than-life artworks that bring a real sense of personality and style.

★**Bistro Francesca** CROATIAN €€
(☑ 099 65 47 538; www.bistrofrancesca.com; Zvonimira 56; mains 59-180KN; ⊗ noon-3.30pm & 6pm-midnight) Quality seafood dishes are on offer here – the black seafood risotto is something of a local institution. Try the scallops with cauliflower cream and the mixed seafood platter, too. Friendly service.

ℹ Information

Tourist Office (☑ 051-856 817; www.tz-baska. hr; Zvonimira 114; ⊗ 8am-9pm Mon-Sat Jun-Aug, to 2pm Mon-Fri Sep-May) Just down the street from the bus station, between the beach and the harbour. Walkers should head here to pick up its hiking-path map. Staff are multilingual.

ℹ Getting There & Away

There are direct services between Baška and Rijeka (84KN, 2¼ hours, four to seven daily).

LIKA

Covering a large swath of the Northern Dalmatian interior between the coastal mountains and the Bosnian border, this lightly populated region has blissful scenery ranging from bucolic farmland to dense forest and craggy uplands. If you're looking for an alternative to beaches and islands, it's a wonderful area to explore. In parts, the karstic nature of the underlying limestone has bequeathed a wonderland of caves, canyons, lakes and waterfalls. The most dramatic of these natural attractions is Plitvice Lakes National Park, one of Croatia's unmissable experiences.

History

Part of the Croatian heartland since the early 7th century, Lika was attacked by the Ottomans in the 16th century and was incorporated into the military frontier *(vojna krajina)*. Vlach and Serb refugees, driven from Bosnia by the encroaching Ottomans, settled in the region with the blessing of the Habsburg monarchy, on the condition that they were prepared to fight to defend their new home. By the 1910 census the population was almost evenly split between the Orthodox and Catholic faiths, with many districts in the east having an outright Serbian majority.

During WWII, Lika's Serbian population suffered greatly at the hands of the Ustaše regime. In 1991, following Croatia's declaration of independence, the Serbs of the Krajina declared themselves an autonomous republic and it was in Lika that the first shots of the war rang out. Much of the local Croatian population was forced to abandon their homes and flee. When Croatian forces regained the area in 1995, most of the Serb population fled – leaving in their wake many abandoned homes and villages. Some, however, chose to return, and today the ethnic make-up of the region is 86% Croat and 12% Serb.

Plitvice Lakes National Park
☑ 053

By far Croatia's top natural attraction and the absolute highlight of Croatia's Adriatic hinterland, this glorious expanse of forested hills and turquoise lakes is exquisitely scenic – so much so that in 1979 Unesco proclaimed it a World Heritage Site. The name

---

WORTH A TRIP

STARA BAŠKA

Many of Krk's best beaches are heavily developed and crowded in summer. For more tranquillity, head south of Punat on the lonely road that heads to **Stara Baška** (not southeast to Baška). It's a superlative drive, through steep, parched hills and lunar scenery. Stara Baška itself is a run-of-the-mill tourist sprawl of holiday homes and caravan parks, but if you pull up 500m before the first campsite there's a series of gorgeous pebble-and-sand coves with wonderful swimming. You'll have to park on the road and then walk down one of the rocky paths for five minutes to get to the coast.

---

is slightly misleading though, as it's not so much the lakes that are the attraction here but the hundreds of waterfalls that link them. It's as though Croatia decided to gather all its waterfalls in one place and charge admission to view them.

The extraordinary natural beauty of the **park** (☑ 053-751 015; www.np-plitvicka-jezera.hr; adult/child Jul & Aug 250/110KN, Apr-Jun, Sep & Oct 150/80KN, Nov-Mar 55/35KN; ⊙ 7am-8pm) merits a full day's exploration, but you can still experience a lot on a half-day trip from Zadar or Zagreb. You must be able to walk a fair distance to get the most out of the place.

🛏 Sleeping & Eating

★ **House Župan**   GUESTHOUSE €
(☑ 047-784 057; www.sobe-zupan.com; Rakovica 35, Rakovica; s/d 250/370KN; ⓟ ❄ 🛜) With an exceptionally welcoming hostess and clean, contemporary and reasonably priced rooms, this is a superb choice. There's even a guest kitchen and plenty of other diversions when you want to relax after a hike. It's set back from the highway in the small town of Rakovica, 11km north of Plitvice Lakes National Park.

Plitvice Backpackers   HOSTEL €
(☑ 053-774 777; www.plitvicebackpackers.com; Jezerce 62, Jezerce; dm/tw 150/340KN; 🛜) Located in Jezerce, the nearest village to the lakes, just 3km from Plitvice Lakes National Park's Entrance 2, this well-run hostel occupies a large house on the main highway. Rooms are clean, lockers are big and there's a fully equipped kitchen. The owners really look after their guests, even shuttling them to and from the park and local supermarket.

ℹ WHEN TO VISIT PLITVICE

While the park is beautiful year-round, spring and autumn are the best times to visit. In spring and early summer the falls are flush with water, while in autumn the changing leaves put on a colourful display. Winter is also spectacular, although snow can limit access and the free park transport doesn't operate. Unquestionably the worst time to visit is in the peak months of July and August, when the falls reduce to a trickle, parking is problematic and the sheer volume of visitors can turn the walking tracks into a conga line and cause lengthy waits for the buses and boats that ferry people around the park.

Plitvice Mirić Inn   GUESTHOUSE €€
(🖉098 93 06 508; www.plitvice-croatia.com; Jezerce 18/1, Jezerce; s/d 550/780KN; ☺Apr-Oct; 🅿️❄🛜) Run by a delightful family, this flower-strewn guesthouse has 13 well-cared-for rooms divided between neighbouring buildings, conveniently located a mere 1.5km from Plitvice Lakes National Park's Entrance 2. Rooms boast slightly more floor space in the newer annex, but they're all very comfortable. Try the home baking if you get a chance.

House Tina   GUESTHOUSE €€
(🖉047-784 197; www.housetina.com; Grabovac 175, Grabovac; d/bungalows 560/875KN; 🅿️❄🛜) Smart and modern, but with a rural ambience, this large, family-run guesthouse offers first-rate family-friendly accommodation both in the main house and in two rustic wooden bungalows in the yard. It's 9km from Plitvice Lakes National Park's Entrance 1, but the owners can organise transport for a relatively small cost.

Villa Lika   GUESTHOUSE €€€
(🖉053-774 302; www.villa-lika.com; Mukinje 63, Mukinje; r from 950KN; ☺Apr-Oct; 🅿️❄🛜🏊) Right by the bus stop in Mukinje, these two large houses have shiny white rooms punctuated with brightly coloured curtains and tiles. There are 15 rooms in total, all set around a beautifully landscaped pool, and a recently opened restaurant offering international and Croatian dishes (portion sizes are small).

Hotel Degenija   HOTEL €€€
(🖉047-782 143; www.hotel-degenija.com; Selište Drežničko 57a, Selište Drežničko; s/d from 700/990KN; 🅿️❄🛜) With a crisp, newish feel, this 20-room roadside hotel, 4km north of Plitvice Lakes National Park's Entrance 1, has smart international-standard rooms and an attractive **restaurant** (🖉047-782 060; mains 55-140KN; ☺7am-11pm; 🛜).

★ Lička Kuća   CROATIAN €€
(🖉053-751 024; Rastovača; mains 70-195KN; ☺11am-10pm Mar-Nov) Built in 1972 and fully rebuilt in traditional stone-walled style in 2015 after burning to the ground three years earlier, Lička Kuća is touristy and extremely busy in high season, but the food is excellent. Specialities include slow-cooked lamb, dry-cured local prosciutto, and mountain trout, making it one of the best places for traditional dishes in the Northern Dalmatian interior.

ℹ Information

Both of the park's two main entrances have parking (7/70KN per hour/day) and an information office stocking brochures and maps. The main park **office** (🖉053-751 014; www.np-plitvicka-jezera. hr; Josipa Jovića 19) is in Plitvička Jezera.

ℹ Getting There & Away

Buses stop at both park entrances; there's a small ticket office at the stop near Entrance 2. Destinations include Šibenik (118KN, four hours, three daily), Split (174KN, 4½ hours, six daily), Zadar (95KN, 2½ hours, seven daily) and Zagreb (89KN, two hours, frequent).

Paklenica National Park
🖉023

Stretching for 145km and creating a natural barrier between inland and coastal Croatia, the rugged peaks of the Velebit Range are an impressive sight. **Paklenica National Park** (🖉023-369 155; www.np-paklenica.hr; adult/child Jun-Sep 60/30KN, Mar-May & Oct 40/20KN, Nov-Feb 20/10KN; ☺entrance booths 6am-8.30pm Jun-Sep, 7am-3pm Oct-May) takes up 95 sq km of these limestone mountains and boasts some of Croatia's most dramatic alpine vistas. It's a superb place to trek gorges, do a bit of climbing or just amble along one of the many streams that score the land.

The park's two biggest attractions are the gorges of Velika Paklenica (Great Paklenica) and Mala Paklenica (Small Paklenica), where cliffs rise 400m into the azure skies. Animals you might spot along the way include golden eagles, striped eagles, peregrine falcons and, if you're extremely lucky, lynx and bears. Chamois gather near the park entrances.

Manita Peć CAVE

(adult/child 30/15KN; ⊙10am-1pm Jul-Sep, reduced days Apr-Jun & Oct) The only cave in Paklenica National Park (p166) that's open to the public, Manita Peć has a wealth of stalagmites and stalactites enhanced by strategically placed lighting in the main chamber (40m long and 32m high). Entry is by 30-minute tour.

Anića Kuk CLIMBING

The best and most advanced climbing in Paklenica National Park, with over 100 routes up to a maximum of 350m.

There's some rustic accommodation for hikers and climbers within the park's boundaries, but most people base themselves in the relative comfort of Starigrad-Paklenica, the small settlement that sprawls along the coastal road near the park entrances. It's neither particularly *stari* (old) or much of a *grad* (town), but it does have access to the sea for a cooling dip after a day's exertions.

Planinarski Dom Paklenica HUT €

(⊘023-301 636; www.pdpaklenica.hr; dm 100KN; ⊙Sat & Sun year-round, daily mid-Jun–mid-Sep) Offering such luxuries as running water, a toilet and electricity, this lodge crams 50 beds into four rooms; bring a sleeping bag. There's also a kitchen and dining room. The hut is a two-hour walk up from the Velika Paklenica gorge. Reservations are recommended on summer weekends.

ℹ Information

Croatian Mountaineering Association

(Hrvatski planinarski savez; ⊘01-48 23 624; www.hps.hr; Kozarčeva 22, Zagreb; ⊙8am-4pm Mon-Fri) Has up-to-date information and publishes a useful map of the park. The association's office is in Zagreb.

Paklenica National Park Office (⊘023-369 155; www.paklenica.hr; Dr Franje Tuđmana 14a, Starigrad-Paklenica; ⊙7am-3pm Mon-Fri) Sells booklets and maps. The *Paklenica National Park* guide gives an excellent overview of the park and details on walks. Rock-climbing permits cost 60KN to 80KN depending on the season; climbers should talk to guides at the park office for advice. Main office in Starigrad-Paklenica; other offices at park entrances.

Starigrad Tourist Office (⊘023-369 245; www.rivijera-paklenica.hr; Trg Tome Marasovića 1, Starigrad-Paklenica; ⊙8am-9.30pm Jul & Aug, to 8pm Jun & Sep, to 2pm Mon-Fri Oct-May) In the Starigrad-Paklenica town centre, across from the small marina.

ℹ Getting There & Away

Most buses travelling along the coastal highway stop at Starigrad-Paklenica. Destinations include Rijeka (135KN, 3¾ hours, five daily), Zadar (28KN, one hour, five daily), Split (118KN, four hours, five daily) and Dubrovnik (from 221KN, nine hours, three daily).

There are generally no taxis in Starigrad-Paklenica. Some hotels will drop off and pick up guests at the park's entrance gates.

DALMATIA

Serving the classic cocktail of historic towns, jewel-like waters, rugged limestone mountains, sun-kissed islands, gorgeous climate and Mediterranean cuisine, Dalmatia is a holidaymaker's dream.

Hot spots include the buzzing Mediterranean-flavoured cities of Zadar and Split, and gorgeous little Hvar Town, where the cashed meet the trashed on the Adriatic's most glamorous party island. Yet one location understandably eclipses any discussion of Dalmatia: the remarkable old town of Dubrovnik. Ringed by mighty defensive walls that dip their feet in the cerulean sea, the city encapsulates the very essence of a medieval fantasy.

If it's relaxation you're after, there are seductive sandy beaches and pebbly coves scattered about islands near and far. Yachties can still sail between unpopulated islands without a shred of development, lost in dreams of the Mediterranean of old, while hikers can wander lonely trails in the mountainous hinterland, where bears and wolves still dwell.

Zadar

⊘023 / POP 75,437

Home to a historic old town of Roman ruins, medieval churches, cosmopolitan cafes and quality museums set on a small peninsula, Zadar is an intriguing city. It's not too crowded and its two unique attractions – the sound-and-light spectacle of the *Sea Organ* and the *Sun Salutation* – need to be seen and heard to be believed.

While it's not a picture-postcard kind of place from every angle, the mix of ancient relics, Habsburg elegance and coastal setting all offset the unsightly tower blocks climbing up the hilly hinterland. It's no Dubrovnik, but it's not a museum town

CROATIA ZADAR

either – this is a living, vibrant city, enjoyed by residents and visitors alike. Zadar is also a key transport hub, with superb ferry connections to the surrounding islands.

History

Zadar was inhabited by the Illyrian Liburnian tribe as early as the 9th century BC. By the 1st century BC it had become a minor Roman colony. Slavs settled here in the 6th and 7th centuries AD, and Zadar eventually fell under the authority of Croatian-Hungarian kings.

The rise of Venetian power in the mid-12th century was bitterly contested – there was a succession of citizens' uprisings over the next 200 years – but the city was finally acquired by Venice in 1409, along with the rest of Dalmatia.

Frequent Veneto-Turkish wars resulted in the building of Zadar's famous city walls in the 16th century, partly on the remains of the earlier Roman fortifications. With the fall of Venice in 1797, the city passed to Austrian rulers, who administered the city with the assistance of their Italianised ruling aristocracy. Italian influence endured well into the 20th century, with Zadar (or Zara, as the Italians call it) captured by Italy at the end of WWI and officially ceded to Italy with the Treaty of Rapallo in 1922.

When Italy capitulated to the Allies in 1943, the city was occupied by the Germans and then bombed to smithereens by the Allies, with almost 60% of the old town destroyed. The city was rebuilt following the original street plan.

History repeated itself in November 1991 when Yugoslav rockets kept Zadar under siege for three months. Few war wounds are now visible, however, and Zadar has reemerged as one of Croatia's most dynamic towns.

◉ Sights

★ Sea Organ   MONUMENT
(Morske orgulje; Istarska Obala) FREE Zadar's incredible *Sea Organ*, designed by local architect Nikola Bašić, is unique. Set within the perforated stone stairs that descend into the sea is a system of pipes and whistles that exudes wistful sighs when the movement of the sea pushes air through it. The effect is hypnotic, the mellifluous tones increasing in volume when a boat or ferry passes by. You can swim from the steps off the promenade while listening to the sounds.

★ Sun Salutation   MONUMENT
(Pozdrav Suncu; Istarska Obala) Another wacky and wonderful creation by Nikola Bašić (the local architect who designed the Sea Organ), this 22m-wide circle set into the pavement is filled with 300 multilayered glass plates that collect the sun's energy during the day. Together with the wave energy that makes the *Sea Organ's* sound, it produces a trippy light show from sunset to sunrise that's meant to simulate the solar system. It also collects enough energy to power the entire harbour-front lighting system.

Roman Forum   RUINS
(Zeleni trg) One of the most intriguing things about Zadar is the way Roman ruins seem to sprout randomly from the city's streets. Nowhere is this more evident than at the site of the ancient Forum, constructed between the 1st century BC and the 3rd century AD. As in Roman times, it's the centre of civic and religious life, with St Donatus' Church dominating one side of it.

St Donatus' Church   CHURCH
(Crkva Sv Donata; Šimuna Kožičića Benje bb; 20KN; ⊙9am-9pm May-Sep, to 4pm Oct-Apr) Dating from the beginning of the 9th century, this unusual circular Byzantine-style church was named after the bishop who commissioned it. As one of only a handful of buildings from the early Croatian kingdom to have survived the Mongol invasion of the 13th century, it's a particularly important cultural relic. The simple and unadorned interior includes two complete Roman columns, recycled from the Forum. Also from the Forum are the paving slabs that were revealed after the original floor was removed.

St Anastasia's Cathedral   CATHEDRAL
(Katedrala Sv Stošije; Trg Sv Stošije; ⊙6.30-7pm Mon-Fri, 8-9am Sat, 8-9am & 6-7pm Sun) FREE Built in the 12th and 13th centuries, Zadar's cathedral has a richly decorated facade and an impressive three-nave interior with the remains of frescoes in the side apses. The cathedral was badly bombed during WWII and has since been reconstructed. On the altar in the left apse is a marble sarcophagus containing the relics of St Anastasia, while the choir contains lavishly carved stalls. A glass vestibule allows you to peer inside when the cathedral's closed, which is often.

Climb the **bell tower** (Široka; 15KN; ⊙9am-10pm Mon-Sat Jun-Aug, shorter hours rest of year) for old-town views.

Archaeological Museum   MUSEUM

(Arheološki Muzej; ☑ 023-250 516; www.amzd.hr; Trg Opatice Čike 1; adult/child 30/15KN; ⊘ 9am-9pm Jun & Sep, to 10pm Jul & Aug, to 3pm Apr, May & Oct, 9am-2pm Mon-Fri, to 1pm Sat Nov-Mar) A wealth of prehistoric, ancient and medieval relics, mainly from Zadar and its surrounds, awaits at this fascinating museum. Highlights include a 2.5m-high marble statue of Augustus from the 1st century AD, and a model of the Forum as it once looked.

Narodni trg   SQUARE

(People's Square) Traditionally the centre of public life, this pretty little square is constantly abuzz with chatter from its many cafe-bars. The western side is dominated by the late-Renaissance City Guard building, dating from 1562; the clock tower was added under the Austrian administration in 1798. Public proclamations and judgments were announced from the loggia opposite (1565), which is now an art-exhibition space.

Museum of Ancient Glass   MUSEUM

(Muzej antičkog stakla; ☑ 023-363 831; www. mas-zadar.hr; Poljana Zemaljskog Odbora 1; adult/child 30/10KN; ⊘ 9am-9pm Mon-Sat May-Sep, to 4pm Oct-Apr) It's baffling that a medium as delicate as glass could survive the earthquakes and wars that have plagued this region over the millennia, but this impressive museum has thousands of objects on display: goblets, jars, vials, jewellery and amulets. Many of the larger glass urns were removed from the local Roman necropolis (cemetery), where they held cremated remains. The layout is superb, with large light boxes and ethereal music to heighten the experience.

St Simeon's Church   CHURCH

(Crkva Sv Šime; Poljana Šime Budinića bb; ⊘ 8.30am-noon & 5-7pm Mon-Fri, 8.30am-noon Sat May-Oct) While this 17th-century baroque church is pretty enough, it's what lies inside that makes it truly noteworthy. Taking pride of place above the main altar, the sarcophagus of St Simeon is a masterpiece of medieval goldsmithery. Commissioned in 1377, the coffin is made of cedar and covered inside and out with finely executed gold-plated silver reliefs.

☞ Tours

Local travel agencies offer boat cruises to Telašćica Bay and the beautiful Kornati Islands; tours generally include lunch and a swim in the sea or a salt lake. Ask around on Liburnska Obala (where the excursion boats are moored) or contact **Aquarius Travel Agency** (☑ 023-212 919; www.aquariuszadar. com; Nova Vrata bb; ⊘ hours vary). Organised trips to the national parks of Paklenica, Krka and Plitvice Lakes are also very popular, making it easy for visitors to access the parks without having to worry about organising transport.

Wine & Food Hedonism   FOOD & DRINK

(Truly Dalmatia; ☑ 095 777 38 89; www.truly dalmatia.com) Food is a big part of the tours on offer here, from wine or olive-oil tastings to cooking classes where you can learn to cook *peka* (roasting meat under a charcoal-covered lid; a real Dalmatian favourite). All tours include a meal featuring traditional local specialities. Prices vary depending on tour, season and number of people.

Zadar Walking Tours   TOURS

(☑ 091 32 79 777; www.zadarwalkingtour.com; per person 100KN; ⊘ 10am, noon & 6pm) These 100-minute tours are a terrific way to get an overview of the city and its history. The guides are excellent and have a full portfolio of Zadar legends and anecdotes, as well as plenty of historical detail. Book in advance or just turn up 10 minutes before the departure time at the lamp post on Narodni trg (People's Sq).

⌷ Sleeping

Windward Hostel   HOSTEL €

(☑ 091 62 19 197; www.facebook.com/windward. hostel.zadar; Gazića 12; dm/d 112/450KN; ✳ 🛜) Just 1.5km from the old town, this 20-bed, yachting-themed hostel is run by a passionate sailor. Rooms are immaculate, with big lockers, electric window blinds and private reading lights. There's a supermarket and bakery nearby, and staff can organise sailing tours and lessons.

Drunken Monkey   HOSTEL €

(☑ 023-314 406; www.themonkeytroophostels. com; Jure Kastriotica Skenderbega 21; dm/r from 175/450KN; ✳ @ 🛜 ✳) Tucked away in a suburban neighbourhood, this friendly little hostel has brightly coloured rooms, a small pool, a guest barbecue and an all-round funky vibe. Staff can arrange trips to the Plitvice Lakes and Krka National Park. When it's full, you can try the Drunken Monkey's nearby sister, the Lazy Monkey, with similar standards and rates.

Boutique Hostel Forum HOSTEL €€
(☑023-253 031; www.hostelforumzadar.com; Široka 20; dm/d/ste from 155/665/725KN) Wonderfully colourful dorm rooms and stylish, white-and-black doubles and suites, some with top skyline and partial water views, make this easily the best hostel and mid-range hotel in the old centre. The location couldn't be better and the rooms are terrific for the price.

Apartments Donat APARTMENT €€
(☑095 82 56 390; www.apartmentsdonat.com; Nadbiskupa Mate Karamana 12; apt from 700KN) Appealing modern apartments in a good old-town location make this an excellent choice. Some are attic rooms and most have artwork feature walls or exposed modern brickwork.

★**Art Hotel Kalelarga** HOTEL €€€
(☑023-233 000; www.arthotel-kalelarga.com; Majke Margarite 3; s/d incl breakfast 1515/1810KN; ❄️🐱) Built and designed under strict conservation rules due to its old-town location, this 10-room boutique hotel is an understated and luxurious beauty. Exposed stonework and mushroom hues imbue the spacious rooms with plenty of style and character. The gourmet breakfast is served in the hotel's own stylish cafe, Gourmet Kalelarga.

★**Almayer - Art &
Heritage Hotel** HERITAGE HOTEL €€€
(☑023-335 357; www.almayer.hr; Braće Bersa 2; d/ste 1745/2200KN; 🅿️❄️@🐱) This elegant hotel, tucked away near the tip of the old town's peninsula, has classy rooms in a wonderful stone-walled heritage building. Discreet service and marvellous breakfasts are all part of the deal.

Hotel Bastion HOTEL €€€
(☑023-494 950; www.hotel-bastion.hr; Bedemi Zadarskih Pobuna 13; r 1320-2730KN; 🅿️❄️🐱) Built over the remains of a Venetian fortress, the Bastion radiates character and sophistication. The 23 rooms and five suites successfully combine a classic early-20th-century feel with a contemporary sensibility. It also boasts a top-drawer restaurant and a basement spa. It's a classy place and the location is brilliant.

✕ **Eating**

Mlinar BAKERY €
(☑091 23 88 620; www.mlinar.hr; Široka 1; snacks from 8KN; ⏲6.30am-11pm Mon-Fri, 7am-11pm Sat & Sun) The Zadar outpost of this nationwide chain is the best bakery in town. It's great for a snack or breakfast on the run, with wholemeal bread, croissants, sweet pastries and *burek* (pastry stuffed with meat, spinach or cheese).

★**Kaštel** MEDITERRANEAN €€
(☑023-494 950; www.hotel-bastion.hr; Bedemi Zadarskih Pobuna 13; mains 70-190KN; ⏲7am-11pm) Hotel Bastion's fine-dining restaurant offers contemporary takes on classic Croatian cuisine (octopus stew, stuffed squid, Pag cheese). France and Italy also make their presence felt, particularly in the delectable dessert list. Opt for the white-linen experience inside or dine on the battlements overlooking the harbour for a memorable evening.

★**Pet Bunara** DALMATIAN €€
(☑023-224 010; www.petbunara.com; Stratico 1; mains 65-160KN; ⏲noon-11pm) With exposed stone walls inside and a pretty terrace lined with olive trees, this is an atmospheric place to tuck into Dalmatian soups and stews, homemade pasta and local faves such as octopus and turkey. Save room for a traditional Zadar fig cake or cherry torte.

4 Kantuna ITALIAN, INTERNATIONAL €€
(☑091 31 35 382; www.restaurant4kantuna.com; Varoshka 1; pizzas 48-63KN, mains 68-175KN; ⏲11am-11pm) With a cool laneway setting as well as a stylish interior dining area, 4 Kantuna gets the simple things right – good service and high-quality cooking without asking you to pay over the odds for the privilege. There's pizza, pasta, risotto and a handful of carefully chosen meat and fish mains.

GourmetKalelarga CAFE €€
(☑023-233 000; www.arthotel-kalelarga.com/gourmet; Široka 23; breakfast 28-60KN, mains 59-155KN; ⏲7am-10pm) Beneath the Art Hotel Kalelarga (p170), this chic little beige cafe is your best option for a cooked breakfast or a decadent cake. As the day progresses, the focus shifts towards more substantial Dalmatian fare. Service is very good.

Restaurant Niko SEAFOOD €€
(☑023-337 888; www.hotel-niko.hr; Obala Kneza Domagoja 9; mains 70-170KN; ⏲noon-midnight) This wildly popular **hotel** (s/d 8250/1140KN; 🅿️❄️🐱) restaurant is great for grilled fish and other seafood, though the menu has red meat and vegetarian dishes, too. It's your best bet down the Borik end of the city.

ZRĆE BEACH: CROATIA'S IBIZA?

The island of Pag is like something from a 1950s Italian film, perfect for a broody black-and-white Antonioni set – it's barren, rocky, and sepia coloured, with vast, empty landscapes. At the island's north, about 3km southeast of the small town of Novalja, is Zrće Beach – often heralded as the Ibiza of Croatia.

Unlike in Ibiza, all of the clubs and bars are right on the beach – but in terms of scale, it's got a long way to go. Basically, there are three main clubs – **Aquarius** (www.aquarius.hr; ☉Jun-Sep), **Kalypso** (www.kalypso-zrce.com; ☉10am-6am Jun-Sep) and **Papaya** (www.papaya.com.hr; ☉10am-6am Jun-Sep) – and a scattering of bars in between, all of which open in June and close by mid-September. Entrance prices very much depend on the event: nights are usually free at the beginning of the season but cost as much as €40 for big-name DJs in mid-August. A series of festivals bring in the crowds, the most notable of which are **Hideout** (www.hideoutfestival.com; ☉late Jun/early Jul), **Fresh Island** (www.fresh-island.org; ☉mid-Jul) and **Sonus** (www.sonus-festival.com; ☉mid-Aug).

The beach itself is a picturesque 1km-long treeless crescent of pebbles overlooking a parched strip of eastern Pag, with the mountains of the mainland rearing up on the horizon – rent an umbrella for shade. Out of season you'll have this otherwise-lonely place to yourself.

Buses connect Novalja with Zadar year-round, with summer-only services to/from Šibenik, Split, Rijeka and Zagreb. In summer, shuttle buses run from Novalja to Zrće Beach (12KN).

★**Corte Vino & More** INTERNATIONAL €€€
(☎023-335 357; www.facebook.com/cortevinomore; Braće Bersa 2; mains 80-180KN; ☉noon-2.30pm & 7-10.30pm) One of the classiest dining experiences in Zadar, Corte Vino & More in the Al Mayer Heritage Hotel has a gorgeous setting, wonderfully attentive service and high-quality food that changes with the seasons, taking Croatian traditional dishes and riffing in subtle, new and creative directions. Fabulous wine list and knowledgeable waiters, too.

Foša SEAFOOD €€€
(☎023-314 421; www.fosa.hr; Kralja Dmitra Zvonimira 2; mains 130-270KN; ☉noon-1am) Classy Foša's gorgeous terrace juts into the harbour, and its sleek interior that combines ancient stone walls with 21st-century style. The main focus of chef Damir Tomljanović is fresh fish, plucked from the Adriatic and served grilled or salt baked; the beef tenderloin with truffles is another star. Also try the Adriatic shrimp with smoked-mussel gnocchi.

🍷 Drinking & Nightlife

★**La Bodega** WINE BAR
(☎099 46 29 440; www.labodega.hr/zadar; Široka 3; ☉7am-1am Sun-Thu, to 1.30am Fri & Sat) With slick, eccentric, semi-industrial decor, a bar with a line of hams and garlic hanging above, Portuguese-style tiles and a welcoming,

open-to-the-street approach, this is one of Zadar's hippest bars. There's a good range of Croatian wines by the glass and an extraordinary selection by the bottle – best enjoyed with a variety of Pag cheese and prosciutto.

Podroom CLUB
(☎099 74 98 451; www.podroom.club; Marka Marulića bb; ☉midnight-6am Fri, 1-6.30am Sat) One of Zadar's biggest clubs, Podroom draws a regular cast of Croatian and international DJs, especially in summer. It's within staggering distance of the old town and really only kicks off around 2am. Live acts also take to the stage to get things going. Admission prices vary depending on who's on the bill.

Cogito Coffee CAFE
(Poljana Pape Aleksandra III B; ☉8am-4pm Tue-Sun) Many locals swear that this is the best coffee in the old town. It also does cocktails and craft beers, and it's far enough off the main tourist drag to feel like a neighbourhood cafe.

Garden Lounge BAR
(☎023-250 631; http://thegarden.hr/the-garden-lounge; Liburnska Obala 6; ☉10am-1am late May-Oct) Perched on top of the old city walls, this exceedingly cool bar-club-garden is very Ibiza-esque, with harbour views, day beds, secluded alcoves, billowing fabric and contemporary electronic music. All. Very. Chilled.

Shopping

★ Natura Zara
FOOD & DRINKS

(☑ 098 888 585; www.facebook.com/Naturazara; Brne Karnarutića 7; ⊙ 8am-9pm Mar-Oct) This gorgeous little shop, tucked away on a quiet old-city street, sells high-quality Croatian wines, olive oils, honeys, truffles and liqueurs, all from small family producers, and all with an ecological focus.

Gligora
FOOD & DRINKS

(☑ 023-700 730; www.gligora.com; Hrvoja Vukčić Hrvatinića 5; ⊙ 7am-8pm Mon-Fri, to 2pm Sat & Sun) Sheep cheese from the island of Pag is a celebrated Croatian culinary tradition. This is the Zadar shopfront for its multi-award-winning cheeses, as well as olive oils, wines and other goodies.

Information

Tourist Office (☑ 023-316 166; www.zadar. travel; Jurja Barakovića 5; ⊙ 8am-11pm May-Jul & Sep, to midnight Aug, 8am-8pm Mon-Fri, 9am-2pm Sat & Sun Oct-Apr; 🖱) Publishes a good colour map and rents audioguides (40KN) for a self-guided tour around the town.

Zadar General Hospital (Opća Bolnica Zadar; ☑ 023-505 505; www.bolnica-zadar.hr; Bože Peričića 5)

Getting There & Away

AIR

Recently upgraded **Zadar Airport** (☑ 023-205 800; www.zadar-airport.hr) is 12km east of the town centre. Croatia Airlines flies to Zadar from Zagreb. There are international flights to Brussels, Dublin, London, Munich, Paris, Warsaw and many more destinations, often with budget airlines.

BUS

The **bus station** (☑ 060 305 305; www.liburnija-zadar.hr; Ante Starčevića 1) is about 1km southeast of the old town. Domestic destinations include Dubrovnik (182KN, eight hours, up to six daily), Rijeka (156KN, 4½ hours, 12 daily), Šibenik (43KN, 1½ hours, at least hourly), Split (86KN, three hours, hourly) and Zagreb (110KN, 3½ hours, hourly).

Getting Around

TO/FROM THE AIRPORT

Timed around all Croatia Airlines flights, buses (25KN one way) depart from outside the main terminal, and from the old town (Liburnska Obala) and the bus station one hour prior to flights.

A taxi will cost around 150KN to the old town and 180KN to Borik.

BUS & BIKE

Liburnija (www.liburnija-zadar.hr) runs buses on 10 routes, which all loop through the bus station. Tickets cost 10KN on board – or 16KN for two from a *tisak* (newsstand). Buses 5 and 8 (usually marked 'Puntamika') head to/from Borik regularly.

Calimero (☑ 023-311 010; www.rent-a-bike-zadar.com; Zasjedanja Zavnoh 1; per hour/day from 40/120KN; ⊙ 8am-8pm Mon-Fri, to 1pm Sat) is Zadar's best place to rent a bicycle. It's an easy walk from the old town.

Krka National Park
☑ 022

Extending along the 73km Krka River, **Krka National Park** (☑ 022-201 777; www.npkrka.hr; adult/child Jul & Aug 200/120KN, Apr-Jun, Sep & Oct 110/80KN, Nov-Mar 30/20KN) runs from the Adriatic near Šibenik inland to the mountains of the Croatian interior. It's a magical place of waterfalls and gorges, with the river gushing through a karstic canyon 200m deep. Sights built by humans are also a major draw of the region, the area's remoteness attracting monks who constructed their monasteries here.

The park has five main entrances, at Skradin, Lozovac, Roški Slap, Krka Monastery and Burnum – all are accessible by car.

Sights & Activities

Skradin
VILLAGE

Skradin is a pretty little riverside town with a combination of brightly painted and bare stone houses on its main street and a ruined fortress towering above. Apart from the opportunity to see the town itself, the advantage to starting your visit to Krka National Park in Skradin is that the park admission fee includes a boat ride through the canyon to Skradinski Buk waterfall. The disadvantage is that there can be long queues for the boats in summer.

Skradinski Buk
WATERFALL

The highlight of Krka National Park, an hour-long loop follows boardwalks, connects little islands in the emerald-green, fish-filled river and terminates at the park's largest waterfall. Skradinski Buk's 800m-long cascade descends by almost 46m before crashing into the lower lake, which is a popular swimming spot. Nearby, a cluster of historic mill cottages have been converted into craft workshops, souvenir stores and places to eat. The whole area gets insanely busy in summer.

From the Lozovac entrance, buses (free with park admission) shuttle visitors from the large car park (also free) down a serpentine road to Skradinski Buk. Neither the free boats nor the buses operate from November to February, but in those months you can drive right down to the falls.

Mother of Mercy Franciscan Monastery MONASTERY
(Franjevački samostan Majke od Milosti; ☎022-775 730) Upstream of Skradinski Buk waterfall the Krka River broadens into Lake Viskovac, a habitat for marsh birds. At its centre is a tree-fringed island, the perfect place for a monastery. Founded in the 14th century by Augustinian hermits, the monastery was expanded in 1445 by Franciscans escaping the Ottoman invasion of Bosnia. The church was extensively remodelled in the 17th century and the bell tower added in 1728. Boat trips head here from Skradinski Buk and include 30 minutes on the island.

★ **Krka Monastery** MONASTERY
(Manastir Krka; ⏲10am-6pm) This isn't just the most important Serbian Orthodox monastery in Croatia; it's one of the faith's most important sites full stop. Featuring a unique combination of Byzantine and Mediterranean architecture, it occupies a peaceful position above the river and a small lake. From mid-June to mid-October a national-park guide is at hand to show you around. At other times you're welcome to visit the church and wander the lakeside path.

Roški Slap WATERFALL
(adult/child Jul & Aug 100/55KN, Apr-Jun, Sep & Oct 60/40KN, Nov-Mar 30/20KN, with Krka National Park entry free; ⏲9am-8pm Jul & Aug, shorter hours rest of year) Beginning with shallow steps and continuing in a series of branches and islets to become 23m-high cascades, this 650m-long stretch is a flamboyantly pretty part of the Krka River. On the eastern side you can visit the water mills that used to grind wheat. Boats leave from Skradinski Buk waterfall (adult/child 140/95KN, 3½ hours).

BIBICh WINE
(☎022-775 597; www.bibich.co; Plastovo; ⏲10am-4.30pm) This wine producer, 9km north of Skradin, offers tasting sessions. Out of season, ring ahead about the cellar-door tastings (mostly reds), just to make sure they're happening. In summer you might find finger food on offer as well. From Skradin, head north, then take the 6075 to Dubravice and follow the signs to Plastovo.

Sleeping

Guest House Ankora GUESTHOUSE €€
(☎095 910 70 68; www.guesthouseankora.com; Mesarska 5a, Skradin; r/apt 490/950KN) Simple but lovingly looked-after rooms and apartments in a good, central Skradin location make this an excellent base for Krka National Park. The stone walls in some rooms, the outdoor hot tub and the friendly service are all bonuses. Three-night minimum stay in summer.

Vila Barbara APARTMENT €€€
(☎095 884 58 01; www.vilabarbara.com; Zagrađe 17, Skradin; apt 1200KN; P 📶) This excellent place has colourful, almost whimsically painted apartments, a quiet terrace and a hot tub. The welcome is warm and the location, not far from the water's edge, is excellent.

Information

There are information offices at each of the park entrances.

Krka National Park Office (☎022-771 688; www.npkrka.hr; Skradin; ⏲8am-8pm) Near the harbour in Skradin; provides good maps and information, and can arrange excursions.

Skradin Tourist Office (☎022-771 329; www.skradin.hr; Trg Male Gospe 3; ⏲9am-5pm Mon-Fri) The main tourist office is in the town hall, but from Easter to October it also staffs a kiosk by the national-park office.

Getting There & Away

Numerous agencies sell excursions to Krka from Šibenik, Zadar and other coastal cities, but it's not difficult to visit independently. In summer seven daily buses (three on Sunday) with **Autotransport Šibenik** (☎022-212 557; www.atpsi.hr) depart from Šibenik for Lozovac and Skradin (28KN, 25 minutes). In winter the only buses are timed around the school run.

Šibenik

☎022 / POP 34,500

Šibenik has a magnificent medieval heart, gleaming white against the placid waters of the bay, something that may not be immediately apparent as you drive through the somewhat shabby outskirts. The stone labyrinth of steep backstreets and alleys is a joy to explore. Šibenik is also an important access point for Krka National Park and the Kornati Islands.

SOKOLARKSI CENTRE

Dedicated to protecting birds of prey in Croatia, the **Sokolarski Centre** (☏091 50 67 610; www.sokolarskicentar.com; Škugori bb, Šibenik; adult/child 50/40KN; ☺9am-7pm Apr-Nov) performs a kind of rescue and rehab service for around 150 injured raptors each year. Visitors are treated to a highly entertaining and educational presentation from centre director Emilo Mendušić, who uses a tame eagle owl and Harris hawks to demonstrate these birds' agility and skills. Rescued native birds aren't used for these shows; they're only kept at the centre until they're healthy enough to be released back into the wild.

Most of the patients at the centre have been involved in a collision on Croatian roads. Other threats to the birds include illegal poisoning, shooting and the use of pesticides.

The Sokolarski Centre is about 7km from Šibenik and is not served by public transport. It's a little tricky to find: to get here, take the road to Krka National Park, turn east at Bilice and look for the signs.

⊙ Sights

★**St James' Cathedral** CATHEDRAL
(Katedrala Svetog Jakova; Trg Republike Hrvatske; adult/child 20KN/free; ☺9.30am-6.30pm) The crowning architectural glory of the Dalmatian coast and the undisputed masterpiece of its principal designer, Juraj Dalmatinac, this World Heritage Site is worth a detour to see. It was constructed entirely of stone quarried from the islands of Brač, Korčula, Rab and Krk, and is reputed to be the world's largest church built completely of stone without brick or wooden supports.

Šibenik City Museum MUSEUM
(Muzej grada Šibenika; ☏022-213 880; www.muzej-sibenik.hr; Gradska Vrata 3; adult/child 30/10KN; ☺8am-8pm Tue-Fri, 10am-8pm Sat & Sun) Housed in the 17th-century Rector's Palace, this well-curated museum focuses on the city and its surrounds. The permanent collection of artefacts dating from prehistory to the end of the Venetian period is split into four clear periods. There are English translations throughout and the odd bit of video to spice things up.

St Michael's Fortress FORTRESS
(Tvrđava Sv Mihovila; adult/child 40/20KN; ☺8am-10pm) Clamber up to the battlements of this large medieval fort for magnificent views – particularly impressive at sunset – over Šibenik, the Krk River and the Adriatic islands. Parts of the fortress date to the 13th century, but the surviving shell has been shored up with a polished-concrete understructure and converted into a summer stage.

St Francis' Church CHURCH
(Crkva Sv Frane; Trg Nikole Tommasea 1; ☺7.30am-7.30pm) The Franciscan monastery's mammoth church dates from the end of the 14th century. It has fine frescoes and an array of Venetian baroque paintings, but the highlight is the painted wooden ceiling, dating from 1674. It's the principal shrine of St Nikola Tavilić, a Franciscan missionary who became the first Croatian saint when he was martyred in Jerusalem in 1391. In the adjacent courtyard you'll find an exhibition on the church's history.

🛏 Sleeping & Eating

★**Indigo** HOSTEL €
(☏022-200 159; www.hostel-indigo.com; Jurja Barakovića 3; dm 129KN; ❋🛜) Lauded by all who stay the night and longer, this friendly little hostel has a four-bed dorm with pine bunks and lockable drawers on each of its four floors. At the very top, the terrace has views over the rooftops to the sea. Blue jeans provide a kooky decoration throughout. Sadly, there's no kitchen.

Hostel Mare HOSTEL €
(☏022-215 269; www.hostel-mare.com; Kralja Zvonimira 40; dm 100-159KN; r 330-450KN; ❋🛜) Pass through the heavy door that opens from the busy road onto a cobbled courtyard, and behind lies this breezy hostel. The decor is fresh, bright and IKEA-style modern, the dorms have backpack-sized lockers and there's one double room with its own bathroom. Breakfast is available (for an extra charge). Bike storage available.

★Medulić Palace Rooms & Apartments APARTMENT €€
(☏095 53 01 868; www.medulicpalace.com; Ivana Pribislavića 4; r 310-630KN; apt 365-815KN; ❋🛜) Central and with exposed stone or brick walls, the Medulic is a fabulous deal. The

standard rooms have less character, but the apartments and superior rooms are well priced and lovely places to spend a night or more.

King Kresimir Heritage Hotel
HERITAGE HOTEL €€€

(☑ 022-427 461; www.hotel-kingkresimir.com; Dobrić 2; r from 1075KN; ✻ @ 🛜) Right on the main square in a former mansion that combines Gothic and baroque touches, the King Kresimir has quietly luxurious rooms. Some rooms have four-poster beds, others have sea views, and the whole place has a classy, professional air.

★ Pelegrini
MEDITERRANEAN €€

(☑ 022-213 701; www.pelegrini.hr; Jurja Dalmatinca 1; mains 79-185KN, 3-/4-/5-course set menu 440/570/700KN; ☺ noon-midnight) Responsible for upping the culinary ante in Šibenik, this wonderful restaurant raids the globe for flavours, with influences from Japan and France, but its heart is in the Mediterranean. Dalmatian offerings are very well represented on the wine list. Call ahead to bag one of the outside tables.

❶ Information

General Hospital Šibenik (Opća bolnica Šibenik; ☑ 022-641 641; www.bolnica-sibenik. hr; Stjepana Radića 83)

NIK Travel Agency (☑ 022-338 550; www.nik. hr; Ante Šupuka 5; ☺ 8am-8pm) Large agency offering excursions to the Kornati Islands and Krka National Park, private accommodation and international bus and air tickets.

Tourist Office (☑ 022-214 411; www.sibenik-tourism.hr; Obala Palih Omladinaca 3; ☺ 8am-9pm May-Oct, to 4pm Mon-Fri Nov-Apr) Helpful tourist office in the heart of the old town.

❶ Getting There & Away

Šibenik's **bus station** (☑ 060 368 368; Draga 14) has plenty of regular services and is only a short walk from the old town. Destinations include Dubrovnik (148KN, 6½ hours, at least two daily), Rijeka (200KN, 6½ hours, at least four daily), Split (48KN, 1½ hours, 12 daily), Zadar (43KN, 1½ hours, at least hourly) and Zagreb (from 132KN, five to seven hours, at least hourly).

Trogir
☑ 021 / POP 13,200

Gorgeous Trogir (called Trau by the Venetians) is set within medieval walls on a tiny island, linked by bridges to both the main-

land and to the far larger Čiovo Island. On summer nights everyone gravitates to the wide seaside promenade lined with bars, cafes and yachts, leaving the knotted, mazelike marble streets gleaming mysteriously under old-fashioned streetlights.

The old town has retained many intact and beautiful buildings from its age of glory between the 13th and 15th centuries. In 1997 its profuse collection of Romanesque and Renaissance buildings earned it World Heritage status.

While it's easily reached on a day trip from Split, Trogir also makes a good alternative base to the big city and a relaxing place to spend a few days.

⦿ Sights

★ St Lawrence's Cathedral
CATHEDRAL

(Katedrala svetog Lovre; ☑ 021-881 426; Trg Ivana Pavla II; 25KN; ☺ 8am-8pm Mon-Sat, noon-6pm Sun Jun-Aug, to 6pm Sep-May) Trogir's show-stopping attraction is its three-naved Venetian cathedral, one of the finest architectural works in Croatia, built between the 13th and 15th centuries. Master Radovan carved the grand Romanesque portal in 1240, flanked by a nude Adam and Eve standing on the backs of lions. At the end of the portico is another fine piece of sculpture: the 1464 cherub-filled baptistery sculpted by Andrija Aleši.

Sacred Art Museum
MUSEUM

(Muzej sakralne umjetnosti; ☑ 021-881 426; Trg Ivana Pavla II 6; 10KN; ☺ 8am-8pm Mon-Sat, 11.30am-7pm Sun Jun-Sep) Highlights of this small museum include illuminated manuscripts; a large painting of St Jerome and St John the Baptist by Bellini; an almost-life-size, brightly painted *Crucifix with Triumphant Christ;* and the darkly lit fragments of a 13th-century icon that once adorned the cathedral's altar.

St Nicholas's Convent
CONVENT

(Samostan svetog Nikole; ☑ 02-881 631; Gradska 2; adult/child 10/5KN; ☺ 10am-1pm & 4.15-5.45pm Jun-Sep, by appointment other times) The treasury of this Benedictine convent is home to a dazzling 3rd-century relief of Kairos, the Greek god of opportunity, carved out of orange marble.

Medena Beach
BEACH

On the Seget Riviera, 4km west of the old town, this stretch of beach has a long promenade lined with bars, tennis courts, minigolf, ice-cream parlours and stands renting jet skis, kayaks and windsurfers. While it's in the grounds of the faded Hotel Medena megaresort, it's open to the general public and there's parking on-site.

Okrug Gornji
BEACH

(Šetalište Stjepana Radića bb) Trogir's most popular beach, Okrug Gornji (aka Copacabana), lies 1.7km south of the old town on the island of Čiovo, and can be reached by road or boat. It's a 2km-long stretch of pebbles, lined with cafe-bars, ice-cream parlours and holiday apartments.

🛏 Sleeping & Eating

Hostel Marina Trogir
HOSTEL €

(✆021-883 075; www.hostelmarina-trogir.com; Cumbrijana 16; dm 175KN; ☉May-Oct; ❄🤶) Run by an expat German couple, this excellent hostel has only four dorms, each sleeping seven or eight people. The custom-built wooden bunks have suitcase-sized lockers underneath, reading lights and privacy curtains for the lower bunk (but not the top one). Plus there's a communal kitchen and separate men's and women's bathrooms.

Villa Moretti
HISTORIC HOTEL €€

(✆021-885 326; www.villamoretti.com; Lučica 1; r €90-120; 🅿❄🤶) Owned by the same family since 1792, this 17th-century palazzo has five spacious, antique-filled rooms accessed by a grand marble and wrought-iron stairway. Two rooms open onto a large rear terrace, but all have million-dollar views over the old town. The bathrooms are large but a tad dated.

Villa Tudor
HOTEL €€

(✆091 25 26 652; www.facebook.com/VillaTudorTrogir; Obala kralja Zvonimira 12; r/apt from €104/171; 🅿❄🤶) With exposed stone offset with baby-blue walls in the stylish bedrooms, and the best water-framed views of Trogir's old town that you could imagine, this little family-run hotel is quite exceptional. The double glazing really does its job on what's a busy strip.

Brown Beach House
HOTEL €€€

(✆021-355 400; www.brownhotels.com; Gradine 66; s/d from €208/260; ☉Mar-Oct; 🅿❄🤶🏊) Much more swanky than the name implies, this luxurious property is the first from this mini chain outside Israel. You would never guess that this vast stone building started life as a tobacco factory; the 42 rooms have style and space to spare. That sense of so-

phisticated glamour continues down to the chequer-board pool and the private beach.

Pizzeria Mirkec
PIZZA €€

(✆021-883 042; www.pizzeria-mirkec.hr; Budislavićeva 15; mains 45-180KN; ☉9am-midnight) With dozens of tables spilling out onto the waterfront promenade and the main restaurant tucked around the corner, this relaxed joint serves tasty wood-fired pizza along with omelettes, steaks, pasta, grilled fish and, if preordered, traditional meals slow-roasted under a *peka* (domed metal lid). There's also a good-value set breakfast option (50KN).

Konoba Trs
DALMATIAN €€€

(✆021-796 956; www.konoba-trs.com; Matije Gupca 14; mains 105-230KN; ☉11am-midnight Mon-Sat, 5pm-midnight Sun) As traditional-looking as they come, this rustic little tavern has wooden benches and old stone walls inside, and an inviting courtyard shaded by grapevines. Yet the menu adds clever, contemporary twists to Dalmatian classics, featuring the likes of panko-crumbed octopus tentacles, and the signature dish, nutmeg-spiced lamb *pašticada* (stew), served with savoury pancakes.

ℹ Information

Atlas Trogir (✆021-881 374; www.atlas-trogir.hr) Arranges private accommodation, runs excursions, and rents cars, scooters, bikes and boats.

Portal Trogir (✆021-885 016; www.portal-trogir.com; Bana Berislavića 3, Trogir; ☉8am-8pm May-Sep, 9am-1pm Mon-Fri Oct-Mar, 9am-4pm Mon-Sat Apr) Organises private accommodation; rents bikes, scooters and kayaks; and books excursions and adventure activities (quad safaris, rafting, diving, canyoning).

Tourist Office (✆021-885 628; www.tztrogir.hr; Trg Ivana Pavla II 1; ☉8am-8pm May-Sep, 9am-5pm Mon-Fri Oct-Apr) Inside the town hall; distributes town maps.

ℹ Getting There & Away

BOAT

Bura Line (✆095 83 74 320; www.buraline.com; Obala kralja Zvonimira bb; adult/child 35/18KN) has a small boat heading backwards and forwards to Split four to six times a day from May to September.

BUS

Intercity buses stop at the **bus station** (✆021-882 947; Kneza Tripimira bb) on the mainland near the bridge to Trogir. Destinations include

Zagreb (148KN, 6½ hours, 10 daily), Rijeka (230KN, 7½ hours, three daily), Zadar (73KN, 2½ hours, 11 daily), Split (20KN, 30 minutes, frequent) and Dubrovnik (137KN, 5½ hours, five daily).

Split city bus 37 (17KN) takes the coastal road through Kaštela every 20 minutes, also stopping at the airport. This is a much slower option than the intercity buses, which take the highway.

ⓘ Getting Around

In summer small passenger **boats** (Obala Bana Berislavića) depart from Obala Bana Berislavića, right in front of Hotel Concordia, heading to the beaches of Okrug Gornji (25KN) and Medena (20KN). The journey takes about 45 minutes.

Split

🖉 021 / POP 178,000

Croatia's second-largest city, Split (Spalato in Italian) is a great place to see Dalmatian life as it's really lived. Always buzzing, this exuberant city has just the right balance between tradition and modernity. Step inside Diocletian's Palace (a Unesco World Heritage Site and one of the world's most impressive Roman monuments) and you'll see dozens of bars, restaurants and shops thriving amid the atmospheric old walls where Split has been humming along for thousands of years.

To top it off, Split has a unique setting. Its dramatic coastal mountains act as the perfect backdrop to the turquoise waters of the Adriatic and help divert attention from the dozens of shabby high-rise apartment blocks that fill its suburbs. It's this thoroughly lived-in aspect of Split that means it will never be a fantasy land like Dubrovnik, but perhaps it's all the better for that.

History

Split achieved fame when the Roman emperor Diocletian (AD 245–313), noted for his restructure of the empire and persecution of early Christians, had his retirement palace built here between 295 and 305. After his death the great stone palace continued to be used as a retreat by Roman rulers. When the nearby colony of Salona (now Solin) was abandoned in the 7th century, many of the Romanised inhabitants fled to Split and barricaded themselves behind the high palace walls, where their descendants live to this day.

First the Byzantine Empire and then Croatia controlled the area, but from the 12th to the 14th centuries medieval Split enjoyed a large measure of autonomy, which favoured its development. The western part of the old town around Narodni trg, which dates from this time, became the focus of municipal life, while the area within the palace walls remained the ecclesiastical centre.

In 1420 the Venetian conquest of Split led to its slow decline. During the 17th century, strong walls were built around the city as a defence against the Ottomans. In 1797 the Austrians arrived, remaining until 1918.

⊙ Sights

The ever-frenetic waterfront promenade – officially called Obala hrvatskog narodnog preporoda (Croatian National Revival Waterfront), but more commonly known as the Riva – is your best central reference point in Split. East of here, past the wharf, are the buzzy beaches of Bačvice, Firule, Zenta and Trstenik bays. The wooded Marjan Hill dominates the western tip of the city and has even better beaches at its base.

★ **Diocletian's Palace**   HISTORIC SITE

(Map p178) Taking up a prime harbourside position, this extraordinary complex is one of the most imposing ancient Roman structures in existence today, and it's where you'll spend most of your time while in Split. Don't expect a palace, though, nor a museum – this is the city's living heart, its labyrinthine streets packed with people, bars, shops and restaurants. Built as a military fortress, imperial residence and fortified town, the palace measures 215m from north to south and 180m east to west.

Although the original structure has been added to continuously over the millennia, the alterations have only served to increase the allure of this fascinating site. The palace was built in the 4th century from lustrous white stone transported from the island of Brač, and construction lasted 10 years. Diocletian spared no expense, importing marble from Italy and Greece, as well as columns and 12 sphinxes from Egypt.

Each wall has a gate at its centre that's named after a metal: the northern **Golden Gate** (Zlatna Vrata; Dioklecijanova bb), the southern **Bronze Gate** (Brončana Vrata; Obala hrvatskog narodnog preporoda bb), the eastern **Silver Gate** (Srebrna Vrata) and the western **Iron Gate** (Željezna Vrata). Between the eastern and western gates there's a straight road (Krešimirova, also known as Decumanus), which separated the imperial residence on the southern side, with its state rooms and

CROATIA SPLIT

Central Split

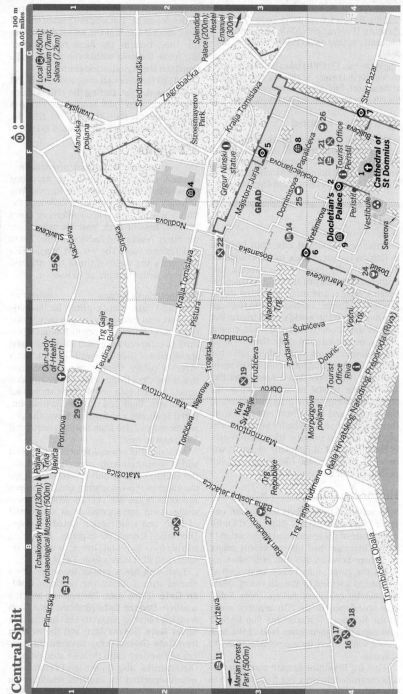

Local (450m);
Tusculum (7km);
Salona (7.2km)

100 m
0.05 miles

Splendida
Palace (200m);
Hostel
Emanuel
(300m)

Stari Pazar

Zagrebačka

Stredmanuška

Livanjska

Manuška
poljana

Strossmayerov
Park

Kralja Tomislava

26

Tourist Office
Peristil

Cathedral of
St Domnius

Grgur Ninski
statue

5

8

12 21

1

Diocletian's
Palace

7

4

Majstora Jurja

Papalićeva

Diokilecijanova

GRAD

Dominisova

25

Nodilova

22

14

9

Vestibule

Peristil

2

Krešimirova

6

Marulićeva

Bosanska

Severova

Dosud

24

Slaviceva

15

Kačićeva

Kralja Tomislava

Sinjska

Pistura

Domaldova

Narodni
Trg

Šubićeva

Trg Gaje
Bulata

Trogirska

Zadarska

Dobrić

Voćni
Trg

Our-Lady-
of-Health
Church

Teutina

Kružićeva

Obrov

Tourist
Office

Obala Hrvatskog Narodnog Preporoda (Riva)

Poljana
Tina
Ujevića

Porinova

Tončićeva

Niščerova

Marmontova

Kraj
Sv Marije

Morpurgova
poljana

Riva

29

Matošića

Ban Mladenova

Bana Josipa Jelačića

Trg
Republike

Trg Franje Tuđmana

19

20

27

Tchaikovsky Hostel (130m);
Archaeological Museum (500m)

Plinarska

Križeva

13

11

Marjan Forest
Park (500m)

17

18

16

Trumbićeva Obala

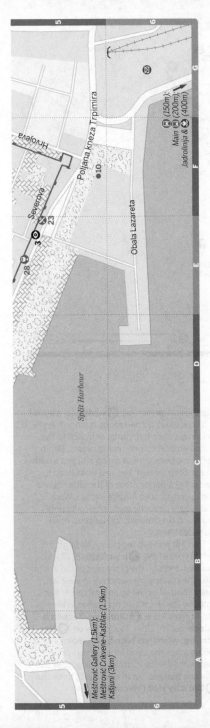

CROATIA SPLIT

Central Split

temples, from the northern side, once used by soldiers and servants.

There are 220 buildings within the palace boundaries, home to about 3000 people. The narrow streets hide passageways and courtyards – some deserted and eerie, others thumping with music from bars and cafes – while residents hang out their washing overhead, kids kick footballs against the ancient walls, and grannies sit in their windows watching the action below.

➡ ★ Cathedral of St Domnius

(Katedrala sv Duje; Map p178; Peristil bb; cathedral/belfry 35/20KN; ⊙ 8am-8pm Jun-Sep, 7am-noon &

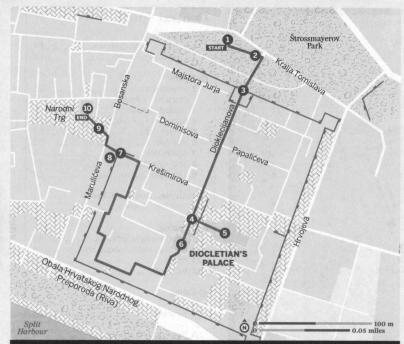

Sight Tour
Diocletian's Palace

START CHAPEL OF ARNERIUS
END NARODNI TRG
LENGTH 500M; ONE HOUR

Begin outside the well-preserved northwest-ern corner tower of Diocletian's Palace at the remains of the ❶ **Chapel of Arnerius**. Head in the direction of the imposing statue of ❷ **Grgur Ninski**, and stop to rub his toe for good luck. Take the stairs down to the ❸ **Golden Gate** (p177), the grandest of the palace's portals. This was the main proces-sional entrance into the palace, decorated with statues, columns and arches, the re-mains of which are still visible.

Enter the palace and walk along its main north–south street, Dioklecijanova, to the ❹ **Peristil**, the ceremonial court at the approach to the imperial apartments. The longer side is lined with six columns, linked by arches and decorated with a stone frieze. Behind this is Diocletian's magnificent mau-soleum, now the ❺ **Cathedral of St Dom-nius** (p179). At the far end, take the stairs up into the well-preserved ❻ **vestibule**, a grand and cavernous domed room, open to the sky, which was once the formal entrance to the retired emperor's personal quarters. Behind here were bedrooms, a dining hall and a bath-house. Step through the vestibule, head to the far right-hand corner of the little square and turn right onto Andrije Aljesija. Work your way around the maze of streets until you reach Krešimirova, the palace's main east–west axis.

Turn left and exit the palace through the high arches of the ❼ **Iron Gate** (p177). As you pass through the outer part of the double gate, the building immediately to your left, easily spotted by the sculptural relief of St Anthony the Hermit on the corner, is the late-Romanesque ❽ **Ciprianis-Beneditti Palace**, built in 1394. You're now on ❾ **Nar-odni trg**, which has been Split's main civic square since medieval times. It was once lined with Venetian Gothic buildings, but the only one that has survived is the 15th-century ❿ **Old City Hall (Vjećnica)**.

5-7pm May & Oct, 7am-noon Nov-Feb, 8am-5pm Mar & Apr) Split's octagonal cathedral is one of the best-preserved ancient Roman buildings still standing. It was built as a mausoleum for Diocletian, the last famous persecutor of the Christians, who was interred here in AD 311. In the 5th century the Christians got the last laugh, destroying the emperor's sarcophagus and converting his tomb into a church dedicated to one of his victims. Note that a ticket for the cathedral includes admission to its crypt, treasury and baptistery (Temple of Jupiter).

➡ Temple of Jupiter

(Jupiterov hram; Map p178; 10KN, free with cathedral ticket; ⊙8am-7pm Mon-Sat, 12.30-6.30pm Sun May-Oct, to 5pm Nov-Apr) Although it's now the cathedral's baptistery, this wonderfully intact building was originally an ancient Roman temple dedicated to the king of the gods. It still has its original barrel-vaulted ceiling and decorative frieze, although a striking bronze statue of St John the Baptist by Ivan Meštrović now fills the spot where Jupiter once stood. The font is made from 13th-century carved stones recycled from the cathedral's rood screen.

➡ Split City Museum

(Muzej grada Splita; Map p178; ☑021-360 171; www.mgst.net; Papalićeva 1; adult/child 22/12KN; ⊙8.30am-9pm Apr-Sep, 9am-5pm Tue-Sat, to 2pm Sun Oct-Mar) Built by Juraj Dalmatinac in the 15th century for one of the many noblemen who lived within the old town, the Large Papalić Palace is considered a fine example of late-Gothic style, with an elaborately carved entrance gate that proclaimed the importance of its original inhabitants. The interior has been thoroughly restored to house this museum, which has interesting displays on Diocletian's Palace and on the development of the city.

➡ Diocletian's Palace Substructure

(Supstrukcije Dioklecijanove palače; Map p178; www. mgst.net; Obala hrvatskog narodnog preporoda bb; adult/child 42/22KN; ⊙8.30am-9pm Apr-Sep, to 5pm Sun Oct, 9am-5pm Mon-Sat, to 2pm Sun Nov-Apr) The Bronze Gate of Diocletian's Palace once opened straight from the water into the palace basements, enabling goods to be unloaded and stored here. Now this former tradesman's entrance is the main way into the palace from the Riva. While the central part of the substructure is now a major thoroughfare lined with souvenir stalls, entry to the chambers on either side is ticketed.

Archaeological Museum   MUSEUM

(Arheološki muzej; ☑021-329 340; www.armus. hr; Zrinsko-Frankopanska 25; adult/child 20/10KN; ⊙9am-2pm & 4-8pm Mon-Sat Jun-Sep, closed Sat afternoon & Sun Oct-May) A treasure trove of classical sculpture and mosaics is displayed at this excellent museum, a short walk north of the town centre. Most of the vast collection originated from the ancient Roman settlements of Split and neighbouring Salona (p182) (Solin), and there's also some Greek pottery from the island of Vis. There are displays of jewellery and coins, and a room filled with artefacts dating from the Palaeolithic Age to the Iron Age.

Meštrović Gallery   GALLERY

(Galerija Meštrović; ☑021-340 800; www.mestrovic.hr; Šetalište Ivana Meštrovića 46; adult/child 40/20KN; ⊙9am-7pm Tue-Sun May-Sep, to 4pm Tue-Sun Oct-Apr) At this stellar art museum you'll see a comprehensive, well-arranged collection of works by Ivan Meštrović, Croatia's premier modern sculptor, who built the grand mansion as a personal residence in the 1930s. Although Meštrović intended to retire here, he emigrated to the USA soon after WWII. Admission includes entry to the nearby Kaštilac (☑021-340 800; Šetalište Ivana Meštrovića 39; ⊙9am-7pm Tue-Sun May-Sep), a fortress housing other Meštrović works.

Marjan Forest Park   PARK

(Park-šuma Marjan; www.marjan-parksuma.hr) Looming up to 178m over Split's western fringes, this nature reserve occupies a big space in Split's psyche. The views over the city and surrounding islands are extraordinary, and the shady paths provide a welcome reprieve from both the heat and the summertime tourist throngs. Trails pass through fragrant pine forests to scenic lookouts, a 16th-century Jewish cemetery, medieval chapels and cave dwellings once inhabited by Christian hermits. Climbers take to the cliffs near the end of the peninsula.

For an afternoon away from the city buzz, consider taking a long walk through the park and descending to Kašjuni beach (Šetalište Ivana Meštrovića bb) to cool off before catching the bus back.

Gallery of Fine Arts   GALLERY

(Galerija umjetnina Split; Map p178; ☑021-350 110; www.galum.hr; Kralja Tomislava 15; adult/child 40/20KN; ⊙10am-6pm Tue-Fri, to 2pm Sat & Sun) Housed in a building that was the city's first hospital (1792), this gallery exhibits 400

CROATIA SPLIT

WORTH A TRIP

SALONA

The ruins of the ancient city of **Salona** (☑021-213 358; Don Frane Bulića bb, Solin; adult/child 30/15KN; ☺9am-7pm Mon-Sat, to 2pm Sun), situated at the foot of the mountains just northeast of Split, are the most archaeologically important in Croatia. Start by paying your admission fee at **Tusculum**, near the northern entrance to the reserve. Built in 1898 by the site's ground-breaking archaeologist Monsignor Frane Bulić as a base for his research, it has a Roman-style drawing room with displays on the early archaeology undertaken here.

---

works of art spanning 700 years. Upstairs is the permanent collection – a chronological journey that starts with religious icons and continues with works by the likes of Paolo Veneziano, Albrecht Dürer and Guido Reni, alongside the work of locals such as Vlaho Bukovac, Ivan Meštrović and Cata Dujšin-Ribar. The temporary exhibits downstairs change every few months.

✨ Festivals & Events

Sudamja   RELIGIOUS

Festivities celebrating Split's patron saint, St Domnius (Sv Duje), start at the beginning of May. They include concerts, poetry readings, exhibitions and a rowing regatta. On the actual 7 May feast day (aka Split Day) there's a religious procession, Mass and fair on the Riva, with fireworks filling the skies.

Ultra Europe   MUSIC

(www.ultraeurope.com; Poljud Stadium; 3-day ticket from €129; ☺Jul) One of the world's largest electronic-music festivals takes over the city's Poljud stadium for three days in July before heading to the islands for the rest of Destination Ultra Croatia Music Week. People from across the world swarm to rave to the tunes of celebrity DJs.

🛏 Sleeping

Hostel Emanuel   HOSTEL €

(☑021-786 533; hostelemanuel@gmail.com; Tolstojeva 20; dm 222KN; ✳@🛜) This hip little hostel in a suburban apartment block has colourful interiors and a relaxed vibe. In the two dorms (one sleeping five, the other 10), each bunk has a large locker, curtains, a reading light and a power outlet.

Tchaikovsky Hostel   HOSTEL €

(☑021-317 124; www.tchaikovskyhostel.com; Čajkovskoga 4; dm 170-240KN; ✳@🛜) Hidden away in a residential block in the Dobri neighbourhood, this converted apartment has four tidy dorms with wooden bunks featuring built-in shelves. There's only one bathroom, and a small kitchen.

★Korta   APARTMENT €€

(Map p178; ☑021-571 226; www.kortasplit.com; Plinarska 31; apt from €94; ✳🛜) Set around a courtyard in the historic Veli Varoš neighbourhood, these simple but elegant apartments have stone-tiled bathrooms and white walls hung with huge TVs and photos of rustic Croatian scenes. Many have balconies.

Apartments Magdalena   APARTMENT €€

(Map p178; ☑098 423 087; www.magdalena-apartments.com; Milićeva 18; apt 465-611KN; ✳🛜) You may never want to leave Magdalena's top-floor apartment once you see the old-town view from the dormer window. The three apartments are comfortable and fully furnished, and the hospitality offered by the off-site owners is exceptional: beer and juice in the fridge, a back-up toothbrush in the cupboard and even a mobile phone with credit on it.

★Heritage Hotel
Antique Split   HERITAGE HOTEL €€€

(Map p178; ☑021-785 208; www.antique-split.com; Poljana Grgura Ninskog 1; r from €267; ✳🛜) Palace living at its most palatial, this boutique complex has eight chic rooms with stone walls and impressive bathrooms. In some you'll wake up to incredible views over the cathedral.

★Villa Split   B&B €€€

(Map p178; ☑091 40 34 403; www.villasplitluxury.com; Bajamontijeva 5; r from €215; P✳🛜) Set into the Roman-built wall of Diocletian's Palace, this wonderful boutique B&B has only three rooms, the best of which is the slightly larger one in the attic. If you're happy to swap the ancient for the merely medieval, there are six larger rooms in a 10th-century building on the main square.

Splendida Palace   BOUTIQUE HOTEL €€€

(☑021-838 485; www.splendidapalace.com; Rokova 26; r incl breakfast from €239; ☺Apr-Oct; P✳🛜🏊) Get in quick to secure one of the 10 rooms in this boutique family-run hotel, occupying a 19th-century house on a quiet side street. Rooms are named after Split landmarks, with large-scale black-and-white photographs to reinforce the theme. The breakfast is buffet-style and there's a small plunge pool in the rear courtyard.

✖ Eating

Kruščić   BAKERY €
(Map p178; ☑ 099 26 12 345; www.facebook.com/Kruscic.Split; Obrov 6; items 6-15KN; ☺ 8am-2pm) Spit's best bakery serves delicious bread, pastries and pizza slices. The focus is more savoury than sweet, although you'll find sweet things, too.

Gušt   PIZZA €
(Map p178; ☑ 021-486 333; www.pizzeria-gust.hr; Slavićeva 1; pizzas 40-62KN; ☺ 9am-11pm Mon-Sat) Split's diehard pizza fans swear by this joint – it's cheap and very local, serving delicious pizza with Neapolitan-style chewy bases. The stone and brick walls make it a cosy retreat in winter.

Makrovega   VEGETARIAN €
(Map p178; ☑ 021-394 440; www.makrovega.hr; Leština 2; mains 60-75KN; ☺ 11am-8pm Mon-Fri, 11am-5pm Sun; 🛜) Hidden away down a lane and behind a courtyard, this meat-free haven serves macrobiotic, vegetarian, vegan and some raw food. Seitan and tofu appear in pasta, curry and salads, and there are excellent cakes. It's somewhat lacking in atmosphere, though.

★ Konoba Fetivi   DALMATIAN, SEAFOOD €€
(Map p178; ☑ 021-355 152; www.facebook.com/KonobaFetivi; Tomića stine 4; mains 70-95KN; ☺ noon-11pm Tue-Sun) Informal and family-run, with a TV screening sports in the corner, Fetivi feels more like a tavern than most that bear the *konoba* name. However, that doesn't detract from the food, which is first rate. Seafood is the focus here. The cuttlefish stew with polenta is highly recommended, but the whole fish is wonderfully fresh, too.

★ Konoba Matejuška   DALMATIAN, SEAFOOD €€
(Map p178; ☑ 021-814 099; www.konobamatejuska.hr; Tomića Stine 3; mains 75-140KN; ☺ noon-11pm Apr-Oct, to 9pm Wed-Mon Nov-Mar) This cosy, rustic tavern, in an alleyway minutes from the seafront, specialises in well-prepared seafood – as epitomised in its perfectly cooked fish platter for two. The grilled squid is also excellent, served with the archetypal Dalmatian side dish, *blitva* (Swiss chard with slightly mushy potato, drenched in olive oil). Book ahead.

Villa Spiza   DALMATIAN €€
(Map p178; Kružićeva 3; mains 50-100KN; ☺ noon-midnight Mon-Sat) A locals favourite, just outside the walls of Diocletian's Palace, this low-key joint offers daily-changing, great-quality Dalmatian mainstays – calamari, risotto, veal – at reasonable prices. The restaurant is split into two spaces across from one another in the same street.

Restoran Perlica   CROATIAN, GRILL €€
(☑ 021-240 004; www.restoran-perlica.hr; Trg Grlo 1, Klis; mains 50-150KN; ☺ 9am-10pm; 🅿🛜♿) When Splićani are after a traditional feast of spit-roasted lamb they head for the hills – to Klis, to be exact. This roadside restaurant, founded in 1877, also serves omelettes, pasta, schnitzels and steaks, but skip straight to the 'Plata Perlica': a big smoky, fatty, garlicky heap of roast lamb, potatoes and vegetables. Combine it with a visit to Klis Fortress (p185).

★ Konoba Marjan   DALMATIAN, SEAFOOD €€€
(Map p178; ☑ 098 93 46 848; www.facebook.com/konobamarjan; Senjska 1; mains 84-160KN; ☺ noon-11pm Mon-Sat; 🛜) Offering great-quality Dalmatian fare, this friendly little Veli Varoš tavern features daily specials such as cuttlefish *brujet* (a flavour-packed seafood stew – highly recommended), *gregada* (fish stew with potato) and prawn pasta. The wine list is excellent, showcasing some local boutique wineries, and there are a few seats outside on the street leading up to Marjan Hill.

★ Zoi   MEDITERRANEAN €€€
(Map p178; ☑ 021-637 491; www.zoi.hr; Obala hrvatskog narodnog preporoda 23; mains 120-180KN; ☺ 6.30pm-midnight) Accessed by a discreet door on the waterfront promenade, this upstairs restaurant serves sophisticated modern Mediterranean dishes that look as divine as they taste. The decor is simultaneously elegant and extremely hip, with the exposed walls of Diocletian's Palace offset with bright bursts of magenta. Head up to the roof terrace for one of Split's most memorable dining spaces.

★ Portofino   ITALIAN €€€
(Map p178; ☑ 091 38 97 784; www.facebook.com/portofinosplit; Poljana Grgura Ninskog 7; mains 95-250KN; ☺ 5-11pm) Spilling onto a surprisingly quiet square at the heart of Diocletian's Palace, Portofino will charm the pants off you with its friendly service, elegant decor, complimentary *amuse-bouches* and delicious

pasta dishes. Other specialities include steak and seafood.

🍷 Drinking & Entertainment

★ Marcvs Marvlvs Spalatensis
WINE BAR

(Map p178; www.facebook.com/marvlvs; Papalićeva 4; ⏰11am-midnight Jun-Aug, to 11pm Mon-Sat Sep-May; 📶) Fittingly, the 15th-century Gothic home of the 'Dante of Croatia', Marko Marulić, now houses this wonderful little 'library jazz bar' made up of small rooms crammed with books and frequented by ageless bohemians, tortured poets and wistful academics. Cheese, chess, cards and cigars are all on offer, and there's often live music.

★ Paradox
WINE BAR

(Map p178; ✆021-787 778; www.paradox.hr; Bana Josipa Jelačića 3; ⏰8am-midnight; 📶) This stylish wine and cheese bar has a fantastic rooftop terrace, a massive selection of Croatian wines (more than 120, including 40 by the glass) and a variety of local cheeses to go with them. The clued-up staff members really know their stuff, and there's live music most weekends.

St Riva
BAR

(Map p178; Obala hrvatskog narodnog preporoda 18; ⏰7am-midnight; 📶) Bad techno and tacky cocktails don't stop St Riva being a great place to hang out. Grab a perch on the narrow terrace built into the walls of Diocletian's Palace and watch the mayhem on the Riva below. Later in the night, a fair bit of booty-shaking happens in the small, clubby space inside.

Academia Ghetto Club
BAR, CLUB

(Map p178; ✆099 6718308; Dosud 10; ⏰4pm-midnight; 📶) Split's most bohemian bar has an ancient Roman walls, a large courtyard with a trickling fountain, a chandelier-bedecked piano lounge and a small red-walled club space with poetry on the walls. The music is great, but the service can be shockingly bad.

D16
CAFE

(Map p178; ✆091 79 00 705; www.d16coffee.com; Dominisova 16; ⏰7am-7pm Mon-Sat, 9am-7pm Sun; 📶) D16's baristas are serious about coffee and they've got the beards to prove it. Hidden away in the back lanes of Diocletian's Palace, this hip little speciality roaster is your best bet for a superbly executed flat white, cold brew or espresso with almond milk. Just be prepared to pay double the price you'd pay at a local-style cafe.

Croatian National Theatre Split
THEATRE

(Hrvatsko narodno kazalište Split; Map p178; ✆021-306 908; www.hnk-split.hr; Trg Gaje Bulata 1) Theatre, opera, ballet and concerts are presented at this gorgeous theatre, built in 1891. Tickets can be bought at the box office or online.

ℹ Information

MEDICAL SERVICES

KBC Split (Klinički bolnički centar Split; ✆021-556 111; www.kbsplit.hr; Spinčićeva 1) Hospital.

TOURIST INFORMATION

Split's tourist offices stock the free 72-hour **Split Card**, which offers free or discounted access to attractions, car rental, restaurants, shops and theatres. You're eligible for the card if you're staying in Split more than four nights from April to September, or staying in designated hotels for more than two nights at other times.

Tourist Office Peristil (Map p178; ✆021-345 606; www.visitsplit.com; Peristil bb; ⏰8am-9pm Jun-Sep, 8am-8pm Mon-Sat, to 5pm Sun Apr, May & Oct, 9am-4pm Mon-Fri, to 2pm Sat Nov-Mar)

Tourist Office Riva (Map p178; ✆021-360 066; www.visitsplit.com; Obala hrvatskog narodnog preporoda 9; ⏰8am-9pm Jun-Sep, 8am-8pm Mon-Sat, to 5pm Sun Apr, May & Oct, 9am-4pm Mon-Fri, to 2pm Sat Nov-Mar)

ℹ Getting There & Away

The bus, train and ferry terminals are clustered on the eastern side of the harbour, a short walk from the old town.

AIR

Split Airport (SPU, Zračna luka Split; ✆021-203 555; www.split-airport.hr; Dr Franje Tuđmana 1270, Kaštel Štafilić) is in Kaštela, 24km northwest of central Split. In summer dozens of airlines fly here from all over Europe (including Austrian Airlines, British Airways, easyJet, Norwegian Air Shuttle and Scandinavian Airlines), but only Croatia Airlines, Eurowings and Trade Air fly year-round.

BOAT

Split's ferry harbour is extremely busy and can be hard to negotiate, so you're best to arrive early. Most domestic ferries depart from Gat Sv Petra, the first of the three major piers, which has ticket booths for both Jadrolinija and Kapetan Luka. The giant international ferries depart from Gat Sv Duje, the second of the piers, where there's a large ferry terminal with ticketing offices for the major lines. In July and August, and at weekends, it's often necessary to appear hours before departure for a car ferry,

KLIS FORTRESS

Controlling the valley leading into Split, the imposing **Klis Fortress** (Tvrđava Klis; ☎ 021-240 578; www.tvrdavaklis.com; Klis bb; adult/child 40/15KN; ⊙ 9.30am-4pm) spreads along a limestone bluff, reaching 385m at its highest point. Its long and narrow form (304m by 53m) derives from constant extensions over the course of millennia. Inside, you can clamber all over the fortifications and visit the small museum, which has displays of swords and costumes and detailed information on the castle's brutal past.

Klis' real history (in a nutshell) goes like this: founded by the Illyrians in the 2nd century BC; taken by the Romans; became a stronghold of medieval Croatian duke Trpimir; resisted attacks for 25 years before falling to the Turks in 1537; briefly retaken in 1596; finally fell to the Venetians in 1648. *Game of Thrones* fans will probably recognise the fortress as Meereen, where Daenerys Targaryen had all those nasty slave-masters crucified in season four. If you're having trouble visualising it, there's a room with stills from the show to jog your memory.

Klis is located 12km northeast of the city centre, and can be reached by city bus 22 (13KN) from Trg Gaje Bulata or Split's local bus station.

and put your car in the line for boarding. There is rarely a problem or a long wait obtaining a space in the low season.

Jadrolinija (☎ 021-338 333; www.jadrolinija. hr; Gat Sv Duje bb) operates most of the ferries between Split and the islands.

➡ Car ferry services per person/car include **Stari Grad on Hvar** (47/310KN, two hours, up to seven daily), **Supetar on Brač** (33/154KN, 45 minutes, up to 14 daily) and **Vela Luka on Korčula** (60/470KN, 2¾ hours, two daily).

➡ Summertime catamaran destinations include **Bol on Brač** (55KN to 80KN, one hour, two daily), **Dubrovnik** (210KN, six hours, daily), **Hvar Town** (55KN to 110KN, one to two hours, up to eight daily) and **Korčula Town** (160KN, 3¾ hours, daily).

Kapetan Luka (Krilo; ☎ 021-645 476; www. krilo.hr) has the following high-speed catamaran services.

➡ Daily to **Hvar** (90KN, one hour) and **Korčula** (130KN, 2½ hours) twice daily June to September.

➡ From April to October, an additional daily boat to **Hvar,** twice daily May to September.

➡ From May to mid-October, daily to **Hvar, Korčula** (130KN, 2¼ hours), **Pomena on Mljet** (140KN, three hours) and **Dubrovnik** (210KN, 4¼ hours).

➡ From June to September, daily to **Bol on Brač** (80KN, 50 minutes), **Makarska** (100KN, 1½ hours), **Korčula** (130KN, 2¾ hours), **Sobra on Mljet** (140KN, four hours) and **Dubrovnik** (210KN, five hours).

BUS

Most intercity and international buses arrive at and depart from the **main bus station** (Autobusni Kolodvor Split; ☎ 060 327 777; www. ak-split.hr; Obala kneza Domagoja bb) beside the harbour. In summer it's best to purchase

bus tickets with seat reservations in advance. If you need to store bags, there's a **garderoba** (left-luggage office; Obala kneza Domagoja 12; 1st hour 5KN, additional hours 1.50KN; ⊙ 6am-10pm May-Sep) nearby.

Domestic destinations include Zagreb (157KN, five hours, at least hourly), Pula (300KN, 10 hours, five daily), Rijeka (244KN, eight hours, eight daily), Zadar (90KN, three hours, at least hourly) and Dubrovnik (127KN, 4½ hours, at least 11 daily). Note that Split–Dubrovnik buses pass briefly through Bosnian territory, so keep your passport handy.

CAR & MOTORCYCLE

Various car-hire companies have desks at the airport, including **Dollar Thrifty** (☎ 021-399 000; www.subrosa.hr; Trumbićeva obala 17), which also has a city office. You can also rent cars, scooters and motorbikes through **Daluma Travel** (☎ 021-338 424; www.daluma-travel.hr; Obala kneza Domagoja 1) and **Split Rent Agency** (Map p178; ☎ 091 59 17 111; www.split-rent. com; Obala Lazareta 3).

TRAIN

Trains head to **Split Train Station** (Željeznica stanica Split; ☎ 021-338 525; www.hzpp.hr; Obala kneza Domagoja 9; ⊙ 6am-10pm) from Zagreb (194KN, 6½ hours, four daily). The station has lockers (15KN per day) that will fit suitcases, but you can't leave bags overnight. There's another **garderoba** (☎ 098 446 780; Obala kneza Domagoja 5; per day 15KN; ⊙ 6am-10pm Jul & Aug, 7.30am-9pm Sep-Jun) nearby, out on the street.

ℹ Getting Around

TO/FROM THE AIRPORT

Airport Shuttle Bus (☎ 021-203 119; www. plesoprijevoz.hr; one way 30KN) Makes the

30-minute journey between the airport and Split's main bus station (platform 1) at least 14 times a day.

City buses 37 & 38 The regular Split–Trogir bus stops near the airport every 20 minutes. The journey takes 50 minutes from the local bus station (p186) on Domovinskog Rata, making it a slower option than the shuttle but also cheaper (17KN from Split, 13KN from Trogir).

Taxi A cab to central Split costs between 250KN and 300KN.

BUS

Promet Split (☑ 021-407 888; www.promet-split.hr) operates local buses on an extensive network throughout Split (per journey 11KN) and as far afield as Klis (13KN), Solin (13KN) and Trogir (17KN). You can buy tickets on the bus, but if you buy from the **local bus station** or from a kiosk, a two-journey (ie return, known as a *duplo*) central-zone ticket costs only 17KN. Buses run about every 15 minutes from 5.30am to 11.30pm.

Makarska Riviera

☑ 021

The Makarska Riviera is a 58km stretch of coast at the foot of the Biokovo mountain range, where a series of cliffs and ridges forms a dramatic backdrop to a string of beautiful pebbly beaches. The foothills are protected from harsh winds and covered with lush Mediterranean greenery, including pine forests, olive groves and fruit trees.

If you're mainly interested in a beach holiday without too many historical sights to distract you, the crystal-clear waters of this strip are hard to beat. However, this is one of the most developed stretches of the Dalmatian coast, and popular with package tours. Note that in July and August the entire riviera is jam-packed with holidaymakers, and many hotels impose a seven-night minimum stay.

Makarska's harbour and historic centre are located on a large cove bordered by Cape Osejava in the southeast and the Sveti Petar peninsula in the northwest. The long pebble town beach, lined with hotels, stretches from the Sveti Petar park northwest along the bay. For a party atmosphere, head past the town beach to Buba beach, near the Hotel Rivijera, where music pumps all day during summer. To the southeast are rockier and lovelier beaches, such as Nugal, popular with nudists.

Punta Rata BEACH
Brela's best beach, Punta Rata is a gorgeous spit of pebbles and pines about 300m northwest of the town centre.

Biokovo Nature Park NATURE RESERVE
(Park Prirode Biokovo; www.biokovo.com; adult/child 50/25KN; ⊙7am-8pm mid-May–Sep, 8am-4pm Apr–mid-May & Oct–mid-Nov) The limestone Biokovo massif offers wonderful hiking opportunities. If you're hiking independently, you have to enter the park at the beginning of Biokovska – the main road that runs up the mountain – and buy an admission ticket there.

Wine Club Croatia WINE
(☑ 091 57 70 053; www.wineclubcroatia.com; workshop 300KN) Enthusiastic and charming wine expert Daniel Čečavac hosts these excellent wine-tasting events in the Park and Osejava hotels (as well as in Baška Voda and Split), pairing five top-notch vintages with local food specialities. He also leads private wine, food and sightseeing tours (two to eight people) to the Pelješac Peninsula (1650KN), Vrgorac (1250KN) and Imotski (850KN).

Makarska and Brela have good accommodation options, but there are large package-holiday resorts and holiday apartments spread all along the coast. If you're travelling in July or August, book well ahead and be prepared for minimum-stay requirements.

★**Maritimo** HOTEL €€€
(☑ 021-679 041; www.hotel-maritimo.hr; Cvitačke 2a; r from 930KN; P❋@☎) Right by the beach, this excellent hotel has friendly staff and modern rooms with fridges, safes, good bathrooms and balconies with sea views. Breakfast on the terrace by the water is a blissful way to start the day.

❶ Getting There & Away

BOAT

Jadrolinija (☑ 021-679 515; www.jadrolinija.hr; Obala kralja Tomislava 15) operates the following car ferries.

➔ Makarska to Sumartin on Brač (passenger/car 30/150KN, one hour) three times daily, increasing to four times in June and September, five times in July and August. Note: bus connections to/from Sumartin are infrequent.

➔ Drvenik to Sućuraj on Hvar (passenger/car 16/108KN, 35 minutes, at least six daily). Note: bus services to/from Sućuraj are extremely limited.

From June to September Kapetan Luka (p185) has a daily high-speed catamaran between Makarska and Dubrovnik (160KN, 3¼ hours), Sobra on Mljet (140KN, 2¼ hours), Korčula Town (130KN, one hour), Bol on Brač (90KN, 35 minutes) and Split (100KN, 1½ hours).

BUS

Makarska is the main transport hub, but most coastal services stop in all the villages and towns along the way. From Makarska there are buses to Dubrovnik (105KN, three hours, eight daily), Split (50KN, 1¼ hours, at least hourly), Šibenik (100KN, three hours, at least four daily), Rijeka (275KN, seven hours, two daily) and Zagreb (175KN, six hours, 10 daily).

Brač Island

021 / POP 14,500

Brač is famous for two things: its radiant white stone, used to build Diocletian's Palace in Split (and, depending on whom you believe, the White House in Washington) and Zlatni Rat, the pebbly beach at Bol that extends languidly into the Adriatic and adorns 90% of Croatia's tourism posters.

It's the largest island in central Dalmatia, with several towns and villages, and a dramatic landscape of steep cliffs, inky waters and pine forests. The interior is scattered with piles of rocks – the result of the back-breaking labour of women who, over hundreds of years, gathered the rocks to clear land for vineyards and orchards. The tough living conditions meant that, over time, a lot of people moved to the mainland for work, leaving the interior almost deserted.

The two main centres, Supetar and Bol, are quite different: Supetar is pleasant if unassuming, while Bol revels in its more exclusive appeal.

🛈 Getting Around

➡ Supetar is the hub for bus transport around the island. Destinations include Milna (30KN, 30 minutes, five daily), Škrip (24KN, 15 minutes, three daily), Pučišća (30KN, 35 minutes, five daily), Bol (43KN, one hour, five daily) and Sumartin (43KN, 1¼ hours, three daily). Services increase in summer and reduce on Sunday.

➡ From Bol, services are much more limited. Aside from the Supetar buses, there are connections to Pučišća (30KN, 35 minutes, three daily).

➡ A car is useful for exploring the smaller settlements on the island. If you want to avoid

the car-ferry charges, it's easy enough to hire a car or scooter from travel agencies in Supetar or Bol when you arrive.

Bol

POP 1630

Gathered around a compact marina, the old town of Bol is an attractive place made up of small stone houses and winding streets dotted with pink and purple geraniums. While it's short on actual sights, many of its buildings are marked with interpretative panels explaining their cultural and historical significance.

The town's major attraction is Zlatni Rat, the seductive pebbly beach that stretches into the Adriatic and draws crowds of swimmers and windsurfers in summer. A long coastal promenade lined with pine trees, sculptures and gardens connects the beach with the old town. Bol is a buzzing place in summer – one of Croatia's favourites – and perennially packed with tourists.

⊙ Sights

★ **Zlatni Rat** BEACH

Croatia's most photographed beach extends like a tongue into the sea for about 400m. Despite the hype and constant crowds, the 'golden cape' is a gorgeous place. Made up of smooth white pebbles, its elegant tip is constantly shuffled by the wind and waves. Pine trees provide shade and rocky cliffs rise sharply behind it, making the setting one of the loveliest in Dalmatia. There's a small nudist section immediately west of the cape.

Stina WINERY

(☑ 021-306 220; www.stina-vino.hr; Riva bb; tastings 75-295KN; ⊙ 11am-7pm Apr, to 9pm May & Oct, to midnight Jun-Sep) This local winery operates a slick, modern tasting room in the First Dalmatian Wine Co-op warehouse (built in 1903), right on the waterfront. Call in at 5pm for a 30-minute tour and leisurely tasting of its top drops, including indigenous Croatian varietals *pošip, vugava, tribidrag* and *plavac mali*. Otherwise, just drop by for a glass of wine in elegant surrounds.

Branislav Dešković Art Gallery GALLERY

(Galerija umjetnina Branislav Dešković; ☑ 021-637 092; Trg Sv Petra 1; adult/child 15/5KN; ⊙ 9am-noon & 6-11pm Tue-Sun Jul & Aug, 9am-3pm Tue-Sat Sep-Jun) Housed in a Renaissance-baroque town house right on the seafront, this excellent gallery displays paintings and sculptures by 20th-century Croatian artists. It's a

DON'T MISS

BLACA HERMITAGE & VIDOVA GORA

Two of Brač's most extraordinary sights lie nestled in the mountains between Nerežišća and the south coast. If you've got your own wheels, they can easily be combined into one trip; look for the signposted turn-off from the main road 4km southeast of Nerežišća.

The journey to **Blaca Hermitage** (Pustinje Blaca; ☑ 091 51 64 671; adult/child 40/10KN; ⊙ 9am-5pm Tue-Sun Jul & Aug, to 3pm Tue-Sun Sep-Jun) is a large part of the experience, involving a rough drive along a narrow, unsealed road and then a 2.5km walk down a steep path (good shoes are recommended).

Things can't have looked too different on the approach to this remote mountain cleft when a small group of priests and their servants, on the run from the Ottoman Turks on the mainland, arrived here in 1551. They initially took shelter in a cave (the walls of which are still visible in the kitchen) and built out from there. You can now take an informative 30-minute tour of the complex, which is full of original furniture, tools and rare manuscripts.

By the 18th century the hermitage ministered to three remote villages, with the priests operating a school from one of the rooms. The school closed in 1963 with the death of the hermitage's last resident priest, the extraordinary Fr Nikola Miličević, who was also a poet and an astronomer of international repute.

If you don't have your own transport, you can arrange a boat from Bol to the bottom of the valley and take a somewhat longer walk up. Otherwise, enquire at the tourist office (p189) about tours.

Vidova Gora is easily reached by a good sealed road through a pine forest, or you can sweat your way up from Bol on foot (two hours) or by mountain bike. At 778m, it's the highest point on the Adriatic islands and the view from the top is astounding. From here the entire island of Hvar is spread out like a map, with Vis and the mountains of the Pelješac Peninsula and Biokovo filling the horizon.

---

surprisingly prestigious collection for such a small town, including works by such luminaries as sculptor Ivan Meštrović and expressionist painter Ignjat Job. The gallery is named after Brač-born Dešković (1883–1939), a sculptor who became famous for his depictions of animals – look for his *Scratching Dog* in the courtyard.

🏃 Activities

Bol is a windsurfing hot spot. Alternatively, if you fancy a challenging **hike**, try the two-hour walk up to Vidova Gora or the four-hour track to Blaca Hermitage. There are also **mountain-biking** trails leading up. The local tourist office (p189) can give you advice and basic maps.

Big Blue Diving   DIVING
(☑ 098 425 496; www.big-blue-diving.hr; Hotel Borak, Zlatnog rata 42; dives with/without equipment 330/220KN; ⊙ 9am-7pm mid-Apr–Oct) Offers introductory courses and has daily trips for qualified divers to sites including reefs, caves and the remains of a submerged Roman villa with mosaics.

Nautic Center Bol   BOATING
(☑ 098 361 651; www.nautic-center-bol.com; Zlatnog rata 9a; ⊙ Jun-Oct) Rents boats from the beach in front of the Bretanide Hotel and offers parasailing, as well as excursions to Hvar, Korčula and Biševo's Blue Grotto.

🛏 Sleeping

Villa Ana   APARTMENT €
(☑ 021-635 022; www.villa-ana-bol.com; David 55a; apt from €51; P❄🌐🏊) A warm welcome awaits at this friendly, family-run set of apartments on the eastern fringes of Bol. The simple but well-equipped units are spread across two blocks, with a small swimming pool and hot tub in between.

Hostel Bol   HOSTEL €€
(☑ 091 50 32 271; www.facebook.com/Hostel Bol; Podan glavica 1d; dm/r from 156/466KN; ⊙ May-Sep; P❄🌐🏊) Even the dorms get their own bathrooms in this well-run, custom-built hostel, right in the heart of the old town. Some of the private rooms have wonderful sea views, and there's even a small indoor pool and a terrace with an outdoor kitchen.

Hotel Bol
BOUTIQUE HOTEL €€€

(☑021-635 660; www.hotel-bol.com; Hrvatskih domobrana 19; r/ste from €137/215; P❄🖥🐕) There's an olive theme running through this contemporary boutique hotel – and we're not just talking about the colour scheme: potted trees grace the balconies and oversized fruit hang on the walls. It's a very slick set-up, with swish rooms (many with sea views), a sauna and a small gym.

🍴 Eating & Drinking

Taverna Riva
DALMATIAN €€€

(☑021-635 236; www.tavernariva-bol.com; Frane Radića 5; mains 95-370KN; ☺noon-3pm & 6-10pm Mar-Oct; 🖉) Bol's most upmarket and expensive restaurant serves fancy Frenchified versions of Dalmatian dishes, including a delicious fish soup, creamy seafood pastas, gnocchi with truffles, lobster and a selection of steaks. Try to leave room for the walnut semifreddo. It's located on a pretty terrace right above the *riva* (seafront promenade).

Varadero
COCKTAIL BAR

(☑091 23 33 471; www.facebook.com/Varadero. Bol; Frane Radića 1; ☺8am-2am May-Nov; 🐕) At this open-air cocktail bar on the seafront you can sip coffee and fresh OJ under straw umbrellas during the day; return in the evening for fab cocktails, DJs and lounging on sofas and armchairs.

ℹ Information

Tourist Office (☑021-635 638; www.bol.hr; Porat Bolskih Pomoraca bb; ☺8.30am-10pm Jul & Aug, 8.30am-2pm & 4-8pm Jun & Sep, 8.30am-2pm & 4-8pm Mon-Sat May & Oct, 8.30am-2pm Mon-Fri Nov-Apr) Housed in a 15th-century Gothic town house, Bol's helpful tourist office is a good source of information on events, sights and activities.

ℹ Getting There & Away

Jadrolinija (☑021-631 357; www.jadro linija.hr; Hrvatskih velikana bb) runs a daily high-speed catamaran between Bol and Split (55KN, one hour). From June to September there's a second daily catamaran from Split (80KN, one hour), Hvar (80KN, 50 minutes), Korčula (130KN, 2½ hours), Makarska (90KN, 35 minutes) and Dubrovnik (210KN, 4¾ hours). Buy your ticket in advance, as these can sell out quickly in high season.

From June to September Kapetan Luka (p185) also runs a fast boat to Bol from Dubrovnik (210KN, four hours), Sobra on Mljet (140KN, three hours), Korčula (120KN, 1¾ hours) and Split (80KN, 50 minutes).

➡ Buses head to the car ferry at Supetar (43KN, one hour, five daily). Services increase in summer and reduce on Sunday.

➡ There's a taxi boat from the harbour to Zlatni Rat (15KN).

Hvar Island
☑021 / POP 11,080

Long, lean Hvar is vaguely shaped like the profile of a holidaymaker reclining on a sunlounger, which is altogether appropriate for the sunniest spot in the country (2724 sunny hours each year) and its most luxurious beach destination.

Hvar Town offers swanky hotels, elegant restaurants and a general sense that, if you care about seeing and being seen, this is the place to be. Rubbing shoulders with the posh yachties are hundreds of young partygoers, dancing on tables at the town's legendary beach bars. The northern coastal towns of Stari Grad and Jelsa are far more subdued and low-key.

Hvar's interior hides abandoned ancient hamlets, craggy peaks, vineyards and the lavender fields that the island is famous for. This region is worth exploring on a day trip, as is the island's southern coast, which has some of Hvar's most beautiful and isolated coves.

Hvar Town
POP 4260

The island's hub and busiest destination, Hvar Town is estimated to draw around 20,000 people a day in the high season. It's amazing that they can all fit in the small bay town, where 13th-century walls surround beautifully ornamented Gothic palaces and traffic-free marble streets, but fit they do.

Visitors wander along the main square, explore the sights on the winding stone streets, swim at the numerous beaches or pop off to the Pakleni Islands to get into their birthday suits – but most of all they come to party. Hvar's reputation as Croatia's premier party town is well deserved.

There are several good restaurants, bars and hotels here, but thanks to the island's appeal to well-heeled guests, the prices can be seriously inflated. Don't be put off if you're on a more limited budget, though, as private accommodation and multiple hostels cater to a younger, more diverse crowd.

◉ Sights

Trg Sv Stjepana
SQUARE

(St Stephen's Sq) Stretching from the harbour to the cathedral, this impressive rectangular square was formed by filling in an inlet that once reached out from the bay. At 4500 sq metres, it's one of the largest old squares in Dalmatia. Hvar Town's walled core, established in the 13th century, covers the slopes to the north. The town didn't spread south until the 15th century.

Fortica
FORTRESS

(Tvrđava Španjola; ☑021-742 608; Biskupa Jurja Dubokovica bb; adult/child 40/20KN; ⊙8am-9pm Apr-Oct) Looming high above the town and lit with a golden glow at night, this medieval castle occupies the site of an ancient Illyrian settlement dating from before 500 BC. The views looking down over Hvar and the Pakleni Islands are magnificent, and well worth the trudge up through the old-town streets. Once you clear the town walls it's a gently sloping meander up the tree-shaded hillside to the fortress – or you can drive to the very top (100KN in a taxi).

⚡ Activities

Most of the swimming spots on the promenade heading west from the centre are tiny, rocky bays, some of which have been augmented with concrete sunbathing platforms. Wander along and take your pick, but check the prices before you settle on a lounger, as some are stupidly expensive (325KN per day at the historic Bonj Les Bains beach club, for instance).

If you don't mind a hike, there are larger pebbly beaches in the opposite direction. A 30-minute walk south and then east from the centre will bring you to the largest of them, Pokonji Dol. From here, a further 25 minutes via a scenic but rocky path will bring you to secluded Mekićevica.

Otherwise, grab a taxi boat to the Pakleni Islands or to one of the beaches further east along the coast such as Milna and Zaraće. Dubovica is particularly recommended: a tiny cluster of stone houses and a couple of cafe-bars set on a gorgeous grin of beach. The juxtaposition of the white pebbles alongside the brilliant blue-green water is dazzling. If you have your own wheels you can park on the highway, not far from where it turns inland towards the tunnel, and reach Dubovica via a rough stony path.

Hvar Adventure
ADVENTURE SPORTS

(☑021-717 813; www.hvar-adventure.com; Jurja Matijevića 20; ⊙Apr-Sep) This agency is a one-stop shop for active travellers, offering kayaking, sailing, cycling, climbing, hiking, skydiving, 4WD safaris, triathlon training and, by way of a breather, wine tours.

🛏 Sleeping

Kapa
HOSTEL €

(☑091 92 41 068; karmentomasovic@gmail.com; Martina Vučetića 11; dm/r from €28/60; ⊙May-Oct; P❄🛜) The advantages of Kapa's south-end-of-town location are the spacious surrounds and the brilliant sunset views. It's run by a young brother-and-sister team, operating out of a large family house. Dorms sleep four to six people, and there are private doubles with their own bathrooms.

Jagoda & Ante Bracanović House
GUESTHOUSE €

(☑021-741 416; www.hvar-jagoda.com; Šime Buzolića Tome 21; r/apt 380/560KN) There are three tidy rooms and one apartment for rent in this large private house on a residential street with very quiet neighbours (it's next to the cemetery). Each room and apartment has its own fridge, balcony and bathroom, and there's a kitchen for guests to use.

Apartments Ana Dujmović
APARTMENT €€

(☑098 838 434; www.visit-hvar.com/apartments-ana-dujmovic; Biskupa Jurja Dubokovića 36; apt from €65; P❄🛜) This brace of comfortable holiday apartments is set behind an olive grove, only a 10-minute walk from the centre of town and, crucially, five minutes from the beach and the Hula-Hula bar. Call ahead and the delightful owner will pick you up from the town centre.

Apartments Komazin
APARTMENT €€

(☑091 60 19 712; www.croatia-hvar-apartments.com; Nikice Kolumbića 2; r/apt from €80/110; ❄🛜) With six bright apartments and two private rooms sharing a kitchen, bougainvillea-draped Komazin is an attractive option near the top of the private-apartment heap. What the apartments may lack in style they more than compensate for in size. And the host couldn't be more welcoming.

Apartments Ivanović
APARTMENT €€

(☑021-741 332; www.ivanovic-hvar.com; Ivana Buzolića 9; r/apt from €87/90; P❄🛜) This large, modern, three-storey house has one double room and five apartments for rent, all with balconies and bathrooms. The hostess speaks

English well and welcomes guests with a drink on the large grapevine-shaded terrace.

Violeta Hvar
APARTMENT €€

(☑ 099 33 44 779; ursa.lavanda@gmail.com; Biskupa Jurja Dubokovića 22; r/apt from €110/156; ❀) White walls are offset with large-scale island images in this stylish apartment block just above the town. All rooms and apartments have large balconies, and the top floor has sea views.

Old Town Hvar Apartments
APARTMENT €€€

(☑ 097 78 03 700; ivanaukic@net.hr; Matije Ivanića 10; apt €150; ❀ 📶) Hidden within Hvar's walled old town, this family-run place has three swish apartments. Apartments 1 and 2 share a 1st-floor terrace, while apartment 3 has a large one all of its own, with sublime views over the rooftops.

✕ Eating

Lola
STREET FOOD €€

(Sv Marak 10; mains 59-119KN; ⊙ 10am-2pm & 6pm-2am; 📶) Hit this buzzing hole-in-the-wall place for top-notch cocktails and a globetrotting range of tasty snacks: everything from empanadas and burgers to pulled-pork steamed buns and lamb curry. Grab a table on the lane and soak up the scene.

Mizarola
PIZZA €€

(☑ 098 799 978; www.facebook.com/mizarolahvar; Vinka Pribojevića 2; mains 55-180KN; ⊙ noon-midnight; 📶) Mizarola has a loyal local following, partly because it's one of the only places to open in the low season, but mainly because of its crowd-pleasing Neapolitan-style pizza. It serves other things (pasta, gnocchi, risotto, grilled meat, fish), but nothing rivals the main attraction. Head up to the roof terrace and tuck in.

Fig
CAFE €€

(☑ 099 26 79 890; www.figcafebar.com; Ivana Frane Biundovića 3; mains 65-100KN; ⊙ 10am-10pm May-Oct; 📶 📶) Run by an Aussie-Croat and an American, this great little place serves up delicious stuffed flatbreads (fig and ricotta, pear and gorgonzola, brie and prosciutto), vegetarian curries and a highly recommended Hvar breakfast: spiced eggs. There are even some vegan options – a rarity in these parts.

Dalmatino
DALMATIAN €€€

(☑ 091 52 93 121; www.dalmatino-hvar.com; Sv Marak 1; mains 80-265KN; ⊙ 11am-midnight Mon-Sat Apr-Nov; 📶) Calling itself a 'steak and fish house', this place is always popular – due,

in part, to the handsome waiters and the free-flowing *rakija* (grappa). Thankfully, the food is also excellent; try the *gregada* (fish fillet served on potatoes with a thick, broth-like sauce).

Grande Luna
DALMATIAN €€€

(☑ 021-741 400; www.grandeluna.hr; Petra Hektorovića 1; mains 75-180KN; ⊙ 11am-2.30pm & 5-10.30pm; 📶) Grande Luna's rooftop terrace doesn't offer views per se, unless you count the blue of the Dalmatian sky offset against the stone of the surrounding buildings. It's an atmospheric setting in which to try traditional dishes, such as *hvarska gregada* (fish stew) and *crni rižoto* (squid-ink risotto). The service is excellent, too.

▼ Drinking & Nightlife

Hula-Hula Hvar
BAR

(☑ 095 91 11 871; www.hulahulahvar.com; Šetalište Antuna Tomislava Petrića 10; ⊙ 9am-11pm Apr-Oct) *The* spot to catch the sunset to the sound of techno and house music, Hula-Hula is known for its après-beach party (4pm to 9pm), where all of young, trendy Hvar seems to descend for sundowner cocktails. Dancing on tables is pretty much compulsory.

Kiva Bar
BAR

(☑ 091 51 22 343; www.facebook.com/kivabar.hvar; Obala Fabrika 10; ⊙ 9pm-2am Apr-Dec) A happening place in an alleyway just off the waterfront, Kiva is packed to the rafters most nights, with patrons spilling out and filling up the lane. DJs spin a popular mix of old-school dance, pop and hip-hop classics to an up-for-it crowd.

3 Pršuta
WINE BAR

(Petra Hektorovića 5; ⊙ 6pm-2am May-Oct) Hvar's best wine bar is an unpretentious little place lurking in an alley behind the main square. Sink into the couch by the bar and feel as if you're in a local's living room while sampling some of the best island wines, paired with Dalmatian snacks.

Carpe Diem
COCKTAIL BAR

(☑ 021-742 369; www.carpe-diem-hvar.com; Obala Riva bb; ⊙ 9am-2am mid-May–Sep) Look no further – you have arrived at the mother of Croatia's glitzy coastal bars. From a groggy breakfast to (pricey) late-night cocktails, there's no time of day when this swanky place is dull. The house music spun by resident DJs is smooth, the drinks well mixed, and the crowd well heeled and jet-setting.

VIS ISLAND

Of all the inhabited Croatian islands, Vis is the furthest from the coast, and the most enigmatic. It spent much of its recent history serving as a Yugoslav military base, cut off from foreign visitors from the 1950s right up until 1989. International and local travellers alike now flock to Vis, seeking authenticity, nature, gourmet delights and peace and quiet. That's only set to increase, following the 2018 release of the movie *Mamma Mia! Here We Go Again*, filmed on the island.

Ancient **Vis Town** sits at the foot of a wide, horseshoe-shaped bay. Ferry arrivals give spurts of activity to an otherwise-peaceful collection of coastal promenades, crumbling 17th-century town houses and narrow lanes twisting gently uphill from the seafront. Vis' long and complicated history has bequeathed it the remains of a Greek cemetery, Roman baths and an English fortress. There are some good places to stay and some excellent restaurants, notably **Pojoda** (☑ 021-711 575; Don Cvjetka Marasovića 10, Kut; mains 50-115KN; ☉ noon-1am Mar-Oct, 6-10pm Nov-Feb; 🖭) and **Lola** (☑ 095 56 33 247; www.lolavis island.com; Matije Gupca 12, Luka; mains 140-170KN; ☉ 6pm-midnight May-Oct).

With a picturesque setting on a bay at the foot of Hum mountain, the town of **Komiža** has a somewhat bohemian, rough-around-the-edges ambience. Narrow backstreets lined with 17th- and 18th-century stone town houses meander up from the port, which has been used by fisherfolk since at least the 12th century. Most visitors head here to catch a boat to the otherworldly but always crowded **Blue Cave** (Modra špilja; adult/child Sep-Jun 70/35KN, Jul & Aug 100/50KN) on the nearby island of Biševo. Boat trips can be arranged through any of the local travel agencies, or simply by walking along the harbour.

While there are beaches scattered around Vis Town and Komiža, some of the island's best are a boat or scooter ride away. The most unspoilt beaches can be found on the southern and eastern sides of the island. Several require some steep downhill walking, so wear comfortable shoes. Tiny **Stiniva** is Vis' most perfect cove, lined with large, smooth pebbles, which blaze white against the blue sea. **Srebrna** has large white pebbles and clear water, and is backed with a nature reserve. Sandy **Milna** has strikingly blue water and several small islands forming an idyllic backdrop. Neighbouring **Zaglav** is even prettier and quieter.

Vis' gastronomic offering isn't limited to its main towns; the interior of the island and its isolated coves are becoming a foodie's dream. Set amid fields 8km south of Vis Town, **Roki's** (☑ 098 303 483; www.rokis.hr; Plisko Polje 17, Plisko Polje; peka per person 150KN; ☉ 7pm-midnight May-Oct) is one of the very best places to try food cooked under a traditional *peka* (metal dome). **Konoba Stončica** (☑ 021-784 7188; www.konoba-stoncica. com; Stončica 11; mains 60-140KN; ☉ 1-11pm May-Oct) is positioned on a pretty sandy beach, serving grilled squid and fish under the shade of palms, pines and a wooden pergola.

Two to three large **Jadrolinija** (☑ 021-711 032; www.jadrolinija.hr; Šetalište stare Isse 2, Luka) car ferries head between Vis Town and Split daily (per person/car 54/340KN, 2¼ hours). There's also a catamaran on this route (55KN, 1½ to 2½ hours, daily), which stops off at Hvar Town (40KN, 50 minutes) on Tuesdays.

ℹ️ Information

Emergency Clinic (Dom Zdravlja; ☑ 021-717 099; Biskupa Jurja Dubokovića 3) About 400m west of the town centre.

Tourist Office (☑ 021-741 059; www.tzhvar. hr; Trg Sv Stjepana 42; ☉ 8am-10pm Jul & Aug, 8am-8pm Mon-Sat, 8am-1pm & 4-8pm Sun Jun & Sep, 8am-2pm Mon-Fri, to noon Sat Oct-May) In the Arsenal building, right on Trg Sv Stjepana.

Tourist Office Information Point (☑ 021-718 109; Trg Marka Miličića 9; ☉ 8am-9pm Mon-

Sat, 9am-1pm Sun Jun-Sep) In the bus station; a summertime annex of the main tourist office.

ℹ️ Getting There & Away

BOAT

Jadrolinija (☑ 021-741 132; www.jadrolinija.hr; Obala Riva bb) operates the following high-speed catamarans.

➜ Daily from Split (55KN, one hour).

➜ From May to September, up to five times a day between Hvar Town and Split (110KN, one hour).

➜ From June to September, daily from Split (110KN, two hours), Bol (80KN, 50 minutes),

Korčula (120KN, 1½ hours) and Dubrovnik (210KN, 3½ hours).

Kapetan Luka (p185) tickets can be purchased from **Pelegrini Tours** (☑ 021-742 743; www.pelegrini-hvar.hr; Obala Riva 20) for the following catamaran services.

➡ Daily from Split (90KN, one hour) and Korčula (110KN, 1¼ hours) – twice daily June to September.

➡ From April to October, daily from Split – twice daily May to September.

➡ From May to mid-October, daily from Dubrovnik (210KN, three hours), Pomena on Mljet (140KN, 1¾ hours), Korčula (110KN, one hour) and Split.

BUS

Hvar Town's **bus station** (Trg Marka Miličića 9) is east of the main square. Buses head to/from the Stari Grad ferry port (27KN, 20 minutes, six daily). Left-luggage, laundry and toilet facilities are available at the **garderoba** (Trg Sv Stjepana bb; per 1/3/12/24hr 20/30/50/60KN; ☺7am-11pm Jun-Sep) on the edge of Trg Sv Stjepana.

❶ Getting Around

In summer taxi boats line Hvar's harbour, offering rides to the Pakleni Islands and isolated beaches further along the coast.

Korčula Island

☑ 020 / POP 15,600

Rich in vineyards, olive groves and small villages, and harbouring a glorious old town, the island of Korčula is the sixth-largest Adriatic island, stretching nearly 47km in length. Dense pine forests led the original Greek settlers to call the island Korkyra Melaina (Black Corfu). Quiet coves and small sandy beaches dot the steep southern coast while the northern shore is flatter and more pebbly.

Tradition is alive and kicking on Korčula, with age-old religious ceremonies, folk music and dances still being performed to the delight of an ever-growing influx of tourists. Oenophiles will adore sampling its wine. Arguably the best of all Croatian whites is produced from the indigenous grape *pošip*, particularly from the areas around the villages of Čara and Smokvica. The *grk* grape, cultivated around Lumbarda, also produces quality dry white wine.

The island's best beach is Pupnatska Luka on the south coast.

Korčula Town

POP 2860

Korčula Town is a stunner. Ringed by imposing defences, this coastal citadel is dripping with history, with marble streets rich in Renaissance and Gothic architecture.

Its fascinating fishbone layout was cleverly designed for the comfort and safety of its inhabitants: western streets were built straight in order to open the city to the refreshing summer *maestral* (strong, steady westerly wind), while the eastern streets were curved to minimise the force of the winter *bura* (cold, northeasterly wind).

The town cradles a harbour, overlooked by round defensive towers and a compact cluster of red-roofed houses. There are rustling palms all around and several beaches are an easy walk away.

◉ Sights & Activities

There are some excellent biking and hiking trails around Korčula; pick up an island map from the tourist office. In the summer, water taxis (p195) offer trips to **Badija Island**, which has a 15th-century Franciscan monastery, a restaurant and a naturist beach.

★**St Mark's Cathedral** CATHEDRAL
(Katedrala svetog Marka; Trg Sv Marka; church 10KN, bell tower adult/child 20/15KN; ☺9am-9pm Jul & Aug, hours vary Sep-Jun) Dominating the little square at Korčula's heart is this magnificent 15th-century cathedral, built from Korčula limestone in a Gothic-Renaissance style by Italian and local artisans. The sculptural detail of the facade is intriguing, particularly the naked squatting figures of Adam and Eve on the door pillars, and the two-tailed mermaid and elephant on the triangular gable cornice at the very top. The bell tower is topped by a balustrade and ornate cupola, beautifully carved by Korčulan Marko Andrijić.

St Mark's Abbey Treasury MUSEUM
(Opatska riznica svetog Marka; Trg Sv Marka; incl cathedral 25KN; ☺9am-7pm Mon-Sat May-Nov) The 14th-century Abbey Palace houses an important collection of icons and Dalmatian religious art. The most outstanding work is the 1431 polyptych of *The Virgin & Child with Saints* by Blaž Jurjev of Trogir. The 20th century is represented by a sketch by Ivan Meštrović and a painting by Đuro Pulitika. There are also liturgical items, jewellery, coins, furniture and ancient documents relating to the history of Korčula.

Korčula Town Museum
MUSEUM

(Gradski muzej Korčula; ☑ 020-711 420; www.gm-korcula.com; Trg Sv Marka 20; adult/child 20/8KN; ⊙9am-9pm Jul-Sep, 10am-1pm Oct-Jun) Occupying the 16th-century Gabriellis Palace, this museum traces the history and culture of Korčula throughout the ages. Displays cover stonemasonry, shipbuilding, archaeology, art, furniture, textiles and examples of Korčulan traditional dress. There are some interesting curios scattered over its four floors – including a tablet recording the Greek presence on the island in the 3rd century BC.

Icon Museum
MUSEUM

(Muzej ikona; Trg Svih Svetih; 15KN; ⊙9am-2pm Mon-Sat May-Sep) This modest museum has a collection of interesting Byzantine icons, painted on gilded wood, and 17th- and 18th-century ritual objects. The real highlight is access to gorgeous 15th-century **All Saints' Church** (Crkva Svih Svetih) next door. This baroque church features a 17th-century painted Cretan crucifix, an extraordinary late-18th-century pietà carved from walnut, and a carved and painted 1439 polyptych altarpiece by Blaž Jurjev of Trogir, considered a Croatian masterpiece.

City Defences
FORT

Korčula's towers and remaining city walls look particularly striking when approached from the sea, their presence warning pirates the town would be no pushover. Originally these defences would have been even more foreboding, forming a complete stone barrier against invaders that consisted of 12 towers and 20m-high walls.

🛏 Sleeping & Eating

Apartments DePolo
GUESTHOUSE €

(☑ 020-711 621; www.family-depolo.com; Sv Nikole 28; r 330KN; P✱🖥) A great budget option, these four simple but comfortable rooms have their own bathrooms and one has a terrace with amazing views. There's a 30% surcharge in the summer for short stays.

★ Korčula Royal Apartments
APARTMENT €€

(☑ 098 18 40 444; www.korcularoyalapartments.com; Trg Petra Šegedina 4; apt €90-115; ⊙May-Sep; ✱🖥) The setting for these smart, well-equipped apartments couldn't be better, occupying an old stone villa facing a little square by the water, just outside the old town.

Guest House Korunić
GUESTHOUSE €€

(☑ 020-715 108; www.guesthousekorunic.com; Hrvatske bratske zajednice 5; r €80; ✱🖥) This little guesthouse consists of three tidy en-suite rooms above the owner's house, one of which has its own kitchenette. They're not overly large, but there's a lovely roof terrace with views over the rooftops if you want to spread out.

Lešić Dimitri Palace
APARTMENT €€€

(☑ 020-715 560; www.ldpalace.com; Don Pavla Poše 1-6; apt from €446; ✱🖥) In a class of its own, this extraordinary place has five impeccable 'residences' in an 18th-century bishop's palace. All are themed after Marco Polo's journeys – China, India etc – while original features (including exposed beams, stone walls and flagstones) reflect the old-town setting.

Hotel Korsal
HOTEL €€€

(☑ 020-715 722; www.hotel-korsal.com; Šetalište Frana Kršinića 80; s/d from €147/194; ⊙May-Oct; ✱🖥) Korsal has 18 comfortable rooms spread among three neighbouring buildings near the marina. The two older blocks have been fully renovated and have sea views, while the new one is set back behind the others and has only partial views.

Marco's
DALMATIAN €€

(☑ 098 275 701; www.marcoskorcula.com; Kaparova 1; mains 65-115KN; ⊙9am-midnight mid-Apr–mid-Oct, 6-11pm Mon-Sat Mar–mid-Apr & mid-Oct–Dec) The hanging tentacles of filament lights over the bar and the big brass fixtures over the tables mark this out as one of Korčula's most fresh and fun restaurants. The menu joins the party, offering traditional specialities such as *žrnovski makaruni* (hand-rolled pasta) alongside the likes of burgers and couscous salads.

LD Terrace
DALMATIAN €€€

(☑ 020-601 726; www.ldrestaurant.com; Šetalište Petra Kanavelića bb; mains 190-240KN; ⊙8am-midnight Apr-Oct; 🖥) The LD stands for Lešić Dimitri and it's no surprise that Korčula's most elegant accommodation should also have its finest restaurant. The setting is magnificent, with a chic upstairs dining room as well as romantic tables set right above the water. The modern Dalmatian menu is well matched by a fine wine list, featuring many high-quality local drops.

🍷 Drinking & Entertainment

Vinum Bonum
WINE BAR

(☑ 091 47 70 236; Punta Jurana 66; ⊙6pm-midnight May-Oct; 🖥) Tucked away on a car-free lane just off the harbour, this casual place allows you to nibble on antipasti while you sample some of the island's best wine and *rakija* (grappa).

Moreška Cultural Club DANCE
(www.moreska.hr; Ljetno kino, Foša 2; 100KN; ☺ shows 9pm Mon & Thu Jul & Aug, shows 9pm Thu Jun & Sep) Enthusiastic townspeople perform the traditional Moreška sword dance, accompanied by a brass band, in an hour-long show. The event usually includes unaccompanied singing by a *klapa* (church-choir) group.

🛍 Shopping

Kutak Knjiga BOOKS
(☑020-716 541; http://kutak-knjiga.blogspot.co.nz; Kovački prolaz bb; ☺9.30am-8pm Mon-Fri May-Oct, to 1.30pm Nov-Apr) It's a mystery how Kutak crams books written in Croatian, English, French, Spanish, Czech, Italian, German, Polish, Swedish and Mandarin into such a small place. It stocks a good selection of Croatian classics translated into English.

ℹ Information

Atlas Korčula (☑020-711 060; www.atlas-korcula.com; Plokata 19 Travnja 1921 bb; ☺8am-8pm Mon-Sat, 8am-3pm Sun Jun-Sep, 8am-3pm Mon-Fri Oct-May) Books excursions and private accommodation, sells souvenirs and operates a currency exchange.

Health Centre (Dom zdravlja; ☑020-711 700; www.dom-zdravlja-korcula.hr; ul 57 br 5)

Tourist Office (☑020-715 701; www.visit korcula.eu; Obala dr Franje Tuđmana 4; ☺8am-8pm Jun-Aug, 8am-3pm Mon-Sat May, Sep & Oct, 8am-2pm Mon-Fri Nov-Apr)

ℹ Getting There & Away

Catamarans stop right by the old town, in the West Harbour, but the main car-ferry terminal is Dominče, 3km east of town. Water taxis depart from the marina to the south of the old town, heading to nearby islets and Lumbarda.

Jadrolinija (☑020-715 410; www.jadrolinija.hr; Plokata 19 travnja 1921 br 19) has car ferries between Orebić and Dominče (passenger/car 16/76KN, 15 minutes), departing roughly every hour (every 90 minutes from October to May). From June to September, a daily catamaran heads from West Harbour to Dubrovnik (130KN, two hours), Hvar (120KN, 1½ hours), Bol (130KN, 2¾ hours) and Split (160KN, 3¾ hours).

Kapetan Luka (☑021-645 476; www.krilo.hr) sails a catamaran to Hvar (110KN, 1¼ hours) and Split (130KN, 2½ hours) daily (twice daily in summer). From May to mid-October there's also a daily boat to/from Dubrovnik (130KN, 1¾

hours), Pomena on Mljet (80KN, 30 minutes), Hvar (110KN, one hour) and Split (130KN, 2¼ hours). From June to September there's another boat to Dubrovnik (130KN, two hours), Sobra on Mljet (80KN, 55 minutes), Makarska (130KN, one hour), Bol (120KN, 1¾ hours) and Split (130KN, 2¾ hours).

In July and August, **G&V Line** (☑020-313 119; www.gv-line.hr; Obala Ivana Pavla II 1, Gruž) has four catamarans per week to Korčula Town from Dubrovnik (90KN, 2½ hours), Polače on Mljet (50KN, 55 minutes) and Sobra (60KN, 1½ hours).

Elafiti Islands

☑020

A day trip to the islands in this archipelago northwest of Dubrovnik makes a perfect escape from the summer crowds. Out of 14 islands only the three largest – Koločep, Lopud and Šipan – are permanently inhabited. You can see all three in one day on a 'Three Islands & Picnic' tour, which is offered by operators that have desks at Dubrovnik's Old Harbour (expect to pay between 250KN and 300KN, including drinks and lunch).

Šipan ISLAND

At 16 sq km Šipan is the largest of the Elafiti Islands and was a favourite with the Dubrovnik aristocracy, who built houses here. Most ferries dock in Suđurađ, a little harbour lined with stone houses and the large fortified Skočibuha villa and tower, built in the 16th century (not open to the public). On the other side of the island, the village of Šipanska Luka has the remains of a Roman villa and a 15th-century Gothic duke's palace.

Lopud ISLAND

Car-free Lopud has the prettiest settlement of all the Elafitis, composed of stone houses surrounded by exotic gardens and overlooked by ruined fortresses. There's a little beach in the town, but you're better off walking across the spine of the island to beautiful sandy Šunj, where a little bar serves griddled fish. The walk takes about 25 minutes, or you can grab a ride in a golf cart for around 20KN.

Koločep ISLAND

The nearest of the Elafitis to Dubrovnik, this sweet island is inhabited by a mere 163 people and is covered in centuries-old pine forests, olive groves and orchards filled with orange and lemon trees. A sandy beach stretches out from the main village past a

MLJET ISLAND

Forest-shrouded Mljet is one of the most seductive of all the Adriatic islands. The establishment of a national park in 1960 at its western end put the island on the tourist map, but Mljet is anything but overrun. Visitors are almost entirely drawn to the tourist enclave around Pomena. The remainder of the island retains the unspoilt air of tranquillity that, according to legend, captivated Odysseus for seven years.

Although it covers 54 sq km of land and sea, including the entire westernmost quarter of the island, when most people talk of **Mljet National Park** (Nacionalni park Mljet; ☑ 020-744 041; www.np-mljet.hr; Pristanište 2; adult/child Jun-Sep 125/70KN, Oct-May 70/50KN; ☺ office 8am-8pm Apr-Oct) they're referring to the small section that's ticketed, taking in the gorgeous saltwater lakes Malo Jezero (Little Lake) and Veliko Jezero (Big Lake). The two are connected to each other by a short channel, while the larger one empties into the sea via the much longer Soline Channel, which makes the lakes subject to tidal flows. Tiny **Sveta Marija Island** lies on Veliko Jezero, not far from its southern shore. Boats (included in the park admission price) head here at least hourly during park opening hours. The island's Benedictine monastery was founded in 1198 but has been rebuilt several times, adding Renaissance and baroque features to the Romanesque structure.

The main hubs of the park are the small villages of **Pomena** and **Polače**, which are packed with visitors on summer days but quieten down again once all the boats leave. Kiosks in both villages sell park admission tickets. From Pomena it's a 400m walk along a forested path to Malo Jezero; from Polače, your ticket includes a transfer to Pristanište on Veliko Jezero, where there's a park information centre.

At Mljet's very eastern tip, the teensy village of **Saplunara** feels sublimely isolated – despite the views towards the bright lights of Dubrovnik. The main drawcards are a trio of sandy beaches and a couple of excellent guesthouses with restaurants attached: **Stermasi** (☑ 098 93 90 362; www.stermasi.hr; Saplunara 2; mains 70-190KN; ☺ 8am-midnight; ☎) and **Villa Mirosa** (☑ 099 19 96 270; www.villa-mirosa.com; Saplunara 26; r from €116; ☺ Mar-Dec; P ✳ 🛜 🏊).

Mljet has three ferry ports: Sobra, near the centre of the island, and Polače and Pomena in the national park. **Mini Brum** (☑ 099 61 15 574; www.rent-a-car-scooter-mljet. hr; ☺ 9am-7pm) rents basic cars (five/12/24 hours from 280/320/390KN) and scooters (five/12/24 hours from 190/220/250KN) from the ferry port in Sobra and from Polače. Bikes can easily be rented in Polače or Pomena (around 20KN per hour).

➡ The quickest connection from the mainland is the **Jadrolinija** (☑ 020-746 134; www. jadrolinija.hr; Zaglavac bb) car ferry from Prapratno to Sobra (passenger/car 28/140KN, 45 minutes, four to five daily).

➡ G&V Line (p195) has a catamaran between Sobra and Dubrovnik daily (55KN, 1¼ hours), stopping first at Šipanska Luka (30KN, 35 minutes). In June a second boat heads directly from Dubrovnik to Sobra and Polače daily. In July and August it also stops at Korčula (80KN, 55 minutes) four times a week.

➡ From May to mid-October **Kapetan Luka** (Krilo; ☑ 021-645 476; www.krilo.hr) has a daily boat to Pomena from Dubrovnik (80KN, 1¼ hours), Korčula (80KN, 30 minutes), Hvar (140KN, 1¾ hours) and Split (140KN, three hours). From June to September a second daily boat heads to Sobra from Dubrovnik (80KN, 55 minutes), Korčula (80KN, 55 minutes), Makarska (140KN, 2¼ hours), Bol (140KN, three hours) and Split (140KN, four hours).

large resort-style hotel. Continue around the corner and you'll reach a pretty but rocky nudist area.

⭐ **Hotel Božica**   HOTEL €€€
(☑ 020-325 400; www.hotel-bozica.hr; Ulica 13 1d, Suđurađ, Šipan; r/apt/ste from €160/290/390;

☺ May-Oct; P ✳ 🛜 🏊) If it's peace and quiet you're after, you could do a lot worse than this modern 30-room hotel on Šipan. Shuffle from the pool to the beach terrace and back again before plotting your next move. The restaurant perhaps? It also rents kayaks and bikes.

Obala DALMATIAN €€€
(☑ 020-759 170; www.obalalopud.com; Obala Iva Kuljevana 18, Lopud; mains 120-165KN; ◷ 10.30am-6pm Apr, to midnight May-Sep) The finest restaurant on Lopud, Obala has been known for its seafood delicacies since 1938. The prices are as fine as the service and the food, but the ambience surpasses it all; you'll be sitting close enough to the sea to dip your feet in. If in doubt, go for the fresh fish baked in salt, a local speciality.

❶ Getting There & Away

Aside from the numerous boat tours, there are regular ferries to the Elafitis from Dubrovnik's Gruž Harbour.

Jadrolinija (☑ 020-418 000; www.jadrolinija. hr; Obala Stjepana Radića 40, Gruž) has four ferries per day to Koločep (23KN, 30 minutes), Lopud (23KN, 55 minutes) and Suđurađ on Šipan (23KN, 1¼ hours); an additional seven to 10 car ferries per week also head to Suđurađ (23KN, one hour), with some stopping at Lopud (23KN, one hour) en route.

G&V Line (p195) has a daily catamaran connecting Šipanska Luka (on Šipan) to Dubrovnik (35KN, 50 minutes) and to Sobra on Mljet (30KN, 35 minutes).

Dubrovnik

☑ 020 / POP 28,500

Regardless of whether you are visiting Dubrovnik for the first time or the hundredth, the sense of awe never fails to descend when you set eyes on the beauty of the old town. Indeed it's hard to imagine anyone becoming jaded by the city's limestone streets, baroque buildings and the endless shimmer of the Adriatic, or failing to be inspired by a walk along the ancient city walls that protected the capital of a sophisticated republic for centuries.

Although the shelling of Dubrovnik in 1991 horrified the world, the city has bounced back with vigour to enchant visitors again. Marvel at the interplay of light on the old stone buildings; trace the peaks and troughs of Dubrovnik's past in museums replete with art and artefacts; take the cable car up to Mt Srđ; exhaust yourself climbing up and down narrow lanes – then plunge into the azure sea.

History

The story of Dubrovnik begins with the 7th-century onslaught of the Slavs, which had wiped out the Roman city of Epidaurum

(site of present-day Cavtat). Residents fled to the safest place they could find, which was the rocky islet of Ragusa, separated from the mainland by a narrow channel. Building walls was a matter of pressing urgency due to the threat of invasion; the city was well fortified by the 9th century when it resisted a Saracen siege for 15 months.

Dubrovnik came under Venetian authority in 1205, finally breaking away again in 1358. By the 15th century the Respublica Ragusina (Republic of Ragusa) had extended its borders to include the entire coastal belt from Ston to Cavtat, having previously acquired Lastovo Island, the Pelješac Peninsula and Mljet Island. Through canny diplomacy the city maintained good relations with everyone – even the Ottoman Empire, to which Dubrovnik began paying tribute in the 16th century.

Centuries of peace and prosperity allowed art, science and literature to flourish, but most of the Renaissance art and architecture in Dubrovnik was destroyed in the earthquake of 1667, which marked the beginning of the economic decline of the town. The final coup de grâce was dealt by Napoleon, whose troops entered Dubrovnik in 1808. The Vienna Congress of 1815 ceded Dubrovnik to Austria.

Dubrovnik was caught in the crosshairs of the war that followed Croatia's declaration of independence in 1991. For no obvious military or strategic reason, Dubrovnik was pummelled with some 2000 shells in 1991 and 1992 by the Yugoslav military, suffering considerable damage and loss of life.

◉ Sights

★ **City Walls & Forts** FORT
(Gradske zidine; Map p200; ☑ 020-638 800; www. wallsofdubrovnik.com; adult/child 200/50KN; ◷ 8am-6.30pm Apr-Oct, 9am-3pm Nov-Mar) No visit to Dubrovnik would be complete without a walk around the spectacular city walls, the finest in the world and the city's main claim to fame. From the top, the view over the old town and the shimmering Adriatic is sublime. You can get a good handle on the extent of the shelling damage in the 1990s by gazing over the rooftops: those sporting bright new terracotta suffered damage and had to be replaced.

★ **Srđ** VIEWPOINT
(Srđ bb) From the top of this 412m-high hill, Dubrovnik's old town looks even more

surreal than usual – like a scale model of itself or an illustration on a page. The views take in all of Dubrovnik and Lokrum, with the Elafiti Islands filling the horizon. It's this extraordinary vantage point that made Srđ a key battleground during the 1990s war. That story is told in **Dubrovnik During the Homeland War** (Dubrovnik u Domovinskom ratu; ☑020-324 856; Fort Imperial, Srđ; adult/child 30/15KN; ⏰8am-10pm; ℗), an exhibition housed in Fort Imperial at the summit.

The easiest and quickest way to get to the top is by cable car, or you can drive (follow the signs to Bosanka), walk via the **Way of the Cross** (Križni put; Jadranska cesta, Srđ), or catch bus 17 from the Pile stop to Bosanka and then walk the final 1.5km.

★**War Photo Limited**   GALLERY
(Map p200; ☑020-322 166; www.warphotoltd. com; Antuninska 6; adult/child 50/40KN; ⏰10am-10pm May-Sep, to 4pm Wed-Mon Apr & Oct) An immensely powerful experience, this gallery features compelling exhibitions curated by New Zealand photojournalist Wade Goddard, who worked in the Balkans in the 1990s. Its intention is to expose the everyday, horrific and unjust realities of war. There's a permanent exhibition on the upper floor devoted to the wars in Yugoslavia; the changing exhibitions cover a multitude of conflicts.

★**Rector's Palace**   PALACE
(Knežev dvor; Map p200; ☑020-321 497; www. dumus.hr; Pred Dvorom 3; adult/child 80/25KN; incl in multimuseum pass adult/child 120/25KN; ⏰9am-6pm Apr-Oct, to 4pm Nov-Mar) Built in the late 15th century for the elected rector who governed Dubrovnik, this Gothic-Renaissance palace contains the rector's office and private chambers, public halls, administrative offices and a dungeon. During his one-month term the rector was unable to leave the building without the permission of the senate. Today the palace has been turned into the **Cultural History Museum**, with artfully restored rooms, portraits, coats of arms and coins, evoking the glorious history of Ragusa.

Cathedral of the Assumption   CATHEDRAL
(Katedrala Marijina Uznesenja; Map p200; Držićeva poljana; treasury 20KN; ⏰8am-5pm Mon-Sat, 11am-5pm Sun Easter-Oct, 9am-noon & 4-5pm Mon-Sat Nov-Easter) Built on the site of a 7th-century basilica, Dubrovnik's original cathedral was enlarged in the 12th century, supposedly funded by a gift from England's King Richard I, the

Lionheart, who was saved from a shipwreck on the nearby island of Lokrum. Soon after the first cathedral was destroyed in the 1667 earthquake, work began on this, its baroque replacement, which was finished in 1713.

St Blaise's Church   CHURCH
(Crkva Sv Vlahe; Map p200; Luža Sq; ⏰8am-noon & 4-5pm Mon-Sat, 7am-1pm Sun) Dedicated to the city's patron saint, this exceptionally beautiful church was built in 1715 in the ornate baroque style. The interior is notable for its marble altars and a 15th-century silver gilt statue of St Blaise (within the high altar), who is holding a scale model of pre-earthquake Dubrovnik. Note also the stained-glass windows designed by local artist Ivo Dulčić in 1971.

Dominican Monastery & Museum   CHRISTIAN MONASTERY
(Dominikanski samostan i muzej; Map p200; ☑020-321 423; www.dominicanmuseum.hr; Sv Dominika 4; adult/child 30/20KN; ⏰9am-5pm) This imposing structure is an architectural highlight, built in a transitional Gothic-Renaissance style and containing an impressive art collection. Constructed around the same time as the city walls in the 14th century, the stark exterior resembles a fortress more than a religious complex. The interior contains a graceful 15th-century cloister constructed by local artisans after the designs of the Florentine architect Maso di Bartolomeo.

Franciscan Monastery & Museum   CHRISTIAN MONASTERY
(Franjevački samostan i muzej; Map p200; ☑020-321 410; Placa 2; 30KN; ⏰9am-6pm Apr-Oct, to 2pm Nov-Mar) Within this monastery's solid stone walls are a gorgeous mid-14th-century cloister, a historic pharmacy and a small museum with a collection of relics and liturgical objects, including chalices, paintings and gold jewellery, and pharmacy items such as laboratory gear and medical books.

Fort Lawrence   FORTRESS
(Tvrđava Lovrjenac; Map p200; www.citywalls dubrovnik.hr; Pile; 50KN, free with city walls ticket; ⏰8am-6.30pm Apr-Oct, 9am-3pm Nov-Mar) St Blaise gazes down from the walls of this large free-standing fortress, constructed atop a 37m-high promontory adjacent to the old town. Built to guard the city's western approach from invasion by land or sea, its walls range from 4m to 12m thick. There's not a lot inside, but the battlements offer

wonderful views over the old town and its large courtyard is often used as a venue for summer theatre and concerts.

Museum of Modern Art   GALLERY
(Umjetnička galerija; ☏020-426 590; www.ug dubrovnik.hr; Frana Supila 23, Ploče; with multimuseum pass adult/child 120/25KN; ⊙9am-8pm Tue-Sun) Spread over three floors of a significant modernist building east of the old town, this excellent gallery showcases Croatian artists, particularly painter Vlaho Bukovac from nearby Cavtat. Head up to the sculpture terrace for excellent views.

🏃 Activities

Sveti Jakov Beach   SWIMMING
(Vlaha Bukovca bb, Viktorija) Head east from the Ploče Gate for 1.7km and you'll come to Sveti Jakov, a gorgeous little beach that doesn't get too rowdy and has showers, a bar and a restaurant.

Bellevue Beach   SWIMMING
(Montovjerna) The nicest beach within an easy walk of the old town is below the Hotel Bellevue. This pebbly cove is sheltered by high cliffs, which provide a platform for daredevil cliff divers but also cast a shadow over the beach by late afternoon – a boon on a scorching day. Public access is via a steep staircase off Kotorska.

Dance Beach   SWIMMING
(Don Frana Bulića bb, Pile) This little rocky stretch has turquoise waters and a series of sunbathing terraces. It's positioned below an old monastery at the foot of **Gradac Park** (Don Frana Bulića bb, Pile), 600m west of the Pile Gate.

Outdoor Croatia   KAYAKING
(☏020-418 282; www.outdoorcroatia.com; day trip 440KN) Rents kayaks and offers day trips around the Elafiti Islands, along with multiday excursions and kayaking-cycling combos.

Adriatic Kayak Tours   KAYAKING, CYCLING
(Map p200; ☏020-312 770; www.adriatickayak tours.com; Zrinsko Frankopanska 6, Pile; half-day from 280KN; ⊙Apr-Oct) Offers sea-kayak excursions (from a half-day paddle to a week-long trip), hiking and cycling tours, and Montenegro getaways (including rafting).

🎉 Festivals & Events

Feast of St Blaise   CULTURAL
(⊙3 Feb) A city-wide bash in honour of the town's patron saint, marked by pageants and

---

ℹ️ MUSEUMS OF DUBROVNIK PASS

Perhaps a cunning plan to get you through the doors of some of the town's more marginal museums, a multimuseum pass (adult/child 120/25KN) allows access to nine of Dubrovnik's institutions. The only must-see among them though is the Rector's Palace (p198), which is also the only one ticketed separately. If you're interested in visiting the excellent Museum of Modern Art, then it's worth buying the pass. The other museums could easily be skipped, but if you want to get your money's worth in a limited amount of time, we suggest you prioritise the rest in the following order: Maritime Museum, Archaeological Museum, Dulčić Masle Pulitika Gallery, Natural History Museum, Ethnographic Museum, Pulitika Studio, Marin Držić House.

---

a procession listed by Unesco as an 'Intangible Cultural Heritage' for remaining largely unchanged for almost a thousand years.

Dubrovnik Summer Festival   CULTURAL
(Dubrovačke ljetne igre; ☏020-326 100; www. dubrovnik-festival.hr; ⊙Jul-Aug) The most prestigious summer festival in Croatia presents a program of theatre, opera, concerts and dance on open-air stages throughout the city from 10 July to 25 August. Tickets are available online, from the festival office just off Placa, and at various venues (up to one hour before the performance).

🛏️ Sleeping

Hostel Angelina   HOSTEL €
(Map p200; ☏091 89 39 089; www.hostelange-linaoldtowndubrovnik.com; Plovani skalini 17a; dm from €49; ❄️🌐) Hidden away in a quiet nook of the old town, this cute little hostel offers bunk rooms, a small guest kitchen and a bougainvillea-shaded terrace with memorable views over the rooftops. Plus you'll get a great glute workout every time you walk up the lane. It also has private rooms in three old-town annexes (from €110).

⭐ Karmen Apartments   APARTMENT €€
(Map p200; ☏020-323 433; www.karmendu.com; Bandureva 1; apt from €95; ❄️🌐) These four inviting apartments enjoy a great location

Dubrovnik Old Town

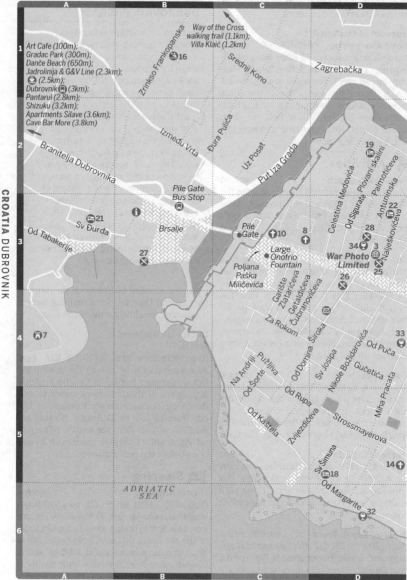

a stone's throw from Ploče harbour. All have plenty of character with art, splashes of colour, tasteful furnishings and books to browse. Apartment 2 has a little balcony, while apartment 1 enjoys sublime port views. Book well ahead.

Villa Klaić B&B €€

(☎091 73 84 673; www.villaklaic-dubrovnik.com; Šumetska 9, Pile; r from €120; P❋🐾🛜) Just off the main coastal highway, high above the old town, this outstanding guesthouse offers comfortable modern rooms and wonderful hospitality courtesy of the owner, Milo Klaić.

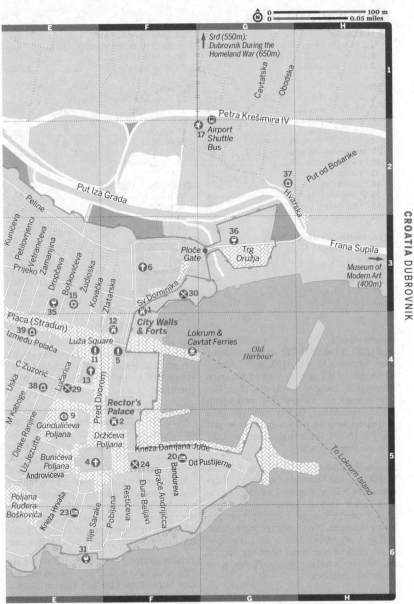

Extras include a small swimming pool, continental breakfast, free pick-ups (for longer stays) and free beer!

City Walls Hostel HOSTEL €€
(Map p200; ☑ 091 79 92 086; www.citywallshostel.com; Sv Šimuna 15; dm/r from €46/104; ﹡@🖙)

Tucked away by the city walls, this classic backpackers is warm and welcoming with a lively character. Downstairs there's a small kitchen and a space for socialising. Upstairs you'll find clean and simple dorms and a cosy double with a sea view.

Dubrovnik Old Town

Rooms Vicelić GUESTHOUSE €€
(Map p200; ☑ 095 52 78 933; www.rooms-vicelic.com; Antuninska 10; r €80-120; ❄☞) Situated on one of the steeply stepped old-town streets, this friendly, family-run place has four atmospheric stone-walled rooms with private bathrooms. Guests have use of a shared kitchenette with a microwave and a kettle. There's also a studio apartment for rent two streets down.

Apartments Silva GUESTHOUSE €€
(☑ 098 244 639; Kardinala Stepinca 62, Babin Kuk; r from 660KN; ℗❄☞) Lush Mediterranean foliage lines the terraces of this lovely hillside complex, a short hop up from the beach at Lapad. The rooms are comfortable and well priced, but best of all is the spacious top-floor apartment (sleeping five). It doesn't have a website, but you'll find it on major booking sites.

★MirÓ Studio Apartments APARTMENT €€€
(Map p200; ☑ 099 42 42 442; www.mirostudioapartmentsdubrovnik.com; Sv Đurđa 16, Pile; apt €145-200; ❄☞) Located in a quiet residential nook only metres from the sea, hidden between the old-town walls and Fort Lawrence, this schmick complex is an absolute gem. The decor marries ancient stone walls and whitewashed ceiling beams with design features such as uplighting, contemporary bathrooms and sliding glass partitions.

Villa Dubrovnik BOUTIQUE HOTEL €€€
(☑ 020-500 300; www.villa-dubrovnik.hr; Vlaha Bukovca 6, Viktorija; r/ste from €720/1260; ℗❄☞☒) Gazing endlessly at the old town and Lokrum from its prime waterfront position, this elegant, low-slung, boutique hotel gleams white against a backdrop of honey-coloured stone. The windows retract completely to bring the indoor pool into the outdoors, but sun seekers can laze on a lounger by the sea or commandeer a day bed in the rooftop prosciutto-and-wine bar.

Villa Sigurata GUESTHOUSE €€€
(Map p200; ☑ 091 57 27 181; www.villasigurata.com; Stulina 4; s/d €110/160) Hidden down a hard-to-find and surprisingly quiet lane behind the cathedral, this 17th-century house has eight atmospheric rooms with exposed stone walls and stylish furnishings. With lanes this tight, it's not surprising that the rooms are dark, but you'll appreciate the shade on hot days. It also has two other old-town annexes.

🍴 Eating

Dolce Vita
SWEETS €

(Map p200; Nalješkovićeva 1a; ice cream/pancakes from 11/22KN; ⊙11am-midnight) Over a dozen different kinds of sumptuous, creamy gelati are on offer at this sweet spot. Alternatively, choose from a substantial menu of cakes and pancakes. You'll have no trouble finding it, as its bright orange chairs and lanterns picturing an ice-cream cone pop out from a narrow side street just off Stradun.

Fast Food Republic
FAST FOOD €

(Map p200; www.facebook.com/RepublicDubrovnik; Široka 4; mains 39-100KN; ⊙10am-midnight) Owned and operated by a friendly young crew, this little burger bar serves a tasty selection of burgers, sandwiches, pizza slices and hot dogs. For a local twist, try an octopus burger.

Shizuku
JAPANESE €€

(☑020-311 493; www.facebook.com/ShizukuDubrovnik; Kneza Domagoja 1f, Batala; mains 70-85KN; ⊙5pm-midnight Tue-Sun; 🛜) Attentive local wait staff usher you to your table in the clean-lined, modern dining room of this popular restaurant, tucked away in a residential area between Gruž Harbour and Lapad Bay. The Japanese owners will be in the kitchen, preparing authentic sushi, sashimi, udon, crispy *karaage* chicken and gyoza dumplings. Wash it all down with Japanese beer or sake.

Nishta
VEGAN €€

(Map p200; ☑020-322 088; www.nishtarestaurant.com; Prijeko bb; mains 98-108KN; ⊙11.30am-11.30pm Mon-Sat; 🍴) The popularity of this tiny old-town restaurant is testament not just to the paucity of options for vegetarians and vegans in Croatia, but also to the imaginative and beautifully presented food produced within. Each day of the week has its own menu with a separate set of cooked and raw options.

Oliva Pizzeria
PIZZA €€

(Map p200; ☑020-324 594; www.pizza-oliva.com; Lučarica 5; mains 74-105KN; ⊙10am-11pm; 🛜🍴) There are a few token pasta dishes on the menu, but this attractive little restaurant is really all about pizza. And the pizza is worthy of the attention. Grab a seat on the street and tuck in.

Bota Šare Oyster & Sushi Bar
SUSHI €€

(Map p200; ☑020-324 034; www.bota-sare.hr; Od Pustijerne bb; mains 62-120KN; ⊙noon-midnight)

WORTH A TRIP

LOKRUM

Lush **Lokrum** (☑020-311 738; www.lokrum.hr; adult/child incl boat 150/25KN; ⊙Apr-Nov) is a beautiful, forested island full of holm oaks, black ash, pines and olive trees, only a 10-minute ferry ride from Dubrovnik's Old Harbour. It's a popular swimming spot, although the beaches are rocky. Boats leave roughly hourly in summer (half-hourly in July and August). The public boat ticket price includes the entrance fee, but if you arrive with another boat, you're required to pay 120KN at the information centre on the island.

It's fair to say that most Croatians don't have much of an interest in or aptitude for Asian cooking, yet fresh seafood is something that they understand very well, as this little place demonstrates. Grab a terrace table with a view of the cathedral and relish Ston oysters (fresh or tempura style) and surprisingly good sushi and sashimi.

⭐Restaurant 360°
INTERNATIONAL €€€

(Map p200; ☑020-322 222; www.360dubrovnik.com; Sv Dominika bb; 2/3/5 courses 520/620/860KN; ⊙6.30-10.30pm Tue-Sun Apr-Sep; 🛜) Dubrovnik's glitziest restaurant offers fine dining at its best, with flavoursome, beautifully presented, creative cuisine, an impressive wine list and slick, professional service. The setting is unrivalled – on top of the city walls with tables positioned so you can peer through the battlements over the harbour.

⭐Nautika
EUROPEAN €€€

(Map p200; ☑020-442 526; www.nautikarestaurants.com; Brsalje 3, Pile; mains 290-360KN; ⊙6pm-midnight Apr-Oct) Nautika bills itself as 'Dubrovnik's finest restaurant' and it comes pretty close. The setting is sublime, overlooking the sea and the city walls, and the service is faultless: black-bow-tie formal but friendly. As for the food, it's sophisticated if not particularly adventurous, with classic techniques applied to the finest local produce. For maximum silver-service drama, order the salt-crusted fish.

⭐Pantarul
MEDITERRANEAN €€€

(☑020-333 486; www.pantarul.com; Kralja Tomislava 1, Lapad; mains 108-180KN, 5-course tasting menus 390-410KN; ⊙noon-4pm & 6pm-midnight Tue-Sun; 🅿🛜) This breezy bistro aligns its menu with the seasons and has a reputation for exceptional homemade bread, pasta and risotto, alongside the likes of steaks, ox cheeks, burgers and various fish dishes. There's a fresh, modern touch to most dishes.

Drinking & Entertainment

★ Bard Mala Buža
BAR

(Map p200; Iza Mira 14; ⊘9am-3am May-Oct) The more upmarket and slick of two cliff bars pressed up against the seaward side of the city walls. This one is lower on the rocks and has a shaded terrace where you can lose a day quite happily, mesmerised by the Adriatic vistas.

Buža
BAR

(Map p200; off Od Margarite; ⊘8am-2am Jun-Aug, to midnight Sep-May) Finding this ramshackle bar-on-a-cliff feels like a real discovery as you duck and dive around the city walls and finally see the entrance tunnel. However, Buža's no secret – it gets insanely busy, especially around sunset. Wait for a space on one of the concrete platforms, grab a cool drink in a plastic cup and enjoy the vibe and views.

Cave Bar More
BAR

(www.hotel-more.hr; Šetalište Nika i Meda Pucića bb, Babin Kuk; ⊘10am-midnight Jun-Aug, to 10pm Sep-May) This little beach bar serves coffee, snacks and cocktails to bathers reclining by the dazzlingly clear waters of Lapad Bay, but that's not the half of it – the main bar is set in an actual cave. Cool off beneath the stalactites in the side chamber, where a glass floor exposes a water-filled cavern.

D'vino
WINE BAR

(Map p200; ☑020-321 130; www.dvino.net; Palmotićeva 4a; ⊘9am-midnight Mar-Nov; 🛜) If you're interested in sampling top-notch Croatian wine, this convivial bar is the place to go. As well as a large and varied wine list, it offers tasting flights presented by cool and knowledgeable staff (three wines from 55KN) plus savoury breakfasts, snacks and platters. Sit outside for the authentic old-town-alley ambience, but check out the whimsical wall inscriptions inside.

Malvasija
WINE BAR

(Map p200; Dropčeva 4; ⊘5pm-1am; 🛜) Named after the white wine produced in the neighbouring Konavle region, this tiny bar is a good spot to sample the local drop. The delicious cheese and charcuterie platters (from 80KN) are a great option for a light, afford-able meal in the often-pricey old town. The service is as charming as it is knowledgeable.

Dubrovnik Beer Factory
CRAFT BEER

(Map p200; www.facebook.com/dubrovnikbeerfactory; Miha Pracata 6; ⊘9am-1am; 🛜) The name might mislead you: this isn't, in fact, a brewery, but the selection of Croatian craft beer is good enough to justify the tag. Still, with huge murals, vaulted ceilings, historic stone details and a large beer garden tucked away in the back, the setting remains the true drawcard. It also serves food and hosts live music.

Revelin
CLUB

(Map p200; www.clubrevelin.com; Sv Dominika 3; ⊘11pm-6am daily Jun-Sep, Sat Oct-May) Housed within the vast vaulted chambers of Fort Revelin, this is Dubrovnik's most impressive club space, with famous international DJs dropping in during summer.

Shopping

★ Kawa
GIFTS & SOUVENIRS

(Map p200; ☑091 89 67 509; www.kawa.life; Hvarska 2, Ploče; ⊘10am-8pm) Selling 'wonderful items made by Croatians', this very cool design store sells everything from wines and craft beers to jewellery, clothing, homewares and even its own line of products under the Happy Čevapi label. Superb service rounds off the experience.

Uje
FOOD & DRINKS

(Map p200; ☑020-321 532; www.uje.hr; Placa 5; ⊘11am-6pm Jan-Mar, 9am-9pm Apr, May & Oct-Dec, 9am-11pm Jun-Sep) Uje specialises in olive oils, along with a wide range of other locally produced epicurean delights, including some excellent jams, pickled capers, local herbs and spices, honey, figs in honey, chocolate, wine and *rakija* (grappa). There's another **branch** (Map p200; ☑020-324 865; Od Puča 2; ⊘9am-9pm Sep-Jun, to midnight Jul & Aug) around the corner.

Information

Dubrovnik's tourist board has offices in **Pile** (Map p200; ☑020-312 011; www.tzdubrovnik.hr; Brsalje 5; ⊘8am-8pm), **Gruž** (☑020-417 983; www.tzdubrovnik.hr; Obala Pape Ivana Pavla II 1; ⊘8am-8pm Jun-Oct, 8am-3pm Mon-Fri, to 1pm Sat Nov-Mar, 8am-8pm Mon-Fri, to 2pm Sat & Sun Apr & May) and **Lapad** (☑020-437 460; www.tzdubrovnik.hr; Dvori Lapad, Masarykov put 2; ⊘8am-8pm Jul & Aug, 8am-noon & 5-8pm Mon-Fri, 9am-2pm Sat Apr-Jun, Sep & Oct) that dispense maps, information and advice.

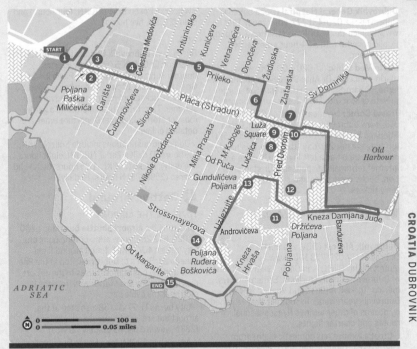

🏃 City Walk
Dubrovnik Old Town

START PILE GATE
END BUŽA BAR
LENGTH 1.2KM; ONE HOUR

Head through the **1 Pile Gate** to the beginning of Placa (aka Stradun), Dubrovnik's marbled main street. Immediately to your right is the **2 Large Onofrio Fountain**, while opposite it is 16th-century **3 Holy Saviour Church**; note the shell damage on its facade.

Continue along past the **4 Franciscan Monastery** (p198) and take any of the narrow lanes to the left. Turn right at the first side street, **5 Prijeko**, lined with restaurants of varying quality but consistently high prices. Turn right onto Žudioska, Dubrovnik's former Jewish ghetto; its 14th-century **6 synagogue** (50KN; ⏲10am-5pm) is the oldest still-functioning Sephardic synagogue in Europe.

Back on Placa, continue to Luža Square, a former marketplace lined with beautiful buildings such as the **7 Sponza Palace** (May-Oct free, Nov-Apr 25KN; ⏲ archives display & cloister 10am-10pm May-Oct; cloister 10am-3pm Nov-Apr) and **8 St Blaise's Church** (p198). Edicts,

festivities and public verdicts were announced from the **9 Orlando Column** at its centre.

Duck through the arch beneath the **10 City Bell Tower** and turn left, and then right at the arch leading to the Old Harbour. Head to the shade of the walls on the far side, then look back for a great view of the Ploče Gate defences.

Scoot through the hole in the wall and turn right; straight ahead is the **11 Cathedral** (p198), with the **12 Rector's Palace** (p198) diagonally across from it. Head down Od Puča, the main shopping strip, and cut through the market on busy **13 Gundulićeva poljana** (Gundulićeva Square), named after the poet whose statue stands at its centre.

At the far end, head up the Jesuit Stairs (the starting point of the notorious 'walk of shame' in *Game of Thrones*) to **14 St Ignatius of Loyola Church** (⏲7am-7pm). Cross the square to its far corner and follow the lane as it curves along the inside of the city walls. When you see a metal gate and a sign saying 'cold drinks', cut through the wall to **15 Buža** (p204).

Dubrovnik General Hospital (Opća bolnica Dubrovnik; ☑ 020-431 777, emergency 194; www.bolnica-du.hr; Dr Roka Mišetića 2, Lapad) Public hospital with a 24-hour emergency department.

Marin Med Clinic (☑ 020-400 500; www.marin-med.com; Dr Ante Starčevića 45, Montovjerna; ⊙ 8am-8pm Mon-Fri, to 1pm Sat) Large private centre with English-speaking doctors.

Travel Corner (Avansa Travel; ☑ 020-492 313; www.dubrovnik-travelcorner.com; Obala Stjepana Radića 40, Gruž; internet per hr 25KN, left luggage per 2hr/day 10/40KN) This handy one-stop shop has a left-luggage service and internet terminals, dispenses tourist information, books excursions and sells Kapetan Luka ferry tickets.

ⓘ Getting There & Away

AIR

Dubrovnik Airport (DBV, Zračna luka Dubrovnik; ☑ 020-773 100; www.airport-dubrovnik.hr; Čilipi) is in Čilipi, 19km southeast of Dubrovnik. Croatia Airlines, British Airways, Iberica, Turkish Airlines and Vueling fly to Dubrovnik year-round. In summer they're joined by dozens of other airlines flying seasonal routes and charter flights.

Croatia Airlines has domestic flights from Zagreb (year-round), Split and Osijek (both May to October only). Trade Air has seasonal flights to/from Rijeka and Split.

BOAT

The **ferry terminal** (Obala Pape Ivana Pavla II 1, Gruž) is in Gruž, 3km northwest of the old town. Ferries for **Lokrum and Cavtat** (Map p200) depart from the Old Harbour.

➜ Jadrolinija (p197) has daily ferries to the Elafiti Islands. From June to September, there's also a daily catamaran to Korčula (130KN, two hours), Hvar (210KN, 3½ hours), Bol (210KN, 4¾ hours) and Split (210KN, six hours).

➜ G&V Line (p195) has a daily catamaran to Šipanska Luka on Šipan (35KN, 50 minutes) and to Sobra on Mljet (55KN, 1¼ hours). In June a second boat heads directly to Sobra and Polače on Mljet (70KN, 1¾ hours). In July and August it also adds a stop at Korčula (90KN, 2½ hours) four times a week. Tickets can be purchased from the kiosk by the harbour 30 minutes prior to departure (an hour prior in July and August). A limited batch is released for online purchase and must be printed to board.

➜ Kapetan Luka (p196) has a daily fast boat from May to mid-October to/from Pomena on Mljet (80KN, 1¼ hours), Korčula (130KN, 1¾ hours), Hvar (210KN, three hours) and Split (210KN, 4¼ hours). From June to September another daily boat goes to Sobra on Mljet (80KN, 55 minutes), Korčula (130KN, two hours), Makarska (160KN,

3¼ hours), Bol on Brač (210KN, four hours) and Split (210KN, five hours).

BUS

Buses from **Dubrovnik Bus Station** (Autobusni kolodvor; ☑ 060 305 070; www.libertas dubrovnik.hr; Obala Pape Ivana Pavla II 44a, Gruž; ⊙ 4.30am-10pm; 🐾) can be crowded, so purchase tickets online or book in advance in summer. The station has toilets, and a *garderoba* for storing luggage. Departure times are detailed online.

Domestic destinations include Split (127KN, 4½ hours, 11 daily), Zadar (182KN, eight hours, five daily), Rijeka (248KN, 12½ hours, daily) and Zagreb (259KN, 11¾ hours, 10 daily).

ⓘ Getting Around

TO/FROM THE AIRPORT

Atlas runs the **airport shuttle bus** (Map p200; ☑ 020-642 286; www.atlas-croatia.com; one-way/return 40/70KN), timed around flight schedules. Buses to Dubrovnik stop at the Pile Gate and the bus station; buses to the airport pick up from the bus station and from the bus stop near the cable car.

City buses 11, 27 and 38 also stop at the airport but are less frequent and take longer (28KN, seven daily, no Sunday service).

Allow up to 280KN for a taxi to Dubrovnik. Dubrovnik Transfer Services (www.dubrovnik-transfer-services.com) offers a set-price taxi transfer service to the city (€30) and Cavtat (€16), and to as far away as Zagreb, Sarajevo, Podgorica and Tirana.

BUS

Dubrovnik has a superb bus service; buses run frequently and generally on time. The key tourist routes run until after 2am in summer, so if you're staying in Lapad, there's no need to rush home. The fare is 15KN if you buy from the driver and 12KN if you buy a ticket at a *tisak* (newsstand). Timetables are available at www.libertasdubrovnik.hr.

To get to the old town from the bus station, take buses 1a, 1b, 3 or 8. To get to Lapad, take bus 7. From the **bus stop** (Map p200) at Pile Gate, take bus 4, 5, 6 or 9 to get to Lapad.

CAR

The entire old town is a pedestrian area, public transport is good and parking is expensive, so you're better off not hiring a car until you're ready to leave the city. All of the street parking surrounding the old town is metered from May to October (40KN per hour). Further out it drops to 20KN or 10KN per hour.

It's a short walk down from the covered **Ilijina Glavica Car Park** (☑ 020-312 720; Zagrebačka bb, Pile; per hr/day/week 40/480/2400KN; ⊙ 24 hour) to the old town, but a hard slog back up. Note that the daily and weekly rates are for prepay only; the machines don't make this clear and we've witnessed people being stung with hefty bills as a result.

All of the usual hire-car companies are represented at the airport and most also have city branches.

Cavtat

☑020 / POP 2150

Set on a petite peninsula embraced by two harbours, the ancient town of Cavtat (pronounced *tsav*-tat) has a pretty waterfront promenade peppered with restaurants, pebbly beaches and an interesting assortment of artsy attractions.

Without Cavtat there would be no Dubrovnik, as it was refugees from Epidaurum (the Roman incarnation of Cavtat) who established the city in 614. The walls of its famous offshoot are visible in the distance and the two are well connected by both boat and bus, making Cavtat either an easy daytrip destination from Dubrovnik, or a quieter (not to mention cheaper) alternative base.

◉ Sights

St Nicholas' Church   CHURCH
(Crkva svetog Nikole; Obala Ante Starčevića bb; ⊙hours vary) Peek inside this 15th-century church to view its impressive wooden altars and the accomplished Bukovac paintings of the four evangelists on either side of the sanctuary. Cavtat landmarks feature prominently in much of the art, including in the 19th-century altarpiece by Carmelo Reggi and in the Stations of the Cross that line the walls.

**Our-Lady-of-the-Snow
Monastery**   MONASTERY
(Samostan Gospe od snijega; ☑020-678 064; www. franjevacki-samostan-cavtat.com; Šetalište Rat 2; ⊙7am-9pm) The church attached to this Franciscan Monastery (founded in 1484) is worth a look for some notable early Renaissance paintings and a wonderful Bukovac canvas depicting the Madonna and Child gazing at Cavtat at dusk. Concerts are regularly held in the cloister.

Bukovac House   MUSEUM
(Kuća Bukovac; ☑020-478 646; www.kuca-bukovac.hr; Bukovčeva 5; 30KN; ⊙9am-6pm Mon-Sat, to 2pm Sun Apr-Oct, 10am-6pm Tue-Sat, 9am-1pm Sun Nov-Mar) The house where Cavtat's most famous son, the painter Vlaho Bukovac (1855–1922), was born and raised has been converted into an interesting little museum devoted to his work. The early-19th-century architecture provides a fitting backdrop to his mementos, drawings and paintings.

Račić Family Mausoleum   MONUMENT
(Mauzolej obitelji Račić; www.migk.hr; Groblje sv Roka, Kvaternikova bb; 20KN; ⊙10am-5pm Mon-Sat Apr-Oct) Built from 1920 to 1921, this octagonal white-stone tomb is the handiwork of preeminent Croatian sculptor Ivan Meštrović. Inside, a heavenly host of angelic faces gazes down on stylised saints. It's located in the town cemetery, in the wooded area near the peak of the peninsula.

🛏 Sleeping & Eating

★**Villa Lukas**   APARTMENT €€
(☑098 549 916; www.villalukas.com; Stjepana Radića 2a; apt from 762KN; 🅿🌂🛜📶❄) Within the peachy shell of this modern block, elegant white-stone stairs lead up to 12 attractive apartments with balconies and sea views. If you get sick of lounging by the little blue-tiled pool, there's a fitness room and a sauna tucked away in the basement.

Castelletto   HOTEL €€
(☑020-479 547; www.dubrovnikexperience.com; Frana Laureana 22; r from €99; 🅿🌂@🛜❄) This very well-run, family-owned place has 13 spacious rooms in a converted villa. All have tea- and coffee-making facilities, a fridge and satellite TV, and some have balconies and sweeping bay views. Airport transfers are free.

Villa Ivy   APARTMENT €€€
(☑020-478 328; www.villaivy-croatia.com; SS Kranjčevića 52; apt from 960KN; 🅿🌂❄) If the location seems a little odd, tucked away in a scruffy neighbourhood at the top of the town, it all makes sense once you see the sea views from the pool terrace. Plus, it's quiet. The four apartments within the apricot-hued block are modern and very comfortable. It only accepts week-long bookings in July and August.

Peco   BAKERY, CAFE €
(Kneza Domagoja 2; pastries 20-30KN; ⊙6am-midnight May-Sep, to 8pm Oct-Apr; 🛜) Few local cafes sell food and even fewer bakeries have seats attached, making Peco a pleasant aberration. Peruse the cabinet then take a seat in the glassed-in terrace and order a sweet or savoury pastry to enjoy with your morning coffee. Return at lunchtime for a sandwich or mini pizza.

★ **Bugenvila**
(☑020-479 949; www.bugenvila.eu; Obala Ante Starčevića 9; mains 90-275KN; ⊘noon-4pm & 6.30-10pm; 🛜🍽) Not just the best place on Cavtat's seafront strip, Bugenvila is one of the culinary trendsetters of the Dalmatian coast. Local ingredients are showcased in adventurous dishes served with artistic flourishes. Visit at lunchtime to take advantage of the three-course special menu (180KN). A separate vegetarian menu is available on request.

ℹ Information

Tourist Office (☑020-479 025; https://visit. cavtat-konavle.com; Zidine 6; ⊘8am-8pm Mon-Sat, to 2pm Sun Apr-Oct, to 3pm Mon-Fri Nov-Mar) Well stocked with leaflets and a free map.

ℹ Getting There & Away

BOAT

During the tourist season at least three different operators offer boats to Cavtat from Dubrovnik's Old Harbour (one-way/return 60/100KN, 45 minutes), with departures at least every half-hour. In winter this reduces to three to five a day, weather dependent.

BUS

Bus 10 runs roughly half-hourly to Cavtat (25KN, 30 minutes) from Dubrovnik's bus station; the closest stop to the Old Town is next to the cable-car terminus.

UNDERSTAND CROATIA

Destination Today

For nigh on a thousand years, Croatia's fortunes were at the mercy of decisions made in Budapest or Venice or Vienna or Belgrade. Now the country's destiny is in its own hands. So the government must have sighed with relief when Croatia's extraordinary achievement of reaching the final of the 2018 FIFA World Cup briefly took other issues out of the headlines: high emigration, border disputes, corruption and far-right nationalism, to name but a handful.

History

Trampled over by invading armies, passed back and forth between empires, split up then put back together again in various different shapes: Croatia's history is more convoluted than most. Post WWII, the creation of the Socialist Federal Republic of Yugoslavia brought some semblance of unity to the south Slavic peoples. Yet it didn't last long.

The Death of Yugoslavia

President Tito left a shaky Yugoslavia upon his death in May 1980. With the economy in a parlous state, a presidency that rotated among the six republics and two semi-autonomous regions could not compensate for the loss of Tito's steadying hand at the helm. The authority of the central government sank along with the economy, and long-suppressed mistrust among Yugoslavia's ethnic groups resurfaced, coinciding with the rise to power of nationalist Slobodan Milošević in Serbia.

With political changes sweeping Eastern Europe and in the face of increasing provocations from Milošević, Slovenia embarked on a course for independence. For Croatia, remaining in a Serb-dominated Yugoslavia without the counterweight of Slovenia would have been untenable.

In the Croatian elections of April 1990, Franjo Tuđman's Croatian Democratic Union (HDZ) came to power. On 22 December 1990, a new Croatian constitution changed the status of Serbs in Croatia from that of a 'constituent nation' to a national minority. The constitution failed to guarantee minority rights and caused mass dismissals of Serbs from the public service. This stimulated Croatia's 600,000-strong ethnic Serb community to demand autonomy. A May 1991 referendum (boycotted by the Serbs) produced a 93% vote in favour of Croatian independence. When Croatia declared independence on 25 June 1991, the Serbian enclave of Krajina proclaimed its independence from Croatia.

War Breaks Out

Under pressure from the EU, Croatia declared a three-month moratorium on its independence, but heavy fighting broke out in Krajina, Baranja and Slavonia. This initiated what Croats refer to as the Homeland War. The Yugoslav People's Army, dominated by Serbs, began to intervene in support of Serbian irregulars under the pretext of halting ethnic violence. When the Croatian government ordered a shutdown of federal military installations in the republic of Croatia, the Yugoslav navy blockaded the Adriatic coast and laid siege to the strategic town of Vukovar on the Danube. During the summer of

1991, a quarter of Croatia fell to Serb militias and the Serb-led Yugoslav People's Army.

In late 1991 the federal army and the Montenegrin militia moved against Dubrovnik, and the presidential palace in Zagreb was hit by rockets from Yugoslav jets in an apparent assassination attempt on President Tuđman. When the three-month moratorium ended, Croatia declared full independence. Soon after, Vukovar finally fell when the Yugoslav army moved in, in one of the more bloodthirsty acts in all of the Yugoslav wars. During six months of fighting in Croatia, 10,000 people died, hundreds of thousands fled and tens of thousands of homes were destroyed.

The UN Gets Involved

Beginning on 3 January 1992, a UN-brokered ceasefire generally held. The federal army was allowed to withdraw from its bases inside Croatia and tensions diminished. At the same time, the EU recognised Croatia. This was followed by US recognition, and in May 1992 Croatia was admitted to the UN.

The UN peace plan in Krajina was intended to bring about the disarming of local Serb paramilitary formations, the repatriation of refugees and the return of the region to Croatia. Instead, it only froze the existing situation and offered no permanent solution.

While attention shifted to the war in neighbouring Bosnia and Hercegovina, the Croatian government quietly began procuring arms from abroad. On 1 May 1995 the Croatian army entered occupied western Slavonia, east of Zagreb, and seized control of the region within days. Belgrade's silence throughout the campaign showed that the Krajina Serbs had lost the support of their Serbian sponsors, encouraging the Croats to forge ahead. On 4 August, the military launched an assault on the rebel Serb capital of Knin. The Serb army fled towards northern Bosnia, along with 150,000 civilians, many of whose roots in the Krajina stretched back centuries. The military operation ended in days, but was followed by months of terror, including widespread looting and burning of Serb villages.

The Dayton Peace Accords signed in Paris in December 1995 recognised Croatia's Yugoslav-era borders and provided for the return of eastern Slavonia. The transition proceeded relatively smoothly, but the two populations still regard each other with suspicion.

Postwar Politics

A degree of stability returned to Croatia after the hostilities. A key provision of the peace agreement was the guarantee by the Croatian government to facilitate the return of Serbian refugees, and although the central government in Zagreb made the return of refugees a priority in accordance with the demands of the international community, its efforts have often been subverted by local authorities intent on maintaining the ethnic singularity of their regions. The most recent census (2011) has Serbs at 4.4% of the population, slightly down on the previous census 10 years earlier, and less than a third of the 1991 numbers.

In the spring of 2008 Croatia was officially invited to join NATO at the summit in Bucharest, which it did in 2009. In 2012 Croats voted in a referendum to join the EU and in 2013 the country officially became a member.

People

With Germanic influences in the north and larger-than-life Mediterranean tendencies on the coast, Croats aren't completely cut from the same mould. Yet from one tip of the Croatian horseshoe to the other, there are constants. Wherever you go, family and religion loom large, social conservatism is the norm, sport is the national obsession and coffee is drunk in industrial quantities.

The vast majority of Croats have a strong cultural identification with Western Europe and draw a distinction between themselves and their 'eastern' neighbours in Bosnia, Montenegro and Serbia. They're quick to point out that Zagreb is actually further west than Vienna; that the nation is overwhelmingly Catholic, rather than Orthodox; and that they use the Latin alphabet, not Cyrillic.

According to the most recent census, 86.3% of the population identifies itself as Catholic, 4.4% Orthodox (this corresponds exactly with the percentage of Serbs), 4% 'other and undeclared', 3.8% atheist and 1.5% Muslim.

Arts

Croatia views itself as a cultured central European nation, steeped in the continent's finest artistic traditions and imbued with its own unique folk styles, but equally unafraid of the avant-garde. Even if they're virtually unknown elsewhere, local artists are highly regarded at home.

The instrument most often used in Croatian folk music is the *tamburica*, a long-necked lute that is plucked or strummed. Translated as 'group of people', *klapa* is an outgrowth of church-choir singing; the form is most popular in Dalmatia and can involve up to 10 voices singing in harmony.

The first literary flowering in Croatia took place in Dalmatia, which was strongly influenced by the Italian Renaissance. The works of the scholar and poet Marko Marulić (1450–1524), from Split, are still venerated. The plays of Marin Držić (1508–67) express humanistic Renaissance ideals and are still performed, especially in Dubrovnik. The epic poem *Osman*, by Ivan Gundulić (1589–1638), celebrated the Polish victory over the Turks in 1621.

Vlaho Bukovac (1855–1922) was the most notable Croatian painter of the late 19th century. However, the most internationally recognised Croatian artist was the sculptor Ivan Meštrović (1883–1962). Antun Augustinčić (1900–79) was another acclaimed sculptor, whose *Monument to Peace* is outside New York's UN building. Đuro Pulitika (1922–2006), known for his colourful landscapes, was a well-regarded Dubrovnik painter, as were Antun Masle (1919–67) and Ivo Dulčić (1916–75).

Environment

Croatia is shaped like a boomerang: from the Pannonian plains of Slavonia between the Sava, Drava and Danube Rivers, across hilly central Croatia to the Istrian peninsula, then south through Dalmatia along the rugged Adriatic coast.

The narrow Croatian coastal belt at the foot of the Dinaric Alps is only about 600km long as the crow flies, but it's so indented that the actual length is 1778km. If the 4012km of coastline around the offshore islands is added to the total, the length becomes 5790km. There are 1244 islands and islets along the tectonically submerged Adriatic coastline; 50 of them inhabited.

Deer are plentiful in the dense forests of Risnjak National Park, as are brown bears, wild cats and *ris* (lynx), from which the park gets its name. Occasionally a wolf or wild boar may appear, but only rarely. Plitvice Lakes National Park, however, is an important refuge for wolves. The rare Eurasian

otter is also protected in Plitvice, as well as in Krka National Park. Two venomous snakes are endemic in Paklenica – the nose-horned viper and the European adder.

The griffon vulture, with a wingspan of 2.6m, has a permanent colony on Cres, and Paklenica National Park is rich in peregrine falcons, goshawks, sparrow hawks, buzzards and owls. Krka National Park is an important migration route and winter habitat for marsh birds as well as rare golden eagles and short-toed eagles.

Food & Drink

Croatian food echoes the varied cultures that have influenced the country over its history. There's a sharp divide between the Italian-style cuisine along the coast and the flavours of Hungary, Austria and Turkey in the continental parts. From grilled sea bass smothered in olive oil in Dalmatia to robust, paprika-heavy meat stews in Slavonia, each region proudly touts its own speciality, but regardless of the region you'll find tasty food made from fresh, seasonal ingredients.

The Istria and Kvarner regions have quickly shot to the top of the gourmet ladder, but other places aren't lagging far behind. Wine and olive-oil production have been revived, and there's now a network of signposted routes around the country celebrating these precious commodities.

Wine

Wine from Croatia may be a novelty to international consumers but *vino* has been an embedded part of the region's lifestyle for more than 25 centuries. Today the tradition is undergoing a renaissance in the hands of a new generation of winemakers with a focus on preserving indigenous varietals and revitalising ancestral estates. Quality is rising, exports are increasing and the wines are garnering global awards and winning the affections of worldly wine lovers thirsty for authentic stories and unique terroirs.

Croatia is roughly divided into four winemaking regions: Slavonia and the Croatian Uplands in the continental zone, with a cooler climate; and Istria/Kvarner and Dalmatia along the Adriatic, with a Mediterranean climate. Within each lie multiple subregions *(vinogorje)*, with 16 distinct areas recognised as Protected Designations of Origin *(Zaštićena oznaka izvornosti)* under EU regulations; wines produced using the specific grape varieties permitted in these geographically defined appellations are marked ZOI on the label.

SURVIVAL GUIDE

ℹ️ Directory A-Z

ACCOMMODATION

Croatia is extremely popular in summer and good places book out well in advance in July and August. It's also very busy in June and September.

Hotels These range from massive beach resorts to boutique establishments.

Apartments Privately owned holiday units are a staple of the local accommodation scene; they're especially good for families.

Guesthouses Usually family-run establishments where spare rooms are rented at a bargain price – sometimes with their own bathrooms, sometimes not.

Hostels Mainly in the bigger cities and more popular beach destinations, with dorms and sometimes private rooms too.

Campgrounds Tent and caravan sites, often fairly basic.

LGBTIQ+ TRAVELLERS

Homosexuality has been legal in Croatia since 1977 and is tolerated but not widely accepted. Public displays of affection between same-sex couples may be met with hostility.

Gay venues are virtually nonexistent outside Zagreb. However, many towns on the coast have an unofficial gay beach – usually a rocky area at the edge of the nudist section.

Zagreb Pride (www.zagreb-pride.net) Usually held on the second Saturday in June.

Split Pride (www.facebook.com/lgbt.pride.split) Also in June.

LORI (www.lori.hr) Lesbian organisation based in Rijeka.

Dating apps Grindr (www.grindr.com) and Planet Romeo (www.planetromeo.com) are very popular with local gay and bisexual men.

MONEY

ATMs are widely available. Credit cards are accepted in most hotels and restaurants. Smaller restaurants, shops and private-accommodation owners only take cash.

OPENING HOURS

Opening hours vary throughout the year. We've provided high-season opening hours; hours generally decrease in the shoulder and low seasons.

Banks 8am or 9am to 8pm weekdays and 7am to 1pm or 8am to 2pm Saturday.

Cafes and bars 8am or 9am to midnight.

Offices 8am to 4pm or 8.30am to 4.30pm weekdays.

Post offices 7am to 8pm weekdays and 7am to 1pm Saturday; longer hours in coastal towns in summer.

Restaurants Noon to 11pm or midnight; often closed Sunday outside peak season.

Shops 8am to 8pm weekdays, to 2pm or 3pm Saturday; some take a break from 2pm to 5pm. Shopping malls have longer hours.

PUBLIC HOLIDAYS

Croats take their holidays very seriously. Shops and museums are shut and boat services are reduced. On religious holidays, the churches are full; it can be a good time to check out the artwork in a church that is usually closed.

New Year's Day 1 January
Epiphany 6 January
Easter Sunday & Monday March/April
Labour Day 1 May
Corpus Christi 60 days after Easter
Day of Antifascist Resistance 22 June
Statehood Day 25 June
Homeland Thanksgiving Day 5 August
Feast of the Assumption 15 August
Independence Day 8 October
All Saints' Day 1 November
Christmas 25 & 26 December

TELEPHONE

➡ To call Croatia from abroad, dial your international access code, then 385 (the country code for Croatia), then the area code (without the initial 0) and the local number.

➡ To call from region to region within Croatia, start with the full area code (drop it when dialling within the same code).

➡ Phone numbers with the prefix 060 can be either free or charged at a premium rate, so watch out for the fine print.

➡ Phone numbers that begin with 09 are mobile-phone numbers. Calls to mobiles are billed at a much higher rate than regular numbers.

ℹ️ Getting There & Away

ENTERING THE COUNTRY/REGION

With an economy that depends heavily on tourism, Croatia has wisely kept red tape to a minimum for foreign visitors.

Passport

Your passport must be valid for at least another three months after the planned departure from Croatia, as well as issued within the previous 10 years. Citizens of EU countries can enter Croatia with only their ID card.

Croatian authorities require all foreigners to register with the local police when they arrive in a new area of the country, but this is a routine matter normally handled by the hotel, hostel, campground or agency securing your private accommodation. If you're staying elsewhere (eg with relatives or friends), your host should take care of it for you.

AIR

There are direct flights to Croatia from a variety of European and Middle Eastern cities year-round, with dozens of seasonal routes and charters added in summer.

Airports & Airlines

Croatia has an astonishing eight airports welcoming international flights, although some of them are highly seasonal. **Croatia Airlines** (OU; ☑ 01-66 76 555; www.croatiaairlines.hr) is the national carrier; it's part of the Star Alliance.

Brač Airport (BWK; ☑ 021-559 711; www.airport-brac.hr) Only operates from April until around September.

Dubrovnik Airport (p206) Croatia Airlines, British Airways, Iberica, Turkish Airlines and Vueling fly here year-round, with numerous other airlines joining them in the tourist season.

Osijek Airport (☑ 060 339 339; www.osijek-airport.hr) Wizz Air flies here year-round from Basel-Mulhouse, while Eurowings has seasonal flights from Cologne/Bonn and Stuttgart.

Pula Airport (p150) Most international services are seasonal except Eurowings, which flies here from Dusseldorf year-round.

Rijeka Airport (p163) On the island of Krk, with year-round flights from Cologne-Bonn on Eurowings, and other airlines offering summer-only services.

Split Airport (p184) Major international airport, with year-round flights from Croatia Airlines and Eurowings, along with many more in summer.

Zadar Airport (p172) International flights in the tourist season only.

Zagreb Airport (p146) Croatia's main air hub, with various airlines flying here year-round from destinations all over Europe and the Middle East.

LAND

Croatia has border crossings with Slovenia, Hungary, Serbia, Bosnia and Hercegovina, and Montenegro.

Bus

Direct bus connections link Croatia to all of its neighbours and to as far afield as Norway. In most cases, passports are collected on the bus and handed over at the border; you usually won't leave the bus unless there's an issue that needs resolving. Useful websites include www.euro lines.com, www.buscroatia.com, www.getbybus. com and www.vollo.net.

Bosnia and Hercegovina Direct buses to Sarajevo from most Croatian cities. Good connections between the Dalmatian coast and popular spots such as Mostar and Međugorje.

Macedonia Direct buses from Skopje all the way to Istria.

Montenegro Regular services between Dubrovnik and the Bay of Kotor.

Serbia Buses from Belgrade to Zagreb, Rovinj and Pula.

Slovenia Buses from Ljubljana to Poreč, Zagreb, Split and Dubrovnik.

Train

Zagreb is Croatia's main train hub but direct international services also head to Rijeka and Pula. In most cases, passports are checked on the train.

Serbia Belgrade to Zagreb.

Slovenia Ljubljana to Zagreb, Rijeka and Pula, and Maribor to Zagreb.

SEA

Regular ferries connect Croatia with Italy; Split is the main year-round hub.

Jadrolinija (www.jadrolinija.hr) Overnight services between Split and Ancona year-round, between Zadar and Ancona from June to September, and between Dubrovnik and Bari from April to November.

SNAV (www.snav.com) Overnight services on the Split–Ancona route from April to October.

Venezia Lines (www.venezialines.com) Ferries ply the Venice–Piran–Poreč–Rovinj route from May to September, continuing on to Pula from June to September, and adding a stop in Umag in July and August.

🛈 Getting Around

AIR

Croatia Airlines is the national carrier, with its main hub in Zagreb. Domestic services head to Brač (summer only), Dubrovnik, Osijek, Pula, Split and Zadar. There are also flights between these regional centres, along with flights to Rijeka from Split and Osijek.

Trade Air (TDR; ☑ 091 62 65 111; www.trade-air.com) has flights from Osijek to Zagreb, Pula and Rijeka; from Rijeka to Split and Dubrovnik; and from Split to Pula and Dubrovnik.

BICYCLE

Bicycles are easy to rent along the coast and on the islands, and cycling can be a great way to explore the islands. Relatively flat islands such as Pag and Mali Lošinj offer the most relaxed biking, but the winding, hilly roads on other islands offer spectacular views. Cycling on the coast or the mainland requires caution: most roads are busy, two-lane highways with no bicycle lanes.

Some tourist offices have maps of routes and can refer you to local bike-rental agencies.

If you have some Croatian-language skills, www.pedala.hr is a great reference for cycling routes around Croatia.

BOAT
Numerous ferries connect the main coastal centres and their surrounding islands year-round, with services extended in the tourist season. Split is the main hub, with the other major ports being Dubrovnik, Šibenik, Zadar and Rijeka.

It's also possible to hire a yacht (with or without a crew) and explore under your own sail. Local boat-hire companies can be found in all of the main coastal towns, alongside the likes of UK-based **Cosmos Yachting** (www.cosmos-yachting.com), which operates out of multiple ports.

Ferry Travel
➡ Locals use the term 'ferry' to refer exclusively to car ferries and 'catamaran' to refer to the faster, passenger-only ferry services.

➡ Ferries operate year-round but additional sailings are added in the busy months (from June to September), with the peak schedule kicking in for July and August. Some catamaran routes only operate in summer.

➡ Boats are comfortable and well equipped, with toilets and seating both inside and out on the deck. The larger boats have restaurants, cafes and bars, and almost all have at least a snack counter. Most offer free wi-fi.

➡ Outside of the busiest times, it's usually possible to simply turn up and purchase your ticket from a kiosk at the wharf.

➡ In most instances you can buy tickets online, although it's not always possible to purchase tickets on the day of travel. Prebooking doesn't guarantee you a space on a particular sailing, so it still pays to get to the wharf early in peak season, especially if you're travelling with a car.

➡ Bikes can be transported on car ferries (but not catamarans) for a fee (13KN to 45KN).

➡ Travelling as a foot passenger gives you more flexibility and is cheaper than travelling with a vehicle. In most cases you can hire a car, scooter or bicycle at your destination.

Ferry Operators
Jadrolinija (p185) The main operator, with car ferries and catamarans on 35 different routes.

Kapetan Luka (p185) Daily fast boats on the Split–Hvar–Korčula route. From mid-April to October there is also a boat between Dubrovnik and Split, stopping at the islands of Mljet, Korčula, Hvar and Brač.

G&V Line (p195) Has a daily catamaran between Dubrovnik and Šipan and Mljet. In July and August some boats continue on to Korčula.

BUS
Bus services are excellent and relatively inexpensive. There are often a number of different companies handling each route, so prices can vary substantially. Luggage stowed in the baggage compartment under the bus costs extra (around 10KN a piece). Note that buses between Split and Dubrovnik pass through Bosnian territory so you'll need to keep your passport handy.

CAR & MOTORCYCLE
Motorways connect Zagreb to Slavonia and Zagreb to Istria via Rijeka. Another major motorway heads from Zagreb to Dalmatia, with turn-offs for Zadar, Šibenik and Split; it continues in the direction of Dubrovnik, but falls short by 110km. Although the roads are in excellent condition, there are stretches where service stations and facilities are scarce.

The **Hrvatski Autoklub** (HAK, Croatian Auto Club; ☑ 24hr roadside assistance 01-1987, traffic information 07-27 77 777; www.hak.hr) offers help, advice and a nationwide roadside-assistance number.

LOCAL TRANSPORT
The main form of local transport is bus (although Zagreb and Osijek also have well-developed tram systems). Buses in major cities such as Dubrovnik, Rijeka, Split and Zadar run regularly; a ride is usually 10KN to 15KN, with a small discount if you buy tickets at a *tisak* (newsstand).

TRAIN
Croatia's train network is limited and trains are less frequent than buses. Delays are also a regular occurrence on Croatian trains, sometimes for a number of hours. For information, contact **HŽPP** (☑ 01-37 82 583; www.hzpp.hr).

No trains run along the coast and only a few coastal cities are connected with Zagreb, notably Rijeka and Split.

Baggage Bringing luggage is free on trains; most stations have left-luggage services.

Classes Domestic trains are either 'express' or 'passenger' (local). Prices quoted by Lonely Planet are for unreserved, 2nd-class seating. Express trains have 1st- and 2nd-class cars; they are more expensive than passenger trains and a reservation is advisable.

Passes Travellers who hold a European InterRail pass can use it in Croatia for free travel. Those travelling only in Croatia are unlikely to do enough train travel to justify the cost.

214

1. Uvac River 2. Predjama Castle, Postojna Cave
3. Waterfalls, Plitvice Lakes National Park
4. Statue at the entrance of Njegoš Mausoleum

Scenic Showstoppers

Plitvice Lakes National Park, Croatia

In a region not short on glorious natural sights, Plitvice Lakes National Park (p165) takes some beating. The focal point is a set of 16 turquoise lakes that empty into each other via cascading waterfalls.

Lake Koman, Albania

Although it was artificially created when the Drin River was dammed in 1978, this large lake provides access to Albania's remote and mountainous north. A scenic three-hour ferry ride takes you deep into the Accursed Mountains (p78), where hiking tracks await.

Lovćen National Park, Montenegro

Lovćen (p261) is the Black Mountain from which Montenegro takes its name, and this national park encircles the nation's historic heartland. Take a vertiginous drive to the striking Njegoš Mausoleum, set atop Lovćen's second-highest peak.

Uvac Canyon, Serbia

The spectacular zigzags of the Uvac River (p360) in southwestern Serbia are best admired from the lookouts high above. Alternatively, book a guided hike and boat ride through the canyon.

Postojna Cave, Slovenia

Not all of the region's best scenery is above ground. Postojna Cave (p405) is one of the world's largest karst cave systems, filled with extraordinary rock formations and featuring the dramatic Predjama Castle (p406).

IOAN F FLORIN ONEJEVIC/SHUTTERSTOCK ©

1. Subotica Synagogue 2. Mural detail, Visoki Dečani Monastery
3. Painted Mosque, Tetovo 4. Blagaj Tekke
5. Domed vestibule, Cathedral of St Domnius

Religious Architecture

ZORAN KARAPANCEV/SHUTTERSTOCK ©

Simultaneously straddling two major religious divides – between Eastern and Western Christianity, and between Christianity and Islam – the Western Balkans has a wealth of architectural treasures from each of the main faiths. Adding to the mix are historic Jewish communities and followers of the Sufi strands of Islamic dervish mysticism.

Cathedral of St Domnius, Croatia

A survivor from ancient Rome's pagan days, the Emperor Diocletian's imposing classical mausoleum is now Split's Catholic cathedral (p179).

Visoki Dečani Monastery, Kosovo

Vivid frescoes fill this Unesco-listed 14th-century Serbian Orthodox monastery (p226), set in an incredibly beautiful spot beneath the mountains of Western Kosovo.

Painted Mosque, North Macedonia

Covered in frescoes, inside and out, Tetovo's Painted Mosque (p301) is the most striking Islamic religious building in the region.

Blagaj Tekke, Bosnia & Hercegovina

The contemplation of nature plays a part in dervish spirituality, and this half-timbered Islamic prayer house (p116) has a peaceful setting above the cave from which the Buna River flows.

Subotica Synagogue, Serbia

Built in 1902, this richly decorated synagogue (p352) in Serbia's Vojvodina region is a showcase of the Hungarian Secession style.

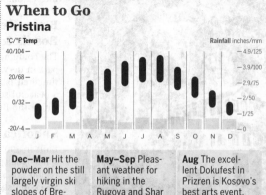

Kosovo

POP 1.92 MILLION

Best Places to Eat

➜ Tiffany (p222)

➜ Renaissance (p222)

➜ Soma Book Station (p222)

➜ Te Syla 'Al Hambra' (p229)

➜ Čaršija e Jupave (p225)

Best Places to Stay

➜ Hotel Prima (p222)

➜ White Tree Hostel (p221)

➜ Dukagjini Hotel (p225)

➜ Driza's House (p228)

➜ Hotel Prizreni (p228)

➜ Hotel Čaršija e Jupave (p225)

Why Go?

Europe's newest country, Kosovo is a fascinating land at the heart of the Balkans rewarding visitors with welcoming smiles, charming mountain towns, incredible hiking opportunities and 13th-century domed Serbian monasteries brushed in medieval art – and that's just for starters.

Kosovo declared independence from Serbia in 2008, and while it has been diplomatically recognised by 111 countries, there are still many nations that do not accept Kosovan independence, including Serbia. The country has been the recipient of massive aid from the international community, particularly the EU and NATO. Barbs of its past are impossible to miss, though: roads are dotted with memorials to those killed in 1999, while NATO forces still guard Serbian monasteries. No matter what many people who've never been to Kosovo might tell you, it's perfectly safe to travel here. Despite this, Kosovo remains one of the last truly off-the-beaten-path destinations in Europe.

When to Go
Pristina

Dec–Mar Hit the powder on the still largely virgin ski slopes of Brezovica.	**May–Sep** Pleasant weather for hiking in the Rugova and Shar Mountains.	**Aug** The excellent Dokufest in Prizren is Kosovo's best arts event.

Entering the Country

Despite Kosovo's slightly ambiguous international status it's well connected with other European countries by air and, with most neighbouring countries, by land. Whichever way you come, entering Kosovo is generally a breeze, with very welcoming and bureaucracy-free immigration and customs. One thing to be aware of, however, is that if you wish to travel between Serbia and Kosovo, you'll need to enter Kosovo from Serbia first.

ITINERARIES

Three Days

Spend a day in cool little Pristina (p220) and get to know Kosovo's charmingly chaotic capital. The next day, visit Visoki Dečani Monastery (p226), then head on to Prizren (p227) to see the old town's Ottoman sights and enjoy the view from the castle.

One Week

After a couple of days in the capital and visits to Gračanica Monastery (p224) and the Bear Sanctuary (p224), loop to lovely Prizren (p227) for a night before continuing to Peja (p225) for monasteries and markets. End with a few days of hiking and climbing in the beautiful Rugova Valley (p226).

Essential Food & Drink

Byrek Pastry with cheese or meat.

Gjuveç Baked meat and vegetables.

Fli Flaky pastry pie served with honey.

Kos Goats-milk yoghurt.

Pershut Dried meat.

Qofta Flat or cylindrical minced-meat rissoles.

Tavë Meat baked with cheese and egg.

Vranac Red wine from the Rahovec (Orahovac) region of Kosovo.

Resources

UN Mission in Kosovo Online (unmik.unmissions.org) A good overview of the UN's work in Kosovo and the latest security situation.

Balkan Insight (www.balkaninsight.com) Quality news and analysis about the Balkans, with a good section on Kosovo.

Kosovo Guide (www.kosovoguide.com) An excellent Kosovo travel wiki.

AT A GLANCE

Area 10,887 sq km

Capital Pristina

Country Code 383

Currency euro (€)

Emergency Ambulance 94; police 92

Language Albanian, Serbian

Population 1.92 million

Time Central European Time (GMT/UTC plus one hour)

Visas Kosovo is visa-free for many travellers for a stay of up to 90 days.

Sleeping Price Ranges

The following price ranges are for a double room with bathroom.

€ less than €40

€€ €40–€80

€€€ more than €80

Eating Price Ranges

The following price categories are for the average cost of a main course.

€ less than €5

€€ €5–€10

€€€ more than €10

Kosovo Highlights

1 Prizren's old town
(p227) Discovering the picturesque, mosque-studded streets of Prizren's charming old quarter and getting a breathtaking view from the fortress.

2 Rugova Valley (p226) Trekking around the stunning landscapes of Kosovo's most impressive mountains, which rise to the west of Peja.

3 Visoki Dečani Monastery (p226) Taking in gorgeous frescoes and then buying monk-made wine and cheese at this serene 14th-century Serbian monastery.

4 Pristina (p220) Exploring Europe's youngest country through its plucky and idiosyncratic capital city and enjoying its excellent dining and nightlife.

5 Patriarchate of Peć (p225) Travelling back in time as you listen to haunting chanting at this medieval church.

6 Bear Sanctuary (p224) Visiting the rescued bears living in excellent conditions at this wonderful lakeside sanctuary that's just a short trip from the capital.

PRISTINA

📞 038 / POP 211,000

Pristina is a fast-changing city that feels full of optimism and potential, even if its traffic-clogged streets and mismatched architectural styles don't make it an obviously attractive place. While the city does have a couple of worthwhile museums and galleries, and serves as a base for interesting nearby sights, for most visitors Pristina is a place where the atmosphere is as much an attraction as any classic tourist sight.

Outside the crowded city centre, with its international restaurants and smart cafes, you'll find yourself in the quaint Turkic hillside neighbourhoods that have defined the city for centuries, where the call to prayer still sounds from minarets overlooking the city's terracotta roofs and where the bustling bazaar remains the focal point of daily life.

⊙ Sights

Central Pristina has been impressively redesigned and is focused on the Ibrahim Rugova Sq, the centrepiece of the city at the end of the attractive, pedestrianised Blvd Nënë Tereza. On summer evenings the square comes alive with strolling families, street performers and little tots racing around on miniature cars.

★ Emin Gjiku

Ethnographic Museum   HISTORIC BUILDING

(Map p223; Rr Iliaz Agushi; ⊙10am-5pm Tue-Sat, to 3pm Sun) FREE This wonderful annex of the Museum of Kosovo (p221) is located in two beautifully preserved Ottoman houses enclosed in a large walled garden. The English-speaking staff will give you a fascinating tour of both properties and point out the various unique pieces of clothing, weaponry, jewellery and household items on display in each. There's no better introduction to Kosovar culture. It's not the easiest place to find and it's not always open during stated hours. The best bet is to ask staff at the Museum of Kosovo.

Museum of Kosovo   MUSEUM

(Map p223; Sheshi Adam Jashari; ⊙10am-6pm Tue-Sun) FREE Pristina's main museum has recently reopened after extensive renovations. Displays begin back in the misty times of the Bronze Age. There are some wonderful statues and monuments to Dardanian gods and goddesses, plus a large stone relief depicting a Dardanian funeral procession.

Bizarrely, the museum then happily skips some 2000 years of history (because clearly nothing at all of note happened between 200 AD and the modern age!) to move straight onto the 19th century and a collection of military weapons which, if nothing else, illustrates how much our technological knowledge has advanced but our intelligence hasn't... Most displays are labelled in English, leaflets giving more detail are also available.

Sultan Mehmet Fatih Mosque   MOSQUE

(Xhamia e Mbretit; Map p223; Rr Ilir Konushevci; ⊙dawn-dusk) The 'imperial mosque', as locals call it, was built on the orders of Mehmed the Conqueror around 1461, and although it was converted to a Catholic church during the Austro-Hungarian era, it was renovated again after WWII and is now the city's most important mosque. The minaret collapsed during an earthquake in 1955; the one standing today is a reconstruction. It has some beautiful interiors, as well as striking painted ceilings over the main entrance.

National Gallery of Kosovo   GALLERY

(Map p223; ☑038 225 627; Rr Agim Ramadani 60; ⊙10am-6pm Mon-Fri, to 5pm Sat & Sun) FREE This excellent space approaches Kosovan art from a contemporary perspective (don't expect to see paintings from the country's history here) and is worth a look around. Exhibitions change frequently and the gallery space is normally given over to a single artist at any one time. At the time of research, the 'art' included a stable of live cows.

It hosts the annual exhibition for the Muslim Mulliqi Prize, the country's leading contemporary visual arts award, around which an exhibition is created each year, guest-curated by a leading art-world figure.

🛌 Sleeping

★ White Tree Hostel   HOSTEL €

(Map p223; ☑049 166 777; www.whitetreehostel.com; Rr Mujo Ulqinaku 15; dm €10-12, d €34; ❄🛜) Pristina's best hostel is run by a group of well-travelled locals who took a derelict house into their care, painted the tree in the courtyard white and gradually began to attract travellers with a cool backpacker vibe. It feels more like an Albanian beach resort than a downtown Pristina bolthole.

Dorms have between four and eight beds plus there are a couple of decent double rooms with private bathrooms. There's also a fully equipped kitchen and it adjoins a very chilled, semi-open-air lounge bar (open to nonguests), which is a perfect place to meet other young travellers. With bicycles attached to the walls and giant metal sculptures, it's all very Instagrammable. The crew also runs a cocktail bar/nightclub in the same building.

Han Hostel   HOSTEL €

(Map p223; ☑044 396 852; www.hostelhan.com; Rr Fehmi Agani 2/4; dm €9-10, d €25; @🛜) Pristina's cheapest hostel is on the 4th floor of a residential building right in the heart of town. Cobbled together from two apartments that have been joined and converted, it all looks a bit grubby from the outside, but in fact this great space has a large communal kitchen, balconies and smart rooms with clean bathrooms. It's well set up for backpackers and run by an extremely friendly local crew.

★ Hotel Prima
BOUTIQUE HOTEL €€
(Map p223; ☑044 111 298; Lldhja e Prizrenit 24; s/d incl breakfast from €30/50; ❄ 🛜) This small family-run hotel on a quiet side street gets pretty much everything right and is easily one of the best sleeps in Pristina. The understated rooms have work desks, wardrobes, and thoughtful extras such as hair-dryers. The beds are solid and comfortable and the showers are always hot. English-speaking staff are full of tips and ideas for Kosovo travel. Excellent value.

Hotel Sirius
BUSINESS HOTEL €€€
(Map p223; ☑044 111 111, 038 222 280; https://siriushotelpristina.reserve-online.net/about; Rr Agam Ramadani; s/d incl breakfast €88/115; ❄ 🛜) The gnarled-tree-branch art in the lobby sets the tone for this smart business-oriented hotel, which sits just steps from Pristina's main square and has spacious and spotless rooms with good bathrooms and fully stocked minibars. There's a gym and business centre, and staff are polite and professional.

The upper levels have great city views; as do the rooftop bar and the restaurant with its all-glass wine cellar.

✖ Eating

Babaghanoush
VEGETARIAN €
(Map p223; Johan V Hahn; mains €2-6; ⏱10.30am-11pm Mon-Sat; 🍴) This tiny, family-run, side-street restaurant is a real delight. The menu is 100% vegetarian and takes its inspiration from the Middle East. The meze includes feta and walnut pâté and red-lentil soup, and the limited but expertly crafted mains include a range of salads or the delicious falafel plate (€5), which mixes falafel with hummus, tabouli and yogurt.

★ Soma Book Station
MEDITERRANEAN €€
(Map p223; ☑038 748818; 4/a Fazli Grajqevci; mains €5-11; ⏱8am-1am Mon-Sat; 🛜) Soma is a local institution among the young, and nearly all visitors to Pristina end up here at some point. The shady garden hums with activity at lunchtime, while the red-brick industrial-chic interior is lined with bookshelves and has a relaxed vibe. Food combines various tastes of the Mediterranean, including tuna salad, beef carpaccio, grilled fish, steaks and burgers.

El Greco
GREEK €€
(Map p223; ☑038 231 550; Meto Bajraktari; mains €5-7; ⏱10am-midnight Mon-Fri, from 11am Sat, from 3pm Sun) Imagine yourself tucked up inside a Greek beachside taverna and that's how you'll feel in this blue-and-white back-street Greek restaurant. You could make a meal out of the many different mezes, which include treats such as feta stuffed peppers or prawns fried in white wine. The main courses focus on meaty mountain fare and include meatballs and steaks.

Liburnia
ALBANIAN €€
(Map p223; ☑044 891 000; Meto Bajraktari; mains €6-8; ⏱8am-11pm Mon-Fri, noon-11pm Sat & Sun) With glowing lamps, traditional Albanian folk music, and tangled vines and flowering plants dripping off the twisted roof beams, this atmospheric backstreet restaurant is an essential pit stop in Pristina. The food is traditional Albanian mountain fare and the restaurant is renowned for its slow-cooked goat, steaming casseroles and home-baked bread.

Renaissance
BALKAN €€€
(Renesansa; ☑044 239 377; Rr Musine Kokollari 35; set meals €15; ⏱6pm-midnight Mon-Sat) This atmospheric place might be Pristina's best-kept secret. Wooden doors open to a traditional stone-walled dining room where tables are brimming with local wine, delicious meze and meaty main courses prepared by the family's matriarch. There's no menu and you'll just be brought a whole array of different dishes. Come with friends and prepare for a long, leisurely meal.

Tiffany
BALKAN €€€
(Map p223; ☑038 244 040; off Rr Fehmi Agani; meals €12; ⏱9am-10.30pm Mon-Sat, from 6pm Sun; 🛜) The organic menu here (delivered by efficient, if somewhat terse, English-speaking staff) is simply dazzling: sit on the sun-dappled terrace and enjoy the day's grilled special, beautifully cooked seasonal vegetables drenched in olive oil, and freshly baked bread. Understandably much prized by the foreign community, this brilliant place is unsigned and somewhat hidden behind a well-tended bush on Fehmi Agani.

🍷 Drinking & Entertainment

Dit' e Nat'
CAFE
(Map p223; ☑038 742 037; www.ditenat.com/en; Rr Fazli Grajqevci 5; ⏱8am-midnight Mon-Sat, from noon Sun; 🛜) 'Day and night' is a home away

KOSOVO PRISTINA

Pristina

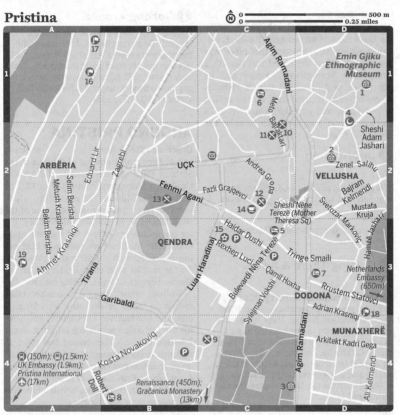

Pristina

◎ Top Sights
1 Emin Gjiku Ethnographic
Museum... D1

◎ Sights
2 Museum of Kosovo D2
3 National Gallery of Kosovo C4
4 Sultan Mehmet Fatih
Mosque.. D1

🛏 Sleeping
5 Han Hostel... C3
6 Hotel Prima..C1
7 Hotel Sirius... D3
8 White Tree Hostel B4

⊗ Eating
9 Babaghanoush C4

10 El Greco... C2
11 Liburnia C2
12 Soma Book Station............................. C2
13 Tiffany B2

🍸 Drinking & Nightlife
14 Dit' e Nat'.. C2

✪ Entertainment
15 Hamam Jazz Bar................................. C3

ℹ Information
16 French Embassy A1
17 German Embassy A1
18 Swiss Embassy D3
19 US Embassy A3

from home for bookish expats and locals alike. There's a great selection of books in English, strong espresso, excellent cocktails, friendly English-speaking staff and occasional live music in the evenings, including jazz. Unusually for meat-loving Kosovo, Dit' e Nat' serves a few vegetarian light lunches and snacks.

Hamam Jazz Bar   JAZZ

(Map p223; ☑038 222 289, 044 222 289; Rr Ha-jdar Dushi 62; ☺6pm-midnight) Easily Pristi-na's most stylish nightspot, this place was also the city's first dedicated jazz bar. It's a fantastically atmospheric lounge, and its impressive post-industrial design includes sheets of cracked dried mud on the ceiling to provide sound isolation, concrete walls and lots of nooks and crannies to enjoy the live music from.

🛈 Information

POST

PTK Post (Map p223; Rr UÇK; ☺8am-8pm Mon-Sat) Post and special delivery services.

MONEY

There are plenty of banks and ATMs throughout the city centre.

🛈 Getting There & Away

AIR

Pristina International Airport (☑038 501 502 1214; www.airportpristina.com) is 18km from the centre of Prilines. There is currently no public transport to and from the airport, so you'll have to get a taxi into the city. Taxis charge €20 for the 20-minute, 18km trip to the city centre, though many will try to ask for more – always agree on a price before you get in. Going from the city to the airport, the cost is normally €13 to 15.

BUS

The **bus station** (Stacioni i Autobusëve; ☑038 550 011; Rr Lidja e Pejes) is 2km southwest of the centre off Blvd Bil Klinton. Taxis to the cen-tre should cost €2, but drivers will often try to charge tourists €5 to €7.

International buses from Pristina include Belgrade (€15.50, seven hours, 11pm) and Novi Pazar (€7.50, three hours, three daily) in Serbia; Tirana, Albania (€10.50, five hours, every one to two hours); Skopje, North Macedonia (€5.50, two hours, hourly from 5.30am to 5pm); Podgorica, Montenegro (€15.50, seven hours, 7pm) and Ulcinj, Montenegro (€15.50, seven hours, 8am and 9pm).

Domestically there are buses to all corners of the country, including Prizren (€4, 75 minutes, every 20 minutes) and Peja (€4, 1½ hours, every 20 minutes).

TRAIN

Trains run from Pristina's small train station in the suburb of Fushë Kosovo to Peja (€3, two hours, twice daily at 8.01am and 4.41pm) and to Skopje in North Macedonia (€4, three hours, 7.22am daily).

🛈 Getting Around

Pristina has a comprehensive bus network. Tick-ets cost 40c and can be bought on board. With the city centre being as small as it is, few travel-lers ever need to make use of these buses. Taxi meters start at €1.50, and most trips around the city can be done for under €3. Try **Radio Taxi Victory** (☑038 555 333).

AROUND PRISTINA

Gračanica Monastery   MONASTERY

(€2; ☺8am-6pm) Southeast of Pristina in the Serbian town of Gračanica is the ancient Gračanica Monastery, completed in 1321 by Serbian king Milutin. The monastery, which is set on large, grassy grounds, is one of the most attractive in Kosovo. You will first en-ter the monastery chapel through the main doors. The medieval-era paintings here are impressive enough but the real treat is saved for the smaller side, chapel, which is an en-chanted cavern of vivid, lifelike murals.

Visitors must dress respectably (that means no shorts or sleeveless tops for any-one, and headscarves for women) and pho-tos are forbidden inside the building. From Pristina, take a Gjilan-bound bus (50c, 15 minutes, every 30 minutes); the monastery's on your left as you enter the centre of town. A taxi from Pristina costs around €7 one-way. It's worth combining a visit here with the nearby Bear Sanctuary.

★ Bear Sanctuary   NATURE RESERVE

(☑045 826 072; www.facebook.com/PylliiArin jvePrishtina; Mramor; adult/child €2/1 Apr-Oct, €1/0.50c Nov-Mar; ☺10am-7pm Apr-Oct, to 4pm Nov-Mar) In a remote, forested spot beyond the village of Mramor, this sanctuary hous-es European brown bears that were rescued from captivity by the charity Four Paws. All the bears here were once kept in tiny cages as restaurant mascots, so although they're hardly out free in the wilderness, the spa-cious, semiwooded enclosures of today are a million times better than the conditions they were once kept in. You can learn more about the bears at the impressive new visitor centre.

From Pristina, board any Gjilan-bound bus and ask to be let off by the Delfina gas sta-tion at the entrance to Mramor. From there, follow the road back past the lakeside, and then around to the right. It's a 3km walk, and the gorgeous countryside and lake make a great spot for a picnic afterwards. Otherwise there's a decent terrace restaurant within the sanctuary (mains around €5.50). A taxi from

Pristina is around €15 and for a couple of euros extra, drivers will stop off at the Gračanica Monastery on the way.

WESTERN KOSOVO

Peja (Peć)

🗹 039 / POP 97,000

Peja (Peć in Serbian) is Kosovo's third-largest city and one flanked by sites sacred to Orthodox Serbians. With a Turkish-style bazaar at its heart, Peja would be a worthwhile stop on its own, but for most visitors the real reason to visit is to use the town as the launch pad to some wonderful mountain adventures in the spectacular nearby Rugova Valley and surrounding mountains. All of this means that Peja is fast becoming Kosovo's international tourism hub.

◉ Sights

★ **Patriarchate of Peć**   MONASTERY
(Pećka Patrijaršija; 🗹 044 150 755; with audio guide €2; ⊙ 8am-6pm) This church and nunnery complex on the outskirts of Peja are a raw slice of Serbian Orthodoxy that has existed here since the late 13th century. Outside in the landscaped grounds, all is bright and colourful, but once inside the church it feels more like you're within a dark cave with magnificent faded frescoes covering the walls and ceiling. The entire complex dates from between the 1230s and the 1330s.

Regional Museum   MUSEUM
(Muzeu Rajonal; 🗹 039 431 976; Sheshi Haxhi Zeka; €1; ⊙ 8am-noon & 1-4pm Mon-Fri, 10am-2pm Sat & Sun) The top-floor of this Ottoman-era house, located behind a rather less-than-traditional petrol station, is filled with local crafts and furniture and has various displays illustrating life in Peja during the Ottoman period. The downstairs floor has a small and more interesting archeological section that does a great job of illustrating the depth of history in these parts. Labelling is poor but some staff members speak English, and when they're working, an animated guided tour is included in your entry fee.

⌖ Tours

★ **Balkan Natural Adventure**   ADVENTURE
(🗹 049 661 105; www.bnadventure.com; Mbreteresha Teute) Balkan Natural Adventure is easily the standout local adventure tour operator. In fact, it was the friendly English-speaking

GJAKOVA
....
Gjakova (also known as Đakovica in Serbian) is a laid-back, likeable and historical town famous for having the longest bazaar in the Balkans. While much of the modern town is fairly unremarkable, its old town and Čaršija (bazaar) are both charming and it's worth an overnight stop as you travel between Prizren and Peja. And, to make your night here even more pleasant, stay at the **Hotel Čaršija e Jupave** (🗹 039 0326 798; www.qarshiaeju pave.com; Rr Ismail Qemali 9; d incl breakfast from €50; 🅿 ❄ 🛜). The beautiful rambling building that the hotel is housed within is all wooden beams, long paper light shades, abstract art and flower-sprinkled bed throws. The service is almost embarrassingly good and there's a memorable in-house restaurant also called **Čaršija e Jupave** (mains €6; ⊙ 7am-11pm; 🕿).

team here who first established many of the trekking trails in the surrounding mountains and put in the via ferrata and zip line. It can also organise caving, rock climbing or snowshoeing, and the crew leads 'Peaks of the Balkans' hiking tours.

🍴 Sleeping & Eating

Stone Bridge Guesthouse   HOTEL €
(🗹 049 797 112; stonebridge.gh@gmail.com; Rr Lidhja e Pejës 6; d €25; 🛜) This new, 10-room hotel in the heart of the town offers superb value for money. The modern, white-and-grey rooms have ubercomfortable mattresses and there are small, modern bathrooms. Try to nab a back room to cut out the worst of the street noise.

★ **Dukagjini Hotel**   HOTEL €€
(🗹 038 771 177; www.hoteldukagjini.com; Sheshi i Dëshmorëve 2; d incl breakfast from €55; 🅿 ❄ ❄ 🛜 ⊛) The regal stone-walled Dukagjini is the smartest address in town. Rooms can be rather small but are grandly appointed and have supremely comfortable beds; many on the 1st floor have huge terraces overlooking the central square. There's a pool and gym and a huge restaurant with views of the river. Free parking.

★ **Art Design**   BALKAN €
(🗹 049 585 885, 044 222 254; Rr Enver Hadri 53; mains €3.50-6; ⊙ 8am-midnight) Despite

sounding flash and modern, Art Design is actually an old house brimming with character and full of local arts and crafts. Choose between dining outside over a little stream or in one of the two rather chintzy dining rooms. Traditional dishes here include *sarma* (meat and rice rolled in grape leaves) and *speca dollma* (peppers filled with meat and rice).

Kulla e Zenel Beut BALKAN €€
(Rr William Walker; mains €3-7; ⊙8am-midnight Mon-Sat; 🔊) This charming option in the centre of town has a pleasant terrace and a cosy dining room. The dishes to go for here are the *tava* (various traditional specialties served in clay pots), though fresh fish, baked mussels, grills and even a breakfast menu are on offer.

ⓘ Getting There & Away

BUS
The town's **bus station** (Rr Adem Jashar) is on Rr Adem Jashari, a 15-minute walk from the town centre. Frequent buses run to Pristina (€4, 1½ hours, every 20 minutes), Prizren (€3, 80 minutes, hourly), Gjakova (€2, 50 minutes, hourly) and Deçan (€1, 20 minutes, hourly). International buses link Peja with Ulclinj (€20, 10 hours, 10am and 8.30pm) and Podgorica in Montenegro (€15, seven hours, 10am).

TRAIN
Trains depart Peja for Pristina (€3, two hours, twice daily) from the town's small **train station** (Rr Emrush Miftari). To find the station, walk away from the Hotel Dukagjini down Rr Emrush Miftari for 1.4km.

Rugova Valley
📷 039

The Rugova Valley and the mountains that hem it in are Kosovo's adventure playground. The serpentine valley itself winds westward out of Peja and climbs steadily upwards toward the border of Montenegro. Narrow side-roads spin off this main route, giving access to high-mountain pastures, glacial lakes and fairy-tale pine forests. Activities include caving, rafting, via ferrata, zip-lining, skiing and snowshoeing, but it's the hiking that really makes this a standout tourist destination. This knot of mountains (which also extends into parts of Albania and Montenegro) is one of the most beautiful mountain ranges in Eastern Europe and remains deliciously unspoiled. Slowly, though, facilities for trekkers are increasing. The world-renowned Peaks of the Balkans long-distance hiking route crosses through the heart of these mountains, and throughout the area, hiking trails are becoming better way-marked.

🏃 Activities

Via Ferrata CLIMBING
(📞 064 9661 105; www.bnadventure.com; via ferrata per person for 2 people €20, via ferrata per person for 3 or more €15) For the brave, two (with a third to come) via ferrata routes have been bolted to the vertical rock face in the lower Rugova Valley. The first goes from the valley floor straight up 450m on a bolted metal rope. The second is a 500m horizontal bolted

KOSOVO RUGOVA VALLEY

WORTH A TRIP

VISOKI DEČANI MONASTERY

Built in the early 14th century by Serbian king Stefan Dečanski, the **Visoki Dečani Monastery** (📞 049 776 254; www.decani.org; ⊙10am-2.30pm & 3.30-5.30pm Mon-Sat, 10am-5.30pm Sun) **FREE** is in a beautiful spot beneath the mountains and surrounded by pine and chestnut trees. If you think the setting is attractive then you'll gasp in wonder as you push open the wooden doors of the church and first lay eyes on the treasures within. With its floor-to-ceiling, Biblical murals it's like stepping into an enormous medieval paintbox. There can be few more beautiful churches in Europe.

Despite the bucolic setting and beauty within, Visoki Dečani also speaks of humanity at its worst. Due to attacks from ethnic Albanians who'd like to see the Serbs leave, the monastery and the 25 monks living here in total isolation from the local community are guarded around the clock by KFOR military forces. You will need to leave your passport or ID card with the soldiers at the entrance gate if you wish to enter the complex.

It's on the outskirts of Dečani, 15km south of Peja (Peć). Buses go to Dečani from Peja (€1, 30 minutes, every 15 minutes) on their way to Gjakova. It's a pleasant 1km walk to the monastery from the bus stop. From the roundabout in the middle of town, take the second exit if you're coming from Peja.

HIKING HAJLA

One of the more popular day-hike trails in the Rugova area is the taxing hike to the summit of Mt Hajla (2403m) on the Kosovo–Montenegro border. A guide is a good idea as the route isn't very well signposted and the ascent to the actual summit is exposed and steep. The trail begins from beside the Ariu Guesthouse in the village of Reka Allages and finishes some six hours later in the village of Drelaj.

The walk starts out through dense, near-pristine forest where bears are sometimes spotted, and then crosses some mountain pastures with seasonal shepherd huts (be careful of the sheep dogs). After a short, fairly flat part you'll need to brace yourself for the steep, lung-bursting zig-zag ascent to the table-like summit of Hajla. As you approach the summit, a little caution is required as you'll be tip-toeing along the edge of an absolutely sheer cliff face, which drops down hundreds of metres into Montenegro. The views from the summit down to the plains of Montenegro are extraordinary.

From the summit, you can either retrace your steps back to where you began or take the longer trail down through forest and then pretty farming country to the village of Drelaj (on the Peaks of the Balkans trail), where you'll find accommodation; transport back to Peja can be arranged. Bring a packed lunch and plenty of water.

trail. Both take about an hour-and-a-half to complete (plus a 30- to 40-minute descent for the first one). All safety gear is provided and guides are there to take you safely along.

Zip-Line ADVENTURE SPORTS
(☑ 064 9661 105; www.bnadventure.com; €10) Hurtle down the Rugova Valley on this new zipline. The route covers 650m and you'll go from start to finish in just over a minute. If we were cleverer, we'd tell you how fast that meant you were travelling... The minimum weight is 25kg and the maximum is 150kg.

🛏 Sleeping

Ariu Guesthouse GUESTHOUSE €
(☑ 04 438 3184, 04 483 1320; Reka Allages; per person full board €25) This farm guesthouse in the idyllic mountain village of Reka Allages sits on the Peaks of the Balkans trail and forms a launch pad for tackling Mt Hajla. The basic accommodation is in six- to 10-person dorms, though a new and more luxurious building was under construction at research time. A stay includes all meals, most of which are made from organic, home-grown food.

Shiqiponja GUESTHOUSE €
(☑ 04 958 6740; Drelaj; per person incl full board €25) On a small farm in the village of Drelaj (the only permanently inhabited village in the upper valley), this welcoming guesthouse has a variety of well-maintained dorm rooms, each of which has its own bathroom. Meals generally utilise home-grown produce. It's on the Peaks of the Balkans trail and is the end point for the Hajla mountain trek.

ℹ Getting There & Away

There is a very limited public transport network along the valley. It's definitely best to have your own car to get around here, or at least hire a taxi in Peja to drive you to your chosen trailhead.

SOUTHERN KOSOVO

Prizren

☑ 029 / POP 185,000

Picturesque Prizren, with its charming mosque- and church-filled old town, shines with an enthusiasm that's infectious. It's Kosovo's second city and most obvious tourist town and is well worth a day or two's lingering exploration. The castle high above the city is a must-see and there's a museum or two, plus the town can be used as a base for day trips to the Shar Mountains. Prizren is equally known for Dokufest, a documentary film festival held each August that attracts documentary makers and fans from all over the world.

The young population means that in the evenings the old town buzzes with revellers and enjoys a very sociable air. However, the town's current glow masks a tragic and divisive past: of the 20,000 Serbs who lived here in 1999, only 20 remain, guarding fiercely the sorrowful remnants of their once strong presence.

SHAR MOUNTAINS

South of Prizren, and tucked into the finger of land extending down into North Macedonia, are the remote and wild Shar Mountains. Topping out (on the Kosovo side of the range) at 2582m, this is one of the least developed and most unknown corners of Kosovo. These undulating, moorland mountains offer fabulous hiking potential, though route way-marking remains sketchy at best. This will likely change in coming years as international tourism grows, especially as in 2017 a new long-distance trail was formally opened. Called the High Scardus Trail, it's a 495km-long route winding through the Macedonian, Kosovan and Albanian parts of the Shar Mountains, although for the moment it remains underdeveloped and little advertised. If this trail is too ambitious, then numerous day walks are possible in the mountains, but for all of them a local guide is recommended. The experienced mountain guides at **E-19 Snowshoeing** (📞 044 201 315; www.snowshoe ing-ks.com; M-99 Hostel, Rr Tabakëve 40) know the trails better than most. The main village in the mountains is Brod, a tiny place (with some limited accommodation) beyond the regional town of Dragash. Suggested one-day hikes from Brod include a walk to a beautiful glacial lake in a deep mountain bowl.

The best place to stay near Brod is the **Hotel Arxhena** (📞 29 285170; Brod; d incl breakfast from €50; ❄ 🛜), which has dark-wood-panelled rooms, completely over-the-top shower units, great mountain views and a restaurant with an outdoor terrace. Walking guides can be arranged, plus there's a spa and an on-site ski lift.

🅞 Sights

Prizren Fortress   CASTLE
(Kalaja; ⊘ dawn-dusk) **FREE** It's well worth making the steep 15-minute hike up from Prizren's old town (follow the road past the Orthodox Church on the hillside; it's well signed and pretty obvious) for the superb views over the city and on into the distance. The fortress itself is a little tumble-down but restoration work is currently underway. In the evening heaps of locals come up here and a slight carnival atmosphere prevails. In the white-heat of day, it can be quite lifeless.

Sinan Pasha Mosque   MOSQUE
(Xhamia e Sinan Pashës; Vatra Shqiptare; ⊘ dawn-dusk) Dating from 1615, the Sinan Pasha Mosque is the most important in Prizren, and it sits right at the heart of the old town, overlooking the river and the town's Ottoman Bridge. Its impressive dome, minaret and colonnaded facade form a fabulous sight from the street, though it's also well worth going inside (outside of prayer times) to see the striking interior.

🎪 Festivals & Events

Dokufest   FILM
(www.dokufest.com; ⊘ early Aug) This superb annual documentary festival has gained a loyal following from documentary makers and lovers around the world. Tickets are easy to come by, and outdoor cinemas are set up around the town, including one stage over the river and another inside the castle.

🛏 Sleeping & Eating

Driza's House   HOSTEL €
(📞 049 618 181; www.drizas-house.com; Remzi Ademaj 7; dm incl breakfast €9-15, tw/tr €25/42; ❄ 🛜) This former family home in a courtyard just off the river embankment retains a welcoming, homey vibe and is full of local charm. It's made up of two (10- and four-bed) dorms with custom-made bunk beds, all of which include curtains, reading lights, personal electricity plugs and lockable storage cupboards; there's also a comfortable private three-bed room.

⭐ Hotel Prizreni   HOTEL €
(📞 029 225 200; www.hotelprizreni.com; Rr Shën Flori 2; s/d incl breakfast from €30/34; 🅿 ❄ 🛜) With an unbeatable location just behind the Sinan Pasha Mosque (though some may be less pleased with the location during the dawn call to prayer), the Prizreni is a pleasant combination of traditional and modern, with 12 small but stylish and contemporary rooms, great views and enthusiastic staff. There's a restaurant downstairs (open 8am to 11pm).

Tiffany   BOUTIQUE HOTEL €€€
(📞 049 281 100; Marin Barleti 16; d from €65; ❄ 🛜) Classy new six-room boutique hotel in an almost overly well-restored old town-house that retains some of the original woodwork.

Modern rooms have plenty of space, the best bathrooms in town, inviting beds, and tubs of flowering geraniums on the window sills. A decent restaurant serving traditional dishes rounds out the deal.

★ **Te Syla 'Al Hambra'** KEBAB €
(☎049 157 400; www.tesyla.com; Shuaib Spahiu; kebabs €2-4; ☺8am-11pm) Unlike most riverside places in Prizren, there's nothing pretentious about this place. It was first established in the 1960s by a street vendor who just sizzled up kebabs on the corner. From such humble beginnings grew this local classic. The kebabs are as sensational as ever, with the meat literally melting in your mouth.

Fish House SEAFOOD €€
(☎045 850 630; www.facebook.com/fishhouseprizren; Shatervan; mains €2.50-8; ☺9am-midnight) Making a light and healthy change from the normal meat-heavy Kosovan diet, the Fish House, which has a quiet garden setting a block back from the river and is easily spotted thanks to the sculpture of a marlin leaping clear of the waves, serves local trout with salad or much-less-local sardines and sea bream. Locals devour the seafood soup.

Restaurant Marashi BALKAN €€
(☎045 225 985; Vatra Shqiptare; mains €3-6; ☺8am-11pm) This renowned riverside restaurant set beside a majestic old sycamore tree serves a range of authentic, traditional Albanian dishes, but it's best-known for its steaks, which you cook yourself on hot stones.

ⓘ Getting There & Away

Prizren is well connected by bus to Pristina (€4, two hours, every 20 minutes), Peja (€3, 80 minutes to two hours, frequent), Skopje in North Macedonia (€10, three hours, two daily) and Tirana in Albania (€12, three hours, seven daily).

The **bus station** is on the right bank of the river, a short walk from the old town: follow the right-hand side of the river embankment away from the castle until you come to the traffic circle, then turn left onto Rr De Rada. The bus station will be on your left after around 200m.

UNDERSTAND KOSOVO

Kosovo Today

Politics in Kosovo is nothing if not a colourful business, and normalcy seems to be a long way off, still. The number-one job for the new Prime Minister is to try to normalise relations with Serbia. Talks are taking place but it's against an atmosphere of mutual distrust. It hasn't helped that Serbian politicians have engaged in some deliberately provocative acts such as launching a new train line between Belgrade and northern Kosovo in January 2017 with the slogan 'Kosovo is Serbian' written on it in 20 different languages.

KOSOVO UNDERSTAND KOSOVO

OFF THE BEATEN TRACK

MOKRA GORA & GAZIVODE LAKE

The northern, predominately Serbian, part of Kosovo is about as off the beaten track as you can get in Europe. For years this intriguing but troubled corner of the country was considered unsafe and most European governments advised their citizens not to visit. In recent years, though, things have started to change as the ethnic Albanian and Serbian communities make efforts to rebuild bridges. This has resulted in a notable decrease in tensions and it's now generally safe to visit the area (do check travel warnings first though).

The highlight of the region is the artificial Gazivode Lake. Stretching over 24km, it's the largest lake in Kosovo. The area surrounding the lake is all bouncy hills and pleasing forest (it's not as rugged and dramatic as mountain ranges elsewhere in Kosovo), and slowly an adventure tourism industry is starting to spring up around the lake and the Mokra Gora mountain. Organised activities on offer include hiking, mountain biking, kayaking, and the challenging **Via Ferrata Berim**. The 3km-long climbing route has an altitude difference of 520m and leads up to the top of **Berim peak** (1731m). The main operator is **Outdoor In** (☎063 855 0929; www.ibarski-kolasin.org; Kolašinskih kneževa bb, Zubin Potok), based in the small town of **Zubin Potok**. It can help organise all these activities and find accommodation (which is limited in the north).

The main town in northern Kosovo is **Mitrovica**. Serbians live in the northern half and ethnic Albanians in the southern half. Tensions often run high in this town and it pays to be cautious. The best advice is actually to look as much like a tourist as possible!

Entrenched corruption at most levels has further helped to create a deeply cynical population on both sides of the ethnic divide. Tensions continue to simmer between the Albanian and Serbian populations, and it's only due to the enormous presence of KFOR (Kosovo Force; the international force responsible for establishing security in Kosovo) in the country that Kosovo can be said to be a functioning and peaceful state.

History

Be aware that Kosovo's history is interpreted very differently depending on who you're talking to, with people of differing ethnic and religious backgrounds tending to be polarised along these lines.

In the 12th century Kosovo was the heart of the Orthodox Christian Serbian empire. This changed when, at the pivotal 1389 Battle of Kosovo, Turkish triumph ushered in 500 years of Ottoman rule and Islam and set the stage for the bitter ethnic and religious conflict that continues to blight the country.

Serbia regained control of Kosovo in the 1912 Balkan War, and the region became part of Yugoslavia when it was created in 1918. In WWII the territory was incorporated into Italian-controlled Albania; it was later liberated and returned to Yugoslavia in October 1944 by Albanian partisans. Following decades of postwar neglect, Kosovo was granted de-facto self-government status as an autonomous province within Serbia in 1974.

Kosovo War

In 1989 the autonomy Kosovo enjoyed under the 1974 constitution was suspended by Slobodan Milošević. Ethnic Albanian leaders declared independence from Serbia in 1990. War in ex-Yugoslavia broke out in 1992, and that same year Ibrahim Rugova was elected as the first president of the self-proclaimed Republic of Kosovo. Ethnic conflict heightened, and the Kosovo Liberation Army (KLA) was formed in 1996.

In March 1999 a US-backed plan to return Kosovo's autonomy was rejected by Serbia, which moved to empty the province of its non-Serbian population. After Serbia refused to desist, NATO unleashed a bombing campaign on 24 March 1999. Nearly 850,000 Kosovo Albanians fled to Albania and Macedonia, telling of mass killings and forced expulsions. In June Milošević agreed to withdraw troops, air strikes ceased, the KLA

disarmed and the NATO-led KFOR took over. From June 1999, Kosovo was administered as a UN-NATO protectorate.

Kosovo caught the world's attention again in 2004 when violence broke out in Mitrovica between the ethnic Serbian and ethnic Albanian communities; 19 people were killed, 600 homes were burnt and 29 monasteries and churches were destroyed in the worst ethnic violence since 1999.

Independence

UN-sponsored talks on Kosovo's status began in February 2006, and Kosovo's parliament declared Kosovo independent on 17 February 2008.

In June 2008 a new constitution transferred power from the UN to the government of Kosovo. Kosovo Serbs established their own assembly in Mitrovica.

In July 2010 the International Court of Justice ruled that Kosovo's declaration of independence did not violate international law; however, Serbia's then president Boris Tadić reiterated that the Serbian government would not recognise the independence of Kosovo. To date, however, Kosovo has been recognised as an independent country by some 111 countries around the world, including most of the EU, the US, Canada, Australia, New Zealand and Japan.

New Leadership – And Again

In 2015 Isa Mustafa became prime minister of Kosovo, ushering in a new era in Kosovan politics. Mustafa's approach to Kosovo's ethnic Serb population was highly controversial, as exemplified by his being pelted with eggs by opposition MPs while giving a speech in Kosovo's parliament shortly after his election. The extraordinary scene followed Mustafa consenting to Kosovo's Serbian communities gaining a degree of self-determination within the country – a move that some nationalists believed would undermine the unity of the young country.

In 2016 former prime minister Hashim Thaçi was elected president of Kosovo. Thaçi has never been far from controversy, having been accused of everything from drug trafficking to selling the organs of Serbian prisoners during his time heading the KLA; he emphatically denies all such charges.

Elections were held again in June 2017 but these only resulted in political deadlock. After much wrangling, in September 2017 Ramush Haradinaj took over as prime minister. As seems to be par for the course in Kosovan politics, Haradinaj is also a man with a controversial past. Accused of war crimes, he was twice put on trial in the Hague and twice acquitted, but that hasn't stopped Serbia from issuing international arrest warrants for him (following through on this, France arrested him in early 2017 when he flew into Basel before he was again released nearly four months later).

People

According to the 2011 census, the population of Kosovo was 1.74 million; 92% are Albanian and 8% are Serb (mostly living in enclaves), Bosniak, Gorani, Roma, Turkish, Ashkali and Egyptian. The main religious groups are Muslim (mostly Albanians), Serbian Orthodox and Roman Catholic.

Arts

Former president Ibrahim Rugova was a significant figure in Kosovo's literary scene; his presidency of the Kosovo Writers' Association was a step towards presidency of the nation. Albanian writer Ismail Kadare's *Three Elegies for Kosovo* is a beautifully written tale of this land's sad history.

Kosovar music bears the imprint of five centuries of Turkish rule; high-whine flutes carry tunes above goatskin drumbeats. Architecture also shows Islamic influence, mixed with Byzantine and vernacular styles.

The visual arts scene is re-emerging after troubled times; visit the National Gallery of Kosovo to check it out.

SURVIVAL GUIDE

ⓘ Directory A-Z

ACCOMMODATION

Accommodation is booming in Kosovo, with most large towns offering a good range of options. There are now backpacker-style hostels in all major cities, and plenty of midrange and even top-end accommodation in Pristina.

EMBASSIES & CONSULATES

There are no embassies for Australia, Canada, New Zealand or Ireland in Kosovo, so consular issues are handled by the respective embassies in Belgrade.

French Embassy (Map p223; ☑ 038 2245 8800; www.ambafrance-kosovo.org; Ismail Qemali 67)

German Embassy (Map p223; ☑ 045 802 734, 038 254 500; www.pristina.diplo.de; Azem Jashanica 17)

Netherlands Embassy (☑ 038 516 103; Xhemajl Berisha 12)

Swiss Embassy (Map p223; ☑ 038 261 261; www.eda.admin.ch/pristina; Adrian Krasniqi 11)

UK Embassy (☑ 038 254 700; www.ukinkosovo.fco.gov.uk; Lidhja e Pejes 177)

US Embassy (Map p223; ☑ 038 5959 3000; https://xk.usembassy.gov; Nazim Hikmet 30)

LGBTIQ+ TRAVELLERS

While legal, homosexuality remains taboo in Kosovo, and it's not a subject that many people will be comfortable broaching. That said, gay and lesbian travellers should generally have no problems, though public displays of affection are definitely inadvisable. There are no gay bars or clubs in the country, though there are a few gay-friendly bars in Pristina and Prizren. Most contact happens online.

MONEY

Kosovo's currency is the euro, despite the country not being part of the eurozone or the EU. ATMs are common, and established businesses accept credit cards.

OPENING HOURS

Opening hours vary, but these are the usual hours of business.

Banks 8am to 5pm Monday to Friday, until 2pm Saturday

Bars 8am to 11pm

Shops 8am to 6pm Monday to Friday, until 3pm Saturday

Restaurants 8am to midnight

PUBLIC HOLIDAYS

Note that traditional Islamic and Orthodox Christian holidays are also observed, including Ramadan.

New Year's Day 1 January

Independence Day 17 February

Kosovo Constitution Day 9 April

Labour Day 1 May

Europe Day 9 May

SAFE TRAVEL

Northern Kosovo Sporadic violence does occur in north Mitrovica and a few other flashpoints where Serbian and Kosovar communities live in close proximity.

Landmines Unexploded ordnance has been cleared from roads and paths, but you should seek KFOR advice (http://jfcnaples.nato.int/kfor) before venturing too remotely. That said, the situation is improving fast, with mine-clearance programmes all over the country.

BORDER CROSSINGS

Albania There are three border crossings between Kosovo and Albania. To get to Albania's Koman Ferry, use the Qafa Morina border crossing west of Gjakova. A short distance further south is the Qafë Prush crossing, though the road continuing into Albania is bad here. The busiest border is at Vërmicë, where a modern motorway connects to Tirana.

North Macedonia Cross into Blace from Pristina and Gllobocicë from Prizren.

Montenegro The main crossing is Kulla/Rožaje on the road between Rožaje and Peja.

Serbia There are six border crossings between Kosovo and Serbia. Be aware that Kosovo's independence is not recognised by Serbia, so if you plan to continue to Serbia but entered Kosovo via Albania, North Macedonia or Montenegro, officials at the Serbian border will deem that you entered Serbia illegally and you will not be let in. You'll need to exit Kosovo to a third country and then enter Serbia from there. If you entered Kosovo from Serbia, there's no problem returning to Serbia.

Driving While it's perfectly legal, it's not a good idea to travel in Kosovo with Serbian plates on your car: you'll potentially leave yourself open to random attacks or vandalism from locals.

TELEPHONE

Kosovo's country code is +383, though many local telephones still use the prefix +381, a hangover from the days before independence. All numbers given are +383 unless otherwise noted.

VISAS

Kosovo is visa-free for EU, Australian, Canadian, Japanese, New Zealand, South African and US passport holders for stays of up to 90 days.

ℹ Getting There & Away

ENTERING THE COUNTRY

Entering Kosovo is generally a breeze, with very welcoming and bureaucracy-free immigration and customs. One thing to be aware of, however, is that if you wish to travel between Serbia and Kosovo, you'll need to enter Kosovo from Serbia first.

AIR

Pristina International Airport (p224) is 18km from the centre of Pristina. Airlines flying to Kosovo include Air Pristina, Adria, Austrian Airlines, easyJet, Norwegian, Pegasus and Turkish Airlines.

LAND

Kosovo has good bus connections between Albania, Montenegro and North Macedonia, with regular services from Pristina, Peja and Prizren to Tirana (Albania), Skopje (North Macedonia) and Podgorica (Montenegro). There's also a train

line from Pristina to Skopje. You can take international bus trips to and from all neighbouring capital cities; note that buses to and from Belgrade in Serbia travel via Montenegro.

ℹ Getting Around

BUS

Buses stop at distinct blue signs but can be flagged down anywhere. Bus journeys are generally cheap, but the going can be slow on Kosovo's single-lane roads.

CAR & MOTORCYCLE

Drivers should carry their licences with them whenever on the road, as police checks are not uncommon. Road conditions in Kosovo are generally good, though watch out for potholes on some poorly maintained stretches. Driving techniques in Kosovo are erratic at best. When driving, keep alert!

European Green Card vehicle insurance is not valid in Kosovo, so you'll need to purchase vehicle insurance at the border when you enter with a car; this is a hassle-free and inexpensive procedure.

It's perfectly easy to hire cars here and travel with them to neighbouring countries (with the exception of Serbia). Note that Serbian-plated cars have been attacked in Kosovo, and rental companies do not let cars hired in Kosovo travel to Serbia, and vice versa.

TRAIN

The train system is something of a novelty, but services connect Pristina to Peja and to Skopje in neighbouring North Macedonia. Locals generally take buses.

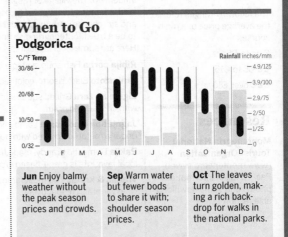

Montenegro Црна Гора

🎵 382 / POP 676,900

Includes ➡

Best Places to Eat

➡ Belveder (p263)
➡ Hotel Soa (p277)
➡ Restaurant Conte (p239)
➡ Konoba Feral (p237)
➡ Antigona (p259)

Best Places to Stay

➡ La Vecchia Casa (p264)
➡ Palazzo Drusko (p244)
➡ Drago (p257)
➡ Palazzo Radomiri (p244)
➡ Old Town Hostel (p243)

Why Go?

Imagine a place with sapphire beaches as spectacular as Croatia's, rugged peaks as dramatic as Switzerland's, canyons nearly as deep as Colorado's, palazzi as elegant as Venice's and towns as old as Greece's. Now wrap it up in a Mediterranean climate and squish it into an area two-thirds the size of Wales and you start to get a picture of Montenegro (Црна Гора).

More adventurous travellers can easily sidestep the peak-season hordes on the coast by heading to the rugged mountains of the north. This is, after all, a country where wolves and bears still lurk in forgotten corners.

Montenegro, Crna Gora, Black Mountain: the name itself conjures up romance and drama. There are plenty of both on offer as you explore this perfumed land, bathed in the scent of wild herbs, conifers and Mediterranean blossoms. Yes, it really is as magical as it sounds.

When to Go
Podgorica

°C/°F Temp   Rainfall inches/mm

Jun Enjoy balmy weather without the peak season prices and crowds.

Sep Warm water but fewer bods to share it with; shoulder season prices.

Oct The leaves turn golden, making a rich backdrop for walks in the national parks.

AT A GLANCE

Area 13,812 sq km

Capital Podgorica

Country Code 🖉 382

Currency euro (€)

Emergency Ambulance 🖉124, fire 🖉123, police 🖉122

Language Montenegrin

Population 676,870

Time Central Europe time zone (GMT/UTC plus one hour)

Visas None for citizens of EU, Canada, USA, Australia, New Zealand and many other countries.

Sleeping Price Ranges

The following price ranges refer to the cheapest option available for a couple.

€ less than €45

€€ €45 to €100

€€€ more than €100

Eating Price Ranges

The following ranges refer to the average price of a main course.

€ up to €5

€€ €5 to €15

€€€ over €15

Resources

Montenegrin National Tourist Organisation (www.montenegro.travel) Packed full of information, photos and some downloadable resources.

Entering the Country

Whether you choose to fly, train, ferry, bus or drive, it's not difficult to get to Montenegro these days. New routes – including those served by low-cost carriers – are continually being added to the busy timetable at the country's two airports. It's also possible to make your way from neighbouring countries, especially Croatia. Dubrovnik's airport is very close to the border and the beautiful city makes an impressive starting point to a Montenegro holiday. Flights, cars and tours can be booked online at lonelyplanet.com/bookings.

ITINERARIES

Five Days

Basing yourself in the atmospheric walled town of Kotor (p240), spend an afternoon in palazzi-packed Perast (p238) and a whole day in buzzy Budva (p249). Allow another day to explore mountainous Lovćen National Park (p261) and the old royal capital, Cetinje (p262).

One Week

For your final two days, head north to the mountains of Durmitor National Park (p272), making sure to stop at the historic Ostrog Monastery (p274) on the way. Spend your time hiking, rafting (in season) and canyoning.

Essential Food & Drink

Loosen your belt; you're in for a treat. By default, most Montenegrin food is local, fresh and organic, and hence very seasonal. The food on the coast is virtually indistinguishable from Dalmatian cuisine: lots of grilled seafood, garlic, olive oil and Italian dishes. Inland it's much more meaty and Serbian-influenced. The village of Njeguši in the Montenegrin heartland is famous for its *pršut* (prosciutto, smoke-dried ham) and *sir* (cheese). Anything with Njeguški in its name is going to be a true Montenegrin dish and stuffed with these goodies. Here are some local favourites.

Riblja čorba Fish soup, a staple of the coast.

Crni rižoto Black risotto, coloured and flavoured with squid ink.

Lignje na žaru Grilled squid, sometimes stuffed *(punjene)* with cheese and *pršut*.

Jagnjetina ispod sača Lamb cooked (often with potatoes) under a metal lid covered with hot coals.

Rakija Domestic brandy, made from nearly anything. The local favourite is grape-based *loza*.

Vranac & krstač The most famous indigenous red and white wine varietals (respectively).

Montenegro Highlights

1 **Kotor** (p240) Roaming the atmospheric streets until you're at least a little lost.

2 **Lovćen National Park** (p261) Driving the vertiginous route from Kotor to the Njegoš Mausoleum.

3 **Perast** (p238) Admiring the baroque palaces and churches.

4 **Ostrog Monastery** (p274) Seeking out the spiritual at this impressive cliff-clinging monastery.

5 **Tara Canyon** (p275) Floating through paradise, rafting between the plunging walls of this canyon.

6 **Cetinje** (p262) Diving into Montenegro's history,

art and culture in the old royal capital.

7 **Ulcinj** (p257) Beaching by day and soaking up the Eastern-tinged vibe on the streets after dark.

8 **Durmitor National Park** (p273) Admiring the mountain vistas reflected in glacial lakes during walks through the wild highlands.

BAY OF KOTOR

Coming from Croatia the Bay of Kotor starts simply enough, but as you progress through fold upon fold of the bay and the surrounding mountains get steeper and steeper, the beauty meter gets close to bursting. It's often described as southern Europe's most spectacular fjord and even though the label's not technically correct, the sentiment certainly is.

Herceg Novi ХЕРЦЕГ НОВИ

♪ 031 / POP 11,100

Standing at the entrance to the Bay of Kotor like an eager host, Herceg Novi welcomes

MONTENEGRO HERCEG NOVI

visitors with bright bouquets, sparkling seas and almost-constant sunshine. Can't find the party? Look down; it's all happening a few dozen wonky steps below the main highway. The Old Town's shiny squares, elegant churches and formidable fortresses echo with the clatter of cafes and bars. Further down, pebbly beaches and concrete terraces offer access to the bay's best – and cleanest – swimming. Follow the pedestrian-only promenade and you'll hit Igalo, famed for its therapeutic mud.

'Novi' means 'new', and while this is indeed one of the newer towns on the bay, it's no spring chicken; it was founded in 1382 by Bosnia's King Tvrtko I. 'Herceg' refers to Herceg (Duke) Stjepan Vukčić Kosača, who fortified the town in the 15th century; the remaining fortifications are a little younger.

◎ Sights

★ Šetalište Pet Danica   WATERFRONT
Named after five young women named Danica who died during WWII, this pedestrian promenade stretches along the waterfront for more than 5km from Igalo to Meljine. It's lined with summer bars, shops, concrete swimming platforms and the odd rocky cove; in places it ducks in and out of tunnels carved through headlands. The strip follows the route of a former train line that once linked the coast to Sarajevo.

Savina Monastery   CHRISTIAN MONASTERY
(Manastir Savina; Braće Grakalić bb; ⊘6am-8pm) Named after Sava, founder of the Serbian Orthodox Church, this peaceful monastery enjoys wonderful coastal views from its location on the town's eastern slopes. It's dominated by the elegant 18th-century **Church of the Dormition** (Crkva uspenja Bogorodice), carved from Croatian pinkish stone. Inside there's a beautiful gilded iconostasis. The smaller church beside it has the same name but is considerably older (possibly 14th century) and has the remains of frescoes.

ⓘ STEP BY STEP

Herceg Novi is extremely hilly and the fastest way from the highway to the beach is via one of the numerous sets of steps. Charming as the stairways (step-enište) are, they make Herceg Novi one of the most challenging towns in Montenegro for the mobility-impaired.

Archangel Michael's Church   CHURCH
(Crkva svetog Arhanđela Mihaila; ⊘7.45am-midnight Jun-Aug, to 9pm Sep-May) Built between 1883 and 1905, this beautifully proportioned, domed, Serbian Orthodox church sits at the centre of gleaming white Trg Herceg Stejpana (known as Belavista to the locals). The archangel is pictured in a mosaic in the lunette above the door, under an elegant rose window.

Kanli Kula   FORTRESS
(I Bokeške brigade bb; adult/child €2/free; ⊘9am-9pm) Kanli Kula means 'bloody tower', and this notorious 16th-century prison more than lived up to its name during Herceg Novi's years of Turkish rule (roughly 1482–1687); in the dungeon below the lower set of flagpoles, you can see where doomed inmates carved into the walls. The huge fort is a far more pleasant place these days, offering stupendous views over the town from its sturdy fortifications. During summer it often hosts musical and theatrical performances.

Forte Mare   FORTRESS
(Save Kovačevića bb; €2; ⊘9am-8pm) The bastion at the town's seaward edge was built between the 14th and 17th centuries but owes its current look to an Austrian makeover in 1833. It's now used for film screenings on summer nights. Downstairs, a 15-minute video tells the story of Ottoman admiral Barbarossa wresting the fort from the Spanish in the 1539 *Siege of Castelnuovo*.

Ulica Njegoševa   STREET
Herceg Novi's Old Town is at its most impressive when approached from the pedestrian-only section of Ulica Njegoševa, which is paved in the same shiny marble as Dubrovnik and lined in elegant, mainly 19th-century buildings. The street terminates in cafe-ringed Trg Nikole Đurkovića, where steps lead up to an elegant crenulated 1667 **clock tower** FREE above the main city gate.

Mirko Komnenović City Museum   MUSEUM
(Gradski muzej; ☎031-340 265; www.rastko.rs/rastko-bo/muzej; Mirka Komnenovića 9; adult/child €3/1; ⊘8am-8pm Mon-Sat May-Sep, 9am-5pm Mon-Sat Oct-Apr) Apart from the building itself (a fabulous bougainvillea-shrouded baroque palace with sea views), the highlight of this little museum is its impressive collection of religious icons. Displays detail Herceg Novi's complicated history, along with archaeological relics and folk costumes. It's named after the former mayor, who donated the building.

🏃 Activities & Tours

Kayak Herceg Novi
KAYAKING

(☑ 067-531 366; www.kayak-hercegnovi.com; Zalo Beach; hire per 1/4/8hr from €7/25/35; ☺ May-Oct) Don't just admire the beautiful bay from the Old Town and along the promenade: hop aboard a kayak and explore it! In addition to rentals, this outfit also runs guided kayaking tours (half-/full day from €30/50) to Rose, Dobreč, Igalo and Mamula Island.

Adriatic Blue
DIVING

(☑ 069-833 043; www.divingmontenegro.com) This friendly group explores the wrecks, underwater caves and islands of Boka Bay. Intro dives (€50), two-tank dives (€70) and PADI courses (from €300) include all gear and boat transfers.

Yachting Club 32
BOATING

(☑ 069-263 888; Šetalište Pet Danica 32) Hires jet skis (€45 per 30 minutes), pedal boats (€5 per hour) and mountain bikes (€3/10 per hour/day), and organises sailing classes and boat trips. If all that sunshine has tuckered you out, it's a top spot to kick back with a drink and do some water-watching.

★ Black Mountain
ADVENTURE

(☑ 067-076 676; www.montenegroholiday.com) 🏄 An excellent full-service agency that can arrange pretty much anything, anywhere in the country, including mountain biking, diving, rafting, hiking, canyoning, boat trips and wine tasting. It can take care of the basics too, such as accommodation, car hire and transfers.

Active Travels Montenegro
ADVENTURE

(☑ 068-658 285; www.activetravelsmontenegro.com) Local guys with excellent English lead rafting, coasteering, hiking and canyoning trips, vineyard visits and sightseeing tours.

🎉 Festivals & Events

Mimosa Festival
PARADE, MUSIC

(www.hercegfest.co.me; ☺ Feb) A mash of yellow blooms, marching majorettes, concerts and sports events.

🛌 Sleeping

Camp Full Monte
CAMPGROUND €

(☑ 067-899 208; www.full-monte.com; Malta-Prijevor Put bb; campsites per person €12, tent rental 3-night minimum €20-25, glamping per person week/fortnight €280/550; ☺ May-Sep) 🏄 Hidden in the mountains near the Croatian border (check online for driving instructions), this campground offers solar-generated hot water, odourless composting toilets and heaps of seclusion. In case the name didn't give it away, clothing is optional. There's a fully equipped kitchen, and meals can be arranged. Customised glamping holidays are available, and include accommodation in a 'mansion' tent.

Hotel Perla
HOTEL €€

(☑ 031-345 700; www.perla.me; Šetalište Pet Danica 98; r/apt from €74/230; 🅿️ ❄️ 📶) It's a 15-minute stroll from the centre but if it's beach you're after, Perla's position is perfect. The helpful staff speak excellent English and the front rooms of this medium-sized modern block have private terraces and sea views. Bikes are available for hire and there's a great kids' playground by the beach.

Stanica Hotel Aurora
BOUTIQUE HOTEL €€

(☑ 067-552 319; www.aurorahotel.me; Šetalište Pet Danica 42; d/apt €70/100; ❄️ 📶) Famous (and famously quirky) Serbian director Emir Kusturica is to thank for converting Herceg Novi's former train station into this seaside inn. The rooms and apartments are characterful (ask for one with a sea view), and it's located in the thick of the action. There's a good but noisy on-site bar and restaurant, and – of course – a small cinema.

🍴 Eating & Drinking

Peter's Pie & Coffee
CAFE €

(☑ 067-148 180; www.peterspie.wordpress.com; Šetalište Pet Danica 18a; mains €3.20-3.80; ☺ 8am-11pm May-Oct, 9am-5pm Nov-Apr; 📶) Peter's is a most un-Montenegrin cafe in that it serves smoothies, juices and a good selection of food: omelettes, sandwiches, grilled vegetables, cakes (including some vegan options) and muffins. The pies in question are something like a cross between a pizza and a savoury tart.

★ Konoba Feral
MEDITERRANEAN €€

(☑ 031-322 232; www.konobaferal.com; Vasa Ćukovića 4; mains €8-20; ☺ 8am-midnight; 📶) A *feral* is a ship's lantern, so it's seafood, not unruly animals, that takes pride of place on the menu. The grilled squid and homemade seafood tagliatelle are excellent, and the wine list includes vintages from the Savina Monastery (p236). This charming place is consistently ranked as the best in town; book ahead if you want to sit on the terrace.

Taverna Splendido
INTERNATIONAL €€

(☑ 067-830 988; www.tavernasplendido.com; Šetalište Pet Danica 77; mains €6-21; ☺ 8am-midnight; 📶🍴) Splendido lives up to its name with a prime spot overlooking the bay, attentive service and a fantastically varied menu (including Bosnian, Dalmatian, Italian, Hungarian, Austrian and Chinese dishes – although it's hard to go past the fish stew and seafood platters). Parents seeking a bit of rare peace while they dine will give thanks for the on-site kids' playground.

Pub Got PUB
(Stepenište 28 Oktobar 8; ☺8am-3am) This awesomely laid-back little hang-out often hosts live blues and classic-rock acts. Chairs are set out on the stepped lane.

Prostorija BAR
(☎069-286 766; www.facebook.com/prostorijahn; Stepenište 28 Oktobar 13; ☺10am-1am) There's a chilled-out Ibiza vibe to this little bar, with an industrial-chic interior and a mirrorball strung over the stepped lane. On summer nights, DJs set up outside.

🛍 Shopping

Town Market MARKET
(Gradska pijaca; Trg Nikole Đurkovića; ☺6am-3pm Mon-Sat, to noon Sun) If you want to take on the locals in a tussle for the best fresh fruit and vegetables, get to this little produce market by around 8am.

ℹ Information

Tourist Office (☎031-350 820; www.hercegnovi.travel; Jova Dabovića 12; ☺9am-4pm Mon-Fri) More of an office than an information centre, this is the main headquarters of Herceg Novi's tourism organisation and it's open year-round. They also operate various seasonal information kiosks scattered around the municipality, including one on the main waterfront **promenade** (Šetalište Pet Danica bb; ☺8am-10pm Jul & Aug, to 8pm Jun & Sep).

ℹ Getting There & Away

BOAT
Taxi boats ply the coast during summer, charging about €10 for a trip to the beaches on the Luštica Peninsula or €15 to the Blue Cave. You'll sometimes get a better rate in Igalo where there's more competition.

BUS
Buses stop at the **station** (☎031-321 225; Dr J Bijelića 1; ☺6am-midnight) just above the Old Town. There are frequent buses to Kotor (€4, one hour), which stop at all of the small towns around the bay. Buses to Budva (€6) either go via Kotor or on the ferry through Tivat

(€3), which is usually quicker depending on the queues. Frequent services head to Cetinje (€8, 2½ hours) and Podgorica (€10, three hours).

International destinations include Dubrovnik, Trebinje, Sarajevo, Belgrade and Skopje.

TAXI
Taxi More (☎19730; www.taximore.com; minimum fare €1.30, per km 90c) Advertises set fares to Dubrovnik Airport (€60), Tivat (€45), Kotor (€50), Budva (€60) and Podgorica Airport (€110). You'll pay extra if there are queues for the Kamenari car ferry.

ℹ Getting Around

BICYCLE
Cyclists should consider leaving the highway at Igalo and pedalling along the waterfront. In summer you'll be slowed by foot traffic but it's a much flatter, safer and more picturesque route than the highway. Apart from a few stretches where you'll be forced back on to the main road, you can travel most of the way to Kamenari alongside the water.

CAR
A tortuous, often gridlocked, one-way system runs through the town. Street parks are divided into two zones charged at either 50c or 80c per hour, or €5 per day; purchase tickets from newsagents or kiosks, circle the time and date, and display them on your dashboard. You can also pay by SMS: follow the directions on the signs.

Perast Пераст
☎032 / POP 270
Looking like a chunk of Venice that has floated down the Adriatic and anchored itself onto the Bay of Kotor, Perast hums with melancholy memories of the days when it was rich and powerful. Despite having only one main street, this tiny town boasts 16 churches and 17 formerly grand palazzi. While some are just enigmatic ruins sprouting bougainvillea and wild fig, others are caught up in the whirlwind of renovation that has hit the town.

The town slopes down from the highway to a narrow waterfront road (Obala Marka Martinovića) that runs along its length. At its heart is St Nicholas' Church, set on a small square lined with date palms and the bronze busts of famous citizens.

Perast's most famous landmarks aren't on land at all: two peculiarly picturesque islands with equally peculiar histories.

◎ Sights

★ Gospa od Škrpjela   ISLAND
(Our-Lady-of-the-Rock Island; ⊙church 9am-7pm Jul & Aug, to 5pm Apr-Jun & Sep-Nov, to 3pm Dec-Mar) This picturesque island was artificially created (on 22 July 1452, to be precise) around a rock where an image of the Madonna was found; every year on that same day, the locals row over with stones to continue the task. In summer, boats line up on the Perast waterfront to ferry people there and back (€5 return); off season, you may need to ask around.

Sveti Djordje   ISLAND
(St George's Island) Sveti Djordje, rising from a natural reef, is the smaller of Perast's two islands. It houses a Benedictine monastery shaded by cypresses and a large cemetery, earning it the local nickname 'Island of the Dead'. Legend has it that the island is cursed...but it looks pretty heavenly to us. The island can only be admired from afar; visitors aren't encouraged.

St Nicholas' Church   CHURCH
(Crkva Sv Nikole; Obala Marka Martinovića bb; treasury €1; ⊙8am-6pm) This large church has never been completed, and given that it was commenced in the 17th century and the bay's Catholic community has declined markedly since then, one suspects it never will be. Its treasury contains beautifully embroidered vestments and the remains of various saints. Climb the imposing 55m bell tower (€1) for impressive views over the bay.

Perast Museum   MUSEUM
(Muzej grada Perasta; ☑032-373 519; www.muzej perast.me; Obala Marka Martinovića bb; adult/child €4/1; ⊙9am-9pm May-Oct, to 3pm Nov-Apr) The Renaissance-baroque Bujović Palace, dating from 1694, has been lovingly preserved and converted into a museum showcasing the town's proud seafaring history. It's worth visiting, less for the portraits of ships and bewhiskered gents, and more for the building itself – and for the wondrous photo opportunities afforded by its balcony.

🛏 Sleeping

Bogišić Rooms & Apartments   APARTMENT €
(☑067-440 062; www.bogisicroomsapartment. com; Obala Marka Martinovića bb; s/apt €25/70; ⊙May-Oct; ✳🗗) This welcoming place offers great value for money and a big serve of genuine Montenegrin hospitality. The rooms aren't massive, but they're comfortable, cute

and right on the waterfront, and they have kitchenettes.

GudCo Apartments   APARTMENT €€
(☑032-373 589; gudco@t-com.me; Perast 152; apt from €75; ✳🗗) There are only two spacious, stone-walled apartments available here, located directly above the extremely welcoming owners' house. Wake up to extraordinary bay views in your spacious Perast pad, then play with the kittens on the rear terrace while you catch up on your laundry (units have washing machines and dishwashers).

Hotel Conte   APARTMENT €€
(☑032-373 687; www.hotelconte.me; Obala Marka Martinovića bb; r/apt from €95/160; ✳🗗) Conte is not so much a hotel as a series of deluxe studio to two-bedroom apartments in historic buildings scattered around St Nicholas' Church. The sense of age resonating from the stone walls is palpable, even with the distinctly nontraditional addition of a Jacuzzi and sauna in the flashest apartment. It's worth paying extra for a sea view.

Palace Jelena   BOUTIQUE HOTEL €€€
(☑032-373 549; www.palacejelena-perast.com; Obala Marka Martinovića bb; r €80-140; ✳🗗) This quaint, family-run hotel isn't suffering from delusions of grandeur; its four atmospheric rooms and lovely restaurant are actually located within a palace (the Lučić-Kolović-Matikola Palace to be precise). It's so close to the shore that you can hear waves lapping from your room. All rooms have gorgeous sea and island views; the most expensive has a balcony.

✗ Eating & Drinking

Konoba Školji   MONTENEGRIN, SEAFOOD €€
(☑069-419 745; www.skolji.com; Obala Marka Martinovića bb; mains €8-24; ⊙10am-midnight; 🗗) This appealing traditional restaurant is all about the thrill of the grill: fresh seafood and falling-off-the-bone meats are barbecued to perfection in full view of salivating diners. Thankfully they're not shy with the portion sizes; the delightful/maddening smell of the cooking and the sea air will have you ravenous by the time your meal arrives. The pasta is good, too.

★ Restaurant Conte   SEAFOOD €€€
(☑032-373 722; www.hotelconte.me; Obala Marka Martinovića bb; mains €10-25; ⊙8am-midnight; 🗗) If you don't fall in love here – with Perast, with your dining partner, with a

random waiter – consider your heart stone; with its island views, table-top flowers and superfresh oysters, this place is ridiculously romantic. You'll be presented with platters of whole fish to select from; the chosen one will return, cooked and silver-served, to your table.

Beach Bar Pirates BAR
(www.facebook.com/BeachBarPirates; Obala Marka Martinovića bb; ⊗8am-9pm Jun-Sep) Tucked under the road on the Risan edge of Perast, this little beach bar serves beers, cocktails and coffees to the beautiful board-shorts-and-bikinis brigade. It often hosts live music acts, DJs and beach parties – and it's the best spot in Perast for a swim.

🛈 Getting There & Away

→ Paid parking is available on either approach to town (per day €2) but, in summer, it's in hot demand.

→ Car access into the town itself is restricted.

→ There's no bus station but buses to and from Kotor (€1.50, 25 minutes) stop at least every 30 minutes on the main road at the top of town.

→ Water taxis zoom around the bay during summer and call into all ports, including Perast.

→ Regular taxis from Kotor to Perast cost around €15.

Kotor KOTOP

📲 032 / POP 13.000
Wedged between brooding mountains and a moody corner of the bay, achingly atmospheric Kotor is perfectly at one with its setting. Hemmed in by staunch walls snaking improbably up the surrounding slopes, the town is a medieval maze of museums, churches, cafe-strewn squares, and Venetian palaces and pillories. It's a dramatic and delightful place where the past coexists with the present; its cobblestones ring with the sound of children racing to school in centuries-old buildings, lines of laundry flutter from wrought-iron balconies, and hundreds of cats – the descendants of seafaring felines – loll in marble laneways. Come nightfall, Kotor's spectacularly lit-up walls glow as serenely as a halo. Behind the bulwarks, the streets buzz with bars, live music – from soul to serenades – and castle-top clubbing.

Budva's got the beaches, and nearby Dubrovnik's got the bling, but for romance, ambience and living history, this Old Town outflanks them all.

History

It's thought that Kotor began as Acruvium, part of the Roman province of Dalmatia. Its present look owes much to nearly 400 years of Venetian rule, when it was known as Cattaro. In 1813 it briefly joined with Montenegro for the first time, but the Great Powers decided to hand it back to Austria, where it remained until after WWI. There's a strong history of Catholic and Orthodox cooperation in the area.

⊙ Sights

The best thing to do in Kotor is to let yourself get lost in the maze of streets. You'll soon know every nook and cranny, but there are plenty of old churches to pop into, palaces to ogle, and many coffees and/or vinos to be drunk in the shady squares.

★**Kotor City Walls** FORTRESS
(Bedemi grada Kotora; Map p242; €8; ⊗24hr, fees apply 8am-8pm May-Sep) Kotor's fortifications started to head up St John's Hill in the 9th century, and by the 14th century a protective loop was completed, which was added to right up until the 19th century. The energetic can make a 1200m ascent up the fortifications via 1350 steps to a height of 260m above sea level; the views from St John's Fortress, at the top, are glorious. There are entry points near the River Gate and behind Trg od Salate. When tackling the walls in summer, avoid the heat of the day and bring lots of water.

St Tryphon's Cathedral CHURCH
(Katedrale Sv Tripuna; Map p242; Trg Sv Tripuna; church & museum €2.50; ⊗9am-8pm Apr-Oct, to 5pm Nov, Dec & Mar, to 1pm Jan & Feb) Kotor's most impressive building, this Catholic cathedral was consecrated in 1166 but reconstructed after several earthquakes. When the entire frontage was destroyed in 1667, the baroque bell towers were added; the left one remains unfinished. The cathedral's gently hued interior is a masterpiece of Romanesque architecture: slender Corinthian columns alternate with pillars of pink stone, thrusting upwards to support a series of vaulted roofs. Look for the remains of Byzantine-style frescoes in the arches.

Maritime Museum of Montenegro MUSEUM
(Pomorski muzej Crne Gore; Map p242; 📲032-304 720; www.museummaritimum.com; Trg Bokeljske Mornarice; adult/child €4/1; ⊗9am-8pm Mon-Sat,

10am-4pm Sun Jul & Aug, 8am-6pm Mon-Sat, 9am-1pm Sun May, Jun & Sep, 9am-5pm Mon-Fri, to noon Sat & Sun Oct-Apr) Kotor's proud history as a naval power is celebrated in three storeys of displays housed in a wonderful early-18th-century palace. An audio guide helps explain the collection of photographs, paintings, uniforms, exquisitely decorated weapons and models of ships.

St Mary's Collegiate Church   CHURCH
(Crkva Sv Marije Koleđate; Map p242; Trg od Drva) Built in 1221 on the site of a 6th-century basilica, this Catholic church is distinguished by impressive 20th-century bronze doors covered in bas-reliefs, the remains of frescoes, a particularly gruesome larger-than-life crucifix, and a glass coffin containing the body of Blessed Osanna of Cattaro (1493–1565). She was what is known as an anchoress, choosing to be walled into a small cell attached to a church so as to devote her life to prayer.

St Luke's Church   CHURCH
(Crkva Sv Luke; Map p242; Trg Sv Luke) Sweet little St Luke's speaks volumes about the history of Croat-Serb relations in Kotor. It was constructed in 1195 as a Catholic church, but from 1657 until 1812 Catholic and Orthodox altars stood side by side, with each faith taking turns to hold services here. It was then gifted to the Orthodox Church.

St Nicholas' Church   CHURCH
(Crkva Sv Nikole; Map p242; Trg Sv Luke) Breathe in the smell of incense and beeswax in this Orthodox church, built in 1909 and adorned with four huge canvasses depicting the gospel writers, a gift from Russia in 1998. The silence, the iconostasis with its silver bas-relief panels, the dark wood against bare grey walls, the filtered light through the dome and the simple stained glass conspire to create a mystical atmosphere.

St Claire's Franciscan Church   CHURCH
(Franjevačka crkva Sv Klare; Map p242; near Trg Sv Luke) Aside from a fine rose window there's not much ornamentation on the facade of this Catholic church, built between the 14th and 17th centuries. But head inside for the full Venetian baroque experience, with cherubs floating around the high altar, holding aloft realistic-looking draperies carved entirely from marble.

Cats Museum   MUSEUM
(Map p242; www.catsmuseum.org; Trg od Kina; adult/child €1/50c; ☺10am-6pm) Crazy cat people and those with a fondness for

BACK ROAD TO MT LOVĆEN ЛОВЋЕН

The journey from Kotor to Mt Lovćen, the ancient core of the country, is one of Montenegro's great drives. Take the road heading towards the Tivat tunnel and turn right just past the graveyard. After 5km, follow the sign to Cetinje on your left opposite the fort. From here, there's 17km of good but narrow road snaking up 25 hairpin turns, each one revealing a vista more spectacular than the last. Take your time and keep your wits about you; you'll need to pull over and be prepared to reverse if you meet oncoming traffic. From the top, the views stretch over the entire bay to the Adriatic. At the entrance to Lovćen National Park you can continue straight ahead through Njeguši for the shortest route to Cetinje or turn right and continue on the scenic road through the park.

whimsical vintage art will adore this charming museum, home to thousands of moggie-themed postcards, lithographs, prints, jewellery and beautiful antique advertisements. The small admission fee goes towards taking care of Kotor's famous felines.

🏃 Activities

Škurda Canyon   ADVENTURE SPORTS
The much-photographed St John's Hill hides a secret in the form of this rugged canyon. In addition to the splendid views of the Old Town, the canyon – about an hour's clamber from Kotor – is riddled with sheer drops, tunnels and waterfalls. Canyoning trips (average €80) are run by **Kotor Bay Tours** (Map p242; ☑069-152 015; www.kotorbaytours.com; Park Slobode) and Montenegro+ (p247).

Ladder of Cattaro   HIKING
(Map p242) FREE The truly vigorous can climb the ancient caravan trail known as the Ladder of Cattaro, which starts near the Škurda River and zigzags up the mountain to join the Coastal Mountain Traversal in Lovćen National Park. The usual requirements of water/sturdy shoes/strong lungs apply.

👉 Tours

Various tour boats leave from opposite the Old Town to explore the bay; expect to pay

Kotor

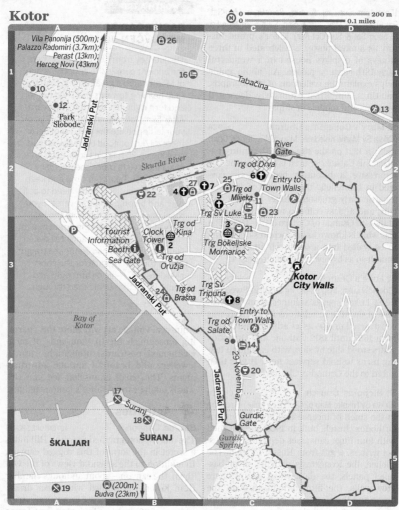

upwards of €15 for a day tour. If you're keen to potter around the Boka on a boat of your own, you'll be disappointed unless you have a boat licence. Most hire companies supply skippers and cater firmly to the top end.

A Day Out On Monty B   BOATING
(Map p242; ☎067-859 309; www.montenegro 4sail.com; per person from €99) If you don't have €1000 to blow on your own luxury yacht, join British ex-pats Katie and Tim (and their two little doggies) for a sail on the 44-ft ketch that doubles as their home (and kennel).

360 Monte   TOURS
(Map p242; ☎032-520 495; www.360monte.me; 29 Novembar bb) Run by the same capable crew as Old Town Hostel, this agency offers a range of tours and cruises. The four most popular are: Great Montenegro (€44, 11½ hours, taking in Njeguši, Lovćen National Park, Cetinje, Rijeka Crnojevića and Sveti Stefan), Tara Rafting (€74, 12½ hours), North Montenegro (€44, 13¼ hours) and the Kotor Bay Cruise (€59, eight hours).

Adventure Montenegro   OUTDOORS
(Map p242; ☎069-049 733; www.adventuremon tenegro.com; Trg od Mlijeka) Rent a kayak and

Kotor

explore the bay on your own terms (single/double kayak €20/25 per day). There are also three-hour kayaking tours (€35), guided full-day hikes up Mt Lovćen (€50), rafting on the Tara River (€80), five-hour speedboat tours of the bay (€280 for up to six people), and a range of sightseeing tours for cruiseboat passengers.

⚜ Festivals & Events

Traditional Winter Carnival   CARNIVAL
(☺Feb) Carrying on the Venetian Renaissance tradition with two weeks of masked balls, parades and performances in the lead-up to Lent.

Kotor Art   PERFORMING ARTS
(www.kotorart.me; ☺late Jun–mid-Aug) Kotor's summer arts festival acts as an umbrella for several established events, including the **Children's Theatre Festival** (Kotorski festival pozorišta za djecu; www.kotorskifestival.me; ☺early Jul), Don Branko's Music Days (featuring international artists performing classical music in Kotor's squares and churches), Perast's Klapa Festival, and assorted workshops, lectures and touring productions.

Boka Night   CULTURAL
(☺mid-Aug) Decorated boats light up the bay, fireworks explode in the sky and the populace parties like there's no tomorrow.

🛏 Sleeping

Although the Stari Grad is a charming place to stay, you'd better pack earplugs. In summer, the bars blast music onto the streets until 1am every night, rubbish collectors clank around at 6am and the chattering starts at the cafes by 8am. Enquire about private accommodation at the tourist information booth (p246).

★Old Town Hostel   HOSTEL €€
(Map p242; ☎032-325 317; www.hostel-kotor.me; 29 Novembar bb; dm from €14, r €75, without bathroom €60; ❋🛜❋) If the ghosts of the Bisanti family had any concerns when their 13th-century palazzo was converted into a hostel, they must be overjoyed now. Sympathetic renovations have brought the place to life, and the ancient stone walls echo with the cheerful chatter of happy travellers. A second building, directly across the road, has modern rooms and a small pool.

Vila Panonija   HOTEL €€
(☎032-334 893; www.vilapanonija.com; Dobrota bb; r €80-110; Ⓟ❋🛜) Set back from the waterfront in Dobrota, this old stone house has been converted into a small hotel – or is it a large guesthouse? The stained glass in the breakfast room is a little 'belle époque' but the bedrooms, with their midnight-blue feature walls, are much more modern. Some have balconies; all have en-suite bathrooms.

Tianis

APARTMENT €€

(Map p242; 032-302 178; www.tianis.net; Tabačina 569; r/apt from €77/83; P✷📶) Well located without being in the midst of the melee, this friendly establishment has a clutch of clean, comfortable apartments of varying sizes, some of which have magical views across the Škurda River to the Old Town from their terraces.

★**Palazzo Drusko**

BOUTIQUE HOTEL €€€

(Map p242; 067-333 172; www.palazzodrusko. me; near Trg od Mlijeka; s/d from €69/139; ✷📶) Loaded with character and filled with antiques, this venerable 600-year-old palazzo is a memorable place to stay, right in the heart of the Old Town. Thoughtful extras include water jugs loaded with lemon and mint, a guest kitchen, 3D TVs and old-fashioned radios rigged to play Montenegrin music.

★**Palazzo Radomiri**

HOTEL €€€

(032-333 176; www.palazzoradomiri.com; Dobrota 220; s/d/ste from €160/180/250; ☺Apr-Oct; P✷📶🏊) This honey-coloured early-18th-century palazzo on the Dobrota waterfront, 4km north of Kotor's Old Town, has been transformed into a first-rate boutique hotel. Some rooms are bigger and grander than others, but all 10 have sea views and luxurious furnishings. Guests can avail themselves of a small workout area, sauna, pool, private jetty, bar and restaurant.

✖ Eating

Ladovina

MONTENEGRIN, DALMATIAN €€

(Map p242; 063-422 472; www.ladovina.me; Njegoševa 209; mains €9-20; ☺8am-1am) Tucked away in the Škaljari neighbourhood, south of the Old Town, this relaxed cafe-restaurant has tables beneath an open-sided pagoda under a canopy of trees. The menu includes veal, lamb and octopus claypots, and a mix of seafood and meat grills. There's a terrific selection of wine by the glass and craft beer. Save room for the Kotor cream pie.

Konoba Galerija

MONTENEGRIN, SEAFOOD €€

(Map p242; 032-322 125; www.restorangalerija. com; Šuranj bb; mains €9-22; ☺11am-11pm) This bustling place on the waterfront excels in both meat and seafood, as well as fast and attentive service (along the coast, you'll find these things are often mutually exclusive). Try the prawns or mixed seafood in buzara sauce, a deceptively simple – yet sublime – blend of olive oil, wine, garlic and mild spices.

Galion

SEAFOOD €€€

(Map p242; 032-325 054; Šuranj bb; meals €12-22; ☺noon-midnight; 📶) With an achingly romantic setting, extremely upmarket Galion gazes directly at the Old Town across the millionaire yachts in the marina. Fresh fish is the focus, but you'll also find steaks, risotto and pasta. It usually closes in winter.

🍷 Drinking & Nightlife

★**Letrika**

COCKTAIL BAR

(Map p242; www.facebook.com/artbarletrika; near Trg Bokeljske Mornarice; ☺8am-1am) By day, Letrika is a quiet place for a sneaky drink, with a steampunk aesthetic and side-alley location. On summer nights DJs set up outside and the lane gets jammed with hip young things dancing and sipping cocktails.

Bokun

WINE BAR

(Map p242; www.facebook.com/BOKUNWINEBAR; near Trg Sv Luke; ☺8am-1am May-Oct, to 11pm Nov-Apr; 📶) This evocative little nook is an ideal place to sample local wines (and perfectly paired meats and cheeses), all to the accompaniment of live music on weekends (think jazz, soul and samba).

Bandiera

BAR

(Map p242; www.facebook.com/bandiera.kotor; 29 Novembar bb; ☺8am-1am; 📶) This cluttered, cavernous old-school bar is a top hang-out, where laid-back conversations and rock music take precedence over texting and techno.

Maximus

CLUB

(Map p242; 067-217 101; www.discomaximus. me; near Trg od Oružja; free-€5; ☺11pm-5am Thu-Sat, nightly in summer) Montenegro's most pumping club comes into its own in summer, hosting big-name international DJs and local starlets. It's set up in the baffling Balkan style, with little high tables covering the dance floor.

🛍 Shopping

Cats of Kotor

GIFTS & SOUVENIRS

(Map p242; 069-249 783; www.catsofkotor. com; near Trg od Mlijeka; ☺9am-9pm) Though you can't bundle them into your backpack (tempting as it may be), you can bring home the cats of Kotor in the form of beautiful, locally made handicrafts with a feline flavour. Part gallery, part boutique, this quirky shop sells everything from cat-themed jewellery and clothes to original artworks.

City Walk
Kotor's Old Town

START SEA GATE
END GURDIĆ GATE
LENGTH 850M; 30 MINUTES

Start at the **1** **Sea Gate**, the main entrance to the Old Town. It was constructed in 1555 when Kotor was under Venetian rule (1420–1797). Look out for the winged lion of St Mark, Venice's symbol, which is displayed prominently on the walls here. Above the gate, the date of the city's liberation from the Nazis is remembered with a communist star and a quote from Tito. As you pass through the gate, look for the 15th-century stone relief of the Madonna and Child flanked by St Tryphon and St Bernard.

The gate opens onto the Old Town's largest square, Trg od Oružja (Armoury Square). Straight ahead is a **2** **clock tower**, built in 1602, with a pyramid-shaped pillory in front of it; unruly citizens were once shackled here for public shaming. Walk left across the square and then take the first lane to the right. In short succession you'll pass the Catholic **3** **St Claire's Franciscan Church** (p241) and Orthodox **4** **St Nicholas' Church** (p241). Pretty **5** **St Luke's Church** (p241) sits on a small square of its own.

Continue on to **6** **St Mary's Collegiate Catholic Church** (p241). Pause to admire the bas reliefs on the bronze doors before cutting across Trd od Drva (Wood Sq) to the **7** **River Gate**, built in 1540. After gazing out on the clear waters of the Škurda River, which forms a moat on the town's northern flank, continue down the main lane back into the Old Town. Duck to the right onto Trg Bokeljske Mornarice (Boka Navy Sq), where you'll find the **8** **Maritime Museum** (p240), and then continue on to Trg Sv Tripuna (St Tryphon's Sq), dominated by the imposing Catholic **9** **cathedral** (p240).

Take the lane to the side of the cathedral, turn right, and continue all the way to the partly 13th-century **10** **Gurdić Gate** and bastion at the southern end of town. The moat here is formed by the gurgling Gurdić Spring.

Kotor Bazaar
MARKET

(Map p242; near Trg Sv Luke; ⊙9am-10pm) Recently opened in the long-abandoned cloister of a Dominican monastery, this little market has stalls selling T-shirts, souvenirs and religious icons. In the back corner there's a little medieval 'museum', where for €3 you can pose with replica weapons and armour, or try your hand with a bow and arrow.

Efesya Souvenir
GIFTS & SOUVENIRS

(Map p242; ☑063-469 624; www.efesyasouvenir. com; near Trg od Mlijeka; ⊙9am-7pm) The best of a crop of Turkish shops to spring up in recent years, Efesya sells colourful glass lamps, ceramics, scarves, bags and even chess sets.

Kamelija
MALL

(Map p242; ☑032-335 380; www.kamelija.me; Trg Mata Petrovića; ⊙9am-11pm; 🛜🅿) This shopping centre, on the highway near the Stari Grad, has a big supermarket, loads of boutiques, a pharmacy, banks and a supervised kids' playground (from €3 per hour). It's a good place to buy a local SIM card.

City Market
MARKET

(Gradska pijaca; Map p242; Jadranski Put; ⊙7am-2pm) Self-caterers can stock up at this food market under the town walls. The vendors are happy to give out free samples of everything, from local *pršut* and cheese to olives and strawberries. On summer evenings stalls spring up selling clothes, jewellery and souvenirs.

ⓘ Information

Kotor Health Centre (Dom zdravlja Kotor; ☑032-334 533; www.dzkotor.me; Jadranski Put bb) Kotor's main clinic.

Tourist Information Booth (Map p242; ☑032-325 951; www.tokotor.me; Jadranski Put; ⊙8am-8pm Apr-Oct, to 6pm Nov-Mar) Stocks free maps and brochures, and can help with contacts for private accommodation.

ⓘ Getting There & Away

The main road to Tivat and Budva turns off the waterfront road at a baffling intersection south of the Stari Grad and heads through a long tunnel.

The **bus station** (☑032-325 809; www.autobuskastanicakotor.me; Škaljari bb; ⊙6am-8pm) is to the south of town, just off the road leading to the tunnel. Buses to Herceg Novi (€4, one hour), Tivat (€1.50, 20 minutes), Budva (€4, 40 minutes), Cetinje (€5, 1½ hours) and Podgorica (€7.50, 2¼ hours) are at least hourly. International destinations include Dubrovnik, Mostar, Belgrade, Tirana and Vienna.

A taxi to Tivat airport should cost around €10.

Tivat Тиват

🖉 032 / POP 9370

Bobbing super yachts, a posh promenade and rows of swanky apartment blocks: visitors to Tivat could be forgiven for wondering if they're in Monaco or Montenegro. The erstwhile-mediocre seaside town has undergone a major makeover – courtesy of the multimillion-dollar redevelopment of its old naval base into a first-class marina – and while it bears no resemblance to anywhere else in the country, Tivat is now attracting the uberwealthy (and less-loaded rubberneckers) in droves.

The town has a reputation as being one of the sunniest spots in the Bay of Kotor. While Tivat will never rival Kotor for charm, it makes a pleasant stop on a trip around the bay, and is a useful base for exploring the Vrmac and Luštica Peninsulas.

◉ Sights

Buća-Luković
Museum & Gallery
MUSEUM

(Muzej i galerija Buća-Luković; ☑032-674 591; www. czktivat.me; Trg od kulture; ⊙8am-2pm & 5-10pm Mon-Fri, 5-10pm Sat & Sun) 𝗙𝗥𝗘𝗘 Aristocratic families from the inner bay once built their summer residences at Tivat to take advantage of its sunnier outlook. One of the few survivors is this 500-year-old fortified enclosure with its own Catholic chapel, which once belonged to Kotor's Buća family. The solid stone defensive tower houses a collection of Roman bits and bobs; next door is a well-presented ethnographical museum with fishing and farming artefacts. Head upstairs for beautiful jewellery and folk costumes.

Porto Montenegro
MARINA

(www.portomontenegro.com) Single-handedly responsible for Tivat's transformation, this surreal 24-hectare town-within-a-town occupies the former Arsenal shipyard and naval base. Primped, preening and planned right down to the last polished pebble, the almost impossibly glamorous complex includes upmarket apartment buildings, a 'lifestyle village' of fancy boutiques, bars, restaurants and leisure facilities, a museum, a resort-style hotel and berths for 450 yachts (with a total of 850 berths planned by completion).

Porto is a phased development – construction is ongoing – but the works don't detract from the surreal feeling of finding yourself in a place usually reserved for those of otherworldly wealth.

Unsurprisingly, the project hasn't been without controversy: 3500 locals took to the streets to protest the sale of the shipyard – a state asset – to foreign investors (an international consortium of the very rich led by the Canadian businessman, the late Peter Munk, who sold the complex to the government of Dubai in 2016) and the loss of 480 jobs. Yet many naysayers have been silenced by the improvements that are evident in the town.

The complex is open to the public and it's a pleasant place to stroll and ogle opulent yachts – if you're not prone to fits of rage at the injustices of contemporary economics. Kids will love the playground shaped like a pirate ship near the maritime museum.

Maritime Heritage Collection
MUSEUM

(Zbirka pomorskog naslijeđa; ☑ 067-637 781; Porto Montenegro; museum/submarine €3/2; ⊙ 9am-4pm Mon-Fri, 1-5pm Sat) Porto Montenegro doffs its hat to its past with this well-curated display (in Montenegrin and English) devoted to the history of the Arsenal shipyard and naval base, housed in one of the site's beautiful old boat sheds. The star exhibits are too big for the museum: the two Yugoslav navy submarines are dry docked outside.

Large Town Park
PARK

(Veliki gradski park) North of the centre, this park is a leafy, peaceful retreat, originally laid out in 1892. It's a serene antidote to the excesses of Porto Montenegro.

Town Beach
BEACH

(Gradska plaža; 21 Novembra bb) You're better off heading to the Luštica Peninsula for a proper swim, but Tivat does offer a couple of options if you're desperate for a dip. Town Beach is a long concrete platform with a 20m pebbly section right by the main promenade. There's another pebbly beach, **Belani** (Plaža Belane; Kalimanjska bb), just past the marina.

🏃 Activities

Montenegro+
OUTDOORS

(☑ 069-190 190; www.montenegroplus.me; ⊙ 9am-7pm) This well-organised group has active pursuits around Tivat covered. It rents stand-up paddleboards (half/full day €25/35), kayaks (€50 per day) and mountain bikes (€25 per day), and offers guided kayaking, hiking and cycling trips, along with diving, canyoning and snowshoeing.

Montenegro Cruising
CRUISE

(☑ 068-330 231; www.montenegrocruising.com; cruises €12; ⊙ May-Sep) Offers daily cruises departing at 9am during the tourist season on boats named *Vesna,* stopping at Žanjic beach, Herceg Novi, Perast's islands and Kotor; the boat returns to Tivat at 6pm. Budva-based travel agents commonly sell this cruise inclusive of bus transfers (€20), with their clients finishing the cruise at Kotor.

Pura Vida
SPA

(☑ 032-540 356; www.puravida-spa.com; Obala bb, Porto Montenegro; massages from €30; ⊙ 7.30am-10pm Mon-Fri, 10am-8pm Sat & Sun) Of course Porto has a day spa, offering all the plucking, pummelling and pampering treatments you'd expect from a luxury resort.

🎉 Festivals & Events

Carnival
CARNIVAL

(⊙ Feb) As in the other bay towns, Tivat's residents don their Venetian masks in February, in the lead-up to Lent.

Žućenica Fest
FOOD & DRINK

(⊙ Jun) Unusual but popular festival celebrating all the weird and wonderful dishes that can be made from wild dandelion (and other local ingredients).

🛏 Sleeping

Hostel Anton
HOSTEL €

(☑ 069-261 182; www.hostelanton.com; Mažina IV bb; dm/r €18/38; 🅿 🛜) This hilltop backpackers is a hostel of the old-school: family-run, oddball art on the walls, instruments waiting to be picked up, and a communal vibe. If glam is your bag, keep moving; amenities are functional but far from flash.

Regent Porto Montenegro
HOTEL €€€

(☑ 032-660 660; www.regenthotels.com; Porto Montenegro; r/ste from €407/619; ❄ 🛜 📶 🏊) Divided into the Italianate 'Venezia' wing and the more contemporary-looking 'Aqua' wing, the Regent is a luxurious place for a splurge. The room decor is remarkably restrained; the designers have left the balcony views to speak for themselves. Facilities – including multiple restaurants and bars, a 20m infinity pool and a first-class spa – are as chic as you'd expect.

MONTENEGRO TIVAT

✗ Eating & Drinking

Bonella
SUPERMARKET €

(www.bonellagreenbazaar.me; Porto Montenegro; snacks 60c-€1.50; ⊙8am-10pm) Bonella is the modern-day jet-settter's take on a grocery store, meaning it's stocked to its stylish rafters with organic produce, fancy health foods and international food brands that you'd be hard-pressed to find anywhere else in the country. It also has a good takeaway food counter selling everything from *burek* (savoury pastries) to gourmet sandwiches, salads and juices.

Giardino
BALKAN, GRILL €€

(✆069-793 611; Nikšićka 11/20; mains €6-18; ⊙2-11pm; 🐾) Hidden away behind a house in a residential street, this charming family-run restaurant is as local as they come. Grab a seat in the garden near the tinkling fountain and tuck into juicy, smoky Balkan favourites such as *pljeskavica* with *kajmak* (a meat patty topped with creamy cheese) or grilled fish.

Big Ben
CAFE, PIZZA €€

(✆067-371 446; www.bigbentivat.com; Obala Filipa Miloševića bb; mains €3.20-15; ⊙8am-1am) If you've got a hankering for a full English breakfast (minus the baked beans), head to this beach cafe where a red phone box and images of Sean Connery's James Bond, Shakespeare, Alfred Hitchcock and Sherlock Holmes sit incongruously against the Adriatic backdrop. Even more incongruous is the rest of the tasty menu: Balkan seafood and meat grills, pasta and pizza.

★One
ITALIAN €€€

(✆067-486 045; www.facebook.com/jettyone; Porto Montenegro; mains €10-22; ⊙8.30am-midnight) This singular brasserie has one of the most expensive views in the country, gazing over trillions of euros' worth of megayachts. The service is a match for the lovely location and the menu is as jet-setting as the clientele – flitting between French, Russian, Indian and American but excelling in Italian. It also does excellent Western-style breakfasts (from €6).

Byblos
LEBANESE €€€

(✆063-222 023; www.byblos.me; Porto Montenegro; mains €16-18; ⊙8am-1am) Byblos' interior is heavy on atmosphere – all lanterns and elegant exotica – while the outdoor 'Mezze and Shisa Terrace' is a billowy hideaway of posh private tents; it's a shame that the toilets don't meet the same standards. The menu offers an upmarket spin on Lebanese cuisine, although it's somewhat hit and miss.

★Black Sheep
PUB

(✆068-900 013; www.facebook.com/tbsgastropub; Ribarski Put bb; ⊙8am-1am; 🐾) This wonderful little gastropub swims against Montenegro's tsunami of wines and *rakija*, serving up lashings of craft beer and cool cocktails. Hip, happening and occasionally hectic (weekends go off with live music and DJs), a night out here is as far from yachtie yahooing as you can get.

Clubhouse
BAR

(✆032-662 722; www.facebook.com/TheClubhousePortoMontenegro; Porto Montenegro; ⊙9am-1am; 🐾) Doing its very best to keep the yacht crews entertained, this lively bar with an upmarket beach-shack vibe hosts live music and kooky themed nights, and screens international football and rugby matches. There's a good selection of imported beer, and visiting Antipodeans can drown their homesickness in Aussie shiraz.

ℹ Information

Tourist Office (✆032-671 324; www.tivat.travel; Palih Boraca 8; ⊙7am-8pm Mon-Fri, 8am-3pm Sat & Sun May-Sep, 8am-3pm Mon-Sat Oct-Apr) Accommodation contacts and information about local sights and walks.

ℹ Getting There & Away

AIR

Tivat airport (TIV; ✆032-670 930; www.montenegroairports.com; Jadranski Put bb) is 3km south of town and 8km through the tunnel from Kotor. The only year-round flights are to Belgrade and Moscow, but dozens of destinations are added in the tourist season.

Taxis charge around €7 for Tivat, €10 for Kotor and €20 for Budva. You'll find car-hire counters at the airport.

BUS

Buses to Kotor (€1.50, 20 minutes) stop outside a silver kiosk on Palih Boraca. The main bus station is inconveniently located halfway between Tivat and the airport. From there, buses head to Herceg Novi (€3, one hour), Budva (€4, 30 minutes), Cetinje (€5, 1¼ hours) and Podgorica (€6, two hours) at least hourly.

CAR

Tivat sits on the western side of the Vrmac Peninsula, which juts out into the Bay of Kotor and divides it in two. The quickest route to Kotor is to take the main road southeast in the direction of Budva, turn left at the major intersection past the airport and take the tunnel. The alternative is the narrow coastal road. For Herceg Novi, take the ferry from Lepetane, 5km northwest of town.

ADRIATIC COAST

Much of Montenegro's determination to re-invent itself as a tourist mecca has focused on this gorgeous stretch of beaches. In July and August it seems that the entire Serbian world can be found crammed onto this less-than-100km stretch of coast. Avoid those months and you'll find a charismatic set of small towns and fishing villages to explore, set against clear Adriatic waters and Montenegro's mountainous backdrop.

Budva БУДВА

☑ 033 / POP 13,400

Budva is the poster child of Montenegrin tourism. Easily the country's most-visited destination, it attracts hordes of holiday-makers intent on exploring its atmospheric Stari Grad (Old Town), sunning themselves on the bonny beaches of the Budva Rivi-era and partying until dawn; with scores of buzzy bars and clanging clubs, it's not nicknamed 'the Montenegrin Miami' for nothing.

Though Budva has been settled since the 5th century BC, you'll be hard-pressed finding much – outside of the Old Town – that isn't shiny and relatively new. Development has run rampant here, and not all of it appears to be particularly well thought out. In the height of the season, Budva's sands are blanketed with package holidaymakers from Russia and Ukraine, while the nouveau riche park their multimillion-dollar yachts in the town's guarded marina. That said, Budva has a hectic charm all of its own.

⊙ Sights

★ Stari Grad   HISTORIC SITE
(Map p252) Budva's best feature and star attraction is the Stari Grad (Old Town) – a mini-Dubrovnik with marbled streets and Venetian walls rising from the clear waters below. Much of it was ruined by two earth-quakes in 1979, but it has since been completely rebuilt and now houses more shops, bars and restaurants than residences.

➜ Trg između crkava
(Map p252) Literally the 'square between the churches', this open area below the citadel provides a visual reminder of the once-cosy relationship between Orthodox and Catholic Christians in this area.

Beautiful frescoes cover the walls and ceiling of **Holy Trinity Church** (Crkva Sv Tro-jice; Map p252; ⊙ 8am-10pm Jun-Sep, 8am-noon & 4-7pm Oct-May), in the centre of the square. Constructed in 1804 out of stripes of pink and honey-coloured stone, this Orthodox church is the only one of the square's interesting cluster of churches that is regularly open.

The largest of the churches is Catholic **St John the Baptist's Church** (Crkva Sv Ivana Krstitelja; Map p252), which was built towards the end of the 12th century and served as a cathedral until 1828 (Budva is now part of the diocese of Kotor). Parts of it possibly date from as early as the 9th century, and the last earthquake revealed the foundations of its predecessor, a 5th-century basilica, beside it. A side chapel houses the *Madonna of Bud-va* – a 12th-century icon venerated by Catholic and Orthodox Budvans alike. There's also a colourful mosaic by Ivo Dulčić behind the altar. Opening hours are sporadic.

Built into the city walls are two tiny churches, which are rarely open. Budva's oldest remaining church is Catholic **St Mary's in Punta** (Crkva Sv Marije; Map p252), dating from 840. Immediately next to it is **St Sava's Church** (Crkva Sv Save; Map p252), named after the founder of the Serbian Or-thodox Church; it once had both Orthodox and Catholic altars.

➜ Citadela
(Map p252; €3.50; ⊙ 9am-midnight May-Oct, to 5pm Nov-Apr) The citadel at the Old Town's seaward end offers striking views, a restau-rant and a library full of model ships, rare tomes and maps displayed safely behind glass. It's thought to be built on the site of the Greek acropolis, but the present incar-nation dates from the 19th-century Austrian occupation.

➜ Town Walls
(Bedemi grada; Map p252; €2; ⊙ 10am-8pm) A walkway about a metre wide leads around the landward walls of the Stari Grad, offer-ing views across the rooftops and down on some beautiful hidden gardens. Admission only seems to be charged in the height of summer; at other times it's either free or locked. The entrance is near the Citadela.

➜ Budva Museum
(Muzej Budve; Map p252; ☑ 033-453 308; Petra I Petrovića 11; adult/child €3/1.50; ⊙ 8am-9pm Tue-Fri, 3-9pm Sat & Sun) This archaeological and ethnographic museum shows off Budva's an-cient and complicated history – dating back to at least 500 BC – over four floors of exhib-its. There's an impressive collection of Greek and Roman jewellery, ceramics, mosaics and

Budva

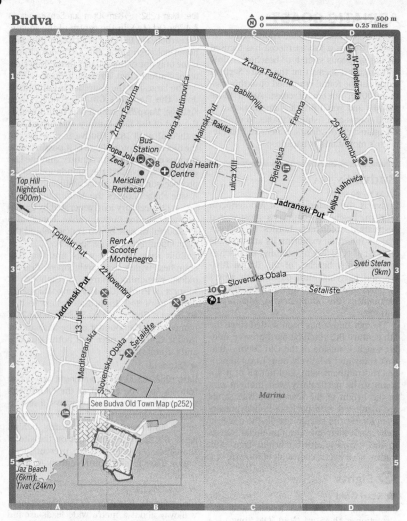

glassware (how it survived in a town so prone to earthquakes and war is anyone's guess), as well as a 5th-century-BC helmet with holes in the back, which suggest that the former owner had at least one very bad day.

➡ **Main Gate**

(Map p252) The remains of the emblem of Venice – the winged lion of St Mark – are still visible over the main entrance to Budva's Old Town.

Ričardova Glava   BEACH
(Richard's Head; Map p252) Immediately south of the Old Town, this little beach has the ancient walls as an impressive backdrop. Wan-

der around the headland and you'll come to a statue of a naked dancer, one of Budva's most-photographed landmarks. Carry on and you'll find the quiet, double-bayed **Mogren Beach**. There's a spot near here where the fearless or foolhardy leap from the cliffs into the waters below.

Slovenska Plaža   BEACH
(Map p250) After the marina, the long sweep of Budva's main beach commences, heralded by blaring local pop and endless rows of sun umbrellas and loungers (available for hire at about €3 each). If you can't get your head around this typically Mediterranean

Budva

⊙ Sights
1 Slovenska Plaža C3

⊟ Sleeping
2 Hotel Oliva... C2
3 Saki Apartmani.....................................D1
4 Villa M Palace....................................... A4

⊗ Eating
5 Forsage Gastro Lounge..................... D2
6 Green Market....................................... A3
7 Jadran kod Krsta................................ B4
8 Mercur Cafe B2
9 Obala.. B3

⊙ Drinking & Nightlife
10 Torch.. C3

concept, there's no charge for spreading out your towel on the patches of beach set aside for the purpose.

Pizana Beach BEACH
(Plaža Pizana; Map p252) By the walls on the northern side of the Old Town, Pizana is a popular 100m stretch of sand and pebbles.

Sveti Nikola ISLAND
Known locally as 'Hawaii', Sveti Nikola is Montenegro's largest island, stretching to nearly 2km. Fallow deer wander about on this uninhabited green spot, which is only a nautical mile away from Budva or Bečići Beach. Its rocky beaches make it a popular destination in summer when taxi boats regularly ferry sunseekers to and fro; those leaving from Slovenska Plaža charge about €3 per person each way (charter your own for €15 to €20).

You'll have more chance escaping the tourist hordes, discarded rubbish and blaring pop music if you hire a kayak and look for a secluded cove on the far side of the island. Local lore has it that the graves scattered around tiny, whitewashed **St Nicholas' Church** (Crkva Sv Nikole) are those of crusaders who died of an unknown epidemic while they camped nearby. The church itself may date to as early as 1096.

Ploče Beach BEACH
(Plaža Ploče; www.plazaploce.com; P) If the sands are getting too crowded in Budva itself, head out to this little pebbly beach at the end of a scrub-covered peninsula, 10km west of town (take the road to Kotor, turn off towards Jaz Beach and keep going). The water is crystal clear but if you prefer fresh water there are little pools set into the

sunbathing terraces. There's a restaurant, a noisy knee-deep pool bar, and inflatable water slides positioned down the quieter, more family-friendly end.

Jaz Beach BEACH
The blue waters and broad sands of Jaz Beach look spectacular when viewed from high up on the Tivat road. While it's not built-up like Budva and Bečići, the beach is still lined with loungers, sun umbrellas and noisy beach bars; head down to the Budva end of the beach for a little more seclusion.

🏊 Activities

Travel agencies on Slovenska Obala peddle every kind of day tour, including Ostrog and Cetinje (€15), the Bay of Kotor (€17) and Dubrovnik (€28). You can hire a kayak (€5 per hour) or paddle boat (€6 per hour) from Mogren Beach. A huge range of boats with skippers are available for hire from the marina. A midsized launch might charge €400 for a day's fishing, while a flash one could be €1200 or more.

Budva Diving DIVING
(Map p252; ☏068-060 416; www.budvadiving. com; Dukley Marina Open Swimming Pool; incl equipment from €40) Based near Pizana Beach, this well-regarded, PADI-certified group offers intro boat dives at 20 locations for experienced divers.

🎭 Festivals & Events

Theatre City PERFORMING ARTS
(☏033-402 935; www.gradteatar.me; ⊙Jul-Aug) Renowned arts festival happening largely in and around the Old Town for seven weeks.

🛏 Sleeping

Freedom Hostel HOSTEL €
(Map p252; ☏067-837 110; www.fb.com/freedom hostelbudva; Cara Dušana 21; dm/tw from €21/55; ⊙Feb-Oct; ❀🛜) In a quieter section of the Old Town, this beloved, sociable hostel has tidy little rooms scattered between three buildings. The terraces and small courtyard are popular spots for impromptu guitar-led singalongs.

Montenegro Hostel HOSTEL €
(Map p252; ☏069-331 031; www.montenegro hostel.com; Vuka Karadžića 12; dm €15-20; ❀🛜) With a right-in-the-thick-of-it Old Town location (pack earplugs), this colourful little hostel provides the perfect base for hitting the bars and beaches. Each floor has its own

Budva Old Town

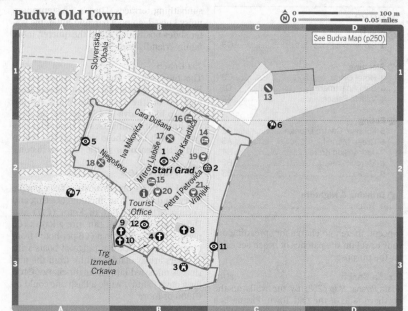

See Budva Map (p250)

Budva Old Town

⊚ Top Sights
1 Stari Grad B2

⊚ Sights
2 Budva Museum B2
3 Citadela B3
4 Holy Trinity Church B3
5 Main Gate A2
6 Pizana Beach C2
7 Ričardova Glava A2
8 St John the Baptist's Church B3
9 St Mary's in Punta B3
10 St Sava's Church B3
11 Town Walls C3
12 Trg između crkava B3

⊕ Activities, Courses & Tours
13 Budva Diving C1

⊟ Sleeping
14 Freedom Hostel B2
15 Montenegro Hostel B2
16 Vila Balkan B1

⊗ Eating
17 Konoba Portun B2
18 Konoba Stari Grad A2

⊜ Drinking & Nightlife
19 Casper B2
20 Greco B2
21 Prince B2

kitchen and bathroom, and there's a communal space at the top for fraternisation.

Hotel Oliva
HOTEL €€

(Map p250; ☎069-551 769; Bjelaštica 16; d/tr from €70/105; ⓟ✳☎) Don't expect anything flashy: just a warm welcome, clean and comfortable rooms with balconies, and a nice garden studded with the olive trees that give this small hotel its name. They no longer have a website; online bookings are handled through the normal sites.

Saki Apartmani
APARTMENT €€

(Map p250; ☎068-453 535; www.facebook.com/SakiHostelBudva; IV Proleterska bb; dm €19, apt from €59; ⓟ✳☎▨) Not quite a hostel and not quite an apartment hotel, this friendly family-run block on the outskirts of town offers elements of both. Individual beds are rented, hostel-style, in a rambling set of rooms. Private apartments have large balconies, but beds have been crammed in where kitchens might otherwise be. Grape and kiwi-fruit vines shade the pleasant communal terrace.

★**Villa M Palace** APARTMENT €€€

(Map p250; ☎032-452 413; www.mpalacebudva.com; Gospoština 25; apt from €170; P❄📶) There's a seductive glamour to this modern block, hemmed in within a rash of new developments near the Old Town. A chandelier glistens in the lift and the walls sparkle in the darkened corridors – and that's before you even reach the luxurious one- to three-bedroom apartments.

Vila Balkan APARTMENT €€€

(Map p252; ☎033-403 564; www.vilabalkan.me; Vuka Karadžića 2; apt from €118; ❄📶) The five apartments of this historic Stari Grad house have a bit of peeling paint here and there but you'll soon forget about it when you see the sea views and parquet floors. Try for the top floor – it's the same price but a little bigger and has a bathtub. Guests score a free lounger set at nearby Ričardova Glava (p250).

Hotel Poseidon HOTEL €€€

(☎033-463 134; www.poseidon-jaz.com; Jaz Beach; r from €112; ⏲Jun-Oct; P❄📶) This glorious seaside hotel has been sitting by the sands of Jaz Beach since 1967, and while the clean, spacious rooms don't show their age, the excellent service certainly echoes decades of experience. The views from every room – many of which have kitchens – are picture-perfect, and the hotel has its own small slice of private beach.

Eating

Mercur Cafe EUROPEAN €

(Map p250; ☎067-570 483; Trg sunca 7; mains €2-7; ⏲5.30am-11pm; 👪) Bus stations and good nosh are usually mutually exclusive territories, but this relaxed restaurant is the exception to the rule. For starters, it sits in a gorgeous green oasis populated by peacocks, chickens and fluffy bunnies; there's also a play space. The menu includes sandwiches, grilled meat, pizza, pasta and cake.

Green Market MARKET €

(Zelena pijaca; Map p250; 22 Novembra bb; ⏲6am-8pm Mon-Sat, to 1pm Sun) This covered market is the place to stock up on fresh produce and domestic cheese, meats and fish.

★**Jadran kod Krsta** MONTENEGRIN, SEAFOOD €€

(Map p250; ☎069-030 180; www.restaurant-jadran.com; Slovenska obala bb; mains €7-20; ⏲7am-1am; 📶) With candlelit tables directly over the water, this extremely popular, long-standing restaurant offers all the usual seafood suspects along with classic Montenegrin dishes from the interior. It may seem incongruous, but there's a rip-roaring bikers' bar out the back.

Forsage Gastro Lounge INTERNATIONAL €€

(Map p250; ☎067-001 008; www.facebook.com/ForsageGastrolounge; 29 Novembra 24; mains €5.20-23; ⏲8am-midnight; ❄📶) Budva's most ambitious restaurant offers the likes of beef Wellington and chateaubriand alongside Asian-inspired chicken and pork dishes. While they don't always get it 100% right – and the dark mirrored ceiling is spectacularly dated – Forsage makes a good alternative to Budva's cookie-cutter seafood restaurants.

Obala EUROPEAN €€

(Map p250; ☎033-402 782; www.restoranobala.me; Slovenska obala bb; mains €5.50-25; ⏲8am-11pm) A crowd-pleasing variety of pasta, pizza, and grilled meat and fish is offered at this waterfront restaurant. The service is hit-and-miss but the grilled squid and steamed mussels are delicious. If you can't get a table with a sea view, opt for one under the wisteria at the rear.

Konoba Stari Grad SEAFOOD €€

(Map p252; ☎033-454 443; www.konobastarigrad.me; Njegoševa 14; mains €10-20; ⏲10am-11pm) With an attractive stone-walled interior and a sunny terrace sandwiched between the Stari Grad's walls and beach, this *konoba* (family-run establishment) isn't short on atmosphere. It's a touch touristy, but the seafood's very good and there's live music most nights.

Konoba Portun MONTENEGRIN, SEAFOOD €€€

(Map p252; ☎068-412 536; Mitrov Ljubiše 5; mains €12-21; ⏲1pm-midnight; 📶) Hidden within the Old Town's tiny lanes, this atmospheric eatery has only three outdoor tables and a handful inside; it feels like you're eating in a long-lost relative's home. The traditional dishes are beautifully presented. Don't miss out on the house speciality, *hobotnica ispod sača* (octopus cooked under a metal lid with hot coals). The grilled squid is excellent too.

Drinking & Nightlife

★**Casper** BAR

(Map p252; www.facebook.com/casper.bar.budva; Petra I Petrovića bb; ⏲10am-2am; 📶) Chill out with a craft beer, cocktail or fair-trade, organic coffee under the pine tree of this picturesque Old Town cafe-bar. It regularly hosts live jazz gigs, and DJs kick off in July and August, spinning everything from soul to house.

Prince
PUB

(Map p252; Vranjak bb; ⊗8am-midnight; ☎) If you're hankering for something slightly more stout than Montenegro's light lagers, pop down to this friendly little hang-out. It bills itself as an 'English pub', and while the inside is indeed dim and cosy, you'd never mistake its sunny, mega-Mediterranean outdoor area for anything you'd find in Blighty. Yes, there's football on the telly.

Torch
BAR

(Map p250; ☎033-683 683; www.budvabeach. com; Slovenksa obala bb; ⊗8am-1am summer; ☎) It's totally scene-y, but Torch is a fun, over-the-top outdoor party palace that epitomises summertime Mediterranean madness. Pool parties, sun-lounge cocktails, water pipes and light noshing are the order of the day.

Top Hill
CLUB

(☎067-478 888; www.tophill.me; Topliški Put bb; ⊗hours vary Jun-Aug) The top cat of Montenegro's summer party scene attracts up to 5000 revellers to its open-air club atop Topliš Hill, offering them top-notch sound and lighting, sea views, big-name touring DJs and performances by local pop stars.

Greco
BAR

(Map p252; Njegoševa 17; ⊗10pm-2am) On summer nights, the little square that Greco shares with its neighbour/rival Jef is packed from wall to wall with revellers.

ℹ Information

Budva Health Centre (Dom zdravlja Budva; Map p250; ☎033-427 200; www.dzbudva.com; Popa Jola Zeca bb; ⊗7am-9pm) Includes an emergency clinic and a pharmacy.

Tourist Office (Map p252; ☎033-452 750; www.budva.travel; Njegoševa 28; ⊗9am-9pm Mon-Sat & 3-9pm Sun Jun-Aug, 9am-8pm Mon-Sat Sep-May) Small but helpful office in the old town.

ℹ Getting There & Away

BUS

The **bus station** (Map p250; ☎033-456 000; Popa Jola Zeca bb) has regular services to Kotor (€4, 40 minutes), Tivat (€4, 30 minutes), Ulcinj (€7, two hours), Cetinje (€4, 40 minutes) and Podgorica (€6, 1½ hours).

International destinations include Dubrovnik, Zagreb, Sarajevo, Belgrade and Tirana.

In summer you can flag down the Mediteran Express from the bus stops on Jadranski Put to head to Jaz Beach (€1.50, at least hourly), Ploče Beach (€2, at least hourly) or Sveti Stefan (€1.50, every 10 minutes).

CAR

There are plenty of well-marked parking areas; expect to pay about €5 per day or around €2 per hour. Tow trucks earn steady business from the Mediteranska shopping strip.

Meridian Rentacar (Map p250; ☎033-454 105; www.meridian-rentacar.com; Popa Jola Zeca 7) offers one-day hire from €26. For something a bit zippier, **Rent A Scooter Montenegro** (Map p250; ☎068-201 095; www. facebook.com/scooterbudva; Jadranski Put bb) has mopeds from €23 per day.

TAXI

Taxis are in ready supply in Budva, but many of those that hang around the nightspots in the early hours are prone to overcharging. You're better off calling a reputable company. Otherwise check that the taxi has a meter and what rate it charges; €4 per kilometre is *not* the going rate.

Eco Taxi (☎19567; www.taxibudva.com)

Terrae-Taxi (☎19717; www.terraecar.com) Advertises set fares to the following airports: Tivat (€15), Podgorica (€40) and Dubrovnik (€90).

Sveti Stefan СВЕТИ СТЕФАН

☎033 / POP 364

Of all the sights along the Adriatic shoreline, Sveti Stefan is the most extraordinary. A fortified island village connected to the mainland by a narrow causeway, its photogenic jumble of 15th-century stone villas overlooks an impeccable pink-sand beach and tempting turquoise waters. The island was nationalised in the 1950s and is now part of the luxurious Aman resort, meaning it's off-limits to all but paying guests. But ogling comes for free; Sveti Stefan has unsurprisingly been named as Montenegro's most photographed site.

Sveti Stefan is also the name of the township that's sprung up onshore. From its steep slopes, you can admire the iconic island to your heart's content. On the downside, parking is difficult, there are lots of steps and there's little in the way of shops. Families will be delighted to discover an excellent (and free) playground near the Olive restaurant.

STARI BAR СТАРИ БАР

The gloriously dilapidated **Stari Bar** (Old Bar; adult/child €2/1; ☺8am-10pm) – the predecessor of the shabby port city of Bar – teeters on a bluff at the foot of Mt Rumija, offering jaw-dropping views and enough enigmatic rubble to get even the dullest imagination running rampant.

Discoveries of pottery and metal suggest that the Illyrians founded the city around 800 BC. In the 10th century, the Byzantine town was known as Antivarium as it is opposite the Italian city of Bari. It passed in and out of Slavic and Byzantine rule until the Venetians took it in 1443 (note the lion of St Mark in the entryway) and held it until it was taken by the Ottomans in 1571. Nearly all the 240 buildings now lie in ruins, mainly as a result of Montenegrin shelling when it captured the town in 1878. An explosion finished off the Franciscan Monastery in 1912 and the 1979 earthquake did still more damage.

A steep, cobbled hill climbs past a cluster of old houses and shops to the fortified entrance, where a short dark passage leads to a large expanse of vine-clad ruins and abandoned streets overgrown with grass and wildflowers. A small **museum** housed in a 17th-century customs building just inside the entrance explains the site and its history. From here, follow the green arrows around the major points of interest. In the western part of the town are the remains of the 13th-century **St Nicholas' Franciscan Monastery**, offering glimpses of Byzantine-style frescoes; it was converted to a mosque in 1595.

The northern corner has an 11th-century **fortress** with much-photographed views showcasing Stari Bar's isolated setting amid mountains and olive groves. Nearby are the foundations of **St George's Cathedral**. Originally a Romanesque church, it was converted into a mosque in the 17th century by the Turks, but the unlucky edifice was ruined after an accidental explosion of gunpowder.

If you're wondering why **St John's Church** is in such good nick, it's because it's been completely reconstructed by one of the families associated with the original church. One of the few other buildings to have an intact roof is **St Verenada's Church**, which contains a few photos from the greater Bar area. The 14th-century **St Catherine's Church**, in a tower above one of the lower gates, was being restored when we last visited.

Ottoman constructions include a solid and charming **Turkish bathhouse** from the 17th or 18th century, the clock tower (1752) and the 17th-century aqueduct that carried water from a spring 3km away; it was reconstructed after the 1979 earthquake.

Stari Bar is 4km northeast of Bar, off the Ulcinj road. Buses marked Stari Bar depart from Ulica Jovana Tomaševića in the centre of 'new' Bar every hour (€1). Apparently every hour, that is: if you're in a rush, you can get a taxi for about €6.

Stari Bar has both an excellent new boutique hotel and a hostel. Some of the restaurants also offer rooms.

⊙ Sights & Activities

Praskvica Monastery   CHRISTIAN MONASTERY
(Прасквица Манастир; Map p256; Jadranska magistrala bb) Just off the highway in the hills slightly north of Sveti Stefan, this humble 600-year-old monastery, named after the peach-scented water of a brook that flows nearby, rests amid an ancient olive grove. It was an important political centre for the Paštrovići, a local tribe whose distinctive cultural traditions have survived along this section of the coast despite numerous foreign occupations.

The monastery was established in 1413 by Balša III of Zeta. The main church, dedicated to St Nicholas (Sv Nikola), originated in that time, although it was substantially destroyed by the French in 1812 as punishment for the monks' support of Montenegro's attempt to overtake the Bay of Kotor. Traces of the original frescoes remain on the left wall, but the rest of the church dates to 1847. The current gilt-framed iconostasis (1863) features paintings by Nicholas Aspiotis of Corfu.

Further up the hill, within a cemetery, are an old schoolhouse and the smaller Holy Trinity Church (Crkva Sv Trojice).

The monastery is well signposted from the main road and an easy walk from either Sveti Stefan or Pržno. It's a working monastery; visitors are welcome, but be sure to dress appropriately.

Sveti Stefan

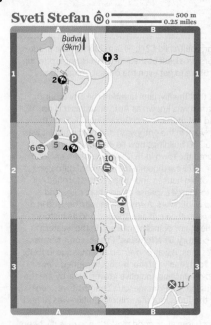

of the Karađorđević royal family, the Serbian monarchs who headed the first Yugoslavia. The whole area is now part of the Aman resort and while you're welcome to walk through, access to the beach itself will cost you a hefty €120.

Crvena Glavica   BEACH
(Map p256) A short hike south of Sveti Stefan will bring you to this collection of small beaches with rocky red sand (*crvena glavica* means 'red head'). It's a steep and bumpy path, but if you're intent on seeking out some peace and quiet (or are a dedicated nudist), it's worth the journey.

Sveti Stefan Island Tour   WALKING
(Map p256; ☑033-420 000; www.aman.com; tours €20; ⊙11am & 2pm) If you're not privileged enough to stay at the Aman resort, the only way to set foot on Sveti Stefan Island is as part of a 40-minute guided tour. Book ahead at the kiosk near the causeway; numbers are strictly limited to 10 people per tour.

🛏 Sleeping & Eating

Many hotels and guesthouses have restaurants attached. For more excellent eating options, take the 20-minute stroll to Pržno.

Crvena Glavica Auto Kamp   CAMPGROUND €
(Map p256; ☑033-468 070; per adult/child/tent/car €2.50/1/3/3.50; ⊙Jun-Sep) You don't need to be a movie star or oligarch to enjoy those million-dollar views. Pitch your tent under the olive trees and stroll past the roving chickens down to the rocky but peaceful shoreline. The toilet block and outdoor showers are very basic.

Sveti Stefan Beach   BEACH
(Map p256) The main point of coming to Sveti Stefan is to spend as much time horizontal as possible, with occasional breaks for a cooling dip. The water here gets deep quickly, as if the surrounding mountains couldn't be bothered adjusting their slope. The sands are pinkish and pebbly, but it's difficult to care about a stray rock in your bathers when you've got a jaw-dropping view of the famous island to squint at from behind your sunnies.

The uncrowded beach on the Budva side of the causeway belongs to the resort. If you don't fancy shelling out €100 for the day-use fee (ie you're not completely insane), the deckchairs on the other side of the causeway get cheaper the further along the beach you go, and there's plenty of rocky – but free – space near the end.

Miločer Beach   BEACH
(King's Beach, Kraljeva Plaža; Map p256) At the northern end of Sveti Stefan Beach, a path leads over a headland draped in pine and olive trees to the turquoise waters and pink sands of Miločer Beach. Set back from the tranquil bay and fronted by a loggia draped in sweet-scented wisteria is the Villa Miločer. This grand two-storey stone building was built in 1934 as the summer residence

★**Drago** B&B €€
(Map p256; ☑033-468 477; www.viladrago.com; Slobode 32; r/apt from €80/155; ❄ 🛜) The only problem with Drago is that you may never want to leave your terrace; the views are *that* sublime. The super-comfy pillows and fully stocked bathrooms are a nice touch. Some rooms and both apartments have kitchens, but it's unlikely you'll use them; the on-site restaurant is excellent (mains €5 to €20), serving specialities from the local Paštrovići clan.

Apartments Dijana APARTMENT €€
(Map p256; ☑069-256 101; www.dijana-montenegro. com; Slobode bb; apt from €75; P❄🛜🌊🌊) Be sure to book far, far ahead if you want to snag one of these comfortable, extremely clean apartments; word of Dijana's warm welcomes has got around, and it's a popular place. Most units have kitchens, balconies and impeccable views to the sea; the flower-strewn communal terrace makes for a beautiful spot to wind down with a vino or three.

Levantin B&B €€
(Map p256; ☑033-468 206; www.levantin.me; Vukice Mitrović 3; r from €60; P❄🛜🌊) Modern and nicely finished, with red stone walls, blue-tiled bathrooms and an attractive plunge pool on the terrace, Levantin has a variety of rooms and apartments at reasonable prices. There's a travel agency attached that can sort you out with tours or rooms in private houses.

Aman Sveti Stefan RESORT €€€
(Map p256; ☑033-420 000; www.aman.com; ste from €1323; P❄🛜🌊) This superlatives-defying resort is one-of-a-kind. Occupying the entire Sveti Stefan Island, it offers 50 luxurious suites that showcase the stone walls and wooden beams of the ancient houses. Amazingly, there's still a village feel here, with cobbled lanes, churches and an open-air cafe on the piazza. Back on the shore, Villa Miločer has a further eight suites by the beach.

Paštrovića Dvori MONTENEGRIN, SEAFOOD €€
(Map p256; ☑033-468 162; Blizikuće bb; mains €8-16; ⊙11am-10pm) With its authentic, homemade Paštrovići cuisine, this happy, hospitable, family-run restaurant ought to be on every traveller's to-try list. It is less flash than most of the other choices in shiny Sveti Stefan (though it does tick the 'divine views' box), but therein lies its charm. The restaurant is well signposted from the main road, south of Sveti Stefan.

🛍 Shopping

Sveti Stefan has a couple of small markets tucked away along the hill leading down to the beach, but it's best to stock up in nearby Budva. There's an ATM and a new strip of shops – including a minimarket and resorty boutiques – near the beach parking lot.

ℹ Getting There & Away

➡ Mediteran Express buses head to and from Budva (€1.50, 20 minutes) every 10 minutes in summer and hourly in winter, stopping on the hill about halfway down to the beach.

➡ Sveti Stefan is all windy, narrow roads, which, of course, the locals tear down with gay abandon; visitors should exercise a touch more caution on the many blind bends.

Ulcinj Улцињ

☑030 / POP 10,700

For a taste of Albania without actually crossing the border, head down to buzzy, beautiful Ulcinj. The population is 61% Albanian (68% Muslim), and in summertime it swells with Kosovar holidaymakers for the simple reason that it's a lot nicer than the Albanian seaside towns. The elegant minarets of numerous mosques give Ulcinj (Ulqin in Albanian) a distinctly Eastern feel, as does the lively music echoing out of the kebab stands around Mala Plaža (Small Beach). Ulcinj's ramshackle Old Town looms above the heaving beach and is a fantastic spot for people-watching without being surrounded by people.

⊙ Sights & Activities

Mala Plaža (Detarët e Ulqinit bb) is the town's main beach, but Ulcinj also has a series of little coves heading southeast along the coast. Each beach has a commercial licence, with seasonal beach bars and eateries. If you value your eardrums, avoid those with names like Ibiza and **Aquarius** (Steva Đakonovića Čiče bb) and head somewhere like **Sapore di Mare** (Steva Đakonovića Čiče bb), where you can either plant yourself on a concrete terrace or find a patch of grass under the pines. **Ladies' Beach** (Steva Đakonovića Čiče bb; €2), true to its name, has a strict women-only policy, while a section of the beach in front of the **Hotel Albatros** (Steva Đakonovića Čiče bb) is clothing-optional. You can even take a dip at the very foot of the Old Town walls at Sunset Beach (p260).

★ **Old Town** AREA

(Stari Grad) The ancient walled town over-looking Mala Plaža is largely residential and somewhat dilapidated, a legacy of the 1979 earthquake. This is part of its charm – this Old Town really *does* feel old, with its uneven cobblestones and paucity of street lighting. Allow at least an hour to simply ramble around to your heart's content. Whatever else you find, spectacular views of Ulcinj and the beach below are guaranteed.

A steep slope leads to the **upper gate**, where just inside the walls there's a small **museum** (Muzej Ulcinj; ☑030-421 419; www.ul-museum.me; adult/child €2/1; ☺8am-8pm Tue-Sun Jun-Sep, to 6pm Apr, May & Oct, 8.30am-3pm Nov-Mar) containing Roman and Ottoman artefacts and a relief map of the town. On the site is a 1510 church that was converted to a mosque in 1693; you can still see the ruined minaret.

Just outside the museum is a 17th-century **fountain** – these days, it's more like a tap – with an Arabic inscription, a crescent moon and flowers carved into the stone.

There has been talk for time immemorial about installing an elevator from Ulcinj's little harbour up to the Old Town, so that everyone – rather than just able-bodied types – can enjoy its ambience. Locals have stopped holding their breath.

St Nicholas' Cathedral CHURCH

(Saborna Crkva svetog Nikole; Buda Tomovića bb) Colourful frescoes fill this Serbian Orthodox cathedral, set among a picturesque grove of gnarled olive trees just below the main gate to the Old Town. It's a relative newbie, having been built in 1890 shortly after the Ottomans were booted out, although it's believed to stand on the site of a 15th-century monastery.

Ulcinj Saltpans BIRDWATCHING

(Ulcinjska solana; www.birdwatchingmn.org; Solanski Put bb) FREE If birds get you all aflutter, you've come to the right place. Founded in 1934 as a commercial salt works, this 1500-hectare private reserve attracts more than 250 species of migratory birds (half of the species registered in all of Europe), including Dalmatian pelicans, Eurasian spoonbills, various birds of prey and – believe it or not – flamingos. Contact the Tourism Information Centre (p260) to arrange a visit.

Commercial activities at the salt works ceased in 2013; when the seawater pumps stopped working, the artificially created salt pans were at risk of disappearing. Environmental groups and volunteers led the fight to save them and have them officially protected by the government. While their fate still hangs in the balance, the reserve does have a birdwatching tower, signposts and information boards.

The salt pans are about 4km east of town. However, the site isn't well set up for visitors; if you turn up without making arrangements, and are prepared to brave the guard dogs at the gate, you may find someone to sign you in and grant you access.

D'Olcinium Diving Club DIVING

(☑067-319 100; www.uldiving.com; Detarët e Ulqinit bb) Local dive sites include various wrecks (this is pirate territory, after all) and the remains of a submerged town. If you've got up-to-date qualifications you can rent gear (€20) here, or head out on their boat for a day's diving (€50). Night dives are also offered (€30).

🛏 Sleeping

★ **Hostel Pirate** HOSTEL €

(☑068-212 552; www.hostel-pirate.com; Nikole Djakonovića bb; dm/r with shared bathroom from €12/30; P❄🛜) Just because it's Ulcinj's only hostel doesn't mean this jolly Pirate rests on its laurels. This is an immaculate, friendly, comfortable and flat-out-wonderful place that installs fierce love and loyalty in its guests. The hostel organises bike rentals, kayaking and boat trips. It also turns on free barbecue dinners fuelled by shots of equally gratis *rakija*.

---

❶ STREET NAMES GALORE

You're unlikely to a find a single street sign in many Montenegrin towns but in Ulcinj, you'll sometimes find three different ones per street: a Montenegrin name, an Albanian version of the Yugoslav-era name, and a new Albanian name. Thus the main boulevard leading east–west at the top of town is either Maršala Tita or Gjergj Kastrioti Skënderbeu, and the main street heading down to the beach is either Ulica 26 Novembra or Rruga Hazif Ali Ulqinaku. We've used the names that were most prominently displayed at the time of research (usually the new Albanian names), but be aware that there is a push to return to the old names.

THE MOSQUES OF ULCINJ

One of Ulcinj's most distinct features is its plethora of mosques. Most are fairly simple structures that are usually more interesting from the inside than out. An exception is the **Sailors' Mosque** (Xhamia e Detarëve, Džamija pomoraca; Detarët e Ulqinit bb), an imposing stone structure right on the waterfront that has some interesting frescoes inside. It was completed in 2012, replacing one (destroyed 1931) that predated the Ottomans and doubled as a lighthouse. Three minutes up the road, the 1719 **Pasha's Mosque** (Xhamija e Pashës, Pašina džamija; Buda Tomovića bb) is an elegant complex with a *hammam* (Turkish bathhouse) attached.

The **Top-of-the-Market Mosque** (Xhamia e Kryepazarit, Džamija Vrhpazara; Gjergj Kastrioti Skënderbeu bb) was built in 1749 at the intersection of the main streets. Within the same block but set slightly back from the road is the 1728 **Mezjah Mosque** (Xhamia në mezgjah, Džamija Namaždjah; Hazif Ali Ulqinaku 71), Ulcinj's main Islamic place of worship. Further north, **Lamit Mosque** (Xhamia e Lamit, Džamija Ljamit; Kadi Hysen Mujali bb) dates from 1689 but was substantially rebuilt after the 1979 earthquake. The ceiling has interesting green-painted geometric wood panelling.

Olive Tree Holiday Park   HOLIDAY PARK €
(☑069-060 026; http://olivetreehp.com; Ćazima Resulbegovića bb; tents €40; ☺ Jun-Sep; P🐾🛜🏊) The tents and bungalows may be new, but they're dotted across a centuries-old olive grove that produces some of Montenegro's finest oil. It's an absolutely wonderful place to get away from the bustle of the beaches below. The pretty, raised tents come with either two singles or a queen bed, along with outdoor relaxing areas and barbecues.

Haus Freiburg   HOTEL €€
(☑030-403 008; www.hotelhausfreiburg.me; Kosovska bb; r/apt from €65/85; P❄🛜🏊) High on the slopes above the town, this family-run hotel has well-kitted-out apartments and rooms, and a particularly attractive roof terrace with sea views, a swimming pool and a small restaurant. Expect to expend 20 minutes walking down to Mala Plaža and a considerable amount of sweat walking back up.

Palata Venezia   HOTEL €€
(☑030-421 004; www.hotelpalatavenezia.com; Stari Grad bb; r/apt from €90/110; ❄🛜🏊) Situated within a centuries-old palazzo with ridiculously good views of Mala Plaža and out to sea, this gorgeously renovated place is the best choice for Old Town digs. While the attentive multilingual staff, excellent facilities, and large rooms and apartments are all very modern, the hotel is steeped in history: be sure to ask them to unlock the small museum.

✖ Eating

If you're keen to cook, hit the traditional **market** (Gjergj Kastrioti Skënderbeu bb) at the top end of town. During summer, uncountable kebab stalls, *pekare* (bakeries) and other fast-food joints operate all along Mala Plaža.

Taphana   SEAFOOD €€
(☑069-235 161; Stari Grad bb; mains €6.50-20; ☺11am-10pm; 🛜) Nautical knick-knacks set the scene for quality seafood, although this upmarket old-town restaurant also serves steaks and other local-style grills. There's a terrific view of Mala Plaža from the covered front terrace.

Bazar   PIZZERIA, SEAFOOD €€
(Hazif Ali Ulqinaku bb; mains €5-14; ☺11.30am-midnight) This upstairs restaurant and pizzeria is a great people-watching perch when the streets below are heaving with tourists. It's the seafood that drags in the locals; the owners catch their own fish every morning. Be sure to try a plate of *lignje na žaru* (grilled squid), one of the restaurant's specialities.

★Antigona   SEAFOOD €€€
(☑069-154 117; Stari Grad bb; mains €8-27; ☺10am-midnight) Antigona's clifftop terrace offers perhaps the most romantic aspect of any restaurant in Ulcinj, and handsome waiters in bow ties only add to the impression. The seafood is excellent too – but be sure to check the price and weight of the fish in advance if you wish to avoid any nasty surprises come bill time. It also rents rooms.

🍷 Drinking & Nightlife

The Mala Plaža promenade buzzes on summer nights. All the bars get packed, people happily whoop it up on the street and sands, and nightclubs spark into life.

★ **Sunset Beach** BAR
(☑069-889 209; www.facebook.com/Sunset
BeachOldTown; Stari Grad bb; ◷9am-midnight
Jun-Sep) Hidden behind the fortifications on
the quiet, western side of the Old Town, this
blissful wee beach bar consists of day beds
and tables perched on rock terraces. You can
swim here during the day and drink here
after dark, but sunset is the time for maximum romance.

Provocateur BAR
(Detarët e Ulqinit bb; ◷10am-2am summer) Part
of a summertime strip of neon-lit doof-doof
beachside bars, Provocateur is actually a lot
more relaxed than it at first appears. It's an
ideal spot to start your night and get the
goss on where to head next.

❶ Information

Accident & Emergency Clinic (☑030-412
433; Majka Tereza bb) There's a pharmacy
attached.

Tourism Information Centre (☑030-412 333;
www.ulcinj.travel; Gjergj Kastrioti Skënderbeu
bb; ◷7am-10pm Jun-Aug, 8am-3pm Mon-Fri
Sep-May) For information, maps, birdwatching
arrangements and accommodation advice for
Ulcinj, Velika Plaža and Ada Bojana.

❶ Getting There & Away

The **bus station** (☑030-413 225; www.bussta
tionulcinj.com; Vëllazërit Frashëri bb; ◷5am-
10pm) is on the northeastern edge of town.
Services head to Herceg Novi (€12, 3½ hours,
daily), Kotor (€9, 2½ hours, daily), Budva (€7, two
hours, nine daily) and Podgorica (€7, two hours,
hourly). International destinations include Tirana, Pristina, Belgrade, Sarajevo and Zagreb.

❶ Getting Around

The roads in Ulcinj – especially leading down
towards the beach – are very narrow and winding. Folks here drive as insanely – if not more
so – as everyone else in the country. Be careful
both when driving and as a pedestrian.

Velika Plaža & Ada Bojana

The appropriately named Velika Plaža (Big
Beach; Велика Плажа) starts 4km southeast
of Ulcinj and stretches for 12 sandy kilometres. It's divided into sections with names
such as Miami, Copacabana and Tropicana;
these beaches don't always live up to their
glamorous names, and the water is mostly
too shallow for proper swimming, but it's

hard not to have fun when everyone else is
clearly having a ball.

The swimming is much better over the
river at peculiar Ada Bojana (Ада Бојана).
This island was formed around a shipwreck
between two existing islands in the river
mouth, which eventually gathered enough
sediment to cover around 520 hectares and
create 3km of beautiful sandy beach. During
its Yugoslav heyday it became one of Europe's premier nudist resorts. If you'd prefer
to keep your gear on, stick to the river mouth
where there is a handful of hip beach bars.

✖ Eating

Miško SEAFOOD €€
(☑069-022 868; www.facebook.com/Misko1953;
Bojana River; mains €10-17; ◷11am-11pm; 🕸)
The most upmarket of the Bojana River restaurants is focused completely on seafood,
including octopus, shrimp, shellfish, a big selection of fresh fish, and, of course, delicious
riblja čorba (fish soup). Its motto, with apol-
ogies to Julius Caesar, is: 'Veni, Vidi, Sjedi,
Jedi', which translates from a mix of Latin
and Montenegrin as 'I came, I saw, Sit! Eat!'

Lovac EUROPEAN €€
(☑030-455 138; www.lovac-azurina.com; Đerane
196; mains €6-15; ◷8am-midnight; 🅿) Serving a
mainly local clientele since 1928, this simple
family restaurant whips up an odd mixture
of traditional Ulcinj specialities, pasta, pizza,
steak tartare, beef stroganoff and a massive
steak and chips. The pizzas are thin-crusted
and delicious, and the *rakija* flows freely. It's
located between the main roundabout leading to Velika Plaža and the Milena Canal.

❶ Getting There & Away

➠ There's a day rate to visit Ada Bojana (€6/1/2
per car/passenger/pedestrian).

➠ You'll need your own car to get here, as public
transport options are few and far between.

CENTRAL MONTENEGRO

Ogle the splendid cap of northern mountains and impeccable drape of glittering
coastline by all means, but to truly get to
know Montenegro, a visit to the country's
core is a must.

Its beating heart is Mt Lovćen, a
1749m-high symbol of national identity and
the very black mountain that gives Crna
Gora its name. To the south, Lake Skadar is
the country's lungs, a clean, green oasis of

lily-strewn waterways and rare bird havens. Swoop north to Ostrog to discover the very soul of the nation in a gravity-defying cliff-face monastery that literally brings pilgrims to their knees. And you'll find character galore in Montenegro's two capitals; the modern-day seat of Podgorica is home to hip bars and a happening arts scene, while the royal city of Cetinje proudly preserves its gallant past in a collection of richly endowed museums and galleries.

Lovćen National Park
Национални Парк Ловћен

Directly behind Kotor is **Mt Lovćen** (Ловћен; 1749m), the black mountain that gave Crna Gora (Montenegro) its name; *crna/negro* means 'black', and *gora/monte* means 'mountain' in Montenegrin and Italian respectively. This locale occupies a special place in the hearts of all Montenegrins. For most of its history it represented the entire nation – a rocky island of Slavic resistance in an Ottoman sea. A striking shrine to Montenegro's most famous son, Petar II Petrović Njegoš, peers down from its heights, with views stretching as far as Albania and Croatia.

The park's main hub is **Ivanova Korita**, near its centre, where there are a few eateries and accommodation providers and, in winter, a beginners ski slope. **Njeguši**, on the park's northern edge, is famous for being the home village of the Petrović dynasty and for making the country's best *pršut* (smoke-dried ham) and *sir* (cheese). Roadside stalls sell both, along with honey.

◉ Sights

Two-thirds of the national park's 62.2 sq km are covered in woods, particularly the black beech that gives the landscape its moody complexion. Even the rockier tracts sprout wild herbs such as St John's wort, mint and sage. The park is home to various types of reptile, 85 species of butterfly and large mammals such as brown bears and wolves. The 200 avian species found here include birds of prey such as the peregrine falcon, golden eagle and imperial eagle (but you'll be looking for a long time for the two-headed variety featured on the Montenegrin flag). Several species migrate between here and Lake Skadar.

★ **Njegoš Mausoleum**   MAUSOLEUM
(Njegošev mauzolej; adult/child €3/1.50; ⊙9am-6pm) Lovćen's star attraction, this magnifi-

cent mausoleum (built 1970 to 1974) sits at the top of its second-highest peak, Jezerski Vrh (1657m). Take the 461 steps up to the entry where two granite giantesses guard the tomb of Montenegro's greatest hero. Inside, under a golden mosaic canopy, a 28-tonne Petar II Petrović Njegoš rests in the wings of an eagle, carved from a single block of black granite.

Njegoš Birth House   HOUSE
(Njegoševa rodna kuća; www.mnmuseum.org; Erakovići bb; adult/child €2/1; ⊙9am-5pm May-Oct) The humble house where Petar II Petrović Njegoš was born has been turned into a small museum. There's not much inside, but it's an interesting insight into how 19th-century Montenegrins lived.

🏃 Activities

The mountains are criss-crossed with hiking paths and mountain-biking trails, which can be accessed from Kotor, Budva or Cetinje. If you're planning on hiking, come prepared; the temperature is, on average, 10 degrees cooler than on the coast and the weather is prone to sudden changes. Water supplies are limited.

Quad Biking   ADVENTURE
(☑033-451 020; www.globtourmontenegro.com; adult/child €87/77) These exhilarating day-long bush-bashing tours leave from Ivanova Korita, bumping up Mt Lovćen to take in some of Montenegro's best mountain and sea views. Prices include pick-ups from coastal towns.

✖ Eating

Konoba kod Radonjića   MONTENEGRIN €€
(☑041-239 820; Njeguši bb; mains €6-13; ⊙8am-7pm; ☎) With stone walls, and meat hanging from the ceiling, this atmospheric family-run tavern serves up delicious roast lamb as well as the local specialities, *pršut* (smoke-dried ham) and *sir* (cheese). Enjoy them along with olives on a Njeguški plate (€9.50) or in sandwiches (€2.50).

ℹ Information

National Park Visitor Centre (☑067-344 678; www.nparkovi.me; Ivanova Korita bb; ⊙9am-5pm) As well as providing information on the national park, this centre also rents bikes (€2/10 per hour/day), offers accommodation in four-bed bungalows (€30) and takes camping bookings (from €3).

❶ Getting There & Away

If you're driving, the park can be approached from either Kotor (20km) or Cetinje (7km); pay the entry fee (€2) at the booths on each approach. Tour buses are the only buses that head into the park. Be aware that this is a *very* twisty-turny and narrow road; the large tour buses that hog it in summer don't make the driving experience any easier. Don't be distracted by the beyond-spectacular views.

Cetinje ЦЕТИЊЕ

☎ 041 / POP 13,900

Rising from a green vale surrounded by rough grey mountains, Cetinje is an odd mix of erstwhile capital and overgrown village, where single-storey cottages and stately mansions share the same street. Several of those mansions – dating from the days when European ambassadors rubbed shoulders with Montenegrin princesses – have become museums or schools for art and music.

The city was founded in 1482 by Ivan Crnojević, the ruler of the Zeta state, after abandoning his previous capital near Lake Skadar, Žabljak Crnojevića, to the Ottomans. A large statue of him stands near the main square. Cetinje was the capital of Montenegro until the country was subsumed into the first Yugoslavia in 1918. After WWII, when Montenegro became a republic within federal Yugoslavia, it passed the baton – somewhat reluctantly – to Titograd (now Podgorica). Today it's billed as the 'royal capital', and is home to the country's most impressive collection of museums.

❍ Sights

Cetinje's collection of four museums (History, King Nikola, Njegoš Biljarda and Ethnographic) and two galleries (Montenegrin Art and its offshoot, Miodrag Dado Đurić) is known collectively as the **National Museum of Montenegro** (www.mnmuseum.org). A joint ticket (€10/5 adult/child) will get you into all of them, or you can buy individual tickets.

Some of the grandest buildings in town are former international embassies from Cetinje's days as Montenegro's capital.

Ulica Njegoševa   STREET
Cetinje's main street is pretty Njegoševa, a partly pedestrianised thoroughfare lined with interesting buildings, cafes and shops.

At the southern end are two shady parks and the elegant **Blue Palace** (Plavi dvorac; Njegoševa bb), built in 1895 for Crown Prince Danilo but recently commandeered by the Montenegrin President – hence the manicured gardens. Its neighbour is the equally graceful former **British Embassy** (Njegoševa bb), built in 1912 but Georgian in its sensibilities; it's now a music academy. Just north of the pedestrian-only section is a striking art-nouveau building covered in glazed tiles, which was once the **French Embassy** (Njegoševa bb).

Miodrag Dado Đurić Gallery   GALLERY
(Galerija; Balšića Pazar; ⊗10am-2pm & 5-9pm Tue-Sun) FREE This edgy establishment is an offshoot of the Montenegrin Art Gallery (p262), and is dedicated to one of Montenegro's most important artists, who died in 2010. Housed in a striking five-storey concrete-and-glass building, it promotes and displays 20th-century and contemporary Montenegrin art.

History Museum   MUSEUM
(Istorijski muzej; ☎ 041-230 310; www.mnmuseum.org; Novice Cerovića 7; adult/child €3/1.50; ⊗9am-5pm Apr-Oct, to 4pm Mon-Sat Nov-Mar) Housed in the imposing former parliament building (1910), this fascinating museum follows a timeline from the Stone Age onwards. Historical relics include the tunic that Prince Danilo was wearing when he was assassinated, and Prince Nikola's bullet-riddled standard from the battle of Vučji Do. It's also the most even-handed museum in the entire region in its coverage of the break-up of Yugoslavia, honestly examining Montenegrin involvement in the bombardment of Dubrovnik and war crimes in Bosnia.

Montenegrin Art Gallery   GALLERY
(Crnogorska galerija umjetnosti; www.mnmuseum.org; Novice Cerovića 7; adult/child €4/2; ⊗9am-5pm Apr-Oct, to 4pm Mon-Sat Nov-Mar) All of Montenegro's great artists are represented here, with the most famous (Milunović, Lubarda, Đurić etc) having their own separate spaces. There's a small collection of icons, the most important being the precious 9th-century *Our Lady of Philermos*, traditionally believed to have been painted by St Luke himself. It's spectacularly presented in its own blue-lit 'chapel', but the Madonna's darkened face is only just visible behind its spectacular golden casing mounted with diamonds, rubies and sapphires.

DELVE DEEP & DINE HIGH

Cetinje may indeed be littered with old-time reminders of its days as Montenegro's capital city, but just 4km away lies an attraction that makes the town look positively modern. Millions of years old, **Lipa Cave** (Lipska pećina; ☑067-003 040; www.lipa-cave.me; adult/child €11/7; ⊙ tours 10am, 11.30am, 1pm, 2.30pm and 4pm May-Oct) is one of the country's largest caves – and the only one open for organised visits – with 2.5km of illuminated passages and halls filled with stalactites, stalagmites and freaky natural pillars. Tours take 60 minutes, including a road-train ride and short walk to the entrance.

Be sure to bring warm clothes, as temperatures hover around 10°C year-round.

If you'd like to delve deeper, call ahead to arrange a 2½-hour Cave Extreme tour (€50/25 adult/child), which includes some abseiling.

Occupying a scenic eyrie, well signposted on the way to Lipa Cave, **Belveder** (☑067-567 217; mains €6-10; ⊙10am-11pm; 🐾) is a wonderful roadside restaurant serving traditional fare including freshwater fish, grilled squid, and lamb and veal slow-roasted *ispod sača* (under a domed metal lid topped with charcoal), accompanied by the smokiest paprika-laced potatoes you could hope for. The views from the wooden-roofed terrace gaze towards Lake Skadar.

King Nikola Museum
PALACE

(Muzej kralja Nikole; www.mnmuseum.org; Dvorski Trg; adult/child €5/2.50; ⊙9am-5pm Apr-Oct, to 4pm Mon-Sat Nov-Mar) Entry to this maroon-and-white palace (1871), home to the last sovereign of Montenegro, is by guided tour (you may need to wait for a group to form). Although looted during WWII, more than enough plush furnishings, stern portraits and taxidermal animals remain to capture the spirit of the court.

Ethnographic Museum
MUSEUM

(Etnografski muzej; Dvorski Trg; adult/child €2/1; ⊙9am-5pm Mon-Sat) The former Serbian embassy houses a well-presented collection of costumes and tools explained by English notations.

Njegoš Museum Biljarda
PALACE

(Njegoš muzej biljarda; www.mnmuseum.org; Dvorski Trg; adult/child €3/1.50; ⊙9am-5pm May-Oct, to 4pm Mon-Sat Nov-Apr) This castlelike palace was the residence of Montenegro's favourite son, prince-bishop and poet Petar II Petrović Njegoš. It was built and financed by the Russians in 1838 and housed the nation's first billiard table (hence the name). Upstairs are Njegoš' personal effects, including his bishop's cross and garments, documents, fabulous furniture and, of course, the famous billiard table.

Relief Map of Montenegro
MUSEUM

(Reljef Crne Gore; €1) This fascinating large-scale 3D map was created by the Austrians in 1917. It's housed in a glass pavilion attached to the side of the Njegoš Museum

Biljarda; if it's closed, you can peer through the windows.

Cetinje Monastery
CHRISTIAN MONASTERY

(Cetinjski manastir; ⊙8am-6pm) It's a case of four times lucky for the Cetinje Monastery, having been repeatedly destroyed during Ottoman attacks and rebuilt. This sturdy incarnation dates from 1786, with its only exterior ornamentation being the capitals of columns recycled from the original building, founded in 1484. The chapel to the right of the courtyard holds the monastery's proudest possessions: a shard of the True Cross (a claim made by many European churches) and the mummified right hand of St John the Baptist.

The hand has a fascinating history, having escaped wars and revolutions and passed through the possession of Byzantine emperors, Ottoman sultans, the Knights Hospitaller, Russian tsars and Serbian kings. It's only occasionally displayed for veneration, so if you miss out you can console yourself with the knowledge that it's not a very pleasant sight.

The monastery treasury (€2) is only open to groups but if you are persuasive enough and prepared to wait around, you may be able to get in (mornings are the best time to try). It holds a wealth of fascinating objects that form a blur as you're shunted around the rooms by an impatient monk. These include jewel-encrusted vestments, ancient handwritten texts, icons (including a lovely Syrian Madonna and Child) and a copy of the 1494 Oktoih (Book of the Eight Voices),

MONTENEGRO CETINJE

A ROYAL ROUND TRIP

From Cetinje, a 53km, day-long, circular mountain-biking route follows roads through Lovćen National Park. You'll ascend 890m in your first 20km to the entrance of the Njegoš Mausoleum, where you can stop for the views and a bite to eat. It's mainly downhill from here, heading in the direction of Kotor before looping through Njeguši and back to Cetinje.

the first book printed in Serbian. The crown of 14th-century Serbian king Stefan Uroš III Dečanski (who was deposed by his son, murdered and became a Serbian saint) is covered in pearls, large precious stones and priceless Byzantine-style enamels.

If your legs, shoulders or cleavage are on display, you'll either be denied entry or given an unflattering smock to wear.

Court Church   CHURCH
(Dvorska crkva; Novice Cerovića bb) Built in 1886 on the ruins of the original Cetinje Monastery, this little church has a lovely gilded iconostasis, but its main claim to fame is as the burial place of Cetinje's founder, Ivan Crnojević, and Montenegro's last sovereigns, Nikola I and Milena. The pair may have been unpopular after fleeing the country for Italy during WWI, but they received a hero's welcome in 1989, when their bodies were returned and interred in these white-marble tombs in a three-hour service.

Vlach Church   CHURCH
(Vlaška crkva; Baja Pivljanina bb) While its present appearance dates from the 19th century, this stone church was actually founded around 1450, thus predating the Montenegrin founding of Cetinje. A sumptuous gilded iconostasis (1878) is the centrepiece of the current church. Take a close look at the churchyard's fence: it's made from 1544 barrels of guns taken from the Ottomans during the wars at the end of the 19th century.

Two 14th-century *stećci* (carved stone monuments) stand in the churchyard, examples of carved tombstones that are found throughout northern Montenegro and neighbouring Bosnia.

Vlach people can be found throughout the Balkans. They're believed to be the remnants of the Roman population (either ethnically Latin or Romanised Illyrians) who retreated into the less accessible areas as the Slavs poured in from the north. In Montenegro they formed seminomadic shepherding communities, moving their flocks between summer and winter pastures. While in neighbouring states they retain their own Latin-based language and customs to a degree, in Montenegro they appear to have been assimilated into the Slavic population.

🛏 Sleeping & Eating

⭐**La Vecchia Casa**   GUESTHOUSE €
(☑067-629 660; www.lavecchiacasa.com; Vojvode Batrica 6; s/d/apt €20/34/38; 🅿❄🛜) With its gorgeous rear garden and pervading sense of tranquillity, this period house captures the essence of old Cetinje. The clean, antique-strewn rooms retain a sense of the home's history, and there's a guest kitchen (stocked with do-it-yourself breakfast supplies) and a laundry.

Green Market   MARKET €
(Zelena pijaca; Baja Pivljanina 24) This zooshed-up local produce market is the best place to stock up on fruit, vegetables, Njeguški cheese and traditional cured meats.

TavèRna   MEDITERRANEAN €€
(☑069-502 503; www.restorantaverna.me; Baja Pivljanina 77; mains €4.50-16; ⊗8am-11pm) Random capitalisation aside, we're big fans of TavèRna's pizza – especially when it's topped with the tastes of the Montenegrin heartland: Njeguši cheese and prosciutto. It's indicative of the pan-Adriatic menu, where Italian pasta and pizza rubs shoulders with spit-roasted meats, stuffed cabbage rolls and grilled fish.

Kole   MONTENEGRIN €€
(☑069-606 660; www.restorantkole.me; Bul Crnogorskih junaka 12; mains €4-16; ⊗7am-midnight) They serve omelettes and pasta at this popular restaurant, but it's worth delving into artery-clogging local specialities such as *Njeguški ražanj* (smoky spit-roasted meat stuffed with prosciutto and cheese) or *popeci na cetinjski način* ('Cetinje-style' veal schnitzel, similarly stuffed, rolled into logs, breaded and deep-fried). Serves are massive; try one between two, with a side salad.

ℹ Information

Accident & Emergency Clinic (Hitna pomoć; ☑041-233 002; Vuka Mićunovića 2)

Tourist Information (☑041-230 250; www.cetinje.travel; Novice Cerovića bb; ⊗8am-6pm

Mar-Oct, to 4pm Nov-Feb) Helpful office that also rents bikes (€2/3 per half-/full day). Short sightseeing tours start from here, taking to Cetinje's streets in golf buggies (€2/3 per 30/45 minutes).

ⓘ Getting There & Away

➔ Cetinje is just off the main Budva–Podgorica highway and can also be reached by a glorious back road from Kotor via Lovćen National Park.

➔ The **bus station** (📞 041-241 744; Trg Golootočkih Žrtava; ⊙ 6am-10pm) has regular services from Herceg Novi (€8, 2½ hours), Tivat (€5, 1¼ hours), Budva (€4, 40 minutes), Kotor (€5, 1½ hours) and Podgorica (€3, 30 minutes).

Lake Skadar National Park НАЦИОНАЛНИ ПАРК СКАДАРСКО ЈЕЗЕРО

Dolphin-shaped Lake Skadar, the Balkans' largest, has its tail and two-thirds of its body in Montenegro and its nose in Albania. On the Montenegrin side, an area of 400 sq km has been protected by a national park since 1983; today, Skadar is renowned as one of Europe's top bird habitats. It's a blissfully pretty area encompassing steep mountains, island monasteries, clear waters, and floating meadows of water lilies. The main – albeit tiny – towns here are Virpazar and Vranjina, though if you've got wheels, you can easily explore the timeless villages sprinkled along the shore.

Lake Skadar is a popular escape for nature lovers, outdoor-activity aficionados and locals fleeing the heat of Podgorica. Legend has it that the lake was created by the tears of a pixie; that may be fanciful, but after one look at magical Skadar, you may find yourself believing in fairy tales, too.

◉ Sights & Activities

Rijeka Crnojevića   VILLAGE

The northwestern end of Lake Skadar thins into the serpentine loops of the Rijeka Crnojevića (Ријека Црнојевића; Crnojević River) and terminates near the pretty village of the same name. It's a charming, tucked-away kind of place set around an arched limestone bridge, built in 1853 by Prince Danilo.

When Montenegro was ruled from Cetinje, this is where the royals came to escape the Black Mountain's winter. The relatively modest house of Vladika Petar I Petrović (St Peter of Cetinje) still stands; you'll recognise it by its ground-floor arches and upper rooms jutting out over the road.

Virpazar   VILLAGE

This tiny town, gathered around a square and a river blanketed with water lilies, serves as the main gateway to Lake Skadar National Park. If you're interested in sampling local wines, you'll find family-run vineyards and tasting cellars in the surrounding hills.

Virpazar (Вирпазар) may be a small speck on the map now, but it was once considered so strategically important that the occupying Turks built the **Besac fortress** (Tvrđava Besac; admission €1) on the hill looming above the village. After their downfall, Virpazar became an important trading town (*pazar* means marketplace) with a lively port; in the early 1900s it was connected to Bar by Montenegro's first narrow-gauge railway. It was also the site of one of the country's first significant uprisings against Axis invaders in WWII, an event commemorated by a striking bronze sculpture near the bridge.

Žabljak Crnojevića   RUINS

FREE For a brief time in the 15th century, between the fall of Skadar (now Shkodra in

---

MONTENEGRO LAKE SKADAR NATIONAL PARK

> ## LAKE SKADAR WILDLIFE
> ....
> Covering between 370 and 540 sq km (depending on the time of year), Lake Skadar is one of the most important reserves for wetland birds in Europe. The endangered Dalmatian pelican nests here along with around 280 other species, including a quarter of the global population of pygmy cormorants. You might spot whiskered terns making their nests on the water lilies.
>
> The average depth of the lake is 5m, with some spots plunging below sea level; these underwater spring holes are called 'eyes', attracting fish by the hundreds. The deepest eye, Radus, sinks down at least 60m. At least 48 species of fish lurk beneath Skadar's smooth surface, the most common of which are carp, bleak and eel. The park offices sell fishing permits; if you join a tour, these will be provided.
>
> Mammals within the park's confines include otters, foxes, weasels, moles, groundhogs and the occasional wolf.

Albania) and the founding of Cetinje, this was the capital of Zetan ruler Ivan Crnojević. Now the enigmatic ruins stand forlornly on a lonely hillside surrounded by lush green plains, with only some rather large snakes and spiders as occupants. The 14m-high, 2m-thick walls look intimidating enough, yet even these couldn't withstand the hammering the Ottoman invaders gave them in 1478.

In summer you can rent quad bikes and jet skis from the small village at the base of the hill. A local family sells drinks and ice creams from their front terrace, near the beginning of the path.

The site's a little hard to find but well worth the effort. Turn off the Virpazar-Podgorica highway towards Vukovci and, after the railway track and the one-way bridge, turn left. Continue for about 4.5km until you see a bridge to your left. Cross the bridge and continue to the car park near the village. Take the stone stairs heading up from the path near the river, follow your nose past the village church and along the overgrown path.

Dodoši   VILLAGE

Although some of the old stone houses date from the 16th century, the main reason to visit this tucked away village is for a dip in the river alongside the floating restaurant. Local lads flaunt their fancy diving skills off the little bridge, but even little kids can leap here with impunity. It's signposted from the road heading east from Rijeka Crnojevića towards Podgorica, around 4.5km past the main river lookout.

★ Undiscovered Montenegro   ADVENTURE

(☑ 069-402 364; www.undiscoveredmontenegro. com; Boljevići bb; week incl accommodation €645-745; ۞ Apr-Oct) This excellent agency specialises in week-long, lake-based itineraries including accommodation in its lovely stone cottage near Virpazar (three-day stays are possible outside of peak season). Guided hikes, kayaking, and wine/gastronomy tours are included in the price, and boat trips, canyoning, horse riding, wilderness canoeing, white-water kayaking and specialist birdwatching can be arranged. Afterwards, relax around the barbecue and pool.

Obod Walking Track   WALKING

Rijeka Crnojevića is the starting point of a two-hour, 7.6km circular walking track that passes a pretty **swimming hole** with icy-cold water, through the ruins of **Obod**, the

site of the region's first printing press, and on to **Obod Cave** (Obodska pećina) at the source of the river. This large cavern is home to over a dozen species of bats, which you'll smell before you see.

🛏 Sleeping & Eating

Four Countesses   APARTMENT €

(☑ 069-255 633; www.facebook.com/fourcount esses; Virpazar bb; s/d/q from €34/36/40; ❀ 🛜) The tongue-in-cheek 'countesses' are a mother and her three friendly daughters who run this unassuming place near the train station. The apartments are clean and well-provisioned, if rather cramped – but at these prices, no one's complaining.

Plavnica Eco Resort   RESORT €€€

(☑ 020-443 700; www.plavnica.me; Donja Plavnica bb; ste from €110; P ❀ 🛜 ☒) Day trippers from Podgorica escape the summer heat at this unusual resort, where there's an impressive pool set within an amphitheatre and a cavernous restaurant with all the ambience of a reception hall. Upstairs are four lavishly furnished suites. The resort has a boat that's used for lake tours, and you can hire catamarans, canoes, kayaks and pedal boats.

Stari Most   SEAFOOD €€

(☑ 067-339 429; Rijeka Crnojevića bb; mains €8-20; ۞ noon-10pm) Perhaps surprisingly – given its sleepy village location – Stari Most is one of Montenegro's finest restaurants. It's well located on the marble riverside promenade, looking to the old bridge from which it derives its name. Fish (particularly eel, trout and carp) is the speciality here and the fish soup alone is enough to justify a drive from Podgorica.

Konoba Badanj   MONTENEGRIN €€

(☑ 069-508 019; www.facebook.com/badanj official; Virpazar bb; mains €5-14; ۞ 10am-midnight; 🛜) A cool stone-walled interior with solid wooden beams, views of the river and interesting art make this an atmospheric eating option. The fish soup comes with big chunks of fish and delicious sconelike homemade bread, or try the eel straight out of Lake Skadar. It also stocks a good range of wine by small, local producers.

❶ Information

National Park Visitor Centre (☑ 020-879 103; www.nparkovi.me; €2, free with national park entry ticket; ۞ 8am-7pm May-Sep, to 4pm Oct-Apr) The main Visitor Centre rests on the opposite side of the causeway leading to Podgorica from Virpazar. It has excellent displays about all of Montenegro's national parks, including lots of taxidermal critters and an ethnographic section with folk costumes and tools. You can buy national park entry tickets (€4) and fishing permits (per day €5) from a kiosk outside.

Virpazar Tourist Office (☑069-091 183; www.visitbar.org; ⊗8am-8pm Mon-Sat, to 2pm Sun May-Sep, 9am-5pm Mon-Fri Oct-Apr; 🛜) This big office on the main square can assist you with arranging anything on the lake, including boat trips, wine tastings and private accommodation. The office operates as a shopfront for the region's small wine producers. Upstairs there are displays about the lake and its environment, illustrated with clever bent-wire sculptures.

❶ Getting There & Away

Virpazar doesn't have a bus station but buses on the Bar–Podgorica route stop on the highway (near Hotel Pelikan). A bus from Podgorica takes 30 minutes (€2.50); you'll have to tell the driver that you want to get off at Virpazar.

The train station is off the main road, 800m south of town. There are several trains to/from Bar (€2, 23 minutes) and Podgorica (€2.20, 30 minutes) every day.

Podgorica Подгорица

☑020 / POP 151,000

Given it's undergone five name changes, passed through the hands of everyone from the Romans to the Turks to the Austro-Hungarians, and twice been wiped off the map entirely, it's little wonder that Podgorica seems permanently gripped by an identity crisis. Its streets are a hotchpotch of Ottoman oddments, Austrian shopfronts, brutalist blocks and shiny new malls, and it has a fraction of the big-smoke buzz other European capitals can claim. But with some excellent galleries, plenty of parks and a vibrant cafe culture, pint-sized Podgorica is worth a look.

The city sits at the confluence of two rivers. West of the Morača is the business district, while the Ribnica divides the eastern side in two. The south side is Stara Varoš, the old Ottoman town, while north is Nova Varoš, home to a lively mixture of shops and bars.

◉ Sights

For a city formerly known as Titograd (literally 'Tito City'), there is an inordinate number of royal sculptures dotted around its many parks. The most imposing is the huge bronze **statue of Petar I Petrović Njegoš**

SECRET WINE

Wine tasting doesn't get more curious than at the **Šipčanik wine cellar** (☑020-444 125; www.plantaze.com; tours & tastings €12-32; ⊗9am-5pm Mon-Fri), 8km southeast of Podgorica, operated by Plantaže, Montenegro's largest wine company. The cellar occupies a 356m-long tunnel which was once a secret underground Yugoslav-era aircraft hangar. Partially destroyed by NATO bombing in 1999 and abandoned immediately afterwards, the revamped hangar now houses millions of litres of wine, ageing gently in bottles, and oak barrels. Call ahead to book a tour.

Four options are available, starting with an hour-long tour and tastings of three standard wines accompanied by cheese and olives. The most expensive tour includes five premium wines paired with food.

(Map p268; Bul Džordža Vašingtona bb), standing on a black marble plinth on the Cetinje edge of town. A large **equestrian statue of Nikola I** (Map p268; Park Ivana Milutinovića) struts grandly at the head of a lovely park with manicured hedges and mature trees. There's also a spectacularly cheesy sculpture of Russian singer-songwriter **Vladimir Visotsky** (Map p268) near the Millennium Bridge (p269), pictured shirtless with a guitar and a skull at his feet. In late 2018 Tito himself made a comeback by way of a bronze statue, reerected in a city park.

Museums & Galleries of Podgorica   MUSEUM

(Muzeji i Galerije Podgoric; Map p268; ☑020-242 543; www.pgmuzeji.me; Marka Miljanova 4; ⊗9am-8pm Tue-Sun) FREE Despite Cetinje nabbing most of the national endowment, Podgorica is well served by this collection of art, artefacts and folk costumes. There's an interesting section on Podgorica's history that includes antiquities exhumed from Doclea, its Roman incarnation, the remains of which are in the northern fringes of the modern city. Look out for Petar Lubarda's large canvas *Titograd* (1956) in the foyer.

Cathedral of Christ's Resurrection   CHURCH

(Saborni hram Hristovog vaskrsenja; Map p268; www.hramvaskrsenja.me; Bul Džordža Vašingtona

Podgorica

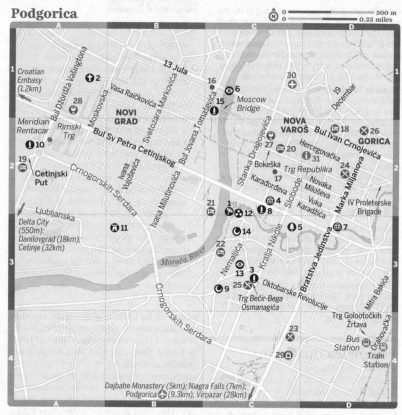

bb) Finally consecrated in 2013 after 20 years of construction, the large dome, white stone towers and gold crosses of this immense Serbian Orthodox cathedral are a striking addition to Podgorica's skyline. The exterior features an unusual contrast between roughly hewn stone at the bottom and intricately carved details above. Inside, huge chandeliers blaze against an overwhelming expanse of gilded frescoes. One controversial image, in the apse above the front door, depicts Tito, Karl Marx and Friedrich Engels burning in hell.

Petrović Palace PALACE
(Dvorac Petrovića; Map p268; ☑ 020-243 914; www.csucg.me; Park Petrovića; ☺ 8am-8pm Mon-Fri, 10am-2pm Sat) FREE The Montenegro Contemporary Art Centre stages high-profile exhibitions in this pale-pink 19th-century palace. The surrounding park is peppered with interesting sculptures and a tiny church.

Temporary exhibitions are also displayed in the small **Galerija Centar** (Map p268; ☑ 020-665 409; Njegoševa 2; ☺ hours vary) FREE in the heart of the city.

Stara Varoš AREA
(Map p268) Podgorica's oldest neighbourhood retains traces of the 400 years in which it was the centre of a bustling Ottoman Turkish town. The blocky **clock tower** (Sahat Kula; Map p268; Trg Bećir-Bega Osmanagića) overlooking the square was useful for signalling Muslim prayer times. In the maze of streets behind it, two mosques remain. You wouldn't know to look at it, but the **Starodoganjska Mosque** (Map p268; Nemaljića bb) has its origins in the 15th century. More impressive is the 18th-century **Osmanagić Mosque** (Osmanagića džamija; Map p268; Spasa Nikolića bb), which Turkish donations have helped to restore.

At the confluence of the two rivers is the ruin of the **Ribnica Fortress** (Tvrđava

Podgorica

na Ribnici; Map p268; Stara Varoš), built by the Ottomans after their conquest in 1474. The best-preserved element is a little arched bridge crossing the Ribnica.

Beach BEACH
(Map p268) The rocky Morača riverbank off Stara Varoš serves as Podgorica's main beach, complete with a summertime bar, deckchairs and sun umbrellas. It's a far cry from the sea beaches Montenegro is famous for – and litter can be a problem – but in the middle of a Podgorica heatwave, it's heavenly.

King's Park PARK
(Kraljev Park; Map p268; Bul Sv Petra Cetinjskog) Rejuvenated in 2013 with Azerbaijani money, this leafy riverside park is one of Podgorica's nicest, and has a great kids' playground.

Millennium Bridge BRIDGE
(Map p268) One of Podgorica's few landmarks, this impressive 173m-long cable-stayed bridge spans the Morača River. The pedestrian-only **Moscow Bridge** runs parallel to it, and is a superb spot for resting your feet and watching the locals go by.

☞ Tours

Montenegro Adventures ADVENTURE
(Map p268; ☏020-208 000; www.montenegro-adventures.com; Jovana Tomaševića 35; ⊗8am-6pm Mon-Fri, 9am-3pm Sat) This well-respected and long-standing agency creates

tailor-made adventure tours, countrywide. It can organise mountain guides, cycling logistics, kitesurfing, hiking, cultural activities, accommodation, flights...you name it.

Montenegro Eco Adventures ADVENTURE
(Map p268; ☏069-123 078; www.montenegro-eco.com; Njegoševa 9; ⊗9am-5pm Mon-Fri) Promoting sustainable 'soft adventure' tours ranging from day trips to countrywide tailored, multiday expeditions.

⌴ Sleeping

Montenegro Hostel HOSTEL €
(Map p268; ☏069-255 501; www.montenegrohostel.com; Spasa Nikolića 52; dm €14-15, r without bathroom €40; P❋@🛜🏊) Tucked behind an old stone gate in Stara Varoš, this welcoming place feels more like a home than a hostel, with an enticing common room (and flop-worthy purple couches), a kitchen and cosy private rooms. Dorms are sparse but sparkling, with privacy curtains on the lower bunks. Note, taxi drivers may be more familiar with the street's old name, Radoja Jovanovića.

Hotel Hemera BOUTIQUE HOTEL €€
(Map p268; ☏020-221 650; www.hotelhemera.com; Njegoševa 17; s/d from €61/81) Exceedingly atmospheric and gorgeously designed, Hemera is a top choice for those who like a bit of chic in their shelter. Rooms and suites have

eclectic art covering the walls and handmade walnut furniture used to fantastic effect. There's a superb restaurant attached, and a common-use library that gives every impression of having apparated straight from Hogwarts.

Athos
APARTMENT €€
(Map p268; ☑067-227 595; www.apartments athos.com; Bul Ivana Crnojevića 58/2; apt €66-115; P✳🖥) Enormous, easy on the eye and close to everything, these exceptional apartments are the best of Podgorica's private pads. All are supremely well equipped (think laundries and dishwashers), come with large terraces (some overlooking the lively cafe below) and have big, comfortable beds. Staff speak English and go out of their way to help guests. There's even a lift.

Hotel Podgorica
HOTEL €€
(Map p268; ☑020-402 500; www.hotelpodgor ica.co.me; Svetlane Kane Radević 1; s/d €90/100; P✳🖥) A wonderful showcase of 1960s Yugoslav architecture, the Podgorica has been modernised yet retains its period charm – right down to the unsmiling staff. The riverstone cladding blends into stone the shade of Montenegro's mountains; the best rooms have terraces facing the river.

★ CentreVille
HOTEL €€€
(Map p268; ☑020-684 000; www.cv-hotel.com; Cetinjski Put 7; s/d from €88/100; P✳🖥) The elegant rooms displaying prints of the New York skyline only emphasise how un-Podgorica-like this slick design hotel actually is. The impression starts in the 'living room lobby', where coloured-glass lamps illuminate dark grey walls, raw-concrete ceilings, leather couches and designer chairs. The hotel is housed within the swish Capital Plaza centre, alongside shops, bars and restaurants.

✗ Eating

Green Market
MARKET €
(Zelena pijaca; Map p268; Bratstva Jedinstva bb; ⊘6am-6pm Mon-Sat, to 3pm Sun May-Oct, 6am-4pm Nov-Apr) Head to this big covered market for fresh fruit and vegetables, or just for a gander; it's always very lively. It's attached to the side of the Mall of Montenegro.

★ Lanterna
MEDITERRANEAN €€
(Map p268; ☑067-361 981; Marka Miljanova 41; mains €3.20-19; ⊘8am-11pm Mon-Sat, noon-11pm Sun; 🖥🚗) Farm implements hang from the rough stone walls creating a surprisingly rustic ambience for the centre of the city. A se-

lection of meat and fish grills and pasta is offered, but it's hard to go past the crispy-based pizza – it's quite possibly Montenegro's best. They also serve breakfasts and sandwiches.

Pod Volat
BALKAN €€
(Map p268; ☑069-618 633; Trg Bećira-Bega Osmanagića; mains €3-11; ⊘7am-midnight) The food on offer here may be kind to the hip pocket, but not so much to the hips themselves; this is gloriously fattening Balkan cuisine at its best. The mixed grill is massive, but it's so good you won't mind loosening your belt a notch. It's a popular locals haunt, and its Stara Varoš location is awesomely atmospheric.

Imanje Knjaz
INTERNATIONAL €€
(☑067-765 800; www.imanje-knjaz.me; Mareza bb; mains €7-20; ⊘8am-midnight; 🖥🍴) On Podgorica's rural northwestern fringe, this large restaurant, reception centre and hotel is an atmospheric meal stop en route to or from Ostrog Monastery. Tables are positioned on terraces set over and around artificial ponds punctuated by fountains. The menu covers the gamut from Wiener schnitzels to spring rolls, with lots of local specialities, too.

Ziya
MIDDLE EASTERN €€€
(Map p268; ☑020-230 690; www.hotelziya.me; Beogradska 10; mains €10-22; ⊘7am-11pm; 🚗) Attached to the boutique hotel of the same name – but welcoming all comers – Ziya serves delectable mains and meze in equally tasty surrounds. It's a bit more upmarket than your hometown kebabery, so be sure to scrub up.

🍷 Drinking & Nightlife

Podgorica's nightlife is centred on Nova Varoš, particularly in the blocks west of Ulica Slobode. The hippest strip right now is Ulica Bokeška. Keep an eye out for posters listing live music events and other happenings.

★ Street Bar
COCKTAIL BAR
(Map p268; ☑067-619 979; www.facebook.com/ StreetBarPodgorica; Bul Džordža Vašingtona bb; ⊘10am-2pm & 6pm-midnight Mon-Fri, 6pm-midnight Sat & Sun; 🖥) The street has come out of the cold in this hip little bar, lined with faux shopfronts and scattered with park-style furniture. Its actual outside area is a surprisingly pleasant tree-lined terrace in a patch of urban wasteland at the centre of a brutalist block. Good cocktails and live music complete the Street scene.

★ **Culture Club Tarantino**   BAR
(Map p268; ☑067-055 333; www.cultureclub.me;
Bokeška 6; ⊗7am-midnight; 🛜) Exemplifying
the offbeat flavour of the Bokeška strip, this
quirky spot promotes local music, art and
other alternative happenings. It's a good
place for a coffee and local-watching by day;
at night it throngs with drinking, dancing
students, creative types and other hip folk.

Buda Bar   BAR
(Map p268; www.facebook.com/Budabarpg; Stanka Dragojevića 26; ⊗8am-3am Mon-Sat) A gold-
en Buddha smiles serenely as you meditate
over your morning coffee or search for the
eternal truth at the bottom of a cocktail
glass. This is one slick watering hole; the
tentlike, semienclosed terrace is the place
to be on balmy summer nights, especially
when there's a local starlet performing.

🛍 Shopping

Delta City   MALL
(☑068-878 637; www.deltacity.me; Cetinjski
Put; ⊗10am-10pm) Megamall with loads of
boutiques, brand names, a good bookshop,
banks, pharmacies, phone companies, supermarkets, a post office and a cinema.

Mall of Montenegro   MALL
(Map p268; ☑067-257 793; www.mallofmontene
gro.com; Bul Save Kovačevića 74; ⊗7am-10pm)
Huge mall with a bowling alley and kids'
play centre.

ℹ Information

Accident & Emergency Clinic (JZU zavod za
hitnu medicinsku pomoć; Map p268; ☑020-
226 081; www.zhmp.org; Vaka Đurovića bb;
⊗24hr)
Tourist Organisation of Podgorica (Map
p268; ☑020-667 535; www.podgorica.travel;
Slobode 47; ⊗8am-8pm Mon-Fri) Operates out
of two offices on the same street; the second is
at Slobode 30.

ℹ Getting There & Away

AIR
Podgorica airport (TGD; ☑020-444 244;
www.montenegroairports.com) is 9km south of
the city. Airlines flying here year-round include
Montenegro, Adria, Air Serbia, Alitalia, Austrian, LOT, Ryanair, Turkish and Wizz.

Taxi fares to the city are about €12; check
the fare before getting in. Trains head between
Podgorica and Aerodrom station (€1.20, seven
minutes, 10 daily), which is a hard-to-find shed
on a scrappy patch of land about 1km from the
airport.

WORTH A TRIP

THE OTHER NIAGARA

They may not be the thundering cascades so beloved by honeymooners
in North America, but the **Niagara
waterfalls** (Nijagarini vodopadi; Rakića
Kuće) make for a fantastic day trip from
Podgorica. The falls are at their dramatic
best after the spring thaws, but you'll find
plenty of locals taking a dip in their somewhat depleted depths in early summer;
by August they're often completely dried
up. There's a good traditional restaurant,
also called Niagara, beside the falls.

Niagara is a 10-minute drive from
Podgorica; you'll need a car as there's
no public transport. Take the signposted
road to Tuzi, then turn right before passing the bridge over the Cijevna River and
follow the signs to Rakića Kuće until you
reach the restaurant's car park.

BUS
Podgorica's **bus station** (Map p268; ☑020-620
430; Trg Golootočkih Žrtava 1; ⊗24hr) has a
left-luggage service, an ATM, a restaurant and
regular services to all major towns, including
Herceg Novi (€10, three hours), Kotor (€7.50,
2¼ hours), Budva (€6, 1½ hours), Ulcinj (€7, two
hours) and Cetinje (€3, 30 minutes).

CAR
Car-hire agencies with counters at Podgorica
Airport include Avis, Budget, Europcar and Sixt.
Local agency **Meridian** (Map p268; ☑020-234
944; www.meridian-rentacar.com; Bul Džordža
Vašingtona 85) also has a city office. The Sozina
tunnel and toll road connects Podgorica to the
Adriatic coast.

TRAIN
From Podgorica's **train station** (☑020-441
209; www.zpcg.me; Trg Golootočkih Žrtava 13)
there are services to Bar (€2.40, one hour, 12
daily), Virpazar (€1.40, 30 minutes, 10 daily) and
Belgrade (€21, 11¾ hours, two daily).

ℹ Getting Around

BUS
It's easy to explore on foot, but if you fancy trying a local bus, they cost 80c for a short journey.

TAXI
Taxis in Podgorica are cheap and reliable, al-
though they can be in short supply late at night.
City Taxi (☑19711; www.citytaxi.com)
Halo Taxi (☑19700; www.facebook.com/Halo
Taxi19700)

MONTENEGRO PODGORICA

NORTHERN MONTENEGRO

The mountainous north is the beefy brawn to the coast's polished pulchritude. Peaking at 2534m, this is the roof of Montenegro, where profound massifs, otherworldly vistas and a picturesque smattering of old-school villages offer a literal and metaphorical breath of fresh air.

The region's main drawcards are its three national parks. Durmitor is a dizzying combination of soaring peaks and the plunging depths of the Tara River Canyon, making for spectacular skiing in winter and rip-roaring rafting in summer. The remote treks and trails of Prokletije's Accursed Mountains are more heaven than hell for serious alpinists, while the less hardcore can catch their breath in Biogradska Gora's gentle lakes and timeless forests.

There's not much in the way of infrastructure outside of Kolašin and Žabljak, but don't let that stop you. Hire a car, steady your nerves, and let the twisty, turny, white-knuckle roads take you where they will.

Biogradska Gora National Park НАЦИОНАЛНИ ПАРК БИОГРАДСКА ГОРА

Nestled within the Bjelasica mountain range, pretty Biogradska Gora has as its heart 16 sq km of virgin woodland – one of Europe's last three remaining primeval forests. If you're knowledgable about such things, you'll be able to spot beech, fir, juniper, white ash, maple and elm trees. Many of the trees in the forest are over half a millennium old, with some soaring to 60m high.

King Nikola is to thank for its survival; on a visit in 1878 he was so taken by the beauty of oh-so-green **Lake Biograd** (Biogradsko jezero) that the locals gifted him the land and he ordered it to be preserved. The park is also home to five high-altitude (1820m) glacial lakes.

Occasional tour buses pull in, but a 10-minute stroll should shake the masses and quickly return you to tranquillity.

Restoran Biogradsko Jezero
MONTENEGRIN €€
(mains €8-9; ☺9am-6pm) Most visitors make a beeline straight for this striking new piece of architecture, perched between the trees on the lake's edge. As well as cooked breakfasts, sandwiches and craft beers, the menu includes a range of stodgy Montenegrin dishes such as *cicvara* (cheesy polenta porridge), *kačamak* (similar, with potato and cream), peasant soup and mountain goulash.

ⓘ Information

Park Office (☑020-865 625; www.nparkovi. me; ☺9am-5pm Sep-May, to 7pm Jun-Aug) A kiosk by the lake sells fishing permits (€20 per day), rents rowing boats (€8 per hour) and kayaks (from €3 per hour), and handles bookings for campsites (€3/5/10 per small tent/ large tent/caravan) and a cluster of 12 small log cabins (€10 per person). There's also a small visitor centre nearby with displays on wildlife and local ethnography.

ⓘ Getting There & Away

The main entrance to the park is between Kolašin and Mojkovac on the Podgorica–Belgrade highway. After paying an entry fee (€3/1.50 adult/child), you can drive the further 4km to Lake Biograd.

Getting here via public transport (plus a bit of hoofing it) is also possible. Buses to/from Kolašin and Mojkovac stop (on request) at Kraljevo Kolo, the entrance to the park. From there it's about an hour's walk to the lake. The nearest train station (Štitarička Rijeka, on the Podgorica–Belgrade route) is a 90-minute walk away.

Durmitor National Park НАЦИОНАЛНИ ПАРК ДУРМИТОР

The impossibly rugged and dramatic Durmitor (Дурмитор) is one of Montenegro's – and Mother Nature's – showpieces. Carved out by glaciers and underground streams, Durmitor stuns with dizzying canyons, glittering glacial lakes and nearly 50 limestone peaks soaring to over 2000m; the highest, **Bobotov Kuk**, hits 2523m. From December to March, Durmitor is a major ski resort, while in summer it's popular for hiking, rafting and other active pursuits.

The national park covers the Durmitor mountain range and a narrow branch heading east along the Tara River towards Mojkovac. West of the park, the mighty Tara marks the border with Bosnia and joins the Piva River near Šćepan Polje.

Durmitor is home to 163 bird species, about 50 types of mammals and purportedly the greatest variety of butterflies in Europe. It's very unlikely you'll spot bears and wolves, which is either a good or bad thing depending on your perspective.

PROKLETIJE NATIONAL PARK

The Prokletije Mountains (Проклетије) are a huge, hulking expanse of wilderness forming the border with Albania and Kosovo. They're the southernmost – and highest – part of the Dinaric Alps. Surreally scenic and eerily remote, this magnificent area may well be one of Europe's least explored corners.

In 2009 a 160-sq-km chunk of the Montenegrin side of the range was declared the country's fifth national park. Ambitious plans are afoot for the entire range to be declared a cross-border Balkans Peace Park (see www.balkanspeacepark.org). The epic Peaks of the Balkans (p38) hiking trail is a 192km circuit that crosses through all three countries.

Both the Montenegrin and the Albanian names for the range (Prokletije and Bjeshkët e Namuna, respectively) translate to the rather ominous-sounding 'Accursed Mountains'. Leave your hoodoo at home; this is a reference to the harsh environment of these sky-punching, jagged peaks rather than any high-altitude jinx.

If you're planning on a serious mountaineering expedition, it's highly recommended that you enlist the services of a local guide; www.peaksofthebalkans.com has a list of trained guides, and the **National Park Visitors Centre** (☑ 051-250 130; www.nparkovi.me; Alipašina bb; ☉ 9am-5pm Jun-Aug, 8am-4pm Mon-Fri Sep-May) in Gusinje also has guides on their books (guides €60/100 per four/eight hours). The centre also stocks the *Prokletije Hiking & Biking* map, as does the **Plav Tourist Office** (☑ 051-250 151; www.toplav.me; Racina bb; ☉ 8am-4pm Mon-Fri, 9am-3pm Sat). *Prokletije Mountains of Plav and Gusinje; 40 Mountain Trails* by local alpinist Rifat Mulić is also useful.

For a taste of the Peaks of the Balkans track, a popular 10-hour hike that stays within Montenegro's boundaries runs from Plav to the village of Vusanje. It takes in 27km of fresh springs, lakes, forests, shepherd communities and a climb up the Bor peak (2106m), offering staggering views of the craggy Karanfil Mountains, nicknamed – with good reason – the 'Dolomites of Montenegro'. Those keen – and equipped with the proper paperwork – to cross the border can overnight at Vusanje and continue on a 21km route to Theth in Albania; the route is particularly fascinating for its communist-era remnants, including an abandoned military post and bunker.

⊙ Sights

★ Black Lake   LAKE

(Crno jezero) Eighteen glittering glacial lakes known as *gorske oči* (mountain eyes) dot the Durmitor range. The spectacular Black Lake, a pleasant 3km walk from Žabljak, is the largest of them and the most visited part of the national park. The rounded mass of **Međed** (the Bear; 2287m) rears up behind it, casting an inky shadow into the pine-walled waters. An easy 3.6km walking track circles the lake.

★ Tara Canyon   CANYON

Slicing through the mountains at the northern edge of the national park, the Tara River forms a canyon that is 1300m deep at its peak (the Grand Canyon plummets a mere 200m deeper). The best views are from the water, and rafting (p275) along the river is one of the country's most popular tourist activities. If you'd rather admire the canyon from afar, head to the top of **Mt Ćurevac** (1625m) – although even this view is restricted by the canyon walls.

The viewpoint isn't well signposted and can be difficult to find. From central Žabljak, take the road north and follow the signs marked 'Panoramic Road 2'. Leave this route at the fork to the right marked 'Tepca'. Eventually there are some small wooden signs pointing to Ćurevac or *vidikovac* (viewpoint). Stop at the grassy parking spot opposite the drink stall and clamber up the small track behind.

Tara Bridge   BRIDGE

(Đurđevića Tara) The elegant spans of the 150m-high Tara Bridge were completed just as WWII was starting. At the time it was the largest concrete arched vehicular bridge in Europe. Its 365m length is carried on five sweeping arches, the largest of which is 116m wide.

Dobrilovina Monastery   CHRISTIAN MONASTERY

Near the eastern boundary of the national park, 28km from Mojkovac, this monastery has an idyllic setting in lush fields hemmed in by the mountains and the Tara River. If

DON'T MISS

OSTROG MONASTERY: 'ST BASIL'S MIRACLE'

Resting improbably – miraculously? – in a cliff face 900m above the Zeta valley, the gleaming white **Ostrog Monastery** (Manastir Ostrog/Манастир Острог; www.manastirostrog.com) FREE is the most important site in Montenegro for Orthodox Christians, attracting up to a million visitors annually. Even with its numerous pilgrims, tourists and souvenir stands, it's a strangely affecting place. A guesthouse near the Lower Monastery offers tidy single-sex dorm rooms, while in summer, sleeping mats are provided for free to pilgrims in front of the Upper Monastery.

The **Lower Monastery** (Donji manastir) is 2km below the main shrine. Stop here to admire the vivid frescoes in the **Holy Trinity Church** (Crkva Sv Trojice; 1824). Behind it is a natural spring where you can fill your bottles with deliciously cold, sweet water (and potentially benefit from an internal blessing as you sup it).

From here the faithful, some of them barefoot, plod up the steep road to the top. Halfway up, the stone walls of the little domed **Church of St Stanko the Martyr** (Crkva Sv Mučenika Stanka) gleam golden in the sunset. Nonpilgrims and the pure of heart may drive directly to the main car park and limit their penitence to just the final 200m.

The **Upper Monastery** (Gornji manastir; the really impressive one) is dubbed 'Sv Vasilije's miracle', because no one seems to understand how it was built. Constructed in 1665 within two large caves, it gives the impression that it has grown out of the very rock. Sv Vasilije (St Basil), a bishop from Hercegovina, brought his monks here after the Ottomans destroyed Tvrdoš Monastery near Trebinje. Pilgrims queue to enter the atmospheric shrine where the saint's fabric-wrapped bones are kept. To enter you'll need to be wearing a long skirt or trousers (jeans are fine), and cover your shoulders. Most women also cover their heads with a scarf. It's customary to back out of the doorways and you'll witness much kissing of lintels and making of signs of the cross from the devout. At the very top of the monastery is another cavelike chapel with faded frescoes dating from 1667.

The monastery is so firmly entrenched in the country's psyche that many Montenegrins – even nonbelievers – commonly 'swear to Ostrog' ('Ostroga mi...') when promising to do something.

There's no direct public transport, but numerous tour buses (€20 to €30 for a day trip) head here from all of the tourist hot spots. There's an Ostrog train station (five daily from Podgorica, 47 minutes, €1.80) way down at the bottom of the hill; it's about a 90-minute hike from there to the Lower Monastery.

If you're driving, we strongly recommend that you take the excellent road through Danilovgrad to the monastery. The old road leaves the main Podgorica–Nikšić highway 19km past Danilovgrad. It's extremely narrow, twisting and steep and in a very poor state of repair; in short, it's terrifying.

you knock at the accommodation wing, a black-robed nun will unlock the church, but only if she's satisfied that you're appropriately attired. The frescoes that remain inside the church, dedicated to St George (Sv Đorđe), are faded but very beautiful.

Stećci Sites   CEMETERY

These mysterious carved stone tomb monuments – dating from between the 12th and 16th centuries – can be found across northern Montenegro and neighbouring Bosnia. There are two extremely significant *stećci* sites in Durmitor National Park (both were added to Unesco's World Heritage list in 2016): the Bare Žugića necropolis, with 300 *stećci*, and Grčko groblje (Greek graveyard), with 49. Many of the stones at both sites are intricately decorated.

🏃 Activities

Hiking

Durmitor is one of the best-marked mountain ranges in Europe, with 25 marked trails making up a total of 150km. Some suggest it's a little *too* well labelled, encouraging novices to wander around seriously high-altitude paths that are prone to fog and summer thunderstorms. Ask the staff at the National Park Visitors Centre (p277) about tracks that suit your level of experience and fitness.

One rewarding route is the hike to the two Škrčka Lakes (Škrčka jezera), in the centre of a tectonic valley, where you can enjoy magnificent scenery and stay overnight in a mountain hut (June to September only). Another popular hike is from the Black Lake to the ice cave *(ledina pećina)* – home in cooler months to stalactite- and stalagmite-like shapes made of ice – on Obla Glava. It's a six- to seven-hour return hike.

If you're considering an assault on **Bobotov Kuk** or a serious winter expedition, it's best to arrange a local guide.

In any case, check the weather forecast before you set out, stick to the tracks, and prepare for rain and sudden drops in temperature. A compass could be a lifesaver. *Durmitor and the Tara Canyon* by Branislav Cerović (€12 from the visitors centre) is a great resource for mountaineers and serious hikers. The **Mountaineering Association of Montenegro** (www.pscg.me) has contacts and info on the peaks and paths of Durmitor.

Rafting

A rafting expedition along the Tara is the best way to revel in glorious river scenery that's impossible to catch from land. Trips are suitable for everyone from the white-water novice to experienced foam-hounds. Though it's not the world's most white-knuckled ride, there are a few rapids; if you're after speed, visit in April and May, when the last of the melting snow revs up the flow. Various operators run trips between April and October.

The 82km section that is raftable starts from Splavište, south of the Tara Bridge, and ends at Šćepan Polje on the Bosnian border. The classic two-day trip heads through the deepest part of the canyon on the first day, stopping overnight at Radovan Luka. Summit Travel Agency (p276) offers a range of rafting trips on this route, with transfers from Žabljak.

Most of the day tours from the coast traverse only the last 18km from Brstanovica – this is outside the national park and hence avoids hefty fees. You'll miss out on the canyon's depths, but it's still a beautiful stretch, including most of the rapids. The buses follow a spectacular road along the Piva River, giving you a double dose of canyon action.

It's important to use a reputable operator; in 2010 two people died in one day on a trip with inexperienced guides. At a minimum make sure you're given a helmet and life jacket – wear them and do them up. Many of the rafting groups also offer other activities, including horse riding, canyoning and jeep safaris.

Camp Grab RAFTING
(☎069-101 002; www.tara-grab.com; half-day incl lunch €44, 3-day all-inclusive rafting trips from €200) In addition to top-notch rafting trips, this excellent outfit offers guided riverboarding (or 'hydrospeed'), canoeing, canyoning, hiking and biking. Grab's lodgings are blissfully located 8km upstream from Šćepan Polje. To get there, you'll need to cross the Montenegrin side of the border crossing and hang a right (tell the guards you're heading to Grab); the last 3.5km is unsealed.

Waterfall Rafting Centre RAFTING
(☎069-310 848; www.raftingmontenegro.com) This crew is a trustworthy choice for Tara River rafting. It offers a variety of trips, ranging in length from a half-day (€45) to three days (from €200). The recently built accommodation centre – 5km from Šćepan Polje – is simple, cosy and wonderfully quiet.

Tara Tour RAFTING
(☎069-086 106; www.tara-tour.com; Šćepan Polje bb) This long-established firm offers an excellent half-day rafting trip (€40, including two meals) and has a cute set of wooden chalets in Šćepan Polje with squat toilets and showers in a separate block.

Skiing

With 120 days of snow cover, Durmitor offers the most reliable – and cheapest – skiing in Montenegro.

Savin Kuk Ski Centar and Javorovača Ski Centar (p276) both rent out equipment and offer lessons. See www.skiresortmontenegro.com (in Montenegrin) for more information on all of Montenegro's ski centres.

Free-riding snowboarders and skiers should check out www.riders.me for off-piste adventure ideas.

Savin Kuk Ski Centar SKIING
(☎052-363 036; www.tcdurmitor.me; ski passes day/week €12/60) Even in the height of summer Savin Kuk (2313m), 5km from Žabljak, wears a pocket of snow. On its slopes you'll find Durmitor's main ski centre. Its 3.5km run starts from a height of 2010m and is best suited to advanced skiers. There are two lifts. Ask about the possibility of skiing **Debeli Namet**, one of Europe's most southern glaciers; it's covered in snow, even in July.

ROAD ROULETTE

The gloriously swooping, zigzaggy roads around the Durmitor area seem to inspire reckless racing-car driver fantasies in many locals, but whatever you do, don't follow their lead. Not only are these roads incredibly dangerous, they're heavily patrolled by the traffic police. We've had reports of people being pulled over for even the most minor infractions, so play it straight and watch your speed.

Javorovača Ski Centar
SKIING

(☏ 067-800 971; www.javorovaca.me; adult/child day passes €8/5, week passes €48/30) On the outskirts of Žabljak, near the bus station, Javorovača Ski Centar has two lifts (550m and 150m), a gentle slope that's good for kids and beginners, year-round accommodation and a restaurant.

Adventure Sports

Red Rock Zipline
ADVENTURE SPORTS

(☏ 069-440 290; www.redrockzipline.com; Đurđevića Tara; adult €10; ⊙ 10am-8pm Apr-Oct) Feel the wind in your hair (and the collywobbles in your stomach) with a 50km per hour flight across the Tara Canyon. The 350m-long zip line is strung alongside the magnificent Tara Bridge with a starting point 170m above the river. It's scary as hell, but fret not: it's run by an extremely professional outfit. Look for the red flags.

Crno Jezero

Avanturistički Park
ADVENTURE SPORTS

(☏ 069-214 110; www.avanturistickipark.me; Black Lake; adult/child €9/8; ⊙ 10am-7pm Jul & Aug, 10am-6pm Sat & Sun Jun & Sep) Want to take flight? Two zip lines have been set up by the shores of Black Lake, offering criminal amounts of fun. The shorter one zips across the forest from a height of 14m, while the longer one will hurtle you for 350m clear across the lake. There are also obstacle courses and plenty of activities set up for kids, including a zip line with toboggan.

Nevidio Canyon
CANYONING

Just south of the national park, near Šavnik, is the remarkable 2.7km-long Nevidio Canyon. Cut by the Komarnica River, at points it is only metres wide, hence the name (*nevidio* means 'invisible'). It's extremely beautiful but equally dangerous. Canyoning expeditions generally take about three to

four hours and participants should be able to swim and have a high level of fitness.

Montenegro Canyoning
ADVENTURE SPORTS

(☏ 069-565 311; www.montenegro-canyoning.com; trips without/with lunch per person €90/100) This highly recommended group focuses solely on expeditions to Nevidio. The guides are extremely experienced canyoners and are members of Alpine Search and Rescue; one of them – Marko – was the first Montenegrin to climb Mt Everest.

Pirlitor
CLIMBING

Two rock walls have been prepared on the side of the mountain here, but you'll need your own ropes. To get to Pirlitor from Žabljak, head towards the Tara Bridge, turn left at Vrela and follow the signs. The access road is very rough and is best attempted with a four-wheel drive.

🚗 Tours

Simply driving in Durmitor is a delight. If you haven't got your own wheels – or are rightfully nervous about braving the precipitous, twisty-turny roads – a jeep safari is an excellent and easy way to take in the region's magnificent scenery. Safaris generally include village visits, traditional lunches and off-road bushwhacks.

Durmitor Adventure
ADVENTURE

(☏ 069-629 516; www.durmitoradventure.com) This well-regarded group offers tandem paragliding (€90), canyoning expeditions to Nevido (€100), climbing at Pirlitor (€50) and a range of guided mountain hikes, including treks to Bobotov Kuk and the ice cave (€70 for a group).

Summit Travel Agency
ADVENTURE

(☏ 068-535 535; www.summit.co.me; Njegoševa 12, Žabljak; half-1-/2-day rafting trips €45/110/200) As well as all-inclusive rafting trips departing from Žabljak, this long-standing agency can arrange jeep tours and canyoning expeditions. It also has accommodation in the form of rental apartments in Žabljak.

🛏 Sleeping & Eating

★ Hikers Den
HOSTEL €

(☏ 067-854 433; www.hostelzabljak.com; Božidara Žugića bb, Žabljak; dm/r from €13/35; ⊙ Apr-Oct; 🛜) Split between three neighbouring houses, this laid-back and sociable place is by far the best hostel in the north. If you're keen on rafting, canyoning or a jeep safari, the charming

English-speaking hosts will happily make the arrangements. They also offer a four-hour 'Durmitor in a day' minivan tour (€20).

★Eko-Oaza Tear of Europe CAMPGROUND €
(Eko-Oaza suza Evrope; ☎069-444 590; www.eko-oaza.me; Gornja Dobrilovina; campsites per 1/2/3 people €7.50/11/15, campervans €13-15, cabins €50, without bathroom €20; ⊙Apr-Oct; 🛜) Consisting of a handful of comfortable wooden cottages with bathrooms (each sleeping five people), small cabins without bathrooms, well-equipped apartments and a fine stretch of lawn above the river, this magical, family-run 'eco oasis' offers a genuine experience of Montenegrin hospitality. Home-cooked meals are provided on request, and rafting, kayaking, canyoning and jeep safaris can be arranged. Truly memorable.

Autokamp Mlinski Potok CAMPGROUND €
(☎069-821 730; www.facebook.com/camp.durmitor.mlinskipotok; Pitomine bb; campsites per person/car €4/2, r €10; ⊙May-Oct; P) With a fabulously hospitable host (there's no escaping the *rakija* shots), this private campsite above the visitors centre is a sociable option. It's a fairly basic set-up but there are hot-water showers and clean sit-down toilets. Private rooms are also available.

Žabljak City Center Apartments APARTMENT €€
(☎052-361 777; www.zabljakapartments.net; Vojvode Mišića bb, Žabljak; apt €52-91) Žabljak is hardly a city, but this set of eight apartments is indeed central. They range from studios to spacious but simple one-bedroom units; the little wood-lined one above the main house has the most character. English isn't a strong point.

Etno Selo Šljeme CABIN €€
(☎063-229 294; www.etnoselosljeme.com; Smrčevo brdo bb; cabins €90; P🛜🐾) Šljeme's two-bedroom A-frame cabins are more swish than some of the other *'etno'* (rustic and vaguely traditional) offerings in the vicinity, and much better than the rooms above the on-site restaurant. There's also a playground, and bikes for hire. It's located 6km south of Žabljak, but less than 3km from the Savin Kuk Ski Centar.

Hotel Soa HOTEL €€€
(☎052-360 110; www.hotelsoa.com; Njegoševa bb, Žabljak; s/ste/apt from €67/105/124; P🛜) The rooms at this snazzy, modern hotel are kitted out with monsoon shower heads, robes and slippers. There's also a playground, bikes for hire and one of the country's best restaurants (mains €5 to €17); try the lamb baked in cream, served with *ajvar* (roasted-red-capsicum dip).

O'ro MONTENEGRIN €€
(Njegoševa bb, Žabljak; mains €8-11; ⊙7am-1am; 🛜) The focus is firmly on local specialities at this appealing wood-and-glass restaurant. In summer grab a seat on the large terrace and tuck into a *Durmitorska večera* (Durmitor dinner) platter featuring air-dried beef, sausages, local cheese, *ajvar* and crispy roast potatoes. It also serve lamb, veal, trout and *kačamak* (polenta, cheese and potato porridge).

ℹ Orientation

All roads (and ski runs and bumpy trails) lead to **Žabljak**, regional capital and – at 1450m – one of the highest towns in the Balkans. Quaintly ramshackle – though slowly smartening up – it's the gateway to Durmitor's mountain adventures. You'll find restaurants, hotels and a supermarket gathered around the car park that masquerades as Žabljak's main square.

ℹ Information

The road to the Black Lake is blocked off just past the National Park Visitors Centre and an entry fee is charged (€3/6/12 per person, per one/three/seven days). Drivers will need to park outside the gates (€2) and walk the remaining 500m to the lake. Keep hold of your ticket, in case you bump into a ranger.

National Park Visitors Centre (☎052-360 228; www.nparkovi.me; Njegoševa bb, Žabljak; ⊙7am-5pm Mon-Fri, 10am-5pm Sat & Sun Jan & Jun–mid-Sep, 7am-3pm Mon-Fri mid-Sep–Dec & Feb-May) On the road to the Black Lake, this centre includes a wonderful micromuseum focusing on the park's flora and fauna. The knowledgeable staff answer queries and sell local craft, maps, hiking guides and fishing permits (€20). The centre also rents bikes (€3/8 per hour/day), assist with accommodation and can organise local guides (€15 to €100, depending on the trail).

Žabljak Tourist Office (☎052-361 802; www.tozabljak.com; Trg Durmitorskih ratnika, Žabljak; ⊙7am-10pm mid-Jun–Sep, 8am-8pm Oct–mid-Jun) Operates in a wooden hut in Žabljak's main square/car park.

The website **www.durmitor.rs** has heaps of information on activities and accommodation in the region, plus the latest news and events listings.

❶ Getting There & Away

All of the approaches to Durmitor are spectacular. The most reliable road to Žabljak follows the Tara River west from Mojkovac. In summer this 70km drive takes about 90 minutes. If you're coming from Podgorica, the quickest way is through Nikšić and Šavnik. The main highway north from Nikšić follows the dramatic Piva Canyon to Šćepan Polje. There's a wonderful back road through the mountains leaving the highway near Plužine, but it's impassable as soon as the snows fall.

The bus station is at the southern edge of Žabljak, on the Šavnik road. Buses head to Podgorica (€8, 2½ hours, eight daily), Belgrade (€21, nine hours, daily) and, in summer, to the Bay of Kotor.

UNDERSTAND MONTENEGRO

Destination Today

When Montenegro chose to part ways from Serbia in 2006, it was a brave move, especially given its tiny population. But toughing it out is something these gutsy people have had plenty of experience in. Montenegro's national identity is built around resisting the Ottoman Empire for hundreds of years in a mountainous enclave much smaller than the nation's current borders. Today, fierce little Montenegro has its sights set on joining an entirely different kind of union: the EU.

NATO & the EU

Shortly after independence in 2006, Montenegro applied to join both the North Atlantic Treaty Organization (NATO) and the European Union (EU). Joining NATO is a contentious issue, as memories of the NATO bombing of Serbia and Montenegro during the Kosovo conflict are still fresh in many people's minds. Anti-NATO protests erupted in Podgorica in late 2015, followed by a split in the ruling coalition in early 2016. The accession to NATO has also upset the historically close relationship between Russia and Montenegro. Some have theorised that Montenegro's NATO membership is a symbolic slap in the face to Russia, proving to them that the organisation's expansion cannot be halted. Nonetheless, in June 2017 Montenegro officially became the 29th member of NATO.

Formal accession negotiations were opened with the EU in June 2012 and Montenegro is tipped to become a member in 2025.

The Serbian Question

Although traditionally the closest of allies, linked by a shared culture and religion, positions have been hardening between Montenegro and Serbia. A recent flashpoint was the 100th anniversary of the Podgorica Assembly which, in 1918, resulted in Montenegro losing its independence and being subsumed within the Serb-ruled Kingdom of Yugoslavia. Commemorations of the event by Serbian organisations were seen as a provocation by the Montenegrin government, which banned a group of Serb academics and politicians from entering the country.

The rhetoric has ratcheted up in recent years, with senior Serbian politicians accusing Montenegro of discrimination against Serbs, and the Serbian Orthodox Patriarch comparing the position of Serbs in Montenegro to their treatment under the Independent State of Croatia during WWII (an era when hundreds of thousands of Serbs were murdered by Croatian fascists). Montenegro's government has described such comments as inaccurate and offensive, and asserted that Serbs never have been and never will be discriminated against in Montenegro.

The Never-Changing Government

Montenegro's 2016 general election was a hugely contentious affair, marked by protests, scandal and intrigue. But for all of the kerfuffle, the results remained the same as they have been since 1990, with the Democratic Party of Socialists (DPS) holding tight to the reins once again. Considering that the DPS was born out of Montenegro's Communist Party, one could argue that it's been in power continuously since 1945 in one form or other. However, today's DPS is a long way from communist, having embarked on an enthusiastic and often controversial campaign of privatisations since the demise of Yugoslavia.

Many of the party's successes and scandals boil down to one man: Milo Đukanović. A charismatic, handsome politician, Đukanović has been the president of the DPS since 1997, and – apart from a few scattered years of 'retirement' – has been either the prime minister or president of Montenegro since 1991. It's a situation redolent of Vladimir Putin and his many power swaps and perennial string-pulling, but don't tell Đukanović that.

Đukanović has alleged that Russia – with a little help from Serbia – was behind a coup plot to derail the 2016 elections due to the DPS's pro-NATO and EU stance. The Montenegrin prosecutor claimed the suspected would-be coup members – 20 of whom were arrested on election day – planned to incite violence on election night, and to have Đukanović assassinated. Đukanović also accused his opposition – the Democratic Front (DF), a coalition comprised mostly of pro-Russian and pro-Serbian groups – of being funded by Russia, a charge the party has denied. The DF – which won 20% of the vote – accused the DPS of faking the attempted coup to improve their vote count. While opposition parties initially refused to accept the election results, the DPS was able to secure support in parliament from social democrats and parties of national minorities.

Organised Crime & Corruption

In the early 2000s Đukanović was investigated by an Italian antimafia unit and charged for his alleged role in a billion-dollar cigarette-smuggling operation; the charges were later dropped. He was named Person of the Year (2015) by the Organized Crime and Corruption Reporting Project for his work in 'promoting crime, corruption and uncivil society'; the OCCRP also called Đukanović's Montenegro 'one of the most dedicated kleptocracies and organized crime havens in the world'.

It's a claim that echoes the 2012 billing of Montenegro as a 'mafia state' by *Foreign Affairs* magazine. The European Commission noted in its 2018 *Report on Montenegro* that 'despite some progress, corruption is prevalent in many areas and remains an issue of concern'.

History

Like all the modern states of the Balkan peninsula, Montenegro has a long, convoluted and eventful history. History is worn on the sleeve here and people discuss 600-year-old events (or their not-always-accurate versions of them) as if they happened yesterday. Events such as the split of the Roman Empire, the subsequent split in Christianity between Catholic and Orthodox, and the

battles with the Ottoman Turks still have a direct bearing on the politics of today.

First Serbian States

In the 9th century the first Serb kingdom, Raška, arose near Novi Pazar (in modern Serbia) followed shortly by another Serb state, Duklja, which sprang up on the site of present-day Podgorica. Raška eventually became known as Serbia and Duklja as Zeta. From the 12th century, Raška/Serbia became dominant over Zeta, which nonetheless remained a distinct area. At its greatest extent Serbia reached from the Adriatic to the Aegean and north to the Danube.

Expansion was halted in 1389 at the battle of Kosovo Polje, where the Serbs were defeated by the Ottoman Turks. By 1441 the Turks had rolled through Serbia and in the late 1470s they took on Zeta. The remnants of the Zetan nobility fled first to Žabljak Crnojevića, near Lake Skadar, and eventually into the mountains. In 1480 they established a stronghold at Cetinje on Mt Lovćen.

Montenegro & the Ottomans

This mountainous area became the last redoubt of Serbian Orthodox culture when all else fell to the Ottomans. It was during this time that the Venetians, who ruled Kotor, Budva and much of the Adriatic Coast, began calling Mt Lovćen the Monte Negro (Black Mountain). The Montenegrins, as they became known, built a reputation as fearsome warriors. The Ottomans opted for pragmatism, and largely left them to their own devices.

With the struggle against the Ottomans, the highly independent Montenegrin clans began to work collaboratively and the *vladika*, previously a metropolitan position within the Orthodox Church, began mediating between tribal chiefs. As such, the *vladika* assumed a political role, and *vladika* became a hereditary title: the prince-bishop.

In the late 18th century the Montenegrins under Vladika Petar I Petrović began to expand their territory, doubling it within the space of a little over 50 years. Serbia achieved independence in 1835 and a similar rebellion against Ottoman control broke out in Bosnia in 1875. Montenegrins joined the insurgency and made significant territorial gains as a result. At the Congress of Berlin in 1878, Montenegro officially achieved independence.

In the early years of the 20th century there were increasing calls for union with

Serbia and rising political opposition to Montenegro's autocratic Petrović dynasty. The Serbian king Petar Karadjordjević was suspected of involvement in an attempt to overthrow King Nikola Petrović, and Montenegrin–Serbian relations reached a low point.

The Balkan Wars of 1912–13 saw the Montenegrins joining the Serbs, Greeks and Bulgarians, and succeeding in throwing the Ottomans out of southeastern Europe. Now that Serbia and Montenegro were both independent and finally shared a border, the idea of a Serbian–Montenegrin union gained more currency. King Nikola pragmatically supported the idea on the stipulation that both the Serbian and Montenegrin royal houses be retained.

The Two Yugoslavias

Before the union could be realised WWI intervened. Serbia quickly entered the war and Montenegro followed in its footsteps. Austria-Hungary invaded Serbia shortly afterwards and swiftly captured Cetinje, with King Nikola escaping to France. In 1918 the Serbian army reclaimed Montenegro, and the French, keen to implement the Serbian–Montenegrin union, refused to allow Nikola to leave France. The following year Montenegro was incorporated in the Kingdom of the Serbs, Croats and Slovenes, the first Yugoslavia.

During WWII the Italians occupied Montenegro. The Communist-led Partisans (headed by Josip Broz Tito) and the Serbian royalist Chetniks engaged the Italians, sometimes lapsing into fighting each other. Ultimately, the Partisans put up the best fight and, with the support of the Allies, they entered Belgrade in October 1944 and Tito was made prime minister. Once the communist federation of Yugoslavia was established, Tito decreed that Montenegro have full republic status and the border of the modern Montenegrin state was set. Of all the Yugoslav states, Montenegro had the highest per-capita membership of the Communist Party and it was highly represented in the armed forces.

Union then Independence

In the decades following Tito's death in 1980, Slobodan Milošević used the issue of Kosovo to whip up a nationalist storm in Serbia and rode to power on a wave of nationalism. The Montenegrins largely supported their Orthodox coreligionists. In 1991 Montenegrin paramilitary groups were responsible for the shelling of Dubrovnik. In 1992, by which point Slovenia, Croatia and Bosnia and Hercegovina (BiH) had opted for independence, the Montenegrins voted overwhelmingly in support of a plebiscite to remain in Yugoslavia with Serbia.

In 1997 Montenegrin leader Milo Djukanović broke with an increasingly isolated Milošević and immediately became the darling of the West. As the Serbian regime became an international pariah, the Montenegrins increasingly wanted to re-establish their distinct identity.

In 2003 Yugoslavia was consigned to the dustbin of history, and Montenegro entered into a state union with Serbia. In theory this union was based on equality between the two republics; however, in practice Serbia was such a dominant partner that the union proved infeasible. In May 2006 the Montenegrins voted for independence.

People

In the last census (2011), 45% of the population identified as Montenegrin, 29% as Serb, 12% as Bosniak or Muslim, 5% as Albanian, 1% as Croat and 1% as Roma. Montenegrins are the majority along most of the coast and the centre of the country, while Albanians dominate in Ulcinj, Bosniaks in the far east, and Serbs in the north and in Herceg Novi. Religion and ethnicity broadly go together in these parts. Over 72% of the population are Orthodox Christians (mainly Montenegrins and Serbs), 19% Muslim (mainly Bosniaks and Albanians) and 3% Roman Catholic (mainly Albanians and Croats).

Montenegrins traditionally considered themselves 'the best of the Serbs', and while most Montenegrins still feel a strong kinship to their closest siblings, this is coupled with a determination to maintain their distinct identity. After negotiating a reasonably amicable divorce from the unhappy state union in 2006, relations between the two countries took a turn for the worse. In 2008 Serbia expelled Montenegro's ambassador after Montenegro officially recognised the Serbian province of Kosovo as an independent country. Diplomatic relations have since resumed, but issues of ethnicity and identity remain thorny.

SURVIVAL GUIDE

ℹ️ Directory A-Z

ACCOMMODATION

Montenegro offers a great variety of accommodation. Booking ahead in the summer – especially on the coast – is essential.

Hotels Range from slick seaside offerings to off-the-beaten-track Yugoslav-style digs. Prices range accordingly.

Hostels Popping up in popular destinations but thin on the ground elsewhere.

Campgrounds Usually offer million-dollar views for penny-pinching prices. Facilities vary wildly.

Private accommodation Almost every town and village has private rooms *(sobe)* and/or apartments *(apartmani)* for rent.

Eco villages Wooden cabins in the countryside.

Seasons & Taxes

Prices are very seasonal, and we've listed prices for the peak season (July and August). Expect to pay less in shoulder season (June and September) and considerably less in the off-season. In the ski resorts, the high season runs from January through to March, with the absolute peak around New Year. Discounts are often available for longer bookings.

All visitors are required to pay a small nightly tourist tax (usually less than €1 per person per night), which is sometimes included in the quoted rate but more often added to the bill at the end. This is almost always collected and paid by the accommodation provider; some private operators may leave it up to the guest to pay, but this is rare. The procedure varies from area to area and it can be nigh on impossible to find the right authority to pay it to. Theoretically you could be asked to provide white accommodation receipt cards (or copies of invoices from hotels) when you leave the country, but in practice this is almost never required.

LGBTIQ+ TRAVELLERS

Where's the party? The answer's nowhere. Although homosexuality was decriminalised in 1977 and discrimination outlawed in 2010, you won't find a single gay or lesbian venue in Montenegro. Don't be fooled by all the men walking arm in arm, or hand in hand in the Albanian areas. Attitudes to homosexuality remain hostile and life for gay people is extremely difficult, exacerbated by the fact that most people are expected to live at home until they're married.

In recent years there have been high-profile incidents of violence against gay activists. The country's first Pride parade was held in Budva in 2013; an Orthodox priest consecrated the town afterwards to 'stop the disease spreading'. Since then, Podgorica has held annual parades, the most recent of which have passed without serious incident.

Many gay men connect via apps or take their chances at a handful of cruisy beaches. These include Jaz Beach near Budva (eastern end), Ada Bojana and below the ruins of Ratac near Bar. Lesbians will find it harder to access the local community.

Check out Queer Montenegro (www.queer montenegro.org) for details on Pride, arts and cultural events, and news updates.

MONEY

ATMs widely available. Credit cards are accepted in larger hotels but aren't widely accepted elsewhere.

OPENING HOURS

Montenegrins have a flexible approach to opening times. Even if hours are posted on the door of an establishment, don't be surprised if they're not heeded. Many tourist-orientated businesses close between November and March.

Banks 8am to 5pm Monday to Friday, 8am to noon Saturday.

Post offices 7am to 8pm Monday to Friday, sometimes Saturday. In smaller towns they may close midafternoon, or close at noon and reopen at 5pm.

Restaurants, cafes & bars 8am to midnight. If the joint is jumping, cafe-bars may stay open until 2am or 3am.

Shops 9am to 8pm. Sometimes they'll close for a few hours in the late afternoon.

PUBLIC HOLIDAYS

New Year's Day 1 and 2 January

Orthodox Christmas 6, 7 and 8 January

Orthodox Good Friday & Easter Monday Date varies, usually April/May

Labour Day 1 and 2 May

Independence Day 21 and 22 May

Statehood Day 13 and 14 July

TELEPHONE

➡ The international access prefix is 00, or + from a mobile phone.

➡ The country code is 382.

➡ Press the *i* button on public phones for dialling commands in English.

➡ Mobile numbers start with 06.

➡ The prefix 80 indicates a toll-free number.

➡ You can make phone calls at most larger post offices. Phone boxes are otherwise few and far between.

VISAS

Many nationalities are entitled to a stay of up to 90 days without a visa.

ⓘ Getting There & Away

ENTERING THE COUNTRY

Entering Montenegro doesn't pose any particular bureaucratic challenges. In fact, the country's dead keen to shuffle tourists in. Unfortunately, Croatia seems less happy to let them go, if the long waits at their side of the Adriatic highway checkpoint are any indication; if you need to be somewhere at a certain time, it pays to allow an hour. The main crossing from Serbia at Dobrakovo can also be slow at peak times.

PASSPORT

Make sure that your passport has at least six months left on it. You'll need a visa if you're not from one of the many countries with a visa-waiver arrangement. There are no particular nationalities or stamps in your passport that will deny you entry. Make sure that your passport is stamped when you enter the country or else there may be difficulties when you leave.

AIR

Montenegro Airlines (www.montenegroairlines.com) is the national carrier, running a small fleet of 116-seater planes.

Montenegro's largest and most modern airport is immediately south of the capital, Podgorica (p271). If you're wondering about the airport code, it's a hangover from Podgorica's previous name, Titograd. Locals sometimes call it Golubovci airport as it's close to a village with that name.

The second international airport, at Tivat (p248), is well positioned for holidaymakers heading to the Bay of Kotor or Budva.

Montenegro's de facto third airport is actually in neighbouring Croatia. Dubrovnik Airport (p206) is a modern facility only 17km from the border and the closest airport to Herceg Novi.

LAND

Montenegro may be a wee slip of a thing but it borders five other states: Croatia, Bosnia and Hercegovina (BiH), Serbia, Kosovo and Albania. You can easily enter Montenegro by land from any of its neighbours.

Border Crossings

Albania There are two main crossings: Sukobin (between Shkodra and Ulcinj) and Hani i Hotit (between Shkodra and Podgorica). If you're paddling about on Lake Skadar, remember that the border runs through the lake and be careful not to cross it. Because of problems with trafficking (of cigarettes, drugs and women), the Montenegro police patrol the lake. The same caution should be applied while hiking in the Prokletije Mountains; you'll need a cross-border permit.

Bosnia & Hercegovina There are four main crossings: Zupci-Sitnica (between Trebinje and Herceg Novi), Klobuk–Ilino Brdo (between Trebinje and Nikšić), Hum–Šćepan Polje (between Foča and Nikšić) and Metaljka (between Sarajevo and Pljevlja). Other more remote crossings are marked on some maps but these may only be open to local traffic (if they are open at all) and we've heard of travellers being turned back at some crossings.

Croatia Expect delays at the busy Debeli Brijeg checkpoint on the Adriatic highway (between Herceg Novi and Dubrovnik). You can avoid them by taking a detour down the Prevlaka Peninsula to the Konfin-Kobila border post, although this has become more popular and sometimes also has queues. To reach it from the Croatian side, turn right off the highway a few kilometres before the main border crossing and pass through Pločice and Vitaljina. The road rejoins the highway on the Montenegro side just before Igalo.

Kosovo There's only one crossing, Kulina, on the road between Rožaje and Peć.

Serbia The busiest crossing is Dobrakovo (north of Bijelo Polje), followed by Dračenovac (northeast of Rožaje) and Ranče (east of Pljevlja). The train crosses at Dobrakovo.

Bus

There's a well-developed bus network linking Montenegro with the major cities of the former Yugoslavia and onward to Western Europe and Turkey. At the border, guards will often enter the bus and collect passports, checking the photos as they go. Once they're happy with them they hand them to the bus conductor who will return them as the driver speeds off. Make sure you get yours back and that it's been stamped.

Useful websites include www.busticket4.me, www.eurolines.com, www.getbybus.com and www.vollo.net.

Albania Direct services from Tirana to Podgorica, Ulcinj, Budva and Kotor.

Bosnia & Hercegovina Buses head from Mostar to Kotor via Trebinje, Podgorica, Cetinje, Budva and Tivat. There are also services from Sarajevo to Herceg Novi, Kotor, Budva, Ulcinj and Podgorica.

Croatia Direct buses from Zagreb to Podgorica via Split, Makarska, Dubrovnik, Herceg Novi, Kotor and Budva.

Kosovo Buses from Pristina to Ulcinj via Peja and Podgorica.

Macedonia Buses head all the way from Skopje to Herceg Novi via Podgorica, Budva, Kotor and Tivat.

Serbia Coaches from Belgrade to Žabljak, Podgorica, Cetinje, Ulcinj, Budva, Tivat, Kotor and Herceg Novi.

Train

Montenegro's main train line starts at Bar and heads north through Podgorica and into Serbia. At least two trains head between Bar and Belgrade daily (€21, 11¾ hours). You'll find timetables on the website of **Montenegro Railways** (www.zcg-prevoz.me).

Sea

Montenegro Lines (www.montenegrolines. com) has boats from Bar to Bari (Italy), at least weekly from May to November (deck ticket €44 to €48, cabin €63 to €210, 11 hours); and from Bar to Ancona (Italy), at least weekly from July to August (deck €60, cabin €80 to €230, 16 hours). Cars cost €56 to €90.

ℹ️ Getting Around

BICYCLE

Cyclists are a rare species even in the cities and there are no special bike lanes on the roads. Don't expect drivers to be considerate; wherever possible, try to get off the main roads. The wearing of helmets is not compulsory. The **National Tourism Organisation** (☑ 080-001 300; www. montenegro.travel) has developed a series of wilderness mountain-biking trails; as most of the country is mountainous, you'll have to be exceedingly fit to attempt them.

BOAT

There are no regular ferry services within Montenegro, but taxi boats are a common sight during summer. They can be hailed from the shore for a short trip along the coast or to one of the islands. They're harder to find outside the high season; look for them at the marinas. Some boats advertise set cruises, but normally they operate on an ad hoc basis.

BUS

The local bus network is extensive and reliable. Buses are usually comfortable and air-conditioned; they're rarely full.

Up-to-date timetable information and online booking can be found on www.busticket4.me. It's usually not difficult to find information on services and prices from the bus station. Most have timetables prominently displayed. As with many service-industry types in Montenegro, some station staff are more helpful than others.

Where English isn't spoken, they'll usually write down the price and time of the bus for you.

It's a bit cheaper to buy your ticket on the bus rather than at the station, but a station-bought ticket theoretically guarantees you a seat. Reservations are only worthwhile for international buses, at holiday times, or where long-distance journeys are infrequent. Luggage carried below is charged at €1 per piece.

Smoking is forbidden on buses and this rule is generally enforced. The standard of driving is no better or worse than that of anyone else on the roads.

CAR & MOTORCYCLE

Independent travel by car or motorcycle is an ideal way to gad about and discover the country; some of the drives are breathtakingly beautiful. Traffic police are everywhere, so stick to speed limits and carry an International Driving Permit.

Allow more time than you'd expect for the distances involved as the terrain will slow you down. You'll rarely get up to 60km/h on the Bay of Kotor road, for instance. The standard of roads is generally fair with conditions worsening in rural areas, especially in winter and after bad weather. A particularly notorious road is the Podgorica–Belgrade highway as it passes through the Morača Canyon, which is often made dangerous by bad conditions and high traffic. It's a good idea to drive defensively and treat everyone else on the road as a lunatic – when they get behind the wheel, many of them are. That said, no matter how much they toot at you or overtake on blind corners, you should avoid confrontation.

The only toll in Montenegro is the Sozina tunnel between Lake Skadar and the sea (€3.50 per car).

TRAIN

Montenegro Railways (Željeznički prevoz Crne Gore; www.zpcg.me) has limited services heading north from Bar and crossing the country before disappearing into Serbia; useful stops include Virpazar, Podgorica, Kolašin, Mojkovac and Bijelo Polje. A second line heads northwest from Podgorica to Danilovgrad and Nikšić.

The trains are old and can be hot in summer, but they're priced accordingly and the route through the mountains is spectacular. Apart from a derailment in 2006 and a crash in 2012, the trains are generally a safe option.

North Macedonia
Северна Македонија

📞 389 / POP 2.08 MILLION

Best Places to Eat

➡ Letna Bavča Kaneo (p308)

➡ Hotel Tutto Restaurant (p299)

➡ Vila Raskrsnica (p311)

➡ Nadžak (p293)

➡ Kebapčilnica Destan (p293)

Best Places to Stay

➡ Vila Raskrsnica (p311)

➡ Villa Dihovo (p312)

➡ Sunny Lake Hostel (p306)

➡ Villa Jovan (p306)

➡ Urban Hostel & Apartments (p291)

Why Go?

Part Balkan, part Mediterranean and rich in Greek, Roman and Ottoman heritage, North Macedonia has a fascinating past and a complex national identity.

Glittering Lake Ohrid and its historic town have etched out a place for North Macedonia on the tourist map, but there is a wealth of natural beauty in this small country.

Dramatic mountains have blissfully quiet walking trails, lakes and riding opportunities. The national parks of Mavrovo, Galičica and Pelister are cultivating some excellent cultural and culinary tourism initiatives; if you want to get off the beaten track in Europe – this is the place.

Skopje's centre has suffered from a building spree of grotesque faux-neoclassical monuments, buildings and fountains, funded by the previous government. Luckily, its Ottoman old town and buzzing modern areas are untouched and remain charming and authentic.

When to Go
Skopje

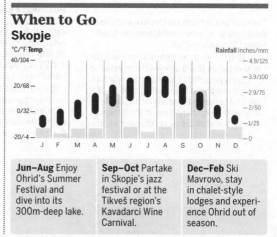

Jun–Aug Enjoy Ohrid's Summer Festival and dive into its 300m-deep lake.

Sep–Oct Partake in Skopje's jazz festival or at the Tikveš region's Kavadarci Wine Carnival.

Dec–Feb Ski Mavrovo, stay in chalet-style lodges and experience Ohrid out of season.

Entering the Country

Skopje and Ohrid are well connected to other Balkan tourist hubs as well as some international destinations further afield. Air connections have increased thanks to the growing number of budget airlines flying here. Buses are generally more frequent and cover a broader range of destinations than trains (they're also just as fast).

ITINERARIES

One Week

Spend a couple of days in Skopje (p286) amid the mind-boggling faux neoclassical architecture and in the Čaršija (p287) with its historic mosques, churches, museums and Ottoman castle. Visit the nearby Canyon Matka (p296) for kayaking and swimming in the cool waters.

Next head to North Macedonia's most charming and historic town, Ohrid (p303), for swimming in the spectacular lake. Visit its frescoed medieval churches, beach-flanked Sveti Naum Monastery (p300), and overwater Bay of the Bones (p301) museum.

Stay in a village guesthouse on the edge of Pelister National Park (p310), with hiking and home cooking. Cross Lake Prespa for the pelican-inhabited, ruin-strewn island of Golem Grad (p309).

Two Weeks

Linger in Pelister National Park (p310) in order to stop in Bitola (p312), loved for its buzz, elegance and ancient Heraclea Lyncestis (p312) ruins.

Next visit Mavrovo National Park (p297) and stay in historic Janče (p298) and Galičnik (p298) villages for superb cuisine and horse riding. Visit the impressive Sveti Jovan Bigorski Monastery (p298).

Make a pit stop in the Tikveš Wine Region (p311) for tastings and a tour.

Essential Food & Drink

Ajvar Sweet red-pepper dip; accompanies meats and cheeses.

Lukanci Homemade chorizo-like pork sausages, laced with paprika.

Pita A pie made of a coil of flaky pastry stuffed with local cheese and spinach or leek.

Rakija Grape-based fruit brandy.

Šopska salata Tomatoes, onions and cucumbers topped with grated *sirenje* (white cheese).

Tavče gravče Baked beans cooked with spices, onions and herbs and served in earthenware.

Vranec and **temjanika** Macedonia's favourite red/white wine varietals.

AT A GLANCE

Area 25,713 sq km

Capital Skopje

Country code 389

Currency North Macedonian denar (MKD)

Emergency Ambulance 194; police 192

Language Macedonian, Albanian

Population 2.08 million

Time East European Time (GMT/UTC plus two hours)

Visas None for EU, US, Australian, Canadian or New Zealand citizens for stays of up to three months

Sleeping Price Ranges

€ less than 3000MKD/€50

€€ 3000MKD/€50 to 5000MKD/€80

€€€ more than 5000MKD/€80

Eating Price Ranges

€ less than 200MKD

€€ 200MKD to 350MKD

€€€ more than 350MKD

Resources

Macedonia Timeless (https://macedonia-timeless.com)

Exploring Macedonia (www.exploringmacedonia.com)

Balkan Insight (www.balkaninsight.com)

North Macedonia Highlights

1 Ohrid's Old Town
(p303) Exploring Ohrid's distinctive historic quarter, right to the end of the boardwalk and pebble beach, and up to the clifftop Church of Sveti Jovan at Kaneo.

2 Skopje (p286) Diving into the historic Čaršija (Old Ottoman Bazaar) of North Macedonia's friendly capital, seeking out its modernist architecture and marvelling

at the supersized riverside monuments.

3 Pelister National Park (p310) Eating your fill at food-focused village tourism initiatives in this underrated national park, then walking it off the next day.

4 Golem Grad (p309) Chasing ghosts, pelicans and tortoises around this eerie Lake Prespa island, fecund with overgrown ruins.

5 Popova Kula (p311) Sipping your way through North Macedonia's premier wine region, Tikveš, using this wonderful winery hotel as your base.

6 Sveti Jovan Bigorski Monastery (p298) Taking tea with monks at this majestic complex teetering in the hills of Mavrovo National Park.

SKOPJE СКОПЈЕ

♪02 / POP 506,930

Skopje has plenty of charm. Its Ottoman- and Byzantine-era sights are focused around the city's delightful Čaršija, bordered by the 15th-century Kameni Most

(Stone Bridge) and Tvrdina Kale Fortress – Skopje's guardian since the 5th century. Don't miss the excellent eating and drinking scene in Debar Maalo, a lovely tree-lined neighbourhood.

For most of its existence, Skopje has been a modest Balkan city known for its rich local life, but the last decade has seen its centre transformed into a bizarre set design for an ancient civilisation. Towering warrior statues, gleaming, enormous neoclassical buildings, marble-clad museums, hypnotic megafountains...and plenty of lions.

This is the result of a controversial, nationalistic project called 'Skopje 2014' implemented by ex–Prime Minister Nikola Gruevski. Some of the buildings along the riverbank are already suffering flooding and have unsteady foundations.

☉ Sights

★ Čaršija
AREA
(Old Ottoman Bazaar; Map p290) Čaršija is Skopje's hillside Ottoman old town, evoking the city's past with its winding lanes filled with teahouses, mosques, craftspeople's shops, and even good nightlife. It also boasts Skopje's best historic structures and a handful of museums, and is the first place any visitor should head. Čaršija runs from the Stone Bridge to the **Bit Pazar** (Map p290; ☉8am-3pm), a big vegetable and household goods market. Expect to get pleasantly lost in its maze of narrow streets.

★ National Gallery of Macedonia
GALLERY
(Daut Paša Amam; Map p290; www.nationalgallery.mk; Kruševska 1a; adult/student & child 50/20MKD; ☉10am-6pm Tue-Sun Oct-Mar, to 9pm Apr-Sep) The Daut Paša Amam (1473) were once the largest Turkish baths outside of İstanbul and they make a magical setting for the permanent collection of Skopje's national art gallery, just by the entrance to the Čaršija. The seven restored rooms house mainly modern art and sculpture from North Macedonia, brought to life by the sun piercing through the small star-shaped holes in the domed ceilings. Two other National Gallery sites – Čifte Amam (p288) and **Mala Stanica** (Map p290; Jordan Mijalkov 18; ☉8am-6pm Tue-Sun Oct-Mar, to 9pm Apr-Sep) – house rotating, temporary exhibitions.

★ Tvrdina Kale Fortress
FORTRESS
(Map p290; Samoilova; ☉7am-7pm) [FREE] Dominating the skyline of Skopje, this *Game of Thrones*–worthy, 6th-century AD Byzantine (and later, Ottoman) fortress is an easy walk up from the Čaršija and its ramparts offer great views over the city and river. Inside the ruins, two mini museums were being built at the time of writing to house various archaeological finds from Neolithic to Ottoman times. This will be a welcome addition to the site, as there are no information boards at the fortress at present.

The entrance is up the hill on Samoilova inside a lovely park; opposite the gateway is a slightly unkempt path that leads across the hill to the Museum of Contemporary Art (p288). En route, you'll get a stellar bird's-eye view of Skopje's futuristic, vortex-like Filip II sports arena in the valley below.

Archaeological Museum of Macedonia
MUSEUM
(Map p290; www.amm.org.mk; Bul Goce Delčev; adult/student & child 300/150MKD; ☉10am-6pm Tue-Sun) This supersized pile of Italianate-styled marble has been a giant receptacle for Skopje's recent splurge on government-led monuments to boost national pride. Inside, there are three floors displaying the cream of Macedonian archaeological excavations beneath the dazzle of hundreds of tiny lights. Highlights include Byzantine treasures; sophisticated 3D reconstructions of early Macedonian faces from skulls; a pint-sized replica of an early Christian basilica showing the life phases of mosaic conservation; and a Phoenician royal necropolis.

Museum of the Macedonian Struggle for Statehood & Independence
MUSEUM
(Map p290; Iljo Vojvoda; adult/child 300/120MKD; ☉10am-6pm, closed 1st Mon of month) Part history museum, part national propaganda machine, this is a formidable memorial to North Macedonia's past occupation, land struggles and revolutionary heroes. The museum is dark, literally (the walls are black and lighting is low) and figuratively (gruesome giant oil paintings depict scenes of battle and betrayal, and physical reconstructions include a bloodied child's cradle and a dead revolutionary hung from the rafters). It's not suitable for children. The guides can be interesting and knowledgable but they do offer a one-sided perspective.

Holocaust Memorial Center for the Jews of Macedonia
MUSEUM
(Map p290; Iljo Vojvoda; ☉9am-7pm Tue-Fri, to 3pm Sat & Sun) [FREE] The mirrored-glass entrance is bizarrely unwelcoming, but once inside this is a moving museum with fascinating displays that commemorate the all-but-lost Sephardic Jewish culture of North Macedonia through a range of photos, English-language wall texts, maps and video. The exhibition

documents the Jewish community's history in the Balkans, ending in WWII when some 98% of Macedonian Jews perished in the Holocaust. At the time of writing, the museum was closed for refurbishment.

Ploštad Makedonija   SQUARE
(Macedonia Sq; Map p290) This gigantic square is the centrepiece of Skopje's audacious nation-building-through-architecture project and it has massive statues dedicated to national heroes, as well as an incongruous Triumphal Arch in the southeast corner. The towering, central warrior on a horse – Alexander the Great – is bedecked by fountains that are illuminated at night. Home to a number of cafes and hotels, it's a popular stomping ground for locals as well as tourists, particularly when the sun goes down.

Museum of Contemporary Art   MUSEUM
(NIMoCA; Map p290; ☑02 311 7734; https://msu.mk; Samoilova 17; 300MKD, free 1st Fri of month; ☺9am-5pm Tue-Sat, to 1pm Sun) Housed in a stunning modernist building with floor-to-ceiling windows and perched atop a hill with wonderful city views, this museum was built in the aftermath of Skopje's devastating 1963 earthquake. Artists and collections around the world donated works to form a collection that includes Picasso, Léger, Hockney, Meret Oppenheim and Bridget Riley. Unfortunately, its collection isn't always on display – you may come here and find its exhibitions extraordinary or mundane, depending on what's been put on display.

Sveti Spas Church   CHURCH
(Church of the Holy Saviour; Map p290; Makarije Frčkoski 8; adult/student 120/50MKD; ☺9am-5pm Tue-Fri, to 3pm Sat & Sun) Partially submerged 2m underground (the Ottomans banned churches from being taller than mosques), this church dates from the 14th century and is the most historically important in Skopje. Its sunken design means it doesn't look like a church, so you might not notice it at first: it's opposite the Old Town Brewery – look for the pretty bell tower that watches over it, built into its outer courtyard wall. Inside the church an elaborate carved iconostasis shines out of the dark.

What you see today is a restoration dating to the early 19th century. The iconostasis (a wooden screen separating the nave of the church from the altar area at the back) is one of North Macedonia's most impressive at 12m long and 7m high. It was built by early-19th-century master craftsmen Makarije

Frčkovski and brothers Petar and Marko Filipovski, and its tiered carvings play out important biblical scenes. Staff will be only too happy to give a brief tour of the church and can speak a number of languages (though be warned, English is not their strong point).

In the church grounds lies the tomb of Goce Delčev – North Macedonia's foremost national hero – and a small exhibition commemorating his life. Delčev is celebrated for his role as leader of the VMRO (Internal Macedonian Revolutionary Organisation) and was killed by Turks in 1903.

Museum of Macedonia   MUSEUM
(Map p290; ☑02 312 9323; Čurčiska; adult/student & child 100/50MKD; ☺9am-4pm Mon-Sat) Sitting inside a concrete brutalist structure – awful to some, fascinating to others – the museum's solid historical and ethnological displays are housed in a sorry state. The museum hosts North Macedonia's biggest ethnographic collection; the display of traditional architecture and the room stuffed with original wood-carved iconostases are highlights. Take advantage of the free guides at reception, because plenty of the displays are only presented in Macedonian.

Note that in summer it's hot as Hades because there's no air-con. Paint is peeling off the walls and the lighting is bad – staff are waiting on a major refurbishment of the building, but have no idea when the budget will materialise. Sadly, it feels like this museum has been superseded by Skopje's over-the-top Archaeological Museum (p287) on the Vardar River.

Mustafa Pasha Mosque   MOSQUE
(Map p290; Samoilova) Standing on a plateau at the very top of Skopje's Čaršija – this working mosque where you can see locals come and go for prayers and chit-chat in the lovely rose garden. Dating to 1492, it was heavily restored over a three-year period from 2008 to 2011 with help from Turkey; its magnificent colonnades, soaring minaret and interior decoration gleam like new.

Čifte Amam   HISTORIC BUILDING
(National Gallery of Macedonia; Map p290; Bitpazarska; adult/student & child 50/20MKD; ☺10am-6pm Tue-Sun Oct-Mar, to 9pm Apr-Sep) The Čifte Amam is a beautiful old Ottoman *hammam* (Turkish bath), now sometimes used as a temporary exhibition space under the stewardship of the National Gallery of Macedonia (p287). You can usually go in, even if there's no exhibition on.

THE STORY OF SKOPJE'S MODERN ARCHITECTURE

After Skopje was hit by a devastating earthquake in 1963, killing 1070 people and destroying around 65% of the city, the Yugoslav government started the reconstruction of the Macedonian capital with help from international governments and the UN. Two years later Japanese architect Kenzo Tange was enlisted to help after the UN set up a master plan for rebuilding Skopje. Tange was one of the 20th-century's most prominent architects and promoter of the 'Metabolist movement' – an architectural movement in postwar Japan that fused the concepts of architectural megastructures and organic biological growth.

A design team of international and Yugoslav architects was formed and lead by Tange's team. Tange's plan included a 'City Gate', designed to concentrate business and traffic communication in the city centre, and residential buildings outside the 'Gate'. The complex plan aimed to build a sophisticated urban structure (which Tange thought was made easier by the lack of private land ownership in socialist Yugoslavia), celebrating the ability to implement progressive design in this 'revolutionary society'.

The plan itself was not entirely accomplished, but several modernist masterpieces survive in Skopje, including the **train station** (Zheleznička Stanica; Bul Kuzman Josifovski Pitu), built by Kenzo Tange, with a vast elevated platform 15m above the ground. Other notable structures are the **Sts Cyril and Methodius University of Skopje** (1974), the country's largest university, designed by Marko Mušič; Janko Konstantinov's otherworldly **Main Post Office** (Map p290; ☎02 314 1141; Orce Nikolov 1; ☉8am-3pm), built in three stages in 1974, 1982 and 1989; his **Telekom Office Building** (1974); **Nikola Karev High School** (1968); the **Cathedral of the Sacred Heart of Jesus** (1977), designed by Blagoje Mickovskiego-Bajo; and the brilliant Macedonian National Opera and Ballet (p295), by Biro 71, completed in 1981.

Memorial House of Mother Teresa
MUSEUM

(Map p290; ☎02 329 0674; ul Makedonija 9; ☉9am-8pm Mon-Fri, to 2pm Sat & Sun) FREE
This extraordinary retro-futuristic memorial is the most unique church you'll see in North Macedonia. Inside the building there's a small 1st-floor museum displaying memorabilia relating to the famed Catholic nun of Calcutta, born in Skopje in 1910. On the 2nd floor there is a mind-boggling chapel, with glass walls wrought in filigree (North Macedonia's revered traditional craft). Silhouettes of doves are worked into the filigree to symbolise peace, as an homage to Mother Teresa.

The memorial sits on the site of a much earlier church, where Mother Teresa was baptised; a plaque around the corner commemorates the spot where she was brought into the world. Look out for the Mother Teresa quotations on plaques around the city centre as well.

Round the back of the memorial, take a peek at the 17th-/18th-century **feudal tower** that housed the nun's memorial before the ultra-contemporary version was built in 2009. The tower, with its stooped wooden balcony, is now crumbling and condemned but it still has city historians confounded:

nobody knows why it was built, as this side of the Vardar River was thought to be uninhabited at the time of its construction. There are gun holes in the tower walls, so it's clear it was used for defence: somebody had something to protect, it's just not clear who or what.

Museum of the City of Skopje
MUSEUM

(Map p290; www.mgs.org.mk; St Kiril & Methodius; ☉9am-3pm Tue-Sun) FREE Occupying the old train station building where the stone fingers of the clock remain frozen in time at 5.17am – the moment Skopje's devastating earthquake struck on 27 July 1963, killing 1070 people – this museum operates as an art gallery for rotating exhibitions, with one area dedicated to a moving exhibition chronicling the horrific events of the earthquake through video footage and photos.

Murat Pasha Mosque
MOSQUE

(Map p290) FREE The original mosque at this site dated to the 15th century and was one of the oldest in the Balkans, but it was ravaged by a fire that devastated the Čaršija in 1689. What you see today is an early-19th-century reconstruction; it features a distinctive, red-tipped clock tower (the clock itself has long been lost, though) and Ottoman *madrasa* (Islamic school) remnants.

Skopje

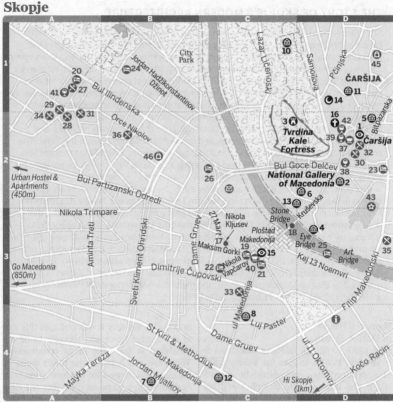

🏃 Activities & Tours

Bicycle Tours & Guides

Macedonia CYCLING

(📱078 982 981; www.bicycle.mk; per day from 800MKD) Skopje's long riverside walkway is a magnet for cyclists, especially at dusk when joggers, kids playing football and anglers all come out too. Rent bikes by the day from this outfit; it'll even drop the bike (including helmet, lights and high-vis vest) at your hotel. Guided Skopje day tours and North Macedonia–wide adventures are also offered.

Skopje Walks WALKING

(Map p290; www.skopjewalks.com; ul Makedonija; donations welcome; ⊘10am) **FREE** These excellent free tours run for three hours and cover every important corner of Skopje's inner city. Highly recommended for insights into the city from local guides who are passionate about Skopje. Tours meet outside the Memorial House of Mother Teresa (p289) – look out for the blue ID badge – at 10am daily.

Macedonia Experience CULTURAL

(Map p290; 📱075 243 944; www.macedoniaexperience.com; ul Nikola Kljusev 3) Can arrange horse riding, bike riding and community tourism forays into Mavrovo National Park from Skopje, often including food tasting. Cultural tours stop at Galičnik or Janče. The business has an office inside the premises of Magelan Travel Service. Day trips around Ohrid and Skopje are also offered.

Skopje Bar Crawl TOURS

(Map p290; www.skopjebarcrawl.mk; Stone Bridge; 600MKD; ⊘9pm) Popular weekend bar crawls that hop between watering holes in and around the Čaršija, tasting local suds and *rakija* (grape-based fruit brandy) and offering drinking games. Check the website for details – the tours meet every Friday or Saturday night.

Go Macedonia TOURS

(📱02 306 4647; www.gomacedonia.com; ul Ankarska 29a) This company focuses on sustainable

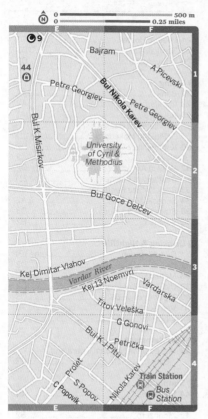

'gourmet beer' weekend features rock acts and DJs, grilled meats and, of course, beer.

Skopje Jazz Festival
MUSIC

(☑02 313 1090; www.skopjejazzfest.com.mk; ☺Oct) The festival features artists from across the globe, always including a world-renowned player or group (Chick Corea, McCoy Tyner, Herbie Hancock and Tito Puente are some past headliners).

Offest
MUSIC

(www.offest.com.mk; ☺early Jun) This world music festival brings together a global range of musicians, groups and other performers in various venues in Skopje in late May and early June each year.

Skopsko Leto
PERFORMING ARTS

(☑02 316 5064; ☺Jun-Jul) Five weeks of summer art exhibitions, performances and concerts. The event organisers don't promote in English, so ask around town to find out what's going on.

🛏 Sleeping

★ Urban Hostel & Apartments
HOSTEL €

(☑02 614 2785; www.urbanhostel.com.mk; Adolf Ciborovski 22; dm/s/d €10/24/35, apt €35-70; ❋ 🛜) In a converted residential house with a sociable front garden for summer lounging, Urban is an excellent budget option on the outskirts of the leafy Debar Maalo neighbourhood, a 15-minute walk west of central Skopje. Decor is eclectic, with a fireplace for cosy winter nights and even a piano. The hostel's modern apartments, on the same road, are great value.

Dorm beds come with curtains and reading lights and the shared bathrooms are large (two have jacuzzi baths!). Breakfast is free, as are the bikes (handy for the schlep into the city centre). There are 10 apartments in total, some near the bus/train stations.

Lounge Hostel
HOSTEL €

(Map p290; ☑076 547 165; www.loungehostel.mk; 1st fl, Naum Naumovski Borče 80; dm €9-10, s/d €25/30; ❋ 🛜 🍴) A lovely large common area, orthopaedic mattresses and bright, breezy balconies attached to every room are some of the highlights of this sociable, retro-styled hostel with a view over City Park. Staff are a little less clued-up here than at some other hostels, but will bend over backwards to help make guests' lives easier.

Hi Skopje
HOSTEL €

(☑02 609 1242; www.hihostelskopje.com; Crniche 15; dm/d from €9/20) In a leafy, affluent

tourism, and can arrange hiking, cycling, caving and winery tours across the country. It also runs a Galičnik Wedding (p299) trip each year, including transport, guided activities, local accommodation and a monastery tour at Sveti Jovan Bigorski (p298).

Macedonia Travel
TOURS

(Map p290; ☑02 311 2408; www.macedoniatravel. com; Orce Nikolov 109/1, 3rd fl) A large agency with lots of experience in running tours, including day trips to Canyon Matka, around Skopje and Ohrid, and to more off-the-beaten-track destinations in the east of the country. Its office is above the Kaj Pero restaurant in Debar Maalo.

🎉 Festivals & Events

Pivolend
BEER

(www.pivolend.com.mk; ☺Aug-Sep) Held at the end of August/beginning of September inside the Tvrdina Kale Fortress (p287), this

Skopje

suburb in the cool shade of Mt Vodno, this hostel's greatest assets are its garden and sprawling layout, which make it feel more spacious. It's a 15-minute walk to Ploštad Makedonija from here (and a 120MKD taxi ride from the bus and train stations), but the trade-off is a relaxing atmosphere.

Unity Hostel HOSTEL €
(Map p290; ☏075 942 494; www.unityhostel.mk; Bul Ilidenska 1, 1st fl; dm €10-12, s/d €25/35; ❋🖧) Housed in an old apartment block, Unity Hostel has a great location – just across the river from Tvrdina Kale Fortress (p287). Inside it's homely and cheerfully run by a young, friendly team. There are just two dorms and one double room, complemented by a balcony, a communal kitchen and a living room.

Hotel Super 8 HOTEL €
(Map p290; ☏02 321 2225; www.hotelsuper8. com.mk; Bul Krste Misirkov 57/3; s/d/tr/f €35/

50/70/80; ❋🖧) Rooms are clean and spacious, and staff very friendly, at this modern hotel just east of the Čaršija. The family who run it have grand ambitions to turn the 1st-floor lounge into a restaurant, and there's also a public cafe on the ground floor.

Bed & Breakfast London BOUTIQUE HOTEL €€
(Map p290; ☏02 311 6146; Maksim Gorki 1; s/d/ste €50/65/105; ❋🖧) The theme here is a little random, but all is forgiven when you see its front-row Ploštad view – rooms at the front are in gawping distance of the Alexander the Great fountain, though the hotel is set back slightly from the main square and windows are thick enough that sound from the cafe/bar below doesn't disturb too much.

Senigallia HOTEL €€
(Map p290; ☏02 322 4044; www.senigallia.mk; Kej 13 Noemvri 5s; s/d from €65/75, ste €90-110; ❋🖧)

This pirate-ship-themed hotel's motto is 'Put your anchor down for the night' – and it's all ersatz antiquity here, with baroque furniture and little round windows from which you can see the river. The interior is wood panelled and neat rooms have mini fridges. Note that a whiff comes off the river sometimes.

Hotel Pelister   HOTEL €€
(Map p290; ☑02 323 9584; www.pelisterho tel.com.mk; Ploštad Makedonija; s/d/apt from €59/69/125; ※@🖨) This six-room hotel enjoys an unbeatable location on the square, overlooking the city's architectural wonders, but its location also has a downside: the bustle of popular Restaurant Pelister (p294) below reverberates through the bones of the building. Rooms vary in size (and are priced accordingly); each comes with a fridge, large windows and slightly tired decor.

★**Hotel Solun**   HOTEL €€€
(Map p290; ☑02 323 2512, 071 238 599; www. hotelsolun.com; Nikola Vapčarov 10; s/d from €83/103; ※@🖨🌡) Accessed through an alley just off the main square, this is a stylish, beautifully designed place, with modern and elegantly decorated rooms, and an excellent art collection on the walls. A spa and an indoor pool beckon downstairs. Hotel Solun sits in a different stratosphere to most of North Macedonia's faded 'high-end' hotels.

The smallest rooms are a little poky. There's a tranquil covered patio where guests love to lounge with coffee. Solun is popular with business travellers, and there are 15% discounts on weekdays, 30% on weekends.

Hotel City Park   HOTEL €€€
(Map p290; ☑02 329 0860; www.hotelcitypark. com.mk; Mihail Cokov 8a, Gradski Park; s/d/ste from €75/90/105; P※🖨) This popular option is in an excellent location opposite City Park and around the corner from a lively strip of neighbourhood cafes and bars on the edge of Debar Maalo. Rooms are fresh, modern and bright, and some have balconies. Guests have free coffee and tea in the rooms and in the downstairs bar.

 Eating

★**Nadžak**   MACEDONIAN €
(Map p290; ☑02 312 8113; Orce Nikolov 105; mains from 100MKD; ☺8am-midnight; 🖨) It doesn't look like much, but the food at Nadžak is excellent, cheap and always fresh. All sorts of Macedonian specialities are on the menu, from *skara* (grilled meat) to liver to peppers

and *tavče gravče* (oven-baked beans in tomato sauce). Everything tastes great – order several dishes and share. Seating is inside and on a covered terrace, in the heart of Debar Maalo.

★**Kebapčilnica Destan**   KEBAB €
(Map p290; ul 104 6; mains 180MKD; ☺8am-11pm) Skopje's best beef kebabs, accompanied by seasoned grilled bread, peppers and a little raw onion, are served at this classic Čaršija place. The terrace is often full. Ten stubby kebabs constitute a serious meat feast (180MKD), or you can ask for a half portion (120MKD). Pair the kebabs with *ajvar* (red-pepper dip) and a cabbage salad.

Destan is Skopje's most famous kebab joint and has been attracting crowds of meat lovers for decades. There's a second, more sanitised, branch tucked away in a corner of Ploštad Makedonija.

Barik   MACEDONIAN €
(Map p290; ☑070 360 601; Mihail Cokov 8; mains from 100MKD; ☺8am-midnight) An excellent little taverna in Debar Maalo, with a great range of Macedonian specialities – try the veal liver with onion with some red wine or the baked cheese. Tables are scattered across the pavement and the whole place has a Mediterranean feel. It's very popular with the locals.

Rock Kafana Rustikana   GRILL €
(Map p290; ☑02 7256 1450; off Dimitrije Čupovski; 140-300MKD; ☺8am-midnight Mon-Sat; 🖨) Just a block from the Ploštad but rocking a decidedly more local vibe, this humble bar-restaurant prides itself on good music, friendly service and simple dishes of grilled meats, sandwiches, and inventive bar snacks such as courgettes with sour cream and garlic. Its setting amid an unkempt, mildly postapocalyptic green space behind the Rekord Hostel only adds to its kooky charm.

Kebapčilnica Destan   KEBAB €
(Map p290; Ploštad Makedonija; mains 180MKD; ☺10am-11pm) Kebapčilnica Destan's other, main restaurant (p293), in Skopje's Čaršija, is more atmospheric and in a better spot for streetside people-watching, but the signature smoky beef kebabs are the same at this central outlet hidden in the southeastern corner of Ploštad Makedonija.

Sushico   ASIAN €€
(Map p290; ☑02 321 7874; www.sushico.com.mk; Aminta Treti 29; mains from 350MKD; ☺11am-11.30pm; 🖨☑) If you fancy a change of palate,

this international chain serves a good range of pan-Asian specialities in an elegant setting (that includes the obligatory large Buddha statues). Try the avocado and quinoa rolls or the staple crispy duck, or choose from noodles, sushi or sashimi. There is a Sunday buffet brunch from noon to 4pm.

Kaj Pero   MACEDONIAN €€
(Map p290; Orce Nikolov 109; mains 120-800MKD; ☺9am-1am) This neighbourhood favourite in Debar Maalo has tables spilling out onto a leafy street, drawing a crowd of casual diners and drinkers. The menu is focused on *skara,* but there are also some inventive nongrill dishes and a good selection of local wines and *rakija*. It's about a 10-minute walk west of central Skopje.

Idadija   GRILL €€
(Map p290; Zhivko Chingo; mains 170-250MKD; ☺noon-midnight) In Debar Maalo's *skara* corner, no-frills Idadija has been serving grilled meats to neighbourhood fans for more than 80 years. Get some meat, a salad and wine, and enjoy the relaxed vibe. Staff speak virtually no English, so make do by pointing at the menu.

Restaurant Pelister   INTERNATIONAL €€
(Map p290; Ploštad Makedonija; mains 260-400MKD; ☺7am-midnight; 🛜) This cafe-restaurant is a real local fixture with a prime spot on Skopje's Ploštad and the feel of a Mitteleuropa grand cafe, attracting a diverse crowd. It's a good spot for coffee and people-watching, and it also serves a vast array of decent pastas.

Skopski Merak   MACEDONIAN €€€
(Map p290; ☏02 321 2215; Debarca 51; mains 200-1000MKD; ☺8am-1am; 🛜) This hugely popular place packs locals in with its pretty timber-framed terrace, live music most evenings and huge menu of *skara* and other Macedonian specialities. Its chef's choice platters of smoked meats, local cheeses and grilled veg are particularly impressive, but not on the menu: ask for *daska* (approximately 500MKD for two people).

Pivnica An   MACEDONIAN €€€
(Beerhouse An; Map p290; ☏02 321 2111; www.pivnicaan.mk; Kapan An; mains 250-750MKD; ☺9am-midnight Mon-Sat, noon-midnight Sun; 🛜) Skopje's Čaršija is still home to a couple of *ans* – ancient Ottoman inns, similar to desert *caravanserai* (inns) – and the Kapan An houses this restaurant. Try butter-soft

sarma (stuffed cabbage leaves) or roasted pork ribs and observe history echoing through the sumptuous central courtyard, where Pivnica's partially covered patio offers a tranquil bolthole.

Stara Gradska Kuća   MACEDONIAN €€€
(Old City House; Map p290; www.starakuka.com.mk; Filip Makedonski 14; mains 300-1000MKD; ☺10am-midnight Mon-Sat; 🛜) Housed in what the owners claim is the oldest functioning house in North Macedonia (now dwarfed by a new government building), this traditional place has a warm ambience, a wide assortment of traditional Macedonian dishes and, sometimes, live music. It's a bit touristy and the food isn't exceptional, but rural village decor still gives it charm in the big city.

🍷 Drinking & Entertainment

★Old Town Brewery   CRAFT BEER
(Map p290; Gradište 1; ☺9am-midnight Sun-Thu, to 1am Fri & Sat; 🛜) The siren call of tasty craft beer sings to locals and tourists alike at Skopje's only microbrewery, which is justifiably popular for its Weiss beer, IPA, golden ale and dark beer – all brewed on-site and accompanied by a dependable menu of international pub grub. The sunny terrace, sandwiched between the walls of Tvrdina Kale Fortress (p287) and Sveti Spas Church, crowns its appeal.

Menada   BAR
(Map p290; ☏070 256 171; Kazandžiska 2; ☺8am-1am) Popular with the local art and culture crowd, Menada often has live music – jazz, rock, folk – and a good atmosphere till the wee hours. The wood-panelled bar and terrace can get quite busy, so grab a table while you can. There are palatable snacks. It's right at the entry into the Čaršija.

Van Gogh Bar   BAR
(Map p290; ☏02 312 1876; Mikhail Cokov 4; ☺8am-1am Mon-Fri, 9am-1am Sat & Sun) Whisky nights, cocktail nights, live-music nights... there's something going on every day of the week at Van Gogh, a poky bar with a lively local crew that spills onto the street. The bar is a local biker haunt, but all sorts of characters drink here and it's always good fun. It's close to City Park in Debar Maalo.

Vinoteka Temov   WINE BAR
(Map p290; Gradište 1a; ☺9am-midnight) Skopje's best wine bar, in a restored wooden building near Sveti Spas Church, is refined and atmospheric. Knowledgeable staff offer

a vast wine list starring the cream of North Macedonia's vineyards, though if you want to taste any of the better wines you'll need to buy a bottle as the glass selection is limited (as it is everywhere in North Macedonia, unfortunately).

K8 CAFE
(Map p290; ☑ 02 7038 3328; Gradište 9; ⊙ 11am-midnight; 🛜) Established by an American expat baker, this quiet little coffee-and-cake spot has a cute terrace tucked up a steep cobbled street in the Čaršija. Its calling card is sweet treats you might not find anywhere else in the country: think Oreos (10MKD) and apple pie.

Trend Lounge Bar CAFE
(Map p290; Ploštad Makedonija; ⊙ 8am-1am Jun-Sep, to midnight Oct-May) Aspiring socialites like this slick place on Skopje's main square, which shares its bar with the adjoining **Bistro London**. The location of both bars is the big draw – with front-row seats for the entrancing fountain-and-lights show beneath the square's giant Alexander the Great statue.

Macedonian National Opera and Ballet OPERA
(Map p290; ☑ 02 311 8451; http://mob.mk; Goce Delčev 4; tickets 400MKD) Set inside the most beautiful modernist building – designed by the Slovene architects Biro 71, completed in 1981 – this is where one can see classic opera and ballet pieces. Check the website for seasonal performances.

🛍 Shopping

★Monozero ARTS & CRAFTS
(Map p290; ☑ 070 255 093; http://mono-zero.com; Kliment Ohridski 30; ⊙ 10.30am-6.30pm Mon-Fri, 10am-4pm Sat) A brilliant local carpentry enterprise, Monozero makes everything out of solid wood sourced from responsibly harvested forests. Each object is handmade using traditional craft techniques. You can pick up cheeseboards, chopping boards and candleholders, each smooth and beautiful, and perfect for remembering North Macedonia, sustainably.

Dželo Filigran JEWELLERY
(Map p290; ☑ 02 311 7769; Beogradska, Čaršija; ⊙ 8.30am-7.30pm) The family behind this highly awarded jewellery business, based in the Čaršija's aptly named 'golden street', are master filigree craftspeople and their works are considered fine examples of this Macedonian art form. Even Salma Hayek (see the picture on the wall behind the counter) has shopped here. Silver filigree is relatively cheap in North Macedonia (even here), and makes a nice souvenir.

ℹ Information

Skopje's tourist information centre (Map p290; Filip Makedonski; ⊙ 8.30am-4.30pm Mon-Fri) has maps and a range of countrywide promotional literature. Note that the advertised opening hours are not kept.

ℹ Getting There & Away

Skopje International Airport (☑ 02 314 8333; www.airports.com.mk; 1043, Petrovec) is located 21km east of the city centre.

Vardar Express (☑ 02 311 8263; www.vardarexpress.com) shuttle bus runs between the airport and the city; check the website for its timetable. Taxis to and from the airport cost 1200MKD.

Skopje's **bus station** (Map p290; ☑ 02 246 6313; www.sas.com.mk; Bul Nikola Karev), with ATM, exchange office and English-language information office, adjoins the train station. Bus schedules are only available online in Macedonian (your hotel/hostel staff should be more than happy to translate for you, though).

ℹ Getting Around

➜ Buses congregate under the bus/train station; for Matka you need bus 60 (70MKD) and for Vodno take the special 'Millennium Cross' bus (35MKD).
➜ Skopje's taxis aren't bad value, with the first kilometre costing just 40MKD, and 25MKD for subsequent kilometres.
➜ Drivers rarely speak English, but they do use their meters (if they don't, just ask/point).

AROUND SKOPJE

Mt Vodno Водно

Framing Skopje to the south, Vodno's towering mass (gondola round-trip 100MKD) – pinpointed by the 66m Millennium Cross – is an enduring symbol of the city. A popular (shaded) hiking trail cuts a swath up its wooded slopes and there's also a gondola that climbs the mountainside from halfway up, where a couple of restaurants cater to day trippers. To get here, take the 'Millennium Cross' special bus (35MKD, 12 daily) from Skopje's bus station to the gondola. A taxi to the gondola costs about 200MKD.

Sveti Pantelejmon Monastery
MONASTERY

(Gorno Nerezi village; 120MKD; ⊙10am-5pm Tue-Sun) Up in the gods around the western side of Vodno, the village of Gorno Nerezi is home to this 1164 monastery, one of North Macedonia's most significant churches. Its Byzantine frescoes, such as the *Lamentation of Christ*, depict a pathos and realism predating the Renaissance by two centuries. It's 5km from Skopje city centre and it takes about 20 minutes to get here by taxi (350MKD, using the meter) because of the steep, windy road. The views from the monastery's terrace are sublime.

Canyon Matka МАТКА

Ah, Matka. Early Christians, ascetics and revolutionaries picked a sublime spot when they retreated into the hills here from Ottoman advances: the setting is truly reverential. Matka means 'womb' in Macedonian and the site has a traditional link with the Virgin Mary.

Churches, chapels and monasteries have long been guarded by these forested mountains, though most have now been left to rack and ruin. Many of the modern-day villages in this area are majority Macedonian Albanian Muslim, though the population is sparse.

These days, locals and tourists alike come to walk the breadth of the canyon and dip a toe in the tempting clear waters of the dammed lake. Brace yourself: the temperature hovers at around 14°C year-round.

Canyon Matka is a popular day trip from Skopje and crowded at weekends; if you want peace and quiet, come very early or stay overnight.

◉ Sights & Activities

★ Sveta Bogorodica Monastery
MONASTERY

(Lake Matka; ⊙8am-8pm) FREE Framed by mountains and with a serene, peaceful atmosphere, Sveta Bogorodica is a special spot. Still home to nuns, this working monastery has 18th-century wooden-balustraded living quarters. The beautiful 14th-century chapel has frescoes from the 1500s. A church has stood on this spot since the 6th century, evident from the crosses on the left-hand side of the entrance.

Bogorodica is clearly signposted from the road that leads to the Canyon Matka car park (buses drop passengers off here); walk up the short, steep hill directly above.

Church of Sveti Andrej
CHURCH

(Lake Matka; ⊙10am-4pm) FREE The most easily accessible of Canyon Matka's 14th-century churches and also one of the finest, the petite Church of St Andrew (1389) is practically attached to the Canyon Matka Hotel and backed by the towering massif of the canyon walls. Inside, well-preserved painted frescoes depict apostles, holy warriors and archangels. Opening hours can be a bit erratic.

Cave Vrelo
CAVE

(Matka boat kiosk; 400MKD; ⊙9am-7pm) A team of scuba divers from Italy and Belgium have explored Matka's underwater caverns to a depth of 212m and still not found the bottom, making these caves among the deepest in Europe. Cave Vrelo is open to the public – you can enter the inky depths of the bat-inhabited cave by boat (popular) or hired kayak.

Canyon Matka Kayaking
KAYAKING

(single/double kayak per 30min 150/250MKD; ⊙9am-7pm) Kayaking through Matka's precipitous canyon is divine. This is a light paddle, where you can enjoy the rock formations and gorgeous sunlight – kayaks are the only watercraft allowed on the lake beside the licensed boat plying the route to Cave Vrelo. You can kayak to the cave and back; count on around two hours in total.

⊨ Sleeping & Eating

Canyon Matka Hotel
LODGE €€

(☏02 205 2655; www.canyonmatka.mk; Lake Matka; d €39-60) The premium lakefront setting by the canyon walls makes this hotel a fine place for a night's rest, but it's more rough around the edges than might be expected and feels like an adjunct to the successful restaurant below. The 2nd-floor rooms have charming wooden beams but are slightly smaller than those on the 1st floor.

Restaurant Canyon Matka
MACEDONIAN €€

(☏02 205 2655; www.canyonmatka.mk/restaurant; Lake Matka; mains from 600MKD; ⊙8am-midnight) With a prime location just above the water, this is fine dining with a focus on the Macedonian and the Mediterranean. Order the grilled trout and salad with any of the good local wines and enjoy the beautiful views. Bring mosquito repellent for evenings.

⊙ Getting There & Away

From Skopje, catch bus 60 from Bul Partizanski Odredi or from the bus/train station (return 70MKD, 40 minutes, nine daily).

WORTH A TRIP

NORTH MACEDONIA'S NORTHEAST

The northeast is a little-visited part of North Macedonia, and indeed it feels like time has stopped here, but there are a couple of sights worth visiting and it works well as a day trip out of Skopje. It's wise to have your own wheels, since it's a tough place to get around on public transport.

Heading out of Skopje and past Kumanovo, you'll find the northeast's crowning jewel – the **Kokino Observatory** (Кокино, Кокино; 60MKD). A Bronze Age, archaeo-astronomical site, this megalithic observatory sits atop a volcanic hill, at an elevation of 1013m; it's a truly marvellous place.

The cracked volcanic rocks were easily shaped for marking the points of the rising sun at the summer and winter solstice, and the spring and autumn equinox. You'll need your own transport to reach Kokino, 19km northeast of Kumanovo: follow the signs for Staro Nagoričane, then for Kokino. The observatory is signposted.

There are some English-language information boards. If you're here in midsummer, remember to bring a hat and sunscreen, since there is very little shade.

Observe the two platforms, upper and lower, and the four 'thrones'. This was where the bonding ritual between the sun god and their representative on earth – the ruler, who sat on one of the thrones – was meant to take place. The ritual took place after the harvest, when the sun's energy was starting to fade and plant life was at its seasonal end. The ruler's power was said to be reinforced by absorbing the sunlight, reuniting them with the sun god and bringing peace and good crops for the community.

The site's primary purpose was for the daily marking of the rising of the sun and the moon, and measuring the length of the lunar months so that a calendar for a periodic cycle of 19 lunar years could be produced. The exceptional complexity of the calendar shows that the people of the time had a keen understanding of astronomy.

On the way back onto the main road, stop off at the **Church of St George** (Staro Nagoričane; ⊙10am-3pm) FREE in the inconspicuous village of Staro Nagoričane, some 15km northeast of Kumanovo; this 14th-century church has some magnificent frescoes and outstanding architecture.

Before heading back to Skopje, visit the rock formations at **Kuklica**. Natural erosion and its varying effects on the area's volcanic rocks are behind the formation of these bizarre 'rock dolls', which are estimated to be nearly 30 million years old.

It is not possible to get to the main section of the lake, where the Canyon Matka Hotel (p296) and boat kiosk are, by car or bus. Taxis (450MKD) and the bus from Skopje will drop you about a 10- to 15-minute walk from there, at the public car park and a couple of riverside restaurants.

If you have your own wheels, the closest public car park to the lake is just before the pedestrian-only walkway, but it's a small car park up a steep hill and fills up quickly in summer and on weekends. Both car parks are free.

WESTERN NORTH MACEDONIA

Mavrovo National Park
Маврово Национален Парк

The gorges, pine forests, karst fields and waterfalls of Mavrovo National Park offer a breath of fresh, rarefied air for visitors travelling between Skopje and Ohrid. Beautiful vistas abound, and the park is home to North Macedonia's highest peak, Mt Korab (2764m). Locally the park is best known for its ski resort (the country's biggest) near Mavrovo town, but by international standards the skiing is fairly average. In summertime, the park is glorious.

One of North Macedonia's most important – and accessible – monasteries, Sveti Jovan Bigorski (p298), is here, as are the atmospheric villages of Galičnik (p298) and Janče (p298), separated by a mountain ridge. The Galičnik traditional village wedding (p299) is one of the country's most popular and quirky summer festivals. Mavrovo is also home to some of North Macedonia's most revered cheesemakers.

Driving in the park is extremely scenic, but a word of caution: car GPS doesn't work well here and signposting is poor.

⊙ Sights & Activities

★ Sveti Jovan Bigorski Monastery

MONASTERY

(⊙ services 5.30am, 4pm & 6pm) **FREE** This revered 1020 Byzantine monastery is located, fittingly, up in the gods along a track of switchbacks off the Debar road, close to Jančе village (p298). Legend attests an icon of Sveti Jovan Bigorski (St John the Baptist) miraculously appeared here, inspiring the monastery's foundation; since then the monastery has been rebuilt often – apparently, the icon has occasionally reappeared too. The complex went into demise during communist rule but has been painstakingly reconstructed and today is as impressive as ever, with some excellent views over Mavrovo's mountains.

The frescoed church also houses what is alleged to be St John's forearm. Bigorski's awe-inspiring iconostasis was the final of just three carved by local craftsmen Makarije Frčkovski and the brothers Filipovski between 1829 and 1835. This colossal work depicting biblical scenes is enlivened with 700 tiny human and animal figures. Gazing up at the enormous, intricate masterpiece is breathtaking. Upon finishing, the carvers allegedly flung their tools into the nearby Radika River – ensuring that the secret of their artistic genius would be washed away forever.

Jančе

VILLAGE

Just a blip on the map, the small village of Jančе is one of the few places in Mavrovo (besides the ski resort) where it's possible to get decent accommodation. It's a picturesque spot; the views from up here are awesome, even if the village itself feels like a forgotten corner of the country. Its cluster of stone houses includes some fascinating examples of decaying rural architecture with *bondruk* wooden frames, packed earthen walls and creaking wooden porches.

Note that although Jančе and Galičnik are very close to each other as the crow flies (6km), there is no road between the two and to visit both involves a drive of about 1½ hours looping through the national park. A picturesque walking trail connects the two villages, climbing up and over the mountain that separates the two, but some parts can be tricky to follow; if at all possible, take a GPS with you if you plan to do this walk.

Galičnik

VILLAGE

Up a winding, tree-lined road ending in a rocky moonscape 17km southwest of Mavrovo, almost depopulated Galičnik features traditional houses along the mountainside. It's also famed for its traditional cheesemaking. The village is placid except during the Galičnik Wedding Festival. A wonderful food and accommodation option is available with one of the few local families that live here year-round, and you can hike in the surrounding area, including to Jančе.

WORTH A TRIP

ILINDEN UPRISING MONUMENT

This 1974 **monument** (Makedonium; Kruševo; 60MKD; ⊙10am-4pm; **P**), commemorating the Ilinden Uprising from 1903, is a marvel of Yugoslav architecture and a fantastic example of abstract historic symbolism. Designed by Prilep architects Iskra and Jordan Grabul, and commonly known as Makedonium, this otherworldly globular structure is meant to represent a 15th-century warrior mace. Inside is a series of stained-glass windows and abstract sculptures, each marking a turning point in North Macedonia's history.

The Ilinden Uprising was the country's first step towards sovereignty. Kruševo became home to the short-lived Macedonian Republic, founded by revolutionaries, on 2 August 1903; the republic was strangled by the Ottoman Empire just 10 days later. The uprising is marked by a celebration known as Ilinden on 2 August each year.

Before you reach the main structure you will pass a series of giant metal chain links being pried apart one by one, representing the loosening of Ottoman shackles on the Macedonian people. After this, progress along a path to a circular field of symbolic concrete cannons engraved with the names of the soldiers and revolutionaries that fell in battle. The monument's guardian will be happy to guide you through more of the symbolism if it's quiet.

Kruševo itself is a pleasant little mountainside town, well off the tourist trail. If you want to stay the night, look for signs advertising *sobi* (rooms) around the old town. Kruševo-Skopje buses run three times a day (410MKD, three hours).

Horse Club Bistra Galičnik HORSE RIDING
(☑077 648 679; www.horseriding.com.mk) You
can go on daily rides (2½ to 5½ hours)
through Mavrovo's mountain valleys, departing from the village of Galičnik and
dropping by traditional villages. The daily
treks have cheese-tasting stops. Multiday
excursions involve camping, cheese tasting
and going up to the Medenica peak.

Zare Lazarevski Ski Centre SKIING
(☑042 489 065; www.skimavrovo.com) This is
North Macedonia's top ski resort (though
the country is not known for its skiing in
general), with average snow cover of 70cm
and 25km of slopes ranging from 1255m to
1860m. A day ticket costs 1100MKD and you
can rent ski gear here.

✯ Festivals & Events

★**Galičnik Wedding Festival** CULTURAL
(www.galichnik.mk; ☺12-13 Jul) The small Mavrovo village of Galičnik is a placid rural
outpost that bursts into life each July with
a traditional wedding festival, when one or
two lucky couples have their wedding here.
It's a big two-day party that you can join,
along with 3000 happy Macedonians. Everyone eats, drinks and enjoys traditional folk
dancing and music.

🛏 Sleeping

Baba i Dede GUESTHOUSE €
(☑070 370 843, 077 854 256; Galičnik; r per person
€20; P 🛜) Baba i Dede means Grandpa and
Grandma – and indeed it's a pair of Galičnik
ancients (more or less the only two people
who live in the village year-round) who welcome you at this charming guesthouse with
a restaurant. The four rooms are spacious
and homely, and the traditional food is delicious, prepared by the ever-smiling Baba.

**Sveti Jovan
Bigorski Monastery** HOSTEL €
(☑Father Serges 070 304 316, Father Silvan 078
383 771; www.bigorski.org; Mavrovo National Park;
dm €15-20; 🟦🛜) For a unique experience,
you can bed down in one of North Macedonia's most famous monasteries for the
night. Rooms are clustered in one wing of
the religious complex and decorated, naturally, with traditional monastic furniture.
Although the sleeping arrangements are effectively dorms, it's a far cry from the hard
wooden bunks you might associate with the
monks' pared-back lifestyle.

Hotel Bistra LODGE €
(☑042 489 027; www.bistra.com; s/d from
€35/50; P 🟦🛜🏊) Near Mavrovo town, the
Bistra has comfortable, clean, rather dated
rooms and some of the park's best amenities. These include a restaurant, bar, pool,
Turkish bath and sauna for cultivating
that ski-lodge glow, plus spas in the deluxe
rooms. Prices are lowest in summer, when
it's a wonderful place to retreat to, with
sweeping views. Add €5 per person onto the
room prices for ski season.

Hotel Tutto HOTEL €€
(☑042 470 999; www.tutto.com.mk; Janče; s/d/
tr €30/50/60, apt €40-50; P 🟦🛜) Welcome
to one of North Macedonia's most enterprising community projects – an eco-hotel with
a restaurant to die for. The setting in Janče
is peaceful and lovely, and there are hiking
trails at the hotel's front door. The 1st-floor
rooms are exceedingly comfy: ask for one at
the front to appreciate the view from your
balcony.

Hotel Radika SPA HOTEL €€€
(☑042 223 300; www.radika.com.mk; S Leunovo;
s/d winter €69/98, summer €59/78; P 🟦🛜🏊)
This ultraposh spa hotel, 5km from Mavrovo town, is perfect for pampering, with
its modern rooms and heavenly lake-view
outdoor pool. Prices fall considerably in
summer, when the hotel can arrange hiking trips and rents out mountain bikes. The
only downside is that it feels quite remote in
summer; in winter a free shuttle bus drops
guests at the ski lifts, 10km away. Bicycles
are available free of charge for guests.

🍴 Eating

★**Hotel Tutto Restaurant** MACEDONIAN €€
(☑042 470 999; www.tutto.com.mk; Janče; mains
from 400MKD; ☺8am-midnight) The owner of
Tutto is a founding member of North Macedonia's Slow Food organisation, and his
enthusiasm for local produce is infused in
the restaurant kitchen. Macedonian specialities such as slow-roast lamb and *pita*
(coiled filo pastry pies stuffed with spinach
and cheese) are a must, and there are always
fresh mushrooms on the menu, picked from
the surrounding forest.

ⓘ Information

Go Macedonia (p290), in Skopje, arranges Galičnik
wedding festival trips including transport, guided
activities, local accommodation and a monastery
tour at Sveti Jovan Bigorski. Book ahead.

Macedonia Experience (p290) can arrange horse riding, bike riding and community tourism forays into the park from Skopje, often including food tastings. Cultural tours stop at Galičnik (p298) or Janče (p298).

Horse Club Bistra Galičnik (p299) runs horse-riding tours from Galičnik.

🛈 Getting There & Away

➤ Without your own wheels, it's difficult to reach the various places of interest in the national park independently, or to do any hiking.

➤ Two buses a day run from Skopje to Mavrovo town, Monday to Saturday (350MKD, 9.30am and 2.45pm).

➤ For Sveti Jovan Bigorski Monastery (p298), buses transiting Debar for Ohrid or Struga will be able to drop you off.

Lake Ohrid ОХРИДСКО ЕЗЕРО

🎵 046

Lake Ohrid, in its vastness and mystery, is a monumentally seductive attraction. Mirror-like and dazzling on sunny days, it's a truly beautiful place – especially in and around the ancient town of Ohrid, with its cobbled streets, distinctive architecture, city beach and lakefront bars.

At 300m deep, 34km long and three million years old, shared by North Macedonia (two-thirds) and Albania (one-third), Lake Ohrid is among Europe's deepest and oldest. The Macedonian portion is inscribed on the Unesco World Heritage list for its cultural heritage and unique nature – it's considered the most biodiverse lake of its size in the world.

To the east of Ohrid lies Galičica National Park with mountain villages and Magaro Peak, which can be summited. To the south, a long, wooded coast has pebble beaches, churches and camping spots. In summer the big, resort-style hotels and beaches can be unpleasantly crowded but there are better spots beyond them.

🔾 Sights & Activities

★ **Sveti Naum Monastery**   MONASTERY

(Lake Ohrid; 100MKD, parking 50MKD; ⊙ 7am-8pm Jun-Aug, closes at sunset rest of year) Sveti Naum, 29km south of Ohrid, is an imposing sight on a bluff near the Albanian border and a popular day trip from Ohrid. Naum was a contemporary of St Kliment, and their monastery an educational centre. The iconostasis inside the church dates to 1711 and the frescoes to

the 19th century; it's well worth paying the fee to enter. Sandy beaches hem the monastery in on two sides and are some of the best places to swim around Lake Ohrid.

Naum's Church of the Holy Archangels (AD 900) was destroyed by the Ottomans in the 15th century and reincarnated as the Church of Sveti Naum when it was rebuilt between the 16th and 17th centuries as a multidomed, Byzantine-style structure on this cliff. Inside, drop an ear to the tomb of Sveti Naum to hear his muffled heartbeat. Then head to the monastery walls for inspiring lake views.

Surrounding the core of the complex is a tranquil garden looped by fountains, with roses and peacocks. Plan to spend half a day here and enjoy the site, stopping for a paddle and lunch or drinks at one of the handful of restaurants and bars outside the main complex. Boat trips to the Springs of St Naum (p302) are also worthwhile, and there's even a good hotel (p302).

If you come by car, you have to pay for parking at the entrance to the monastery. From Ohrid town harbour, boats run to Sveti Naum (€10 return) every day at 10am, returning at 4pm, and it's 1½ hours each way; taxis take half an hour and cost €16 one way or €32 return, and for that price the driver will stop at the Bay of Bones as well. There's also a bus from Ohrid, which runs six to seven times daily (110MKD to 150MKD), stopping at the bus station and running along Bul Turtsticka.

Vevčani   VILLAGE

(Lake Ohrid) Keeping one sleepy eye on Lake Ohrid from its mountain perch, Vevčani dates to the 9th century and is a quiet rural settlement beloved by locals for its traditional restaurants and natural springs (p302). The old brick streets flaunt distinctive 19th-century rural architecture and the village is watched over by the Church of St Nicholas. Vevčani lies 14km north of Struga, at the northerly edge of the lake. Buses from Struga run hourly (50MKD); a taxi should cost around 400MKD.

Start at the bottom of the village and stroll upwards through the narrow lanes to see Vevčani's higgledy-piggledy two-storey stone houses, stabilised by a *bondruk* system of wooden frames and finished off with stooped wooden porches. In the upper part of the village, the Vevčani Springs are a delightful, leafy retreat for strolling, picnicking and cooling off in the company of a couple

WORTH A TRIP

MONASTERIES AND MOSQUES

The 13th-century **Treskavec Monastery** (Manastir Treskavec, Манастир Тресkавец; off R1303) FREE rises from Mt Zlato (1422m), a bare massif replete with imposing twisted rock formations. One doesn't know which is more impressive – the bare granite boulder mountainside or the half-ruined monastery. Vivid frescoes, including a rare depiction of Christ as a boy, line the 14th-century Church of Sveta Bogorodica, built over a 6th-century basilica. Restoration work is slowly progressing, following a fire that ravaged much of the structure.

Earlier Roman remains are inside, along with graves, inscriptions and monks' skulls. The monastery is not always staffed, so you may find yourself completely alone atop the hill. At such times, an echo of Indiana Jones can accompany a wander through the site as the sense of abandonment, silence save for the wind, and birds flapping through dusty eaves make it a very eerie place to explore.

Treskavec is 10km above Prilep and there's no public transport, so driving or hiking are the only options. A pristine asphalt road zips you up to the monastery along a steep and winding route that must have been a real test of faith a few centuries back. Start from Prilep's cemetery and turn uphill at the sign marked 'Manastir Sveta Bogorodica, Treskavec'. It takes about 10 minutes to drive up from there.

Tetovo's beautiful **Painted Mosque** (Pasha's Mosque, Шарена Џамија; cnr Ilindenska & Brajka Milladinovi, Tetovo; ⊙6am-10pm) FREE is like something out of the Arabian Tales and quite unique in the Balkans. First built in the 15th century, it was razed to the ground two centuries later in a great fire that annihilated half the city; the design and architecture you see today is a 19th-century reconstruction. The facade is a patchwork of rectangular panels worked in a fresco technique; inside, the decoration becomes rich and floral, with geometric and arabesque ornamentation.

The mosque's design was masterminded by Abdurrahman Pasha of Tetovo, hence the name Pasha's Mosque (though it is much more widely known simply as the Painted Mosque).

The mosque sits on the southern bank of the Pena River, which bisects Tetovo. The town itself is a largely modern place and there's little to keep you here. Buses run every hour, if not more frequently, from Skopje and the journey takes 40 minutes to an hour. Tetovo is 43km west of Skopje.

of small shrines and gushing rivers. At the mouth of the spring, it's possible to see the water bubbling irrepressibly up from beneath the moss-covered rocks.

Once you've visited the springs, take the steep track just outside the site entrance to Kutmičevica (p302) restaurant for inventive traditional cuisine such as nettle pie, *jufki* (homemade pasta with cheese) and *lukanci* (homemade paprika-laced pork sausage). Its creaking wood-beamed dining room has spectacular views over the mountain – you can even stay here if you wish to spend the night in the village.

Visit in January and you will stumble upon one of the largest pagan festivals in the Balkans, the Vevčani Carnival (p302), which is celebrated annually with elaborate costumed revelry and lots of noise.

A network of signposted mountain walking trails, set up by Balkan Hiking Adventure (www.balkanhikingadventure.com) to develop mountain tourism in the border ar-

eas between North Macedonia, Kosovo and Albania, also passes through Vevčani. Check online for details.

If driving, pay close attention to signposting from Struga, because it can be easy to miss; you should enter the settlement through a stone gate in the lower village.

Museum on Water – Bay of Bones

MUSEUM

(☏078 909 806; adult/student & child 100/30MKD; ⊙9am-7pm Jul-Aug, to 4pm Sep-Jun, closed Mon Oct-Apr) In prehistoric times Lake Ohrid was home to a settlement of pile dwellers who lived literally on top of the water, on a platform supported by up to 10,000 wooden piles anchored to the lake bed. The remains of the settlement were discovered at this spot and were gradually excavated by an underwater team between 1997 and 2005; the museum is an elaborate reconstruction of the settlement as archaeologists think it would have looked between 1200 and 600 BC.

Vevčani Springs
SPRING

(Vevčani, Lake Ohrid; adult/child 20/10MKD; ⊙9am-5pm) The small mountain village of Vevčani, 14km north of Struga on Lake Ohrid, is celebrated for these natural springs, which writhe and wriggle through leafy forests at the top of the village. The area includes a number of paths and boardwalks, and is popular with locals for picnics and as a place to cool off on hot days, though it's a beautiful, contemplative spot at any time of year.

Trpejca
VILLAGE

Cupped between a sloping hill and a tranquil bay, Ohrid's last traditional fishing village features clustered houses with terracotta roofs and a white-pebble beach. At night, the sounds of crickets and frogs are omnipresent. Trpejca has limited services, though in midsummer its small beach gets very crowded. Locals like to swim here, but the frogs and flotsam and jetsam are a bit off-putting.

Springs of St Naum
BOATING

(Sveti Naum Monastery; per boat 600MKD) Inside the Sveti Naum Monastery (p300), colourful covered motorboats sit waiting to whisk visitors over the lake to see the Springs of St Naum. The water here is fed by Lake Prespa and is astoundingly clear – at some points it is 3.5m deep and still you can see the bottom.

Diving Center Amfora
DIVING

(⌀071 359 810; www.amfora.com.mk; 1hr dives €55) This Lake Ohrid outfit can take you diving under the Museum on Water (p301) to see the remains of an ancient lake settlement that sits in a watery grave at the Bay of Bones. Bones, teeth, amulets and fragments of pottery can be seen at depths between 5m and 8m, and the instructor is happy to take beginners as well as certified divers. Book at least a day ahead.

🎉 Festivals & Events

Vevčani Carnival
CARNIVAL

(⊙mid-Jan) This traditional pagan carnival is thought to have existed for 1400 years, and is celebrated in Vevčani with great pomp. The elaborate costumes are reminiscent of Halloween and locals go to great lengths to design their own gory costumes. There's food, wine, music and general revelry.

🛌 Sleeping

Robinson Sunset House
HOSTEL €

(⌀075 727 252; Lagadin, Lake Ohrid; dm/d/apt €12/30/45; ❋🛜) Sweeping lake views, free surfboards (for paddling) and a sprawling garden with lots of relaxing nooks and crannies make this ramshackle hostel a winner if you don't fancy the bustle of Ohrid itself. It sits on a hill above the village of Lagadin, a short bus ride south of Ohrid town. Rooms are spacious and charming, if quite basic.

Gradište Camping
CAMPGROUND €

(per tent €10, parking 100MKD; ⊙Jun–mid-Sep, 24hr reception) Gradište Camping is popular with city dwellers who keep cabins as summer houses – evenings are dedicated to barbecues and Macedonian music at top volume. Camping is in a prime spot on a hill on the western edge of the site, and the beach is nice and long. Gradište is on the road to Sveti Naum, about 16km south of Ohrid town.

Hotel Sveti Naum
HOTEL €

(⌀046 283 080; www.hotel-stnaum.com.mk; Sveti Naum; s/d/ste from 1890/2500/4990MKD; 🛜) Inside the grounds of the Sveti Naum Monastery (p300), some of this hotel's rooms and suites have lovely lake views. Designed in line with traditional building principles, the rooms feature monastic-style furniture and are quite spacious, if a little dated. It's also right by one of Lake Ohrid's best beaches. For the price, it's a steal.

🍴 Eating & Drinking

Restoran Ribar
SEAFOOD €

(Trpejca; 120-160MKD; ⊙8.30am-10pm, skara till 8.30pm) Right on Trpejca's waterfront, Ribar serves local fish, *skara* and coffee. If you're passing in summer, this is a great spot to stop for lunch under the shady patio and watch kids jump off the pier on the small pebble beach nearby. To get here, take the left-hand path opposite Villa De Niro heading downwards.

Restaurant Ostrovo
MACEDONIAN €€

(Sveti Naum Monastery; mains 120-850MKD; ⊙8am-9pm) Of all the restaurants at Sveti Naum (p300), this one has the prettiest setting by the water. Cross the little bridge and there's a seemingly endless garden for dining as well as a unique feature: moored pontoons that you can eat on. Staff speak very little English but are friendly and helpful. Fish features heavily on the menu and breakfast here is good. Note that the signage for this place is in Cyrillic only – look for 'Остpoвo'.

Kutmičevica
MACEDONIAN €€

(⌀046 798 399; www.kutmicevica.com.mk; Vevčani; mains 250-900MKD; ⊙9am-midnight)

This restaurant, which reverberates with the chatter of locals, is a great find: the views from its dining room are immense, right out over the village. It spills onto a terrace on sunny days. The traditional wood-beamed setting matches the menu, where you'll see some Macedonian specialities you won't find in Ohrid, and some inventive takes on classic foods.

Orevche Beach Bar BAR
(Orevche, Lake Ohrid; ⊙10am-8pm; 🛜) A twisted cliffside path sloping steeply downwards into the unknown makes Orevche feel like a secret hideaway, and really it is because hardly anybody knows it's here. The Lake Ohrid water is clear and it would be easy to lose a few hours lounging on the rustic beach bar's day beds and swimming, particularly at sunset.

❶ Information

Once you leave Ohrid town, ATMs are surprisingly hard to find. There's a reliable one in the foyer of Hotel Bellevue, a giant waterfront high-rise just south of Ohrid town.

❶ Getting There & Away

The major regional bus hub is Ohrid town, and the northerly lake town of Struga also has some bus connections to other Macedonian towns.

❶ Getting Around

Bus Frequent buses ply the Ohrid–Sveti Naum route (€1) in summer, stopping off at various points along the lake road, including the village of Lagadin and the Bay of Bones (p301).
Boat Transfers from Ohrid to Sveti Naum (€10 return) run every day in summer.

Ohrid Охрид

🖉 046 / POP 55,750

Sublime Ohrid is North Macedonia's most seductive destination. It sits on the edge of serene Lake Ohrid, with an atmospheric old quarter that cascades down steep streets, dotted with beautiful churches and topped by the bones of a medieval castle. Traditional restaurants and lakeside cafes liven up the cobblestone streets, which in high summer can be very lively indeed. Outside of July and August, the tourist circus subsides and the town becomes more lived in.

Ohrid is small enough to hop from historic monuments into a deck chair and dip your toes in the water – a lovely little town beach and boardwalk make the most of the town's natural charms. A holiday atmosphere prevails all summer, when it's a good idea to book accommodation in advance. Ohrid's busiest time is from mid-July to mid-August, during the popular summer festival (p306).

◉ Sights & Activities

★Ohrid Boardwalk
& City Beach BEACH
(Map p304) Skimming the surface of the water along Ohrid's shore, snaking towards Kaneo fishing village and the town's most famous church, this over-water boardwalk takes you to a beautiful outcrop of rocky beaches and a handful of small restaurants and bars. On a hot day the area is thronged by bathers, drinkers and diners. The cool waters are translucent and inviting, the cliff-backed setting is sublime, and strolling this stretch of coast up to the Church of Sveti Jovan at Kaneo is an Ohrid must.

★Church of
Sveti Jovan at Kaneo CHURCH
(Map p304; Kaneo; 100MKD; ⊙9am-6pm) This stunning 13th-century church is set on a cliff over the lake, about a 15-minute walk west of Ohrid's port area, and is possibly North Macedonia's most photographed structure. Peer down into the azure waters and you'll see why medieval monks found spiritual inspiration here. The small church has original frescoes behind the altar.

Plaošnik CHURCH
(Map p304; adult/student & child 100/30MKD; ⊙8am-7pm) Saluting the lake from Ohrid's hilltop, Plaošnik is home to the multidomed medieval Church of Sveti Kliment i Pantelejmon, the foundations of a 5th-century basilica and a garden of intricate early Christian flora-and-fauna mosaics. The central church was restored in 2002; though it lacks the ancient wall frescoes of many other Macedonian churches, it is unusual in having glass floor segments revealing the original foundations and framed relics from the medieval church, which dated to the 9th century.

Sveta Bogorodica Bolnička
& Sveti Nikola Bolnički CHURCH
(Map p304; off Car Samoil; admission to each church 50MKD; ⊙9am-1pm) *Bolnica* means 'hospital' in Macedonian; during plagues visitors faced 40-day quarantines inside the walled confines of these petite churches,

Ohrid

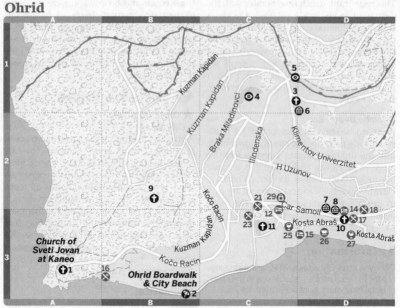

Ohrid

which are thought to date to the 14th century. Sandwiched between Car Samoil and Kosta Abraš in the heart of the Old Town, the churches have somewhat irregular opening hours, but don't miss going in if they are open. Both are small and low-lying, but have intricate interiors heaving under elaborate icons.

The dining terrace of **Pizzeria Leonardo** (Map p304; Car Samoil 33; pizzas 170-350MKD;

10am-midnight) actually backs onto the grounds of Sveti Nikola Bolnički.

National Workshop for Handmade Paper
MUSEUM

(Map p304; Car Samoil 60; 8.30am-9pm Mon-Sat, 9am-4pm Sun) FREE Here's a slightly random fact for you: Ohrid has been printing paper since the 16th century and this museum-cum-shop has one of only two copies of the Gutenberg Press in the world. Staff are on hand to give a demonstration of the paper-making process (in excellent English), and the teeny museum also sells handmade paper products such as pretty gift bags and notebooks.

Church of Sveta Bogorodica Perivlepta
CHURCH

(Map p304; Klimentov Univerzitet; 100MKD; 9am-4pm) Just inside the **Gorna Porta** (Upper Gate; Map p304; Ilindenska), this 13th-century Byzantine church, whose name translates as 'Our Lady the Most Glorious', has vivid biblical frescoes (newly restored in 2017) painted by masters Michael and Eutychius, and superb lake and Old Town views from its terrace. There's also an icon gallery highlighting the founders' artistic achievements.

National Museum
MUSEUM

(Robev Family House Museum; Map p304; Car Samoil 62; adult/student & child 100/50MKD; 9am-3pm Tue-Sun) Ohrid's National Museum is housed over three floors of this remarkably well-preserved Old Town house, which dates from 1863 and was once owned by the Robev family of merchants. The creaking timbered building has just been renovated; on the top two floors displays include Roman archaeological finds, a 5th-century golden mask from Ohrid and local woodcarving, while the ground floor is reserved for art exhibitions. Across the road the Urania Residence, part of the museum, has an ethnographic display.

Sveta Sofija Cathedral
CHURCH

(Map p304; Car Samoil; adult/student & child 100/30MKD; 9am-7pm) Ohrid's grandest church, 11th-century Sveta Sofija is supported by columns and decorated with elaborate, if very faded, Byzantine frescoes, though they are still well preserved and very vivid in the apse. Its superb acoustics mean it's often used for concerts. To one side of the church there's a peaceful, manicured garden providing a small oasis of green in the heart of the Old Town.

Icon Gallery
GALLERY

(Map p304; 046 251 935; Klimentov Univerzitet; 100MKD; 10am-2pm & 6-9pm Tue-Sun) This small museum contains an impressive collection of Macedonian religious icons, from the 13th to the 18th century. It's right by the Church of Sveta Bogorodica Perivlepta, near the Gorna Porta.

Classical Amphitheatre
AMPHITHEATRE

(Map p304; Braka Miladinovci; 24hr) FREE Ohrid's impressive amphitheatre was built in the Hellenistic period (around 200 BC); the Romans later removed 10 rows to accommodate gladiators and used it as a site for Christian executions. Today it's incongruously hemmed in by residential housing and a little underwhelming as a historic attraction. In summer it is brought to life as a venue for Ohrid's Summer Festival (p306) performances.

★ Free Pass Ohrid
TOURS

(Map p304; 070 488 231; www.freepassohrid. mk; Kosta Abraš 74) Run by twin sisters and offering a whole array of tailored tours – from hiking in Galičica National Park, to wine touring around Tikveš, and boat trips and paragliding around Lake Ohrid, among others – this is local enterprise and alternative tourism at its best. They also run stacks of cultural and adventure tours from their Ohrid base.

✨ Festivals & Events

★ Ohrid Summer
Festival PERFORMING ARTS
(📞 046 262 304; http://ohridskoleto.com.mk; Kej Maršal Tito; ⏰ box office 9am-10pm Jul & Aug) This is Ohrid's most celebrated festival and one of the biggest cultural events in North Macedonia. It hits town in late July and features classical and opera concerts, theatre and dance staged at venues all over the city, including the Classical Amphitheatre (p305). Buy tickets from the box office kiosk on Kej Maršal Tito, next to the Jazz & Blues cafe-bar.

🛏 Sleeping

★ Villa Jovan HISTORIC HOTEL €
(Map p304; 📞 076 236 606; vila.jovan@gmail.com; Car Samoil 44; s/d/ste €27/59/98; 🅿🕸🛜) By far the most charming place to stay in Ohrid, this 1856 mansion offers nine rooms in the heart of the Old Town. There are old-world furnishings, creaky floors and wooden beams, and a cosy atmosphere. The two top-floor rooms have quirky sunken baths sitting behind a glass wall, looking out onto the tiny sun-trap terraces.

There are no communal areas at all in this hotel, but on the plus side this means breakfast is served down by the harbour at the owners' lakeside restaurant – Restoran Čun (p308). Ask for discounts October to May.

★ Sunny Lake Hostel HOSTEL €
(Map p304; 📞 075 629 571; www.sunnylakehostel.mk; 11 Oktomvri 15; dm €10-12, d €24; 🕸🛜) This excellent hostel is a bustling hub for backpackers. Though it could be more spacious, nobody cares because they have such a good time here. The common areas are a highlight: a snug upstairs terrace with lake views and a garden down below for beer drinking. Facilities include a laundry, free breakfast, a kitchen, lockers and bike hire (€5 per day).

Villa Lucija GUESTHOUSE €
(Map p304; 📞 046 265 608, 077 714 815; Kosta Abraš 29; s/d/tr/apt €30/35/45/55; 🕸🛜) Lucija is in the thick of the Old Town with possibly the town's most enviable location: right on the lakefront with a patio and decking by the water's edge, complete with lounge chairs. A homely feel pervades, with

a communal kitchen and lovingly decorated, breezy rooms with lake-view balconies. Rooms cost €5 less per night from mid-September to mid-June.

City Hostel HOSTEL €
(📞 078 208 407; jedidooel@yahoo.com; Bul Makedonski Prosvetiteli 22; dm/d €10/30; 🕸🛜) In a modern block 10 minutes' walk north of Ohrid's harbour, everything at this family-run hostel feels fresh and new. The quirky interior takes inspiration from Ohrid's timbered Old Town houses – even down to the lanterns. The common area is a little dark and there's no communal outside chilling space, but the rooms are bright and all have balconies and en-suite bathrooms.

★ Jovanovic Guest House GUESTHOUSE €€
(Map p304; 📞 070 589 218; jovanovic.guesthouse@hotmail.com; Boro Šain 5; apt €40-65; 🕸🛜) This property has two studio apartments, both of which sleep four, set in the heart of the Old Town. Each is well equipped and comes with a shady balcony. The apartment on the 1st floor is slightly bigger, but the top-floor apartment's balcony is more private and has one of the best views in town, right over the lake and Sveta Sofija Cathedral.

🍴 Eating

Via Sacra PIZZA €
(Map p304; 📞 075 440 654; Ilindenska 36; mains 160-350MKD; ⏰ 10am-midnight; 🛜) Pleasantly fusing the best of Italian and Macedonian fare, Via Sacra offers up crisp and tasty pizzas as well as a good selection of Macedonian national cooking and wines. Service is excellent and its location is a big draw too: facing the lovely Sveta Sofija Cathedral on a cobbled Old Town street. Breakfast is also served.

Green Market MARKET €
(off Goce Delčev; ⏰ 7am-9pm Mon-Sat, to 2pm Sun, closes 7pm Mon-Sat in winter) Ohrid's main outdoor fruit and vegetable market is great for self-caterers and sells everything from local produce to electronics and kids' toys. Enter directly behind the fountain on Goce Delčev, near the Činar tree. Monday is the market's biggest day, when traders come from around Ohrid to sell.

Tinex Supermarket SUPERMARKET €
(Map p304; Bul Makedonski Prosvetiteli; ⏰ 8am-10pm) There are no food shops in the Old Town, so if you're self-catering you'll have to walk here to get supplies. Tinex is one of two supermarkets that sit just back from the

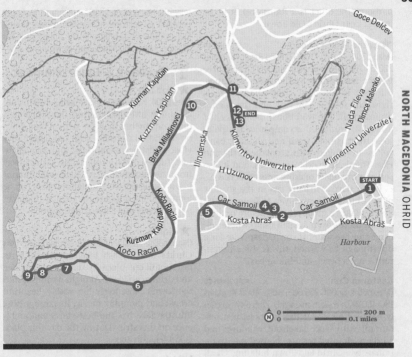

Town Walk
Ohrid Old Town

START: CAR SAMOIL
END: CHURCH OF SVETA BOGORODICA PERIVLEPTA
LENGTH: 3KM; 1½ HOURS

Begin at the eastern end of **1 Car Samoil street**, lined with beautiful traditional architecture. Pop down to see the tiny **2 Sveta Bogorodica Bolnička & Sveti Nikola Bolnički** (p303) churches and admire the frescoes stretching across the domed ceilings. Return to Car Samoil and look inside the **3 National Workshop for Handmade Paper** (p305). Further up the street, see the work of **4 Marta Pejoska** (p309), a local artist who practises the traditional technique of silver filigree. As you reach the end of Car Samoil street, you will come out onto the main town square and **5 Sveta Sofija Cathedral** (p305) – best visited if there is a concert on.

From here go to the **6 Ohrid boardwalk** (p303) to admire the rock formations that frame the lake. The boardwalk will take you to

the old fishing neighbourhood of **7 Kaneo**, once totally cut off from the rest of Ohrid. Have a coffee or meal break at **8 Letna Bavča Kaneo** (p308) and check out the restaurant's old photographs of the fishing community from the 19th century.

From here, head uphill (there's a lot of uphill in Ohrid!) to one of North Macedonia's most scenic structures, the **9 Church of Sveti Jovan at Kaneo** (p303). Go uphill again, along Kočo Racin street and glance down at the **10 Classical Amphitheatre** (p305), mostly quiet except for Summer Festival performances, then follow the winding street past the **11 Gorna Porta** (p305) towards the **12 Church of Sveta Bogorodica Perivlepta** (p305). The ancient frescoes have been recently renovated and shine in their fresh coats of paint. Pop into the **13 Icon Gallery** (p305) to see the depictions of Byzantine saints. Before heading back down the hill, take in the sweeping views of Lake Ohrid and the cascading town from up above – it's a magical sight.

harbour (the other is a Ramstore). It is the largest near Ohrid's Old Town.

★ Letna Bavča Kaneo   SEAFOOD €€

(Map p304; ☑ 070 776 837; Kočo Racin 43; mains 220-500MKD; ☺ 8am-midnight; ☎) Of the three terrace restaurants by the water at Kaneo, this one is the best – the atmosphere is right, the food is fantastic and the service professional. The traditional menu has had a facelift; truffle oil accompanies the potatoes, trout is both fresh and smoked, courgettes are stuffed with aromatic herbs and rice. There are good local wines, and it also serves a breakfast of croissants and cheese.

Letna Bavča virtually sits in the shadow of the Church of Sveti Jovan at Kaneo (p303) and it makes a great pit stop before or after a visit; there's even a small ramp where you can enter the water if you're desperate for a dip (though be warned, this is still a restaurant – not a beach-and-bikini bar).

Restoran Čun   MACEDONIAN €€

(Map p304; ☑ 046 255 603; Kosta Abraš 4; mains 180-480MKD; ☺ 8am-midnight) There's a vaguely nautical air about this whitewashed restaurant with large lakefront windows and a breezy elevated terrace, housed in a traditional-style Ohrid Old Town building. Of all the restaurants on this prime strip, Čun is the classiest.

Restaurant Antiko   MACEDONIAN €€

(Map p304; Car Samoil 30; mains 200-800MKD; ☺ 11am-11pm) In an old Ohrid mansion in the middle of the Old Town, the famous Antiko has great traditional ambience and is a good place to try classic dishes such as *tavče gravče*, and top-quality Macedonian wines.

Restaurant Belvedere   GRILL €€

(Map p304; Kej Maršal Tito 2; mains 240-1400MKD; ☺ 9am-1am; ☎) This place, just outside the Old Town on the lakeside promenade of the New Town, is a great place for *skara*, as well as many other Macedonian specialities, including lake-plucked fish (the range of dish prices is vast). In warmer months the large outdoor terrace makes this a very popular dining spot.

Restoran Sveta Sofija   MACEDONIAN €€€

(Map p304; Car Samoil 88; mains 300-1000MKD; ☺ 10am-11pm; ☎) This upmarket restaurant opposite the Sveta Sofija Cathedral couldn't have a better location, and in the warmer months you can dine al fresco across the road on a little terrace. Local trout, eel and 'monas-

tery cheese' (cheese with garlic and *bukovec* pepper) all feature on the traditional menu. Oenophiles will delight in its staggering list of more than 100 Macedonian wines.

🍷 Drinking & Entertainment

★ Jazz Inn   BAR

(Map p304; Kosta Abraš 74; ☺ 9pm-1am) This unassuming little jazz-themed bar sways to a different rhythm than the strip of bars down on Ohrid's lakefront, with an alternative vibe, a distinct soundtrack and arty clientele. Tucked down a cobbled backstreet away from the touristy hubbub, the low-lit interior has a speakeasy feel, though revellers can be found spilling out onto the road by midnight on weekends and throughout summer.

★ Liquid   CAFE

(Map p304; Kosta Abraš 17; ☺ 8am-1am; ☎) Ohrid's most stylish lakefront bar is a relaxed chill-out place by day, serving coffee and drinks (no food). At night it morphs into the town's most lively bar with a beautiful crowd and pumping music. Its patio jutting into the lake has the best views and ambience on this strip. During the day this place is kid-friendly too.

NOA Lounge Bar   BAR

(Map p304; Kosta Abraš 38; ☺ 9am-1am; ☎) You'll find just as many people eating as drinking at this sleek cafe-bar on the lively Kosta Abraš strip in Ohrid's Old Town. At night, the music is kept to a sociable level (meaning you can hear yourself talk, if that's what you want on an evening out). The lakefront terrace has lovely views and there's a full cocktail and wine list.

Havana Club   BAR

(Map p304; www.cubalibreohrid.com; Partizanska 2; ☺ 1am-5am) Popular nightclub right by Ohrid's harbour. During the summer months it opens nightly and is normally standing-room only, with DJs from all over the Balkans coming to play; expect to queue to get in as it's the only place in town open this late. Entrance is around the back and the club is on the 2nd floor.

Dom na Kultura
Grigor Prličev   ARTS CENTRE

(Map p304; Bul Makedonski Prosvetiteli) Holds cultural events such as traditional song and dance during festivals, and houses Ohrid's movie theatre.

Shopping

★Atelier Marta Pejoska JEWELLERY

(Map p304; ☎070 691 251; whatisfiligree.tumblr.com/; Car Samoil 52; ⊙noon-6.30pm) Ohrid-born Marta trained as an architect and decided to dedicate herself to the traditional Macedonian craft of filigree – silver thread weaving that has the appearance of silver lace (pieces from €25). Marta is a charming host and works to order as well as displaying and selling her existing designs. She often has exhibitions in her small shop.

Information

Ohrid does not have an official tourist office (despite the fact that many city maps suggest it does); www.visitohrid.org is the municipal website. Free Pass Ohrid (p305) Can arrange tours around the lake and beyond.

Getting There & Away

Ohrid's **St Paul the Apostle Airport** (☎046 252 820; www.airports.com.mk) is 10km north of the town.

There is no public transport to and from the airport. Taxis cost 500MKD one way (don't bother haggling because it's a set fare) and are easy to pick up without pre-booking.

Ohrid's **bus station** (cnr 7 Noemvri & Klanoec) is 1.5km northeast of the town centre. Tickets can either be bought at the station itself or from the **Galeb** (Map p304; ☎046 251 882; www.galeb.mk; Partizanska; ⊙9am-5pm) bus company ticket office just outside Ohrid Old Town. A taxi to Ohrid's bus station from the port area on the edge of the Old Town is a set fare of 150MKD.

It's also possible to cross into Albania by taking the bus or a taxi to Sveti Naum (p302), from where you can cross the border and take a taxi (€5, 6km) to Pogradeci.

Galičica National Park

Галичица Национален Парк

The rippling, rock-crested massif of Galičica separates Lakes Ohrid and Prespa, and is home to Magaro Peak (2254m), a handful of mountain villages and 1100 species of plant, 12 of which can be found only here. Lake Prespa is home to the island of Golem Grad. The whole area is protected as a 228-sq-km national park, stretching down to Sveti Naum.

Sights

★Golem Grad ISLAND

(Lake Prespa) Adrift on Lake Prespa, Golem Grad was once the king's summer playground but is now home to wild tortoises, cormorants and pelicans, and perhaps a few ghosts. A settlement endured here from the 4th century BC to the 6th century AD and during medieval times there was a monastery complex. The ruins, birdlife and otherworldly beauty make it well worth exploring. Vila Raskrsnica (p311) or Dzani Dimovski (☎070 678 123), who owns the cafe at Dupeni Beach, organise trips.

The island is part of the Galičica National Park, though it's easier to access from the eastern side of Lake Prespa, near Pelister National Park. Ongoing excavations have unearthed dozens of ruins, many of which have been marked out for visitors with information boards (in English). The battered **church of St Peter**, which dates to the 14th century and bears remnants of frescoes, is the closest historic structure to the boat docking area and just a short way along the marked path. After that, you'll find the remaining stumps of a **Roman house**, the overgrown foundations of a couple of early Christian **basilicas** dating to the 5th and 6th centuries, and an impressive waterside ruin of a 4th-century **Roman cistern** (though the last is a little off the marked track).

Golem Grad is only 750m long and 450m wide, so very walkable. If you felt like it, you could even camp out here overnight. The boat trip is worth doing in itself, as the sight of the pelicans in the water and on the shore as you approach the island is magical. Note that the shoreline is backed by high rocks and cliffs 20m to 30m high, so it's not much of a swimming spot – particularly as it's also home to a high concentration of (harmless) water snakes. Its nickname is 'snake island'; wear hiking boots as there are also some poisonous land snakes to watch out for.

Dzani Dimovski is a reliable boat driver – though he doesn't speak much English. An hour or so on the island and return boat transfers from Dupeni Beach costs €65 for up to three to four people. The boat driver will happily lead you ashore and through the island, or you can explore alone – note that the walking trail markers do occasionally become a little hard to follow.

Lake Prespa LAKE

Prespa is separated from its sister lake, Ohrid, by Galičica National Park and a road crosses the ridge of the park, linking the two. Prespa's mirrorlike surface stretches for 176.8 sq km and it is the highest tectonic lake on the Balkans (853m) – the borders of

North Macedonia, Albania and Greece converge in its centre. In Prespa's centre lies the island of Golem Grad (p309) – undoubtedly its greatest attraction. **Dupeni Beach**, near the Greek border on its eastern side, is a (sandy!) spot for swimming.

ℹ️ Information

There is a park entry toll of 80MKD from the Ohrid side.

ℹ️ Getting There & Away

If you're driving from Ohrid in the direction of Pelister National Park or Bitola, you can also take a winding mountain road that turns off just after the village of Trpejca and connects the two lakes, curling up and over the park and spitting you out at Prespa. You can drive up as high as 1600m using this road.

CENTRAL NORTH MACEDONIA

Pelister National Park
ПЕЛИСТЕР НАЦИОНАЛЕН ПАРК

North Macedonia's oldest national park, created in 1948, Pelister covers 171 sq km of the country's third-highest mountain range, the quartz-filled Baba massif. Eight peaks top 2000m, crowned by Mt Pelister (2601m). Two glacial lakes, known as 'Pelister's Eyes', sit at the top. Summiting both Mt Pelister and the lakes is one of the park's biggest hiking attractions.

Pelister's 88 tree species include the rare five-leafed *molika* pine. It also hosts endemic Pelagonia trout, deer, wolves, chamois, wild boars, bears and eagles.

In WWI, the foothills were used by the Macedonian Front, and it was here and Bitola that bore the brunt of the country's involvement in the war – now commemorated in a moving history trail (p311) within the park.

Pelister has excellent village guesthouses nearby and is just 30 minutes away by car from historic Bitola. With its fresh alpine air and good day hikes, the park is an underrated Macedonian stopover.

◎ Sights

Dihovo   VILLAGE

Propping up the base of Pelister, just 5km from Bitola, the 830m-high mountainside hamlet of Dihovo is a charming spot, surrounded by thick pine forests and rushing mountain streams. The village's proximity to the main access road into the Pelister National Park makes it a popular base for walkers, and locals have shown impressive initiative in developing their traditional community into a pioneering village tourism destination.

Dihovo's pretty coil of stone houses includes three guesthouses, a beekeeper, the icon-rich Church of Sveti Dimitrije (1830) and access to mountain paths, plus a waterfall to cool off in on hot summer days. The beekeeper offers honey tastings; book through Villa Dihovo (p312), whose owner Petar can also arrange other local community activities.

The waterfall isn't signposted and can be tricky to find: follow signs for the now-defunct open-air swimming pool, take the forest track that veers off the paved road to the left, head past the pool down the field track to the left of the pool, and keep walking for about 10 minutes to reach the falls. A taxi from Bitola to Dihovo costs about 150MKD.

Brajčino   VILLAGE

Cradled by the foothills on the western edge of Pelister, little Brajčino's lungs are fit to bursting with fresh mountain air, making it a thoroughly idyllic place to pitch up. Rushing water resounds around the village, cherry trees blossom in spring and migrating swallows stop by; traditional rural architecture adds further charm. There are five churches and a monastery hidden in the leafy environs circling this well-kept village and a two- to three-hour, well-marked trail takes in all of them.

🏃 Activities

★ Bee Garden BN   FOOD

(📞 097 526 9535; www.pcelarnikbn.com; Dihovo; ⊙ by appointment) A fantastic opportunity to learn about beekeeping and taste local honey, pollen and royal jelly. The friendly apiarist will demonstrate the workings of the hives, and you can buy some of the delicious products – perfect for gifts back home. The beekeeper's family also do excellent traditional home cooking, which can be booked by phoning in advance.

Mt Pelister & Lakes   WALKING

Pelister's signature hike is the full-day ascent to the national park's highest peak (2601m) and nearby mountain lakes – Big Lake and Small Lake – that puncture the mountaintop like a pair of deep blue eyes, hence their nickname, 'Pelister's Eyes'. There are numerous

DON'T MISS

TASTING TIKVEŠ WINES AT THE SOURCE

Five hundred years of Ottoman rule buried North Macedonia's ancient winemaking culture (the Ottomans, being Muslim, generally did not drink), and the practice was confined to monasteries for centuries. But these days you'll hear plenty of references to Tikveš – the country's most lauded (and developed) wine region.

None of the wineries accept walk-ins, so you'll need to plan appointments to taste and tour by calling ahead (if you're not driving, arrange a taxi at a cost of about €25 per car for five or so hours). **Tikveš Winery** (☑043 447 519; www.tikves.com.mk; 29 Noemvri 5; wine tasting per person from 300MKD; ◷10am-6pm Mon-Sat), one of the largest and most celebrated, can be virtually impossible to get an appointment at unless you plan way in advance.

Most vineyards – with the exceptions of **Bovin** (☑043 365 322; http://bovin.com.mk/; Industriska, 1440 Negotino; ◷8am-4pm Mon-Fri) and **Popova Kula** (☑043 367 400; www. popovakula.com.mk; bul Na Vinoto 1, Demir Kapija), both of which are well signposted – are extremely difficult to find on your own. Boutique Bovin offers an informative run through its winery and cellars, but some of the winery 'tours', such as the one at **Stobi Winery** (☑078 221 427; www.stobiwinery.mk; Autopat 2, 1420 Gradsko; ◷9am-6pm) FREE, are really not worth bothering with. In short, Tikveš' reputation and Macedonian enthusiasm somewhat oversell the experience.

Happily, **Popova Kula** (☑043 367 400; www.popovakula.com.mk; Bul Na Vinoto 1, Demir Kapija; s €35-45, d €50-110; P❄🛜) in Demir Kapija, the region's only winery hotel and restaurant, is worth the effort. The owner took inspiration from the winery experiences of California and what he's achieved here is in a different league to everything else in the region. Tours of the property are held four times a day for guests and nonguests, with fascinating insight into the history of the site thrown in.

A stay at Popova Kula is highly recommended, but it's also possible to take a tour of the region from Ohrid (a long day) with Free Pass Ohrid (p305).

North Macedonia's key unique grape varietal is *vranac* (a full-bodied red), while Popova Kula in particular prizes a little-known grape called *stanushina*.

---

starting points for the hike but none are reliably marked so it's advisable to take a guide.

Guides can be arranged for about €50 through Villa Dihovo (p312) and Vila Raskrsnica (p311) and most speak English. If your budget won't stretch to a guide, at the very least take a detailed map, which can be purchased from the national park information centre (p312) for 120MKD.

The road from Dihovo that leads into the park will get you up as high as 1400m and it's about 4½ hours uphill from there to the summit of Mt Pelister. From the other side of the park (near Brajčino) the hike will take longer as you start from a lower base: plan for about a seven-hour climb and up to five hours to get back down – you'll need to start very early to make it back down again in a day.

To get to the lakes is further still, as it's an extra 6.5km (two to 2½ hours) on top of the 11km to 13km it takes to get to the top of Mt Pelister (the distance depends on which route you take, as there are several trails). If you start very early, both the mountain and lakes can be seen in a day hike, but if you aren't confident there's also a mountain hut at Big

Lake (June to September) you can stay at, or you can trek back from Big Lake to the village of Nizhepole, which cuts the walk a bit short.

First World War Trail   WALKING

This gentle trail starting at the national park's headquarters meanders uphill through Pelister's cool alpine forests, and is accompanied by engaging information boards (in English) exploring this area's experiences during WWI. The trail is easy enough to follow without a map or GPS.

🛏 Sleeping

★**Vila Raskrsnica**   BOUTIQUE HOTEL €

(☑075 796 796; vila.raskrsnica@gmail.com; Brajčino; r per person €25; P❄🛜) It's worth detouring from the tourist trail just to stay at this utterly lovely village hotel, which offers four rooms in a chalet-style house and lipsmacking country food. Rooms are comfortable and elegant, with exposed stone walls and wooden floors, but it's the expansive mountain-backed garden, rustic picnic tables and a peeping view of Lake Prespa that make Raskrsnica so special.

Villa Patrice   VILLA €

(📞 075 466 878; Dihovo; s/d €12/18; 🛜) This house is used for overspill when Villa Dihovo is full, but it's a gorgeous little 1970s chalet in itself, with spacious rooms, a large garden and a big front balcony with pretty views. It feels more like a home than a hotel, with a communal lounge and kitchen and '70s furniture.

Villa Ilinden 1903   GUESTHOUSE €

(📞 076 697 909; Dihovo; s/d/tr/q €15/25/36/45; 🅿🛜) This beautiful, old stone house has creaking wooden floors, a secluded patio fortified by high stone walls and old country paraphernalia that continues into the four bedrooms. There are a few too many cobwebs kicking about and the shared bathrooms are a little old-fashioned, but this place is a lovely tranquil spot in Dihovo village. Guests share a communal kitchen.

⭐ **Villa Dihovo**   GUESTHOUSE €€

(📞 070 544 744, 047 293 040; www.villadihovo. com; Dihovo; room rates at your discretion; 🛜) A remarkable guesthouse, Villa Dihovo comprises three traditionally decorated rooms in a historic house that's home to former professional footballer Petar Cvetkovski and family. There's a big, private flowering lawn and cosy living room with an open fireplace for winter. The only fixed prices are for the homemade wine, beer and *rakija;* all else, room price included, is your choice.

The rooms are a bit of a mountain-lodge-style affair, with a new extension above the restaurant area; bedrooms in the extension don't have doors for the en-suite bathrooms, so beware if planning to share.

Petar himself is a mine of information, deeply involved in the Slow Food movement, and can arrange everything from food tastings to hikes to Pelister's lakes, to mountain-bike rides to an evening of wine tasting in his cellar. Ask about cooking classes (€20 per person).

Book as far ahead as possible, because this place is popular. When it's full, Petar is more than happy to help arrange accommodation elsewhere in the village, such as at Villa Ilinden 1903, and to provide meals.

ℹ️ Information

Pelister National Park Information Centre
(📞 047 237 010; www.park-pelister.com; Nizhepole; ⏰ 9am-3pm Tue-Sun) sells a detailed map of the park and its trails (120MKD). The centre is accessible from the Dihovo road shortly after you enter the park.

ℹ️ Getting There & Away

There is one main road into Pelister, which enters from the eastern side coming from Bitola and skirts very close to the village of Dihovo. If you enter the park in your own car, you'll be stopped at a checkpoint and charged 50MKD.

Public transport does not service the park. If you're staying in one of the surrounding villages, your host will be able to organise transfers. A taxi from Bitola or Dihovo costs 360MKD one way.

Bitola Битола

📞 047 / POP 95,390

Buttressing Pelister National Park, elevated Bitola (660m) has a sophistication inherited from its Ottoman days when it was known as the 'City of Consuls'. Macedonians wax lyrical about its elegant buildings, nationally important ruins and cafe culture – yet as far as tourists are concerned, it's still a little off the beaten track.

Crumbling and colourful 18th- and 19th-century townhouses, coupled with an authentic, workaday Čaršija (Old Ottoman Bazaar), make Bitola worth a day trip or an overnight stay if you've made it as far as Pelister's westerly mountains for some hiking.

Join the locals in sipping a coffee and people-watching along pedestrianised Širok Sokak, the main promenade and heart of the city, and explore the wonderful Čaršija (p314). Don't miss visiting the ancient ruins of Heraclea Lyncestis, one of the country's best archaeological sights.

◎ Sights & Activities

⭐ **Heraclea Lyncestis**   ARCHAEOLOGICAL SITE
(adult/child 100/20MKD; ⏰ daylight-8pm) Located 1km south of central Bitola, Heraclea Lyncestis is among North Macedonia's best archaeological sites, though the neglected state of the on-site museum might make you think otherwise. See the Roman baths, portico and amphitheatre, and the striking early Christian basilica and episcopal palace ruins, with beautiful, well-preserved floor mosaics – they're unique in depicting endemic trees and animals. There's a small shady cafe in the grounds and the setting is bucolic.

Founded by Philip II of Macedon, Heraclea became commercially significant before the Romans arrived (168 BC), and its position on the Via Egnatia kept it prosperous. In the 4th century, Heraclea became an episcopal seat, but it was sacked by Goths and then Slavs.

Bitola

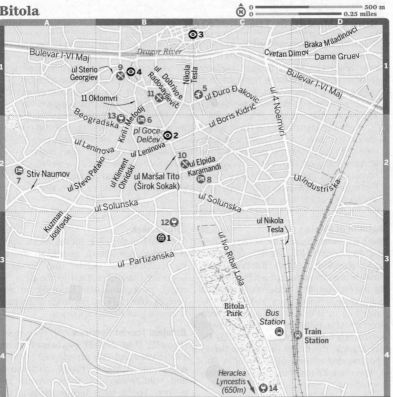

Bitola

◉ Sights
1 Museum of Bitola B3
2 Širok Sokak B2
3 Stara Čaršija C1
4 Yeni Mosque & Clock Tower B1

✪ Activities, Courses & Tours
5 Balojani Tourist Services C1

🛏 Sleeping
6 City House B2
7 Hotel Teatar A2

8 Via Apartments C2

✕ Eating
9 Art Caffè B1
10 El Greko B2
11 Vino Bar Bure B1

🍷 Drinking & Nightlife
12 Jagoda B3
13 Porta Jazz B2
14 Sun Love Happiness C4

Taxis from central Bitola cost 80MKD but they don't hang around at the site – ask the staff at the entrance desk if they wouldn't mind calling one for you when you want to leave. Alternatively, there's a bus stop back on the main road heading north into central Bitola. The city's main bus and train stations are no more than a 15-minute walk

from Heraclea Lyncestis, so if you're passing through town, it's easy enough to visit on foot: turn left onto the main road in front of the stations, walk for 500m with the park on your right and then past it, and take the right-hand signposted turn-off to the ruins. Follow the narrow road past the cemetery (on your right) until you reach the site.

BURIAL MOUND OF THE UNBEATEN

This magnificent **monument** (Park na revolucijata, Car Samoil, Prilep) FREE to Prilep's Partisan soldiers who died in WWII is the 1961 work of one of the former Yugoslavia's most brilliant architects, Bogdan Bogdanović, who specialised in mixing up the historical with the antic and celestial. The eight marble monoliths, each between 3m and 5m tall, depict what is thought to be a traditional circle dance, with feminine bodies and double faces representing a continuity between beginnings and ends. Simultaneously modern and ancient, this is a treat.

The town's high number of Partisans and their activism during WWII gave Prilep the status 'Town of National Heroes' in Yugoslavia, hence Bogdanović's prestigious commission. As you enter the park, you will see stone plaques marking the town's most celebrated Partisans. The marble carving of the monument's figures was done by Prilep's stonemasons, and there was a great emphasis on local workers and stone.

Set in Prilep's Revolution Park, just out of town on the road to Bitola, this is also a wonderful place to have a picnic.

Museum of Bitola   MUSEUM
(Map p313; www.muzejbitola.mk; ul Kliment Ohridski; adult/student 100/20MKD; ⊙8am-4pm Tue-Fri, 10am-4pm Sat-Mon) Bitola's history museum is a little unkempt but has interesting displays on local archaeology, regional architecture, revolutionary history and the area's role in WWI. There's even a reconstruction of a 19th-century Bitola drawing room and a memorial room to Mustafa Kemal Ataturk, the father of modern Turkey, who attended military high school in Bitola. There are English-language translations throughout.

Stara Čaršija   BAZAAR
(Old Ottoman Bazaar; Map p313) Bitola's Stara Čaršija boasted about 3000 clustered artisans' shops in Ottoman times; today, only about 70 different trades are conducted, but it's still an interesting place to wander – particularly as it's got a much more lived-in feel to it than the Čaršija in Skopje. Here, you'll see locals zipping about buying provisions, clothes and so on; one of the most interesting sections of the bazaar is the food market in the eastern corner.

Yeni Mosque
& Clock Tower   HISTORIC SITE
(Map p313; Širok Sokak) Bitola's 16th-century Yeni Mosque and 17th-century stone clock tower sit at the top of Širok Sokak, Bitola's main pedestrianised thoroughfare, before the Dragor River and gateway to the Stara Čaršija (p314). Today the site is a pretty park where locals come to cool off under umbrellas of shady trees. The clock tower still chimes at 6am, noon, 6pm and midnight.

Širok Sokak   STREET
(ul Maršal Tito; Map p313) Bitola's Širok Sokak is the city's best-known, most lively street – its multicoloured facades and European honorary consulates attest to the city's Ottoman-era sophistication. Enjoying the cafes here, as colourful local life promenades past, is an essential Bitola experience.

Balojani Tourist Services   OUTDOORS
(Map p313; ☑047 220 204; www.balojani.com.mk; 1 Vlatko Milenkoski) This experienced operator offers guided hiking, biking, gastronomy and wildlife-watching tours around the country. Foodie tours include visits to traditional markets and cooking lessons with the locals, while conservation expeditions are a chance to join national park rangers and see bears, wolves and (if you're lucky) the endangered Balkan lynx in their natural habitat.

🎭 Festivals & Events

Manaki Brothers Film Festival   FILM
(www.manaki.com.mk) In mid-September the Manaki Brothers Film Festival screens independent foreign films. It honours Yanaki and Milton Manaki, the Balkans' first film-makers, who began using the medium in 1905 and documented the quotidian life of Manastir – as Bitola was then known. The country's National Archive has thousands of films and photographs left by the prolific brothers.

Bit Fest   PERFORMING ARTS
(www.bitfest.mk; ⊙Jun-Aug) Features concerts, literary readings and art exhibits.

🛏 Sleeping & Eating

★ Hotel Teatar
BOUTIQUE HOTEL €
(Map p313; ☑ 047 610 188; Stiv Naumov 35; s/d/tr from €24/40/55; ⓟ ❉ ⓡ) Sensitively designed in the image of a traditional Macedonian (Ottoman) house, Hotel Teatar is without doubt one of the loveliest hotels in the country. Rooms are spacious, simple and stylish, with large comfortable beds. The common areas display ethnographic costumes, and there's a secluded central courtyard with tables for drinks and breakfast.

City House
HOTEL €
(Map p313; ☑ 047 553 060; Vienska 20; d/apt €35/60; ❉ ⓡ) If you're after a plush and modern room in Bitola, you'll find it at this family-run minihotel. It's in an excellent spot just off Širok Sokak and has a friendly atrium-enclosed cafe-bar. There are six rooms in total, including two apartments with balconies, and a complimentary big breakfast; all rooms come with a fridge.

Via Apartments
APARTMENT €
(Map p313; ☑ 075 552 343; www.via.mk; off ul Elpida Karamandi 4; s/d/tr/q €13/24/31/40; ❉ ⓡ) Set back from the road, hidden away down a dingy alley, Via's lovely front garden/patio is a surprising oasis. Inside, the well-designed, modern apartments share a kitchen, laundry and lounge. The location is excellent: just off Širok Sokak.

Art Caffè
CAFE €
(Map p313; ☑ 047 610 139; Širok Sokak 25; pastries from 40MKD; ⊙8am-1am; ⓡ) This modern 'Made in Bitola' brand has three cafes around town, seducing patrons with cakes, croissants, coffee and delicious sweet and savoury local pastries. Everything is baked in-house and it's a lovely spot for breakfast; try the out-of-this-world *kolač*, a sweet flaky pastry layered with curd, raisins, apple, poppy seeds and walnuts. The nicest branch is this one, opposite the clock tower park.

Vino Bar Bure
MEDITERRANEAN €
(Map p313; ☑ 047 227 744; Širok Sokak 37; mains from 90MKD; ⊙8am-midnight; ⓡ) Positioned at the end of Širok Sokak, overlooking the street and the square, this restaurant specialises in Macedonian and Turkish cuisine, and good local wines. It has a modern terrace with a bustling atmosphere and a cosy interior. Order a *pide* – a flatbread with toppings of meat and/or cheese – or a *lahmacun* (Turkish pizza) and watch the world go by.

El Greko
PIZZA €
(Map p313; cnr Širok Sokak & ul Elpida Karamandi; mains 150-350MKD; ⊙9am-1am; ⓡ) This taverna and pizzeria with pavement space on Bitola's main pedestrianised strip has a great beer-hall ambience and a menu geared towards comfort food (there's nothing particularly Greek about it).

🍸 Drinking & Nightlife

★ Porta Jazz
BAR
(Map p313; Kiril i Metodij; ⊙8am-1am, to midnight Sep-May; ⓡ) There's a notably bohemian vibe at this popular place that's packed every night in summer, and when live jazz and blues bands play during the rest of the year (September to May). It's located near the Church of Sveti Dimitrij, one block back from Širok Sokak.

Jagoda
BAR
(Map p313; ☑ 047 203 030; Širok Sokak 154; ⊙7am-midnight; ⓡ) Right at the end of Širok Sokak, this is a great place for coffee, beer and DJ parties – the red-and-white chequered tablecloths, the good music and the airy terrace opposite the little park mean you can spend quite a few hours hanging out here. It's where the local art crowd goes. It serves meze, too.

Sun Love Happiness
BAR
(Map p313; City Park; ⊙10am-1am Jun-Sep) Located by the city stadium in the park, this fun-loving bar occupies a poolside spot inside the swimming-pool complex. To access it you literally have to cross the pool using planks: quite a bizarre experience. It doesn't usually get busy until 10.30pm – locals come here before diving into Positive Summer Club (midnight to 5am), to the right as you enter the complex.

ℹ Information

Bitola Tourist Office has no walk-in office. There is a decent website – http://bitola.info/ – with information about the town.

ℹ Getting There & Away

The **bus** (Map p313; ul Nikola Tesla) and **train stations** (ul Nikola Tesla) are adjacent, 1km south of the centre.

UNDERSTAND NORTH MACEDONIA

North Macedonia Today

North Macedonia has dealt with many crises in recent years, including the plight of migrants crossing the country on their way to northern Europe.

In 2016 Prime Minister Nikola Gruevski – the man behind the 'revamping' of Skopje's centre – stood down as the EU brokered a deal to end months of political crisis; in 2018, Gruevski was sentenced for corruption and money laundering but then escaped to Hungary, where he was granted political asylum. Social Democrat Zoran Zaev formed a ruling coalition with ethnic Albanian groups in 2017.

Greece had blocked North Macedonia from negotiating EU accession since 1991, objecting to its former name 'Macedonia' as it potentially lays claim to the Greek region of Macedonia. After a referendum in September 2018 failed to change the country's constitutional name to North Macedonia, in January 2019 the Macedonian Parliament voted to go ahead with the name change. Soon after, the Greek Parliament also voted to ratify the agreement and in February 2019 North Macedonia – as the country is now officially called – signed the NATO accession agreement.

In the meantime, Turkey has become North Macedonia's best regional ally in recent years – it's revisiting its former Balkan colonies and investing heavily in the region, both financially and culturally.

History

Historical or geographical Macedonia is divided between the Republic of North Macedonia (38%), Greek Macedonia (51%) and Bulgaria's Pirin Macedonia (11%). For its people, their history is a source of great pride but also a heavy burden. The post-Yugoslav experience has seen existential pressure from neighbours constantly challenging the Macedonian identity. North Macedonia's history is too complex for simple answers, but many have strong opinions.

Ancient Macedonians & Romans

The powerful Macedonian dynasty of King Philip II (r 359–336 BC) dominated the Greek city-states. Philip's son, Alexander the Great, spread Macedonian might to India.

After his death (323 BC), the empire dissolved amid infighting. In 168 BC, Rome conquered Macedonia; its position on the Via Egnatia, from Byzantium to the Adriatic, and the Axios (Vardar River) from Thessaloniki up the Vardar Valley, kept cities prosperous.

Christianity reached Macedonia with the Apostle Paul. The Roman Empire's AD 395 division brought Macedonia under Byzantine Constantinople and Greek-influenced Orthodox Christianity.

The Coming of the Slavs & the Macedonian Cars

The 7th-century Slavic migrations intermingled Macedonia's peoples. In 862, two Thessaloniki-born monks, St Cyril and St Methodius, were dispatched to spread orthodoxy and literacy among Moravia's Slavs (in modern-day Czech Republic). Their disciple, St Kliment of Ohrid, helped create the Cyrillic alphabet. With St Naum, he propagated literacy in Ohrid (the first Slavic university).

Byzantium and the Slavs could share a religion, but not political power. Chronic wars unfolded between Constantinople and the expansionist Bulgarian state of Car Simeon (r 893–927) and Car Samoil (r 997–1014). After being defeated in today's Bulgaria, Prespa and Ohrid in Macedonia became their strongholds. Finally, Byzantine Emperor Basil II defeated Samoil at the Battle of Belasica (near today's Strumica, in eastern Macedonia) in 1014, and Byzantium retook Macedonia.

Later, the Serbian Nemanjic dynasty expanded into Macedonia. After Emperor Stefan Dušan (r 1331–55) died, Serbian power waned. The Ottoman Turks soon arrived, ruling until 1913.

Ottoman Rule & the Macedonian Question

The Ottomans introduced Islam and Turkish settlers. Skopje became a trade centre, and mosques, *hammams* (Turkish baths) and castles were built. However, Greeks still wielded considerable power. In 1767, Greece caused the abolition of the 700-year-old Ohrid archbishopric. Greek priests opened schools and built churches, to the resentment of locals. Bulgaria and Serbia also sought Macedonia. The lines were drawn.

In Macedonia, Western European ethnic nationalism collided with the Ottomans' civil organisation by religion (not ethnicity). Europe's powers intervened after the 1877–78 Russo-Turkish War, when the Treaty of San Stefano awarded Macedonia to Bulgaria. Fearing Russia, Western powers reversed this with the Treaty of Berlin, fuelling 40 years of further conflict.

Although Macedonia remained Ottoman, the 'Macedonian Question' persisted. Various Balkan powers sponsored revolutionary groups. In 1893, the Internal Macedonian Revolutionary Organisation (Vnatrešna Makedonska Revolucionerna Organizacija, or VMRO) was formed. VMRO was divided between 'Macedonia for the Macedonians' propagandists and a pro-Bulgarian wing.

In the Ilinden Day Uprising (2 August 1903), Macedonian revolutionaries declared the Balkans' first democratic republic, in Kruševo; it lasted just 10 days before the Turks crushed it. Although leader Goce Delčev had died months earlier, he's considered a Macedonian national hero. The uprising is commemorated at the Ilinden Uprising Monument (p298) in Kruševo.

In 1912 the Balkan League (Greece, Serbia, Bulgaria and Montenegro) fought Turkey (the First Balkan War), with Macedonia a prime battleground. The Turks were expelled, but a dissatisfied Bulgaria turned on its allies in 1913 (the Second Balkan War). Defeated, Bulgaria allied with Germany in WWI, reoccupying Macedonia and prolonging local suffering.

The Yugoslav Experience

When Bulgaria withdrew after WWI, Macedonia was divided between Greece and the new Kingdom of Serbs, Croats and Slovenes (Royalist Yugoslavia). Belgrade banned the Macedonian name and language, and disgruntled VMRO elements helped Croat nationalists assassinate Serbian King Aleksandar in 1934.

During WWII, Josip Broz Tito's Partisans resisted the Bulgarian–German occupation and socialist Yugoslavia was formed in 1945, with Macedonia as a republic. Some ethnic Macedonians joined the communists fighting royalists in the 1946–49 Greek Civil War. The communist defeat forced thousands, including many children (known as the *begalci*, meaning 'refugees'), to flee Greece.

In Yugoslavia, Macedonia became more urbanised and Macedonian grammar was established in 1952. The 1963 earthquake destroyed around 65% of Skopje and the city was rebuilt with Yugoslav and international donations. Macedonia's Orthodox Church was created in 1967 – the 200th anniversary of the Ohrid archbishopric's abolition.

After Independence

In a 1991 referendum, 74% of Macedonians voted to secede, making Macedonia the only Yugoslav republic to do so peacefully. However, the withdrawing Yugoslav army took everything, leaving the country defenceless. Greece's fears of an invasion from the north thus seemed unfounded to everyone but them; nevertheless, Macedonia changed its first flag (with the ancient Macedonian Vergina star) to appease Athens, after it had already accepted a 'provisional' name, the Former Yugoslav Republic of Macedonia (FYROM), in order to join the UN in 1993. When the USA (following six EU countries) recognised 'FYROM' in 1994, Greece defiantly announced an economic embargo.

This crippling embargo coincided with wars in other former Yugoslav states, creating ideal conditions for high-level schemes for smuggling fuel and other goods. The 1990s 'transition' period created a political/business oligarchy amid shady privatisations, deliberate bankrupting of state-owned firms and dubious pyramid schemes.

During the 1999 Kosovo crisis and NATO bombing of Serbia, Macedonia sheltered more than 400,000 Kosovo Albanian refugees. In 2001 Ushtria Člirimtare Kombetare (UČK; National Liberation Army) was created demanding equal rights for Macedonia's large ethnic Albanian minority, which brought the country to the brink of a civil war. The conflict-ending Ohrid Framework Agreement granted minority language and national symbol rights to the Albanians, along with quota-based public-sector hiring.

Macedonians found the conflict a humiliating defeat. Albanians saw it as the first step to a full ethnic federation. Foreign powers have argued that this may well occur, if Macedonia cannot join NATO and the EU.

People

The 2011 census was delayed indefinitely and no new census has been scheduled. The issue that makes a census such a delicate procedure is the proposal to exclude people who have been absent from the country for over a year. A large proportion of the Albanian population has left the country to work abroad and they fear being under-represented in such a census.

In 2004, the population of 2,022,547 was divided thus: Macedonians (64%), Albanians (25%), Turks (4%), Roma (2.7%), Serbs (1.8%) and others (2.5%), including Vlachs – alleged descendants of Roman frontier soldiers.

Religion

Most Macedonians are Orthodox Christians, with some Macedonian-speaking Muslims (the Torbeši and Gorani). Turks are Muslim, as are Albanians and (nominally, at least) the impoverished Roma. Social and ethnic complexities relating to religion have caused concern over Islamic fundamentalism, as seen in protests and violent attacks on Christians.

A 200-strong Jewish community, most of whom live in Skopje, descends from Sephardic Jews who fled Spain after 1492. More than 7200 people – 98% of their ancestors – were deported to Treblinka by Bulgarian occupiers in WWII. The community holds a Holocaust commemoration ceremony every 11 March, and the Holocaust Memorial Center for the Jews of Macedonia (p287) in Skopje is a must-see for anyone interested in this grim part of North Macedonia's modern history.

The Macedonian Orthodox Church isn't recognised by some neighbouring Orthodox countries, but it's active in church-building and restoration work. Although Macedonians don't attend church services in large numbers, they do stop to light candles, kiss icons and pray.

Arts

Macedonian folk instruments include the *gajda* (a single-bag bagpipe) and *zurla* (a double-reed horn), often accompanied by the *tapan* (drum). Other instruments include the *kaval* (flute) and *tambura* (small lute with two pairs of strings).

Traditional dancing includes the *oro* circle dance, the male-only *Teškoto oro* (difficult dance), *Komitsko oro* (symbolising the anti-Ottoman struggle), and the *Tresenica,* performed by women from the mountainous region of Mariovo.

Macedonian musicians have won international acclaim, including pianist Simon Trpčeski, opera singer Boris Trajanov, jazz guitarist Vladimir Četkar and percussionists the Tavitjan Brothers. Especially beloved was Toše Proeski, a charismatic singer admired for both his music and humanitarian work who died tragically in 2007, aged just 26.

Milcho Manchevski is North Macedonia's best-known film director. *Before the Rain* (1994) was nominated for an Academy Award for Best Foreign Language Film and won the Golden Lion at the Venice Film Festival. The *New York Times* included *Before the Rain* in its *Guide to the Best 1000 Films Ever Made.*

Food & Drink

North Macedonia's specialities are part Ottoman, part Central European. The tomato is king and grows abundantly here: the national salad, *šopska salata,* features tomatoes, peppers, onions and cucumbers topped with tangy *sirenje* (white cheese). *Tavče gravče* (oven-cooked white beans in a tomato sauce) and *lukanci* (homemade chorizo-like pork sausages) are divine.

Skara (grilled meat) includes spare ribs, beef *kebapci* (kebabs) and *uviač* (rolled chicken or pork stuffed with yellow cheese). *Skara* in particular is ubiquitous.

For breakfast, try *burek* (cheese, spinach or minced meat in filo pastry) with drinking yoghurt, or *mekici* (fried dough) with homemade jam.

Skopsko Pivo and Zlaten Dab are the two local beers; they're both lagers, but Zlaten Dab has more flavour. The national firewater, *rakija,* is a strong fruit brandy typically made from grapes (recipes vary across the Balkan countries) and most locals have their own homemade stash. Liquors made from cherries and plums are also popular – Macedonians will try to make the most of what they can find locally; cherry trees are everywhere and laden with fruit in summer.

Environment

The Continental and Mediterranean climate zones converge in North Macedonia (25,713 sq km). Although mostly plateau (600m to 900m above sea level), it features more than 50 mountain peaks topping 2000m. The Vardar River starts in the west, passes Skopje and runs into Greece's Aegean Sea. Lakes Ohrid and Prespa are among Europe's oldest tectonic lakes (three million years old); Ohrid is the Balkans' deepest. International borders are largely mountainous, including Shar Mountain, near Kosovo in the northwest; Mt Belasica, in the southeast, bordering Greece; and the Osogovski and Maleševski ranges near Bulgaria. North Macedonia's highest peak, Mt Korab (2764m), borders Albania in the Mavrovo National Park.

Flora & Fauna

North Macedonia's eastern Mediterranean and Euro-Siberian vegetation contains pine-clad slopes. Lower mountains feature beech and oak. Vineyards dominate the central plains. Endemic flora includes the *molika* tree, a subalpine pine unique to Mt Pelister, and the rare *foja* tree on Lake Prespa's Golem Grad island.

North Macedonia's alpine and low Mediterranean valley zones have bears, wild boars, wolves, foxes, chamois and deer. The rare lynx inhabits Shar Mountain and Jasen Nature Reserve. Blackcaps, grouse, white Egyptian vultures, royal eagles and forest owls inhabit woodlands. Lake birds include rare Dalmatian pelicans, herons and cormorants. Storks (and their huge nests) are prominent. North Macedonia's national dog, the *šar planinec*, is a 60cm-tall sheepdog that protects sheep from predators.

Lakes Ohrid, Prespa and Dojran are separate fauna zones, due to territorial and temporal isolation. With more than 200 endemic species, Ohrid is a living fossil-age museum – its endemic trout predates the last ice age. Ohrid also has whitefish, gudgeon and roach, plus a 30-million-year-old snail genus, and the mysterious Ohrid eel, which arrives from the Sargasso Sea to live for 10 years before returning to breed and die.

National Parks

Pelister (near Bitola) and Galičica (between Lakes Ohrid and Prespa) National Parks are in a tri-border protected area involving Albania and Greece. Both are laced with walking trails and Galičica is home to a number of mountain villages. Mavrovo National Park (in North Macedonia's west, between Debar and Tetovo) offers great hiking in summer and skiing in winter. All parks are accessible by road.

Environmental Issues

Lake Ohrid's endemic trout *(Salmo letnica)* is an endangered species and protected from fishing. Locals take the warning quite seriously these days and farm trout to put on their menus instead.

More broadly, the lake's growing popularity as a stop-off on the tourist circuit has become cause for concern among conservation groups. Plans were drawn up to create a marina, artificial Mediterranean-style beaches and new apartments by draining an important marshland that acts as a natural filter to the lake. A local initiative called Ohrid SOS was set up in 2015 to help challenge the proposals, and these plans have been shelved. The struggle to find a balance between commercial desires and conservation imperatives continues.

SURVIVAL GUIDE

❶ Directory A–Z

ACCESSIBLE TRAVEL

Historic sites and old quarters aren't wheelchair-friendly, and generally neither are buses and trains. Expensive hotels may provide wheelchair ramps and have lifts.

Download Lonely Planet's free Accessible Travel guides from http://lptravel.to/Accessible Travel.

ACCOMMODATION

The accommodation scene in North Macedonia is slowly improving and though some hotels can be bad value for money, there are many charming places to stay. Village guesthouses are best in the mountains, and there are lovely small hotels, as well as the occasional monastery room. Be aware that 'apartment' usually just means a larger room rather than an actual apartment.

ACTIVITIES
Hiking

Hiking trails are scribbled across the landscape from north to south and east to west (particularly in Galičica, Pelister and Mavrovo National Parks), but invariably the trail markers are not well maintained. Proceed with caution at all times.

Hiking guides cost from between €50 and €80 a day, or consider investing in a GPS if you want to do any serious walking in the country. **Balkan Hiking Adventures** (www.balkanhikingadventure.com) is a network of 37 cross-border trails between North Macedonia, Kosovo and Albania, and an excellent online resource with downloadable maps for a number of trails around Lake Ohrid and in the Baba Mountains (Pelister National Park). A good organisation for tailored tours with professional guides is **Hiking The Balkans** (www.hikingthebalkans.com).

The new 495km **High Scardus Trail** crosses the border triangle between Albania, Kosovo and North Macedonia. It takes around 20 days to hike.

North Macedonia is chronically affected by summer wildfires. Hikers should check conditions in advance – if you get stuck in the wrong patch of forest, it could not only be dangerous, it could also be illegal if firefighters or park wardens have closed the area. Information on wildfires is communicated on the news service.

Other Activities

Mountain biking This activity is usually organised only as multiday trips. Some of the walking trails in Pelister National Park are used by mountain bikers; Petar at Villa Dihovo (p312) can arrange rides there. **Ride MK** (☑ 075 341 131; www.ride.mk; Angel Dinev 3b, Skopje; ☺8am-4pm Mon-Fri) is a professional outfit that can organise tours anywhere in the country.

Paragliding Daredevils unfurl their parachutes over Mt Galičica; Free Pass Ohrid (p305) can organise this activity.

Horse riding Short and long rides run by Horse Club Bistra Galičnik (p299) trot through valleys in Mavrovo National Park and include cheese tasting. Multiday treks are also organised June to October.

Kayaking Kayaks can be rented without pre-booking at Canyon Matka (p296), but you don't get long on the water and it's very tame in summer – for beginners only.

Scuba diving Lake Ohrid's Diving Center Amfora (p302) can organise basic dives to check out Neolithic settlement remains at the Bay of Bones.

Skiing North Macedonia's premier ski resort is Zare Lazarevski (p299) in Mavrovo, though there are also some ski runs in Pelister. It is now possible to ski from North Macedonia into Kosovo on Shar Mountain with specialised skiing guides. **Shar Outdoors** (www.sharout doors.com) organises cross-border skiing tours so you can glide between North Macedonia, Kosovo and Albania.

INTERNET ACCESS

Wi-fi is widely available in restaurants, cafes, hotels and hostels – sometimes you just have to ask for the password.

LGBTIQ+ TRAVELLERS

Macedonians are religious conservatives and the country's LGBT scene is very small. The Rainbow Europe Index continues to rank the country's gay rights among the worst in the region.

MONEY

North Macedonia's national currency is the denar (MKD), but many tourist-related prices (such as transport and hotel costs) are quoted in euros – you may even find that the business owner doesn't immediately know the denar price if you ask for it. Hence Lonely Planet lists prices as they are quoted rather than in denars only.

Carrying some euros into North Macedonia can be handy for larger outgoings such as hotel bills, but note that it usually works out better if you pay for smaller costs in denars. Motorway tolls, for example, are about 30% more expensive if you pay in euros.

Taxi drivers hate it when you pay with a 1000-denar note, and may make you go into a shop to get change.

Macedonian exchange offices (*menuvačnici*) work commission-free. ATMs are widespread. Credit cards can be used in larger cities (especially in restaurants), but don't rely on them outside Skopje.

OPENING HOURS

Banks 7am to 5pm Monday to Friday

Cafes 8am to midnight

Museums Many close on Mondays

Shops 9am to 6pm

PUBLIC HOLIDAYS

New Year's Day 1 January

Orthodox Christmas 7 January

Orthodox Easter Week March/April/May

Labour Day 1 May

Sts Cyril and Methodius Day 24 May

Ilinden Day 2 August

Independence Day 8 September

Revolution Day 11 October

St Clement of Ohrid Day 8 December

TELEPHONE

Drop the initial zero in city codes and mobile prefixes (07) when calling from abroad. Within North Macedonia, intercity calls require the city code; this is dropped for within-city calls.

TOURIST INFORMATION

Travel agencies and hotels are the best sources of tourist information in North Macedonia, as most of the official tourist offices have been shut down. You won't find any in Ohrid or Bitola, for example; those in Skopje don't keep to their opening hours. The country's official website is **Macedonia Timeless** (www.macedonia-timeless.com).

VISAS

Citizens of former Yugoslav republics, Australia, Canada, the EU, Iceland, Israel, New Zealand, Norway, Switzerland, Turkey and the USA, and many other countries, can stay for three months, visa-free. Check the Ministry of Foreign Affairs website (www.mfa.gov.mk) if unsure.

ⓘ Getting There & Away

Skopje and Ohrid are well connected to other Balkan tourist hubs as well as some international destinations further afield. Air connections have increased thanks to the growing number of budget airlines flying here. Buses are generally more frequent and cover a broader range of destinations than trains (they're also just as fast).

ENTERING THE COUNTRY

Some travellers have reported being denied entry to Serbia from North Macedonia if they have a stamp from Kosovo in their passport.

AIR

Budget airlines have improved Skopje's modest number of air connections, and it's now connected pretty well to major European cities. Wizz Air still flies Skopje–London, but has stopped its Ohrid–London flights, and the Skopje–Barcelona connection was stopped in autumn 2018.

BORDER CROSSINGS

Albania North Macedonia and Albania have four border crossings; the busiest are Kafasan–Qafa e Thanës, 12km southwest of Struga, and Sveti Naum–Tushëmishti, 29km south of Ohrid. Blato, 5km northwest of Debar, and Stenje, on Lake Prespa's southwestern shore, are the least used.

Bulgaria For Bulgaria, Deve Bair (90km from Skopje, after Kriva Palanka) accesses Sofia. The Delčevo crossing (110km from Skopje) leads to Blagoevgrad, while the southeastern Novo Selo crossing, 160km from Skopje beyond Strumica, reaches Petrich.

Kosovo Blace, 20 minutes north from Skopje, reaches Pristina in Kosovo, while Tetovo's Jazince crossing is closer to Prizren.

Serbia Tabanovce is the major road/rail crossing for Belgrade.

See the Airports of Macedonia website (www.airports.com.mk) for information about flying in and out of North Macedonia, including timetables, carriers and weather conditions.

LAND
Bus

International routes generally arrive at and depart from Skopje or Ohrid. Pristina, Tirana, Sofia, Belgrade and Thessaloniki are the most common connections.

From Skopje it's also possible to get to Ljubljana, İstanbul and Zagreb; some Ohrid buses travel to various destinations in Montenegro.

Car & Motorcycle

Bringing your own vehicle into North Macedonia is hassle free, though you do need a Green Card (proof of third-party insurance, issued by your insurer). You also need to bring the vehicle registration/ownership documents.

Note that petrol stations are not always located within spitting distance of the border crossings, but the country isn't large and you're unlikely to go more than 25km or so without finding a pump.

Train

→ Macedonian Railway runs antiquated trains. They are often the cheapest mode of transport and the most iconic way to travel, passing through wild terrain. However, the network is limited and trains are less frequent than buses.

→ Trains connect Skopje to Pristina, Belgrade and Thessaloniki (though the last is via a train-and-bus combo because of the fraught relationship with Greece).

→ Timetables and fares are viewable online (http://mktransport.mk/en).

❶ Getting Around

BICYCLE

→ Helmets are not compulsory in North Macedonia but always advisable.

→ Bicycle lanes are only present in big towns such as Skopje and Bitola.

→ It is illegal to cycle on motorways, though locals may tell you otherwise.

→ The website www.bicycle.mk is a good source of information for cycling in North Macedonia.

BUS

→ Skopje serves most domestic destinations.

→ Larger buses are new and air-conditioned; kombis (minibuses) are usually not.

→ During summer, pre-book for Ohrid.

→ Sunday is often the busiest day for intercity bus travel among locals, so best book ahead.

CAR & MOTORCYCLE

There are occasional police checkpoints; make sure you have the correct documentation. Call 196 for roadside assistance.

Car Hire

→ Skopje's rental agencies include international biggies and local companies. Ohrid has many options, other cities have fewer.

→ Economy cars (small) average €25 a day, including basic insurance, but you can negotiate down to €20 to €21 a day if you're renting for one to two weeks.

→ Bring your passport, driver's licence and credit card.

Road Rules

→ Drive on the right.

→ Speed limits are 120km/h on motorways, 80km/h for open road and 50km/h to 60km/h in towns. Speeding fines start from 1500MKD.

→ Seatbelt and headlight use is compulsory (yes – headlights even during the day).

→ Drivers will be fined if caught using mobile phones while driving.

→ Police also fine for drink driving (blood alcohol limit 0.05%). Fines are payable immediately.

TRAIN

Domestic trains are reliable but slow. From Skopje, one train line runs to Negotino and another to Bitola via Veles and Prilep. A smaller line runs Skopje–Kičevo. Ohrid does not have a train station.

Serbia Србија

POP 7.11 MILLION

Best Places to Eat

➡ Iris New Balkan Cuisine (p337)

➡ Šaran (p338)

➡ Bela Reka (p338)

➡ Ambar (p338)

➡ Pasent (p351)

Best Places to Stay

➡ Mama Shelter (p334)

➡ Savamala Bed & Breakfast (p333)

➡ Yugodom (p332)

➡ Vrdnička Kula (p351)

Why Go?

Diverse, welcoming and a hell of a lot of fun – everything you never heard about Serbia is true. Best of all, this landlocked country in the heart of the Balkans is still delightfully off the tourist trail. While the feisty Serbian spirit is embodied in Belgrade's world-class nightlife and Novi Sad's epic EXIT Festival, look beyond these historic metropolises and you'll discover a crucible of cultures and unsullied outdoors ripe for exploration.

The art nouveau town of Subotica revels in its Austro-Hungarian heritage, bohemian Niš echoes to the clip-clop of Roma horse carts, and minaret-studded Novi Pazar nudges the most sacred of Serbian Orthodox monasteries. Established wine regions and thermal spas cradled in rolling hills date back to Roman times. On the slopes of Kopaonik, Zlatibor and Stara Planina, ancient traditions coexist with après-ski bling, while super-scenic Tara and Đerdap National Parks brim with hiking, biking, rafting and kayaking opportunities.

When to Go
Belgrade

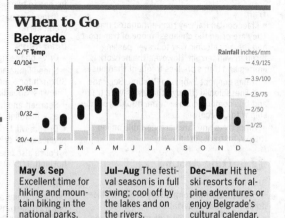

May & Sep Excellent time for hiking and mountain biking in the national parks.

Jul–Aug The festival season is in full swing; cool off by the lakes and on the rivers.

Dec–Mar Hit the ski resorts for alpine adventures or enjoy Belgrade's cultural calendar.

Entering the Country

Getting to Serbia is a cinch; it's connected to Europe by main roads, there are no seas to cross and its two airports welcome flights from across the continent and the world. All of Europe is accessible from Belgrade: Budapest, Zagreb, Sofia and Thessaloniki are a train ride away, and regular buses serve destinations including Vienna, Sarajevo and Podgorica.

ITINERARIES

One Week
Revel in three days of cultural and culinary exploration in Belgrade (p325), allowing for at least one night of hitting the capital's legendary nightspots. Carry on north to laid-back Novi Sad (p345) and the vineyards and monasteries of Fruška Gora National Park (p350) and Sremski Karlovci (p350). Complete the Vojvodina tour with a day trip to Subotica (p352) to admire its art nouveau architecture.

Two Weeks
Follow the above itinerary, then head to southern Serbia. Start in the west with hiking and rafting in Tara National Park (p354) en route to Turkish-flavoured Novi Pazar (p358). Hop over to bohemian Niš (p363) in the east and return to Belgrade after cycling or a boat trip through Đjerdap National Park (p367).

Essential Food & Drink

Ajvar Spread made from roasted peppers, aubergines and garlic.

Burek Flaky meat, cheese or vegetable pie eaten with yoghurt.

Ćevapi These skinless sausages are the national fast food.

Gomboce Potato-dough dumplings, usually stuffed with plums.

Kajmak Dairy delight akin to a salty clotted cream.

Karađorđeva šnicla Similar to chicken Kiev, but with veal or pork and lashings of kajmak and tartar.

Pljeskavica Spicy hamburger, usually served with onions.

Rakija Strong distilled spirit made from fruit – the most common variety is šljivovica, made from plums.

Ražnjići Pork or veal shish kebabs.

Riblja čorba Fish soup, most commonly from carp, spiced with paprika.

Svadbarski kupus Sauerkraut and hunks of smoked pork slow-cooked in giant clay pots.

Urnebes Creamy, spicy peppers-and-cheese spread.

AT A GLANCE

Area 77,474 sq km

Capital Belgrade

Country code 381

Currency Dinar (RSD)

Emergency Ambulance 194, fire 193, police 192

Language Serbian

Population 7.11 million

Time East European Time (GMT/UTC plus one/two hours in winter/summer)

Visas None for citizens of the EU, UK, Australia, New Zealand, Canada and the USA

SERBIA

Sleeping Price Ranges

The following price categories are based on the cost of a high-season double room including breakfast. Although accommodation prices are often quoted in euro, you must pay in dinar. City tax (130RSD to 155RSD per person per night) is levied on top of lodging bills.

€ less than 3000RSD

€€ 3000RSD to 8000RSD

€€€ more than 8000RSD

Eating Price Ranges

The following price categories are based on the cost of a main course.

€ less than 600RSD

€€ 600–1000RSD

€€€ more than 1000RSD

Serbia Highlights

1 **Belgrade** (p325) Revelling in the melange of faded Yugonostalgia and cutting-edge Balkan cool.

2 **Tara National Park** (p354) Hiking or rafting around the most scenic slice of Serbia.

3 **EXIT Festival** (p347) Joining the revellers in July.

4 **Đerdap National Park** (p361) Cycling or cruising through the Danube's mighty Iron Gates gorge.

5 **Studenica Monastery** (p358) Admiring ancient frescoes in a white-marble 12th-century monastery.

6 **Uvac Canyon** (p360) Looking for griffon vultures as

you glide along the zigzagging Uvac River.

7 **Subotica** (p352) Gawking at the art nouveau architecture of a leafy Vojvodinian town.

8 **Rajac Wine Cellars** (p362) Tasting the native drops in Negotin's 19th-century wine villages.

BELGRADE БЕОГРАД

📱 011 / POP 1.6 MILLION

Outspoken, adventurous, proud and audacious: Belgrade ('White City') is by no means a 'pretty' capital, but its gritty exuberance makes it one of Europe's most happening cities. While it hurtles towards a brighter future, its chaotic past unfolds before your eyes: socialist blocks are squeezed between art nouveau masterpieces, and remnants of the Habsburg legacy contrast with Ottoman relics and socialist modernist monoliths. This is where the Sava and Danube Rivers kiss, an old-world culture that at once evokes time-capsuled communist-era Yugoslavia and new-world, EU-contending cradle of cool.

Grandiose coffee houses and smoky dives pepper Knez Mihailova, a lively pedestrian boulevard flanked by historical buildings all the way to the ancient Belgrade Fortress. The riverside Savamala quarter has gone from ruin to resurrection, and is the city's creative headquarters (for now). Deeper in Belgrade's bowels are museums guarding the cultural, religious and military heritage of the country.

History

Belgrade has been destroyed and rebuilt countless times in its 2300-year history. Celts first settled on the hill at the confluence of the Sava River and the Danube, the Romans came in the 1st century BC, and havoc was wreaked by Goths and Huns until the area was colonised by Slavic tribes in the 6th century.

In 1403, Hungary gave Belgrade to Despot Stefan Lazarević, making it the Serbian capital. The 1400s saw waves of Turkish attacks; it was conquered in 1521 and the city's population was shipped to İstanbul. In 1807 Belgrade was briefly liberated from the Turks, who finally relinquished control in 1867.

In 1914 the Austro-Hungarian Empire captured Belgrade; it was soon driven out, only to return in 1915, staying for three years. In 1918 Belgrade became the capital of Yugoslavia. The city was under German occupation and bombed by both Nazis and Allies during WWII.

In the 1990s Belgrade became the site of strong local resistance against Serbian president Slobodan Milošević, with thousands of Belgradians taking part in large-scale peaceful protests – often broken up by force – demanding the end of his rule. Milošević stayed on, and in 1999 NATO forces bombed Belgrade for three months after the president's refusal to end the repression of Albanians in Kosovo; the campaign killed dozens of Serbian civilians and destroyed not only military targets but also a hospital, residential buildings and, for still inexplicable reasons, the Chinese Embassy. In Belgrade's centre, the bombed building that housed the Yugoslavian Ministry of Defence has been left in ruins as a grim reminder of the city's darkest days.

◉ Sights

★ **Belgrade Fortress**   FORTRESS
(Beogradska tvrđava; Map p334; www.beogradskat vrdjava.co.rs; ⏱24hr) **FREE** Some 115 battles have been fought over imposing, impressive Belgrade Fortress (aka Kalemegdan); the citadel was destroyed more than 40 times throughout the centuries. Fortifications began in Celtic times, and the Romans extended it onto the flood plains during the settlement of 'Singidunum', Belgrade's Roman name. Much of what stands today is the product of 18th-century Austro-Hungarian and Turkish reconstructions. The fort's bloody history, discernible despite today's jolly cafes and funfairs, only makes the fortress all the more fascinating.

Audio guides in six languages with a map (300RSD plus ID as deposit) are available from the souvenir shop within the Inner Stambol Gate, which is also where you must purchase tickets for the Clock Tower, Roman Well and Big Gunpowder Magazine.

★ **Museum of Yugoslavia**   MUSEUM
(Map p328; www.muzej-jugoslavije.org; Botićeva 6; 400RSD, incl entry to Marshal Tito's Mausoleum, 4-6pm 1st Thu of month free; ⏱10am-6pm Tue-Sun) This must-visit museum houses an invaluable collection of more than 200,000 artefacts representing the fascinating, tumultuous history of Yugoslavia. Photographs, artworks, historical documents, films, weapons, priceless treasure: it's all here. It can be a lot to take in; English-speaking guides are available if booked in advance via email, or you can join a free tour on weekends (11am in English, Serbian at noon). **Marshal Tito's Mausoleum** (Kuća Cveća, House of Flowers; 400RSD, includes entry to Museum of Yugoslavia; ⏱10am-6pm Tue-Sun) is also on the museum grounds; admission is included in the ticket price.

The museum's main building, known as the May 25 Museum, has undergone extensive renovations, and should have reopened the the time you read this. Take trolleybus 40 or 41 at the south end of Parliament on Kneza Miloša; ask the driver to let you out at Kuća Cveća.

SERBIA BELGRADE

★ **Mt Avala**   TOWER

(Mt Avala; tower 300RSD; ⊙ tower 9am-8pm Mar-Sep, to 5pm Oct-Feb) Looming over Belgrade and topped with the tallest tower in the Balkans (204.5m), Mt Avala is a city landmark that makes for a pleasant break from the capital's bustling streets. The **broadcasting tower**, originally completed in 1965 but levelled by NATO bombs in 1999, was rebuilt in 2010 and now offers picture-perfect panoramas over Belgrade and beyond from viewing platforms and a cafe. Nearby, the **Monument to the Unknown Hero** by Ivan Meštrović honours Serbian victims of WWI.

Mt Avala is 16km from the city centre; on weekends in summer, bus 400 runs to the top of Avala from the **Voždovac** (Joakima Rakovca) stop.

★ **Museum of Contemporary Art**   MUSEUM

(Map p328; www.msub.org.rs; Ušće 10; 300RSD, free Wed; ⊙ 10am-6pm Mon, Wed & Fri-Sun, 10am-10pm Thu) One of Belgrade's top cultural sights, this recently renovated museum is a treasure trove of 20th-century art from the ex-Yugoslav cultural space. The 1960s concrete-and-glass modernist building, surrounded by a sculpture park, has great views towards the Belgrade Fortress across the Sava River.

Conceptual art features prominently, including a 1970s video called *Freeing the Memory* from the region's most famous artist (and Belgrade native), Marina Abramović. One section is dedicated to the 1920s Yugoslav avant-garde magazine *Zenit* and the Zenitism art movement associated with it.

★ **National Museum**   MUSEUM

(Narodni Muzej; Map p334; www.narodnimuzej. rs; Trg Republike 1a; adult/child 300/150RSD, Sun free; ⊙ 10am-6pm Tue, Wed, Fri & Sun, Thu & Sat noon-8pm) Lack of funding for renovations kept Serbia's National Museum mostly shuttered for 15 years, but its much ballyhooed 2018 reopening has been a great source of national pride – it awoke from the dead on Vidovdan (28 June), the country's national day – and for good reason. Built in 1903 and reconstructed multiple times over the years, the museum's latest €12 million makeover frames some 5000 sq metres of exhibition space over three floors.

Highlights include works by Croatian Ivan Meštrović, the most celebrated sculptor of the Kingdom of Yugoslavia; archaeological treasures from Roman-era Serbia; and extensive galleries dedicated to both 18th- and 19th-century Serbian art and 20th-century Yugoslavian art. Don't miss the museum's most haunting corner, where Stevan Aleksić's *The Burning of the Remains of St Sava* (1912) sits sidesaddle to Đorđe Krstić's *The Fall of Stalać* (1903), two hyper-realistic and menacing oils on canvas.

★ **Nikola Tesla Museum**   MUSEUM

(Map p328; www.nikolateslamuseum.org; Krunska 51; admission incl guided tour in English 500RSD; ⊙ 10am-8pm Tue-Sun) Meet the man on the 100RSD note at one of Belgrade's best museums, where you can release your inner nerd with some wondrously sci-fi-ish interactive elements. Tesla's ashes are kept here in a glowing, golden orb: debate has been raging for years between the museum (and its secular supporters) and the Church as to whether the remains should be moved to Sveti Sava Temple.

Zepter Museum   GALLERY

(Map p334; ☑ 011 328 3339; www.zeptermuseum. rs; Knez Mihailova 42; 200RSD; ⊙ 10am-8pm Tue, Wed, Fri & Sun, noon-10pm Thu & Sat) This impressive collection of works by contemporary Serbian artists became Serbia's first private museum in 2010, but remains somewhat hidden even though it's housed in a magnificent 1920s building in the heart of pedestrianised Knez Mihailova. The eclectic interior is a fitting backdrop to the range of styles on display. The permanent collection is a great overview of the main trends in Serbian art from the second half of the 20th century. The museum also hosts temporary exhibitions and events.

Sveti Sava Temple   CHURCH

(Map p328; www.hramsvetogsave.com; Krušedolska 2a; ⊙ 7am-7pm) Sveti Sava is the Balkans' biggest (and the world's second biggest) Orthodox church, a fact made entirely obvious when looking at the city skyline from a distance or standing under its dome. The church is built on the site where the Turks apparently burnt relics of St Sava. Work on the church interior (frequently interrupted by wars) continues today as the cupola is being adorned with a 1248-sq-metre mosaic, one of the world's largest on a curved surface.

Work is expected to continue through 2020 – until then, visit the astonishing gold-ceilinged crypt and its stunning ornate chandeliers, Murano glass mosaics and vibrant frescoes.

BELGRADE'S HISTORIC 'HOODS

Skadarska or 'Skadarlija' is Belgrade's Montmartre. This cobblestoned strip east of Trg Republike was the bohemian heartland at the turn of the 20th century; local artistes and dapper types still gather in its legion of cute restaurants and cafes.

Savamala, a once cool, now clinging-to-life destination *du jour*, spreads west of the old town along the Sava River. Constructed in the 1830s for Belgrade's smart set, it now boasts cultural centres, ramshackle architecture, nightspots galore and a buzzing vibe.

Dorćol, an Ottoman-era multicultural marketplace, stretches northeast from the old town to the Danube. Today it's a leafy, hip neighbourhood dotted with sidewalk cafes, boutiques and cocktail bars.

Zemun, 6km northwest of central Belgrade, was the most southerly point of the Austro-Hungarian Empire when the Turks ruled Belgrade. These days it's known for its fish restaurants and quaint, nonurban ambience.

Royal Compound   PALACE

(Map p328; ☑011 263 5622; www.royalfamily. org; Bul Kneza Aleksandra Karađorđevića, Dedinje; 650RSD; ⊙10am Wed, 10am & 1pm Sat & Sun Apr-Oct) Commissioned between the two world wars by soon-to-be-assassinated King Alexander I of Yugoslavia, the Royal and White Palaces in Belgrade's exclusive Dedinje neighbourhood were residences of King Peter II and used by the communist regime after WWII. Today they are home to the descendants of the Karađorđević dynasty and can be visited only by guided tour. The two-hour tour (book through the Tourist Organisation of Belgrade; www. tob.rs) leaves from Nikola Pašić Square Wednesday and weekends from April through to October.

Covered in white marble, the Royal Palace was built in 1929 in the Serbian-Byzantine style. Its most impressive rooms are the Entrance Hall, the baroque Blue Drawing Room and the Renaissance-style Dining Room and Gold Drawing Room. The classicist White Palace has several rooms furnished in the style of Louis XV and Louis XVI. The palaces house a large art collection from the Karađorđević family.

Sveti Marko Church   CHURCH

(Map p334; www.crkvasvetogmarka.rs; Tašmajdan Park; ⊙hours vary) This huge five-domed church, based on the design of Kosovo's Gračanica Monastery, houses priceless Serbian icons and the tomb of Emperor Dušan 'The Mighty' (1308–55). Behind it is a tiny **Russian Church** (Church of the Holy Trinity; Map p334; Tašmajdan Park) erected by refugees who fled the October Revolution.

Orthodox Cathedral   CHURCH

(Saborna crkva; Map p334; www.saborna-crkva. com; Kneza Sime Markovića 3; ⊙7am-8pm) Dedicated to Archangel Michael, this cathedral was constructed between 1837 and 1841 on the site of an earlier 18th-century church; it's opposite the **Museum of the Serbian Orthodox Church** (Map p334; Kralja Petra 5; 200RSD; ⊙9am-4pm Mon-Fri). Built mainly in classicist style, it has a baroque tower and an impressive Romanticist iconostasis. Inside the crypt are the tombs of Prince Miloš and his son Prince Mihailo, while great 19th-century Serbian scholars Vuk Stefanović Karadžić and Dositej Obradović are buried in the church's graveyard.

Bajrakli Mosque   MOSQUE

(Map p334; Gospodar Jevremova 11; ⊙24hr) The last remaining – and functioning – mosque *(džamija)* in Belgrade was built around 1575. It's small and fascinating, and you're on your own here; leave your shoes just inside to the right and dress modestly.

Residence of Princess Ljubica   PALACE

(Map p334; www.mgb.org.rs; Kneza Sime Markovića 8; 200RSD; ⊙10am-5pm Tue-Thu & Sat, to 6pm Fri, 10am-2pm Sun) This preserved Oriental-style residence was built between 1829 and 1831 for the wife of Prince Miloš and houses a permanent collection of 19th-century Belgrade interiors on the 1st and 2nd floors, while the basement hosts events and temporary exhibitions.

Topčider Park   PARK

(Map p328; Bulevar Vojvode Mišića; ⊙24hr) The vast Topčider (named after the Turkish word for cannons, as this is where the Turks cast their cannons for the 1521 attack on Belgrade) has been a favourite picnic area for

SERBIA BELGRADE

Greater Belgrade

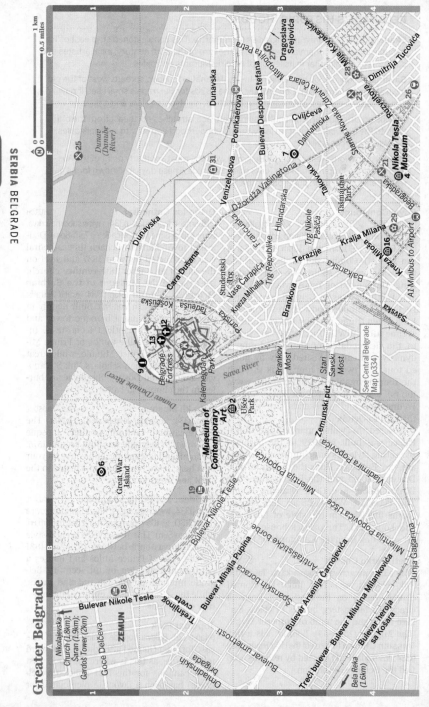

1 km
0.5 miles

N

Dunav (Danube River)

Dunav (Danube River)

Sava River

Great War Island

ZEMUN

Belgrade Fortress

Kalemegdan Park

Museum of Contemporary Art

Ušće Park

Nikolajevska Church (1.8km);
Šaran (1.9km);
Gardoš Tower (2km)

Nikola Tesla Museum

See Central Belgrade Map (p334)

A1 Minibus to Airport

Bela Reka (1.6km)

Bulevar Nikole Tesle

Bulevar Nikole Tesle

Bulevar Mihaila Pupina

Bulevar Arsenija Čarnojevića

Bulevar Milutina Milankovića

Bulevar heroja sa Košara

Treći bulevar

Bulevar umetnosti

Milentija Popovića Ušće

Milentija Popovića

Vladimira Popovića

Antifašističke borbe

Španskih boraca

Zemunski put

Jurija Gagarina

Goce Delčeva

Trešnjino cveta

Omladinskih brigada

Stari Savski Most

Brankov Most

Brankova

Kneza Miloša

Kralja Milana

Terazije

Savska

Balkanska

Takovska

Beogradska

Tasmajdan Park

Trg Nikole Pašića

Hilandarska

Trg Republike

Kneza Mihaila

Vase Čarapića

Studentski Trg

Francuska

Džordža Vašingtona

Cara Dušana

Tadeuša Košćuška

Venizelosova

Dunavska

Poenkaerova

Bulevar Despota Stefana

Mitropolita Petra

Dalmatinska

Cvijićeva

Starine Novaka Zdravka Čelara

Ruzveltova

Dragoslava Srejovića

Nilje Kovačevića

Dimitrija Tucovića

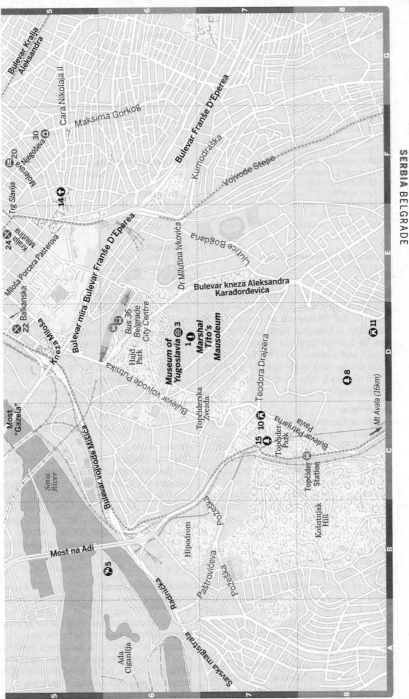

Greater Belgrade

Belgraders since the 19th century, when its gigantic sycamore tree was planted. It's home to the **Residence of Prince Miloš** (Map p328; ⊙10am-8pm Tue-Sun Apr-Sep, 11am-4pm Tue-Sun Oct-Mar), the small Topčider Church and a restaurant. The park is south of the centre, next to the upmarket Dedinje neighbourhood; take tram 3 from the former main railway station.

Jevremovac
Botanical Gardens GARDENS
(Botanička bašta Jevremovac; Map p328; https://jevremovac.bio.bg.ac.rs; Takovska 43; 250RSD; ⊙9am-7pm) Belgrade's beautiful botanic gardens are a peaceful oasis in the hectic city; it's an exceedingly pleasant place to picnic, stroll or just loiter under any of the shady trees. Be sure to check out the Victorian-style greenhouse and the tranquil Japanese garden.

Ada Ciganlija BEACH
(Map p328; www.adaciganlija.rs; parking 250RSD; ⊙24hr) **FREE** In summertime, join the hordes of sea-starved locals (up to 250,000 a day) for sun and fun at this artificial island on the Sava. Cool down with a swim, kayak or windsurf after a leap from the 55m bungee tower. Take bus 52 or 53 from Zeleni Venac.

Great War Island ISLAND
(Veliko ratno ostrvo; Map p328; ⊙24hr) **FREE** Despite the name, this island at the confluence of the Sava and Danube Rivers is a peace-

ful retreat from bustling Belgrade. Once a strategic defence point in various battles for the city, it's been left to run gloriously wild, offering a haven to almost 200 bird species (and a handful of locals who've set up *vikendice* – holiday shacks – in its overgrown interior). Lido Beach at its northern tip is a popular swimming spot.

During summer, a temporary bridge is set up between Zemun and the island, though getting here by kayak is a lot more fun; Belgrade Adventure (p331) offers tours.

Gardoš Tower TOWER
(Tower of Sibinjanin Janko; www.kulanagardosu.com; Gardoš fortress; 200RSD; ⊙10am-7pm) This splendid brick tower (1896) has been renovated to house a free gallery, which hosts regular exhibitions. The views from the top, especially at sunset, are breathtaking. Somewhat confusingly, it's also known as the Millennium Tower. From Zemun's buzzy Sinđelićeva, the tower is a five-minute walk up the cobbled street of Grobljanska.

Nikolajevska Church CHURCH
(Hram Svetog Oca Nikolaja; Njegoševa 43, Zemun; ⊙hours vary) Goggle at the astounding baroque iconostasis at this church in the Zemun neighbourhood, believed to be the oldest in Belgrade. It's thought to have been built in 1570, but its current facade dates to the 1750s. Its ruined interior, full of faded paintings and murals, is one of the spookiest you'll see.

Museum of Illusions
MUSEUM

(Map p334; www.muzejiluzija.rs; Nušićeva 11; adult/child 600/400RSD; ⊚9am-10pm) This 2018 newcomer is a delight for the kiddos. Spread over two floors of hands-on, interactive illusions – explained in English, German and Spanish in addition to Serbian – it will confuse, thrill and entertain visitors. Great photo ops (the Beuchet Chair, which evokes those Bolivian salt-flat photos you always see on Instagram; the Upside Down room etc) keep the laughs going.

Yugoslavian Ministry of Defence
HISTORIC BUILDING

(Map p328; www.mod.gov.rs; Kneza Miloša 33) The most dramatic ruin from NATO's 1999 bombing of Yugoslavia is this masterpiece of postwar architecture that once held the Ministry of Defence of Yugoslavia. The bombed-out site lies mostly untouched after three direct hits (two in April and a third nine days later) and is considered a make-shift monument (the Cyrillic banner reads, 'Serbian Ministry of Defence and Army'). There are plans for a Nemanjić dynasty museum here, but for now, it's a grim reminder of the Yugoslav Wars.

🖝 Tours & Activities

★ Yugotour
DRIVING

(☑066 801 8614; www.yugotour.com; tours per person 2900-8900RSD; ⊚from 11am) Yugotour is a mini road trip through the history of Yugoslavia and the life of its president Tito. Belgrade's communist years are brought to life in the icon of Yugo-nostalgia: a Yugo car!

Tours are led by young locals happy to share their own perceptions of Yugoslavia; they take in the communist-era architecture of Novi Beograd, the Museum of Yugoslavia and Marshal Tito's Mausoleum, among other locations.

★ Taste Serbia
FOOD & DRINK

(☑065 236 4866; www.tasteserbia.com; tours 4130-35400RSD) Take your taste buds on a holiday with these deliciously diverse tasting tours run by three local foodies. Explore Belgrade's gourmet scene, head north on a bacon-centric Vojvodinian voyage, stuff yourself in western Serbia and more; all tours are customisable, informative and fun. Pack your stretchy pants. Minimum two people and maximum of 16 people per group; advance bookings essential.

Finovino
WINE

(Map p334; ☑011 403 0962; www.finovino.rs; Pop Lukina 6; ⊚10am-10pm) This excellent top-end wine shop is a must stop for Serbian and Balkan wines, but before committing you can indulge in a six-wine tasting of local wines for 2950RSD. The tastings include pairing with three cheeses (*sjenički, homoljski* and goat) and pork cold cuts, including coveted Mangalica. Reservations at least one day in advance are required.

Belgrade Underground
HISTORY

(Map p334; ☑011 328 4323; www.go2serbia.net; Gračanička 11; per person from 1900RSD; ⊚9am-8pm Mon-Fri, to 3pm Sat) Delve into Belgrade's tumultuous past – from Roman times until the Cold War – on this fascinating 2½-hour tour of subterranean caves, bunkers and secret passageways. Bookings are a must. English tours run Tuesday (10am), Saturday (11.30am) and Sunday (2.30pm) and are handled by Eurojet, a travel agency at Gračanička 11.

Belgrade Adventure
KAYAKING

(Map p328; ☑060 014 0117; www.belgradeadventure.com; Zemunski kej, Barakuda (boat); per person from 2400-3600RSD; ⊚tours noon & 5pm daily) This relatively light kayaking tour takes in a number of riverside destinations with stunning views of the city. The standard tour to Great War Island starts from the Kalemegdan Fortress, complete with a crash course on its history. Plenty of activities are ensured at each stop, including rope swings or beach football (BBQs can also be tacked on).

iBikeBelgrade
CYCLING

(Map p334; ☑066 900 8386; www.ibikebelgrade.com; Braće Krsmanović 5; 1 hr/day €2/€8; ⊚Apr-Oct) Wheel around town on tailored cycle tours that take in everywhere from Ada Ciganlija to Zemun. Daily tours (2000RSD to 2600RSD per person) are available, as are customised multiday journeys through other parts of Serbia.

Belgrade Alternative Guide
WALKING

(☑063 743 3055; www.belgradealtguide.com; tours per person 1700-9800RSD) Run by passionate locals, these tours explore Savamala rooftop hang-outs, central art galleries, street art, the history of Zemun, farmers markets, secret eateries and surrounding villages. Tours generally run between three and four hours.

Nightlife Academy CULTURAL

(☎ 064 662 2956; www.nightlifeacademy.com; tour incl drinks from 1200RSD; ⊙ Thu, Fri & Sat) Take in Belgrade's famous nightlife and learn how to party like a local. Excellent value for money; reservations essential.

⚒ Festivals & Events

Belgrade Dance Festival DANCE

(www.belgradedancefestival.com; ⊙ Mar) From Akram Khan Company and Compañía Nacional de Danza to Sylvie Guillem and Mikhail Baryshnikov, Belgrade Dance Festival showcases the most important dancers and dance companies from around the world.

Mikser Festival ART

(www.festival.mikser.rs; ⊙ Apr/May) The hyper-hipster Mikser Festival brings Belgrade's creative side into the spotlight, with a full program devoted to the latest in music, design, sustainable development and quirky innovation.

Night of Museums CULTURAL

(Noć Muzeja; www.nocmuzeja.rs; ⊙ May) Explore the best of Belgrade's museums and galleries after dark (5pm to 1am); a huge range of cultural and artistic programs are held in conjunction with the event. In addition to the capital, a further 45 towns in Serbia take part.

Public transport is free on the night for anyone holding a festival ticket (book at www.eventim.rs).

Ring Ring MUSIC

(www.ringring.rs; ⊙ May) The bill of this lively world-music festival is crammed with eclectic acts from around the Balkans and the planet.

Belgrade Summer Festival ART

(BELEF; www.belef.rs; ⊙ Jul-Aug) A dynamic sampling of innovative music, dance, theatre and visual arts displays held around the streets and squares of the city each July/August.

Belgrade Beerfest BEER, MUSIC

(www.belgradebeerfest.com; ⊙ Aug) Held over five nights each August, this is an unrivalled revelry of live rock shows, carousing crowds of over half a million people, and of course, beer, beer, beer.

Belgrade International Theatre Festival THEATRE

(BITEF; https://festival.bitef.rs; ⊙ Sep) Week-long showcase of experimental and traditional European theatre, going strong for 50 years.

October Salon ART

(Oktobarski Salon; www.oktobarskisalon.org; ⊙ Sep-Oct) Prestigious biennial exhibition of contemporary visual arts featuring dozens of local and international artists.

Belgrade Music Festival MUSIC

(BEMUS; www.bemus.rs; ⊙ Sep-Oct) Serbia's longest-running music festival (1969) hosts local and international classical music artists.

⌂ Sleeping

★ Hostel Bongo HOSTEL €

(Map p334; ☎ 011 268 5515; www.hostelbongo. com; Terazije 36; dm/d with shared bathroom 1800/4800RSD; ❄ @ ☎) Guests at the modern, brightly painted and meticulously maintained Bongo can take their pick: plunge into the tonnes of attractions, bars and restaurants nearby, or hide from it all in the hostel's sweet garden terrace. Fantastic staff with oodles of hostelling experience.

Hostelche HOSTEL €

(Map p334; ☎ 011 263 7793; www.hostelchehos tel.com; 1st fl, Kralja Petra 8; dm 1500RSD, s/d 4200/4800RSD; ❄ @ ☎) Bend-over-backwards staff, a homey atmosphere and super location make this award-winner popular for all the right reasons. Dorm beds are all floor level (no bunks), set on hardwood flooring with lockers and cabinets for guests. There is also a branch in Smederevo.

YOLOstel HOSTEL €

(Map p334; ☎ 063 382 813; www.yolostel. rs; Apartment 6, 3rd fl, Uzun Mirkova 6; dm/d from 1200/3600RSD; ❄ ☎) This designer hostel enjoys an awesome location just a short stumble from Savamala. With custom-made furniture, quirky, gorgeous decor and a hip, refined air, this is not your usual backpacker flophouse. Private corner room number 1 features an epic balcony for gazing down at Belgrade going about its business.

★ Yugodom GUESTHOUSE €€

(Map p334; ☎ 065 984 6366; www.yugodom.com; Strahinjica Bana 80; d/ste 4200/8400RSD; ❄ ☎) This evocative two-room guesthouse offers more than a comfortable bed; it's also a vessel for time travel. Billed as a 'stayover museum', Yugodom (*dom* means 'house' in Serbian) is decked out with gorgeous art and Yugoslavian mid-century modern furnishings from the Tito era (though you'll find all the mod cons and self-catering facilities you need disguised among the retro trappings).

BELGRADE WATERFRONT

Some might argue that much of Belgrade's appeal is in its derelict, communist-era buildings and Cold War feel. A large swath of the city, especially around Novi Beograd and the Sava River waterfront, are almost a time capsule of brutalist architectural might. Its streets harbour crumbling concrete blocks, faded façades and a general vibe that makes one wonder if Belgradians got the memo: Yugoslavia died in 1992! Others might have a point in saying the city needs to modernise and a bit of urban renewal might do it some good. But few bargained for what they are getting: an Emirati-funded (and Emirates-evoking) development project known as the **Belgrade Waterfront** (www. belgradewaterfront.com), a rather controversial and grandiose makeover of nearly 2 million square metres of land on the southern bank of the Sava River in Savamala, (once) the city's most cutting-edge and bohemian district.

The €3.5 billion mixed-use residential, office and retail scheme includes office and luxury apartment buildings, a park and promenade, five-star hotels, a shopping mall, a Buddha Bar and Belgrade Tower (Kula Beograd), a 168m-high mixed-use skyscraper that will house The St Regis Belgrade Hotel and The Residences at The St Regis Belgrade. The numbers are striking by Serbian standards: 5700 housing units, 2200 hotel rooms and capacity to accommodate 12,700 office workers, all done up in the glitziest and most un-Balkan of ways (it looks a lot like Dubai, though!). The polarising project has already claimed some casualties: the city's historic late-19th-century main train station was decommissioned in mid-2018; the Bristol Hotel nearby, a marvel of Secession architecture and a Serbian cultural monument, was shuttered shortly thereafter; and several *splavovi* (river-barge nightclubs) and housing office complexes have been relocated.

Those who helped turn Savamala into a cradle of cool are now writing the neighbourhood's eulogy. The project has sparked widespread protests around the city, frequently organised by **Ne Davimo Beograd** ('Don't Drown Belgrade'; @nedavimobgd on Twitter), the project's main opposition movement. Regardless of which side one might fall, one thing is indisputable: the 21st century is arriving in the White City.

The location is as impeccable as the surrounds: on a newly pedestrianised street smack in the middle of Dorćol and across the road from Bajloni Market .

⭐ **Savamala Bed & Breakfast**　B&B €€
(Map p334; ☏ 011 406 0264; www.savamalaho tel.rs; Kraljevića Marka 6, Savamala; s/d/tr from 6000/7200/9000RSD; ✳🛜) This brilliant B&B is all early-1900s charm out the front and nouveau-Savamala graffiti-murals out the back. As hip as you'd expect from its location in Belgrade's coolest quarter, the digs here are furnished with a mix of period furniture and the work of up-and-coming Belgrade designers. It's close to the city's main sights, and there are tonnes of happening bars and restaurants within staggering distance.

Smokvica Bed & Breakfast　B&B €€
(Map p334; ☏ 069 446 4002; www.smokvica.rs; Gospodar Jovanova 45, Dorćol; d 7700RSD; ✳🛜) Smokvica's shabby-chic cafe and accommodation empire has expanded to Dorćol, where the line-up's second B&B occupies a grand whitewashed 19th-century mansion. Spacious rooms with vaulted ceilings and hardwood floors are decked out in trademark sky blue, with supersonic showers. The designer cafe at this location is also a charming retreat just steps from the six rooms.

San Art Floating Hostel　HOSTEL €€
(Map p328; ☏ 063 238 278; www.sanarthostel.rs; Ušće bb; d/tr/q from 5300/5800/7700RSD; ✳🛜) This wooden house-raft on the Danube offers river-top relaxation with airy, cosy rooms (all with private bathrooms) and tranquil terraces. If you'd rather rave than retreat, it's an easy walk to summer's *splavovi* (river-barge nightclubs). Get here by bus 15 or 84 from Zeleni Venac; ask to be let out at Ušće Park.

Hotel Jugoslavija　HISTORIC HOTEL €€
(Map p328; ☏ 011 402 2222; www.hoteljugoslavi ja.rs; Bulevar Nikole Tesle 3, Zemun; s/d/ste from 4403/5738/8179RSD; 🅿✳🛜) One of Belgrade's most famous buildings, this monolithic communist relic was *the* happening place in its Yugoslavia heyday; everyone from Tina Turner to Queen Elizabeth II had a turn beneath its sheets. Bombed during the 1990s NATO campaign, it remained shuttered for decades. It's now back in full

Central Belgrade

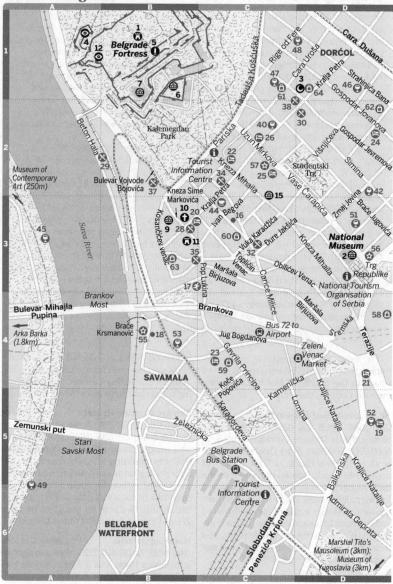

SERBIA BELGRADE

swing, and though it's been renovated, the feel remains delightfully old-school Yugo.

★ **Mama Shelter**   BOUTIQUE HOTEL €€€
(Map p334; ☎ 011 333 3000; www.mamashel ter.com/en/belgrade; Kneza Mihaila 54a; d from 8300RSD; P🅿❄@🛜) Belgrade is just the seventh city worldwide to receive one of Philippe Starck's whimsical designer Mama Shelter hotels – the city's hottest – this one sitting on prime real estate at the Belgrade Fortress end of Kneza Mihaila, on the top floor of the glitzy Rajićeva Shopping Centre.

★**Hotel Moskva**   HISTORIC HOTEL €€€

(Hotel Moscow; Map p334; ☎011 364 2000; www.hotelmoskva.rs; Terazije 20; s/d/ste from 10,500/12,800/24,700RSD; 🅿❄@🛜) Art nouveau icon and proud symbol of the best of Belgrade, the majestic 123-room Moskva has been wowing guests – including Albert Einstein and Alfred Hitchcock – since 1906. Laden with ye olde glamour, this is the place to write your memoirs at an old desk.

Square Nine   DESIGN HOTEL €€€

(Map p334; ☎011 333 3500; www.squarenine.rs; Studentski Trg 9; d/ste from 35,000/27,500RSD; 🅿❄@🛜) Behind a copper-toned facade overlooking pleasant Studentski Park, Square Nine cradles a vintage, mid-century modern motif – the work of top Brazilian architect Isay Weinfeld – in its spacious and hip lobby. Grainy dark hardwood hallways lead to luxury rooms equipped with limestone bathrooms, Italian linens and espresso machines; there's also a spa, lobby bar and rooftop Japanese restaurant.

🍴 Eating

★**Pekara Trpković**   BAKERY €

(Map p328; www.facebook.com/pekaratrpkovic; Nemanjina 32; burek per 100g 32-55RSD; ⊙6am-8.30pm Mon-Sat, to 4pm Sun) The fact that this family business has existed for over a century in the competitive bakery market is quite an achievement. The Serbian tradition of making pastries has reached its peak in this case. Trpković delicacies and sandwiches are extremely popular, so you can often see queues, especially for breakfast and lunch breaks.

Sometimes there are two queues – one just for *burek* (heavenly filo pastries stuffed with veal, cheese, spinach etc).

Crna Ovca   GELATO €

(Map p334; www.crnaovca.rs; Kralja Petra 58; small/medium/large 160/270/380RSD; ⊙10am-midnight; 🛜) This cheerful and always busy gelato shop sells some of Belgrade's best and boasts some wacky flavours (Gorgonzola, peanut butter and chocolate-covered pretzels) in addition to top sellers crème brûlée and caramelised walnuts, pistachio and Plazma (a Serbian biscuit). With 26 options per day, there's always something new and quirky to try.

★**To Je To!**   BALKAN €

(Map p334; www.sarajevski-cevapi.com; Bul Despota Stefana 21; mains 218-744RSD; ⊙10am-midnight; 🛜) The name means 'that's it', and

Rooms are funky and fun, but the real coup here is the 1000-sq-metre rooftop restaurant, bar and hang-space, complete with arcade games, outdoor fire pit, stupendous views and oodles of beautiful people – one of the few places in Belgrade to get an aerial perspective with a cocktail in hand. Go at sunset!

Central Belgrade

in this case, they're talking about meat. Piles of the stuff, grilled in all its juicy glory, make up the menu here in the form of Sarajevo-style *ćevapi* (minced veal or pork sausages), turkey kebabs, sweetbreads and more. It serves homemade *sarma* (stuffed cabbage rolls) on weekends. Cheap, scrumptious and highly recommended by locals.

Ferdinand Knedle   DUMPLINGS €
(Map p334; www.facebook.com/ferdinandknedle; Cara Lazara 19; dumplings 80-170RSD; ⊘10am-11pm) You'll feel like a kid in a candy store if this fun cafe is your intro to *gomboce* (dumplings), served here in all manner of delectable sweet and savoury combinations that take the traditional plum-stuffed ver-

sion to new heights. Are you feeling like ham, rocket and mozzarella or dark chocolate and cherries? Go for both, they're small!

Hummus Bar   ISRAELI €
(Map p328; www.hummusbar.rs; Beogradska 66; mains 200-620RSD; ⊘24hr; ✎) If you've had your fill of Serbian fast food, make your way to this little joint for fresh, flavoursome falafel rolls and shawarma. As you might expect, the hummus is heavenly.

★**Ribnjak**   SERBIAN €€
(Map p328; ✆011 331 8894; Jojkićev Dunavac bb; mains 400-1000RSD, fish per kg 600-2900RSD; ⊘noon-10pm) An unremarkable houseboat moored far enough from the city centre that

few people know about it (or ever see it!), this undeniably simple *restoran* (restaurant) does remarkable, extra effort-worthy things with river fish.

The speciality is rarely seen fish *mućkalica* (spicy stew) – order that as an appetiser (after the fish soup!) and follow with a perfectly griddle-seared whole zander *(grillovani smuđ)* and sides of Dalmatian-style potato and mangel (chard). No English menu. It's a 600RSD or so CarGo ride from Trg Republike.

Mayka
VEGETARIAN €€
(Map p334; ☑ 011 328 8401; www.facebook.com/ maykabeograd/; Kosančićev venac 2; mains 785-1050RSD; ⊗ 11am-midnight; 🖘🍴) Among Belgrade's slim offerings for vegetarians, here's a gem right in the city centre. Mayka serves up worldly vegetarian specialities in a Serbian way. Listen to the waiter's recommendations and don't miss dishes featuring its house-made seitan or stir-fried veggies with smoked sunflower cheese. Indian and Thai curries go down a treat as well, especially on the rustic front patio.

★ Manufaktura
BALKAN €€
(Map p334; ☑ 011 218 0044; www.restoran-manu faktura.rs; Kralja Petra 13-15; mains 410-1480RSD; ⊗ 9am-midnight; 🖘) Just off pedestrianised Knez Mihailova (look for the red umbrellas in the patio), Manufaktura offers Balkan dining in a modern ambience resembling an exquisite pantry. It has a good choice of meze dishes, and a separate deli section. Homegrown ingredients are sourced from across Serbia, while the *rakija* (strong distilled spirit made from fruit) and wine lists feature small family producers. There's live music in the evenings.

Mezestoran Dvorište
MEDITERRANEAN €€
(Map p334; ☑ 011 324 6515; www.restorandvoriste. rs; Svetogorska 46; mains 790-1290RSD; ⊗ 9am-midnight; 🖘) You'll wonder how many folks stroll right by this unremarkable residential building in Belgrade, not knowing this lovely Mediterranean restaurant is hidden away behind, it as soon as you lay your eyes on the lovely courtyard (a lot, that's how many). The food – Greek-leaning but with Turkish and Italian peppered about – is excellent.

?
SERBIAN €€
(Znak Pitanja; Map p334; Kralja Petra 6; mains 850-2100RSD; ⊗ 10am-midnight) Belgrade's oldest *kafana* (tavern) has been attracting the bohemian set since 1823 with dishes such as stuffed chicken and mushroomy

house-speciality pork *mućkalica* (spicy stew) with bacon and onion served in a bread bowl. Its quizzical name follows a dispute with the adjacent church, which objected to the boozy tavern – originally called 'By the Cathedral' – referring to a house of God.

Dva Jelena
SERBIAN €€
(Two Deer; Map p334; ☑ 011 723 4885; www.dva jelena.rs; Skadarska 32; mains 640-1680RSD; ⊗ 11am-1am; 🖘) A local icon, Dva Jelena has been dishing up huge portions of hearty fare amid painted wood panelling, kitschy portraits and antique musical instruments for over 180 years. Rustic, homespun and with the obligatory violin serenades, it ticks all the Skadarlija boxes.

Radost Fina Kuhinjica
VEGETARIAN €€
(Map p334; ☑ 060 603 0023; www.facebook.com/ RadostFinaKuhinjica; Pariska 3; mains 670-720RSD; ⊗ 2pm-midnight Tue-Sat, 1-9pm Sun; 🖘🍴) Barbecue-obsessed Serbia isn't the easiest place for vegetarians, but thanks to this candlelit eatery you'll never have to settle for eating garnish and chips again. Its limited menu features veg burgers and lasagne, shiitake quesadillas and a few other meat substitutes, some of which are vegan. The back courtyard is lovely.

Smokvica
CAFE €€
(Map p334; www.smokvica.rs; Kralja Petra 73, Dorćol; mains 650-2100RSD; ⊗ 9am-midnight Sun-Thu, to 1am Fri-Sat; 🖘) With its winsome courtyard terrace, arty crowd and with-it gourmet menu, to stumble across Smokvica ('little fig') is to forget you're in hustling, bustling Belgrade. Nibble innovative salads, gourmet tasting plates and cosmopolitan mains, or just sip good coffee in an atmosphere both rare and rarified.

Smokvica's **Molerova** (Map p328; ☑ 069 444 6403; Molerova 33; s/d from 6142/6969RSD; ❋🖘) and **Jovanova** (p333) branches have hip B&Bs attached.

★ Iris New Balkan Cuisine
SERBIAN €€€
(Map p328; ☑ 064 129 6377; www.newbalkancui sine.com/iris; Sarajevska 54; tasting menus veg/ nonveg 3000-3700RSD, with wine 5600/6300RSD; ⊗ 12.30-10pm Wed-Sat; 🖘🍴) 🍃 Belgrade's best foodie bang for the buck is this newcomer clandestinely occupying a 1st-floor apartment south of the old train station. Courses from the tasting menu are based around a single ingredient – whatever head chef Vanja Puškar has procured from organic farmers

SERBIA BELGRADE

that week – and taken to new heights without leaving behind their Serbian origins.

Memorable examples when we dined: a stunning Buša beef carpaccio with yoghurt, olive oil and fried sourdough; a perfectly crisp pork schnitzel doused in green pea and mint cream with sage-perfumed zucchini foam; and a delightful fig-stuffed chicken roulade on triple-fried potato, with salty caramel and hop-orange foam. Natural wines often accompany the eight-course menus. Welcome to the New Balkans!

★ Little Bay EUROPEAN €€€

(Map p334; www.littlebay.rs; Dositejeva 9a; mains 695-1590RSD; ⊙9am-1am; 🕾) Little wonder locals and visitors have long been singing the praises of this gem: it's one of the most interesting dining experiences in Belgrade. Tuck yourself into a dramatic private opera box and let any of the meaty treats melt in your mouth as a live opera singer does wonderful things to your ears. It does a traditional English roast lunch (795RSD to 995RSD) on Sundays.

★ Šaran SEAFOOD €€€

(☑011 261 8235; www.saran.co.rs; Kej Oslobođenja 53, Zemun; mains 1050-2090RSD; ⊙noon-11pm Sun & Mon, to 1am Tue-Sat; 🕾) Šaran (meaning 'carp') is rightfully renowned as Zemun's best quayside fish restaurant for its exceptional fish dishes, professional service and welcoming atmosphere. Freshwater river fish dishes like Smederevo-style pike (grilled, then baked under an astonishingly flavourful smothering of tomatoes, garlic, onions and red peppers) and pricier whole saltwater options (6100RSD to 8400RSD) are absolute standouts. Live Balkan music most nights.

★ Bela Reka SERBIAN €€€

(☑011 655 5098; www.restoranbelareka.rs; Tošin bunar 79, Novi Beograd; mains 630-1890RSD; 🕾) One of Belgrade's best new restaurants, Bela Reka is modern and sophisticated, but fiercely dedicated to the traditional craft of Serbian cuisine, and is well worth a trek to Novi Beograd, 5.5km west of Brankov Most. Gorgeously presented, meat-leaning dishes are some of Belgrade's best: perfectly spiced, Pirot-style uštipci (meatballs), walnut-and-hazelnut-crusted monastery chicken and homolje (sausage stuffed with cheese) are outstanding.

An award-winning baker fires up traditional somun flatbread in a clay oven and the goat's cheese comes direct from their own farm (you can pick some up in their artisan market). But wait, dessert! Go for ledene kocke, a dead-simple, dead-delicious sponge cake resurrected from Yugoslavian recipe books.

Lorenzo & Kakalamba INTERNATIONAL €€€

(Map p328; ☑011 329 5351; www.lk.rs; Cvijićeva 110; mains 820-3600RSD, pizzas 690-960RSD; ⊙noon-midnight; 🕾) Covered from floor to ceiling in a riot of out-there artworks and marvellous miscellany, and staffed (and frequented) by peculiar characters, to step inside here is to fall down the rabbit-hole to Wonderland.

★ Ambar BALKAN €€€

(Map p334; ☑011 328 6637; www.ambarrestaurant. com; Karađorđeva 2-4, Beton Hala; small plates 310-1150RSD; ⊙10am-2am; 🕾) Upmarket, innovative small-plate takes on Balkan cuisine are the go to at this chic spot – the best of a handful of trendy options overlooking the river. Everything from ajvar (spread made from roasted peppers, aubergines and garlic) to mixed grills has been given a contemporary spin; even the pljeskavica (spicy hamburger, usually served with onions) gets the five-star treatment. Put your meal choices in the hands of the excellent and well-versed staff and you won't be disappointed, right down to the Serbian wines. You can try everything for 2990RSD.

🍷 Drinking & Nightlife

★ Restoran Tabor TAVERNA

(☑011 241 2464; www.restorantabor.com; Bulevar Kralja Aleksandra 348; ⊙noon-2am Mon-Sat; 🕾) If you want an authentic Serbian Friday-night experience, this wildly popular (reserve several days ahead) kafana in Zvezdara has it all: captivating folk music, great traditional food (don't skip the mak pita – a baklava-like dessert made with poppy seeds), sexy lighting and a room full of good-time-seeking locals (and celebs) who will eventually be dancing on the tables! It's 5.5km west of Knez Mihailova (a 300RSD or so CarGo ride from Savamala).

★ Kafana Pavle Korčagin TAVERNA

(Map p328; ☑011 240 1980; www.kafanapavlekor cagin.rs; Ćirila i Metodija 2a; ⊙7.30am-2am Mon-Fri, 10am-2am Sat, 11am-midnight Sun) Raise a glass to Tito at this frantic, festive kafana. Lined with communist memorabilia and packed to the rafters with revellers and grinning accordionists, this table-thumping throwback fills up nightly; reserve a table via the website in advance.

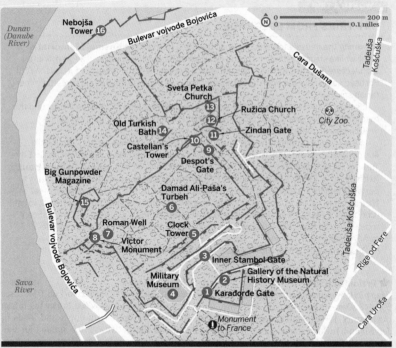

🏃 Site Tour
Belgrade Fortress Београдска Тврђава

START KARAĐORĐE GATE
END NEBOJŠA TOWER
LENGTH TWO HOURS

From Kalemegdan Park, enter the Upper Town of the fortress across the bridge of the 18th-century **1 Karađorđe Gate**. Straight ahead is the **2 Gallery of the Natural History Museum**, housed in a 19th-century Turkish guardhouse. From the **3 Inner Stambol Gate** (1750) you'll reach the **4 Military Museum** where you can get a crash course in the military history of the region.

Nearby is the 27.5m-high **5 Clock Tower**; climb the narrow stairs for panoramic views of Kalemegdan Park. Further along is the 1784 **6 Damad Ali-Paša's Turbeh**, a mausoleum of an Ottoman-era governor. Continue on to the **7 Roman Well**, a mysterious 60m-deep cistern of dubious origin and shrouded in legends. Looming beside it is the **8 Victor Monument** by Ivan Meštrović, erected in 1928 to commemorate Serbia's WWI victories.

The Lower Town slopes down towards the mouth of the Sava and the Danube.

Enter through the 15th-century **9 Despot's Gate**, consisting of inner and outer ramparts. The tall **10 Castellan's Tower** beside it today houses the Observatory of Belgrade's Astronomical Society. Next is the massive 15th-century **11 Zindan Gate**, with two rounded towers and a bridge. Below the ramparts, the ivy-swathed **12 Ružica Church** has chandeliers made by WWI Serbian soldiers from bullet casings, swords, rifles and cannon parts. Nearby is the small but lovely **13 Sveta Petka Church**, built above a spring that's believed to have miraculous powers.

The next stop towards the river is the 18th-century **14 Old Turkish Bath** (Hammam), now home to the Planetarium of Belgrade's Astronomical Society. To the west, the **15 Big Gunpowder Magazine** (1718) was set up by the Austrians; it has a collection of Roman sarcophagi, tombstones and altars. The **16 Nebojša Tower** (1460), a former dungeon and now museum, sits on the riverbank on the northeastern ramparts.

WORTH A TRIP

DAY TRIPS FROM BELGRADE

Crowning the densely forested Kosmaj mountain (626m), the **Kosmaj Memorial** is an alien-like structure that is a prime example of Yugoslav-era *spomenik* (memorial) architecture. Five fins form a huge star-shaped monument that honours the fallen WWII Partisan soldiers of the Kosmaj Detachment and symbolises the Šumadija region's libertarian spirit.

It's a great spot for hiking and cycling (particularly the path forming a loop around the memorial), well marked, with picnic areas that are popular on summer weekends.

Kosmaj lies 50km south of Belgrade and is best visited by car.

In the town of Topola is the **Oplenac Royal Complex** (www.oplenac.rs; adult/child 400/300RSD; ⊙8am-7pm), where Karađorđe plotted the Serbian insurrection against the Turks in 1804. One ticket grants access to all attractions, including **King Peter's House** (with the royal family's portrait gallery), **Karađorđe's Fort** (now a museum housing period artefacts and personal effects), **Karađorđe's Church** and the **Winegrower's House** (now a gallery). The most impressive is the white-marble **Church of St George** (Crkva Svetog Djordja; www.oplenac.rs; adult/child 400/300RSD), adorned with magnificent mosaics made from 40 million pieces of coloured glass; its crypt is the Karađorđević family mausoleum.

Buses connect Topola with Belgrade (660RSD, 1½ hours, 11 daily).

★**Pržionica D59B**　CAFE
(Map p334; www.przionica.tumblr.com; Dobračina 59; ⊙8.30am-5.30pm Mon-Sat; 🛜) Throughout history Lower Dorćol, with dozens of Jewish and Turkish stores, has had a special relationship with coffee. It's no wonder that the tradition lives on in places like Pržionica, where the city's best coffee goes hand in hand with industrial design and meticulous baristas, who prepare espresso (170RSD) with the care and precision usually reserved for an archaeological dig.

Zaokret　CAFE
(Map p334; www.facebook.com/zaokret; Cetinjska 15; ⊙9am-midnight; 🛜) Indie-music lovers will feel right at home with carefully selected playlists of resident and guest DJs at Zaokret. Thematic evenings, occasional gigs and live radio shows make this place packed almost every evening. If you prefer quiet hours, drop by in the early afternoon for slow coffee and craft beers Kabinet and Santo (on draught).

★**Bar Central**　COCKTAIL BAR
(Map p334; www.facebook.com/BarCentral011; Kralja Petra 59; ⊙9am-midnight Sun-Thu, to 1am Fri & Sat; 🛜) This is the HQ of Serbia's Association of Bartenders, a fact made evident after one sip of any of the sublime cocktails (515RSD to 1165RSD) on offer. With an interior as polished as a bottle flip-pour, this ain't the place for tacky tikis and those little umbrellas – this is serious mixology territory.

★**Klub 20/44**　RIVER BARGE
(Map p334; www.facebook.com/klub2044; Ušće bb; ⊙5pm-2am Sun, Tue & Wed, to 4am Thu, to 5am Fri & Sat; 🛜) Retro, run-down and loads of fun, this alternative *splav* is named for Belgrade's map coordinates. Open year-round, it has become an electronica reference for top European DJs – despite its shabby appearance. Swimming up from the back might be your easiest way in!

★**Centrala**　BAR
(Map p334; Simina 6; ⊙9am-1am; 🛜) Centrala is one of those neighbourhood haunts that immediately feels like home, if home was a lively, jam-packed, but somehow laid-back, bar on a street corner. Owned by a local painter, there are occasionally exhibitions held here, but the main attraction is its hospitable, happy crowd and a noticeable absence of the pretentiousness that often plagues 'cool' Belgrade bars.

Krafter　CRAFT BEER
(Map p334; www.facebook.com/kftbeerbar; Strahinjića Bana 44, Dorćol; ⊙9am-midnight Mon-Thu, to 1pm Fri & Sat, 10am-midnight Sun; 🛜) Hopheads seeking local salvation should settle in at this intimate, industrial-chic craft beer bar featuring 14 rotating offerings on draught (pints 295RSD to 385RSD) – always Serbian – along with a small international selection in bottles. The menu is heavily weighted towards hoppy pale and India pale ales, and the lovely English-speaking staff are passionate about their suds devotion.

★**Blaznavac** BAR
(Map p334; www.facebook.com/blaznavac; Kneginje Ljubice 18, Dorćol; ⊙9am-1am Sun-Thu, to 2am Fri & Sat; 🛜) Part-cafe, part-bar, part-wonderfully-wacky-gallery, this pocket-sized place is one of the city's best spots for pre-drink drinks. Plastered with murals and quirky collectables, it's used as an exhibition space for young artists. It also hosts live music and spoken-word events. Blaznavac's appeal isn't limited to night-time jams and cocktails: it's charming for coffee or a snack.

Samo Pivo BAR
(Map p334; www.samopivo.rs; Balkanska 13; ⊙noon-midnight Sun-Thu, to 1am Fri & Sat; 🛜) Hidden up an out-of-service escalator that leads to an abandoned shopping arcade, Samo Pivo – 'just beer' in Serbian – feels like a brash, unconventional war room catering equally to a chain-smoking mix of craft beer fiends and Lav or Jelen devotees. It's Belgrade's most extensive selection (23 draught beers and over 200 brands in bottles) and boasts an ace patio.

Povetarac RIVER BARGE
(Map p334; www.facebook.com/povetaracbrod; Brodarska bb; ⊙11pm-5am Mon-Sat, 8pm-late winter; 🛜) This rusting cargo ship attracts a fun indie crowd for its eclectic playlist, cheap drinks and exceedingly welcoming atmosphere. Open year-round.

Kafeterija CAFE
(Map p334; www.kafeterija.com; Kralja Petra 16; ⊙8am-midnight Mon-Thu, to 1am Fri-Sat, 9am-midnight Sun; 🛜) Part of a popular chain, this Kafeterija branch occupies the early-20th-century building that's one of Belgrade's finest examples of Secession-style architecture and was once home to the city's first department store. It offers more than 10 types of international coffee (espresso from 145RSD), as well as tasty (though a bit pricey) snacks and light meals (145RSD to 695RSD).

Dvorištance BAR
(Map p334; www.facebook.com/klub.dvoristance; Cetinjska 15; ⊙9am-1am Sun-Thu, to 2am Fri & Sat; 🛜) Rainbow-bright cafe by day and an absolute ripper of a bar/performance space by night, whimsical little Dvorištance is textbook Cetinjska 15. It regularly hosts live gigs and alternative/indie DJ parties.

Leila Records BAR
(Map p334; www.leila.rs; Gospodar Jevremova 6; ⊙8am-midnight Sun-Thu, to 1am Fri-Sat; 🛜) Oozing vintage cool, this part-bar/part-vinyl-record-shop is a magnet for indie scenesters, bohemian artists and vinylphiles. During the day, it's a great spot for sidewalk people-watching along this hip corner of Gospodar Jevremova, while on winter weekends it's perfect for plopping down on gorgeous furniture and grooving to vinyl-only DJs.

Vinoteka WINE BAR
(Map p334; www.facebook.com/vinotekasavamala; Karađorđeva 57, Savamala; ⊙11am-midnight Sun-Thu, to 1am Fri & Sat; 🛜) If you want to take a deep dive into Serbian wine, this cosy Savamala wine bar boasts 40 domestic wines by the glass (290RSD to 450RSD) and nearly 300 ex-Yugoslavian regional wines by the bottle (it's a bottle shop by day). It's not a wild place but rather perfect for a bit of juice and a conversation in a more intimate setting.

Miners Pub PUB
(Map p334; www.facebook.com/minerspub; Rige od Fere 16, Dorćol; ⊙2pm-midnight Sun-Thu, to 1am Fri-Sun; 🛜) Grungy and cavernous, this blue-collar craft beer pub features 15 Serbian beers on draught and a slew in bottles as well. Under brick archways, stake out a corner for yourself alongside cool art on the walls; or go for a bit of pinball and drinking mixed in with the classic rock'n'roll or oldies soundtrack. *Živeli!*

Rakia Bar BAR
(Map p334; www.rakiabar.com; Dobračina 5, Dorćol; ⊙9am-midnight Sun-Thu, to 1am Fri & Sat; 🛜) An ideal spot for *rakija* rookies to get their first taste of the spirit of Serbia. English-speaking staff will gently guide you through the 51 options, both traditional plum varieties as well as all manner of other fruits, several of which emerge from its own distillery (discerning palates should head straight for Stara Sokolova 12 year, however).

Buyer beware: this is stiff stuff. If you love something, pick up a bottle at **Rakia & Co** (Map p334; www.shop.rakiabar.com; Terazije 42; ⊙9am-9pm Mon-Fri, 10am-6pm Sat, 11am-5pm Sun), its sister shop.

☆ Entertainment

★**KC Grad** CULTURAL CENTRE
(Map p334; www.gradbeograd.eu; Braće Krsmanović 4, Savamala; ⊙noon-1am Mon-Thu, to 5.30am Fri & Sat, 2pm-midnight Sun; 🛜) A Savamala stalwart (it's been running since 2009), this wonderful warehouse space promotes local creativity with workshops, exhibitions, a restaurant and nightly music events.

SERBIA BELGRADE

Kvaka 22
ARTS CENTRE

(Map p328; ☑ 062 811 0071; www.kvaka22.com; Ruzveltova 39; ⊙ hours vary) A collective of young and restless artists scouted, cleaned up and created a three-storey art space in an abandoned building next to the New Cemetery. Kvaka 22 (Catch 22) features a gallery, event space and artists' ateliers. Gig nights are most popular, when the place turns into a real living-room guerrilla club.

Bitef Art Cafe
LIVE MUSIC

(Map p328; www.bitefartcafe.rs; Mitropolita Petra 8; ⊙ 9am-4am; 🐾) There's something for everyone at this delightful hotchpotch of a cafe-club. Funk, soul and jazz get a good airing, as do rock, world and classical music. In summer, Bitef moves its stage to Belgrade Fortress.

Yugoslav Cinematheque
CINEMA

(Map p334; ☑ 011 328 6723; www.kinoteka.org.rs; Uzun Mirkova 1; films 200RSD; ⊙ hours vary) The Yugoslav Cinematheque's impressive and recently renovated building across from the Ethnographic Museum screens everything from the classics of world cinema to arthouse productions and cult Yugoslav-era movies. There are also regular screenings in its other building on Kosovska.

Yugoslav Drama Theatre
THEATRE

(Jugoslovensko Dramsko Pozorište; Map p328; ☑ 011 306 1957; http://jdp.rs; Kralja Milana 50; ⊙ box office 10am-3pm & 5pm-performance time Mon-Sat, 7pm-performance time Sun) Founded in 1947, the highly regarded and much awarded JDP has three stages. The repertoire ranges from innovative interpretations of the classics of world theatre to thought-provoking avant-garde drama. English subtitles are included for some performances.

National Theatre
THEATRE

(Map p334; ☑ 011 262 0946; www.narodnopozoriste.rs; Francuska 3; ⊙ box office 11am-3pm & 5pm-performance time) This glorious 1869 building hosts operas, dramas and ballets during autumn, winter and spring.

🛍 Shopping

★ Makadam
ARTS & CRAFTS

(Map p334; www.makadam.rs; Kosančićev venac 20; ⊙ noon-8pm Tue-Sun; 🐾) Make your way to Makadam across the original Turkish cobblestones of Kosančićev venac, a lovely slice of old Belgrade. The concept store only sells handmade products from across Serbia. Shoppers will find an impressive selection of carefully chosen items by local craftspeople and designers, with the accent on the use of natural and traditional materials.

The bistro (9am to midnight daily) serves local wines, beers and more. The sidewalk seating here – in fact along a large swath of Kosančićev venac – draws a lively, in-the-know happy hour crowd.

★ Parfimerija Sava
PERFUME

(Sava Perfumery; Map p334; www.facebook.com/parfemisava; Kralja Petra 75; ⊙ 10am-1pm & 4-7pm Mon-Fri, to 2pm Sat; 🐾) With its old-fashioned interior, gorgeous vintage bottles and delectable scents wafting throughout, this traditional perfumery is a doorway into the Belgrade of yore. Established in 1954 by the father of current owner, Nenad, this is the last of its kind in Belgrade, where scents are mixed by hand in a mysterious room behind a heavy curtain and labelled by typewriter.

Expect to spend around 570RSD to 985RSD for a small bottle – and leave the shop doused in various scents dispersed from a 1930s hand pump!

★ Belgrade Design District
FASHION & ACCESSORIES

(Čumićevo Sokače; Map p334; www.belgradedesigndistrict.blogspot.com; Čumićeva 2; ⊙ noon-8pm Mon-Fri, to 5pm Sat) Once Belgrade's first mall and later abandoned, this revitalised complex is now home to more than 30 boutiques showcasing up-and-coming local fashionistas, jewellers, artists and designers. It's a great place to pick up original pieces you won't find elsewhere. It's in the middle of the city hidden behind buildings; follow the marked passage from Nušićeva by Trg Terazije.

Jane Doe Concept Store
DESIGN

(Map p334; www.janedoeshop.net; Cara Uroša 19, Dorćol; ⊙ 10am-midnight Mon-Thu, to 1am Fri-Sat, noon-10pm Sun) The newest edition from Jane Doe – real name Bojana! – expands from the vintage realm of the Kapetan Mišina shop (Kapetan Mišina 17; ⊙ noon-8pm Mon-Fri, to 5pm Sat) to include designer jewellery, clothing and art, mostly from Serbia but also from further afield in the Balkans. This hip shop also pulls quintuple-duty as a bar, gallery, community art space, cinema and theatre.

★ Dechkotzar Clothing Co.
CLOTHING

(Map p334; www.dechkotzar.com; Gračanička 16; ⊙ 10am-9pm Mon-Fri, to 7pm Sat) The domain of hipster graphic artists, this small boutique does the city's best designer T-shirts, trucker

ⓘ TRAM 2

Belgrade is a tram fan's ultimate playground – the city is home to all manner of streetcar delights spanning a colourful arsenal of models (West German, Czechoslovakian, Swiss and Spanish) and eras. And while we wouldn't quite say it's as cinematic as Lisbon's famous Tram 28E, none of Belgrade's lines are more fascinating than Tram 2. The iconic, Czechoslo-vakian-built Tatra KT4 tram shakes, rattles and rolls along a circular route around Belgrade's Old Town, taking in some of the city's most iconic sights, neighbourhoods and architecture along the way – just as it did in the former Yugoslavia. The 17-stop, 8km ride takes in Brankov Most, the Belgrade Cooperative Building, Hotel Bristol and the former Central Train Station in Savamala; the bombed-out Yugoslavian Ministry of Defence (p331) and other historic government buildings along regal Kneza Miloša; and the imposing Belgrade Fortress (p325) near Dorćol, among other cinematic architectural gems. The full route takes about 40 minutes and costs 89RSD (Tram 2 drivers do not sell tickets on board).

hats, canvas bags, art prints and other design-forward souvenirs. With the exception of the French sunglasses, it's all local.

Bombondžija Bosiljčić FOOD & DRINKS
(Map p334; www.ratluk-bosiljcic.co.rs; Gavrila Princi-pa 14; ⊙7am-7pm Mon-Fri, 8am-2pm Sat) Literally the last of its kind, this family-owned store is the only remaining one in Belgrade selling handmade sweets. The Bosiljčić family has kept the tradition alive by handing it down for three generations. The sweets include lollipops, all handmade to 1930s recipes, but the speciality is Turkish delight; it's usually made the same day and there are 14 varieties.

★Yugovinyl MUSIC
(Map p334; www.facebook.com/recordstorebel grade; Cetinjska 15; ⊙noon-9pm Sun-Thu, to 10pm Fri-Sat; ☎) Crate-diggers will find plenty to paw through at Yugovinyl, hailed as one of the best record stores in Europe. It's got about 20,000 records in about as many genres, though there's a big focus on Yugoslavia-era prog, punk and new wave. It's worth a visit just to listen to whatever tunes the owners are spinning from the prime people-watching patio.

Kalenić Market MARKET
(Map p328; cnr Maksima Gorkog & Njegoševa; ⊙6am-7pm) In the heart of the refined Vračar neighbourhood, near the Sveti Sava Temple, this bustling green market with produce brought from all over Serbia is Belgrade's biggest and the locals' favourite. Come here to try national delicacies, chat with the vendors, browse the bric-a-brac section and chill out in the surrounding cafes.

Palmas Boutique FASHION
(Map p328; www.facebook.com/palmasboutique; Mihizova 11; ⊙noon-8pm Mon-Sat, noon-3pm Sun)

One of Belgrade's trendiest and most stylish boutiques, Palmas is a treasure trove of Serbian-designed pop culture, from art prints and hipster hoodies to themed socks and designer tees. Hip, Belgrade-based urban streetwear brands like Shinobi, Street Fashion Belgrade and VVE LOVE RED are finely represented. Music is expectedly hip as well.

Vojvođanski Dućan FOOD
(Vojvodina Shop; Map p334; www.vojvodjanski ducan.com; Dobračina 28; ⊙9am-8pm Mon-Fri, to 6pm Sun) Set up to promote and preserve the traditional culture and cuisine of Vojvodina province, this beautiful little shop stocks its shelves with locally grown and made speciality meats, cheeses, alcohol, honey, jams, sweets, and art and handicrafts. Tastings are available. It's a wonderful, welcoming spot and a great introduction to the tastes and treats of northern Serbia.

ⓘ Information

The Tourist Organisation of Belgrade hosts tourist information centres at **Nikola Tesla Airport** (Turistički informativni centri; ☎011 209 7828; www.tob.rs; Aerodrom Beograd 59, Belgrade Nikola Tesla Airport; ⊙9am-9.30pm), (shared with National Tourism Organisation of Serbia, **Knez Mihailova** (☎011 263 5622; Knez Mihailo-va 56, Belgrade City Library; ⊙9am-8pm) and the now decommissioned **Central Train Station** (☎011 361 2732; Central Train Station; ⊙9am-2pm Mon-Sat). The National Tourism Organisation of Serbia operates the information centres at **Trg Republike** (Map p334; ☎011 328 2712; www.serbia.travel; Trg Republike 5; ⊙10am-9pm Mon-Fri, to 6pm Sun) and **Mt Avala** (☎011 390 8517; www.serbia.travel; Mt Avala Tower; ⊙9am-8pm Mar-Sep, to 5pm Oct-Feb). More info points are planned.

Emergency Medical Assistance (☑ 011 361 5001; www.beograd94.rs; Bul Franše D'Eperea 5; ⊙24hr) For emergency medical situations.

Prima 1 (☑ 011 361 099; www.primax.rs; Nemanjina 2; ⊙24hr) All-hours pharmacy. The website has listings of other branches across the city.

ℹ Getting There & Away

AIR

Belgrade Nikola Tesla Airport (☑ 011 209 4444; www.beg.aero; Aerodrom Beograd 59) is 18km from Belgrade. **Air Serbia** (www.airserbia.com) is Serbia's domestic carrier.

BUS

Belgrade's **bus station** (Glavna Beogradska autobuska stanica; Map p334; ☑ 011 263 6299; Železnička 4) is near the eastern banks of the Sava River: **BAS** (www.bas.rs) and **Lasta** (www.lasta.rs) are the two main carriers. Departures and ticketing are in the main building; arrivals are at a separate platform 300m east on the other side of the park.

Sample international routes include Sarajevo (2510RSD, eight hours, six daily), Ljubljana (4770RSD, 7½ hours, three daily) and Pristina (2020RSD, seven hours, five daily). For Vienna (2470RSD to 4570RSD, nine hours, three daily) and some other international destinations, tickets must be purchased at **Basturist** (☑ 011 263 8982; www.basturist.com; Železnička 4) at the eastern end of the station.

Frequent domestic services include Subotica (1270RSD to 1440RSD, three hours, nine daily), Novi Sad (750RSD, one hour, every 15 minutes), Niš (1280RSD, three hours, every 30 minutes) and Novi Pazar (1470RSD, three hours, every 45 minutes).

TRAIN

Most local and international trains depart from **Belgrade Centar** (Prokop Station; ☑ 011 397 5533; www.srbvoz.rs; Prokupačka), while trains for Bar (Montenegro), Sofia (Bulgaria) and Thessaloniki (Greece) leave from **Topčider Station** (☑ 011 360 2899; www.srbvoz.rs; Topčiderska, Topčider), south of the city centre. See www.serbianrailways.com for updates.

Frequent trains go to Novi Sad (from 388RSD, 1½ hours, eight daily), Subotica (from 660RSD, three hours, six daily) and Niš (from 884RSD, four hours, six daily). International destinations include Bar, Montenegro (from 2833RSD, 11½ hours, 9.05pm), Budapest (from 1770RSD, eight hours, three daily), Sofia (from 2821RSD, 12 hours, 9.06am), Thessaloniki (from 4400RSD, 15 hours, 6.21pm) and Zagreb (from 2243RSD, seven hours, 10.20am and 9.19pm).

ℹ Getting Around

TO/FROM THE AIRPORT

Local bus 72 (Map p334; Jug Bogdanova, Zeleni Venac; 89RSD to 150RSD, half-hourly, 4.50am to midnight from airport, 4am to 11.40pm from town) connects the airport with Zeleni Venac (note the stop where passengers alight *from* the airport is different from the stop going *to* the airport); the cheapest tickets must be purchased from news stands. The **A1 minibus** (Map p328; Kralja Milutina, Trg Slavija) also runs between the airport and the central Trg Slavija (300RSD, 5am to 3.50am from airport, 4.20am to 3.20am from the square).

Don't get swallowed up by the airport taxi shark pit. Head to the taxi information desk (near the baggage claim area); they'll give you a taxi receipt with the name of your destination and the fare price (fixed according to six zones). A taxi from the airport to central Belgrade (Zone 2) is 1800RSD (a CarGo ride-share is about 500RSD less).

PUBLIC TRANSPORT

GSP Belgrade (www.gsp.rs) runs the city's trams and trolleybuses, which ply limited routes, but buses chug all over town. Rechargeable **BusPlus** (www2.busplus.rs) smart cards can be bought (250RSD) and topped up (89RSD per ticket) at kiosks and other outlets (eg Maxi supermarkets) across the city; tickets are 150RSD if you buy from the driver. Fares are good for 90 minutes. Unlimited paper BusPlus passes relevant to tourists are available for one, three and five days for 250RSD, 700RSD and 1000RSD, respectively.

Tram 2 (p343) connects Belgrade Fortress with Trg Slavija and the bus stations.

Belgrade Centar train station in Prokop is connected by **bus 36** (Map p328; Prokupačka) with Trg Slavija and the bus stations, and by trolleybus 40 or 41 with the city centre.

Zemun is a 45-minute walk from central Belgrade (across Brankov Most, along Nikole Tesle and the Kej Oslobođenja waterside walkway). Alternatively, take bus 15 or 84 from Zeleni Venac market.

TAXI

Move away from obvious taxi traps and flag down a distinctly labelled cruising cab, or get a local to call you one. Flag fall is 170RSD; reputable cabs should charge about 65RSD per kilometre between 6am and 10pm Monday to Friday, 85RSD between 10pm and 6am, and weekends and holidays. Make absolutely sure the meter is turned on.

Naxis Taxi (☑ 011 19084; www.naxis.rs) Order a car by phone, text, Twitter or mobile app. Rates are fixed, drivers speak English and major credit cards are accepted. You can also rent a driver for a day trip out of the city. **CarGo** (www.appcargo. net) is a popular ride-share app.

VOJVODINA ВОЈВОДИНА

Home to more than 25 ethnic groups, six official languages and the best of Hungarian and Serbian traditions, the pancake plains of the northern Vojvodina province mask a diversity unheard of in the rest of the country. Affable capital Novi Sad hosts the eclectic EXIT Festival, the largest music festival in southeastern Europe, while the hills of Fruška Gora National Park keep the noise down in hushed monasteries and ancestral vineyards. Charming Subotica, 10km from Hungary, is an oasis of art nouveau architectural gems.

Novi Sad Нови Сад

☑ 021 / POP 341,600

Novi Sad is a chipper town with all the spoils and none of the stress of the big smoke. Locals sprawl in pretty parks and outdoor cafes, and laneway bars pack out nightly. The looming Petrovaradin Fortress keeps a stern eye on proceedings, loosening its tie each July to host Serbia's largest music festival. You can walk to all of Novi Sad's attractions from the happening pedestrian thoroughfare, Zmaj Jovina, which stretches from the main square (Trg Slobode) to Dunavska.

Novi Sad isn't nicknamed the 'Athens of Serbia' for nothing: its history as a vibrant, creative city continues today in its established galleries, alternative music scene and a vibe that's generally more liberal than that of other Serbian cities. Novi Sad is 2019's European Youth Capital, and in 2021, it will become the first non-EU city to spend a year with the prestigious title of European Capital of Culture.

◉ Sights

★ Petrovaradin Fortress   FORTRESS
(Petrovaradinska Tvrdjava; Map p346; Beogradska; ☺24hr) Towering over the river on a 40m-high volcanic slab, this mighty citadel, considered Europe's second-biggest fortress (and one of its best preserved), is aptly nicknamed 'Gibraltar on the Danube'. Constructed using slave labour between 1692 and 1780, its dungeons have held notable prisoners including Karađorđe (leader of the first Serbi-

an uprising against the Turks and founder of a royal dynasty) and Yugoslav president Tito.

Have a good gawk at the iconic clock tower: the size of the minute and hour hands are reversed so far-flung fisherfolk can tell the time. Within the citadel walls, a museum (p346) offers insight into the site's history; it can also arrange tours (in English; 3500RSD) of Petrovaradin's 16km of creepy, but cool, unlit underground tunnels *(katakombe)*. Petrovaradin hosts Novi Sad's wildly popular EXIT Festival (p347) each July.

★ Gallery of Matica Srpska   MUSEUM
(Map p346; www.galerijamaticesrpske.rs; Trg Galerija 1; 100RSD; ☺10am-8pm Tue-Thu, to 10pm Fri, to 6pm Sat & Sun) First established in Pest (part of modern Budapest) in 1826 and moved to Novi Sad in 1864, this is one of Serbia's most important and long-standing cultural institutions. It's not a mere gallery but rather a national treasure, with three floors covering priceless Serbian artworks from the 18th, 19th and 20th centuries in styles ranging from Byzantine to modernist, with countless icons, portraits, landscapes and graphic art (and more) in between.

★ Štrand   BEACH
(50RSD; ☺8am-7pm) One of Europe's best by-the-Danube beaches, this 700m-long stretch morphs into a city of its own come summertime, with bars, stalls and all manner of recreational diversions attracting thousands of sun- and fun-seekers from across the globe. It's also the ultimate Novi Sad party venue, hosting everything from local punk gigs to EXIT raves. It's great for kids (watch them by the water: the currents here are strong), with playgrounds, trampolines and dozens of ice-cream and fast-food stalls.

Museum of Vojvodina   MUSEUM
(Muzej Vojvodine; Map p346; www.muzejvojvodine. org.rs; Dunavska 35-7; 200RSD; ☺9am-7pm Tue-Fri, 10am-6pm Sat & Sun) This worthwhile museum houses historical, archaeological and ethnological exhibits. The main building covers Vojvodinian history from Palaeolithic times to the late 19th century. Nearby, at building 37, which also houses the Museum of Contemporary Art Vojvodina (p346), the story continues to 1945 with harrowing emphasis on WWI and WWII. The highlights include three gold-plated Roman helmets from the 4th century, excavated in the Srem region not far from Novi Sad, and one of the city's first bicycles, dating from 1880.

Novi Sad

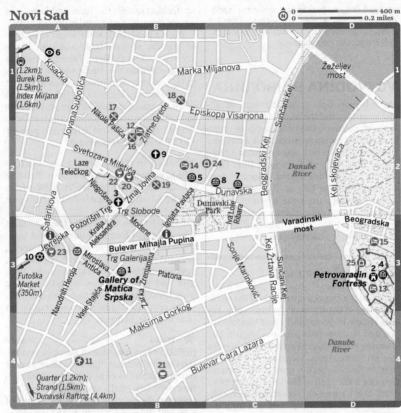

Fisherman's Island
ISLAND

(Ribarsko Ostrvo; ⊙24hr) **FREE** This small but exceedingly pleasant 'island' (it's technically a peninsula) is a wonderful spot for a Danube-side picnic or lazy stroll. More restaurants, hotels and *splavovi* are opening all the time; for now it remains a low-key city getaway for those in the know.

You can cross over to the island from the western end of the Štrand when the tide is very low; otherwise catch a taxi (around 300RSD) from the centre.

City Museum of Novi Sad – Foreign Art Collection
GALLERY

(Map p346; www.museumns.rs; Dunavska 29; 150RSD; ⊙10am-6pm Tue-Sat, noon-8pm Sun) Once the private collection of famed Novi Sad mayor and physician Branko Ilić, this special part of the City Museum's collection displays paintings by Western European artists alongside fine pieces of applied art, some of which date back to the 15th century. The Ilić col-

lection has hundreds of paintings, including several notable pieces of Venetian and other Italian Renaissance and baroque masters.

Museum of Contemporary Art Vojvodina
GALLERY

(Map p346; ☑021 526 634; www.msuv.org; Dunavska 37; ⊙10am-6pm Tue-Thu, Sat & Sun, to 8pm Fri) **FREE** Near to the Museum of Vojvodina (p345)'s main building is this annexe. It is home to the city's premier collection of Serbian (particularly Vojvodinian) and international contemporary art from the second half of the 20th century and early 21st century, including sculptures, paintings, drawings and photography, installations, conceptual and digital art and design. It hosts thematic exhibitions, featuring local provocative artists or international celebrities such as Damien Hirst.

Synagogue
SYNAGOGUE

(Map p346; Jevrejska 11; ⊙hours vary) The 1909 Synagogue of Novi Sad, designed by

Novi Sad

Hungarian architect Lipót Baumhorn, was built as the fifth one on the same location to serve the city's once large Jewish community, and is nowadays used as a concert hall due to its fine acoustics. Its art nouveau facade, yellowed bricks, stained-glass windows and sheer size make it a desirable photo and film location.

St George Church   CHURCH
(Crkva Svetog Georgija; Map p346; Pašićeva; ⊙7am-9pm) This baroque-style Orthodox church adjacent to the Bishop's Palace dates from 1734; pop inside to check out its stained-glass interior and the iconostasis, which was painted by the main artist of Serbian realism, Paja Jovanović.

🏃 Activities

Dunavski Rafting   WATER SPORTS
(☎063 825 1982; www.dunavskirafting.org; Špic Ribarskog ostrva, Fisherman's Island (eastern end); canoes or kayaks per hr/day 300/1800RSD, tours from 700RSD) Dunavski Rafting rents out canoes and kayaks and runs paddling tours to various sites along the Danube as well as a daily sunset cruise on the river. Its 'Floating Island' catamaran can be chartered for private sightseeing tours.

NS Bike   CYCLING
(Map p346; www.nsbike.rs; Sutjeska 2, Spens Stadium; user card 600RSD, bicycles per hr/day 30/170RSD; ⊙registration 8am-4pm Mon-Fri) With 13 pickup/drop-off stations around town, NS Bike makes it easy to explore (mostly flat) Novi Sad by pedal power. To rent bikes, you need to get a user card first by registering with your ID at one of the sales points.

🎭 Festivals & Events

EXIT Festival   MUSIC
(www.exitfest.org; ⊙Jul) The Petrovaradin Fortress is stormed by thousands of revellers each July during this epic festival. The first edition, in 2000, lasted 100 days and galvanised a generation of young Serbs against the Milošević regime. The festival has since been attended by the eclectic likes of Prodigy, Gogol Bordello and Motörhead...plus about 200,000 merrymakers from around the world each year.

Gradić Fest   CULTURAL
(⊙early Sep) A joint effort of Cinema City, International Festival of Street Musicians and several other events, Gradić Fest transforms the streets of the picturesque 18th-century Lower Town beneath the Petrovaradin Fortress through a series of free events featuring local and international artists from various genres. It all takes place during the first three days of September.

🛏 Sleeping

⭐**Varad Inn**   HOSTEL €
(Map p346; ☎021 431 400; www.varadinn.com; Štrosmajerova 16, Petrovaradin; dm/d/q from 1230/3960/4820RSD; ⊛🌐) Sitting in the shadow of Petrovaradin Fortress, this excellent budget option is housed in a gorgeous

yellow baroque-style building constructed in 1714. Completely renovated but making beautiful use of salvaged historical bits and bobs, the Varad Inn (get it?) has beautiful feel-at-home rooms (all with their own bathrooms, lockers and towels), a lovely cafe and garden, and communal kitchen.

★ **Narator** APARTMENT €€
(Map p346; ☑ 060 676 7886; www.en.narator. rs; Dunavska 17/Trg Republike 16; s/d apt from 3600/4800RSD; ✲ ♠) The super-central designer digs at Narator do indeed tell a story; four of them, in fact, one for every themed, individually decorated apartment. With names like 'Chambermaid from Eden', 'The Bookworm' and 'Captain Honeymoon', each room's tale unfolds via a series of exquisite, original naive-style portraits scattered across the walls. All apartments are self-contained.

★ **Hotel Veliki** HOTEL €€
(Map p346; ☑ 021 472 3840; www.hotelveliki novisad.com; Nikole Pašića 24; s/d incl breakfast from 4300/6000RSD; ✗✲♠) Sitting atop an absolutely stupendous Vojvodinian restaurant of the same name, the Veliki ('Big') lives up to its name: some of the rooms are truly huge and pleasantly modern. Staff are delightful, and the location, around the corner from Zmaj Jovina, is top-notch.

Leopold I LUXURY HOTEL €€€
(Map p346; ☑ 021 488 7878; www.leopoldns.com; Petrovaradin Fortress; 1st-fl r/ste incl breakfast from 16,800/24,000RSD, 2nd-fl r/ste incl breakfast from 10,800/16,800RSD; ✗✲♠) This rock-top, 59-room hotel in the Petrovaradin complex is split into two sections, with two different names: the 1st floor, **Leopold I**, is given over to indulgent baroque-style digs while the 2nd floor, **Garni Hotel Leopold I**, comprises modern, (slightly) economical rooms. The location is unbeatable, and breakfast at the terrace restaurant is a princely way to start the day.

✕ Eating

★ **Toster Bar** BURGERS €
(Map p346; www.tosterbar.rs; Zmaj Jovina 24; burgers 320-860RSD; ☉ 10am-11pm Mon-Thu, to 1am Fri & Sat, 11am-11pm Sun; ♠) There are likely better Serbian-style *pljeskavica* in Novi Sad, but there certainly aren't better American-style burgers, and the beauty of wildly popular Toster is that it does both!

Tucked away in a jam-packed *pasaž* (passage), it's a Croatian-owned, cash-only joint doing fat, juicy and spicy (Carolina Reaper spicy!) burgers along with a wise devotion to craft beer.

Burek Plus BAKERY €
(Rumenačka 106; pastries 90-160RSD; ☉ 5am-5pm Mon-Fri, 5pm-midnight Sat) Get in line with the locals at Novi Sad's best bet for *burek* – this dead-simple spot churns out delicious meat, cheese, potato and plain versions until they run out (usually around noon).

Index Mirjana FAST FOOD €
(Braće Popović 8; sandwiches 200-290RSD; ☉ 7am-11pm Sun-Thu, to midnight Fri & Sat) The consensus among Novosadjani is that this hole-in-the-wall of a sandwich shop produces the best version of the locally famous Index sandwich – an indulgent, sauce-laden spin on a ham-and-cheese sandwich – in the friendliest of manners.

★ **Fish i Zeleniš** MEDITERRANEAN €€
(Fish and Greens; Map p346; ☑ 021 452 002; www. fishizelenis.com; Skerlićeva 2; mains 696-2900RSD; ☉ noon-11pm; ♠✐) This character-filled, snug little nook serves up the finest vegetarian and pescatarian meals in northern Serbia. Organic, locally sourced ingredients? Ambient? Ineffably delicious? Tick, tick, tick. Check the daily specials or spring for one of its excellently prepared Mediterranean staples, guided by the affable staff.

★ **Project 72** SERBIAN €€
(Map p346; ☑ 021 657 2720; www.wineanddeli. rs; Kosovska 15; small plates 242-898RSD, mains 725-1692RSD; ☉ 9am-11pm Mon-Thu, to 1am Fri & Sat; ♠) ✐ This smart bistro with lovely sidewalk seating is brought to Novi Sad by the same owners as the excellent Fish i Zeleniš (p348), but here the concentration is on creative tapas and heartier, Mediterranean/Serbian meat dishes, which pair wonderfully with the deep wine list featuring 21 Serbian wines by the glass.

Café Veliki SERBIAN €€
(Map p346; ☑ 021 533 420; www.cafeveliki.com; Nikole Pašića 24; mains 550-1450RSD; ☉ 8am-11pm Sun-Thu, to midnight Fri-Sat; ♠) ✐ Far from Novi Sad's standard hotel restaurants, Café Veliki – inside Hotel Veliki – is a go-to destination for Vojvodinian cuisine in a hip, industrial-chic environment, with sustainable architecture throughout.

RURAL ESCAPES

Hang your crown at **Dvorac Fantast** (Дворац Фантаст; 🖋 021 691 5200; www.pikbecej.
rs/dvorac-fantast; Potes Salaši 1, Bečej; s/d/tr/apt from 3220/4570/5580/5770RSD; 🅿 🛜),
a dreamy mansion in Vojvodina's north. Built in 1919 by Bogdan Dunđerski, a famous
Vojvodinian landowner, the gleaming castle is set on lavish grounds, complete with a
working thoroughbred stable and a small chapel. Rooms are furnished with period pieces. The opulent **restaurant** (mains 450RSD to 900RSD) focuses on Vojvodinian cuisine.
The castle is open to visitors (tours 120RSD). It's 60km east of Novi Sad.

While **Salaš 137** (🖋 021 714 497; www.salas137.rs; Čenej; mains 550-1650RSD) is perfect
for rustic repose, it's the traditional Vojvodinian-style feasting and the activities that
draw the crowds. Work in the organic garden, go for a carriage ride, feed the animals –
you'll work up an appetite worthy of the famously huge meals they serve here. Sleep it
off in charming **rooms** (single/double/triple 4500/5350/6350RSD) furnished in Alt
Deutsche style. Salaš 137 is 10km north of Novi Sad, just off the E75 motorway.

🍷 Drinking & Nightlife

★ Kafeterija
COFFEE

(Map p346; www.kafeterija.com; Lovćenska 9;
⏱ 7am-11pm Mon-Sat, from 8am Sun; 🛜) Belgrade-based Kafeterija produces Novi Sad's
best 'Third Wave' java in this cosy coffeehouse chock-full of plush lounge furniture
and exposed cement support beams. Lovely
patio as well.

PUBeraj
BAR

(Map p346; www.facebook.com/puberajcafee; Mite
Ružića; ⏱ 8am-11pm Mon-Thu, to 1am Fri & Sat,
noon-11pm Sun; 🛜) The hippest and certainly the most local of the smattering of bars
around Laze Telečkog, PUBeraj is the brain-
child of local Andrija Nikitović, who figured
a stylish cocktail bar sandwiched between a
barbershop (Berberaj) and salon (FeniRaj)
was just what Novi Sad needed. It features
at least 30 whiskies, and hosts DJs and live
music several times per week.

Škripa Pub
CRAFT BEER

(Map p346; www.facebook.com/skripapub; Jevrejska 1; ⏱ 3-11pm Sun-Thu, to 1am Fri & Sat; 🛜)
Tucked away in a former home that sits in
a residential parking lot 450m southwest of
Trg Slobode, 'Screech' pub is just far enough
from the centre to feel like a find. Six taps
of mostly local craft beer – including Novi
Sad's own 3Bir and Razbeerbriga, as often
as possible – go down too easy with the cool
tunes and laid-back ambience.

Beer Store
CRAFT BEER

(Map p346; www.beerstore.rs; Svetozara Miletića
17; ⏱ 4pm-midnight Sun-Thu, to 1am Fri & Sat; 🛜)
Don't let the name confuse you, Novi Sad's
top craft beer destination features 20 mostly
Serbian brews on draught, along with another 180 or so in bottles. Expect several pale
ales and IPAs from Novi Sad's finest, 3Bir,
which can be enjoyed on the outdoor patio
along this atmospheric pedestrianised street.

Quarter
CLUB

(www.clubquarter.net; Bul Despota Stefana 5, Chinese Quarter; ⏱ hours vary; 🛜) Hosting regular
exhibitions, live music gigs and all manner
of avant-garde performances, the Quarter
is also a top spot for a drink and hanging
out with the offbeat locals that the Chinese
Quarter attracts. Pop next door to club Fabrika, the neighbourhood's arty-crew HQ.

🛍 Shopping

Galerija ITD
ART

(Map p346; www.design-radosevic.com/galerija-itd;
Petrovaradin Fortress; ⏱ 10am-10pm) For unique
Novi Sad and Yugoslavia-centric screen
printed T-shirts, art prints and posters, head
to this gallery featuring the work of famed
local artist Branislav Radošević, whose iconic designs have interpreted Novi Sad pop
culture for four decades.

Futoška Market
MARKET

(Futoška pijaca; Žike Popovića 4; ⏱ 6am-6pm Mon-
Sat, to 2pm Sun) This century-old market – the
city's largest – is often said to be even busier
than the main street in Novi Sad. You can
find pretty much anything here, from fruit
and veg to local meats and sweets, clothes
and other kinds of stuff (sometimes all on a
single stall). A fascinating place to explore.

ℹ Information

The centre of town is awash with free wi-fi: the
network is 'Evropska Prestonica Kulture 2021'
and the password is 'opens2019'.

WORTH A TRIP

HISTORIC BAČ

For a concentrated hit of Vojvodina's history, head to **Bač Fortress** (Bačka tvrđava, Бачка Тврђава; www.turizam.bac.rs; Bač; ⏰ 4-8pm Mon-Fri, noon-8pm Sat & Sun) FREE, 65km west of Novi Sad. The town's star attraction is its partially ruined fortress. Records indicate it was first built in AD 873, before being annexed, renovated and destroyed repeatedly by various empires until the 18th century. These days you can visit the main tower and check out a small archaeological exhibition.

Buses from Novi Sad run to Bač (710RSD, 1¾ hours, 12 daily).

Bač town's other highlights include a recently renovated **Franciscan monastery** (first established by Knights Templar in 1169) and the ruins of a 16th-century **hammam**, the only surviving Turkish bath in Vojvodina.

The Tourist Organisation of the City of Novi Sad operates two tourist information centres; one at **Jevrejska** (Turistički info centri; Map p346; ☐ 021 661 7343; www.novisad.travel; Jevrejska 10; ⏰ 7.30am-5pm Mon-Fri, 10am-3pm Sat) on the way to the main bus and railway stations; and on **Bulevar Mihajla Pupina** (☐ 021 421 811; Bul Mihajla Pupina 9; ⏰ 7.30am-5pm Mon-Fri, 10am-5pm Sat) near the Petrovaradin Fortress, Belgrade Quay and the Danube.

Apoteka Bulevar (www.apotekanovisad.co.rs; Bul Mihajla Pupina 7; ⏰ 24hr) This 24hr-art deco pharmacy is nearly an attraction in and of itself!

Klinički Centar Vojvodine (☐ 021 484 3484; www.kcv.rs; Hajduk Veljkova 1) Novi Sad's hospital.

Magelan Travel (☐ 021 420 680; www.magelantravel.rs; Nikole Pašića 7; ⏰ 8am-5pm Mon-Fri, to 2pm Sat) An established operator offering a range of small-group day and two-day excursions around Serbia, including sightseeing, wine and spa tours and more. All trips can also be booked through the **Serbian Adventures** (☐ 062 737 242; www.serbianadventures.com) website.

❶ Getting There & Away

The **bus station** (Međumesna autobuska stanica Novi Sad; ☐ 021 444 022; Bul Jaše Tomića 6) has regular departures to Belgrade (700RSD, one hour, every 10 to 30 minutes) and Subotica (790RSD, 1¾ hours). There are a dozen or so buses to Niš (1780RSD, 5½ hours). Two buses go daily to Budapest (3130RSD, 5¾ hours, 9.15am and 10.15pm).

Frequent trains leave the **train station** (Železnička stanica Novi Sad; ☐ 021 420 700; www.srbvoz.rs; Bul Jaše Tomića 4), next door to the bus station, for Belgrade (400RSD, 1¾ hours) and Subotica (490RSD, 2½ hours). At least three trains go daily to Budapest (1500RSD, 6½ hours, 9.26am, 1.17pm and 11.30pm).

❶ Getting Around

From the Novi Sad train station, city bus 4B (65RSD) will take you to the town centre.

Crveni i Red Taxi (www.crvenitaxi.co.rs/aplikacija) is the most reliable taxi app for Novi Sad.

Novi Sad has a long history with bicycle transport (its first bicycle club was founded in 1886). The city counts approximately 80km of bike paths with expansion plans in the works.

Fruška Gora National Park ФРУШКА ГОРА & Sremski Karlovci СРЕМСКИ КАРЛОВЦИ

Serbia's oldest national park, Fruška Gora is an 80km stretch of rolling hills where cloistered life has endured since monasteries were built between the 15th and 18th centuries to safeguard Serbian culture from the Turks. Of the 35 original monasteries, 16 remain and they're open to visitors. Fruška Gora is also famous for its small but select wineries; grapes were first planted here in AD 3 by the Romans.

Almost 100 million years ago, Fruška Gora was an island in the Pannonian Sea; its highest peak is Crveni Čot (539m). Today its forests make for pleasant hikes and off-road bike rides. The region is dotted with photogenic villages – none more so than baroque-style Sremski Karlovci, the gateway to the park.

◉ Sights

Little Sremski Karlovci is a lovely place to simply wander. Most of its architectural and historical sights are scattered in and around the main square, including **St Nicholas Orthodox Cathedral** (1762; its splendid iconostasis is the work of Serbia's leading baroque painter, Teodor Kračun), the **Patriarchy residence**, the working **Karlovci Theological School** (1794) and **Karlovci Grammar School** (1791), Serbia's oldest. The round yellow **Chapel of Peace** (1817) at the southern end of the village is where the Turks and Austrians signed the 1699 Peace Treaty;

famously, this is where the round table was used for the first time in the history of diplomacy. Local rumour has it that if one drinks from the magnificent **Four Lions fountain**, they'll return to Karlovci to be married.

⚡ Activities

A 9.5km circular **hiking** path starts and ends at the National Park Office on Iriški Venac; most of the route is through the forest and it's well signposted.

Fruška Gora hosts a **mountaineering marathon** (www.fruskogorski-maraton.com) each May, with 19 trails ranging in character from recreational to competitive and in length from 4km to 133km. The website has downloadable trail maps.

In summer you can rent bikes/canoes (per day 600/2000RSD) at these locations in Sremski Karlovci: bikes at Mitropolita Stratimirovića 5, and canoes from Naša Čarda restaurant next to Hotel Dunav (p351).

★ Museum of Beekeeping & Wine Cellar Živanović   WINE
(Muzej pčelarstva i vinski podrum Živanović; ☑ 021 881 071; www.muzejzivanovic.com; Mitropolita Stratimirovića 86b, Sremski Karlovci; tour 250RSD, degustation 450RSD, tour & degustation 650RSD; ⏲ 8am-4pm) This small museum covers, unsurprisingly, beekeeping and winemaking. While you're here, it'd be a crime not to try (and buy) a few glasses of the local wine, *bermet*. The wine degustation includes seven different wines and three types of honey.

The opening hours are flexible, so it's a good idea to phone before visiting.

Kovačević Wine House   WINE
(Vinska kuća Kovačević; ☑ 022 463 137; www.vinskakucakovacevic.com; Krstašice bb, Irig; ⏲ 8am-11pm) This is one of the most famous wineries in Fruška Gora. For over 100 years, it has produced top-shelf reds and whites; trying the local *bermet* is a must. The winery's take on Vojvodinian cuisine is gorgeously gourmet. Degustations are organised at the restaurant (Wine House) and best booked ahead; the winery itself is a short drive away in Irig.

🛏 Sleeping & Eating

Hotel Dunav   HOTEL €€
(☑ 021 884 008; www.hoteldunav.co.rs; Dunavska 5, Sremski Karlovci; s/d/tr 3850/4450/6170RSD; apt 5200-8890RSD; P ❄ 🞉 ☰) Smack on the Danube, the flower-draped Dunav is a good all-rounder, with comfortable large rooms (though slightly dated bathrooms), a sauna,

outdoor pool, huge entertainment room and a terrace restaurant that's worth a visit in its own right. The management can assist with day trips, wine tastings and boat trips.

★ Vrdnička Kula   CABIN €€€
(☑ 063 495 319; www.etnoselo-vk.rs; Potes pod kulom bb, Vrdnik; cabin s/d/tr 9950/9950/12,050RSD; hotel from s/d/apt 6150/8600/30,500RSD; P ❄ 🞉) Looking for a green getaway? Put this forest oasis at the top of your list. The sprawling complex is modelled on an *etno selo* (traditional village), with quaint wooden buildings (including a chapel), restaurant, wine cellar, wellness centre and playground. The compound has two parts: the 'village' offers traditional cabins, while the hotel has modern rooms.

Brankov Čardak   SERBIAN €€
(☑ 021 298 3530; Stražilovo; mains 400-1700RSD; ⏲ noon-10pm) Tucked away at the end of a forest road and perpetually shrouded in barbecue smoke, this is a Fruška Gora institution. Its setting, in the idyllic Stražilovo valley, can't be beaten. Though the menu is simple, the Serbian classics are grilled, basted and baked to perfection. It's only 5km from Sremski Karlovci.

★ Pasent   EUROPEAN €€€
(☑ 021 881 696; Dunavska 7, Sremski Karlovci; mains 490-3100RSD; ⏲ 9am-11pm) Down by the Danube, with a huge lantern-decorated garden and a soundtrack of chillout bossa nova tunes, gorgeous Pasent is an unmissable dining experience in Sremski Karlovci. Naturally, the fish (choose between carp, trout, sterlet, catfish and pike) is delicious, and served grilled, smoked, in a soup or a stew. Don't miss the *kuglof*, the famous Austro-Hungarian dessert popular in Vojvodina.

ℹ Information

Fruška Gora National Park Office (☑ 021 463 666; www.npfruskagora.co.rs; Iriški Venac; ⏲ 8am-4pm Mon-Fri, from 10am Sat) Drop in for accommodation assistance as well as maps and books covering the region.

Sremski Karlovci Tourist Organisation (☑ 021 882 127; www.karlovci.org.rs; Patrijarha Rajačića 1; ⏲ 8am-6pm Mon-Fri, 10am-6pm Sat & Sun) The helpful staff speak English and can find private accommodation or organise tours.

ℹ Getting There & Away

The park is an easy 11km drive from Novi Sad. Alternatively, catch a bus in Novi Sad bound for

DON'T MISS

BIRDWATCHING IN CARSKA BARA ЦАРСКА БАРА

Carska Bara's name translates as 'Imperial Swamp' and this **nature reserve** (☑063 325 868; www.carskabara. rs; Beloblatski put bb; walking trail adult/ child 150/100RSD, 2hr boat tour adult/child 450/400RSD, canoe hire per hr 500RSD, birdwatching per 2hr 2000RSD; ☺boat tours 1pm & 3pm Sat & Sun) is indeed one of the country's most important protected areas. Among its 250 bird species are the white-tailed eagle and all 10 species of the European heron. There are also 24 registered fish species, as well as mammals, such as otters and wild boar, and 500 types of plants.

Activities include walking along a 4km signposted trail, birdwatching and boat tours; you can also rent canoes. Maps and brochures are available from the **visitors centre** at the start of the walking trail. There's a **restaurant** with parking 250m from the reserve (across the road).

Carska Bara is located 60km east of Novi Sad; it's easily accessed by car.

Irig (175RSD, 40 minutes) and ask to be dropped off at Novo Hopovo Monastery. From here, catch local buses to other points such as Vrdnik and Iriški Venac. Stražilovo is only 5km from Sremski Karlovci; a taxi ride is 500RSD.

Local buses 61 and 62 (135RSD, 25 minutes) run frequently between Sremski Karlovci and Novi Sad.

❶ Getting Around

Having your own car is the best option for exploring the park's monasteries and wineries. The Iriški Venac crossroads connects the villages of Fruška Gora with Novi Sad and all points south.

Public transport gets you to villages within the park, from where you can walk between sights. Buses between Novi Sad and the villages of Fruška Gora display two-digit numbers, usually starting with a 7; ask the driver to let you off where you want to go. Private buses, which you can hail, also run through the region.

Subotica Суботица

☑ 024 / POP 97,910

Sugar-spun art nouveau marvels, a laid-back populace and a sprinkling of Serbian and Hungarian flavours make this leafy town – the second largest in Vojvodina and practically at the Hungarian border – a worthy day trip or stopover. Once an important and wealthy hub of the Austro-Hungarian Empire, Subotica attracted some of the region's most influential architects and artists; their excellently preserved handiwork is today the town's biggest drawcard. It's also one of Serbia's most multicultural towns, with more Hungarians than Serbs, and a sizeable population of Croats.

◉ Sights

★Synagogue   SYNAGOGUE
(Sinagoga; www.en.josu.rs; Trg Sinagoge 2; adult/ child 250RSD/free; ☺10am-6pm Tue-Fri, to 2pm Sat & Sun) Subotica's first art nouveau building is the splendid 1902 synagogue designed by Marcell Komor and Deszö Jakab. Its stylised decorations in the form of tulips and peacock feathers are typical of the Hungarian Secession style; it also features stained-glass windows from Miksa Róth's studio and roof tiles made of Zsolnay ceramics. The synagogue was restored to its full glory inside and out in 2018.

City Hall   HISTORIC BUILDING
(Gradska kuća; ☑024 555 128; Trg Slobode; tour with/without tower 300/150RSD; ☺tours noon Tue-Sat) Built in 1910 and designed by Marcell Komor and Deszö Jakab, this behemoth is a curious mix of art nouveau and something Gaudí may have had a playful dab at. The council chambers – with exquisite stained-glass windows, Zsolnay ceramics and elaborate decor – are not to be missed. A guided tour of the building takes place at noon; you can also opt to climb its soaring, 76m-high tower for fantastic views.

Modern Art Gallery Subotica   GALLERY
(Savremena galerija Subotica; www.sgsu.org.rs; Park Ferenca Rajhla 5; adult/child 100/50RSD; ☺8am-7pm Mon-Fri, 9am-1pm Sat) This mansion, also known as Raichle Palace, was built in 1904 as the home and design studio of architect Ferenc Raichle, and it shows. One of the most sumptuous buildings in Serbia, it's inspired by Transylvanian folk art in a vibrant flourish of mosaics, ceramic tiles, floral patterns and stained glass. Varying exhibitions are hosted here, but even if there's nothing on, the palace offers eye candy in spades.

City Museum Subotica   MUSEUM
(Gradski muzej Subotica; www.gradskimuzej.subotica.rs; Trg Sinagoge 3; 150RSD; ☺10am-6pm Tue-Sat) Eclectic exhibitions are the highlights

in this 1906 art nouveau residence of the Dömötör family designed by Budapest's Vago brothers. The building's geometric elements are typical of the Viennese Secession style. An entire gallery is dedicated to the Hungarian fine arts in Vojvodina (1830–1930), including a huge portrait of Empress Maria Theresa by Mór Than.

Lake Palić LAKE
(Palićko jezero; www.palic.rs; bike per hr/day 200/1000RSD, kayak/pedalboat/motorboat per 30min 200/500/1000RSD) The resort town of Palić, 8km from Subotica, is home to a 5-sq-km lake popular with boaters, fisherfolk and afternoon amblers; its water isn't approved for swimming, but there's an outdoor thermal pool. The park is graced with villas, restaurants and fine examples of Hungarian art nouveau, including the 1912 **Grand Terrace**, the mushroom-like **water tower** and the folksy wooden **Women's Lido** (with a cafe). There's a 3km birdwatching trail, plus bikes and boats for hire.

🛌 Sleeping

Pansion Mali Hotel GUESTHOUSE €€
(☑024 552 977; www.malihotelsubotica.com; Harambašićeva 25; s/d/tr 2720/4140/5560RSD; P❄ 🛜) A great choice for a no-fuss stay, this comfortable, modern guesthouse with friendly staff is located in a quiet street near the town centre. The rooms are spacious and bright (if a little bland) and the bathrooms are spick and span. Breakfast is available for €3.

Hotel Galleria HOTEL €€€
(☑024 647 111; www.galleria-center.com; Matije Korvina 17; s/d 7330/9460RSD, apt/ste from 10,640/22,460RSD; ❄🛜) These four-star rooms resemble a 'gentleman's den', with warm mahogany-looking fittings and beds lined with bookshelves. The hotel also houses a gigantic wellness centre and several restaurants. It's inside the Atrium shopping plaza; the parking costs €6 per day.

🍴 Eating & Drinking

Ravel DESSERTS €
(www.ravel.rs; Branislava Nušića 2; cakes 135-220RSD; ☺9am-10pm Mon-Sat, from 11am Sun) Don't miss this adorable art nouveau classic for a fab selection of cakes, from Hungarian *doboš torta* and sugar-soaked *šampita* to heavenly chestnut puree and the ubiquitous baklava.

Kafana Bates EASTERN EUROPEAN €€
(☑024 556 008; www.batessubotica.com; Vuka Karadžića 17; mains 540-1350RSD; ☺10am-10pm

Mon-Sat, 11am-4pm Sun) This isn't a place for a light nibble: the chefs ladle up huge portions of belt-busting Serbian and Hungarian dishes, from grilled meats and fish to goulash. The restaurant's interior is a tad twee (in a good way), and the garden terrace is perfect on summer evenings (or for escaping the smoke indoors). Expect live *tamburaši* (mandolin-like music) on Friday nights.

Bodis & Porto CAFE
(Rudić ulica 1; ☺7am-11pm Sun-Thu, to midnight Fri & Sat) A slick, colourful lounge that plays the likes of Lou Reed on one of Subotica's leafy streets, Bodis & Porto has a small but creative selection of sandwiches, pastas and salads; there's even a vegetarian burrito. It doubles as a bar in the evenings.

★Klein House Social Bar & Art Gallery BAR
(☑063 709 3636; www.kleinhousegallery.com; Štrosmajerova 9; ☺10am-11pm Mon-Thu, to midnight Fri, 6pm-midnight Sat) Part gallery, part bar, part avant-garde exhibition space, this is a cool, cultured place to spend an evening. It's a favourite haunt for local and visiting creatives. The wine list isn't bad either, and the place often hosts tasting nights.

ℹ Information

Tourist Information Office (☑024 670 350; www.visitsubotica.rs; Trg Slobode; ☺8am-4pm Mon-Fri, 9am-1pm Sat) Friendly, English-speaking staff provide advice and brochures at the City Hall.

ℹ Getting There & Away

From the **bus station** (www.sutrans.rs; Senćanski put 3) there are hourly services to Novi Sad (760RSD, two hours) and Belgrade (1060RSD, 3½ hours).

Subotica's **train station** (Bose Milećević bb) has three daily trains to Budapest (2430RSD, four hours). Trains to Belgrade (560RSD, 3½ hours, six daily) stop at Novi Sad (384RSD, 1½ hours).

WESTERN & CENTRAL SERBIA

Great adventures await southwest of Belgrade. The thickly forested Tara National Park is arguably the country's most scenic slice, with an enormous canyon, resplendent river and wildlife galore. The rolling green hills of Šumadija (meaning 'forest land') encircle the first capital of modern Serbia, historic Kragujevac. Pressed against Balkan neighbours are the melding cultural heritages of Novi Pazar and the Raška region (aka 'Sandžak'), the last to be liberated from Ottoman rule.

Tara National Park & Around

With 220 sq km of forested slopes, dramatic ravines, jewel-like waterways and rewarding views, Tara National Park (Национални Парк Тара; part of the Dinaric Alps) is scenic Serbia at its best. The park's main attraction is the vertigo-inducing Drina River canyon, the third largest of its kind in the world. The gloriously green river slices through the cliffs, offering prime panoramas and ripper rafting; Tara's two lakes, Perućac and Zaovine, are ideal for calm-water kayaking.

Serbia's largest population of endangered brown bears is found within Tara's woods, though you'd be lucky to bump into any. The park is also home to foxes, lynxes, otters and 130-plus types of birds, as well as over 1000 flora species, including the rare Pančić spruce.

○ Sights

Lake Perućac   LAKE
(Jezero Perućac) Lake Perućac was created in 1966 by the damming of the Drina, and has been a favourite with families and fisherfolk ever since. Marking the border between Serbia and Bosnia and Hercegovina, it's dotted with pontoons, houseboats and paddleboats, though given the lake is 52km long, it's easy to find your own secluded spot. The visitors centre (p356) on its shores rents out **kayaks** (per hour/day 200/800RSD); boat tours are another popular way to explore the calm blue waters.

Lake Zaovine   LAKE
(Zaovinsko jezero) Surrounded by thick woods dotted with quaint villages, the artificial Lake Zaovine is a serene spot in Tara's south. Almost preternaturally peaceful, it's a top spot for doing nothing – as well as taking a dip. For more active exploration, rent a **kayak** (per hour/day 200/800RSD) from the Mitrovac visitors centre (p356).

Drvengrad   VILLAGE
(Küstendorf; ☑ 064 883 0213; www.mecavnik.info; Mećavnik hill, Mokra Gora; adult/child 250/100RSD; ⊙ 7am-7pm) Drvengrad ('Timbertown') in Mokra Gora was built by enigmatic film-

maker Emir Kusturica in 2002 for his film *Life Is a Miracle.* Quirky flourishes are everywhere: the Stanley Kubrick cinema shows Kusturica's films, and vintage cars are parked on twisting streets named after celebrities such as Bruce Lee and Diego Maradona (about whom Kusturica made a fascinating documentary). Drvengrad hosts the international **Küstendorf Film and Music Festival** (www.kustendorf-filmandmusicfestival.org) each January. The village is 40km from Tara National Park.

★**Kadinjača
Memorial Complex**   MEMORIAL
(Spomen kompleks Kadinjača; ⊙ memorial hall 8am-4pm Mon-Fri, 10am-4pm Sat) Serbia's most grandiose *spomenik* (Yugoslav-era memorial), Kadinjača commemorates the Partisans from the Workers' Battalion who perished on this spot fighting the Germans in November 1941. Rising on a green hill like some futuristic Stonehenge, the arresting series of white granite monoliths of various heights and angles culminates in two 14m-high pillars that together form a symbolic 'bullet hole' sculpture. The 15-hectare complex comprises a stone pyramid with a crypt for the fallen soldiers.

The memorial complex is located 14km northwest of Užice, accessed from the road to Bajina Bašta. If visiting from Bajina Bašta, a return taxi should cost around 1300RSD.

🏃 Activities

Tara offers more than spectator scenery; there are countless ways to get your pulse rate up in the park's glorious mountains, forests, canyons and waterways. The visitors centres (p356) can help with any outdoor activities that float your boat. **Wild Serbia** (☑ 063 273 852; www.wildserbia.com) runs canyoning and kayaking trips.

★**Šargan Eight**   RAIL
(Šarganska osmica; ☑ Mon-Fri 031 510 288; www.sarganskaosmica.rs; Mokra Gora; adult/child 600/300RSD; ⊙ 3 daily Jul & Aug, 2 daily Apr-Jun, Sep & Oct, daily Dec-Feb) The Šargan Eight tourist train, stationed in Mokra Gora, was once part of a narrow-gauge railway linking Belgrade with Sarajevo and Dubrovnik. The joy of the 2½-hour round-trip is in its disorienting twists, turns and tunnels (all 22 of them). The vintage train chugs past some stupendous mountain scenery; but hang on to your camera; it's a long way down. Mokra Gora is located 40km from Tara National Park.

DON'T MISS

ZLATIBOR ЗЛАТИБОР

A romantic region of gentle mountains, traditions and hospitality, Zlatibor (meaning 'golden pine') is located south of Tara National Park. Not far beyond the resort centre – which has become overdeveloped and commercialised in recent years – are quaint villages that feel a million miles away; it's a road-tripping wonderland.

Sirogojno Open-Air Museum (Muzej na otvorenom Sirogojno; ☑ 031 380 2291; www.siro gojno.org.rs; adult/child 150/100RSD; ☺ 9am-7pm Apr-Oct, to 4pm Nov-Mar) Tumble back in time at this wonderful village-museum. High-roofed, fully furnished wooden houses are spread across a pleasant mountainside; each contains displays and artefacts covering various aspects of life in 19th-century Serbia.

Stopića Cave (Stopića pećina; adult/child 250/150RSD; ☺ 9.30am-4.30pm Nov-Mar, to 6pm Apr-Oct) This limestone cave with a massive entrance is a 4km drive north of Sirogojno. The underground river that runs through it has created fantastic pools and waterfalls, illuminated by coloured lights to magical effect.

Gostilje Waterfall (Vodopad Gostilje; www.gostiljevodopad.rs; adult/child 150/100RSD; ☺ 9am-8pm) A popular picnic spot on the outskirts of Zlatibor is dominated by a 20m-high waterfall that morphs into a series of scenic miniature cascades accessed by steps and footbridges. It's an enjoyable 12km drive from Sirogojno.

Express buses connect Zlatibor with Belgrade (1350RSD, four hours, 10 daily) and Novi Sad (1250RSD, 6½ hours, four daily). Without your own car, the easiest way to go exploring is on a tour; **Zlatibor Tours** (☑ 063 245 943; www.zlatibortours.com; Tržni centar bb; ☺ 8am-10pm) offers accommodation and tour bookings.

Hiking

The park has 25 hiking trails, five of which are billed as 'educational paths', with signposts and seating along the way; see the park website (www.nptara.rs) for information or drop into the visitors centres for maps.

Easy paths lead to Tara's five official lookouts, the most popular of which is **Banjska Stena** for its spectacular views of Lake Perućac, the Drina canyon and mountains stretching across the border to Bosnia. The 6km gravel trail starts in Mitrovac and is open to hikers as well as drivers. Another is **Crnjeskovo**, which is 3km from Kaluđerske Bare and also has fantastic views of the Rača River canyon and Bajina Bašta.

Mountain Biking

The Tara region is criss-crossed with mountain-biking trails (many of which are also shared with hikers). Routes include a mountainous 29km loop through the forest (starting and ending at Šljivovica village, near Kaluđerske Bare) and the incredibly scenic, only semi-gruelling 42km 'Empress Tara' journey through the heart of the park (Kaludjerske Bare to Perućac). If you don't have your own bike, the visitors centre in Mitrovac (p356) rents them out (one hour/day 150/600RSD). Maps are available at the visitors centres or online at www.mapa.iz.rs.

☞ Tours

Tara Tours ADVENTURE
(☑ 031 861 501; www.taratours.rs; Svetosavska 80, Bajina Bašta; ☺ 9am-4pm Mon-Fri, to noon Sat) This local agency offers adventures in and around Tara, including boat trips (per person 2200RSD, five times weekly in July and August, on weekends in June and September), Drina rafting, bear-watching, sightseeing excursions and hosted visits to the annual **Bajina Bašta Regatta** (Drinska regata; www.regata.rs; ☺ Jul). Staff can also help with finding private accommodation in the area.

🛏 Sleeping & Eating

Vila Drina HOTEL €€
(☑ 031 859 300; Perućac; s/d/ste 4700/6500/8800RSD; P ❖ 🕏) This cute hotel sits beside the tiny Vrelo River (365m long) and the mighty Drina; it's a good base for Tara activities or for simply escaping from the world. The building itself – more like a stately home than a hotel – is old, but has been renovated; rooms aren't posh, but they're comfortable and modern enough.

Hotel Omorika HOTEL €€
(☑ 031 315 0050; www.hotelitara.mod.gov.rs; Kaluđerske Bare; s/d incl breakfast & dinner from 4200/7600RSD; P ❖ 🕏 ≋) High up in the hills (1059m), this huge hotel sits right in

the heart of the national park. Run by the Serbian army and with a fantastic Yugoslav-retro lobby, it's nevertheless a great choice both for its location and the tremendous list of facilities on offer, including an indoor pool, a sauna, a movie theatre and a bowling alley.

★ Restoran Vrelo   SERBIAN €€
(✆ 031 859 095; Perućac; mains 520-800RSD; fish 2200-2900RSD; ⊙ 7am-10pm) Next door to Vila Drina (p355), this large restaurant that dishes up classic Serbian fare gets top marks for location: its wooden terrace, tucked into the greenery, sits atop the tiny Vrelo River's lovely waterfall on the Drina (a view best admired from a boat). It's well worth ordering the (pricier) fresh fish here.

Javor   SERBIAN €€
(Kaluđerske Bare; mains 530-1200RSD; ⊙ 10am-midnight) Across the road from Hotel Omorika (p355), Javor is true to its mountain setting with large outdoor bench-style tables in the shade of tall pine trees. It's the place to go if you're up for some local game specialities such as wild boar goulash or venison ragout, although there are plenty of standard Serbian dishes on the menu. The service can be slow.

❶ Information

Tara National Park Visitors Centre (✆ 031 863 644; www.nptara.rs; Milenka Topalovića 3, Bajina Bašta; ⊙ 8am-4pm Mon-Fri, 10am-4pm Sat) The main park management office and visitors centre is in Bajina Bašta. There are other visitors centres in **Mitrovac** (⊙ 9am-4pm; 🛜) and **Perućac** (⊙ 9am-4pm Jun-Aug).

❶ Getting There & Around

Buses (1040RSD, 4½ hours, five daily) run between Belgrade and **Bajina Bašta bus station** (✆ 031 865 485; Svetosavska 3, Bajina Bašta).

Bajina Bašta, on the park's eastern edge, is the gateway to the area. From Bajina Bašta, there are buses to Mitrovac within Tara National Park (190RSD, three daily) as well as to Kaluđerske Bare and Perućac. If you're driving, the roads to Perućac, Mitrovac and Kaluđerske Bare are signposted.

Kragujevac Крагујевац

📲 034 / POP 150,800

Sheltered by the rolling green hills of Šumadija region, industrial Kragujevac might not be of huge tourist appeal but it's an important destination for anyone with an interest in history. This was the first capital (1818–41) of the modern Serbian state, the birthplace of its industrial revolution, and the location of one of the greatest tragedies the country suffered during WWII – these important stories are told in the town's three worthwhile museums. Today Kragujevac is Serbia's fourth-largest city, a lively place with a significant student population and an up-and-coming music festival; it's also a good base for exploring the region.

◉ Sights

★ **Memorial Museum '21st October'**   MUSEUM
(Muzej 'Kragujevački oktobar'; www.spomenpark. rs; Desankin venac bb, Memorijalni park Šumarice; 100RSD; ⊙ 8am-6pm Mon-Fri, 9am-4pm Sat & Sun) Šumarice Memorial Park is home to a sombre museum that tells the harrowing

---

ALPINE ADVENTURES

Clustered around Pančić Peak (Pančićev Vrh; 2017m), **Kopaonik** (Копаоник; www.tckopao nik.com; day/3-day/weekly ski pass 3200/8590/15050RSD) has 200 sunny days a year, snow cover from November to May, 70km of ski slopes and 24 lifts. About 120 sq km of the mountain range is a protected park. Organise passes through your accommodation, at signposted shops in town, the tourist centre or online at www.skijalistasrbije.rs.

Large-scale hotels with restaurants, gym facilities, pizzerias, discos and shops are the norm in Kopaonik, but there are some lower-key options. There are three daily buses from Belgrade (1700RSD, five hours) and one from Niš to Brus (795RSD, 1½ hours, 3pm). From Novi Pazar, pick up an infrequent connection in Raška; taxis cost around 2400RSD.

Though primarily a winter sports destination, Kopaonik is a beautiful place for hiking and mountain biking in summer; other activities include horse riding, rafting on the Ibar River, paragliding, a zipline and tours to nearby monasteries or wineries; contact the tourist centre or check www.eng.infokop.net for details. Prices plummet in the off-season, though many places open arbitrarily during this time.

story of the 1941 massacre of around 3000 Kragujevac civilians during the German occupation of Serbia. A 7km circular road leads through the 352-hectare park, past the locations of 30 mass graves and 10 memorials. A gallery of paintings by renowned Yugoslav artist Petar Lubarda is part of the permanent exhibition, as are the personal effects and heartbreaking farewell messages of those who were executed.

There are audio guides in five languages; the exhibition includes English translations.

Old Foundry Museum
MUSEUM

(Muzej Stara livnica; ☑034 337 786; www.muzej-topolivnica.rs; Trg Topolivaca 4, Knežev arsenal; ⊙7am-3pm Mon-Fri) **FREE** This fascinating museum is housed in the 1882 building of Kragujevac's old cannon factory *(topolivnica)*. Part of the Prince's Arsenal industrial complex, it hosts a permanent exhibition of machinery, firearms and other equipment produced in the factory in the 19th and 20th centuries. The exhibition is well curated, but unfortunately there's no English signage for now. Ring the bell to be let inside.

Kragujevac National Museum
MUSEUM

(Narodni muzej Kragujevac; www.muzej.org.rs; Vuka Karadžića 1; 100RSD; ⊙10am-5pm Tue-Fri, to 2pm Sat & Sun) A complex of several modest buildings, the National Museum is centred around the former *konak* (residence) of Prince Miloš, built in 1860. The Oriental-style **Amidža's Mansion** (Amidžin konak), which dates from 1818, represents the only surviving building from the old court complex. The **art gallery** has a worthwhile collection of 20th-century paintings and sculptures and features some of the most acclaimed Serbian artists, such as expressionist Sava Šumanović and surrealist Leonid Šejka.

★ Festivals & Events

Fića Fest
CAR SHOW

(⊙Jun) This annual automobile show brings together hundreds of Fića fans from Serbia and abroad. The popular small model was the first car produced in the former Yugoslavia (back in 1955); over three decades Kragujevac's Crvena Zastava factory rolled out nearly a million vehicles. Fića was the first family car for many Yugoslavs and is still fondly remembered across the Balkans.

Arsenal Fest
MUSIC

(www.arsenalfest.rs; Knežev arsenal; ⊙late Jun) With its main stage located in Kragujevac's disused 19th-century industrial zone, this three-day alternative music festival features some of the most prominent Serbian, ex-Yugoslav and international bands. In 2018, The Kills, Editors and Morcheeba were among the headlining acts.

🛏 Sleeping

Hotel Kragujevac
HOTEL €€

(☑034 335 811; www.hotelkragujevac.com; Kralja Petra 21; s/d/apt 3930/5000/7220RSD; P❋🛜) It may look like a socialist-era monolith eyesore from the outside, but this eight-storey hotel has been completely refurbished (the glass elevator is kind of cool) and now offers good value for money with all the mod cons and a central location. The rooms have plenty of natural light and spotless bathrooms; the rooftop restaurant (p357) boasts the best view in town.

Hotel Zelengora
HOTEL €€

(☑034 336 254; www.hotelzelengora.com; Branka Radičevića 22; s/d/apt 3200/4800/7000RSD; P❋🛜) One of Serbia's oldest hotels, Zelengora occupies a strategic corner in the town's pedestrian zone (it can get noisy at night). The 19th-century building with flowerpots in the windows now has a modern lobby and is decorated with abstract artworks. The rooms are on the small side and the top-floor ones are attic-style. The restaurant serves Italian and Chinese cuisine.

✕ Eating & Drinking

Panorama
INTERNATIONAL €€

(☑034 335 533; www.panoramakg.com; Kralja Petra 21; mains 620-1500RSD; ⊙10am-midnight) For some refreshingly non-Balkan dining in an elegant setting with impeccable service – and unbeatable views of the city – head straight to the rooftop restaurant of the eight-storey Hotel Kragujevac (p357). The chef's focus is on the use of ingredients and spices (think salmon in dill sauce, lamb in dijon mustard and honey, chicken with prunes, or turkey fillet in blackcurrant sauce).

Kafana Balkan
SERBIAN €€

(www.kafana-balkan.rs; Kralja Aleksandra 94; mains 490-890RSD; ⊙7am-midnight Sun-Thu, to 1am Fri & Sat) The locals' favourite, this historic *kafana* (going strong since 1890) ticks all the boxes: red-chequered tablecloths and black-and-white photos of old Kragujevac on the

WORTH A TRIP

EXCURSIONS FROM KRAGUJEVAC

A forlorn guardian of the Ibar valley (20km south of Kraljevo), **Maglič** (Tvrđava Maglič, Тврђава Маглич) is one of Serbia's best-preserved medieval fortifications. Built in the 13th century to protect the nearby Studenica and Žiča Monasteries, it was conquered by the Turks in 1438. The rectangular, 2m-thick defensive walls with seven towers and a 20m-high keep stand on a ridge above the curving river, offering fantastic views over the green hills; within the 2000-sq-metre area are the remains of a church and a palace.

One of Serbia's most sacred sites, Unesco-listed **Studenica Monastery** (Manastir Studenica, Манастир Студеница; ☑ 064 646 7492; www.manastirstudenica.rs; ⊙ 8am-7pm) was established in 1196 by the founder of the Serbian empire (and future saint) Stefan Nemanja and developed by his sons Vukan, Stefan and Rastko (St Sava). Two well-preserved churches lie within the monastery's impressive white-marble walls. **Bogorodičina Crkva** (Church of Our Lady) contains Stefan Nemanja's tomb. The smaller **Kraljeva Crkva** (King's Church) houses the acclaimed Birth of the Virgin fresco and other masterpieces.

Famous for its curative spas since AD 2, **Vrnjačka Banja** (Врњачка Бања ; www.vrnjackabanja.co.rs; Vrnjačka Banja; Roman Font wellness centre per 2hr 1500RSD) is home to the world's only hot spring with a temperature exactly the same as the average human body (36.5°C). It attracts health-seekers looking to take to the same therapeutic waters as the ancient Romans, 19th-century socialites and communist bigwigs before them. A huge range of wellness treatments is available.

The centre of the Župa wine region, Aleksandrovac is situated in the West Morava River valley, north of Kopaonik National Park. While sauvignon, semillon and riesling grapes are all grown here, it's the centuries-old *prokupac* and *tamjanika* varietals that shine. **Ivanović Winery** (☑ 063 528 246; www.ivanovicvino.com; 10. avgusta 18, Aleksandrovac; ⊙ noon-8pm Mon-Fri, to 5pm Sat & Sun), founded in 1919, welcomes visitors (but book ahead); sample a sip or three in the rustic garden.

---

walls, somewhat surly staff, large portions of perennial Balkan classics paired with select Šumadija wines, and traditional harmonica-and-violin live music in the evenings.

Kafemat 27 CAFE
(www.facebook.com/kafemat27; Karađorđeva 19; ⊙ 7am-midnight Mon-Thu, to 1am Fri & Sat, 8am-midnight Sun) For arguably the best coffee blends in town, join the trendy locals at this street-corner hang-out with modern industrial-style decor and a casual outdoor terrace.

Cafe Oblomov BAR
(www.facebook.com/caffeoblomov; Branka Radičevića 14; ⊙ 8am-midnight Mon-Thu, to 1am Fri & Sat, 10am-midnight Sun) A chilled-out garden cafe by day and a hip bar spinning indie tunes in the evening, subdued Oblomov is set up in an old townhouse on a quiet street and feels like a hang-out for arty types. The high-ceilinged rooms are decked out with vintage knick-knacks, and there's a small but satisfying cocktails menu.

❶ Information

The well-stocked **tourist information centre** (☑ 034 335 302; www.gtokg.org.rs; Zorana Đinđića 11; ⊙ 8am-8pm Mon-Fri, 9am-3pm Sat)

has maps, brochures, souvenirs and private accommodation listings.

❶ Getting There & Away

Kragujevac is located 120km south of Belgrade. From the **bus station** (☑ 034 354 659; Šumadijska bb), there are frequent services to Belgrade (800RSD, two hours, 12 daily), Novi Sad (1145RSD, four hours, six daily) and Niš (800RSD, 2¾ hours, three daily).

Novi Pazar Нови Пазар

☑ 020 / POP 66,500

Novi Pazar (meaning 'new marketplace') is the cultural centre of southern Serbia's Sandžak region with a majority Muslim population, which is immediately obvious on the approach to town from the lanky minarets that dot the hilly cityscape. Turkish coffee, cuisine and customs abound; the old bazaar's hectic lanes are chock-full of cafes and shops peddling Turkish goods from jewellery to jeans. And yet, some of the most sacred Orthodox sights – a Unesco-listed monastery and the oldest church in the country – are on the outskirts of Novi Pazar: this was the heartland of the medieval Serbian state of Raška.

⊙ Sights

★ Sopoćani Monastery
MONASTERY

(Manastir Sopoćani; foreigners €2; ⊘8am-7pm)
Built around 1265 by King Stefan Uroš I (who is buried here), this Unesco-listed monastery was destroyed by the Turks in 1689 and restored in 1926. Frescoes inside the Romanesque church are prime examples of medieval art; the *Assumption of the Virgin Mary* fresco is one of Serbia's most renowned.

The monastery is 14km west of town. There are three daily buses from the bus station (110RSD, 30 minutes); the return times allow for about an hour at the monastery.

Museum Ras Novi Pazar
MUSEUM

(Muzej Ras Novi Pazar; www.muzejnp.rs; Stevana Nemanje 20; adult/child 100/50RSD; ⊘8am-8pm Mon-Fri, 10am-2pm Sat) This wonderful regional museum occupies a mid-19th-century Oriental-style building. Its permanent collection covers the archaeology, ethnology, history and applied art of the Raška (Sandžak) region and features old coins, weapons, jewellery, folk clothing, traditional tools, furniture and writings in Arabic, Hebrew and Old Church Slavonic. One of the highlights is the skeleton of an Iron Age warrior. There are Roman and Islamic tombstones in the yard and a collection of black-and-white drawings of Novi Pazar on the ground floor.

Church of St Peter
CHURCH

(Petrova crkva; ☎060 059 8401; foreigners €2; ⊘8am-3pm) Dating from the 9th century (according to the oldest written sources) but with 6th-century foundations, this small stone basilica located on a hill 3km from town is the oldest intact church in Serbia. Inside, remnants of frescoes cling to the ancient archways; there's a fascinating, photogenic cemetery outside that dates from the 19th century. If it's locked, phone or ask at the nearby house to be let in.

Altun-Alem Mosque
MOSQUE

(Altun-Alem džamija; 1.maja 79) This renovated mosque (named after a miracle-working gemstone) was built in the mid-16th century, and is one of the oldest Islamic buildings surviving in Serbia. It's a working mosque, so be sure to dress modestly and ask permission before going inside.

⫤ Sleeping

Hotel Tadž
HOTEL €€

(☎020 311 904; www.hoteltadznd.com; Rifata Burdževića 79; s/d/tr 3500/5000/6000RSD;

Ⓟ ☀ ⓦ) This relatively modern, upmarket hotel just minutes away from the town centre has friendly staff, reliable wi-fi and a high-quality restaurant that serves international cuisine. There's one double room with a jacuzzi (7000RSD).

Hotel Vrbak
HOTEL €€

(☎020 314 844; www.hotelvrbak.com; 37. Sandžačke divizije 2; s/d/tr/apt 2500/4500/5500/5000RSD; Ⓟ ☀ ⓦ) The Vrbak, a motley mash-up of socialist-modernist and Oriental architectural styles, is an unmissable landmark in the centre of town. Though the lofty lobby atrium with a cupola hints at Napoleonic delusions, the rooms are clean but basic. It's worth staying here just so you can say you did.

✕ Eating & Drinking

Šadrvan
GRILL €

(28. Novembra 12; meals 180-460RSD; ⊘24hr) Of all the fast-food spots in the town centre, this no-frills joint (also known as 'Kod Jonuza') right by the *sebilj* (fountain) is the best for greasy-chinned grill gourmandising. Order *ćevapi* as a portion of five or 10 and wash them down with yoghurt.

★ Sve pod Sač
PIES €

(1. maja 20; pies 600-1400RSD; ⊘7.30am-8pm) A tiny family-owned cafe, Sve pod Sač is Novi Pazar's go-to place for must-try *mantije* (bite-sized, square-shaped pastries with meat), as well as four types of pies (with meat, cheese, spinach and potatoes).

★ Isa-Beg's Hammam
CAFE

(⊘8am-midnight) The cosy open-roofed cafe set up in one part of the semi-ruined Isa-Beg's Hammam is an atmospheric place to have a Turkish coffee or a lemonade along with a *kadaif* (traditional dessert soaked in syrup), especially if a soothing violin instrumental is playing. It's on the street corner across from Sve pod Sač cafe.

Caffe Art
BAR

(www.facebook.com/caffeart.90; Stevana Nemanje 116; ⊘8am-midnight) The closest thing Novi Pazar has to a real bar is this snug, atmospheric cafe with retro low lighting and loud music that's a mix of rock, indie and electro tunes. It's one of the rare places in town that serves alcohol.

AROUND NOVI PAZAR

The Uvac River's spectacular meanders are the highlight of the 75-sq-km **Uvac nature reserve** (☑ 033 64 198; www.uvac.org.rs; boat tour with/without hike per person 1500/1100RSD; ⊙ bookings 8am-4pm Mon-Fri) in southwestern Serbia. The incredibly green river snakes through steep limestone rock in a zigzag manner – a feat of nature that's best admired from high above, at Molitva or Veliki vrh lookouts. The reserve, which also comprises a 6km-long cave system, owes its protected status to 219 species of plants, 24 types of fish and 130 bird species including the endangered *beloglavi sup* (griffon vulture).

A number of **hiking trails** lead around the canyon and past the lookouts, from 2km to 10km, offering plenty of birdwatching opportunities along the way – you can't miss the mighty bird of prey with its 3m wingspan! The 2km-long **Ice Cave** (with a permanent temperature of 8°C) has several galleries and is rich in ornaments. A boat trip through the canyon with a park ranger includes a tour of the cave and a hike up to a lookout (call to book ahead; the trip with/without a hike takes roughly five/three hours). Wild Serbia (p354) offers Uvac **kayaking** and caving tours.

The easiest way to reach Uvac is with your own wheels.

Secluded 13th-century **Crna Reka** (Manastir Crna Reka; Ribariće; ⊙ 5am-7pm), (meaning 'black river'), has a unique setting among Serbian monasteries: it's built into caves, seemingly hanging off a steep cliff above the abyss of a sinking river. Staircases connect the cells within the four-level cave system. Protected by forested mountains and accessed via a narrow wooden footbridge, the monastery started as a hermitage and served as a refuge during Ottoman times. The frescoes inside the tiny cave church are the work of famous 16th-century painter Longin.

Crna Reka is located near Ribariće vilage, just off the Ibar highway 30km south of Novi Pazar. Frequent buses from Novi Pazar stop at the village. Cross the bridge over Gazivode lake, then follow the paved road that leads through the forest to the monastery (it's about 3km uphill).

❶ Information

Novi Pazar Tourist Organisation (☑ 020 338 030; www.tonp.rs; Mitrovačka bb; ⊙ 7.30am-3pm Mon-Fri) The helpful staff can provide brochures, help with private accommodation and check when the Church of St Peter is open.

❶ Getting There & Away

Frequent buses leave the **bus station** (☑ 020 318 354; www.sandzaktrans.rs; Omladinska bb) for Belgrade (1300RSD, four hours); there is one daily bus to Niš (1200RSD, four hours, 7.30am) and services to Pristina (850RSD, 2½ hours, three daily).

EASTERN & SOUTHERN SERBIA

Heading southeast of the capital, you'll experience some of Serbia's least visited yet most exhilarating destinations. To the far east, the 'Iron Gates' of Đerdap National Park serve as a dramatic natural border with Romania. Southern Serbia's urban heart is historic Niš, home of the acclaimed Nišville International Jazz Festival. Nearby Stara Planina, dotted with secluded villages, ravines and countless waterfalls, offers wonderful hiking and a chance to conquer Serbia's highest peak, Midžor.

Đerdap National Park & Around

Serbia's largest national park (Национални Парк Ђердап; 636 sq km) is also one of its most dramatic, with arresting attractions both natural and human-made. The astounding Iron Gates gorge (Đerdapska klisura) is the park's main draw; its formidable cliffs – some of which soar over 500m – dip and dive for 100km along the Danube to form a natural border with Romania. The medieval Golubac Fortress, the Mesolithic settlement of Lepenski Vir and the Roman-era Tabula Traiana (commemorating a bridge across the Danube) are testimony to old-time tenacity.

The park itself is home to plenty of critters, including bears, lynxes, wolves, eagles and owls. With marked paths and signposted viewpoints, Đerdap is an excellent hiking destination; the EuroVelo 6 cycling path runs through here.

◉ Sights

★ Lepenski Vir ARCHAEOLOGICAL SITE

(www.lepenski-vir.org; adult/child 400/250RSD; ◷9am-8pm) What is now Đerdap National Park was once a major centre for Mesolithic- and Neolithic-era fishing communities, a past that has been wonderfully preserved in this unsung museum overlooking the Danube. Housed – somewhat ironically – within a space-age building, religious and workaday artefacts, sculptures and skeletons dating back as far as 7000 BC are on display here. Perhaps the most impressive is the world-famous Foremother and several other stone sculptures of fish-like idols with human faces.

There's no public transport to the archaeological site; if you're not driving, catch a taxi from Donji Milanovac (it's 16km upstream).

Golubac Fortress FORTRESS

(Tvrđava Golubački Grad; www.tvrdjavagoluback igrad.rs; Golubac; adult/child 600/120RSD; ◷10am-7pm Tue-Sun Apr-Aug, to 6pm Sep, to 5pm Oct, to 4pm Nov-Mar) The remains of this 10-tower fortified town brood majestically by the entrance to Đerdap National Park. Originally a Roman settlement, the fortress was built around the 14th century, passing through the hands of the Ottomans, Hungarians, Bulgarians and Austrians before the Serbs secured it once and for all in 1867. Today, it's a fabulous place to wander around and gasp at the lofty views of the ramparts and the mighty Danube (which looks more like a sea from here).

Silver Lake LAKE

(Srebrno jezero; www.srebrnojezero.com) Evocatively named after its shimmering surface, Silver Lake in Serbia's east makes for a good stop if travelling from Belgrade to Đerdap National Park. The 14km-long, oxbow-shaped lake was created by damming an arm of the Danube and is well populated with fish. Tourist facilities include a marina, beaches, swimming pools and sports courts. In summer, **Silver Star boat tours** (three hours, adult/child 990/450RSD) go to Ram and Golubac Fortresses.

Silver Lake is 4km from the town of Veliko Gradište, which is connected by bus with Belgrade (1050RSD, two hours, seven daily). Contact **Veliko Gradište Tourist Information Centre** (☏012 716 0020; www. tovg.org; Karpatska 3a, Silver Lake; ◷8am-9pm Mon-Sat) for assistance with accommodation.

☆ Activities

Hiking

Hiking in the national park is possible as long as you register with the visitors centre at least three days before setting off. There are nine marked trails; a 4km path starts just above Lepenski Vir Hotel (p362). Two trails lead from the Đerdap highway to the highest peaks of Mt Miroč: a 7.6km path to **Veliki Štrbac** (768m), which offers dramatic views over the narrowest part of the Iron Gates gorge; and a 7.1km path to **Mali Štrbac** (626m), from where you can admire the massive Decebalus rock sculpture on the Romanian bank of the Danube.

Cycling

The **EuroVelo 6** (www.eurovelo.com) cycling path runs along the Danube for 110km through Đerdap National Park and is fully signposted.

☞ Tours

Wild Serbia (p354) offers one-day kayaking trips (€70) through Đerdap including a visit to Golubac Fortress and Lepenski Vir. You can also see the highlights of the gorge by **speedboat** (060 2323 056; per person 1200RSD) from Tekija; the trip takes one hour.

★ Golubac from a Boat BOATING

(☏064 254 7539; www.golubacizbrodica.rs; 2hr-tour 1200RSD) Local historian, Đerdap enthusiast and author of two books about Golubac, Jovan Kocmanović offers informative and entertaining one- or two-hour boat tours through the Iron Gates gorge and around the fortress; cycling and walking tours through surrounding forests, nearby caves and along the Danube; boat rental (for up to five people); as well as customised trips around eastern Serbia.

⌅ Sleeping & Eating

★ Vila Dunavski Raj B&B €€

(☏012 639 616; www.viladunavskiraj.rs; Vinci bb, Golubac; d/tr/f from 4500/5700/6050RSD; ⓟ⬠) A family-owned villa tucked away deep in a pine forest near the banks of the Danube, Dunavski Raj gets a gold star for location. Lovely hosts, organic breakfast, swings, hammocks and large terraces for each room all conspire to keep you in this secluded spot. The downside: small, slightly dated bathrooms and no air-con. If you're not driving, catch a taxi from Golubac.

THE TREASURES OF NEGOTIN REGION

Eastern Serbia's Negotin (Неготин) region has been producing wine since the 3rd century and is known for native *bagrina* and *začinak* varietals. Its 19th-century 'wine-cellar villages', or *pimnice*, are unique architectural complexes of stone **wine cellars** (Rajačke pimnice; Rajac) partially buried into the ground. Some are open for visitors and offer lodgings; try **Pimnica Perić** (☑ 064 1943 065), owned by the sixth generation of the same family.

Rajac village has the largest number of preserved cellars (196), followed by neighbouring Rogljevo (122). You'll find the compound on a hill 2km from the centre of the village. Don't miss the old village **cemetery**, with intriguing tombstones displaying unique shapes and ornaments, made of the same material as the cellars.

Rajac is located 25km from the town of Negotin, which is connected with Belgrade by bus (1200RSD, five hours, seven daily). There's a signposted walking trail (8km) between Rajac and Rogljevo. Contact **Negotin Tourist Organisation** (☑ 019 547 555; www.toon. org.rs; Kraljevića Marka 6, Negotin; ⊙ 7am-4pm Mon-Fri) for tours and accommodation.

The remote Negotin region hides one of the country's more dramatic **natural phenomena** (Vratnjanske kapije). Three gigantic stone arches – known as Small Gate (Mala kapija), Big Gate (Velika kapija) and Dry Gate (Suva kapija) – were moulded by erosion in the Vratna River canyon; the last one is the most impressive but also the least accessible and recommended for more experienced hikers. Signposted trails (1km to Small and Big Gates, 5km to Dry Gate) lead uphill through the forest from Vratna Monastery.

As the area is a hunting ground for mouflon and deer, hikers have high chances of spotting some of these majestic animals. The monastery is located about 35km from Negotin.

Lepenski Vir Hotel HOTEL €€
(☑ 030 590 210; www.hotellepenskivir.co.rs; Radnička bb, Donji Milanovac; s/d 2100/3400RSD; P❄️📶🏊) The interior has an eery 1960s Yugoslavia vibe and the wi-fi doesn't reach past the lobby, but this is your best bet as a base for exploring Đerdap National Park and the Lepenski Vir archaeological site. There's a huge restaurant – encircled by an actual iron curtain! – and an indoor pool. Ask for a room with Danube views.

★**Kapetan Mišin Breg** BALKAN €€
(☑ 063 452 201; www.kapetanmisinbreg.rs; Majdanpečki put bb, Donji Milanovac; set menu 950-1500RSD) Fantastic views of the Đerdap gorge and an introduction to traditional Vlach cuisine from eastern Serbia are reason enough to visit this hillside complex. Bonus: you can hear about the region's history and admire the owner's open-air wood and stone sculpture gallery. The set menu includes homemade cornbread, fried nettles, stewed chicken livers, honey brandy and more. Call to book ahead.

Zlatna Ribica SERBIAN €€
(☑ 012 638 603; www.kafanazlatnaribica.com; Cara Dušana 28, Golubac; mains 690-990RSD, fish 950-2400RSD; ⊙ noon-11pm) Book a seat on the outdoor terrace at Zlatna Ribica ('Goldfish') for a thoroughly seaside feel: the restaurant occupies a prime spot by the Danube, which is at its widest point here (7km), with Golubac Fortress looming in the distance. Its grilled-meat and fish specialities come in huge portions, so you can take your time enjoying the panoramic views.

ℹ️ Information

The English-speaking staff at the national park **visitors centre** (☑ 030 590 778; www. npdjerdap.org; Kralja Petra 14, Donji Milanovac; museum 150RSD; ⊙ 7am-3pm Mon-Fri) can assist with all park enquiries. If you plan on hiking in the park, you must register here before setting off.

For maps, brochures and accommodation listings, visit the tourist information centres at **Golubac** (☑ 012 638 613; www.togolubac. rs; Cara Lazara 15, Golubac; ⊙ 7am-9pm) and **Kladovo** (☑ 019 801 690; http://tookladovo.rs; Kralja Aleksandra 15, Kladovo; ⊙ 7am-3pm).

ℹ️ Getting There & Around

Đerdap National Park is 190km west of Belgrade. Buses run from Belgrade to Golubac (1100RSD, 2½ hours, seven daily) and Donji Milanovac (1450RSD, 3½ hours, six daily). Timetables can be sporadic; it's best to have your own wheels to fully explore the region. The Đerdap highway (M 25-1, aka Đerdapska magistrala) is a wonderfully scenic drive; some sections of the road are in poor shape, however, so make sure you drive carefully.

Niš Ниш

☑ 018 / POP 183,000

Serbia's third-largest metropolis is a lively city of curious contrasts, where Roma in horse-drawn carriages trot alongside new cars, and posh cocktails are sipped in antiquated alleyways. It's a buzzy kind of place, with a high number of university students, packed-out laneway bars, a happening live-music scene, and pop-up markets and funfairs come summertime.

Niš was settled in pre-Roman times, but hit its peak during the years of the empire. Constantine the Great (AD 280–337) was born here, as were two other Roman emperors, Constantius III and Justin I. Turkish rule lasted from 1386 until 1877, despite several Serb revolts; Ćele Kula (Tower of Skulls) and Niš Fortress are reminders of Ottoman dominion. Niš also suffered during WWII; the Nazis built one of Serbia's most notorious concentration camps here.

◉ Sights

★ Orthodox Cathedral CATHEDRAL
(Saborni hram; Map p364; Prijezdina 7; ⊙7am-7pm) Second only in size to Belgrade's St Sava Temple, this huge Orthodox cathedral, completely restored after being destroyed in a fire in 2001, was consecrated. The church is a curious mix of Byzantine, Oriental and Western architectural styles and famous for the iconostasis with 48 paintings by Serbian artist Đorđe Krstić – to say nothing of its elaborate, colourful, floor-to-ceiling paintwork.

Bubanj Hill Memorial Park MEMORIAL
(Spomen park Bubanj; Vojvode Putnika; ⊙24hr) Bubanj Hill, located 3km from the city centre, is the location of one of Serbia's most recognisable Yugoslav-era *spomeniks*. Three gigantic fists rising from the ground are the work of sculptor Ivan Sabolić and symbolise the resistance and suffering of men, women and children (or, according to other interpretations, Serbs, Jews and Roma) during WWII. This was the site of mass executions of prisoners from the concentration camp by the Nazis. It's a sombre place for reflection.

Red Cross
Concentration Camp MUSEUM
(Crveni Krst; Map p364; Bul 12 Februar; 200RSD, with Archaeological Hall & Ćele Kula 300RSD; ⊙9am-7pm Tue-Sun) One of the best-preserved Nazi camps in Europe, the deceptively named Red Cross (named after the adjacent train station) held about 30,000 Serbs, Roma, Jews and Partisans during the German occupation of Serbia (1941–45). Harrowing displays tell their stories, and those of the prisoners who attempted to flee in the biggest-ever breakout from a concentration camp. This was a transit camp, so few were killed on the premises – they were taken to Bubanj (p363), or on to Auschwitz, Dachau or other concentration camps.

Ćele Kula MONUMENT
(Tower of Skulls; Bul Zoran Đinđić; 200RSD, with Red Cross Concentration Camp & Archaeological Hall 300RSD; ⊙9am-7pm Tue-Sun) With Serbian defeat imminent at the 1809 Battle of Čegar, the Duke of Resava kamikazed towards the Turkish defences, firing at their gunpowder stores, killing himself, 4000 of his men and 10,000 Turks. The Turks triumphed regardless, and to deter future acts of rebellion, they beheaded, scalped and embedded the skulls of the dead Serbs in this tower. Only 58 of the initial 952 skulls remain. Contrary to Turkish intention, the tower serves as proud testament to Serbian resistance. Catch bus 1 across the street from tourist information on **Vožda Karađorđa** (60RSD).

Mediana RUINS
(Bul Cara Konstantina; 200RSD; ⊙9am-7pm Tue-Sun) Mediana is what remains of Constantine the Great's luxurious 4th-century Roman palace. The recently unveiled 1000 sq metres of gorgeous mosaics are the highlight here; they were hidden from public view until protective renovations were completed in 2016. Digging has revealed a palace, a forum, a church and an expansive grain-storage area. The ruins have been closed for more renovations, but should have reopened by the time you read this. Mediana is on the eastern outskirts of Niš and a short walk from Ćele Kula.

Archaeological Hall MUSEUM
(Map p364; Nikole Pašića 59; 200RSD, with Red Cross Concentration Camp & Ćele Kula 300RSD; ⊙9am-7pm Tue-Sun) Though it's small, this museum is worth a gander for its collection of prehistoric, Roman and medieval artefacts, including coins, jewellery, religious pieces and a truly extraordinary, partially bronzed 4th-century Roman gate. It doesn't get many visitors, and the friendly curator is extremely keen to talk about the displays and the fascinating history of Niš.

SERBIA NIŠ

Niš

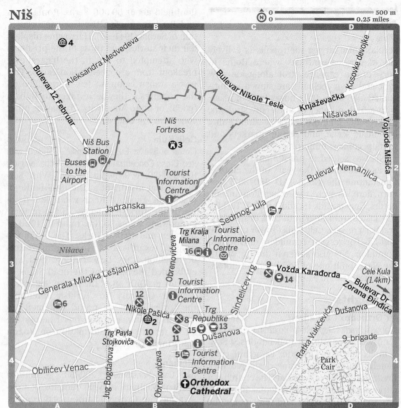

Niš

Niš Fortress FORTRESS
(Niška tvrđava; Map p364; Đuke Dinić; ⊙24hr)
Though its current incarnation was built
by the Turks in the 18th century, there have
been forts on this site since ancient Roman
times. Today it's a sprawling recreational
area with restaurants, cafes, market stalls
and ample space for moseying, as well as
the 16th-century **Bali-beg Mosque**. The
fortress hosts the Nišville International Jazz
Festival each August and Nišomnia, featuring rock and electro acts, in September. The

city's main pedestrian boulevard, Obreno-vićeva, stretches before the citadel.

⭐ Festivals & Events

Nišville International
Jazz Festival
MUSIC

(www.nisville.com; Niš Fortress; from 3550RSD; ☉Aug) This jazz festival, held at Niš Fortress, attracts big-name musos from Serbia and around the world.

Nišomnia
MUSIC

(www.facebook.com/festivalnisomnia; Niš Fortress; ☉Sep) Serbian and global rock and electro acts descend on Niš Fortress each September.

🛏 Sleeping

Aurora Hostel
HOSTEL €

(Map p364; ☎063 109 5820; www.aurorahostel. rs; Dr Petra Vučinića 16; dm/r from 1120/4560RSD; ✴🛜) Set within a 19th-century former Turkish consulate, Aurora offers charm and comfort by the ladle-load. Though the building has been renovated, its wood-heavy interiors and hospitable host are redolent of a more gentle era. Rooms are spick and span – all with private bathrooms – and there's a good communal kitchen, and a lovely garden area for socialising.

⭐ ArtLoft Hotel
BOUTIQUE HOTEL €€

(Map p364; ☎018 305 800; www.artloftho tel.com; Oblačića Rada 8a/7; s/d/ste from 5612/6466/7320RSD; ✴🛜) Central and chic, this designer hotel takes its name literally, with original murals and paintings by local artists dominating every room. The modern feel extends to the professional staff, who take service to the next level by offering friendly assistance, advice and little touches including complimentary fruit and drinks. It's a short stroll from here to Trg Republike and Kopitareva.

⭐ Hotel Sole
HOTEL €€

(Map p364; ☎018 524 555; www.hotelsole.rs; Kralja Stefana Prvovenčanog 11; s/d from 5782/6844RSD, incl breakfast; P✴🛜) Sitting pretty right in the heart of Niš, this refurbished hotel has modern, super-spacious rooms with boutique furnishings; ceiling murals are a very cool touch. Hotel Sole also dishes up one of the best breakfasts you'll find anywhere and the staff were the best we met in Serbia's cities. They'll even throw in laundry at no extra charge.

🍴 Eating

⭐ Pekara Anton Plus
BAKERY €

(Map p364; www.pekara-brankovic.com; Trg Pavla Stojkovića 17; burek 45-120RSD; ☉6am-8pm Mon-Fri, to 4pm Sat, to 2pm Sun) Prepare to hurry up and wait for the Serbian breakfast of champions: *burek*. This slick *pekara* (bakery) does the best in Niš. Four versions are available – veal, cheese, spinach and pizza (ham, cheese and mushroom) – and the Nišlije can't get enough of them.

Kod Lafa
FAST FOOD €

(Map p364; Vožda Karađorđa bb; burgers from 160RSD; ☉24hr) On the left at this glorified fast-food stall, an army of perfectly grilled *pljeskavica*; on the right, a colourful array of tempting trimmings, all of which dares you to walk by without throwing yourself at the mercy of these carnivorous takeaway delights.

Kafana Galija
SERBIAN €€

(Map p364; www.kafanagalija.com; Nikole Pasica 35; mains 260-1700RSD; ☉10am-midnight Mon-Thu, to 2am Fri & Sat, 11am-7pm Sun; 🛜) The chefs here grill to thrill, with exceptional takes on classics, including spicy meat platters and a good *pljeskavica*. Rouse yourself from your food coma by sticking around for the rollicking live music and associated crowd carousing – the patio spills out onto bustling Kopitareva. Save room for the wet and wonderful baklava.

Pleasure
INTERNATIONAL €€

(Map p364; www.pleasure.rs; Kopitareva 7; mains 230-1520RSD; ☉8.30am-11.30pm Mon-Sat, 10am-10pm Sun; 🛜) This hip spot on busy Kopitareva, with a hilariously empty non-smoking section, has a more varied (and vegetarian-friendly) menu than the traditional *kafane* that make up the bulk of the Niš culinary landscape. The gourmet pastas are exceptional, and the gambles on unusual ingredient combinations have paid off (try the turkey with pistachio sauce and beetroot risotto).

⭐ Stambolijski
SERBIAN €€€

(Map p364; ☎018 300 440; www.restoranstam bolijski.rs; Nikole Pašića 36; mains 390-1950RSD; ☉noon-10.30pm; 🛜) This upscale, standout New Balkan restaurant elegantly occupies the oldest preserved home in Niš (dating to 1878) and is easily the city's top dining destination. The accolades were quickly showered on Chef Saša Mišić for his modern takes on classics like *jagnjetina ispod sača* (lamb cooked in a clay pot), coupled with creative dishes like pork neck with beer and honey.

🍷 Drinking & Nightlife

★**Ministarstvo Beer Bar**   CRAFT BEER

(Map p364; www.facebook.com/pg/ministarstvo beerbar; Vojvode Vuka 12; ⊗8.30am-midnight Mon-Thu, to 1.30am Fri, 10.30am-1.30am Sat, 5pm-midnight Sun; 🛜) Ministarstvo is one of Niš' go-to craft beer destinations, with 15 options on draught (mostly Serbian, a bit of mainstream German and Czech) and a gaggle more by the bottle. A fantastic soundtrack, lively patio and a fun, suds-swilling crowd make this a solid choice for hopheads who want to steer clear of more crowded areas such as Kopitareva.

Vespa Bar   BAR

(Map p364; www.vespabar.com; Trg Republike; ⊗8am-midnight Mon-Thu, to 2am Fri & Sat, 9am-midnight Sun; 🛜) There are literally Vespas coming out of the woodwork at this happy, happening bar in the centre of town. Chat with the friendly 'bikies' over beer (local and international) or something from the extensive cocktail list (195RSD to 420RSD). Ace people-watching.

Kafeterija Biro   COFFEE

(Map p364; www.facebook.com/birokafeterijanis; Koste Stamenkovića 1; 8am-11pm Mon-Sat, from 10am Sun; 🛜) Niš isn't as accustomed to barista-driven coffee as Belgrade and Novi Sad, but this little coffeehouse was the first in town to brew and prepare next-level jitter juice. With its picket-fenced sidewalk seating and winding staircases leading to two upper floors of industrial-chic cosiness, it's a great spot to dig in for a while.

ℹ️ Information

The Tourist Organisation of Niš runs several tourist information centres, including one within the **Niš Fortress** (Turistički info centri; Map p364; ☑ 018 250 222; www.visitnis.com; Tvrđava; ⊗9am-8pm Tue-Fri, 9.30am-2.30pm Sat & Sun). Other convenient branches in the city centre include **Vožda Karađorđa** (Map p364; ☑ 018 523 118; Vožda Karađorđa 7; ⊗9am-8pm Mon-Fri, to 2pm Sat), **Obrenovićeva** (Map p364; ☑ 018 520 207; Obrenovićeva 38; ⊗9am-8pm Mon-Fri, to 2pm Sat) and **Dušanova** (Map p364; ☑ 018 505 688; Dušanova 30; ⊗8am-4pm Mon-Fri).

ℹ️ Getting There & Away

The **bus station** (Autobuska stanica Niš; Map p364; ☑ 018 255 177; www.nis-ekspres.rs; Bul 12 Februar) has frequent services to Belgrade (1118RSD, three hours, hourly), and one daily bus each to Brus (795RSD, 1½ hours, 3pm) and Novi Pazar (1280RSD, four hours, 3.15pm). **Niš Ekspres** (www.nis-ekspres.rs) heads to Sofia, Bulgaria (1225RSD, five hours, 4.30am) and Skopje, North Macedonia (1234RSD, four hours, six daily).

From the **train station** (Železnička stanica Niš; ☑ 018 264 625; www.srbvoz.rs; Dimitrija Tucovića bb), there are four daily trains to Belgrade (from 900RSD, 4½ hours), one to Sofia

---

DON'T MISS

THE SACRED & THE SUBTERRANEOUS

Hemmed in by mammoth walls with 11 towers, **Manasija Monastery** (Manastir Manasija, Манастир Манасија; www.manasija.rs; Despotovac; ⊗8am-7pm May-Oct, to 4pm Nov-Apr), built in 1418, was a fortified hideout for artists and writers fleeing the Turkish invasion. Many consider its frescoes to be predecessors to the Serbian equivalent of Renaissance art; Holy Warriors is among those that survived the monastery's Ottoman-era decimations and rebuildings with startling vitality and colour.

Buses run from Belgrade to Despotovac (1100RSD, 2½ hours, six daily). From there, it's 3.5km to the monastery.

A winding 20km beyond Despotovac, the eight-million-year-old **Resava Cave** (Resavska pećina; www.resavskapecina.rs; adult/child 300/250RSD; ⊗guided tours 9am-5pm Apr-Nov) has 40-minute guided tours through impressive underground halls, featuring natural formations with names like 'Hanged Sheep' and 'Thirst for Love'. Temperatures average just 7°C; bring a jumper, even in summer.

Only 10km from Resava, with a lovely forest setting at the base of Veliki Buk waterfall (50m), **Vodopad tavern** (Lisine; ☑ 035 881 9084; www.vodopad-lisine.com; mains 700-2000RSD; ⊗8am-11pm Mon-Fri, to midnight Sat & Sun) is a perfect spot for lunch.

A taxi will take you to both the cave and Manasija Monastery (p366) from Despotovac; the return trip is around 2000RSD.

WORTH A TRIP

THE RUINS OF GAMZIGRAD ГАМЗИГРАД

Unesco-listed **Felix Romuliana** (Gamzigrad; adult/student incl National Museum Zaječar 400/300RSD; ⊗8am-8pm Apr-Oct, to 4pm Nov-Mar) was built for the Roman emperor Galerius and completed around AD 313. Ravaged by the Huns in the 5th century and abandoned following the arrival of the Slavs, who named it Gamzigrad ('Slither Town'), today the palace lies in ruins. Most archaeological findings from the site, including a bust of Galerius, are kept in Zaječar's **National Museum** (Narodni muzej Zaječar; Dragoslava Srejovića 2, Zaječar; adult/student incl Felix Romuliana 400/300RSD; ⊗8am-6pm Mon-Fri, 9am-6pm Sat & Sun). Still, the sprawling grassy mounds and the remains of massive ramparts, gates, towers and Corinthian pillars are impressive.

The palace had two temples, a 4th-century Christian basilica, public baths and mausoleums where Galerius and his mother Romula were buried. The most interesting surviving floor mosaics are the ones depicting the Labyrinth and god of wine Dionysus; they can be seen in the Zaječar museum.

Gamzigrad is 11km west of Zaječar in eastern Serbia. Local buses from Zaječar run to Gamzigrad every hour, or it's a 15-minute taxi ride from town. Buses run from Belgrade to Zaječar (1400RSD, four hours, 10 daily).

(from 1100RSD, six hours, 2.16pm) and one to Skopje (from 900RSD, five hours, 11.19pm).

The **Niš Constantine The Great Airport** (☎018 458 3336; www.nis-airport.com; Vazduhoplovaca 24) is 4km from downtown Niš; destinations include Germany, Italy, Slovakia and Switzerland. **Bus 34B** (Map p364; Bul 12 Februar) heads from the bus station to the airport (60RSD, 10 minutes), leaving from a stop just outside the station. From the airport, it's 34A.

A taxi to/from the airport to town is around 400RSD – be wary of solo taxis waiting for passengers and changing the tariff period from 'one' to far more expensive 'three' (reserved for long-distance trips out of town).

Stara Planina Стара Планина

Stretching along the border with Bulgaria, Stara Planina (Old Mountain) nature park is one of Serbia's most scenic regions – and yet it receives far fewer tourists than the mountains in the west. Part of the Balkan mountain range, this is prime hiking territory with Serbia's highest peak, Midžor (2169m), a third of the country's waterfalls and out-of-time stone villages tumbling down mountain slopes. The whole area is incredibly rich in flora, with 115 endemic plant species; its similarly diverse fauna includes white and golden eagles, bustard owls, bears, wolves, wild boar, foxes, deer, otters, chamoix and others.

◉ Sights & Activities

The marked **hiking** trails in Stara Planina's north include a 2km route from Babin Zub mountain lodge to Babin Zub (1758m) peak,

and an 8.6km route from the mountain lodge to Midžor. The southern side is dotted with secluded nature spots; the best-known are Tupavica waterfall, Rosomačko grlo canyon, Vladikine ploče cave and **Kozji kamik** viewpoint (with great views of 17km-long Lake Zavoj). **Nature Travel Office** (☎069 201 0180; www.naturetraveloffice.com; tours per group €35-80) offers small-group guided tours including hikes and kayaking.

Gostuša   VILLAGE

Situated in the heart of Stara Planina, Gostuša is one of the oldest and most remote villages in the Pirot region. The main attractions are its remarkable houses, rising on a hillside and covered – from base to roof – with plates made of authentic Stara Planina stone.

The village is located east of Lake Zavoj, 25km from Pirot. Some households offer homestays; contact **Pirot Tourist Information Centre** (☎010 320 838; www.topirot.com; Srpskih Vladara 77, Pirot; ⊗8am-4pm Mon-Fri) for assistance.

🛏 Sleeping & Eating

Hotel Sin-Kom   HOTEL €€

(☎010 322 505; www.hotel-sinkom.com; Nikole Pašića bb, Pirot; s/d from 2900/3900RSD; ☐❄☎) If transport from Pirot is not an issue, Sin-Kom is a solid choice for visiting Stara Planina, with friendly staff and a convenient location around the corner from the bus station. While not exactly brimming with character, the 'comfort' rooms are huge, with leather armchairs and hydromassage showers.

★**Ladna Voda**   SERBIAN **€€**
(Nikole Pašića 45, Pirot; mains 350-910RSD; ☺1-11pm Mon-Fri, 9am-11pm Sat) Grab an outdoor table at this renowned *kafana* that backs onto the courtyard of the regional Ponišavlje Museum to enjoy the view of its 19th-century Ottoman-style facade. A selection of quality Serbian (and the odd Macedonian) wines by the glass go well with Stara Planina delicacies, *peglana kobasica* (flattened spicy sausage) and *Pirotski kačkavalj* (hard sheep's-milk cheese).

ⓘ Getting There & Around

Stara Planina is about 70km from Niš and 50km from the town of Pirot, which is the gateway to the mountain. **Pirot Bus Station** (☑ 010 342 548; Trg Republike, Pirot) has services to and from Niš (550RSD, 1½ hours, hourly) and Belgrade (1600RSD, four hours, four daily).

A local English-speaking taxi driver (and former photojournalist) who knows Stara Planina inside out, **Foto Rota** (☑ 064 346 2731; rotaizpirota@gmail.com; Pirot) is the person to contact for transport or private tours from Pirot into all corners of the mountain. You can negotiate prices depending on the destination and length of the trip.

UNDERSTAND SERBIA

Serbia Today

Independent once again since the 2006 breakup of its short-lived union with Montenegro, Serbia is now an official candidate for EU membership. Accession talks started in late 2015, but it remains to be seen how the EU-facilitated dialogue with its former province of Kosovo – which declared independence in 2008, a move that Serbia refuses to recognise – will affect these aspirations.

Serbia joined NATO's Partnership for Peace in 2006. However, it maintains an official policy of military neutrality and doesn't aspire to join the alliance, which is extremely unpopular – to say the least – among the local population due to the 1999 NATO bombing campaign over Kosovo.

In addition to its struggling economy and a 16% unemployment rate, Serbia's challenges include an aging population (partly due to low natality but also because younger people continue the decades-long trend of emigration in search of a better life abroad), and declining press standards, according to

the Reporters Without Borders 2018 index on media freedom.

History

Events that took place centuries ago are as personal to many Serbs as if they happened last week. The history of present-day Serbia is defined by foreign invasions, from the time the Celts supplanted the Illyrians in the 4th century BC followed by the arrival of the Romans 100 years later and the Slavs in the 6th century AD.

Enter the Ottomans

Medieval Serbia flowered under the Nemanjić dynasty from the second half of the 12th century. It was recognised as a kingdom in 1217 during the rule of Stefan Prvovenčani, whose brother Sava became the first archbishop of the independent Serbian Orthodox Church. The 'golden age' was reached during Stefan Dušan's reign as emperor (1346–55).

Serbia declined after his death, and at the pivotal Battle of Kosovo in 1389 – much mythologised in Serbian national consciousness – the Turks defeated the Serbs, ushering in nearly 500 years of Islamic rule. Early revolts were crushed, but the 1815 uprising led to de facto independence that became complete in 1878 under the Obrenović royal dynasty.

During the Balkan Wars (1912–13), the Ottomans were driven out of present-day North Macedonia and Kosovo and these territories were incorporated into the Kingdom of Serbia.

The Land of South Slavs

On 28 June 1914, Austria-Hungary used the assassination of Archduke Franz Ferdinand by Bosnian Serb Gavrilo Princip in Sarajevo as cause to invade Serbia, sparking WWI: almost 60% of Serbia's male population (or a quarter of its total population) perished. In 1918 – emerging victorious from WWI – the Kingdom of Serbia and Kingdom of Montenegro united with the former Austro-Hungarian territories of present-day Croatia, Slovenia, Bosnia & Hercegovina (BiH), plus Serbia's modern-day Vojvodina province, to form the Kingdom of Serbs, Croats and Slovenes under the rule of the Serbian Karađorđević dynasty. The country was renamed Yugoslavia (Land of South Slavs) in 1929.

An anti-Axis coup in March 1941 led to the Nazi bombing of Belgrade and the German occupation of Serbia. Royalist Četniks and communist Partisans fought the Germans,

Croatia's pro-Nazi, genocidal Ustaše regime and each other, with Josip Broz Tito's Partisans finally gaining the upper hand. In 1945 they formed the government, abolished the monarchy and declared a federal republic including Serbia and its two autonomous provinces, Kosovo and Vojvodina.

Tito broke with former ally Stalin in 1948, and in 1961 founded the nonaligned movement. Within Yugoslavia, growing regional inequalities and burgeoning Serbian expansionism fuelled demands for greater autonomy. Tito's death in 1980 signalled the beginning of the rise of nationalism, stifled but long-simmering, within the republics.

The Yugoslav Wars

By 1986 Serbian nationalists were espousing a 'Greater Serbia', an ideology that would encompass Serbs from all republics into one state. Appropriated by Serbia's Communist Party leader Slobodan Milošević, the doctrine was fuelled by claims of oppression of Serbs by Kosovo Albanians, leading to the abolishment of self-rule in Kosovo in 1990. Croatia, Slovenia, BiH and Macedonia seceded from the federation, sparking a series of violent conflicts known collectively as the Yugoslav Wars.

Bitter, bloody and monstrously complex, the wars – Slovenia's Ten-Day War, the Croatian War of Independence and the Bosnian War – were fought not just between breakaway forces and the majority-Serb Yugoslav National Army and paramilitaries, but along fractious ethnic and religious lines as well. Due to the Milošević regime's role in the conflict and support for Croatia's Krajina Serbs and Bosnia's Republika Srpska, between 1992 and 1995 Serbia was under UN sanctions. The embargo had a devastating impact on the country's economy and caused rampant hyperinflation (the highest in the world), a flourishing black market and mass migration, particularly of highly educated young people.

In April 1992 the remaining republics, Serbia and Montenegro, formed the rump Yugoslav federation without provision of a satisfying level of autonomy for Kosovo given its Albanian majority. The guerrilla Kosovo Liberation Army was formed and violence erupted in 1998. In March 1999 peace talks failed when Serbia rejected the US-brokered Rambouillet Agreement (which called for an international military presence in Kosovo). In response to organised resistance in Kosovo, Serbian forces cracked down on its Albanian population, galvanising the US and NATO into a 78-day bombing campaign; hundreds of thousands of Albanians fled to Macedonia and Albania. On 12 June 1999 Serbian forces withdrew from Kosovo. The bombing resulted in still unconfirmed numbers of civilian deaths, destruction of industrial and transport infrastructure and large-scale environmental pollution.

European Dawn

In the 2000 presidential elections, opposition parties led by Zoran Đinđić and Vojislav Koštunica declared victory, a claim denounced by Milošević. Opposition supporters from all over Serbia swarmed Belgrade and stormed the Parliament. Milošević had to acknowledge defeat and Koštunica became the new president. Serbia restored ties with Europe and rejoined the UN. In April 2001, Milošević was arrested and extradited to the international war crimes tribunal in The Hague; he died in prison in March 2006.

In 2003, a loose union of Serbia and Montenegro replaced the rump Yugoslavia. The next year, Serbia was shaken by the assassination of reformist Prime Minister Zoran Đinđić – who had been instrumental in overthrowing Milošević and extraditing him to The Hague – by members of an organised crime group. In June 2004, Serbia gained a new president in pro-European Boris Tadić. In May 2006, 55% of Montenegrins voted for independence from Serbia and the union was abolished. In February 2008, the EU- and NATO-controlled Kosovo province declared independence, a move that Serbia holds to be illegal.

In the 2012 elections, Tadić lost the presidency to Tomislav Nikolić, a former member of the far-right Serbian Radical Party. In 2014 and 2016, Aleksandar Vučić was elected prime minister. A former ultra-nationalist member of the Serbian Radical Party, Vučić about-faced and joined the more liberal Serbian Progressive Party in 2008. In 2017, Vučić succeeded Nikolić as president, and Serbia gained a new prime minister in Ana Brnabić – the first female and first openly LGBT head of government in Serbia.

People

The population of Serbia is estimated at 7.11 million people, made up of Serbs (83%), Hungarians (3.5%), Bosniaks (2%), Roma (2%)

and a mix of other nationalities including Croats, Albanians, Romanians, Bulgarians, Slovaks and Vlachs. Around 85% of the population identify as Orthodox. The 5% Catholic population are mostly Vojvodinian Hungarians. Muslims (Albanians and Slavic) comprise around 3% of the country's population. Serbia's Jewish population largely perished during the Nazi occupation in WWII.

The Arts

Literature

Long-time Belgrade resident and Yugoslav diplomat Ivo Andrić (1892–1975) was awarded the Nobel prize in 1961 for his historical novel *Bridge on the Drina*. Miloš Crnjanski (1893–1977) was a leading poet of Serbian modernism but is equally well known for his novels *The Journal of Carnojevic* (1921), *Migrations* (1929) and *A Novel about London* (1972).

The huge opus of Borislav Pekić (1930–92) includes novels, dramas, science fiction, essays and political memoirs. Only his early novels *The Time of Miracles* (1965), *The Houses of Belgrade* (1970) and *How to Quiet a Vampire* (1977) are available in English. Danilo Kiš (1935–89) was an acclaimed author of the Yugoslav period whose novels translated into English include *Hourglass* (1972) and *A Tomb for Boris Davidovich* (1976).

Renowned postmodernist Milorad Pavić (1929–2009) used nonlinear narrative forms: *Dictionary of the Khazars* (1984) can be read in random order, while *The Inner Side of the Wind* (1998) can be read from the back or the front. In recent years, works by contemporary Serbian novelists have been translated into English as part of the excellent 'Serbian Prose in Translation' series. Recommended reads include: *Estoril* by Dejan Tiago-Stanković, *Hamam Balkania* by Vladislav Bajac, *Fear and Servant* by Mirjana Novaković, and *Destiny, Annotated* by Radoslav Petković.

Cinema

The Yugoslav-era 'black wave' *(crni talas)* of the 1960s and early '70s is internationally lauded for its creativity, nonconformism and subtle critique of the socialist regime. Notable movies of this group include *I Even Met Happy Gypsies* (Skupljači perja; 1967) by Aleksandar Petrović, *Early Works* (Rani radovi; 1969) by Želimir Žilnik and *Mysteries of the Organism* (Misterije organizma; 1971) by Dušan Makavejev. Serbian black humour gets a good workout in Yugo-classics *Who's That Singing Over There?* (Ko to tamo peva; 1980), *The Marathon Family* (Maratonci trče počasni krug; 1982), *The Elusive Summer of '68* (Varljivo leto '68; 1984) and *Balkan Spy* (Balkanski špijun; 1984).

Two-time Palme d'Or winner Emir Kusturica, originally from Bosnia, is known for his raucous approach to storytelling. Check out *Underground* (1995), the surreal tale of seemingly never-ending Balkan conflicts, or *Time of the Gypsies* (Dom za vešanje; 1989). Watch *Premeditated Murder* (Ubistvo s predumišljajem; 1995), *Cabaret Balkan* (Bure baruta; 1998), *Sky Hook* (Nebeska udica; 2000) and *Thunderbirds* (Munje; 2001) for a great snapshot of the 1990s in the Serbian capital. *Parade* (Parada; 2011) brilliantly chronicles the furore over Belgrade's early pride parades.

Music

Wild sounds of brass bands called *trubači* are the national music; the best ones are Roma ensembles from southern Serbia. Popular examples are albums by trumpet player extraordinaire Boban Marković. *Trubači* get an orgiastic outing at Guča's Trumpet Festival each August. You'll no doubt come across the violin-heavy *tamburaši* at romantic restaurants, particularly in Vojvodina province.

For crooning and swooning, check out Novi Sad's favourite son, Đorđe Balašević. Some of Serbia's best representatives of world music are the late Roma singer Šaban Bajramović and Hungarian violinist Lajkó Félix. The most authentic name on the scene in recent years is Kralj Čačka, seen by many as the Serbian version of Tom Waits; his music is usually described as a mix of jazz, blues, rock and chansons.

Cross traditional folk with techno and you get *turbofolk* – controversial during the Milošević era for its nationalist overtones, these days it's more mainstream fun. Serbia's major 1980s rock bands – including Idoli, Električni Orgazam, EKV and Partibrejkers – were hugely popular across Yugoslavia; you'll still hear them getting a good blasting in bars today. Since the 1990s, alternative bands such as Darkwood Dub and Kanda Kodža i Nebojša have become stalwarts of Belgrade's music scene.

Food & Drink

Serbia's regional cuisines range from spicy Hungarian goulash in Vojvodina to Turkish kebabs in Novi Pazar. The country is famous for *roštilj* (grilled meats). The ubiquitous snack is *burek,* a filo-pastry pie usually made with *sir* (cheese) or *meso* (meat). Vegetarians should try asking for *posna hrana* (literally 'fasting food'); this is also suitable for vegans. Otherwise, there's always *srpska salata* (raw peppers, onions and tomatoes), *šopska salata* (tomatoes, cucumber and onion with grated white cheese), *gibanica* (cheese pie) or *zeljanica* (cheese pie with spinach).

Viscous *domaća/turska kafa* (Turkish coffee) is omnipresent. Many people distil *rakija* (akin to schnapps) from plums *(šljivovica),* grapes *(lozovača)* or other fruits; the delicious *medovača* is made from honey. Serbia's long tradition of viniculture goes back to Roman times; top wine routes include Sremski Karlovci and Fruška Gora National Park in Vojvodina, eastern Serbia's Negotin region and central Serbia's Župa region around Aleksandrovac.

SURVIVAL GUIDE

ℹ️ Directory A–Z

ACCOMMODATION
You'll find hotels and hostels in Serbia's cities and most towns. The **Serbian Youth Hostels Association** (Ferijalni Savez Beograd; ☎ 011 322 0762; www.hostels.rs; Makedonska 22/2, Belgrade) can help with hostel information and advice. Private rooms *(sobe)* and apartments *(apartmani)* offer good value and can be organised through tourist offices. 'Wild' camping is possible outside national parks; **Camping Association of Serbia** (www.camping.rs) lists official campsites. In rural areas, look out for *etno sela* (traditional village accommodation); in Vojvodina, *salaši* (farmsteads) make for a memorable stay. **Rural Tourism Serbia** (www.selo.co.rs) can organise village sleepovers.

LGBTIQ+ TRAVELLERS
As evidenced by the furore over Belgrade's early pride parades (chronicled in the 2011 film *Parada*), life is not all rainbows for homosexuals in this conservative country. Discretion is highly advised. Check out www.gay-serbia.com and www.gej.rs for the latest news in the Serbian LGBT community, or to make local connections.

MONEY
ATMs are widespread and cards are accepted by established businesses. There's an exchange office *(menjačnica)* on every street corner. Exchange machines accept euros, US dollars and British pounds.

OPENING HOURS
Banks 9am to 5pm Monday to Friday, 9am to 1pm Saturday
Bars 8am to midnight (later on weekends)
Restaurants 8am to midnight or 1am
Shops 8am to 6pm or 7pm Monday to Friday, 8am to 3pm Saturday

PUBLIC HOLIDAYS
New Year 1 and 2 January
Orthodox Christmas 7 January
Statehood Day 15 and 16 February
Orthodox Easter April/May
Labour Day 1 and 2 May
Armistice Day 11 November

SAFE TRAVEL
Travelling around Serbia is generally safe for visitors who exercise the usual caution. The exceptions can be border areas, particularly the southeast Kosovo border where Serb–Albanian tensions remain. Check the situation before attempting to cross overland, and think thrice about driving there in Serbian-plated cars.

TELEPHONE
The country code is 381. To call abroad from Serbia, dial 00 followed by the country code. Press the *i* button on public phones for dialling commands in English. Long-distance calls can also be made from booths in post offices. A variety of local and international phonecards can be bought in post offices and news stands.

VISAS
None required for citizens of the EU, UK, Australia, New Zealand, Canada and the USA.

ℹ️ Getting There & Away

AIR
Belgrade's Nikola Tesla Airport (p344) handles most international flights. The airport website has a full list of airlines servicing Serbia. In the south, Niš Constantine the Great Airport (p367) links Niš with countries including Germany, Italy, Slovakia and Switzerland.

Serbia's national carrier is **Air Serbia** (www.airserbia.com). It code-shares with airlines including Etihad, Aeroflot, Alitalia and KLM.

LAND
Border Crossings

Because Serbia does not acknowledge crossing points into Kosovo as international border crossings, it may not be possible to enter Serbia from Kosovo unless you first entered Kosovo from Serbia. If you wish to enter Serbia from Kosovo, consider taking a route which transits another nearby country. Check with your embassy for updates.

Bus

Bus services to Western Europe and Turkey are well developed. When crossing borders, officers will usually board the bus, take everyone's passports, then return them after processing them; passengers wait in their seats.

Car & Motorcycle

Drivers need International Driving Permits. If you're in your own car, you'll need your vehicle registration and ownership documents and locally valid insurance (such as European Green Card vehicle insurance). Otherwise, border insurance costs about €150 for a car, €95 for a motorbike; www.registracija-vozila.rs has updated price lists. Check your hire-car insurance cover to be sure it covers Serbia.

Driving Serbian-plated cars into Kosovo is not a good idea, and is usually not permitted by rental agencies or insurers anyway.

Train

International rail connections leaving Serbia originate in Belgrade. Heading north, most call in at Novi Sad and Subotica. Heading southeast, they go via Niš. The scenic route to Bar on the Montenegrin coast passes through Užice in the southwest.

At border stops, officials will board the train to stamp your passport and check for relevant visas. For more information, visit the website of **Serbian Railways** (www.serbianrailways.com).

❶ Getting Around

BICYCLE

Bicycle paths are improving in larger cities. Vojvodina is relatively flat, but main roads can make for dull days. Mountain biking in summer is popular in regions including Tara National Park, Fruška Gora and Zlatibor. Picturesque winding roads come with the downside of narrow shoulders.

The international **Euro Velo 6** (www.eurovelo.com) route runs through parts of Serbia including Novi Sad, Belgrade and Đerdap National Park.

BUS

Bus services are extensive, though outside major hubs, sporadic connections may leave you in the lurch for a few hours. In southern Serbia particularly, you may have to double back to larger towns.

Reservations are only worthwhile for international buses and during festivals. Tickets can be purchased from the station before departure or on board.

CAR & MOTORCYCLE

The **Automobile & Motorcycle Association of Serbia** (Auto-Moto Savez Srbije; 📞 011 333 1100, roadside assist 1987; www.amss.org.rs; Ruzveltova 18; ⊙ 8am-4pm Mon-Fri) provides roadside assistance and extensive information on its website. A great resource for drivers is the **Planplus** (www.planplus.rs) interactive online road atlas; *Intersistem Kartografija* publishes a useful road map of Serbia (1:550,000).

Several car-hire companies have offices at Nikola Tesla Airport in Belgrade. Small-car hire typically costs €25 to €45 per day. Check where you are not able to take the car. In Belgrade and other large towns you may have to purchase parking tickets from machines, kiosks or via SMS (in Serbian only).

Traffic police are everywhere and accidents are workaday. As of 2018, the BAC limit is 0.02%. You must drive with your headlights on, even in the daytime. An International Driving Permit is required.

TRAIN

Serbian Railways (www.serbianrailways.com) links Belgrade, Novi Sad, Subotica, Niš and Užice in the west; check the website for smaller stations between the cities. Train enthusiasts will enjoy the scenic Šargan 8 railway (p354) in Mokra Gora.

Trains usually aren't as regular and reliable as buses, and can be murderously slow, but they're a fun way to met locals and other travellers.

Slovenia

POP 2 MILLION

Best Places to Eat

➡ Hiša Franko (p404)

➡ Castle Restaurant (p392)

➡ Monstera Bistro (p385)

➡ Pri Mari (p416)

Best Places to Stay

➡ Linhart Hotel (p395)

➡ Jazz Hostel & Apartments (p391)

➡ Design Rooms Pr' Gavedarjo (p400)

➡ DomKulture MuziKafe (p420)

Why Go?

It's a pint-sized place, with a surface area of just over 20,000 sq km, and two million people. But 'good things come in small packages', and never was that old chestnut more appropriate than in describing Slovenia. The country has everything – from beaches, snow-capped mountains, and hills awash in grape vines to Gothic churches, baroque palaces and art nouveau buildings. Its incredible mixture of climates brings warm Mediterranean breezes up to the foothills of the Alps, where it can snow in summer. The capital, Ljubljana, is a culturally rich city that values sustainability over unfettered growth. This sensitivity towards the environment extends to rural and lesser-developed parts of the country.

When to Go
Ljubljana

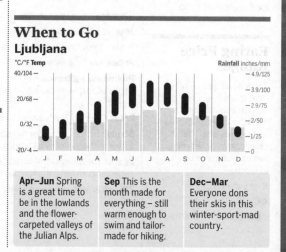

Apr–Jun Spring is a great time to be in the lowlands and the flower-carpeted valleys of the Julian Alps.

Sep This is the month made for everything – still warm enough to swim and tailor-made for hiking.

Dec–Mar Everyone dons their skis in this winter-sport-mad country.

SLOVENIA

Sleeping Price Ranges

The following price ranges refer to a double room with en-suite toilet and bath or shower, and include tax and breakfast.

€ less than €50

€€ €50–100

€€€ more than €100

Eating Price Ranges

The following price ranges refer to a two-course, sit-down meal, including a drink, for one person. Many restaurants also offer an excellent-value set menu of two or even three courses at lunch.

€ less than €15

€€ €15–30

€€€ more than €30

Entering the Country

Entering Slovenia is usually a straightforward procedure. If you're arriving from an EU Schengen country, such as Austria, Italy or Hungary, you will not have to show a passport or go through customs, no matter which nationality you are. If you're coming from any non-Schengen country, ie outside of the EU but also including Croatia, full border procedures apply.

ITINERARIES

Three Days

Spend a couple of days in Ljubljana (p375), then head north to unwind in romantic Bled (p389) or Bohinj (p396) beside idyllic mountain lakes. Alternatively, head south to visit the caves at Škocjan (p408) or Postojna (p405).

One Week

A full week will allow you to see the country's top highlights. After two days in the capital, head for Bled and Bohinj. Depending on the season, take a bus or drive over the hair-raising Vršič Pass (p401) into the valley of the vivid-blue Soča River and take part in some adventure sports in Bovec (p401). Continue south to the caves at Škocjan and Postojna and then to the sparkling Venetian port of Piran (p412) on the Adriatic.

Essential Food

Little Slovenia boasts an incredibly diverse cuisine, with as many as two dozen different regional styles of cooking. Here are some highlights:

Gibanica Layer cake stuffed with nuts, cheese and apple.

Jota Hearty bean-and-cabbage soup.

Postrv Trout, particularly from the Soča River, is a real treat.

Potica A nut roll eaten at teatime or as a dessert.

Prekmurska gibanica A rich concoction of pastry filled with poppy seeds, walnuts, apples and cheese and topped with cream.

Pršut Air-dried, thinly sliced ham from the Karst Region.

Štruklji Scrumptious dumplings made with curd cheese and served either savoury as a main course or sweet as a dessert.

Žganci The Slovenian stodge of choice – groats made from barley or corn but usually *ajda* (buckwheat).

Žlikrofi Ravioli-like parcels filled with cheese, bacon and chives.

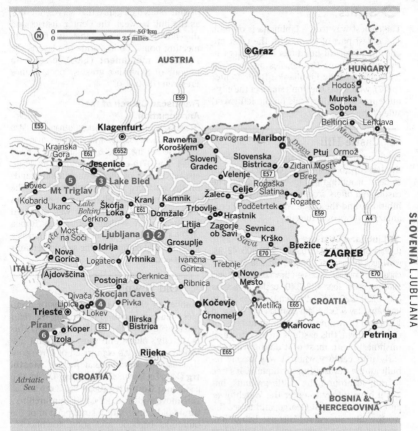

Slovenia Highlights

1 Ljubljana Castle (p376) Enjoying a 'flight' on the funicular up to this spectacular hilltop castle.

2 National & University Library (p377) Considering the genius of architect Jože Plečnik at Ljubljana's historic library.

3 Lake Bled (p389) Gazing at the naturalperfection of this crystal-green lake.

4 Škocjan Caves (p408) Gawking in awe at the 100m-high walls of this incredible cave system.

5 Mt Triglav (p396) Climbing to the top of the country's tallest mountain.

6 Piran (p412) Getting lost wandering the narrow Venetian alleyways of this seaside town.

LJUBLJANA

♪ 01 / POP 279,750 / ELEV 297M

Slovenia's capital and largest city is one of Europe's greenest and most liveable capitals. Car traffic is restricted in the centre, leaving the banks of the emerald-green Ljubljanica River, which flows through the city's heart, free for pedestrians and cyclists. In summer, cafes set up terrace seating along the river; it almost feels like a street party. Slovenia's master of early-modern, minimalist design, Jože Plečnik, graced the capital with beautiful bridges and buildings as well as dozens of urban design elements, such as pillars, pyramids and lamp posts. Some 50,000 students support an active clubbing scene, and Ljubljana's museums and restaurants are among the best in the country.

◉ Sights

The easiest way to see Ljubljana is on foot. The oldest part of town, with the most important historical buildings and sights (including Ljubljana Castle), lies on the right (east) bank of the Ljubljanica River. Center (p377), which has the lion's share of the city's museums and galleries, is on the left (west) side of the river.

◉ Castle Hill

Begin an exploration of the city by making the trek up to Castle Hill (Grajska Planota) to poke around grand Ljubljana Castle. The castle area offers a couple of worthwhile exhibitions, and the castle watchtower affords amazing views over the city.

★ Ljubljana Castle   CASTLE
(Ljubljanski Grad; Map p382; ☑ 01-306 42 93; www.ljubljanskigrad.si; Grajska Planota 1; adult/child incl funicular & castle attractions €10/7, incl Time Machine tour €12/8.40, castle attractions only €7.50/5.20; ⊙ castle 9am-11pm Jun-Sep, to 9pm Apr, May & Oct, 10am-8pm Jan-Mar & Nov, to 10pm Dec) Crowning a 375m-high hill east of the Old Town, this castle is an architectural mishmash, with most of it dating from the early 16th century when it was largely rebuilt after a devastating earthquake. It's free to ramble around the castle grounds, but you'll have to pay to enter the Watchtower and the Chapel of St George, and to see the worthwhile Slovenian History Exhibition, visit the Puppet Theatre and take the Time Machine tour.

◉ Prešernov Trg & Around

Triple Bridge   BRIDGE
(Tromostovje; Map p382) Running south from Prešernov trg to the Old Town is the much celebrated Triple Bridge, originally called Špital (Hospital) Bridge. When it was built as a single span in 1842 it was nothing spectacular, but between 1929 and 1932 superstar architect Jože Plečnik added the two pedestrian side bridges, furnished all three with stone balustrades and lamps, and forced a name change. Stairways on each of the side bridges lead down to the poplar-lined terraces along the Ljubljanica River.

Prešernov Trg   SQUARE
(Prešeren Sq; Map p382) The centrepiece of Ljubljana's wonderful architectural aesthetic is this marvellous square, a public space of understated elegance that serves not only as the link between the Center district and the Old Town but also as the city's favourite meeting point. Taking pride of place is the **Prešeren monument** (1905), erected in honour of Slovenia's greatest poet, France Prešeren (1800–49).

Franciscan Church of the
Annunciation   CHURCH
(Frančiškanska cerkev Marijinega oznanjenja; Map p382; ☑ 01-242 93 00; www.marijino-oznanjenje. si; Prešernov trg 4; ⊙ 6.40am-noon & 3-8pm) **FREE** The 17th-century salmon-pink Franciscan Church of the Annunciation stands on the northern side of Prešernov trg. The interior has six side altars and an enormous choir stall. The main altar was designed by the Italian sculptor Francesco Robba (1698–1757). To the left of the main altar is a glass-fronted coffin with the spooky remains of St Deodatus.

◉ Old Town

Ljubljana's Old Town (Staro Mesto) occupies a narrow swath of land along the right (eastern) bank of the Ljubljanica River. This is the city's oldest and most important historical quarter. It's comprised of three contiguous long squares that include **Mestni trg** (Town Sq; Map p382), **Stari trg** (Old Sq; Map p382) and **Gornji trg** (Upper Sq; Map p382) as you move south and east. It's an architectural gold mine, with a large portion of the buildings baroque and some townhouses along Stari trg and Gornji trg retaining their medieval layout.

Town Hall   HISTORIC BUILDING
(Mestna Hiša; Map p382; ☑ 01-306 30 00; Mestni trg 1; tours €5; ⊙ 8am-5pm Mon-Fri) **FREE** The seat of the city government and sometimes referred to as the Magistrat or Rotovž, the town hall was erected in the late 15th century and rebuilt in 1718. The Gothic courtyard inside, arcaded on three levels, is where theatrical performances once took place; it contains some lovely graffiti. One-hour guided tours are offered in English on Saturdays at 1pm. Tours must be booked in advance through the Ljubljana TIC (p387).

Robba Fountain   FOUNTAIN
(Map p382; Mestni trg) The three titans with their gushing urns on this fountain represent the three rivers of the historic Slovenian province of Carniola: the Sava, Krka and Ljubljanica – but are modern copies.

The original fountain, worn down by time and eaten away by urban pollution, is now housed in the National Gallery (p379).

Cobblers' Bridge   BRIDGE
(Čevljarski Most; Map p382) In the midst of the Old Town, a small street running west from Stari trg (p376) called Pod Trančo (Below Tranča) leads to this evocatively named footbridge. During the Middle Ages this was a place of trade, and a tolled gateway led to the town. Craftspeople worked and lived on bridges (in this case 16 shoemakers) to catch the traffic and avoid paying town taxes – a medieval version of duty-free.

⊙ Central Market Area

The market area extends east of the Triple Bridge (p376) along the eastern edge of the Ljubljanica River, following Adamič-Lundrovo nabrežje. There are not many traditional sights here, but it's a great place for a stroll and to pay a visit to the **Central Market** (Centralna Tržnica; Map p382; Vodnikov trg; ⊙ open-air market 6am-6pm Mon-Fri, to 4pm Sat summer, to 4pm Mon-Sat winter), where you can stock up on fresh local produce, fish and deli items.

Cathedral of St Nicholas   CHURCH
(Stolna Cerkev Sv Nikolaja; Map p382; ☑ 01-234 26 90; www.lj-stolnica.rkc.si; Dolničarjeva ulica 1; ⊙10am-noon & 3-6pm) FREE A church has stood here since the 13th century, but the existing twin-towered building dates from the start of the 18th century. Inside, it's a vision of pink marble, white stucco and gilt and contains a panoply of baroque frescoes. Have a look at the magnificent carved choir stalls, the organ and the angels on the main altar.

Dragon Bridge   BRIDGE
(Zmajski Most; Map p382) The much-loved Dragon Bridge, topped with four scary-looking dragons on each corner, stands northeast of the Old Town, just beyond Vodnikov trg. The bridge was built in Viennese Secession (art nouveau) style and dates from 1900–01.

⊙ Center

This large district on the left bank of the Ljubljanica is the nerve centre of modern Ljubljana. It is filled with shops, commercial offices, government departments and embassies. Center is divided into several distinct neighbourhoods centred on squares.

National & University Library   ARCHITECTURE
(Narodna in Univerzitetna Knjižnica, NUK; Map p382; ☑ 01-200 12 09; www.nuk.uni-lj.si; Turjaška ulica 1; ⊙8am-8pm Mon-Fri, 9am-2pm Sat) FREE This library is architect Jože Plečnik's masterpiece, completed in 1941. To appreciate this great man's philosophy, enter through the main door (note the horse-head doorknobs) on Turjaška ulica – you'll find yourself in near darkness, entombed in black marble. As you ascend the steps, you'll emerge into a colonnade suffused with light – the light of knowledge, according to the architect's plans.

City Museum of Ljubljana   MUSEUM
(Mestni Muzej Ljubljana; Map p382; ☑ 01-241 25 00; www.mgml.si; Gosposka ulica 15; adult/child €6/4; ⊙10am-6pm Tue, Wed & Fri-Sun, to 9pm Thu) The excellent city museum, established in 1935, focuses on Ljubljana's history, culture and politics via imaginative multimedia and interactive displays. The reconstructed street that once linked the eastern gates of the Roman colony of Emona (today's Ljubljana) to the Ljubljanica River, and the collection of well-preserved classical artefacts in the basement treasury, are worth a visit in themselves. So too are the models of buildings that the celebrated architect Jože Plečnik never got around to erecting.

⊙ Museum Area

Four of Ljubljana's most important museums are located in this area, which is only a short distance to the northwest of **Trg Republike** (Republic Sq; Map p378).

Museum of Modern Art   MUSEUM
(MG, Moderna Galerija; Map p378; ☑ 01-241 68 34; www.mg-lj.si; Cankarjeva cesta 15; adult/student €5/2.50, with Museum of Contemporary Art Metelkova €7.50; ⊙10am-6pm Tue-Sun, to 8pm Thu Jul & Aug) This gallery houses the very best in modern Slovenian art. Keep an eye out for works by painters Tone Kralj *(Family)*, the expressionist France Mihelič *(The Quintet)* and the surrealist Stane Kregar *(Hunter at Daybreak),* as well as sculptors including Jakob Savinšek *(Protest)*. The museum also owns works by the influential 1980s and 1990s multimedia group Neue Slowenische Kunst (NSK; *Suitcase for Spiritual Use: Baptism under Triglav*) and the artists' co-operative Irwin *(Capital)*.

Ljubljana

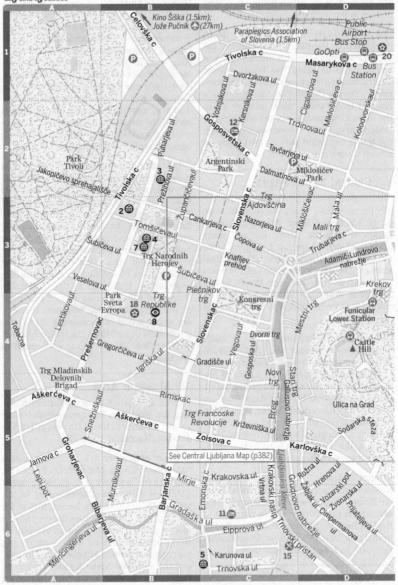

See Central Ljubljana Map (p382)

National Museum of Slovenia

MUSEUM

(Narodni Muzej Slovenije; Map p378; ☏ 01-241 44 00; www.nms.si; Prešernova cesta 20; adult/student €6/4, with National Museum of Slovenia–Metelkova or Slovenian Museum of Natural History €8.50/6, lapidarium free; ⊙10am-6pm, to 8pm Thu) Housed in a grand building from 1888 – the same building as the Slovenian Museum of Natural History (p379) – highlights include the highly embossed *Vače situla* – a Celtic pail from the 6th century BC that was unearthed in a town east of Ljubljana.

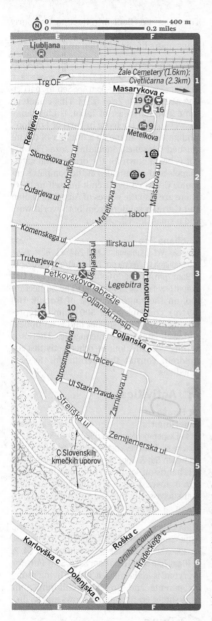

Slovenian Museum of Natural History MUSEUM
(Prirodoslovni Muzej Slovenije; Map p378; ☑01-241 09 40; www.pms-lj.si; Prešernova cesta 20; adult/student €4/3, with National Museum of Slovenia €8.50/6, 1st Sun of month free; ☺10am-6pm Fri-Wed, to 8pm Thu) This museum shares the same building as the National Museum of Slovenia (p378), and contains reassembled mammoth and whale skeletons, stuffed birds, reptiles and mammals. The mineral collections amassed by the philanthropic Baron Žiga Zois in the early 19th century and the display on Slovenia's unique salamander *Proteus anguinus* are worth the visit. Note the entrance to both museums is on the eastern side of the building, facing the park.

National Gallery of Slovenia MUSEUM
(Map p378; ☑01-241 54 18; www.ng-slo.si; Prešernova cesta 24; adult/child €7/3, 1st Sun of month free; ☺10am-6pm Tue, Wed & Fri-Sun, to 8pm Thu) Slovenia's foremost assembly of fine art is housed over two floors in an old building

There's also a Stone Age bone flute discovered near Cerkno in western Slovenia in 1995. You'll find examples of Roman jewellery found in 6th-century Slavic graves, as well as a glass-enclosed Roman lapidarium outside to the north.

SLOVENIA LJUBLJANA

(1896) and a modern wing. It exhibits copies of medieval frescoes and wonderful Gothic statuary as well as Slovenian landscapes from the 17th to 19th centuries (check out works by Romantic painters Pavel Künl and Marko Pernhart). Other noteworthies: impressionists Jurij Šubic *(Before the Hunt)* and Rihard Jakopič *(Birches in Autumn)*, the pointillist Ivan Grohar *(Larch)* and Slovenia's most celebrated female painter, Ivana Kobilca *(Summer)*.

◉ Trubarjeva Cesta & Tabor

This bustling street, lined with watering holes and eateries, gives way to leafy, residential Tabor, home to some world-class museums and Metelkova Mesto, Ljubljana's centre of alternative culture.

Museum of Contemporary Art Metelkova   GALLERY
(MSUM, Muzej Sodobne Umetnosti Metelkova; Map p378; ☑ 01-241 68 00; www.mg-lj.si; Maistrova ulica 3; adult/student €5/2.50, with Museum of Modern Art €7.50; ⊙ 10am-6pm Tue-Sun, to 8pm Thu Jul & Aug) This gallery, housed in a sleekly redesigned block building, picks up the thread from its sister institution, the Museum of Modern Art (p377), with Eastern European (mostly ex-Yugoslav) works from the 1960s till today. Plenty of obscure material here, but just as much of it is challenging and thought-provoking.

Slovenian Ethnographic Museum   MUSEUM
(Slovenski Etnografski Muzej; Map p378; ☑ 01-300 87 45; www.etno-muzej.si; Metelkova ulica 2; adult/child €4.50/2.50, 1st Sun of month free; ⊙ 10am-6pm Tue-Sun) Housed in the 1886 Belgian Barracks on the southern edge of Metelkova, this museum has a permanent collection on the 2nd and 3rd floors. There's traditional Slovenian trades and handicrafts – everything from beekeeping and blacksmithing to glass-painting and pottery making – and some excellent exhibits directed at children.

◉ Outside the Centre

Plečnik House   MUSEUM
(Hiša Plečnik; Map p378; ☑ 01-241 25 06; www.mgml.si; Karunova ulica 4-6; adult/child €6/4; ⊙ 10am-6pm Tue-Sun) This small house in Trnovo is where local architect Jože Plečnik lived and worked for almost 40 years.

There's an excellent introduction by hourly guided tour to this almost ascetically religious man's life, inspiration and work.

Žale Cemetery   CEMETERY
(Pokopališče Žale; ☑ 01-420 17 00; www.zale.si; Med Hmeljniki 2; ⊙ 7am-9pm Apr-Sep, to 7pm Oct-Mar; ☐ 2, 7 or 22 to Žale) **FREE** This cemetery, some 2km northeast of Tabor, is Ljubljana's answer to Père Lachaise in Paris or London's Highgate. It is 'home' to a number of distinguished Slovenes, including Jože Plečnik, but is best known for the ornamental gates, chapels and colonnades at the complex's entrance designed by Plečnik himself in 1940. There are also the graves of Austrian, Italian and German soldiers from both world wars and a small Jewish section.

Ljubljana Zoo   ZOO
(Živalski Vrt Ljubljana; ☑ 01-244 21 82; www.zoo-ljubljana.si; Večna pot 70; adult/child €8/5.50; ⊙ 9am-7pm Apr-Aug, to 6pm Sep, to 5pm Mar & Oct, to 4pm Nov-Feb; ☐ 18 Večna pot) The 20-hectare zoo, on the southern slope of **Rožnik Hill** (394m), contains some 500 animals representing almost 120 species and is an upbeat and well-landscaped menagerie. There's a petting zoo and lots of other activities for children; consult the website for feeding schedules.

🏃 Activities

★ House of Experiments   AMUSEMENT PARK
(Hiša Eksperimentov; Map p382; ☑ 01-300 68 88; www.he.si; Trubarjeva cesta 39; €6; ⊙ 4-8pm Wed, 11am-7pm Sat & Sun) A super place for kids, this hands-on science centre has almost four dozen inventive and challenging exhibits that successfully mix learning with humour. There's a science adventure show at 5pm.

Mala Ulica   PLAYGROUND
(Little Street; Map p382; ☑ 01-306 27 00; www.malaulica.si; Prečna ulica 7; family/child €4/2; ⊙ 10am-7pm Mon-Fri, to 6pm Sat & Sun) Fun for everyone is Mala Ulica, a 'public living room' for parents and preschool children, with workshops, crafts, puppet shows and so on.

👉 Tours

The Ljubljana Tourist Information Centre (p387) offers a number of guided tours of the city organised around modes of transport or themes, such as food and drink. See the website for a list.

Ljubljana Free Tour WALKING
(Map p382; ☑040 604 476; www.ljubljanafreetour.
com; Prešernov trg; donation expected; ⊙11am
year-round & also 3pm May-Oct) Highly rec-
ommendable 'free' city tour (the name is a
misnomer because you are expected to tip).
Groups meet up in Prešernov trg (p376);
tours last about 2½ hours and cover most
of the major sights (except the castle). Check
the website for fixed-price themed tours on
the communist era and medieval Ljubljana
(both €10).

LjubljanaNjam TOURS
(☑041 878 959; www.ljubljananjam.si; 3-4hr tours
€55-65) Among the best of several companies offering food walking tours in Ljubljana. The name 'LjubljanaNjam' translates
roughly as 'Ljubljana Yum', and epicure Iva
Gruden will have you eating out of bakers'
hands, nibbling goat cheese in the market,
scoffing Carniola sausage and slurping fair-
trade espresso. Also runs tours focused on
wines and craft beers.

🎉 Festivals & Events

Druga Godba MUSIC
(Another Story; https://drugagodba.si; ⊙May)
This festival of alternative and world music
takes place in the Križanke (p386).

Ljubljana Pride LGBT
(www.ljubljanapride.org; ⊙Jun) Annual gay
pride parade and festival, with a week of
conferences, movies, performances and
discussions at venues around town. See the
website for calendar.

**Ana Desetnica International Street
Theatre Festival** THEATRE
(www.anamonro.si/ana-desetnica; ⊙Jun-Jul) Organised by the Ana Monró Theatre in late
June/early July, this festival is not to be
missed.

Ljubljana Festival MUSIC
(www.ljubljanafestival.si; ⊙Jul-Aug) The number-
one event on Ljubljana's social calendar is the
Ljubljana Festival, a celebration from early
July to late August of music, opera, theatre
and dance held at venues throughout the
city, but principally in the open-air theatre
(p386) at the Križanke.

🛏 Sleeping

⭐**Hostel Vrba** HOSTEL €
(Map p378; ☑064 133 555; www.hostelvrba.si;
Gradaška ulica 10; dm €22-30, d €65-75; @🛜)

Definitely one of our favourite budget digs
in Ljubljana, this nine-room hostel on the
Gradiščica Canal is just opposite the bars
and restaurants of delightful Trnovo. There
are three twin doubles, dorms with four to
eight beds (including a popular all-female
dorm), hardwood floors and an always
warm welcome. Free bikes in summer.

Celica Hostel HOSTEL €
(Map p378; ☑01-230 97 00; www.hostelcelica.
com; Metelkova ulica 8; dm €18-26, s/d cell €58/62;
@🛜) This stylishly revamped former prison (1882) in Metelkova (p386) has 20 'cells',
designed by different artists and architects,
and complete with original bars. There are
nine rooms and apartments with three to
seven beds and a packed, popular 12-bed
dorm. The ground floor is home to a cafe
and restaurant (set lunch around €7). Bikes
cost €3/6 for a half-/full day.

Hostel 24 Center HOSTEL €
(Map p378; ☑040 780 036; https://hostel24.si/
center; Poljanska cesta 15; dm €16-20, d €50-58;
🎮@🛜) One of three hostels in a chain, this
one is just east of the central market (p377)
and Dragon Bridge (p377) on a street that
seems to be gaining momentum (and a few
bars and restaurants). Hostel 24 offers dorm
accommodation in six- to 12-bed rooms, as
well as several private apartments for two to
four people.

Hotel Galleria BOUTIQUE HOTEL €€
(Map p382; ☑01-421 35 60; www.hotelgalleria.eu;
Gornji trg 3; s €70-110, d €90-130; 🎮@🛜) This
attractive boutique hotel has been cobbled
together from several Old Town townhouses. There are 16 spacious rooms and a multi-
tiered back garden. The decor is kitsch with
a smirk and there are fabulous touches
everywhere. Among our favourites are the
enormous room 8, with views of the **Her-
cules Fountain** (Map p382; Levstikov trg), and
room 13, with glimpses of Ljubljana Castle.

Slamič B&B B&B €€
(Map p378; ☑01-433 82 33; www.slamic.si; Ker-
snikova ulica 1; s €65-75, d €95-110, ste from €135;
🅿🎮🛜) It's slightly away from the action
but Slamič, a B&B above a famous cafe and
teahouse, offers 17 bright, refurbished rooms
with en-suite facilities and large, comfortable beds. Choice rooms include those looking on to a back garden, and the one just
off an enormous terrace used by the KavaČaj
(CoffeeTea), a gem of a cafe on the ground
floor.

Central Ljubljana

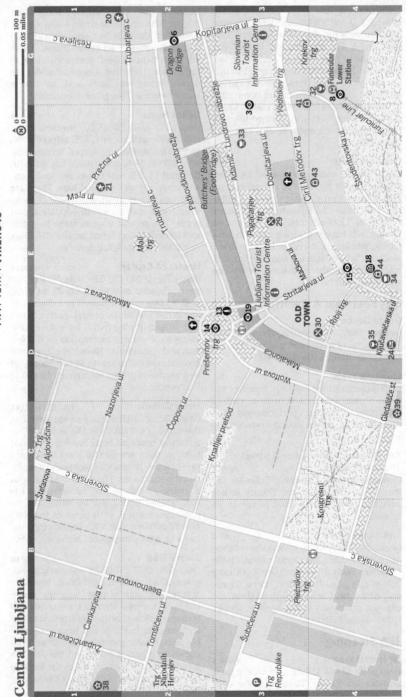

N
0   100 m
0   0.05 miles

Map labels:

Reslieva c

20
6
Kopitarjeva ul
Dragon Bridge
Slovenian Tourist Information Centre
Krekov trg
Vodnikov trg
32
Funicular Lower Station
41
8
3
33
Adamič - Lundrovo nabrežje
Dolničarjeva ul
2
Ciril Metodov trg
43
Trubarjeva c

Trubarjeva c
Prečna ul
21
Mala ul
Petkovškovo nabrežje
Butchers' Bridge (Footbridge)
Pogačarjev trg
29

Mali trg
Makova ul
18
44
15
34

Miklošičeva c
Ljubljana Tourist Information Centre
Stritarjeva ul
OLD TOWN
Ribji trg
30
7
13
19
Prešernov trg
14
35
Ključavničarska ul
24

Nazorjeva ul
Wolfova ul
Mačkalonca
Gledališče st
39

Čopova ul
Knaflev prehod

Trg Ajdovščina
Štefanova ul
Slovenska c

Kongresni trg

Beethovnova ul
Slovenska c
Plečnikov trg

Cankarjeva c
Tomšičeva ul
Šubičeva ul
Trg Narodnih Herojev
Trg Republike

Župančičeva ul
38

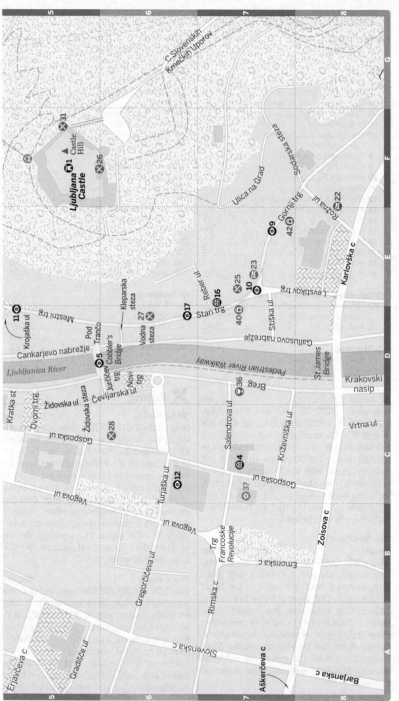

Central Ljubljana

★ **Adora Hotel**   HOTEL €€€
(Map p382; 📱082 057 240; www.adorahotel.si;
Rožna ulica 7; s €115, d €125-155, apt €135-165;
P ❋ @ 🛜) This small hotel below Gornji trg
is a welcome addition to accommodation in
the Old Town. The 10 rooms are small but
fully equipped, with lovely hardwood floors
and tasteful furnishings. The breakfast room
looks out onto a small garden, bikes are free
for guests' use, and the staff are overwhelmingly friendly and helpful.

Vander Urbani
Resort   BOUTIQUE HOTEL €€€
(Map p382; 📱01-200 90 00; www.vanderhotel.
com; Krojaška ulica 6-8; r €130-210; ❋ @ 🛜 ❋)
This stunning boutique hotel in the heart
of Ljubljana's Old Town is formed from four
17th-century buildings. But history stops
there, for this hostelry – with 16 rooms over
three floors – is as modern as tomorrow.
Designed by the trendsetting Sadar Vuga
architectural firm, the rooms are not huge
but each is unique and makes use of natural
materials.

✗ Eating

★ **Ek Bistro**   INTERNATIONAL €
(Map p378; 📱041 937 534; www.facebook.com/
ekljubljana; Petkovškovo nabrežje 65; breakfasts
€8-10; ⊙8am-8pm Mon-Thu, to 9pm Fri & Sat,
to 3pm Sun; 🛜🗩) Ljubljana's top spot for
brunch, meaning in this case big slices of
avocado toast on homemade bread, bowls
of muesli and yoghurt, and eggs Benedict
on fresh-baked English muffins. Wash it
down with a glass of freshly squeezed something or a flat white. The fresh-cut flowers
on the tables look great against the dis-
tressed brick walls.

Pop's Place   BURGERS €
(Map p382; 📱059 042 856; www.facebook.com/
popsplaceburgerbar; Cankarjevo nabrežje 3; burgers €8-10; ⊙noon-midnight; 🛜) Centrally located craft-beer and burger bar that's evolved
into a must-visit. The burgers, with locally
sourced beef and brioche-style buns, are excellent, as are the beers and cocktails. The
dining area feels festive, with an open kitch-
en behind the bar and communal tables out

front for diners to rub elbows and compare burgers. Avoid traditional meal times: Pop's gets busy.

Druga Violina
SLOVENIAN €

(Map p382; ☑ 082 052 506; www.facebook.com/drugaviolina; Stari trg 21; mains €6-10; ☺8am-midnight; ☏) Just opposite the Academy of Music, the 'Second Fiddle' is an extremely pleasant and affordable place for a meal in the Old Town. There are lots of Slovenian dishes, including *ajdova kaša z jurčki* (buckwheat groats with ceps) and *obara* (a thick stew of chicken and vegetables), on the menu. It's a social enterprise designed to help those with disabilities.

Gostilna Dela
INTERNATIONAL €

(Map p378; ☑ 059 925 446; www.facebook.com/gostilnadela; Poljanska cesta 7; mains €5-7; ☺8am-4pm Mon-Fri; ☏🖉) This delightful bistro serves tasty homestyle cuisine, only much better. From the soups and the meat and vegetarian main courses to the shop-made *štruklji* (cheese dumplings), it's all memorable. The breakfast omelettes stretch off the plate. What's more, 'Dela' (Work) is helping to create job opportunities for local youth otherwise excluded from the working world. Breakfast and lunch only.

Odprta Kuhna
MARKET €

(Open Kitchen; Map p382; www.odprtakuhna.si; Pogačarjev trg; mains €8-15; ☺10am-9pm Fri mid-Mar–Oct, up to 11pm in summer) The 'Open Kitchen' is an amazing food fair, with local and international specialities cooked on-site from many of the best restaurants around the city and beyond. Try to time your arrival away from traditional meal times, or prepare for long lines.

Gostilna na Gradu
SLOVENIAN €€

(Inn at the Castle; Map p382; ☑ 031 301 777; www.nagradu.si; Grajska planota 1; mains €12-18; ☺10am-midnight Mon-Sat, noon-6pm Sun; ☏) Right within the Ljubljana Castle (p376) complex, Na Gradu is much too stylish to be just a *gostilna* (inn-like restaurant). The award-winning chefs use only Slovenian-sourced breads, cheeses and meats, and age-old recipes to prepare a meal to remember. If you really want to taste your way across the country, try the five-course gourmet tasting menu for €42.20.

Julija
MEDITERRANEAN €€

(Map p382; ☑ 01-425 64 63; http://julijarestaurant.com; Stari trg 9; mains €10-20; ☺11.30am-midnight; ☏) Arguably the best of several restaurants standing side by side on touristy Stari trg. The menu revolves around risottos and pastas, with plenty of tempting meat and fish options. The atmosphere is casual, though the relatively formal baroque setting makes Julija a solid choice for a fancy meal or a date. The three-course set lunches (around €9) are good value.

Gostilna Jakob Franc
SLOVENIAN €€

(Map p378; ☑ 051 616 000; www.facebook.com/gostilnaJakobFranc; Trnovski pristan 4a; mains €8-20; ☺11am-11pm Mon-Sat, to 4pm Sun; ☏) This small place in Trnovo is great for lunch, particularly if you're in the mood for pork. Jakob Franc is a Slovenian wunderkind who's taken concepts such as farm-fresh and whole-animal and applied them to local pig varieties. The results are satisfying dishes including the smoked pork neck on buckwheat porridge with mushrooms. The wine list is excellent.

★Monstera Bistro
SLOVENIAN €€€

(Map p382; ☑ 040 431 123; http://monsterabistro.si; Gosposka ulica 9; 3-course lunch €19, 7-course tasting menu €55; ☺11.30am-5pm Mon-Wed, to 11pm Thu-Sat; ☏🖉) 🖉 The concept bistro of star TV chef Bine Volčič delivers 'best-meal-of-the-trip' quality using locally sourced, seasonal ingredients and zero-waste food-prep concepts. Most diners opt for the three-course lunch (starter, main course, dessert), though the multicourse dinners are consistently good. The light-infused dining room, with white-brick walls and light woods, feels dressy without being overly formal. Book in advance.

Strelec
SLOVENIAN €€€

(Archer; Map p382; ☑ 031 687 648; www.kaval-group.si/strelec.asp; Grajska Planota 1; mains €15-30; ☺noon-10pm Mon-Sat; ☏) This is haute cuisine from on high – the Archer's Tower of Ljubljana Castle (p376), no less – with a menu that traces the city's history chosen by ethnologist Janez Bogataj and prepared by Igor Jagodic, recognised as one of the top chefs in Slovenia. Tasting menus are priced from €32 to €77 for between three and nine courses.

🍷 Drinking & Nightlife

★Magda
CAFE

(Map p382; ☑ 01-620 26 10; https://barmagda.si; Pogačarjev trg 1; ☺7am-1am Mon-Sat, from 10am

Sun; 🕐) It's hard to put a finger on what makes Magda so special. Maybe it's the expertly prepared espresso (just €1 a cup purchased at the bar) or the unique 'tapas-style' breakfast menu, where you choose from local meats and cheeses, or the craft gins and local homemade brandies on offer. It's a great choice to start or end the day.

Wine Bar Šuklje   WINE BAR

(Map p382; 📞 040 654 575; www.winebar.suklje. com; Breg 10; ⊙ 9am-midnight Mon-Sat, to 4pm Sun; 🕐) This central upscale tasting room is the perfect choice for sampling wines from around Slovenia. The owner is a winemaker and has a knowledgeable palate for assembling tasting flights plus meat and cheese plates to space the tastings. It also sells bottles from the family winery in the southeastern region of Bela Krajina and from select wineries around the country.

Slovenska Hiša   COCKTAIL BAR

(Slovenian House; Map p382; 📞 083 899 811; www. slovenskahisa.si; Cankarjevo nabrežje 13; ⊙ 8am-1am Sun-Thu, to 3am Fri & Sat; 🕐) Our favourite boozer along the river is so cute it's almost twee. Choose from artisanal coffees, wines, lemonades, cocktails and spirits, featuring ingredients sourced only in Slovenia. Order one of the inventive meat and cheese plates (€4 to €7) to soak up the alcohol.

Klub Daktari   BAR

(Map p382; 📞 064 166 212; www.daktari.si; Krekov trg 7; ⊙ 7.30am-1am Mon-Fri, 8am-1am Sat, 9am-midnight Sun; 🕐) This rabbit warren of a watering hole at the foot of the **funicular** (Map p382; 📞 01-306 42 00; www.ljubljanskigrad. si; Krekov trg; adult/child €4/3 return, €2.20/1.50 one-way; ⊙ 10am-6pm) to Ljubljana Castle (p376) is so chilled there's practically frost on the windows. The decor is retro-distressed, with shelves full of old books and a piano in the corner. More a cultural centre than a club, Daktari hosts live music and an eclectic mix of other cultural events.

Pritličje   CAFE

(Ground Floor; Map p382; 📞 082 058 742; www. pritlicje.si; Mestni trg 2; ⊙ 9am-1am Sun-Wed, to 3am Thu-Sat; 🕐) The ultra-inclusive 'Ground Floor' offers something for everyone: cafe, bar, live music, cultural centre and comic-book shop. Events are scheduled almost nightly and the location next to the Town Hall (p376), with good views across Mestni trg (p376), couldn't be more perfect.

Q Cultural Centre   GAY & LESBIAN

(Kulturni Center Q; Map p378; 📞 01-430 35 35; www.kulturnicenterq.org; Metelkova Mesto, Masarykova cesta 24) Works together with ŠKUC (Galerija Škuc; Map p382; 📞 01-251 65 40; www.galerijaskuc.si; Stari trg 21; ⊙ noon-7pm Tue-Sun) FREE and **Klub Tiffany** (Map p378; www. kulturnicenterq.org; Metelkova Mesto, Masarykova cesta 24; ⊙ 11pm-5am Fri & Sat); it shares space with the latter in Metelkova Mesto. Check the website for dance parties, cultural events, discussions etc.

Metelkova Mesto   CLUB

(Metelkova Town; Map p378; www.metelkovamesto. org; Masarykova cesta 24) This ex-army garrison – taken over by squatters in the 1990s and converted into a free-living commune – is home to several clubs, bars and concert venues. It generally comes to life after 11pm daily in summer, and on Friday and Saturday the rest of the year. The quality of the acts varies, though there's usually a little of something for everyone.

☆ Entertainment

★ Kino Šiška   LIVE MUSIC

(📞 030 310 110, box office 01-500 30 00; www. kinosiska.si; Trg Prekomorskih brigad 3; ⊙ box office 3-8pm Mon-Fri, pub 8am-midnight, events 8pm-2am; 🕐; 🚊 1, 3, 5, 8, 22, 25) This renovated old movie theatre now houses an urban cultural centre, hosting mainly indie, rock and alternative bands from around Slovenia and the rest of Europe. Buy tickets at the box office or at **Eventim** (Map p378; 📞 090 55 77; www. eventim.si; Trg Osvobodilne Fronte 6; ⊙ 8am-4pm) offices around town.

Križanke   PERFORMING ARTS

(Map p382; 📞 01-241 60 00, box office 01-241 60 26; www.ljubljanafestival.si; Trg Francoske Revolucije 1-2; ⊙ box office 10am-8pm Mon-Fri, to 2pm Sat May-Sep, noon-5pm Mon-Fri, 10am-2pm Sat Oct-Apr, 1hr before performance) The open-air theatre seating more than 1200 spectators at this sprawling 18th-century monastery, remodelled by Jože Plečnik in the 1950s, hosts the events of the summer Ljubljana Festival (p381). The smaller Knights Hall (Viteška Dvorana) is the venue for chamber concerts.

Slovenia Philharmonic Hall   CLASSICAL MUSIC

(Slovenska Filharmonija; Map p382; 📞 01-241 08 00; www.filharmonija.si; Kongresni trg 10; tickets €8-16; ⊙ box office 11am-1pm & 3-6pm Mon-Fri) Home to the Slovenian Philharmonic, founded in 1701, this small but atmospheric venue at the southeast corner of Kongresni trg also stages concerts and hosts performances of the Slovenian Chamber Choir (Slovenski Komorni Zbor). Haydn, Beethoven and Brahms were honorary Philharmonic members, and Gustav Mahler was resident conductor for a season (1881–82).

Opera Ballet Ljubljana
OPERA

(Map p382; ☑ 01-241 59 00, box office 01-241 59 59; www.opera.si; Župančičeva ulica 1; ⊙ box office 10am-1pm & 2-6pm Mon-Fri, 10am-1pm Sat, 1hr before performance) Home to the Slovenian National Opera and Ballet companies, this historical neo-Renaissance theatre has been restored to its former glory. Enter from Cankarjeva cesta.

Gala Hala
LIVE MUSIC

(Map p378; ☑ 01-431 70 63; www.galahala.com; Metelkova Mesto, Masarykova cesta 24; tickets €3-10) Metelkova (p386)'s biggest and best venue to catch live alternative, indie and rock music several nights a week. There's an open-air performance space from May to September.

Channel Zero
LIVE MUSIC

(Map p378; www.ch0.org; Metelkova Mesto, Masarykova cesta 24; tickets from €3; ⊙ hours variable; 🎧) Venue at Metelkova Mesto (p386) featuring reggae, dub, punk and hardcore music.

Cvetličarna
LIVE MUSIC

(☑ 040 689 559; www.cvetlicarna.info; Kranjčeva ulica 20; ⊙ 9pm-4am Fri & Sat, other times according to event; 🚌13, 20) Cavernous concert hall hosting live acts and DJs most weekends, as well as a variety of other types of performances, including comedy, on some weeknights. Check the website for an up-to-date calendar of events.

Cankarjev Dom
CLASSICAL MUSIC

(Map p378; ☑ 01-241 71 00, box office 01-241 72 99; www.cd-cc.si; Prešernova cesta 10; ⊙ box office 11am-1pm & 3-8pm Mon-Fri, 11am-1pm Sat, 1hr before performance) Ljubljana's premier cultural and conference centre has two large auditoriums (the Gallus Hall is said to have perfect acoustics) and a dozen smaller performance spaces offering a remarkable smorgasbord of performance arts.

🛍 Shopping

★ Kraševka
FOOD & DRINKS

(Map p382; ☑ 01-232 14 45; www.krasevka.si; Vodnikov trg 4; ⊙ 9am-7pm Mon-Fri, to 3pm Sat) This fantastic delicatessen with more than 300 products from farms (mostly) in the Karst stocks *pršut* (air-dried ham, not unlike prosciutto) in all its variations and cheeses, as well as wines and spirits, oils and vinegars, and honeys and marmalades.

Vinoteka Movia
DRINKS

(Map p382; ☑ 051 304 590; www.movia.si; Mestni trg 2; ⊙ noon-midnight Mon-Sat) As much a wine shop as a wine bar, this is always our first port of call when buying a bottle. Although Movia is its own label, the knowledgeable staff here will advise you on and sell you wine from other vintners.

3 Muhe
ARTS & CRAFTS

(3 Flies; Map p382; ☑ 01-421 07 15; www.3muhe.si; Stari trg 30; ⊙ 10am-7.30pm Mon-Fri, to 2pm Sat) Only fair-trade products make it to the shelves of this socially conscious enterprise, be it coffee from Uganda, spices from Sri Lanka, baskets from Ghana or stemware from Guatemala. You'll feel good just walking in.

Lina
FASHION & ACCESSORIES

(Map p382; ☑ 01-421 08 92; www.svila-lina.net; Gornji trg 14; ⊙ 10am-1pm & 3-7pm Mon-Fri, to 1pm Sat) Dušanka Herman's scrumptious painted silk accessories include unevenly cut ties and scarves for men and daringly coloured dresses for women. Just try to leave without buying something!

Trgovina IKA
GIFTS & SOUVENIRS

(Map p382; ☑ 01-232 17 43; www.trgovina-ika.si; Ciril Metodov trg 13; ⊙ 9am-7.30pm Mon-Fri, to 6pm Sat, 10am-2pm Sun) This gift shop-cum-art gallery-cum-fashion designer opposite the cathedral and Central Market sells handmade items that put a modern spin on traditional forms and motifs. More than 100 designers have clothing, jewellery, porcelain etc on sale here.

ℹ Information

ATMs are everywhere, including several outside the Ljubljana TIC (p387). Full-service banks are all around the centre; they're the best places to exchange cash.

Ljubljana Tourist Information Centre (TIC; Map p382; ☑ 01-306 12 15; www.visitljubljana.com; Adamič-Lundrovo nabrežje 2; ⊙ 8am-9pm Jun-Sep, to 7pm Oct-May) Knowledgeable and enthusiastic staff dispense information, maps and useful literature and help with accommodation. Offers a range of interesting city and regional tours and maintains an excellent website.

Slovenian Tourist Information Centre (STIC; Map p382; ☑ 01-306 45 76; www.slovenia.info; Krekov trg 10; ☺ 8am-9pm daily Jun-Sep, 8am-7pm Mon-Fri, 9am-5pm Sat & Sun Oct-May; ☎) Good source of information for travel to the rest of Slovenia, with internet and bicycle rental also available.

⚊ Getting There & Away

BUS

Buses to destinations both within Slovenia and abroad leave from the **bus station** (Avtobusna Postaja Ljubljana; Map p378; ☑ 01-234 46 00; www.ap-ljubljana.si; Trg Osvobodilne Fronte 4; ☺ 5am-10.30pm Mon-Fri, 5am-10pm Sat, 5.30am-10.30pm Sun) just next to the **train station** (Železniška Postaja; ☑ 01-291 33 32; www.slo-zeleznice.si; Trg Osvobodilne Fronte 6; ☺ 5am-10pm). The station website has an excellent timetable for checking departure times and prices. At the station, you'll find multilingual information phones and a touchscreen computer next to the ticket windows. There's another touchscreen computer outside. You do not usually have to buy your ticket in advance; just pay as you board the bus. But for long-distance trips on Fridays, just before the school break and public holidays, you run the risk of not getting a seat. To be safe, book the day before and reserve a seat.

Some sample one-way fares (return fares are usually double) from the capital:

DESTI-NATION	PRICE (€)	DURA-TION (HR)	DIS-TANCE (KM)	FREQUENCY
Bled	7.80	1½	57	hourly
Bohinj	9.80	2	91	hourly
Koper	11.10	2½	122	5 daily with more in season
Maribor	11.40	2-3	141	2-4 daily
Novo Mesto	7.20	1	72	up to 7 daily
Piran	12	3	140	up to 7 daily
Postojna	6	1	53	up to 24 daily

TRAIN

Domestic and international trains arrive at and depart from central Ljubljana's train station (p388), where you'll find a separate information centre on the way to the platforms. The website has an excellent timetable with departure times and prices. Buy domestic tickets from windows No 1 to 8 and international ones from either window No 9 or the information centre.

The following are one-way, 2nd-class domestic fares, travel times, distances and frequencies from Ljubljana. Return fares are double the price, and there's a surcharge of €1.80 on domestic InterCity (IC) and EuroCity (EC) train tickets.

DESTI-NATION	PRICE (€)	DURA-TION (HR)	DIS-TANCE (KM)	FREQUENCY
Bled	€6.60	55min	51	up to 21 daily
Koper	€9.60	2½	153	up to 4 daily, with more in summer
Maribor	€9.60	1¾	156	up to 25 daily
Murska Sobota	€13	3¼	216	up to 5 daily
Novo Mesto	€6.60	1½	75	up to 14 daily

⚊ Getting Around

TO/FROM THE AIRPORT

The cheapest way to Jože Pučnik Airport (p425) is by public bus (€4.10, 50 minutes, 27km) from **stop No 28** (Map p378; €4.10 one way; ☺ 5.20am-8.10pm) at the bus station (p388). These run at 5.20am and hourly from 6.10am to 8.10pm Monday to Friday; at the weekend there's a bus at 6.10am and then one every two hours from 9.10am to 7.10pm. Buy tickets from the driver.

Two airport shuttle services that get consistently good reviews are **GoOpti** (Map p378; ☑ 01-320 45 30; www.goopti.com; Trg Osvobodilne Fronte 4; €9 one way) and **Markun Shuttle** (☑ reservations 041 792 865; www.prevozi-markun.com; €9 one way), which will transfer you from Brnik (where the airport is) to central Ljubljana in half an hour. Book by phone or online.

A taxi from the airport to Ljubljana will cost €35 to €45.

BICYCLE

Ljubljana is a pleasure for cyclists, and there are bike lanes and special traffic lights everywhere.

Ljubljana Bike (☑ 01-306 45 76; www.visit ljubljana.si; Krekov trg 10; per 2hr/day €2/8; ☺ 8am-7pm Mon-Fri, 9am-5pm Sat & Sun Apr, May & Oct, 8am-9pm Jun-Sep) rents two-wheelers in two-hour or full-day increments from April through October from the Slovenian Tourist Information Centre (p388).

For short rides, you can hire bicycles as needed from 38 **Bicike(lj)** (www.bicikelj.si;

subscription weekly/yearly €1/3, plus hourly rate; ⊘24hr) stations with 300 bikes located around the city. To rent a bike requires pre-registration and subscription over the company website plus a valid credit or debit card.

PUBLIC TRANSPORT

Ljubljana's city buses, many running on methane, operate every five to 15 minutes from 5am (6am on Sunday) to around 10.30pm. There are also a half-dozen night buses. A flat fare of €1.20 (good for 90 minutes of unlimited travel, including transfers) is paid with a stored-value magnetic Urbana card, which can be purchased at news stands, tourist offices and the public-transport authority's **Information Centre** (📲01-430 51 74; www.lpp.si/en; Slovenska cesta 56; ⊘6.30am-7pm Mon-Fri) for €2; credit can then be added (from €1 to €50).

THE JULIAN ALPS

This is the Slovenia of tourist posters: mountain peaks, postcard-perfect lakes and blue-green rivers. Prepare to be charmed by Lake Bled (with an island and a castle!) and surprised by Lake Bohinj (how does Bled score all that attention when down the road is Bohinj?). The lofty peak of Mt Triglav, at the centre of a national park of the same name, may dazzle you enough to prompt an ascent.

Lake Bled

📲04 / POP 5100 / ELEV 481M

Yes, it's every bit as lovely in real life. With its bluish-green lake, picture-postcard church on an islet, a medieval castle clinging to a rocky cliff and some of the highest peaks of the Julian Alps and the Karavanke as backdrops, Bled is Slovenia's most popular resort, drawing everyone from honeymooners lured by the over-the-top romantic setting to backpackers, who come for the hiking, biking, water-sports and canyoning possibilities.

That said, Bled can be overpriced and swarming with tourists in July and August. But as is the case with many popular destinations around the world, people come in droves – and will continue to do so – because the place is so special.

◉ Sights

★ **Lake Bled**   LAKE
(Blejsko jezero; Map p390) Bled's greatest attraction is its exquisite blue-green lake,

measuring just 2km by 1.4km. The lake is lovely to behold from almost any vantage point, and makes a beautiful backdrop for the 6km walk along the shore. Mild thermal springs warm the water to a swimmable 22°C (72°F) from June through August. The lake is naturally the focus of the entire town: you can rent rowing boats, splash around on stand-up paddleboards (SUPs) or simply snap countless photos.

Bled Castle   CASTLE
(Blejski Grad; Map p390; 📲04-572 97 82; www.blejski-grad.si; Grajska cesta 25; adult/child €11/5; ⊘8am-9pm Jun-Aug, to 8pm Apr-May & Sep-Oct, to 6pm Nov-Mar) Perched atop a steep cliff more than 100m above the lake, Bled Castle is how most people imagine a medieval fortress to be, with towers, ramparts, moats and a terrace offering magnificent views. The castle houses a **museum collection** that traces the lake's history from earliest times to the development of Bled as a resort in the 19th century.

Bled Island   ISLAND
(Blejski Otok; ⊘9am-7pm) Tiny, tear-shaped Bled Island beckons from the shore. There's the **Church of the Assumption** (Cerkev Marijinega Vnebovzetja; 📲04-576 79 79; www.blejskiotok.si; adult/child €6/1; ⊘9am-7pm May-Sep, to 6pm Apr & Oct, to 4pm Nov-Mar) and a small museum, the **Provost's House** (📲04-576 79 78; www.blejskiotok.si; adult/child €6/1, incl with admission to Church of the Assumption; ⊘9am-7pm May-Sep, to 6pm Apr & Oct, to 4pm Nov-Mar), but the real thrill is the ride out by *pletna* (gondola). The *pletna* will set you down on the south side at the monumental **South Staircase** (Južno Stopnišče), built in 1655. The staircase comprises 99 steps – a local tradition is for the husband to carry his new bride up them.

Vintgar Gorge   PARK
(Soteska Vintgar; 📲031 344 053; www.vintgar.si; adult/child €5/2.50; ⊘8am-7pm late Apr-Oct) One of the easiest and most satisfying half-day trips from Bled is to Vintgar Gorge, some 4km to the northwest of Bled village. The highlight is a 1600m wooden walkway through the gorge, built in 1893 and continually rebuilt since. It criss-crosses the swirling Radovna River four times over rapids, waterfalls and pools before reaching 16m-high Šum Waterfall.

Bled

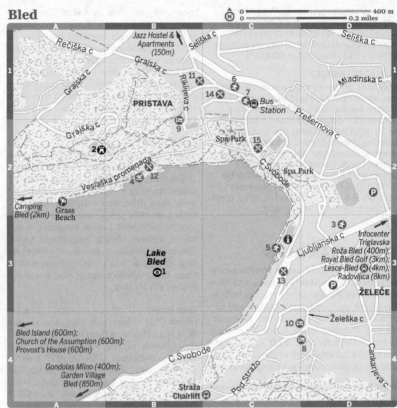

SLOVENIA LAKE BLED

Bled

🏃 Activities

Several local outfits organise outdoor activities in and around Bled, including trekking (p393), mountaineering, rock climbing, ski touring, cross-country skiing, mountain biking, rafting, kayaking, canyoning, horse riding, paragliding and ballooning.

Adventure Sports

★ **3glav Adventures**   ADVENTURE SPORTS
(Map p390; ☎ 041 683 184; www.3glav.com; Ljubljanska cesta 1; ☺ 9am-noon & 4-7pm mid-Apr-Oct) Bled's number-one adventure-sport specialist. Its most popular trip is the Emerald River Adventure (from €80), an 11-hour hiking

and swimming foray into Triglav National Park and along the Soča River that covers a sightseeing loop of the region (from Bled over the Vršič Pass and down the Soča Valley, with optional rafting trip). Book by phone or via the website.

Life Adventures ADVENTURE SPORTS
(Map p390; ☑ 040 508 853; www.lifeadventures.si; Grajska cesta 10; ⊗ 8am-7pm May-Sep) Offers a wide range of adventure activities, including a demanding but fun full day of canyoning from €148 and three hours of snorkelling in the Soča River gorge (from €68). Can help arrange self-guided itineraries for Slovenia and Croatia (walking, cycling, driving, activity-based), and has comprehensive winter options: backcountry skiing, snowshoeing, ice climbing, sledding and other snow sports in the Julian Alps.

Mamut ADVENTURE SPORTS
(Map p390; ☑ 040 121 900; www.slovenija.eu.com; Cesta Svobode 4; ⊗ 8am-7pm May-Sep) Offers a full menu of outdoor activities (rafting, canyoning, hiking, paragliding etc), plus rental of bikes and SUP boards. It also offers guided trips to Vintgar Gorge (€4 per person) as well as convenient transfers to Ljubljana city centre (€9 per person) and to Jože Pučnik Airport (€12 per person).

Boating & Swimming

Gondola Ride BOATING
(Pletna; ☑ 041 427 155; www.bled.si; per person return €14; ⊗ 8am-9pm Mon-Sat, to 6pm Sun Jul & Aug, 8am-7pm Mon-Sat, 11am-5pm Sun Apr-Jun, Sep & Oct, 8am-6pm Mon-Sat, to 1pm Sun Nov-Mar) Riding a piloted *pletna* out to Bled Island is the archetypal tourist experience. There is a convenient jetty just below the TIC (Pletna; Map p390; ☑ 041 427 155; www.bled.si; per person return €14; ⊗ 8am-9pm Mon-Sat, to 6pm Sun Jul & Aug, 8am-7pm Mon-Sat, 11am-5pm Sun Apr-Jun, Sep & Oct, 8am-6pm Mon-Sat, to 1pm Sun Nov-Mar) and another in Mlino on the south shore, with the same contact details and opening hours. You get about half an hour to explore the island. In all, the trip to the island and back takes about 1¼ hours.

Castle Lido SWIMMING
(Grajsko Kopališče; Map p390; ☑ 04-578 05 28; www.kopalisce-bled.si; Veslaška promenada 11; day pass adult/child €8/6; ⊗ 9am-8pm Jul-Aug, to 7pm Jun) The popular grass beach below the castle offers lake swimming behind protected enclosures as well as water slides and other family-friendly amusements. You

can rent lockers, deckchairs and umbrellas. Note that it's normally closed on rainy days. There are slightly cheaper tickets if you arrive after 5pm.

🛏 Sleeping

Bled has a wide range of accommodation, but book well in advance if you're travelling in July or August. Private rooms and apartments are offered by many homes in the area. Prices indicated are for peak season (July and August); there may be discounts in quieter periods. If you're driving, ask about parking at or near your accommodation.

⭐ **Jazz Hostel & Apartments** HOSTEL, GUESTHOUSE €
(☑ 040 634 555; www.jazzbled.com; Prešernova cesta 68; dm €35, d €80, without bathroom €60, apt d/q €90/100; 🅿 @ 🛜) If you don't mind being a little way (a short walk) from the action, this is a first-class budget choice. Guests rave about Jazz, mainly thanks to Jani, the superbly friendly owner who runs a sparkling, well-kitted-out complex. There are dorms (bunk-free, and with under-bed storage) and colourful en-suite rooms, plus family-sized apartments with a full kitchen. Book well in advance.

Camping Bled CAMPGROUND €
(☑ 04-575 20 00; www.sava-camping.com; Kidričeva cesta 10c; campsites from €23, glamping huts from €90; 🅿 @ 🛜) Bled's hugely popular, amenity-laden campground is in a rural valley at the western end of the lake, about 4km from the bus station. There's a rich array of family-friendly activities available, and a restaurant and a store on-site.

Old Parish House GUESTHOUSE €€
(Stari Farovž; Map p390; ☑ 04-576 79 79; www.blejskiotok.si; Riklijeva cesta 22; s/d from €80/120; 🅿 🛜) In a privileged position, the Old Parish House belonging to the Parish Church of St Martin has been transformed into a simple, welcoming guesthouse, with timber beams, hardwood floors and neutral, minimalist style. Pros include car parking, lake views and waking to church bells.

Garni Hotel Berc HOTEL €€
(Map p390; ☑ 04-576 56 58; www.berc-sp.si; Pod Stražo 13; s/d €70/90; ⊗ Apr-Oct; 🅿 🛜) Not to be confused with Penzion Berc across the road, this charming 15-room hotel is reminiscent of a Swiss chalet, with a cosy traditional feel and lots of pine wood in its simple, appealing rooms. It's one of a great

pocket of guesthouses in a quiet location above the lake. Free bikes are a bonus.

Garden Village Bled
RESORT €€€

(☑ 083 899 220; www.gardenvillagebled.com; Cesta Gorenjskega odreda 16; pier tent €130, tree house €320, glamping tent €370; ☺ Apr-Oct; P@🛜🌊) Garden Village embraces and executes the eco-resort concept with aplomb, taking glamping to a whole new level and delivering lashings of wow factor. Accommodation ranges from small two-person tents (with shared bathroom) on piers over a trout-filled stream, to family-sized tree houses and large safari-style tents. Plus there are beautiful grounds, a natural swimming pool and an organic restaurant.

Penzion Berc
PENSION €€€

(Map p390; ☑ 04-574 18 38; www.penzion-berc. si; Želeška cesta 15; r €160-190; P🛜) Rooms at this snug pension are in demand, and it's not hard to see why: a quiet position a few minutes' walk from town, a delightful 19th-century farmhouse aesthetic and a garden that's also home to a great restaurant. There's also the chance to arrange small-group sightseeing trips.

🍴 Eating & Drinking

Slaščičarna Zima
CAFE €

(Map p390; ☑ 04-574 16 16; www.smon.si; Grajska cesta 3; kremna rezina €3; ☺ 7.30am-9pm) Bled's culinary speciality is the delicious *kremna rezina*, also known as the *kremšnita*: a layer of vanilla custard topped with whipped cream and sandwiched between two layers of flaky pastry. While this patisserie may not be its place of birth, it remains the best place in which to try it – retro decor and all.

Grajska Plaža
SLOVENIAN €€

(Castle Beach Restaurant; Map p390; ☑ 031 813 886; www.grajska-plaza.com; Veslaška promenada 11; mains €8-20; ☺ 9am-11pm May–mid-Oct; 🛜) Even the locals say that dining here feels like a summer holiday. It's built on a terrace over the Castle Lido and has a relaxed vibe, helpful service and an easy all-day menu that stretches from morning coffee to end-of-day cocktails. Meal options like grilled trout or octopus salad are generous and tasty.

Gostilna Murka
SLOVENIAN €€

(Map p390; ☑ 04-574 33 40; www.gostilna-murka. com; Riklijeva cesta 9; mains €10-20; ☺ 10am-10pm Mon-Fri, noon-11pm Sat & Sun; 🛜) This

traditional restaurant set within a large, leafy garden may at first appear a bit theme-park-ish – but this is one of the first places locals recommend and the food is authentic (lots of old-school national dishes). Offers good-value lunch specials for around €6 (but you'll have to ask the server).

Ostarija Peglez'n
SEAFOOD €€

(Map p390; ☑ 04-574 42 18; Cesta Svobode 19; mains €9-23; ☺ 11am-11pm; 🛜) Fish is the main game at the lovely, central 'Iron Inn'. Enjoy the cute retro decor with lots of antiques and curios, and choose from a tempting menu of trout from local rivers, John Dory from the Adriatic coast, and a host of calamari, seafood pasta and fish soup options. Meaty mains and veggie options also offered. Book in advance.

Špica
INTERNATIONAL €€

(Map p390; ☑ 04-574 30 27; www.restavracija-spica.si; Cesta Svobode 9; mains €11-18; ☺ 9am-midnight; 🛜) If you don't mind the occasional tour bus filing through, this is a reliable standby for good grilled meats, pastas, burgers and the odd Mexican dish, like burritos and fajitas. There's a big terrace for dining in the sunshine and a more secluded terrace towards the back. Unusual for Bled, it serves big breakfasts (€9 to €10) from 9am until noon.

★ Finefood – Penzion Berc
SLOVENIAN €€€

(Map p390; ☑ 04-574 18 38; www.penzion-berc. si; Želeška cesta 15; mains €18-40; ☺ 5-11pm May-Oct; 🛜) In a magical garden setting, Penzion Berc sets up a summertime restaurant, with local produce served fresh from its open kitchen. Try sea bass with asparagus soufflé, homemade pasta with fresh black truffle, deer entrecôte or Black Angus steak. Finefood's reputation for high-class flavour and atmosphere is well known: book ahead.

Castle Restaurant
SLOVENIAN €€€

(Map p390; ☑ advance booking 04-620 34 44; www.jezersek.si/en/bled-castle-restaurant; Grajska cesta 61; mains €20-40, tasting menu from €50; ☺ 10.30am-10pm; 🛜) It's hard to fault the superb location of the castle's restaurant, with a terrace and views straight from a postcard. What a relief the food is as good as it is: smoked trout, roast pork, poached fish. Note advance booking by phone is compulsory for dinner and only the multicourse tasting menu is available.

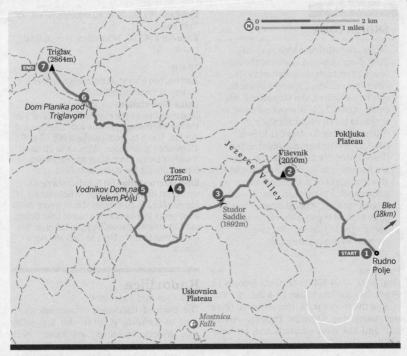

🏃 Walking Tour
Summiting Mt Triglav from Lake Bled

START RUDNO POLJE
END RUDNO POLJE
LENGTH 26KM; TWO DAYS

The shortest (and considered the easiest, though still challenging) ascent of Mt Triglav starts from **1** **Rudno Polje** (1347m) on the Pokljuka Plateau, in a remote area 18km west of Bled. An experienced climber could do this in under 12 hours out and back, but most mortals choose to stay overnight.

If you have your own wheels, the trailhead is accessible to motor vehicles and there are parking spots for you to leave the car overnight. Otherwise, you'll have to arrange a drop-off and pickup from someone in Bled. If you're climbing with a guide or have arranged your tour through an adventure agency, these details will be sorted out for you.

The route follows a well-marked trail under **2** **Viševnik** (2050m), considered to be the most popular of Slovenia's 2000m peaks because of the views. The trail heads northwest and then bends sharply south before passing over the **3** **Studor Saddle** (1892m). From

here, the path contours around the slopes of towering **4** **Tosc** (2275m).

Around three hours of hiking from the Studor Saddle brings you to the welcome sight of the **5** **Vodnikov Dom na Velem Polju** mountain hut, at 1817m. The hut has around 60 beds and a restaurant. You can sleep here or continue on for another two hours, heading north and west, to the **6** **Dom Planika pod Triglavom**, at 2401m, which offers another chance to bed down or grab a bite to eat. Always pre-book a bed, since neither hut has emergency overflow in case all the beds are taken.

From this hut, it's 1½ hours of steep climbing and scrambling along the summit ridge, grabbing hold of metal spikes and grips, to the **7** **top of Triglav**.

The descent follows the same path in the reverse direction. The way down is easier and quicker than the climb, though trickier in part due to loose rocks or potentially wet (and slippery) paths. Provided you've reached the summit in the early morning, you'll be back on the ground in Rudno Polje by the late afternoon.

WORTH A TRIP

ŠKOFJA LOKA

Škofja Loka (Bishop's Meadow), just 26km from Ljubljana, is among the most beautiful and oldest settlements in Slovenia. Its evocative 13th-century castle, now home to the **Loka Museum** (Loški muzej; 📞 04-517 04 00; www.loski-muzej.si; Grajska pot 13; adult/child €5/3; ⏰ 10am-6pm Tue-Sun May-Oct, to 5pm Nov-Apr), and picturesque **Mestni Trg** (Town Square) can be explored as a day trip from the capital or as an overnight stay (though book accommodation in advance since there's just a handful of lodging options). When the castle and other old buildings are illuminated on weekend nights, Škofja Loka takes on the appearance of a fairy tale.

Pub Bled   PUB

(Map p390; 📞 04-574 26 22; Cesta Svobode 19; ⏰ 9am-1am Sun-Thu, to 3am Fri & Sat; 🛜) The pick of the town's pubs, this convivial place sits above the Ostarija Peglez'n restaurant and has great cocktails and, on some nights, a DJ.

ℹ Information

Good online sources of info include Turizem Bled (www.bled.si) and In Your Pocket (www.inyourpocket.com/bled).

Infocenter Triglavska Roža Bled (📞 04-578 02 05; www.tnp.si; Ljubljanska cesta 27; ⏰ 8am-6pm mid-Apr–mid-Oct, to 4pm mid-Oct–mid-Apr; 🛜)

Tourist Information Centre (Map p390; 📞 04-574 11 22; www.bled.si; Cesta Svobode 10; ⏰ 8am-9pm Mon-Sat, 9am-5pm Sun Jul & Aug, reduced hours Sep-Jun; 🛜) Open year-round: outside high season until at least 6pm Monday to Friday, to 3pm Sunday.

ℹ Getting There & Away

BUS

Bled is well connected by bus; the **bus station** (Map p390; Cesta Svobode 4) is a hub of activity at the lake's northeast. **Alpetour** (📞 04-201 32 10; www.alpetour.si) runs most of the bus connections in the Julian Alps region, so check its website for schedules.

Popular services:

Kranjska Gora (€4.70, 50 minutes, 40km, up to 12 daily)

Lake Bohinj (€3.60, 37 minutes, 29km, up to 12 daily)

Ljubljana (€7.80, 70 to 80 minutes, 57km, up to 15 daily)

Radovljica (€1.80, 14 minutes, 7km, at least half-hourly)

TRAIN

Bled has two train stations, though neither one is close to the town centre:

Lesce-Bled station Four kilometres east of Bled township on the road to Radovljica. It's on the rail line linking Ljubljana with Jesenice and Austria. Trains to/from Ljubljana (€5.20 to €7, 40 minutes to one hour, 51km, up to 20 daily) travel via Škofja Loka, Kranj and Radovljica. Buses connect the station with Bled.

Bled Jezero station On Kolodvorska cesta northwest of the lake. Trains to Bohinjska Bistrica (€1.85, 20 minutes, 18km, seven daily), from where you can catch a bus to Lake Bohinj, use this smaller station. You can travel on this line further south to Most na Soči and Nova Gorica.

Radovljica

📞 04 / POP 5922 / ELEV 490M

The town of Radovljica (sometimes shortened to Radol'ca) is filled with impossibly cute, historic buildings and blessed with scenic views of the Alps, including Triglav. It was settled by the early Slavs, and by the 14th century had grown into an important market town centred on a large rectangular square, today's Linhartov trg, and fortified with high stone walls. Much of the original architecture, amazingly, is still standing and looks remarkably unchanged from those early days.

◎ Sights

★ Linhartov Trg   SQUARE

Radovljica's colourful main square is the town's leading attraction, lined with houses from the 16th and 17th centuries. Look especially for **Thurn Manor** (Linhartov trg 1), a baroque palace that is home to museums and a school of music, and **Koman House** (Komanova Hiša; Linhartov trg 23), identified by a baroque painting of St Florian on its facade. **Mali House** (Malijeva Hiša; Linhartov trg 24) has a barely visible picture of St George slaying the dragon. **Vidič House** (Vidičeva Hiša; 📞 04-029 63 62; www.vidichouse.com; Linhartov trg 3; coffee €2; ⏰ 9am-10pm; 🛜) has a corner projection and is painted in red, yellow, green and blue.

Beekeeping Museum   MUSEUM

(Čebelarski Muzej; 📞 04-532 05 20; www.mro.si; Linhartov trg 1; adult/child €3/2; ⏰ 10am-6pm Tue-Sun May-Oct, 8am-3pm Tue, Thu & Fri, 10am-noon

& 3-5pm Wed, Sat & Sun Mar, Apr, Nov & Dec, 8am-3pm Tue-Fri Jan & Feb) More interesting than it sounds, this apiculture museum takes a closer look at the long tradition of beekeeping in Slovenia. The museum's collection of illustrated beehive panels from the 18th and 19th centuries, a folk art unique to Slovenia, is the largest in the country, and there are some rather astounding beehives in improbable shapes: (life-sized) people, a miniature mansion, even a lion. You can also observe a live beehive in action, filled with a family of indigenous Carniolan bees.

🛏 Sleeping

There are several very nice options right on central Linhartov trg, though they are all small and normally require a reservation. If you're travelling during the festival season in August, you may need to book your room months in advance. The TIC lists private accommodation options on its website.

Vidic House   HOSTEL €
(Vidičeva Hiša; ☑ 031 810 767; www.vidichouse.com; Linhartov trg 3; per person €25; ☎) This 400-year-old historic townhouse on the main square offers accommodation in four large, homely apartments, with postcard views over Linhartov trg. There's a kitchen in each apartment, and access to a laundry, plus a cool cafe downstairs. Breakfast costs €4.

★Linhart Hotel   HOTEL €€
(☑ 059 187 547; www.linharthotel.com; Linhartov trg 17; r €70-90, ste €110; P ☎) Opened in 2017, the Linhart goes for a toned-down version of elegance, occupying a sensitively restored 17th-century townhouse on central Linhartov trg. Many of the original features, including the stone staircase leading to the rooms, arched ceilings and exposed wood beams have been preserved. The rooms are simply furnished but exude real quality. The family that owns the property couldn't be friendlier.

Gostilna Lectar   PENSION €€
(☑ 04-537 48 00; www.lectar.com; Linhartov trg 2; s/d €75/110; ❊ ☎) This delightful B&B on the main square has nine individually decorated rooms done up in folk motifs – painted headboards and room signs made of *lect* (gingerbread) – that could have ended up kitsch but instead feel like those in a village farmhouse from the 19th century, although

with modern creature comforts. Note: prices are reduced outside August.

🍴 Eating & Drinking

Gostilna Avguštin   SLOVENIAN €€
(☑ 04-531 41 63; www.gostilna-avgustin.si; Linhartov trg 15; mains €10-18; ⊘ 9am-10pm) The huge portions match the big welcome at this delightful central restaurant (the name is often anglicised to Augustin). It serves excellent Slovenian dishes to order. Don't miss the cellar dining room, which was once part of a prison (and may have seen an execution or two), and the wonderful back terrace with views of Triglav.

Gostilna Lectar   SLOVENIAN €€
(☑ 04-537 48 00; www.lectar.com; Linhartov trg 2; mains €12-20; ⊘ 11am-10pm; ☎) Take your time to peruse the huge, multilingual menu of local specialities here. Some items may not immediately appeal (eg pickled beef tongue, sausage in hog's grease), while others boast of a long family pedigree and almost demand to be sampled: the homemade *štruklji* and *žlikrofi* (ravioli of cheese, bacon and chives), for example, and the Lectar strudel.

★Vila Podvin   SLOVENIAN €€€
(☑ 083 843 470; www.vilapodvin.si; Mošnje 1; mains €22-32; ⊘ noon-10pm Tue-Sat, to 5pm Sun; ☎) Winning plaudits from diners local and foreign, this elegant establishment is 3km east of Linhartov trg, on the 14th-century Grad Podvin Estate. Kitchen creativity combines with quality local produce and some time-honoured techniques to produce plates that match the beauty of the setting. Lunch is great value (three courses for €18), as is the chef's tasting menu (four/six courses €40/60).

ℹ Information

Tourist Information Centre (TIC; ☑ 04-531 51 12; www.radolca.si; Linhartov trg 9; ⊘ 9am-7pm Jun-Sep, to 4pm Oct-May; ☎) Centrally located, helps book rooms, sells good local hiking and cycling maps, rents bikes and has a computer on hand for gratis surfing. The office also sells local souvenirs.

ℹ Getting There & Away

BUS
The **bus station** (Kranjska cesta) is 300m northwest of Linhartov trg. There's a timetable posted on a board outside the station, or check bus schedule info online at www.alpetour.si.

SLOVENIA RADOVLJICA

TRIGLAV NATIONAL PARK

Triglav National Park (Triglavski Narodni Park; commonly abbreviated as TNP), with an area of 840 sq km (over 4% of Slovenian territory), is one of the largest national reserves in Europe. It is a pristine, visually spectacular world of rocky mountains – the centrepiece of which is **Mt Triglav** (2864m; p393), the country's highest peak – as well as river gorges, ravines, lakes, canyons, caves, rivers, waterfalls, forests and Alpine meadows. The limestone peak called Triglav (Three Heads) has been a source of inspiration and object of devotion for Slovenes for more than a millennium – it even appears on the country's flag. The early Slavs believed the mountain to be the home of a three-headed deity who ruled the sky, the earth and the underworld.

The park has information centres in Bled (p394), Stara Fužina (p398) in Bohinj, and **Trenta** (Dom Trenta; ☑ 05-388 93 30; www.tnp.si; ☺ 9am-7pm Jul-Aug, 10am-6pm May, Jun, Sep & Oct, 10am-2pm Mon-Fri Jan-Apr, closed Nov-Dec) on the Vršič Pass. These centres have displays on park flora and fauna and are well worth a stop. They have a good program of activities in summer and can put you in touch with mountain guides.

Good online starting points for learning about the park are www.tnp.si and www. hiking-trail.net. Several hiking maps are available from TICs. Two decent options: the laminated 1:50,000-scale *Triglavski Narodni Park* (€9.10; buy online from shop.pzs. si) from the Alpine Association of Slovenia (PZS), and Kartografija's widely available 1:50,000-scale *Triglavski Narodni Park* (€8; www.kartografija.si).

Roughly half-hourly services depart for Bled (€1.80, 14 minutes, 7km) from around 5am to 11pm (hourly on weekends). Services to Ljubljana are also frequent, running half-hourly or hourly from 5am to 9pm (€5.60, one hour, 50km). There are also regular buses to Lake Bohinj (€4.70, 50 minutes, 36km) and Kranjska Gora (€5.20, 53 minutes, 41km).

TRAIN

The train station is 100m below the Old Town on Cesta Svobode. International trains use the nearby station at Lesce-Bled.

Radovljica is on a main rail line linking Ljubljana (€4.28, one hour, 48km) with Jesenice (€1.95, 17 minutes, 16km) via Škofja Loka, Kranj and Lesce-Bled. At least 10 trains a day pass through the town in each direction.

Lake Bohinj

☑ 04 / POP 5100 / ELEV 542M

Many visitors to Slovenia say they've never seen a more beautiful lake than Bled...that is, until they've seen the blue-green waters of Lake Bohinj, 26km to the southwest. Admittedly, Bohinj lacks Bled's glamour, but it's less crowded and in many ways more authentic. It's an ideal summer holiday destination. People come primarily to chill out or to swim in the crystal-clear water, with leisurely cycling and walking trails to occupy them as well as outdoor pursuits like kayaking, hiking and horse riding.

◉ Sights

★ Church of St John the Baptist
CHURCH

(Cerkev Sv Janeza Krstnika; ☑ 04-574 60 10; Ribčev Laz 56; church & bell tower €4, church only €2.50; ☺ 10am-4pm Jun-Aug, group bookings only May & Sep) This postcard-worthy church and bell tower, at the head of the lake and beside the stone bridge, dates back at least 700 years and is what every medieval church should be: small, surrounded by natural beauty and full of exquisite frescoes. The nave is Romanesque, but the Gothic presbytery dates from about 1440. Many walls and ceilings are covered with 15th- and 16th-century frescoes.

Savica Waterfall
WATERFALL

(Slap Savica; ☑ 04-574 60 10; www.bohinj.si; Ukanc; adult/child €3/1.50; ☺ 8am-8pm Jul & Aug, 9am-7pm Apr-Jun, to 5pm Sep-Nov) The magnificent Savica Waterfall, which cuts deep into a gorge 78m below, is 4km from Ukanc and can be reached by a walking path from there in 1½ hours. By car, you can continue past Ukanc via a sealed road to a car park beside the Savica restaurant, from where it's a 25-minute walk up more than 500 steps and over rapids and streams to the falls. Wear decent shoes for the slippery path.

Vogel
MOUNTAIN

(☑ 04-572 97 12; www.vogel.si; cable car return adult/child €20/10; ☺ cable car 8am-7pm) The glorious setting and spectacular panoramas make it worth a trip up Vogel – during winter, when it's a popular **ski resort** (04-572 97 12; www.vogel.si; day pass adult/child €32/16; mid-Dec–Mar), but also in its 'green season', when walks and photo ops abound. The cable car runs every 30 minutes or so from its base near Ukanc – the base station is at 569m, the top station at 1535m.

🏃 Activities

Lake Bohinj is filled with activities of all sorts, from active pursuits like canyoning and paragliding from Vogel to more-sedate pastimes like hiking, cycling and horse riding. The TIC in Ribčev Laz maintains a list of tour operators and equipment-rental outfits, and can help arrange trips and tours.

Tourist Boat – Ribčev Laz   BOATING
(Turistična Ladja; 041 353 064; www.tourist-boat. eu; adult/child one-way €9/6.50, return €10.50/7.50; May-Sep) An easy family-friendly sail from Ribčev Laz to Camp Zlatorog in Ukanc (and back). It's worth checking the timetable online – boats depart Ribčev Laz at 80-minute intervals from 10.50am to 5.30pm.

Mrcina Ranč   HORSE RIDING
(041 790 297; www.ranc-mrcina.com; Studor; 1/4hr from €25/60) Pretty Mrcina Ranč in Studor offers a range of guided tours on horseback through unspoiled countryside. Tours can last from one to seven hours; in spring and autumn overnight trips are possible. Tours are on sturdy Icelandic horses; kids can be catered to. Bookings required.

Alpinsport   ADVENTURE SPORTS
(04-572 34 86; www.alpinsport.si; Ribčev Laz 53; 10am-6pm) Rents equipment: canoes, kayaks, SUPs and bikes in summer; skis and snowboards in winter. It also operates guided rafting and canyoning trips. Its base is opposite Hotel Jezero in Ribčev Laz.

PAC Sports   ADVENTURE SPORTS
(Perfect Adventure Choice; 04-572 34 61; www. pac.si; Hostel Pod Voglom, Ribčev Laz 60; 8am-10pm Jun-Sep, to 8pm Oct-May) Popular sports and adventure company, based in Hostel Pod Voglom, 2km west of Ribčev Laz; also has a summertime lakeside kiosk at Camp Zlatorog. Rents bikes, canoes, SUPs and kayaks, and operates guided canyoning, rafting and caving trips. In winter, it rents sleds and offers ice climbing and snowshoeing.

🛏 Sleeping

From May through September, many houses in Stara Fužina, Studor and Srednja Vas, north of Ribčev Laz, offer private accommodation. Look for the signs 'sobe' or 'apartma', indicating the owners have a room to let.

Camp Zlatorog   CAMPGROUND €
(059 923 648; www.camp-bohinj.si; Ukanc 5; per person €11-15.50; May-Sep; P📶) This tree-filled campground can accommodate up to 750 guests and sits photogenically on the lake's southwestern corner, 5km from Ribčev Laz. Prices vary according to site location, with the most expensive (and desirable) sites right on the lake. Facilities are very good – including a restaurant, a laundry and water-sport rentals – and the tourist boat docks here. Tents can be hired.

Pension Stare   PENSION €€
(040 558 669; www.bohinj-hotel.com; Ukanc 128; s/d €60/90; P📶) This sweet 10-room pension is on the Savica River in Ukanc, surrounded by a large, peaceful garden. If you really want to get away from it all without having to climb mountains, this is your place. Rooms are no-frills; there's a half-board option too.

Hotel Bohinj   HOTEL €€
(059 113 354; www.hotelbohinj.si; Ribčev Laz 45; s/d €70/90; P@📶) This Alpine lodge has arguably seen better days but nevertheless offers very good value and is more than likely to have a free room. Simply furnished rooms are large and clean. Many have balconies. Ask for a room overlooking the mountains at the back. The staff is young and eager to please. There's a small garden terrace at the front for coffee.

★ Vila Park   BOUTIQUE HOTEL €€€
(04-572 33 00; www.vila-park.si; Ukanc 129; d €100-120; P📶) Vila Park creates a great first impression, with sunloungers set in expansive riverside grounds, and balconies overflowing with flowers. The interior is equally impressive, with eight elegant rooms plus a handsome lounge and dining area. Note: it's a kid-free zone.

🍴 Eating

Many of the better restaurants are spread out to the north and east of Ribčev Laz, which will require a modest hike, or car or bike to reach. There's a **Mercator** (04-572 95 32; Ribčev Laz 49; 7am-7pm Mon-Sat, to noon Sun) supermarket next to the TIC in Ribčev Laz.

★ **Štrud'l** SLOVENIAN €
(📱 041 541 877; www.facebook.com/gostilnica.trgo
vinica.strudl; Triglavska cesta 23, Bohinjska Bistrica;
mains €6-12; ⊘8am-10pm; 🛜) This modern
take on traditional farmhouse cooking is a
must for foodies keen to sample local specialities. Overlook the incongruous location in
the centre of Bohinjska Bistrica, and enjoy
dishes like *ričet s klobaso* (barley porridge
with sausage and beans).

Foksner BURGERS €
(www.facebook.com/foksner; Ribčev Laz 49; burgers €7-10; ⊘4-10pm; 🛜) Easily a candidate for
the best burger joint in Slovenia, and centrally located, within easy walking distance
of the TIC in Ribčev Laz. The burgers are
grilled on the deck and served with a side
of potato wedges and a locally brewed craft
beer or a decent domestic wine. Simple food
done very well. Dinner only.

Gostilna Mihovc SLOVENIAN €
(📱04-021 61 06; www.gostilna-mihovc.si; Stara
Fužina 118; mains €8-15; ⊘9am-11pm) This place
in Stara Fužina is popular – not least for its
homemade brandy. Try the *pasulj* (bean
soup) with sausage (€7) or the beef *golaž*
(goulash; €7). Live music on Friday and Saturday evenings. In summer book in advance
to secure a garden table.

Gostilna Pri Hrvatu SLOVENIAN €€
(📱031 234 300; Srednja Vas 76; mains €10-
18; ⊘10am-11pm Wed-Mon) Get an eyeful of
mountain views from the sweet creek-side
terrace of this relaxed inn in Srednja Vas.
Flavourful homemade dishes include buckwheat dumplings, polenta with porcini,
local chamois in piquant sauce, and grilled
trout.

ℹ Information

There are two main TICs in the Bohinj area: the
office in **Ribčev Laz** (TIC; 📱04-574 60 10; www.
bohinj-info.com; Ribčev Laz 48; ⊘8am-8pm
Mon-Sat, to 6pm Sun Jul & Aug, 9am-5pm Mon-
Sat, to 3pm Sun Nov & Dec, 8am-7pm Mon-Sat,
9am-3pm Sun Jan, Feb, May, Jun, Sep & Oct;
🛜) is closer to the lake and handier for most
visitors than the office in **Bohinjska Bistrica** (LD
Turizem; 📱04-574 76 00; www.ld-turizem.si;
Mencingerjeva ulica 10; ⊘8am-7pm Mon-Sat, to
1pm Sun Jul & Aug, 9am-noon & 2-6pm Mon-Fri,
9am-1pm Sat, to noon Sun Sep-Jun; 🛜). Both
have a wealth of free material and sell souvenirs
and local products.

The **national park centre** (📱04-578 02 45;
www.tnp.si; Stara Fužina 38; ⊘8am-6pm Jul

& Aug, 9am-5pm Apr-Jun, Sep & Oct) in Stara
Fužina is well worth a stop.

ℹ Getting There & Away

BUS

The easiest way to get to Lake Bohinj is by **bus**
(Ribčev Laz) – services run frequently from Ljubljana, via Bled and Bohinjska Bistrica. **Alpetour**
(📱information 04-201 32 10; www.alpetour.si)
is the major bus operator for the region.

Services from Lake Bohinj (departing from
Ribčev Laz, near the TIC):
Bled (€3.60, 40 minutes, 29km, up to 12 daily)
Bohinjska Bistrica (€1.80, eight minutes, 7km,
up to 20 daily)
Ljubljana (€9.80, two hours, 86km, up to nine
daily)

TRAIN

Several trains daily make the run to Bohinjska
Bistrica from Ljubljana (€7.30, two hours, six
daily), though this route requires a change in
Jesenice. There are also trains between Bled's
small Bled Jezero station and Bohinjska Bistrica
(€1.85, 20 minutes, 18km, seven daily).

From Bohinjska Bistrica, passenger trains to
Nova Gorica (€5.80, 1¼ hours, 61km, up to eight
daily) make use of a century-old, 6.3km tunnel
under the mountains that provides the only
direct option for reaching the Soča Valley.

Kranjska Gora

📱04 / POP 1491 / ELEV 806M
Nestling in the Sava Dolinka Valley some
40km northwest of Bled, Kranjska Gora
(Carniolan Mountain) is among Slovenia's
largest and best-equipped ski resorts. It's at
its most perfect under a blanket of snow, but
its surroundings – nudging both the Austrian and Italian borders – are wonderful to explore at other times, too. There are endless
possibilities for hiking, cycling and mountaineering in Triglav National Park, which
is right on the town's doorstep to the south,
and few travellers will be unimpressed by a
trip over the Vršič Pass, the gateway to the
Soča Valley.

◎ Sights

Slovenian Alpine Museum MUSEUM
(Slovenski Planinski Muzej; 📱083 806 730; www.
planinskimuzej.si; Triglavska cesta 49, Mojstrana;
adult/child €6/3.60; ⊘9am-7pm Jun–mid-Sep, to
5pm mid-Sep–May) This modern, interactive
museum dedicated to mountain exploration is a great rainy-day activity, especially
for kids. There are movies showing off the

beauty of the peaks, lots of climbing gear and even an escape room. The museum is located in Mojstrana, about 15km south of Kranjska Gora. It's the traditional starting point for the northern approaches to Mt Triglav.

Jasna Lake LAKE
(Jezero Jasna) Jasna Lake lies just south of Kranjska Gora, and if you're heading over the Vršič Pass it's the first spot of interest. It's a small, blue glacial lake with white sand around its rim and the little Pišnica River flowing alongside. Standing guard is a bronze statue of Zlatorog. The lake is a popular recreation area; there's a pocket of accommodation on the hill above.

Zelenci NATURE RESERVE
(⊙24hr) **FREE** About 5km west of Kranjska Gora, signed just off the main road, is this idyllic nature reserve and wetlands. It's the perfect leg-stretcher, with a short path to a turquoise-coloured lake that is the source of the Sava River. You can easily walk here in about an hour on a path from Kranjska Gora via Podkoren following the signs towards Rateče.

Liznjek House MUSEUM
(Liznjekova Domačija; ☑04-588 19 99; www.gmj.si; Borovška cesta 63; adult/child €2.50/1.70; ⊙10am-6pm Tue-Sat, to 5pm Sun) The endearing 17th-century Liznjek House contains a good collection of traditional household objects and furnishings peculiar to this area. Among the various exhibits are some excellent examples of trousseau chests covered in folk paintings, some 19th-century icons painted on glass and a collection of linen tablecloths (the valley was famed for its flax and for its weaving).

🏃 Activities

Skiing
Skiing is Kranjska Gora's bread and butter and the resort can get very crowded in January and February. The season usually lasts from mid-December through March.

There are a number of ski schools and ski-rental outlets – a good source of information is the website www.kranjska-gora.si.

Kranjska Gora Ski Centre SKIING
(RTC Žičnice; ☑04-580 94 00; www.kr-gora.si; Borovška cesta 103a; day pass adult/child €34/22; ⊙Dec-Mar) Kranjska Gora's main ski area is just five minutes' walk from the town centre. The slopes of Vitranc mountain run for several kilometres west to Podkoren and Planica, making effectively one big piste. All up, there are 18 slopes of varying technical difficulty, at altitudes of 800m to 1215m. There's also 40km of cross-country trails, and a fun park for snowboarders.

Adventure Sports

Planica Zipline ADVENTURE SPORTS
(☑041 828 151; www.planica-zipline.si; Planica Nordic Centre, Rateče; individual/tandem €25/40; ⊙by appointment only from 11am & 1.30pm daily Jul & Aug, Sat & Sun only Jun & Sep) The operators claim this is the world's steepest zipline, and with a path that glides over the towering Planica Ski-Jump Centre, who are we to argue? The descent runs 566m and takes under a minute. The altitude differential is about 200m. Note: it's mandatory to prebook your spot via the website. The location is 6km west of Kranjska Gora.

Bike Park Kranjska Gora MOUNTAIN BIKING
(☑041 706 786; www.bike-park.si; Borovška cesta 107; day pass €26, bike rental per day €55; ⊙9am-5pm daily Jun-Aug, Fri-Sun May, Sep & Oct) On the central slopes of Vitranc, this park is a mecca for mountain bikers – a chairlift takes you up the hill and you descend on trails of varying difficulty. The park offers rental of bikes and protective gear, plus guided and shuttle tours into the surrounding mountains.

Hiking
The area around Kranjska Gora and into Triglav National Park is excellent for hikes and walks, ranging from the very easy to the difficult. Before heading out, buy the 1:30,000-scale *Kranjska Gora* hiking map published by LTO Kranjska Gora and available at the TIC for €6.50 – it details 20 walking routes and 15 cycling tracks.

There's a well-marked trail from Planica to the Category II, 50-bed mountain hut, **Planinski dom Tamar** (Dom v Tamarju; ☑04-587 60 55; www.en.pzs.si; per person €10-20), at 1108m in the Tamar Valley – reserve ahead. The one-hour walk here from the Planica Ski-Jump Centre is spectacular, and lies in the shadow of Mojstrovka (2332m) to the east and Jalovec (2645m) to the south. From the hut, the Vršič Pass is about three hours away on foot.

🛏 Sleeping
Accommodation demand (and prices) peak from December to March and in midsummer. There are a number of large chain

hotels but these are generally pricey and uninspiring; there are some real gems in the smaller, family-run places, though.

Natura Eco Camp
CAMPGROUND €

(☑ 064 121 966; www.naturaecocamp.si; sites per adult/child €15/10, safari tent €150, tree tent €80; ⊙ Jun-Sep; P 🐾 🛜) 🦮 This back-to-nature campground some 600m north of the highway (signposted) sits in a green glade and is as close to paradise as we've been for a while. Pitch a tent or stay in one of the safari tents or the unique tree tents (great teardrop pods suspended from branches, with mattresses on a platform inside).

★ Design Rooms Pr' Gavedarjo
B&B €€

(☑ 031 479 087; www.prgavedarjo.si; Podkoren 72; s €60-80, d €80-150; P 🛜) 🦮 There's a lot to love about this incarnation of a century-old homestead, especially the clever design that celebrates Slovenian heritage and melds old with new in each of its five guest rooms. Added bonus: its location on a pretty village square in Podkoren, 3km west of Kranjska Gora. This place is popular and you'll need to reserve weeks in advance.

Hotel Lipa
PENSION €€

(☑ 04-582 00 00; www.hotel-lipa.si; Koroška cesta 14; s €60-80, d €70-90; P 🛜) Arguably the best hotel in terms of size (just 11 rooms), quality of the room furnishings, views out over the mountains and location – close to the town centre but far enough away to feel removed from the crowds. The restaurant is excellent, as are the buffet breakfasts. Find it just north of the TIC, beside the small bus station.

Hotel Kotnik
HOTEL €€

(☑ 041 671 980; www.hotel-kotnik.si; Borovška cesta 75; s €70-90, d €90-110; P 🛜) This charming, bright-yellow, flower-adorned hotel sits plumb in the heart of town. It has 15 cosy rooms, friendly staff, a great restaurant and pizzeria downstairs, and bikes for hire (€17 per day).

Hotel Miklič
HOTEL €€€

(☑ 04-588 16 35; www.hotelmiklic.com; Vitranška ulica 13; s €80-110, d €120-160; P 🛜) There's warm, personalised service at this pristine 17-room, family-run hotel south of the town centre. Most of the rooms are large, with living space, and families are well accommodated (there's a kids' playroom). Half-board is possible at the high-quality on-site restaurant. The location is within comfortable walking distance of Jasna Lake.

✗ Eating

Pick up picnic supplies at the Mercator (☑ 04-583 45 78; Borovška cesta 92; ⊙ 8am-7pm Mon-Sat, to 1pm Sun) supermarket, located west of the town centre, next to the post office.

Gostilna Pri Martinu
SLOVENIAN €

(☑ 04-582 03 00; Borovška cesta 61; mains €6-15; ⊙ 10am-11pm) Ask a local where to eat and they'll invariably suggest here: it's an atmospheric tavern-restaurant with a country farmhouse vibe, and you will certainly not leave hungry. Dishes are old-school (house specialities include roast pork, beef goulash, river trout, and sausage with sauerkraut) and the portions are huge.

★ Skipass Hotel Restaurant
INTERNATIONAL €€

(☑ 04-582 10 00; www.skipasshotel.si; Borovška cesta 14c; mains €15-21; ⊙ 5-10pm Mon-Fri, from 1pm Sat & Sun; 🛜) Easily the most upscale dining option in town. The geometric timber feature above the bar creates a fresh first impression and the menu follows its lead. It's an appealing combination of influences from across the nearby Italian and Austrian borders, the food given a local twist and sharp presentation. The three-/five-course chef's menu is €28/45.

Hotel Lipa Restaurant
SLOVENIAN €€

(☑ 04-582 00 00; www.hotel-lipa.si; Koroška cesta 14; mains €8-20; ⊙ noon-11pm; 🛜 ☑) The in-house restaurant of the Hotel Lipa offers excellent value, with a solid range of pastas and pizzas, plus excellent and affordable up-market main dishes (oven-baked octopus, beefsteak with black truffles). Still relatively rare for Slovenia, it has vegan and gluten-free pizza options. Eat in or out on the terrace in nice weather.

ℹ Information

Tourist Information Centre (TIC; ☑ 04-580 94 40; www.kranjska-gora.si; Kolodvorska ulica 1c; ⊙ 8am-8pm Jun-Sep, to 6pm Oct-May; 🛜) Well-stocked, central TIC, with a cafe and a computer for short-term use. Sells hiking and cycling maps.

ℹ Getting There & Away

Buses are your best option; these are mainly run by Alpetour (www.alpetour.si). The small **bus stop** (Avtobusna postaja; ☑ 04-201 32 15; www.alpetour.si; Koroška cesta) is located 100m north of the TIC.

CROSSING THE VRŠIČ PASS

A couple of kilometres from Kranjska Gora is one of the road-engineering marvels of the 20th century: a breakneck, Alpine road that connects Kranjska Gora with Bovec, 50km to the southwest. The trip involves no fewer than 50 pulse-quickening hairpin turns and dramatic vistas as you cross the Vršič Pass at 1611m.

The road was commissioned during WWI by Germany and Austria-Hungary in their epic struggle with Italy. Much of the hard labour was done by Russian prisoners of war, and for that reason, the road from Kranjska Gora to the top of the pass is now called the Ruska cesta (Russian Road).

The road over the pass is usually open from May to October and is easiest to navigate by car, motorbike or bus (in summer, buses between Kranjska Gora and Bovec use this road). It is also possible – and increasingly popular – to cycle it.

Popular bus routes:

Bled (€6, 64 minutes, 43km) Only two direct services daily – however, there are hourly buses to Lesce-Bled train station (€4.70, 50 minutes, 40km).

Ljubljana (€9, two hours, 91km, up to nine daily)

Vršič Pass Alpetour runs buses to Bovec (€7, one hour 40 minutes, 46km) via Trenta (€5, 70 minutes, 25km) from late June through August. Check the website for timetables.

SOČA VALLEY

The Soča Valley region (Posočje) stretches west of Triglav National Park and includes the outdoor activity centres of Bovec and Kobarid. Threading through it is the magically aquamarine Soča River. Most people come here for the rafting, hiking and skiing, though there are plenty of historical sights and locations, particularly relating to WWI, when millions of troops fought on the mountainous battlefront here; between the wars, the Soča Valley fell under Italian jurisdiction. Another big drawcard is the food – Kobarid is the epicentre of the region's growing culinary reputation.

Bovec

⏱ 05 / POP 3150 / ELEV 456M

Soča Valley's de facto capital, Bovec offers plenty for adventure-sports enthusiasts. With the Julian Alps above, the Soča River below and Triglav National Park (p396) all around, you could spend a week here rafting, hiking, kayaking, mountain biking and, in winter, skiing, without ever doing the same thing twice. It's beautiful country and Bovec's a pleasant town in which to base yourself for these activities.

◉ Sights

★ **Boka Waterfall**   WATERFALL

(Slap Boka) With a sheer vertical drop of 106m (and a second drop of 30m), Boka is the highest waterfall in Slovenia – and it's especially stunning in the spring, when snowmelt gives it extra oomph. It's 5.5km southwest of Bovec – you can drive or cycle to the area and park by the bridge, then walk about 15 minutes to the viewpoint.

Kanin Cable Car   CABLE CAR

(☎ 05-917 93 01; www.kanin.si; adult €10-34, child €8-28; ⏱ hours vary) This cable car whisks you up to the Bovec Kanin Ski Centre in a number of stages. It's most often used as an access for winter skiing or summer activities, but it's equally rewarding for sightseers – the views from the top station and en route are sweepingly beautiful. In summer, in particular, the last departure heading up the mountain can be as early as 2pm, so it's usually best to visit in the morning.

Kluže Fortress   CASTLE

(Trdnjava Kluže; ☎ 05-388 67 58; www.kluze.net; adult/student/child €3/2/1.50; ⏱ 9am-8pm Jul & Aug, 10am-5pm Sun-Fri, to 6pm Sat Jun & Sep, 10am-5pm Sat & Sun May & Oct) Built by the Austrians in 1882 on the site of a 17th-century fortress above a 70m ravine on the Koritnica River, Kluže Fortress is 4km northeast of Bovec. It was the site of an Austro-Hungarian garrison during WWI, right behind the front line of the Isonzo battlefield. Exhibitions outline its turbulent history. Even more dramatic is the upper fortress, Fort Hermann, built in 1900 halfway up Mt Rombon to the west.

🏃 Activities

Adventure Sports

There are dozens of adrenaline-raising companies in Bovec; some specialise in one activity (often rafting), while others offer multiday packages so you can try various activities (rafting, canyoning, kayaking, paragliding, climbing, caving, ziplining). Some agencies offer winter sports too, like dog-sledding and snowshoeing.

Nature's Ways ADVENTURE SPORTS
(☑031 200 651; www.econaturesways.com; Čezsoča) Right by the river around 2km from Bovec, this company runs all the usual Bovec activities, including canyoning, rafting, kayaking, ziplining, caving and mountain biking. Reducing plastic pollution is part of its mantra.

Soca Rider ADVENTURE SPORTS
(☑041 596 104; www.socarider.com; Trg Golobarskih Žrtev 40) Does all of the usual trips, but distinguishes itself by making families and beginners a key part of its offering.

Bovec Rafting Team ADVENTURE SPORTS
(☑041 338 308; www.bovec-rafting-team.com; Mala Vas 106) On-the-water specialists (rafting, minirafting, kayaking, hydrospeeding, canyoning). Prices start from €50/40 per adult/child for a three-hour rafting trip to €270 for a three-day rafting course. Also offers caving, paragliding and winter activities like snowshoeing and dog-sledding.

Aktivni Planet ADVENTURE SPORTS
(☑040 639 433; www.aktivniplanet.si; Trg Golobarskih Žrtev 19) Professional outfit that offers multiday packages so you can try all its various activities (rafting, canyoning, kayaking, caving, ziplining, biking, hiking). Affiliated with Hostel Soča Rocks (p402).

Hiking & Walking
The 1:25,000-scale *Bovec z Okolico* (Bovec and Surrounds; €7) map lists a number of walks, from two-hour strolls to the ascent of Mt Rombon (2208m), a good five hours one way. Other great areas to explore include Lepena, en route to Trenta; the spectacular Mangart Saddle (at 2072m, reached by Slovenia's highest road); and the Alpine valley of Loška Koritnica. Ask for more info at the TIC.

Closer to town, a number of trails begin and end in Bovec itself. Pick up the free *Hiking Trails in Bovec Land* from the TIC for more information.

🛏 Sleeping

Bovec has some excellent accommodation, across a range of budgets. In addition to hotels and hostels, the TIC has dozens of private rooms and apartments (from €20 per person) on its lists. Don't discount the many scenic options along the road to Trenta towards the Vršič Pass, especially if you have a campervan.

Adrenaline Check
Eco Place CAMPGROUND €
(☑041 383 662; www.adrenaline-check.com; Podklopca 4; campsite per person €15, s/d tent from €40/50, safari tent €120-150; ⊙May-Sep; P🛜) About 3km southwest of town, this fun, fabulous campground makes camping easy: hire a tent under a lean-to shelter that comes with mattresses and linen, or a big, furnished safari-style tent. Cars are left in a car park, and you walk through to a large, picturesque clearing (so it's not for campervans).

Hostel Soča Rocks HOSTEL €
(☑041 317 777; www.hostelsocarocks.com; Mala Vas 120; dm €13-18, d €35-50; P@🛜) Hostel Soča Rocks is a new breed of hostel: colourful, spotlessly clean and social, with a bar that never seems to quit. Dorms sleep a maximum of six; there are also a few doubles (all bathrooms shared). Cheap meals are served (including summertime barbecue dinners), and a full activity menu is offered: the hostel is affiliated with Aktivni Planet (p402).

Hotel Sanje ob Soči HOTEL €€
(☑05-389 60 00; www.sanjeobsoci.com; Mala Vas 105a; s/d €80/110; P🛜) 'Dream on the Soča' is an architecturally striking hotel on the edge of town. Interiors are minimalist and colourful, and room sizes range from 'economy' on the ground floor to studios and family-sized apartments (named after the mountain you can see from the room's windows). There's friendly service, a sauna area and a great breakfast spread (€12).

★ Pristava Lepena RESORT €€€
(☑041 671 981, 05-388 99 00; www.pristava-lepena.com; Lepena 2; r from €126; ⊙mid-May–mid-Oct; P🛜🏊) This positively idyllic 'hotel village' is set in an Alpine meadow above the Lepena Valley. It's a small collection of rustic houses and rooms, run by a charming Slovenian-Uruguayan couple. In a beautiful setting, there's a pool, a high-quality restaurant (open to all), a sauna and a tennis court, and fishing and horse-riding opportunities.

Dobra Vila   BOUTIQUE HOTEL €€€
(☑05-389 64 00; www.dobra-vila-bovec.si; Mala
Vas 112; r €140-270; P ❄ @ 🖥) This stunning
10-room boutique hotel is housed in an erstwhile telephone-exchange building dating
from 1932. Peppered with art deco flourishes, interesting artefacts and *objets d'art*, it
has its own library and a wine cellar, and a
fabulous restaurant with a winter garden
and an outdoor terrace.

✕ Eating & Drinking

You won't go hungry in Bovec, and there's
a handful of good choices sprinkled around
the town centre. That said, it lacks the
choice of Kobarid or, a little further afield,
the appealing local specialities of Idrija.

Felix   CAFE €€
(☑05-388 67 33; Mala Vas 16; mains €7-16; ⊙7am-
10pm Mon-Thu, to 11pm Fri-Sun) This endur-
ingly popular streetside cafe is known for its
grilled meat and fish dishes and breakfasts,
and the cool vibe at large on the terrace at
most hours of the day.

Gostilna Sovdat   SLOVENIAN €€
(☑05-388 60 27; www.gostilna-sovdat.si; Trg Golobarskih Žrtev 24; mains €7-22; ⊙10am-10pm) Sovdat isn't strong on aesthetics and its outdoor
terrace isn't as pretty as others in town, but
the crowd of locals attests to its popularity
and value. Lots on the menu falls under €10,
including plentiful pastas and bumper burgers. You can go upmarket, too, with the likes
of gnocchi in a truffle sauce or roast beef
with Gorgonzola.

Dobra Vila Restaurant   SLOVENIAN €€€
(☑05-389 64 00; www.dobra-vila-bovec.si; Mala Vas
112; 4-/6-course set menu €45/60) Easily the best
place to eat in town is the polished restaurant at Dobra Vila – preferably in the pretty
garden in summer. A carefully constructed
menu of local, seasonal ingredients is served
to an appreciative crowd. Setting, service and
food are first-class; bookings are essential.

★ Črno Ovca   PUB
(www.facebook.com/crnaovca.bovec; Trg Golobarskih Žrtev 18; ⊙4pm-midnight Mon-Thu, 10am-3am
Fri & Sat, to 11pm Sun) You may have to search
for this tucked-away bar, but the Black
Sheep is worth the hunt (hint: it's close to
Hotel Kanin). Enjoy the relaxed atmosphere,
occasional live music and the activities available (kids' playground, petanque, tennis
courts for hire) – or just sit and drink in the
mountain views.

❶ Information

Tourist Information Centre (TIC; ☑05-302
96 47; www.bovec.si; Trg Golobarskih Žrtev 22;
⊙8am-8pm Jul & Aug, 9am-7pm Jun & Sep,
8.30am-12.30pm & 1.30-5pm Mon-Fri, 9am-
5pm Sat & Sun May, shorter hours Oct-Apr) The
TIC is open year-round. Winter hours will depend on the reopening of the local ski centre –
expect long hours when the ski season is fully
operating.

❶ Getting There & Away

Popular bus routes:
Kobarid (€3.30, 30 minutes, 22km, five daily)
Ljubljana (€14, 3¾ hours, 151km, three daily)
Vršič Pass Busline **Alpetour** (☑04-532 04 45;
www.alpetour.si) runs buses to Kranjska Gora
(€7, 1¾ hours, 46km) via Trenta (€2.90, 30
minutes, 20km) from May through September.
Check the website for timetables; there are five
or six departures daily.

Kobarid

☑05 / POP 4143 / ELEV 231M
Charming Kobarid is quainter than nearby
Bovec, and despite being surrounded by
mountain peaks it feels more Mediterranean than Alpine, with an Italianate look (the
border at Robič is only 9km to the west).

On the surface not a whole lot has
changed since Ernest Hemingway described
Kobarid (then Caporetto) in *A Farewell to
Arms* (1929) as 'a little white town with a
campanile in a valley', with 'a fine fountain
in the square'. The bell in the tower still rings
on the hour, but, sadly, the fountain has disappeared.

◉ Sights

★ Kozjak Waterfall   WATERFALL
(Slap Kozjak) One of the region's loveliest
short walking trails (approximately 30
minutes) leads to the photogenic, 15m-high
Kozjak Waterfall, which gushes over a rocky
ledge in a cavern-like amphitheatre, into a
green pool below. Access the trail from various spots: from a footbridge from Kamp Lazar campground or from a car park opposite
Kamp Koren.

Kobarid Museum   MUSEUM
(Kobariški Muzej; ☑05-389 00 00; www.koba
riski-muzej.si; Gregorčičeva ulica 10; adult/child
€6/2.50; ⊙9am-6pm Apr-Sep, 10am-5pm Oct-
Mar) This museum is devoted almost entirely to the Soča Front and the 'war to end all
wars'. Themed rooms describe powerfully

the 29 months of fighting, and there's a 20-minute video (available in 10 languages) that gives context. There are many photos documenting the horrors of the front, military charts, diaries and maps, and two large relief displays showing the front lines and offensives through the Krn Mountains and the positions in the Upper Soča Valley.

🏃 Activities

Kobarid doesn't quite keep to the same frenetic pace as nearby Bovec, but it still has a handful of operators who can get you active (and usually rather wet). There's also good hiking in the area.

X Point
ADVENTURE SPORTS
(☑05-388 53 08; www.xpoint.si; Trg Svobode 6) Operates from its base at X Point Hostel, with the usual waterborne activities (rafting, kayaking etc) and mountain biking, and it's the place to come for tandem-paragliding.

Positive Sport
ADVENTURE SPORTS
(☑040 654 475; www.positive-sport.com; Trg Svobode 15) Offers rafting, canyoning, kayaking and mountain biking. Bookings can be made online or at its office on the main square.

🛏 Sleeping

Kobarid has tidy in-town accommodation, but for those with their own wheels, Hiša Franko and Nebesa are two stellar choices out in the surrounding hills and valleys.

Kamp Koren
CAMPGROUND €
(☑05-389 13 11; www.kamp-koren.si; Drežniške Ravne 33; campsite per adult/child €13.70/6.85, chalet €65-190; P☈) The oldest campground in the valley, this lovely green site is about 500m northeast of Kobarid, by the Soča River and the road to Drežnica. There are loads of activities and facilities, and some quite luxurious log-cabin chalets that sleep six in comfort.

Hemingway House
APARTMENT €€
(☑040 774 106; www.hemingwayhouseslove nia.com; Volaričeva ulica 10; apt €40-70; ☈) A good-value option in the town centre, honouring Papa Hemingway and owned by Marie, a Canadian. The house has five apartments (each with a bathroom and a kitchen) over three floors – they sleep between two and five people, and share a lovely garden where breakfast (€5) can be served. In the

rooms, we like the exposed wooden beams. Off-season and weekly rates too.

★Nebesa
CHALET €€€
(☑05-384 46 20; www.nebesa.si; Livek 39; d €185-275; P☈) The name translates as 'Heaven', and it's fitting. These four heavenly mountain retreats sit at the top of a 7km winding road from Idrsko village (2km south of Kobarid) and enjoy stupendous views. Each sleeps two and is large and self-contained, with a kitchenette and a terrace; there's also a communal house with a kitchen and a wine cellar, plus saunas.

Hiša Franko
GUESTHOUSE €€€
(☑05-389 41 20; www.hisafranko.com; Staro Selo 1; r €120-150; P☈) This foodie favourite is in an old farmhouse 3km west of Kobarid in Staro Selo, halfway to the Italian border. Here 10 rooms ooze character, with rich colours and fabrics and interesting artworks. A handful of rooms have huge bathtubs; others have terraces. All partake in a sumptuous breakfast (€20 per person). And best of all: the acclaimed restaurant downstairs.

🍴 Eating

There are plenty of restaurants around the main square – they're easy to find and all have extensive menus. However, the best places to eat are out of town and are well worth the detour to get to. While you're here, make sure you try the local dessert, *kobariški štruklji* (little dumplings stuffed with walnuts and raisins).

Restaurant Lazar
SLOVENIAN €€
(☑05-388 53 33; www.lazar.si; Trnovo ob Soči 1b; mains €7-22; ⊗8am-10pm Apr-Oct, shorter hours Nov-Mar) Where do top locals chefs recommend for a casual meal? This fun, rustic outdoor restaurant-bar at the riverside Lazar holiday centre (camping and quality rooms also available). Its menu ranges from cheap, filling pancakes to Black Angus steaks, and fire-roasted lamb and pork ribs. It's well placed for the walk to/from Kozjak Waterfall.

★Hiša Franko
SLOVENIAN €€€
(☑05-389 41 20; www.hisafranko.com; Staro Selo 1; 6-/8-course set menu €125/150, wine pairing €50/75; ⊗noon-4pm Mon, 5-11pm Wed-Fri, noon-4pm & 7-11pm Sat & Sun Jun-Sep, closed Mon Oct-May) Provenance is everything at this restaurant in Staro Selo, just west of town

and one of the best in the country. Menus change with the seasons and showcase produce from Chef Ana's garden, plus berries, trout, mushrooms, cheese, meat and fish delivered by local farmers. The resulting dishes are innovative and delicious, and ably paired with top-notch wines. Service is first class.

Topli Val SEAFOOD €€€
(☑ 05-389 93 00; www.hotelhvala.si; Trg Svobode 1; mains €11-46; ☺ noon-3pm & 6-10pm; ☑) Seafood is the focus of the menu, and it's excellent, from the carpaccio of sea bass to the Soča trout and signature lobster with pasta. It's not exclusively aquatic – the 'mountains meet the sea' here: venison is also a speciality, and vegetarians will fare well. For dessert, try the *kobariški štruklji*.

ⓘ Information

Tourist Information Centre (TIC; ☑ 05-380 04 90; www.soca-valley.com; Trg Svobode 16; ☺ 9am-8pm Jul & Aug, 9am-1pm & 2-7pm Mon-Fri, 9am-1pm & 4-7pm Sat & Sun May, Jun & Sep, 9am-4pm Mon-Fri, 10am-4pm Sat Oct-Apr) Good local maps and brochures, plus information on Triglav National Park (p396).

ⓘ Getting There & Away

The closest train station is at Most na Soči (22km south, and good for trains to/from Bohinjska Bistrica and Bled Jezero).

Buses stop in front of the Cinca Marinca bar-cafe at Trg Svobode 10. Popular bus services from Kobarid include:

Bovec (€3.30, 30 minutes, 22km, five daily) In July and August, two of these services connect with buses over the Vršič Pass to Kranjska Gora.

Ljubljana (€12.20, 3¼ hours, 131km, four daily)

SLOVENIAN KARST

The Karst Region (*Kras* in Slovenian) of western Slovenia is a limestone plateau stretching inland from the Gulf of Trieste. Rivers, ponds and lakes can disappear and then resurface in the Karst's porous limestone through sinkholes and funnels, often resulting in underground caverns like the fabulous caves at Škocjan and Postojna. Along with caves, the Karst is rich in olives, fruits, vineyards producing ruby-red *teran* wine, *pršut*, old stone churches and red-tiled roofs.

Postojna

☑ 05 / POP 9420 / ELEV 546M

The karst cave at Postojna is one of the largest in the world, and its stalagmite and stalactite formations are unequalled anywhere. Among Slovenia's most popular attractions, it's a busy spot – the amazing thing is how the large crowds at the entrance seem to get swallowed whole by the size of the cave, and the tourist activity doesn't detract from the wonder. It's a big, slick complex, and it doesn't come cheap. But it's still worth every minute you can spend in this magical underground world. The adjacent town of Postojna serves as a gateway to the caves and is otherwise a fairly attractive provincial Slovenian town.

⊙ Sights

★**Postojna Cave** CAVE
(Postojnska Jama; ☑ 05-700 01 00; www.postojnska-jama.eu; Jamska cesta 30; adult/child €25.80/15.50, with Predjama Castle €35.70/21.40; ☺ tours hourly 9am-6pm Jul & Aug, to 5pm May, Jun & Sep, 10am, noon & 3pm Nov-Mar, 10am-noon & 2-4pm Apr & Oct) The jaw-dropping Postojna Cave system, a series of caverns, halls and passages some 24km long and two million years old, was hollowed out by the Pivka River, which enters a subterranean tunnel near the cave's entrance.

Visitors get to see 5km of the cave on 1½-hour tours; 3.2km of this is covered by a cool electric train. Postojna Cave has a constant temperature of 8°C to 10°C, with 95% humidity, so a warm jacket and decent shoes are advised.

Vivarium Proteus MUSEUM
(☑ 05-700 01 00; www.postojnska-jama.eu; adult/child €9.90/5.90, with Postojna Cave €31.80/19.10; ☺ 8.30am-6.30pm Jul & Aug, to 5.30pm May, Jun & Sep, 9.30am-5.30pm Apr, to 4.30pm Oct, to 3.30pm Nov-Mar) Just near the entrance to the Postojna Cave is the Vivarium, the cradle of a special branch of biology: speleobiology. Postojna provides shelter to dozens of cave-dwelling animal species – visitors can get to know some of the most interesting ones in more detail here, including the 'human fish', as well as the slenderneck beetle, cave squid and cave centipede.

Planina Cave CAVE
(Planinska Jama; ☑ 041 338 696; www.planina.si; Planina; adult/child €10/7; ☺ 3pm Sat, 3pm & 5pm Sun Apr-Sep) Planina Cave, 12km to the

WORTH A TRIP

PREDJAMA CASTLE

Predjama Castle (Predjamski Grad; ☑ 05-700 01 00; www.postojnska-jama. eu; Predjama 1; adult/child €13.80/8.30, with Postojna Cave €35.70/21.40; ⊙ 9am-7pm Jul & Aug, to 6pm May, Jun & Sep, 10am-5pm Apr & Oct, to 4pm Nov-Mar), 9km from Postojna, is one of Europe's most dramatic castles. It teaches a clear lesson: if you want to build an impregnable fortification, put it in the gaping mouth of a cavern halfway up a 123m cliff. Its four storeys were built piecemeal over the years from 1202, but most of what you see today is from the 16th century. It looks simply unconquerable.

northeast of Postojna Cave, is the largest water cave in Slovenia and a treasure-trove of fauna (including *Proteus anguinus*). The cave's entrance is at the foot of a 100m rock wall. It's 6.5km long, and you are able to visit about 900m of it in an hour. There are no lights, so take a torch.

🏃 Activities

As you'd imagine, proper caving is an option here, although experienced spelunkers will find what's on offer to be pretty tame – it's a safe adventure for your average punter.

The forested hills to the east and southeast of Postojna are rich in brown bears and a couple of operators offer tours in search of these soulful creatures.

Slovenia4Seasons WILDLIFE WATCHING
(☑ 040 387 887; www.slovenia4seasons.com; per person from €195; ⊙ May-Oct) This upmarket operator runs bear-watching excursions – it claims a 90% success rate and offers a 50% discount on a second tour if the first one is unsuccessful. It can pick you up from your hotel or the tourist office in Postojna.

**Forest
Adventures** WILDLIFE WATCHING
(☑ 040 187 309; www.forest-adventures.eu; Ulica Vilka Kledeta 6; per person from €60; ⊙ May-Oct) This Postojna-based outfit offers a handful of bear-watching excursions, which range from three to seven hours and involve a mix of hiking and time spent in a hide. It also offers hiking.

🛏 Sleeping

**Youth Hostel
Proteus Postojna** HOSTEL €
(☑ 05-850 10 20; www.proteus.sgls.si; Tržaška cesta 36; dm/s/d €15/23/34; P @ 🛜) Don't be fooled by the institutional exterior – inside, this place is a riot of colour. It's surrounded by parkland and is a fun, chilled-out space, with three-bed rooms (shared bathrooms), kitchen and laundry access, and bike rental. The year-round hostel shares the building with student accommodation, so facilities are good. It's about 500m southwest of Titov trg.

★**Lipizzaner Lodge** GUESTHOUSE €€
(☑ 040 378 037; www.lipizzanerlodge.com; Landol 17; s/d/q from €55/80/100; P 🛜) In a relaxing rural setting 9km northwest of Postojna Cave, a Welsh-Finnish couple established this very hospitable, affordable guesthouse. They offer seven well-equipped rooms (including family-sized, and a self-catering apartment); great-value, three-course evening meals on request (€20); brilliant local knowledge (check out their comprehensive website for an idea); forest walks (including to Predjama in 40 minutes); and bike rental.

Hotel Jama HOTEL €€€
(☑ 05-700 01 00; www.postojnska-jama.eu; Jamska cesta 30; r from €129) This huge, concrete, socialist-era hotel is part of the Postojna Cave complex and has undergone a stunning renovation, reopening in 2016 with slick, contemporary rooms with striking colour schemes and lovely glass-walled bathrooms. It's worth paying extra (anywhere between €10 and €30) for a room with a view. There's also a restaurant and a bar, and the excellent buffet breakfast costs €12.

🍴 Eating

★**Restaurant Proteus** SLOVENIAN €€
(☑ 081 610 300; Titov trg 1; mains €12-22; ⊙ 8am-10pm) The fanciest place in town: inside is modern and white, with booths fringed by curtains, while the terrace overlooking the main square is a fine vantage point. Accomplished cooking showcases fine regional produce – house specialities include venison goulash and steak with *teran* sauce. It's hard to go past the four-course Chef's Slovenian Menu (€38) for value and local flavour.

Modrijan Homestead SLOVENIAN €€
(☑ 05-700 01 00; www.postojnska-jama.eu; Postojna Cave complex; mains €12-22; ⊙ 10am-6pm

Apr-Sep) As you'd imagine, eating at the touristy complex surrounding Postojna Cave is not cheap, but here you'll get some very tasty grilled meats to fuel exploration. The menu lists an impressive seven languages and includes grilled trout, salmon and veggies. The meats – roast suckling pig, *klobasa* (sausage) and *čevapčiči* (spicy meatballs) – are excellent.

❶ Information

Tourist Information Centre Galerija (TIC; ☑ 040 122 318; www.visit-postojna.si; Trg Padlih Borchev 5; ⊙ 9am-5pm Mon-Sat, to 3pm Sun) Well-stocked tourist office in the town centre.

Tourist Information Centre Postojna (TIC; ☑ 064 179 972; www.visit-postojna.si; Tržaška cesta 59; ⊙ 8am-4pm Mon-Fri, 10am-3pm Sat) A smart new pavilion has been built in the town's west, on the road into Postojna. It's handy for those driving into town and there's adequate parking.

❶ Getting There & Away

BUS

Postojna's **bus station** (Titova cesta 2) is 200m southwest of Titov trg. Note some intercity buses will stop at the cave complex too (on timetables this is Postojnska jama). Destinations from Postojna include:

Cerknica (€2.90, 27 minutes, seven daily)
Divača (for Škocjan; €3.90, 30 minutes, seven daily)
Koper (€7.50, 1¼ hours, up to eight daily)
Ljubljana (€6.80, one hour, hourly)
Piran (€9.60, 1¾ hours, four daily)

TRAIN

The train station is on Kolodvorska cesta about 800m east of the square.

Postojna is on the main train line linking Ljubljana (€5.80, one hour) with Sežana and Trieste via Divača, and is an easy day trip from the capital. As many as 20 trains a day make the run from Ljubljana to Postojna and back.

You can also reach Koper (€6.99, 1½ hours) on the coast. There are up to six trains a day; some may require a change at Divača.

Cerknica
☑ 01 / POP 4018 / ELEV 572M

Cerknica is the largest town on a lake that isn't always a lake – one of Slovenia's most unusual natural phenomena. It's a good springboard for the gorge at Rakov Škocjan

and Notranjska Regional Park as a whole, not least because it's a quiet little place that gets none of the tourist buses that can plague nearby Postojna. If you'll be in the area in the week before Ash Wednesday, don't miss Cerknica's fun carnival celebrations.

◉ Sights

Notranjska Regional Park   NATURE RESERVE
(Notranjski Regijski Park; www.notranjski-park. si) This 222-sq-km park is a real biodiversity hotspot and holds within its borders a good deal of the region's karst phenomena, including the intermittent Lake Cerknica, forests, meadows, wetlands, caves (including Križna Cave) and Rakov Škocjan gorge. There is also a wealth of cultural heritage in the form of orchards, preserved buildings and old hayracks. Great hiking, cycling and birdwatching lie within its borders. The area's tourist office (p408) can provide info.

Lake Cerknica   LAKE
(Cerniško Jezero) Since ancient times, periodic Lake Cerknica has baffled and perplexed people, appearing and disappearing with the seasons. Cerknica is a *polje*, a field above a collapsed karst cavern riddled with holes like a Swiss cheese. During rainy periods, usually in the autumn and spring, water comes rushing into the *polje*. As the water percolates between the rocks, the sinkholes and siphons can't handle the outflow underground, and the *polje* becomes Lake Cerknica – sometimes in less than a day.

✳ Festivals & Events

★ Pust v Cerknici   RELIGIOUS
(www.pust.si; ⊙ Feb-Mar) Cerknica is famous for its pre-Lenten carnival, Pust, which takes place for four days over the weekend before Ash Wednesday. Mask-wearing merrymakers and witches parade up and down while being provoked by *butalci* (hillbillies) with pitchforks.

🛏 Sleeping & Eating

Prenočišča Miškar   GUESTHOUSE €
(☑ 081 602 284; www.miskar.si; Žerovnica 66; s/d/tr €35/50/66; ⓟ ⓢ) This four-room guesthouse is a very good choice, on forested grounds about 7km southeast of town (and only about 5km from Križna Cave). The owners are friendly, the balcony views superb. Bears wander the surrounding woods.

BEAR-WATCHING IN THE LOŽ VALLEY

The secluded Lož Valley (Loška Dolina), southeast of Cerknica, is a green and tranquil taste of rural Slovenia. In summer look out for its trademark *ostrnice* (tall slender haystacks). There's also a world-class cave experience, **Križna Cave** (Križna Jama; ☑041 632 153; www.krizna-jama.si; adult/child €9/6; ⊗tours 11am, 1pm, 3pm & 5pm Jul & Aug, 11am, 1pm & 3pm Sep, 3pm Sat & Sun Apr-Jun), and stirring **Snežnik Castle** (Grad Snežnik; ☑01-705 78 14; www.nms.si; Kozarišče 67; adult/child €5/3; ⊗tours hourly 10am-6pm Apr-Sep, to 4pm Tue-Sun Oct-Mar) to visit. But the main reason to come here is one of the best chances in Europe to see brown bears. The **tourist information centre** (TIC; ☑081 602 853; www.loskadolina.info; Cesta 19 Oktobra 49, Lož; 1/2/3 people €100/130/165) can arrange an evening with a local guide at an elevated wildlife observation lookout. Gostišče Mlakar offers customised nature programs, from multiday wildlife photography workshops to seasonal bear-watching tours. There is little public transport through the Lož Valley, and certainly none at the after-sunset time when you're likely to be returning from watching bears – you'll need your own wheels to explore the area.

Valvasorjev Hram SLOVENIAN €
(☑01-709 37 88; Partizanska cesta 1; mains €8-17; ⊗8am-11pm Mon-Sat, 3-10pm Sun) This simple eatery serves hearty dishes like *jota* (bean soup) and *klobasa* as well as pizza. It has its own wine cellar, and outside seating in summer.

❶ Information

Tourist Information Centre (TIC; ☑01-709 36 36; ticerknica@cerknica.si; Tabor 42; ⊗8am-4pm Mon-Sat, to noon Sun) For local information, including for Notranjska Regional Park. Bike rental available.

❶ Getting There & Away

Bus connections from Cerknica:
Ljubljana (€6.50, 1¼ hours, up to 17 daily)
Postojna (€2.90, 27 minutes, six daily)
Ratek (€1.40, nine minutes, nine daily) The closest train station.

Škocjan Caves

Touring the huge, spectacular subterranean chambers of the 6km-long **Škocjan Caves** (Škocjanske Jame; ☑05-708 21 00; www.park-skocjanske-jame.si; Škocjan 2; cave tour adult/child Jul & Aug €20/10, Mar-Jun, Sep & Oct €18/9, Nov-Feb €16/7.50; ⊗tours hourly 10am-5pm Jun-Sep, 10am, noon, 1pm & 3.30pm Apr, May & Oct, 10am & 1pm Mon-Sat, 10am, 1pm & 3pm Sun Nov-Mar) is a must. This remarkable cave system was carved out by the Reka River, which enters a gorge below the village of Škocjan and eventually flows into the Dead Lake, a sump at the end of the cave where it disappears. It surfaces again as the Timavo River at Duino in Italy, 34km northwest, before emptying into the Gulf of Trieste. Dress warmly and wear good walking shoes.

🏃 Activities

Škocjan Education Trail WALKING
If you have time before or after your cave tour, follow the circular, 2km Škocjan Education Trail around the collapsed dolines of the cave system and into nearby hamlets. If time is short, take the path leading north and down some steps from the caves' ticket office – after 250m you'll reach a **viewpoint** that enjoys a superb vista of the Velika Dolina and the gorge where the Reka starts its subterranean journey.

🛏 Sleeping & Eating

Pr' Vncki Tamara GUESTHOUSE €€
(☑05-763 30 73, 040 697 827; pr.vncki.tamara@gmail.com; Matavun 10; d €70; ℗) This welcoming, relaxed spot in Matavun is just steps south of the entrance to the caves. It has four traditionally styled rooms with a total of 10 beds in a charming old farmhouse; we love the rustic old kitchen with the open fire. Bikes can be rented; meals can be arranged (and are highly praised).

Etna ITALIAN €€
(☑031 727 568; www.etna.si; Kolodvorska ulica 3a, Divača; mains €8-19; ⊗11am-11pm Tue-Sun) Etna takes the classic pizza-pasta-meat menu and gives it a creative twist, with surprisingly tasty (and beautifully presented) results. All the essentials are homemade (pasta, pizza

dough from wholemeal flour); pizza choices are divided between classic or seasonal. The desserts are pretty as a picture.

❶ Getting There & Away

The Škocjan Caves are about 4.5km by road southeast of Divača. A bus connection runs from Divača's neighbouring train and bus stations to the caves a couple of times a day – the caves office recommends you call for times, as these change seasonally. Alternatively, there's a one-hour signed walking trail to the caves.

Buses between Ljubljana and the coast stop at Divača. Destinations include:

Koper (€5, 45 minutes, up to 11 daily)
Ljubljana (€8.50, 1½ hours, seven daily)
Postojna (€3.90, 30 minutes, seven daily)

Train destinations from Divača:

Koper (€4.28, 50 minutes, five daily)
Ljubljana (€7.70, 1½ hours, up to 14 daily)
Postojna (€3.44, 35 minutes, up to 14 daily)

WESTERN WINE REGIONS

Welcome to one of our favourite corners of Slovenia. This collection of wine regions out west, close to the Italian border, is a wonderful place to spend a few days. The wineries and excellent dining options are reason enough to visit the Vipava Valley, while the neighbouring Karst Wine Region is a well-kept secret that's worth discovering. But the crowning glory is Goriška Brda, a Tuscany-like land of fortified villages atop rolling hills with boutique family wineries in between.

Goriška Brda

📷 05 / ELEV UP TO 800M

Picture-perfect Goriška Brda (Gorica Hills) is a tiny wine-producing region that stretches from Solkan west to the Italian border. It's a charmer, reminiscent of Tuscany, full of rolling hills topped with small settlements and churches, its hillsides lined with grapevines and orchards. In short, it's one of Europe's best-kept secrets. A good place to start is **Dobrovo**, 18km northwest of central Nova Gorica, where there's a castle, *vinoteka* (wine bar) and information centre. In addition to its grapes and wine, Goriška Brda is celebrated for its fruit, cheeses and olive oil, and especially its cherries (usually available from early June).

⦿ Sights & Activities

Wine tasting is the main activity in these parts, although you could also go for a hike or two-wheeled ride in the hills, stopping in pretty villages at regular intervals as you go.

Dobrovo Castle CASTLE
(Grad Dobrovo; 📞 05-395 95 86; Grajska cesta 10; adult/child €3/1.50; ⦿ 8am-4pm Tue-Fri, 1-6pm Sat & Sun) The Renaissance-style Dobrovo Castle, dating from 1606, has a handful of rooms filled with artworks and period furnishings (limited labelling). There's a decent restaurant here, and **Vinoteka Brda** (📞 05-395 92 10; www.vinotekabrda.si; tastings from €7; ⦿ noon-8pm Wed-Sat) for wine tasting.

★ **Vinska Klet Goriška Brda** WINE
(📞 05-331 01 44; www.klet-brda.si; Zadružna cesta 9, Dobrovo; ⦿ 10am-4pm Mon-Sat) This wine cooperative, just downhill from Dobrovo Castle, has the largest wine cellar in Slovenia.

SLOVENIA GORIŠKA BRDA

WORTH A TRIP

THE LIPICA STUD FARM

The impact of the tiny town of Lipica, 2km from the Italian border, has been far greater than its size would suggest. This tiny village lives for and on its white Lipizzaner horses, which were first bred here for the Spanish Riding School in Vienna in the late 16th century. Horses remain the main appeal of a visit here. The **Lipica Stud Farm** (📞 05-739 15 80; www.lipica.org; Lipica 5; tour adult/child €16/8, incl performance €23/12; ⦿ tours 10am-5pm Apr-Oct, 10am-3pm Nov-Mar, live performances 3pm Tue, Fri & Sun, 11am Sat Jun-Aug, 3pm Tue, Fri & Sun May & Sep, 3pm Sun Apr & Oct) can be visited on popular, 50-minute guided tours. The interesting, informative tours are available in a number of languages; a tour covers the farm's unique heritage and the breeding of the horses, and visits the pastures and stables. It ends at the very good, hands-on museum called Lipikum (entrance included in tour). A highlight is the performance of these elegant horses as they go through their complicated paces, pirouetting and dancing to Viennese waltzes with riders en costume.

HRASTOVLJE'S 'DANCE OF DEATH'

The tiny Karst village of Hrastovlje is one of southwestern Slovenia's most rewarding excursions. The small Romanesque **Church of the Holy Trinity** (Cerkev Sv Trojice; ☑ 031 432 231; adult/child €3/1.50; ☺ 9am-noon & 1-5pm Wed-Mon) here is a dramatic sight, surrounded by medieval stone walls with corner towers, and covered inside with extraordinary 15th-century frescoes, including the famous *Dance of Death*. Getting here involves a few twists and turns – you'll really need your own vehicle – but it's worth it many times over.

It offers an excellent 90-minute 'Sommelier Tasting' (€20), which includes a tasting of six wines, a quick sommelier primer, a visit to the wine cellar, and cheese and nibbles. Advance bookings essential; other tours and tastings are also on offer.

Scurek WINE
(☑ 05-304 50 21; www.scurek.com; Pleshivo 44; ☺ by appointment) Almost within sight of the Italian border (some of the vineyards even lie across the border), this family-run producer is known for its full-bodied white and red Stara Brajda blends. If you contact them in advance, they're usually happy to show you around (check out the colourful barrels decorated by artists) and give you a tasting.

Bjana WINE
(☑ 05-395 92 30, tastings 031 339 931; www.bjana.si; Biljana 38; ☺ by appointment) One of the longest-standing wineries in the area, Bjana has won numerous awards for its sparkling wines. There are two gorgeous rooms if you're keen to stay overnight, and they arrange tastings if you contact them in advance.

🛏 Sleeping & Eating

There are apartments and private rooms for rent across the region – bookings can be made through tourist information centres and booking websites. Šmartno in particular has a few standout options. A number of wineries engage in *agriturismo* (farm stays), with rooms and meals available – Bjana is one of the best.

★ **Hotel San Martin** HOTEL €€
(☑ 05-330 56 60; www.sanmartin.si; Šmartno 11; r/ste/apt €90/110/140; ℗ ❄ ☎) To stay in the area, atmospheric Šmartno is a top choice. This hotel is close to the entrance to the fortified village and has polished service, bright, good-value rooms (including family-sized) and a highly regarded restaurant (Tuesday to Sunday) showcasing regional produce and enjoying a view-enriched terrace.

Hiša Marica GUESTHOUSE €€
(☑ 05-304 10 39; www.marica.si; Šmartno 33; s/d €70/100; ❄ ☎) This charming old inn lies within the fortified walls of Šmartno and offers four excellent, spacious rooms. Also here is a wine bar (Wednesday to Monday) serving up local flavours, including home-cured hams and salamis, and Soča Valley cheeses.

Hotel San Martin SLOVENIAN €€
(☑ 05-330 56 60; www.sanmartin.si/en/gastronomy; Šmartno 11; mains €11-20; ☺ noon-3pm & 6-10pm Tue-Thu, noon-10pm Fri & Sat, to 4pm Sun) With fine views from the terrace, a thoughtfully prepared seasonal menu and a commitment to local ingredients, the restaurant of the hotel of the same name in Šmartno comes highly recommended. Watch for classic mountain dishes like venison ragout or mountain trout, while the desserts are heavenly or sinful, depending on your perspective. Fab wines, too.

ℹ Information

Tourist Information Centre (☑ 05-395 95 94; www.brda.si; Grajska cesta; ☺ 9am-5pm Mon-Fri, 10am-6pm Sat & Sun Mar-Oct, 9am-4pm Mon-Fri Nov-Feb) Information on the Goriška Brda region.

ℹ Getting There & Away

Public transport out here is nearly nonexistent – your own wheels (two or four) are recommended for explorations.

SLOVENIAN COAST

Slovenia has just 47km of coastline on the Adriatic Sea, but it certainly makes the most of it. Seaside towns like Koper, with its medieval core, and glorious Piran are full of important Venetian Gothic architecture, and have clean beaches, boats for rent and rollicking bars. That said, the coast is overbuilt, and jammed with tourists from May to September.

Koper

📖 05 / POP 25,500

Coastal Slovenia's largest town, Koper (Capodistria in Italian) is something of a well-concealed secret. At first glance, it appears to be a workaday port that scarcely gives tourism a second thought. Your first impression may be even more underwhelming as you see all the industrial areas and shopping malls on the outskirts. But Koper's central core is delightfully medieval and far less overrun than its ritzy cousin, Piran.

◉ Sights

Although the city has no standout attractions, it's a great place to wander and enjoy its architectural riches. The easiest way to see Koper's Old Town is to walk from the marina on Ukmarjev trg east along Kidričeva ulica to Titov trg and then south down Čevljarska ulica, taking various detours along the way.

★ Titov Trg   SQUARE

In the centre of old Koper, Titov trg is a Venetian-influenced stunner; mercifully, like much of the Old Town's core, it is closed to traffic. On the north side is the arcaded Venetian Gothic **Loggia** (Loža; Titov trg 1) built in 1463 (a perfectly placed cafe lives here!); attached is the **Loggia Gallery**, with changing art exhibits.

Praetorian Palace   NOTABLE BUILDING

(Pretorska Palača; 📞 05-664 64 03; Titov trg 3; adult/child €4/2.50; ⊙ tours 10am, noon, 2pm, 4pm & 6pm Jul-Sep, 11am, 1pm & 3pm Oct-Jun) On the southern side of Titov trg is the white Praetorian Palace, a mixture of Venetian Gothic and Renaissance styles dating from the 15th century and the very symbol of Koper. Now serving as the town hall, it contains a reconstructed old pharmacy and the tourist information office on the ground floor, plus exhibits on the history of Koper and a ceremonial hall for weddings on the 1st floor. Access is via guided tour.

Cathedral of the Assumption   CATHEDRAL

(Stolnica Marijinega Vnebovzetja; Titov trg) Plumb on Titov trg is the Cathedral of the Assumption and its 36m-tall belfry, now called the **City Tower** (adult/child €3/2; ⊙ 9am-1pm & 4-8pm Jul-Sep, 9am-5pm Oct-Jun), with 204 climbable stairs to superb views. The cathedral, partly Romanesque and Gothic but mostly dating from the mid-18th century, has a white classical interior with a feeling of space and light that belies the sombre exterior.

Kidričeva Ulica   STREET

On the north side of Kidričeva ulica are several churches from the 16th century, including the **Church of St Nicholas** (Cerkev Sv Nikolaja; Kidričeva ulica 30; ⊙ hours vary), plus some restored Venetian houses and the 18th-century baroque **Totto Palace** (Palača Totto; Kidričeva ulica 22a), with winged lion relief. Opposite the palace are wonderful **medieval townhouses** (Kidričeva ulica 33), with protruding upper storeys painted in a checked red, yellow and green pattern.

Trg Brolo   SQUARE

Linked to Titov trg to the east, Trg Brolo is a wide and leafy square of fine old buildings, including the late-18th-century baroque **Brutti Palace** (Palača Brutti; Trg Brolo 1), now the central library, to the north. On the eastern side is the 17th-century **Vissich-Nardi Palace** (Palača Vissich-Nardi; Trg Brolo 3) containing government offices and the **Fontico** (Fontiko; Trg Brolo 4), a granary where the town's wheat was once stored, with wonderful medallions and reliefs. Close by is the disused **Church of St James** (Cerkev Sv Jakoba; Martinčev trg) dating from the 14th century.

🛏 Sleeping & Eating

Hostel Histria   HOSTEL €

(📞 070 133 552; www.hostel-histria.si; Ulica pri Velikih Vratih 17; dm €15-23; ✳ @ 🕏) Supremely placed in the core of the Old Town, this cosy place is in a 200-year-old house, with decent facilities (including air-con and laundry). Dorms have six or eight beds; bathrooms are shared.

★ Hostel Villa Domus   HOSTEL €€

(📞 030 468 777; www.villa-domus.si; Vojkovo Nabrežje 12; dm from €17, r €54-77; ✳ 🕏) On the southern fringe of the old city, this well-regarded hostel has simple but modern dorms and doubles or twins that put most hotels in the area to shame. Some rooms from the upper floors have fine views and the rooms themselves, though on the small side, are terrific value.

Fritolin   FISH & CHIPS €

(Pristaniška ulica 2; dishes €2.50-8) There's an outdoor fresh-food market not far from the shore, and it's surrounded by cheap eating

SLOVENIA KOPER

WORTH A TRIP

PORTOROŽ: SLOVENIA'S SWISH RESORT

Every country with a coast needs a swish beach resort and Portorož (Portorose in Italian) is Slovenia's. There is a sense that this could be anywhere in the northern Mediterranean, which is fine if that generic experience is what you're looking for. But Slovenia's other coastal towns have significantly more charm and character.

Portorož's beaches are relatively clean (if wall-to-wall with people in summer), and there are spas and wellness centres where you can take the waters or cover yourself in curative mud. The vast array of accommodation options makes Portorož a useful (if less atmospheric) fallback if everything's full in Piran, which is only 4km up the road.

spots and cafe-bars popular with locals. We love tiny Fritolin for its fish and chips: calamari fried or grilled, sardines, portions of seabass or bream, or *fritto misto* (mixed fried seafood). There are benches out front, or a park nearby.

★ **Capra** MEDITERRANEAN €€
(☑ 041 602 030; www.capra.si; Pristaniška ulica 3; mains €9-23; ☺noon-11pm) Capra is a sexy new indoor–outdoor venue with a touch of Scandi style. Its appeal extends all day, from coffee to lounge-y cocktails, and the creative, ambitious menu covers many bases with great seafood, salad and pasta options (how's homemade pasta with scampi and truffle?). Presentation is first-class, as are the desserts.

❶ Information

Tourist Information Centre (TIC; ☑ 05-664 64 03; www.koper.si; Titov trg 3; ☺9am-8pm Jul-Sep, to 5pm Oct-Jun) Friendly office on the ground floor of the Praetorian Palace.

❶ Getting There & Away

The joint bus and train station is 1.5km southeast of the Old Town on Kolodvorska cesta.

There's a handy central **bus stop** (Piranška ulica) for local services (including to other coastal cities) on Piranška ulica (just south of the market).

Piran

📞 05 / POP 3800

One of the loveliest towns anywhere along the Adriatic coast, picturesque Piran (Pirano in Italian) sits prettily at the tip of a narrow peninsula. Its Old Town – one of the best-preserved historical towns anywhere in the Mediterranean – is a gem of Venetian Gothic architecture, but it can be a mob scene at the height of summer. In quieter times, it's hard not to fall instantly in love with the atmospheric winding alleyways, the sunsets and the seafood restaurants.

◉ Sights

★ **Tartinijev Trg** SQUARE
(Map p414) The pastel-toned Tartinijev trg is a marble-paved square (oval, really) that was the inner harbour until it was filled in 1894. The **statue** of a nattily dressed gentleman in the centre is of native son, composer and violinist Giuseppe Tartini (1692–1770). East is the 1818 **Church of St Peter** (Cerkev Sv Petra; Map p414; Tartinijev trg). Across from the church is **Tartini House** (Tartinijeva Hiša; Map p414; ☑05-671 00 40; www.pomorskimuzej. si; Kajuhova ulica 12; adult/child €2/1; ☺9am-noon & 6-9pm Jul & Aug, shorter hours Sep-Jun), the composer's birthplace. The **Court House** (Sodniška Palača; Map p414; Tartinijev trg 1) and the porticoed 19th-century **Municipal Hall** (Občinska Palača; Map p414; Tartinijev trg 2), home to the tourist information centre, dominate the western edge of the square.

Cathedral of St George CATHEDRAL
(Župnijska Cerkev Sv Jurija; Map p414; www.zupnija-piran.si; Adamičeva ulica 2) A cobbled street leads from behind the red Venetian House Tartinijev trg on to Piran's hilltop cathedral, baptistery and bell tower. The cathedral was built in baroque style in the early 17th century on the site of an earlier church from 1344.

The cathedral's doors are usually open and a metal grille allows you to see some of the richly ornate and newly restored interior, but full access is via the **Parish Museum of St George** (Map p414; ☑05-673 34 40; Adamičeva ulica 2; adult/child €2/1; ☺9am-1pm & 5-7.30pm Mon-Fri, 9am-2pm & 5-8pm Sat, from 11am Sun), which includes the church's treasury and catacombs.

Mediadom Pyrhani MUSEUM
(Map p414; ☑08-205 52 72; www.mediadom-piran. si; Kumarjeva 3; adult/child €5/2; ☺9am-noon &

6-10pm Jul & Aug, 9am-noon & 4-7pm May & Jun, 10am-5pm Apr & Sep, to 4pm Oct-Mar) This exciting new multimedia, interactive museum takes you on an innovative journey through Piran's historical story, with a 'time machine' and numerous exhibits that take a fresh look at the town's fascinating history. Archaeological finds and restored interiors add to the atmosphere.

Bell Tower TOWER

(Zvonik; Map p414; Adamičeva ulica; €1; ⊙10am-8pm summer, shorter hours rest of year) The Cathedral of St George's free-standing, 46.5m bell tower, built in 1609, was clearly modelled on the campanile of San Marco in Venice and provides a fabulous backdrop to many a town photo. Its 147 stairs can be climbed for fabulous views of the town and harbour. Next to it, the octagonal 17th-century baptistery contains altars and paintings. It is now sometimes used as an exhibition space. To the east is a 200m-long stretch of the 15th-century **town wall**.

🏃 Activities

Piran is more for seeing than for doing, but waterborne activities – boat trips, swimming and diving – are all possible.

Sailing Piran BOATING

(Map p414; ☑040 669 961; sailingpiran@gmail.com; 4/8hr excursions per person €55/75, boat rental per 4/8hr €240/320; ⊙9am-1pm & 2-6pm) Take to the Adriatic aboard a yacht for a lovely day or half-day out. The views back towards Piran are worth every euro.

Subaquatic BOATING

(Map p414; ☑041 602 783; www.subaquatic.si; Piran Marina; adult/child €15/10; ⊙cruises 10am, 2pm, 4.15pm & 6.30pm Apr-Sep) Subaquatic offers 1½-hour coastline cruises from Piran to Fiesa and Strunjan (and back). Panoramas are enjoyed above and under the water, with windows under the deck. Check tour schedules online – in cooler months, there may be only two a day.

🛏 Sleeping

Piran has a number of atmospheric choices and an unusually stable accommodation offering. Prices are higher here than elsewhere along the coast, and you'd be crazy to arrive without a booking in summer. If you're looking for a private room, start at **Maona Tourist Agency** (☑05-674 03 63; www.maona.si; Cankarjevo nabrežje 7; ⊙9am-8pm Mon-Sat,

10am-1pm & 5-7pm Sun) or **Turist Biro** (☑05-673 25 09; www.turistbiro-ag.si; Tomažičeva ulica 3; ⊙9am-1pm & 4-7pm Mon-Sat, 10am-1pm Sun).

Max Piran B&B €€

(Map p414; ☑041 692 928; www.maxpiran.com; Ulica IX Korpusa 26; d €70-88; ❀🛜) Piran's most romantic accommodation has just six handsome, compact rooms, each bearing a woman's name rather than a number, in a delightful, coral-coloured, 18th-century townhouse. It's just down from the Cathedral of St George, and is excellent value.

Miracolo di Mare B&B €€

(Map p414; ☑051 445 511, 05-921 76 60; www.miracolodimare.si; Tomšičeva ulica 23; r €60-80; 🛜) A lovely and decent-value B&B, the Wonder of the Sea has a dozen charming (though smallish) rooms, some of which (like No 3 and the breakfast room) give on to a pretty garden. Floors and stairs are wooden and original.

★**PachaMama** GUESTHOUSE €€€

(PachaMama Pleasant Stay; Map p414; ☑05-918 34 95; www.pachamama.si; Trubarjeva 8; r €80-175; ❀🛜) Built by travellers for travellers, this excellent guesthouse sits just off Tartinijev trg and offers 12 fresh rooms, decorated with timber and lots of travel photography. Cool private bathrooms and a 'secret garden' add appeal. There are also a handful of studios and family-sized apartments dotted around town, of an equally high standard.

Art Hotel Tartini HOTEL €€€

(Map p414; ☑05-671 10 00; www.hotel-tartini-piran.com; Tartinijev trg 15; s €130, d €150-220; ❀🛜) This attractive, 45-room property faces Tartinijev trg and manages to catch a few sea or square views from the upper floors. A 2018 overhaul has turned the rooms into some of Piran's best – stylish, whitewashed and ever so comfortable. The staff are especially friendly and helpful. The summertime rooftop terrace is a winner.

Hotel Piran HOTEL €€€

(Map p414; ☑05-666 71 00; www.hotel-piran.si; Stjenkova ulica 1; d €120-180; ❀🛜) The town's flagship hotel has a commanding waterside position, great service and a century of history. There are 74 modern rooms and 15 suites – sea view is the way to go, if you can. Downstairs is a wellness centre, cafe and restaurant with large terrace; on the rooftop is a fab summertime champagne bar for hotel guests only.

Piran

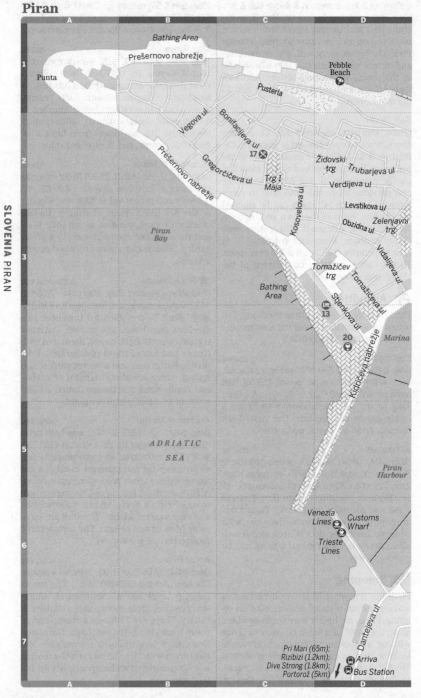

SLOVENIA PIRAN

Bathing Area

Prešernovo nabrežje

Punta

Pebble Beach

Pusterla

Vegova ul

Bonifacijeva ul

Gregorčičeva ul

Prešernovo nabrežje

17

Trg 1 Maja

Židovski trg

Trubarjeva ul

Verdijeva ul

Kosovelova ul

Levstikova ul

Obzidna ul

Zelenjavni trg

Vidalijeva ul

Piran Bay

Tomažičev trg

Bathing Area

Tomažičeva ul

Stjenkova ul

13

20

Marina

Kidričeva nabrežje

ADRIATIC SEA

Piran Harbour

Venezia Lines

Customs Wharf

Trieste Lines

Dantejeva ul

Pri Mari (65m); Rizibizi (1.2km); Dive Strong (1.8km); Portorož (5km)

Arriva Bus Station

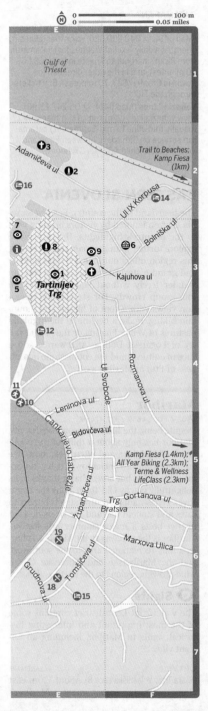

Piran

✖ Eating & Drinking

One of Piran's attractions is its plethora of fish restaurants, especially along Prešernovo nabrežje. Most cater to the tourist trade and are rather overpriced, but there are some gems worth tracking down. The seafood pairs well with the local *malvazija* white wine.

Cantina Klet   SEAFOOD €
(Map p414; Trg 1 Maja 10; mains €5-10; ⊙10am-11pm) This small wine bar sits pretty under a grapevine canopy on Trg 1 Maja. You order drinks from the bar (cheap local wine from the barrel or well-priced beers), but we especially love the self-service window (labelled 'Fritolin pri Cantini') where you order from a small blackboard menu of fishy dishes, like fish fillet with polenta, fried calamari or fish tortilla.

Pirat   SEAFOOD €€
(Map p414; ☎041 327 654; www.facebook.com/PiratPiran; Župančičeva ulica 26; mains €9-21; ⊙11am-10pm) It's not the fanciest place in

town, but the atmosphere is top-notch and Rok and his crew do their best to ensure you have a good time. Seafood is king, from the fresh fish carpaccio to pasta with lobster and grilled seabass filleted at the table. It's all nicely accompanied by local *malvazija*.

★ **Pri Mari**   MEDITERRANEAN €€
(☑041 616 488, 05-673 47 35; www.primari-piran.com; Dantejeva ulica 17; mains €8-24; ⊙noon-4pm & 6-10pm Tue-Sun Apr-Oct, noon-4pm & 6-10pm Tue-Sat, noon-6pm Sun Nov-Mar) This stylishly rustic and welcoming restaurant run by an Italian-Slovenian couple serves the most inventive Mediterranean and Slovenian dishes in town – lots of fish – and a good selection of local wines. Space is limited, so it pays to book ahead.

Gostilna Park   SLOVENIAN €€
(Map p414; ☑05-992 17 51; Župančičeva 21; mains €9-19; ⊙noon-11pm) Tucked a little away from the main tourist drag, this fine little place doesn't mess with the basics: fresh seafood, grilled or lightly fried; *čevapčiči* and excellent meat platters; and light salads to keep things fresh. It's all nicely cooked and served with a smile.

★ **Café Teater**   BAR
(Map p414; ☑041 638 933; Stjenkova ulica 1; ⊙9am-midnight) With a grand waterfront terrace and faux antique furnishings, this is where anyone who's anyone in Piran can be found. Perfect for sundowners. During the day, it's as much coffee as cocktails, but the latter take over late afternoon.

ⓘ Information

Tourist Information Centre (TIC; Map p414; ☑05-673 44 40; www.portoroz.si; Tartinijev trg 2; ⊙9am-10pm Jul & Aug, to 7pm May, to 5pm Sep-Apr & Jun) Your first stop for information on Piran and Portorož. It's in the impressive Municipal Hall.

ⓘ Getting There & Away

BUS

Arriva (Map p414; ☑090 74 11; www.arriva.si) buses serve the coast; see the website for schedules and prices. From the **bus station** (Map p414; Dantejeva ulica) south of the centre, buses run frequently to Portorož (€1.40, eight minutes), and up to four times an hour to Izola (€2.50, 30 minutes) and Koper (€3, 45 minutes). Three buses daily make the journey to Ljubljana (€13, three hours), via Divača and Postojna.

CATAMARAN

From late June through August, **Trieste Lines** (Map p414; ☑040 200 620; www.triestelines.it) operates a daily (except Wednesday) catamaran from Piran's harbour to Trieste in Italy (€9.60, 30 minutes), and in the other direction to Rovinj in Croatia (€23, 70 minutes). Buy tickets through the TIC.

Venezia Lines (Map p414; ☑05-242 28 96; www.venezialines.com) runs a summer-only (usually mid-June to mid-September) catamaran service on Saturdays between Piran and Venice (adult/child €67/42, 3¾ hours).

EASTERN SLOVENIA

The heartland of the country, Eastern Slovenia is often ignored by visitors heading west to the country's highlights. If you want to explore further than the main tourist routes, this region offers outdoor activities aplenty and grand historical centres, where you can wander freely without squeezing between tour-group crowds. For stupendous mountain views with a spot of hiking and mountain biking, make a beeline to the highland pastures of Velika Planina or the glacial valley of Logarska Dolina. Afterwards, add a slice of culture amid the cobblestone quaintness of Ptuj or Maribor's cafes.

Maribor

☑02 / POP 94,650 / ELEV 266M

Despite being the nation's second-largest city, Maribor has only about a third of the population of Ljubljana and often feels more like an overgrown provincial town. It has no unmissable sights but oozes charm thanks to its delightfully patchy Old Town along the Drava River. Pedestrianised central streets buzz with cafes and student life, and the riverside Lent district hosts a major summer arts festival. Maribor is the gateway to the Maribor Pohorje, a hilly recreational area to the southwest, and the Mariborske and Slovenske Gorice wine-growing regions to the north and east.

◉ Sights

The waterfront Lent district contains some of the most important and interesting historical sights in Maribor, including an ancient vine.

Old Vine   LANDMARK
(Stara Trta; Vojašniška ulica 8) About 150m east along the Pristan embankment is Maribor's

WORTH A TRIP

ALPINE PASTURES OF VELIKA PLANINA

Loosely translated as 'Great Highlands', **Velika Planina** (www.velikaplanina.si) is a pretty mountaintop pasture that combines stunning scenery with traditional heritage; the herding and dairy economy here has changed little for hundreds of years. It's a popular day trip from Ljubljana or Kamnik for everyone from dog walkers and amblers to more serious hikers.

The journey to the top of Velika Planina unfolds in two stages: first a dramatic **cable-car ride** (☑ 031 680 862; www.velikaplanina.si; adult/child return incl chairlift €15/11, cable car only €13/9; ☺ twice hourly 8.30am-6pm Jun-Sep, 9am, 10am, noon, 2pm & 4pm Mon-Thu, hourly 9am-5pm Fri-Sun Oct-May), and then a choice of either a 15-minute chairlift or hiking the rest of the way. Once on the pastures, there's little to do except walk the pristine fields and drink in the views, surrounded by snow-capped mountains.

To get there with your own wheels, take the road north from Kamnik for 9.5km, beside the Kamniška Bistrica River, to arrive at the lower station, from where you access Velika Planina by cable car. Three daily buses also travel from Kamnik to Kamniška Bistrica via the cable-car stop for Velika Planina.

While on top of Velika Planina, have a meal at **Zeleni Rob** (Velika Planina; mains €5.50-8.50; ☺ 8am-4pm Mon-Thu, to 5pm Fri-Sun), known for its hearty stews and said by some to serve Slovenia's best *štruklji* (cheese dumplings).

---

most celebrated attraction, the so-called Old Vine, which still produces between 35kg and 55kg of grapes and about 25L of red wine per year, despite being planted more than four centuries ago. It is tended by a city-appointed viticulturist, and the dark-red Žametna Črnina (Black Velvet) is distributed to visiting dignitaries as 'keys' to Maribor in the form of 0.25L bottles.

Old Vine House   MUSEUM
(Hiša Stare Trta; ☑ 02-251 51 00; www.maribor-pohorje.si; Vojašniška ulica 8; wine tasting €4; ☺ 9am-8pm May-Sep, to 6pm Oct-Apr) FREE Learn about Maribor's 400-year-old vine and Slovenian viniculture at Old Vine House, where you can taste local wine from its enormous collection. And don't miss the lovely new floor mosaic tracing Maribor's history.

Synagogue   SYNAGOGUE
(☑ 02-252 78 36; Židovska ulica 4; €1; ☺ 8am-4pm Mon-Fri) Just north of the pentagonal 16th-century Water Tower on the waterfront, a set of steps leads up to Židovska ulica (Jewish St), the centre of the Jewish district in the Middle Ages, and home to this 15th-century synagogue. It contains Gothic key stones and tomb fragments; the special exhibitions and 15-minute video are enlightening.

Glavni Trg   SQUARE
Maribor's marketplace in the Middle Ages, Glavni trg is just north of the river and the main bridge crossing it. In the centre of the square is Slovenia's most extravagant

plague pillar, erected in 1743. Behind it is the **town hall** (Glavni trg 14), built in 1565 by Venetian craftsmen.

National Liberation Museum   MUSEUM
(Muzej Narodne Osvoboditve; ☑ 02-235 26 00; www.muzejno-mb.si; Ulica Heroja Tomšiča 5; adult/child €3/2; ☺ 8am-5pm Mon-Fri, 9am-noon Sat) Housed in a stunning 19th-century mansion, the collections here document Slovenia's struggle for freedom throughout the 20th century, with particular emphasis on the work of the Pohorje Partisans during the Nazi occupation. Riveting.

🛏 Sleeping

Much of Maribor's accommodation veers towards the business traveller. For a city, midrange and budget options are thin on the ground; it pays to book ahead. The TIC (p418) can organise private rooms (single/double from €25/40) and apartments.

★ **Hostel Pekarna**   HOSTEL €€
(☑ 059 180 880; www.mkc-hostelpekarna.si; Ob Železnici 16; dm/s/d €21/30/54; P @ 🛜) Part of Maribor's Pekarna alternative cultural centre, this bright and welcoming hostel south of the river is housed in a converted army bakery (*pekarna* is 'bakery' in Slovene). Accommodation is mostly in four-bed dorms but there are also private studios and apartments with kitchenette. Facilities include a communal balcony, kitchen, cosy TV room and laundry, plus free bike rental.

Hotel Maribor   APARTMENT €€€

(☑02-234 56 00; www.hotelmaribor.si; Glavni trg 8; apt s/d/f from €109/139/149; P❄🖥) This 18th-century brewery building has been sensitively converted into the nicest digs in town. Spacious, white-on-white apartments (the biggest has four bedrooms) have bags of sleek minimalist style. Some have original stone wall features, while all come with full kitchens, big balconies, repurposed factory lamps swinging over tables and sumptuous bathrooms with walk-in showers. There's a small sauna on-site.

✗ Eating & Drinking

Malca   EUROPEAN €

(☑059 100 397; www.malcamimogrede.si; Slovenska ulica 4; dishes €4.90-6.60; ☺10am-4pm Mon-Fri; 🖉) This lunchtime bistro serves some of the freshest dishes based on seasonal ingredients in Maribor. The daily changing menu takes inspiration from across Europe (such as paella and moussaka) as well as including Slovenian favourites like nettle soup and *žlikrofi*.

★ Restavracija Mak   EUROPEAN €€

(☑02-620 00 53; www.restavracija-mak.si; Osojnikova ulica 20; set lunch/dinner from €25/45; ☺noon-3pm & 6-9.30pm Tue-Sat) The restaurant itself, in Obrežje across the Drava River, may not look like much, but you're here for the food not some grand dining hall. Owner-chef David Vračko will guide you through a multiple-course food experience (there's no menu) of creative European cuisine. Booking is highly recommended, and don't expect to eat and run. This is a three- to four-hour affair.

Gostilna Maribor   SLOVENIAN €€

(Glavni trg 8; mains €6-26; ☺7.30am-11pm Mon-Thu, to 2am Fri & Sat, 9am-4pm Sun) This great new addition to Maribor's dining scene focuses on bringing contemporary tweaks to traditional Styrian dishes with mains like wild boar with carrot *štruklji* and *spätzle* (small pasta dumplings) with smoked curd. For lunch it's known for its *žemljica* (traditional bun) sandwiches (€6 to €7) stuffed with ingredients such as beef, horseradish and sauerkraut.

Luft Bar   BAR

(☑040 413 514; www.luftbar.si; Ulica Vita Kraigherja 3; ☺8am-midnight Mon-Fri, 9am-4am Fri & Sat, 10am-10pm Sun; 🖥) Always suckers for views and recycling, we love that the old Slavija Hotel is now an office building with a two-level rooftop cafe-bar. Floor 11 has a slick bar; go one floor up to the open terrace and you'll be bowled over by the sweeping views of the city and mountains. Service is friendly, the cocktails out of this world.

Čajek Cafe   CAFE

(www.cajek.com; Slovenska ulica 4; ☺7.30am-10pm Mon-Fri, 9am-10pm Sat, 3-9pm Sun; 🖥) Our favourite cafe in Maribor has an old-fashioned, cosy interior with lots of dark wood and eclectic decor. The menu concentrates on tea (in umpteen different flavours), though there's decent coffee, cold drinks and beer too, as well as homemade cake.

ℹ Information

Tourist Information Centre Maribor (TIC; ☑02-234 66 11; www.maribor-pohorje.si; Partizanska cesta 6a; ☺9am-7pm Mon-Fri, to 5pm Sat & Sun) Helpful TIC in a large kiosk opposite the Franciscan church. Staff can organise city tours with local guides; between June and October they run group city tours (€8, 1½ hours) on Friday at 4pm and Saturday at 11am.

ℹ Getting There & Away

BUS

You can reach virtually any town in Slovenia (and certain international destinations) from Maribor's huge **bus station** (Minska ulica).

DESTINATION	PRICE (€)	DURATION (HR)	FREQUENCY
Celje	6.70	1½	5 daily weekdays, 1 daily weekends
Ljubljana	12.40	2-3	7 daily weekdays, 2-3 daily weekends
Munich (Germany)	48	6	9.50pm & 11.45pm daily
Murska Sobota	6.30	1¼	8 daily weekdays, 3-5 daily weekends
Ptuj	3.60	¾	At least hourly weekdays, 5-7 daily weekends
Sarajevo (Bosnia)	45	9	6.40pm daily & 9.15pm Mon-Thu, Sat & Sun
Slovenj Gradec	7.20	2	3 daily
Vienna (Austria)	23	3½	8.25am & 8pm daily

TRAIN

As well as direct services, there are many more possible connections to Ljubljana and Ptuj by changing in Pragersko.

International connections to Belgrade (€29, 8½ hours) and Zagreb (€12, three hours) are possible by changing in Zidani Most.

Ptuj

☑ 02 / POP 17,800 / ELEV 225M

Rising gently above a wide valley, Ptuj (p-too-ee) forms a symphony of red-tile roofs best viewed from across the Drava River. One of the oldest towns in Slovenia, Ptuj equals Ljubljana in terms of historical importance. The compact medieval core, with its cobblestone alleys rimmed by interesting facades, scattered with ornate monasteries and topped by a grand whitewashed castle, may be easily seen in a day, but the laid-back ambience, cafe culture and great hotels may convince you to base yourself here for a while longer. There are plenty of interesting side trips and activities in the area if you do decide to linger.

☉ Sights

★ Ptuj Castle   CASTLE

(Grad Ptuj; ☑ castle 02-748 03 60, museum 02-787 92 30; www.pmpo.si; Na Gradu 1; adult/child €5/3; ☉ 9am-6pm Mon-Fri, to 8pm Sat & Sun Jul & Aug, 9am-6pm May-Jun & Sep–mid-Oct, to 5pm mid-Oct–Jun) Ptuj Castle is an agglomeration of styles from the 14th to the 18th centuries, but it is nonetheless a majestic sight, sitting high on the hill overlooking the red-roofed burger houses of Ptuj and the Drava River. It houses the **Ptuj-Ormož Regional Museum**, but is equally worth the trip for the views of Ptuj and the river. The shortest way to the castle is to follow narrow Grajska ulica, east of the Hotel Mitra, which leads to a covered wooden stairway and the castle's Renaissance **Peruzzi Portal** (1570).

Dominican Monastery   MONASTERY

(Dominikanski Samostan; Muzejski trg 1; adult/child/family €4/2/9; ☉ 10am-6pm Tue-Sun Apr-Sep) Carefully restored and newly reopened to the public, Ptuj's Dominican Monastery was first established in 1230, though much of its original medieval character was replaced by baroque features during the 18th century. Inside, the walls of the Gothic cloister still hold on to scraps of faded frescoes, while the baroque powder-pink refectory is home to swirling plasterwork and colourful murals. The entrance fee includes an audio guide with some good basic historical information on the building.

Slovenski Trg   SQUARE

Funnel-shaped Slovenski trg is the centre of old Ptuj. The 16th-century **City Tower** (Mestni Stolp) dominates the square's eastern side. Roman tombstones and sacrificial altars from Poetovio were incorporated into the walls in the 1830s – check the reliefs of Medusa's head, dolphins, a lion and a man on horseback.

In front of the tower stands the 5m-tall **Orpheus Monument** (Orfejev Spomeni), a 2nd-century Roman tombstone with scenes from the Orpheus myth. It was used as a pillory in the Middle Ages.

Prešernova Ulica   STREET

Pedestrian Prešernova ulica was the town's market in the Middle Ages. The arched spans above some of the narrow side streets support older buildings. The **Late Gothic House** (Prešernova ulica 1), dates from about 1400. Opposite is the sombre **Romanesque House** (Prešernova ulica 4), the oldest building in Ptuj. The renovated yellow pile called the **Little Castle** (Mali Grad; Prešernova ulica 33-35) was the home of the Salzburg bishops and various aristocratic families over the centuries.

🏃 Activities

Kobal Wine Shop   WINE

(Vinoteka Kobal; ☑ 041 348 596; www.kobalwines.si; Prešernova ulica 4; wine tasting €9; ☉ by appointment 10am-6pm Mon-Sat) Kobal is one of the Haloze area's most notable boutique wineries, producing a completely luscious sauvignon as well as a richly bodied *šipon*. Its wine shop, inside the Romanesque House (p419) is a suitably atmospheric place to get stuck into some tasting. Phone beforehand to make sure the shop is open.

Ptuj Wine Cellar   WINE

(Ptujska Klet; ☑ 02-787 98 27, 041 486 258; www.pullus.si; Vinarski trg 1; tours €7-12; ☉ by appointment 9am-noon & 1-5pm Mon-Fri, to noon Sat) One of the oldest cellars in Slovenia, this is the place to go if you want to learn about local wine, especially Haloze sauvignon, *šipon* or *laški rizling* (Laški riesling). Book tours in advance. It also holds Slovenia's oldest vintage: Zlata Trta, the 'Golden Vine' sweet wine dating from 1917. You can sample local wines at the attached **Pullus Vinoteka** (☑ 02-787 98 10; Vinarski trg 1; ☉ 9am-5pm Mon-Fri, to 1pm Sat).

Terme Ptuj
THERMAL BATHS

(www.sava-hotels-resorts.com; Pot v Toplice 9; adult/child Mon-Fri €15/9.90, Sat & Sun €16/10.50; ⊙ indoor complex 8am-10pm Mon-Fri, from 7am Sat & Sun, outdoor complex 9am-8pm May-Sep) Kids need to cool off after trudging the cobblestones? Bring them here. The outdoor complex is a family-fun set-up with a range of water slides, a wave pool and a slow-current 'river' for those who just want to relax on an inner tube. Outside of summer, the indoor complex has seven pools with one water slide.

🛏 Sleeping

Ptuj has some of the most interesting places to stay in Eastern Slovenia, much of them slap bang in the historic central city area. The TIC can arrange private rooms (per person €20 to €25) both in the centre and on the south side of the Drava near Terme Ptuj.

Panorama Guesthouse
GUESTHOUSE €

(☑02-787 75 70; www.panorama-krapsa.si; Maistrova ulica 19; s €30-35, d €45-50, studio €60; 🛜)
With a countryside setting, yet still only a 10-minute walk into the centre, this rambling guesthouse has bright, homey rooms, all with fridges, satellite TVs and kettles. The mammoth garden, with chickens and an area set up with playground equipment, makes this a good choice for those travelling with little ones. Bonus points for the beautiful, friendly dog.

★ DomKulture MuziKafe
BOUTIQUE HOTEL €€

(☑02-787 88 60; www.muzikafe.si; Vrazov trg 1; s €42-67, d €57-81, f €115, studio €90; 🛜) This quirky cracker of a place is tucked away off Jadranska ulica. Each room is idiosyncratically decorated with lashings of retro chic by the hotel's designer owners; we especially love rooms 1 and 7. There's a small kitchen for guest use, plus Ptuj's best cafe downstairs with a terrace and vaulted brick cellar that hosts musical and artistic events.

Hotel Mitra
BOUTIQUE HOTEL €€€

(☑051 603 069, 02-787 74 55; www.hotel-mitra.si; Prešernova ulica 6; s €62-69, d €106; 🅿🌀🛜) With Turkish carpets on the wooden floors and walls hung with specially commissioned paintings plus a wellness centre off a tranquil internal courtyard, the Mitra is one of provincial Slovenia's more interesting small hotels. The 25 good-sized rooms each come with their own name and theme; rooms on the top floor have mansard ceilings.

🍴 Eating & Drinking

Teta Frida
CAFE €

(☑02-771 02 35; Mestni trg 2; cakes €3.10-4.40; ⊙7am-10pm Mon-Thu, to midnight Fri, 8am-midnight Sat, 10am-10pm Sun; 🛜) Resign yourself to a trip to the dentist when you get home. Based in the 18th-century Corner House, Teta Frida's chocolate torte and kremšnita (millefeuille-style custard pastry) with fruity twists are worth it. There's a good amount of dairy and gluten-free cake options as well.

★ Gostilna Grabar
EUROPEAN €€

(☑02-778 21 40; Rabelčja vas 15; mains €14-24; ⊙10am-10pm Mon-Sat, to 7pm Sun) This unassuming restaurant in the suburbs whips up the most creative modern European cooking in the area. The menu changes daily, based on what's in season and what they've pulled fresh from the garden. Expect seriously good eating dressed up with a dash of foamscrumbs-purees frippery, but never just for the sake of style; it's all about flavour here.

Gostilna Ribič
SLOVENIAN €€

(☑02-749 06 35; Dravska ulica 9; mains €12-30; ⊙10am-11pm Sun-Thu, to midnight Fri & Sat; 🛜🍴) Ptuj's fanciest restaurant is in a prime position, with a shady terrace facing the river. The speciality here is fish – particularly trout and pike-perch – and local chicken dishes, but it deserves serious kudos for the small but way more inventive than most vegetarian menus (the black risotto with tofu is divine) and the kids' menu. Service is exceptional.

Legend Pub
PUB

(☑02-749 32 50; Murkova ulica 6; ⊙7am-11pm Mon-Thu, to 1.30am Fri & Sat, 8am-11.30pm Sun) Great for a sundowner, this pub attracts a youngish crowd and is one of Ptuj's most popular hang-outs after dark. As well as all the usual offerings, there's a small menu of global craft beers.

ℹ Information

Tourist Information Centre Ptuj (☑02-779 60 11; www.ptuj.info; Slovenski trg 5; ⊙9am-8pm May–mid-Oct, to 6pm mid-Oct–Apr) Housed in the 16th-century **Ljutomer House** and with plenty of maps and brochures. Check out the side room with a video of the **Kurentovanje festival** (www.kurentovanje.net; ⊙Feb).

ℹ Getting There & Away

BUS

Ptuj's **bus station** (Osojnikova cesta) has decent connections to nearby towns on weekdays.

LOGARSKA DOLINA

Squeezed between craggy snow-capped peaks, this narrow glacial valley (7.5km long and no more than 500m wide) is the archetype vision of Slovenia's Alpine countryside. Hikers, bikers and fresh-air fiends flock here through the warmer months to soak up the lush green meadows, thick forest-clad hills and majestic mountain panoramas.

This 'pearl of the alpine region' was declared the Logarska Dolina Country Park in 1987 and its mere 24 sq km are scattered with caves, springs, peaks, rock towers and waterfalls to explore as well as endemic flora (golden slipper orchids) and rare fauna (mountain eagles, peregrine falcons) to spot. It's one of the most magically pretty corners of the country. Bedding down here – such as at the town's **Lenar Farmhouse** (☑ 03-838 90 06, 041 851 829; www.lenar.si; Logarska Dolina 11; d/tr/q €80/114/127, apt €80-120, hayloft per person €12; P ⓢ) – is one of the great joys of any Slovenia journey.

Maribor (€3.60, one hour) One or two per hour weekdays, five to six services daily on weekends.

TRAIN

Ptuj train station is on Osojnikova cesta, 1km east of the centre.

Ljubljana (€10 to €14.80, 1¾ to 2½ hours) Two to four direct services daily. Several other trains require a transfer at Zidani Most or Pragersko.

Maribor (€3.45 to €5.25, 50 minutes) Nine direct trains daily on weekdays and five daily on weekends. More services with a change in Pragersko.

SOUTHEASTERN SLOVENIA

Slovenia's southeast doesn't announce itself as loudly as other parts of the country, preferring subtle charms over big-ticket attractions. This is a region where life slows down considerably – all the better to enjoy meandering rivers and rolling hills covered with forest, orchards and grapevines. Here, villages cluster around church spires, and distinctive *toplarji* (double-linked hayracks) shelter neat woodpiles. Low-key tourist attractions come in the shape of grand monasteries, restored castles, local wines and health spas.

Dolenjske Toplice

☑ 07 / POP 810 / ELEV 176M

Within striking distance of Novo Mesto, this small thermal resort is one of Slovenia's oldest spa towns. The pools are its main attraction, and while a large proportion of Dolenjske Toplice's visitors are here for medical purposes, the very swish Hotel Balnea (p422) and connected wellness centre are geared towards pampering and have brought spa-break tourism to town.

Located in the karst valley of the Sušica (a tributary of the Krka River) and surrounded by the wooded slopes of **Kočevski Rog**, it's also an excellent place in which to hike and cycle if you can pull yourself away from massages, sweat baths and thermal water soaks.

🏃 Activities

Balnea Wellness Centre THERMAL BATHS
(☑ 07-391 97 50; www.terme-krka.com; ZdravLiški trg; pools day pass adult/child/family Mon-Thu €10/8/32, Fri-Sun €14/12/42; ☺ lagoon 9am-9pm Sun-Thu, to 11pm Fri & Sat) The main reason people come to Dolenjske Toplice is this attractive, well-run spa centre. The **Lagoon** has outdoor (May to September) and indoor (year-round) pools with thermal water between 27°C and 32°C; the **Oasis** section hosts saunas, a Japanese sweat bath and a chill-out terrace; and the swish **Treatment** section is where you go for pampering facials and rejuvenating massages.

🛏 Sleeping & Eating

Hotel Oštarija GUESTHOUSE €€
(☑ 031 413 588; www.ostarija.si; Sokolski trg 2; s/d €40/60, apt d/q €65/72; P ❄ ⓢ) Don't fancy staying at one of the big spa-hotels? Then this super-friendly guesthouse is by far the top choice, with the bonus of the town's best restaurant (p422) downstairs. Spotless rooms have a bright, contemporary feel and are comfortably kitted out. When we last pulled through town, management was adding a dash of character by giving each room individual herbal themes.

WORTH A TRIP

THE JERUZALEM-LJUTOMER WINE ROAD

The Jeruzalem-Ljutomer Wine Road begins at Ormož, 23km east of Ptuj, and continues for 18km north to Ljutomer, the main seat in the area, via the delightful hilltop village of Jeruzalem. The rural vistas of rolling hills, speckled with wineries predominantly producing white wines, make for a scenic cycle tour or easygoing country drive.

Jeruzalem Ormož Winery (☑ 02-741 57 25; www.visitjeruzalem.com; Kolodvorska 11, Ormož; tasting tour per person €15; ⊙ by appointment 8am-4pm Mon-Fri, to noon Sat) Wine shop and cellar of the Puklavec family, which has been producing wine since the 1930s. Wines include a peppery pinot grigio and the interestingly spicy sweet *traminec*. Pre-book tours two days in advance.

Malek Vineyard Cottage (Zidanica Malek; www.visitjeruzalem.com; Svetinje 22; tasting tour per person 3/4/5 wines €6/7/8; ⊙ 11am-6pm May-early Nov) Tasting room and wine shop run by the family behind the Jeruzalem Ormož Winery. Tastings don't require pre-booking, so just pull in along the road between Svetinje and Jeruzalem to sample some local produce.

Vino Kupljen (☑ 02-719 41 28; www.vino-kupljen.com; Svetinje 21; tastings 5/10 wines €10/25, min 4 people; ⊙ 10am-4pm) This boutique winery produces the excellent Stars of Stiria label, including an intense pinot noir and a full-bodied sauvignon blanc. The 10-wine tasting includes a cellar tour.

★ **Hotel Balnea**　　　　SPA HOTEL €€€
(☑ 07-391 94 00; www.terme-krka.com; Zdraviliški trg 11; r s/d €126/182, ste s/d €141/232; P ✳
🛰 ❄) Few newly built hotels in Slovenia can compare with this sleek 63-room four-star in terms of design and facilities. Heavy on timber, natural materials and nature-inspired colours, the spacious contemporary rooms (nearly all with big balconies complete with sun loungers) are just the ticket for a relaxing getaway. Bag a back-facing room for views over the park.

★ **Oštarija**　　　　SLOVENIAN €€
(☑ 051 262 990; www.ostarija.si; Sokolski trg 2; mains €9-25; ⊙ noon-11pm Tue-Sat, to 4pm Sun; ✳ 🛰) There are few eating options in town, so it's a joy to find this place, a foodie's treat with a menu based around seasonal local produce. Drop in for its three-course lunches (Monday to Friday €10, Saturday €12, Sunday €14) and marvel at the bargain of a five-course dinner for €27 (eight courses for €38).

ℹ Information

Tourist Information Centre Dolenjske Toplice (TIC; ☑ 07-384 51 88; www.dolenjske-toplice.si; Sokolski trg 4; ⊙ 9am-noon & 2-6pm Mon-Fri, 10am-noon & 2-4pm Sat & Sun) Well-informed and friendly office with plenty of maps and information on sights and activities in the area.

ℹ Getting There & Away

The main bus stop is right in the centre of town.
Ljubljana (€7.20, 1½ hours, 73km) Two daily.

UNDERSTAND SLOVENIA

History

Early Years

Slovenes can make a credible claim to having invented democracy. By the early 7th century, their Slavic ancestors had founded the Duchy of Carantania (Karantanija), based at Krn Castle (now Karnburg in Austria). Ruling dukes were elected by enobled commoners and invested before ordinary citizens.

This unique model was noted by the 16th-century French political philosopher Jean Bodin, whose work was a reference for Thomas Jefferson when he wrote the American Declaration of Independence in 1776.

Carantania (later Carinthia) was fought over by the Franks and Magyars from the 8th to 10th centuries, and later divided up among Austro-Germanic nobles and bishops.

The Habsburgs & Napoleon

Between the late 13th and early 16th centuries, almost all the lands inhabited by Slovenes, with the exception of the Venetian-controlled coastal towns, came under the domination of the Habsburgs, ruled from Vienna.

Austrian rule continued until 1918, apart from a brief interlude between 1809 and 1813 when Napoleon created six so-called Illyrian Provinces from Slovenian and Croatian regions and made Ljubljana the capital.

Napoleon proved a popular conqueror as his relatively liberal regime de-Germanised the education system. Slovene was taught in schools for the first time, leading to an awakening of national consciousness. In tribute, Ljubljana still has a French Revolution Sq (Trg Francoske Revolucije) with a column bearing a likeness of the French emperor.

World Wars I & II

Fighting during WWI was particularly savage along the Soča Valley – the Isonzo Front – which was occupied by Italy then retaken by German-led Austro-Hungarian forces. The war ended with the collapse of Austria-Hungary, which handed western Slovenia to Italy as part of postwar reparations.

Northern Carinthia, including the towns of Beljak and Celovec (now Villach and Klagenfurt), voted to stay with Austria in a 1920 plebiscite. What remained of Slovenia joined fellow south (jug) Slavs in forming the Kingdom of Serbs, Croats and Slovenes, later Yugoslavia.

Nazi occupation in WWII was for the most part resisted by Slovenian Partisans, though after Italy capitulated in 1943 the anti-partisan Slovenian Domobranci (Home Guards) were active in the west. To prevent their nemeses, the communists, from taking political control in liberated areas, the Domobranci threw their support behind the Germans.

The war ended with Slovenia regaining Italian-held areas from Piran to Bovec, but losing Trst (Trieste) and part of Gorica (Gorizia).

Tito's Yugoslavia

In Tito's Yugoslavia in the 1960s and '70s, Slovenia, with only 8% of the national population, was the economic powerhouse, creating up to 20% of the national GDP.

But by the 1980s the federation had become increasingly Serb-dominated, and Slovenes feared they would lose their political autonomy. In free elections, Slovenes voted overwhelmingly to break away from Yugoslavia and did so on 25 June 1991. A 10-day war that left 66 people dead followed; Yugoslavia swiftly signed a truce in order to concentrate on regaining control of coastal Croatia.

From Independence to Today

Shortly after the withdrawal of the federal army from Slovenian soil on 25 October 1991, Slovenia got a new constitution that provided for a bicameral parliamentary system of government.

The head of state, the president, is elected directly for a maximum of two five-year terms. Milan Kučan held that role from independence until 2002, when the late Janez Drnovšek (1950–2008), a former prime minister, was elected. Diplomat Danilo Türk has been president since 2007, having been re-elected in 2012.

Executive power is vested in the prime minister and their cabinet. The current premier is Janez Janša, who was returned to power in early 2012 after 3½ years in opposition.

Slovenia was admitted to the UN in 1992 as the 176th member-state. In May 2004, Slovenia entered the EU as a full member and less than three years later adopted the euro, replacing the tolar as the national currency.

People

The population of Slovenia is largely homogeneous. Just over 83% are ethnic Slovenes, with the remainder Serbs, Croats, Bosnians, Albanians and Roma; there are also small enclaves of Italians and Hungarians, who have special deputies looking after their interests in parliament.

Slovenes are ethnically Slavic, typically hardworking, multilingual and extrovert. Around 60% of Slovenes identify themselves as Catholics.

Arts

Slovenia's most cherished writer is the Romantic poet France Prešeren (1800–49). His patriotic yet humanistic verse was a driving force in raising Slovene national consciousness. Fittingly, a stanza of his poem 'Zdravljica' (A Toast) forms the lyrics of the national anthem.

Many of Ljubljana's most characteristic architectural features, including its recurring pyramid motif, were added by celebrated Slovenian architect Jože Plečnik (1872–1957), whose work fused classical building principles and folk-art traditions.

Postmodernist painting and sculpture were more or less dominated from the 1980s by the multimedia group NeueSlowenische Kunst (NSK) and the artists' cooperative Irwin. It also spawned the internationally known industrial-music group Laibach, whose leader, Tomaž Hostnik, died tragically in 1983 when he hanged himself from a *kozolec*, the traditional (and iconic) hayrack found only in Slovenia.

Slovenia's vibrant music scene embraces rave, techno, jazz, punk, thrash-metal and chanson (torch songs from the likes of Vita Mavrič); the most popular local rock group is Siddharta, formed in 1995 and still going strong. There's also been a folk-music revival: keep an ear out for Katice and Katalena, who play traditional Slovenian music with a modern twist, and the vocalist Brina.

Environment

Slovenia is amazingly green; indeed, 58% of its total surface area is covered in forest and it's growing. Slovenia is home to almost 3200 plant species – some 70 of which are indigenous.

Triglav National Park is particularly rich in native flowering plants. Among the more peculiar endemic fauna in Slovenia is a blind salamander called *Proteus anguinus* that lives deep in Karst caves, can survive for years without eating and has been called a 'living fossil'.

Food & Drink

Slovenia boasts an incredibly diverse cuisine. Though it's not always possible to find regional favourites such as *žlikrofi* (pasta stuffed with cheese, bacon and chives) and *jota* (hearty bean soup), and rich desserts like *gibanica* (a layer cake stuffed with nuts, cheese and apple), on restaurant menus, they're worth ordering when you do see them.

Dishes like *brodet* (fish soup) from the coast, *ajdovi žganci z ocvirki* (buckwheat 'porridge' with pork crackling) and salad greens doused in *bučno olje* (pumpkinseed oil) are generally eaten at home.

A *gostilna* or *gostišče* (inn) or *restavracija* (restaurant) more frequently serves *rižota* (risotto), *klobasa* (sausage), *zrezek* (cutlet/steak), *golaž* (goulash) and *paprikaš* (piquant chicken or beef 'stew'). *Riba* (fish) is excellent and usually priced by the *dag* (100g). Common in Slovenia are such Balkan favourites as *čevapčiči* (spicy meatballs) and *pljeskavica* (spicy meat patties), often served with *kajmak* (a type of clotted cream).

You can snack cheaply on *burek* (€2), flaky pastry stuffed with meat, cheese or apple. Alternatives include *štruklji* (cottage-cheese dumplings) and *palačinke* (thin sweet pancakes).

Wine, Beer & Brandy

Distinctively Slovenian wines include peppery red *teran* (made from Refošk grapes in the Karst Region), *cviček* (a dry light red – almost rosé – wine from eastern Slovenia) and m*alvazija* (a straw-colour white from the coast that is light and dry). Slovenes are justly proud of their top vintages, but cheaper bar-standard *odprto vino* (open wine) sold by the decilitre (100mL) is just so-so.

Pivo (beer), whether *svetlo* (lager) or *temno* (porter), is best on *točeno* (draught) but always available in cans and bottles too.

There are dozens of kinds of *žganje* (fruit brandy) available, including *češnjevec* (made with cherries), *sadjevec* (mixed fruit), *brinjevec* (juniper), *hruška* (pears, also called *viljamovka*) and *slivovka* (plums).

SURVIVAL GUIDE

❶ Directory A–Z

ACCESSIBLE TRAVEL

Slovenia is reasonably accessible for travellers with disabilities. Facilities include public telephones with amplifiers, pedestrian crossings with beepers, Braille on maps at bus stops, sloped pavements and ramps in government buildings, and reserved spaces in many car parks. Helpful organisations:

Paraplegics Association of Slovenia (Zveza Paraplegikov Republike Slovenije; ☑ 01-432 71 38; www.zveza-paraplegikov.si/eng; Štihova ulica 14, Ljubljana; ⊙7am-3pm Mon-Fri) Produces a guide for members in Slovene only (although the English-language website is fairly complete).

Slovenian Association of Disabled Students (Društvo Študentov Invalidov Slovenije; ☑ 01-565 33 51; www.dsis-drustvo.si; Kardeljeva ploščad 5, Ljubljana; ⊙9am-4pm Mon-Fri) Active group for those with special needs.

ACCOMMODATION

Slovenia has all manner of places to bed down. You'll need to book well in advance if you're travelling during peak season (July and August on the coast and at Bled or Bohinj; spring and autumn in Ljubljana). At other times, you'll have little trouble finding accommodation to fit your budget.

Hotels Runs the gamut from family-run operations to five-star boutiques.

Hostels Both indie hostels and HI-affiliated affairs are plentiful.

Pensions & Guesthouses Often family-owned and good value.

Private Rooms Single rooms or fully furnished flats. Locate via tourist information centres.

Mountain Huts Simple beds, with or without facilities, near hiking trails.

LEGAL MATTERS

Persons violating the laws of Slovenia may be expelled, arrested or imprisoned. Penalties for possession, use or trafficking of illegal drugs in Slovenia are strict, and convicted offenders can expect heavy fines and even jail terms. The permitted blood-alcohol level for motorists is 0.05%, and it is strictly enforced, especially on motorways. Fines start at €300.

Alcohol may not be purchased from a shop, off-licence or bar for consumption off the premises between 9pm and 7am.

LGBTIQ+ TRAVELLERS

Slovenia has a national gay-rights law in place that bans discrimination on the basis of sexual preference in employment and other areas. In recent years, a highly visible campaign against homophobia has been put in place across the country, and same-sex marriage is allowed.

Several organisations are active in promoting gay rights and fostering cultural and social interaction. Foremost among these are ŠKUC (Študentski Kulturni Center, Student Cultural Centre; www.skuc.org) and **Legebitra** (Map p378; ✆ 01-430 51 44; https://legebitra.si; Trubarjeva cesta 76a, Ljubljana; ☉ noon-4pm Mon, to 6pm Tue & Fri, to 9pm Wed & Thu).

MONEY

ATMs are widely available or you can exchange money at banks. Credit and debit cards are accepted by most businesses throughout the country.

OPENING HOURS

Opening hours can vary throughout the year. We've provided high-season opening hours.
Banks 8.30am to 12.30pm and 2pm to 5pm Monday to Friday
Bars 11am to midnight Sunday to Thursday, to 1am or 2am Friday and Saturday
Restaurants 11am to 10pm
Shops 8am to 7pm Monday to Friday, to 1pm Saturday

PUBLIC HOLIDAYS

Slovenia celebrates 14 *prazniki* (holidays) each year. If any of them fall on a Sunday, the Monday becomes the holiday.
New Year's 1 and 2 January
Prešeren Day (Slovenian Culture Day) 8 February
Easter & Easter Monday March/April
Insurrection Day 27 April
Labour Day holidays 1 and 2 May
National Day 25 June
Assumption Day 15 August
Reformation Day 31 October
All Saints' Day 1 November
Christmas Day 25 December
Independence Day 26 December

TELEPHONE

Slovenia's country code is 386. Slovenia has six area codes (01 to 05 and 07). Ljubljana's area code is 01.

➤ To call a landline within Slovenia, include the area code if the number you are calling is outside the area code.

➤ To call abroad from Slovenia, dial 00 followed by the country and area codes, and then the number.

➤ To call Slovenia from abroad, dial the international access code, 386 (the country code for Slovenia), the area code (minus the initial zero) and the number.

TOURIST INFORMATION

The **Slovenian Tourist Board** (www.slovenia. info), based in Ljubljana, is the umbrella organisation for tourist promotion in Slovenia, and produces a number of excellent brochures and booklets in English. The organisation oversees dozens of tourist information centres (TICs) across the country.

ⓘ Getting There & Away

Most travellers arrive in Slovenia by air, or by rail and road connections from neighbouring countries. Flights, cars and tours can be booked online at lonelyplanet.com/bookings.

AIR

Ljubljana's **Jože Pučnik Airport** (Aerodrom Ljubljana; ✆ 04-206 19 81; www.lju-airport.si; Zgornji Brnik 130a, Brnik), 27km north of the capital, is the only air gateway for travelling to and from Slovenia. The arrivals hall has a branch of the **Slovenia Tourist Information Centre** (STIC; www.visitljubljana.si; Jože Pučnik Airport; ☉ 8am-7pm Mon-Fri, 9am-5pm Sat & Sun Oct-May, 8am-9pm Jun-Sep) and a bank of ATMs (located just outside the terminal).

Adria Airways (✆ flight info 04-259 45 82, reservations 01-369 10 10; www.adria.si) The Slovenian carrier serves more than 30 European destinations on regularly scheduled flights; there are useful connections to other former Yugoslav capitals.

Budget carriers include **EasyJet** (www.easyjet. com) and **Wizz Air** (✆ Slovenia call centre 090 100 206; www.wizzair.com).

LAND

Slovenia is well connected by road and rail with its four neighbours – Italy, Austria, Hungary and Croatia. Bus and train timetables sometimes use Slovenian names for foreign cities.

Bus

Several long-haul coach companies operate in Slovenia, connecting the country to destinations around Europe. This service is often cheaper and faster than trains. Buses are also useful for reaching areas where train connections from Slovenia are deficient, including to points in Italy and BiH.

Most international services arrive and depart from Ljubljana's main bus station (p388). Maribor is an important departure point for trips north to Vienna and south to Zagreb and Belgrade. Slovenia's coastal cities, Piran, Koper and Izola, from June to September, have regular direct bus connections to points on the Croatian coast and to Trieste, Italy.

Car & Motorcycle

Good roads and highways connect Slovenia with all four of its neighbours. Even though borders are open with Italy, Austria and Hungary, motorists must still carry with them the vehicle's registration papers and liability insurance and a valid driver's licence. Expect to show these documents at highway crossings with Croatia.

From the moment your vehicle enters Slovenia, you're obligated to display a road-toll sticker (*vinjeta*). A sticker should already be in place on rental cars, but if it's not, try to buy a sticker at a petrol station near the border before you enter Slovenia or at the first big service plaza you see on the highway once you're in Slovenia.

Stickers cost €15/30/110 for a week/month/year for cars and €7.50/30/55 for motorbikes, and are available at petrol stations, post offices and TICs. Failure to display a sticker risks a fine of up to €300.

Train

The **Slovenian Railways** (Slovenske Železnice, SŽ; ☑ info 1999; www.slo-zeleznice.si) network links up with the European railway network via Austria (Villach, Salzburg, Graz, Vienna), Italy (Trieste), Germany (Munich, Frankfurt), Czech Republic (Prague), Croatia (Zagreb, Rijeka), Hungary (Budapest), Switzerland (Zürich) and Serbia (Belgrade). The Slovenian Railways website has full information in English on current international connections.

SEA

During summer it's possible to travel by sea between Piran and the Italian ports of Venice and Trieste. Purchase tickets and obtain information through the Tourist Information Centre (p416).

🟢 Getting Around

BICYCLE

➡ Cycling is a popular way to get around.

➡ Bikes can be transported for €3.50 in the baggage compartments of IC and regional trains. Larger buses can also carry bikes as luggage.

➡ Cycling is permitted on all roads except motorways. Larger towns and cities have dedicated bicycle lanes and traffic lights.

➡ Bicycle-rental shops are generally concentrated in the more popular tourist areas, such as Ljubljana, Bled, Bovec and Piran, though a few cycle shops and repair places hire them out as well. Expect to pay from €3/17 per hour/day; you will usually be asked to pay a cash deposit or show some ID as security.

BUS

➡ The Slovenian bus network is extensive and coaches are modern and comfortable. You can reach every major city and town, and many smaller places, by bus.

➡ A range of companies serve the country, but prices tend to be uniform: around €4/6/10/17 for 25/50/100/200km of travel.

➡ Buy your ticket from ticket windows at the bus station (*avtobusna postaja*) or pay the driver as you board. There are normally enough seats. The exception is for Friday and weekend travel, where it's best to book your seat (€1.50) a day in advance. Bus services are limited on Sundays and holidays.

CAR & MOTORCYCLE

Roads in Slovenia are good. Tolls are not paid separately on motorways. Instead, cars must display a *vinjeta* (road-toll sticker) on the windscreen. The sticker costs €15/30/110 for a week/month/year for cars and €7.50/30/55 for motorbikes and is available at petrol stations, post offices and tourist information centres. Failure to display a sticker risks a fine of up to €300.

Rentals from international firms such as Avis, Budget, Europcar and Hertz are broadly similar; expect to pay from €40/200 per day/week, including unlimited mileage, insurance and taxes. Some smaller agencies have more competitive rates; booking on the internet is usually cheaper.

For emergency roadside assistance, call 1987 anywhere in Slovenia.

TRAIN

Domestic trains are operated by Slovenian Railways. The network is extensive and connects many major cities and towns. Trains tend to offer more space and are more comfortable than buses, and can occasionally be cheaper. Trains are useful mainly for covering long distances. The railways website has a timetable and extensive information in English.

➡ Purchase tickets at the train station (*železniška postaja*) or buy them from the conductor on the train (costs an extra €2.50).

➡ An 'R' next to the train number on the timetable means seat reservations are available. If the 'R' is boxed, seat reservations are obligatory.

Understand
the Western
Balkans

The Western Balkans Today

The Balkans have long been a byword for political turbulence, and in that respect, nothing much has changed. Armed conflict may have ceased but relations between states – and between differing groups within states – remain exceedingly complicated. Tourism is booming, however, and visitors can easily sail through this fascinating and strikingly beautiful region, blissfully unaware of the deep divisions that are bubbling away and, in some cases, threatening to boil over.

Best in Print

The Bridge on the Drina (Ivo Andrić; 1945) The Nobel Prize winner's key work; a multigenerational saga of life in Ottoman-ruled Bosnia.

Chronicle in Stone (Ismail Kadare; 1971) Albania's pre-eminent writer lyrically describes his hometown, Gjirokastra.

Death and the Dervish (Meša Selimović; 1966) Yugoslav-era classic detailing with the psychological struggles of a Muslim cleric dealing with the harsh Ottoman regime.

The Houses of Belgrade (Borislav Pekić; 1970) Unusual tale of a reclusive landlord stepping out of his postwar isolation.

The Encyclopedia of the Dead (Danilo Kiš; 1983) A collection of nine short stories by the internationally acclaimed Yugoslav author.

Best on Film

No Man's Land (2001) Oscar winner focusing on a Bosnian Serb and Bosniak sharing a trench.

Battle of Neretva (1969) Epic war movie celebrating a major WWII Partisan victory.

Before the Rain (1994) Beautifully shot Macedonian masterpiece.

Neighbourly Relations

The rise of nationalism throughout Europe has been felt in the Western Balkans too, with various politicians courting support from homegrown nationalists at the expense of regional stability.

Croatia currently has minor territorial disputes with four of its five neighbours, and also stands accused of meddling in Bosnia's affairs after protesting the 2018 election of a moderate to the Croatian position in Bosnia's tripartite presidency (Croatia argues that he only won the position due to the votes of Bosniaks, leaving Bosnia's Croats unrepresented). The Bosnian election highlighted the deep ethnic divisions in the country, which remains divided into two entities along the former wartime frontline (frozen at the time of the 1995 Dayton Agreement). The new Bosnian Serb member of the presidency is a nationalist who has openly called for independence for the Republika Srpska, Bosnia's Serb-dominated entity.

Relations between Serbia and Montenegro, once the staunchest of allies, have also soured. Montenegro has accused Serbia of interfering in its affairs, and perhaps even assisting an attempted coup during its 2016 elections. Serbia accuses Montenegro of discriminating against its Serbian citizens and undermining the Serbian Orthodox Church (Montenegro is seeking official recognition for its own Montenegrin Orthodox Church).

However, the most seemingly intractable regional dispute remains that between Serbia and Kosovo. Serbia regards Kosovo as an intrinsic part of Serbia (many Serbs consider it a kind of spiritual heartland), and refuses to recognise its 2008 declaration of independence. Kosovo retaliated in 2018 by imposing 100% tariffs on Serbian and Bosnian goods (Bosnia is the only other Western Balkans nation not to recognise Kosovo).

On a positive note, North Macedonia and Greece have resolved their long-standing conflict over the former country's name. The unwieldy 'Former Yugoslav Republic of Macedonia', which Greece had previously insisted upon in a bid to differentiate the country from its own region of Macedonia, was consigned to history books in February 2019.

The European Union Carrot

The prospect of membership of the EU has been an important factor in promoting peace between the Western Balkans nations and encouraging them to deal with issues of corruption, organised crime and war crimes. Key figures in the 1990s wars were handed over to the UN's International Criminal Tribunal for the former Yugoslavia (ICTY). The ICTY was dissolved at the end of 2017, but war criminals continue to be tried in individual jurisdictions. Of the 161 individuals indicted by the ICTY, 90 were convicted and sentenced, including notorious figures such as Radovan Karadžić and Ratko Mladić.

Slovenia was accepted into the EU in 2004 and Croatia joined in 2013. Slovenia has adopted the euro and joined the border-free Schengen Area; Croatia has yet to do so. However, with the EU grappling with Brexit and the appetite for expansion waning, the membership progress for the remaining 'Western Balkans Six' has stalled. Montenegro is widely considered to be the most advanced of the aspirants, with membership tipped for 2025. However, it still has a long way to go in terms of dealing with corruption, media freedom and organised crime.

There are fears that, with the prospect of EU membership so distant, there's less incentive to keep a lid on nationalism and to heal the wounds of the past. In some instances, things have even gone backwards; in 2018 the Republika Srpska's parliament rescinded their own previous acceptance of the Srebrenica massacre, for instance.

Balancing Tourism

In 2017, 18.5 million travellers visited Croatia; by head of population, that puts it among the most overtouristed countries in the world. The places most feeling the strain of overtourism include the Unesco World Heritage Sites of Dubrovnik and Kotor, both compact walled towns groaning under the weight of visitors, particularly the daily influx of cruise-ship passengers. Montenegro continues to develop its tiny coast at an extraordinary rate and has even mooted resorts on environmentally sensitive sites such as Lake Skadar National Park.

However, other parts of the region have plenty of room for more visitors, and economies in desperate need of the boost. Serbia will be hoping that Novi Sad's role as European Capital of Culture in 2021, the first non-EU city to be given that title, will attract attention to its Vojvodina province.

AREA: **284,630 SQ KM**

POPULATION: **24.5 MILLION**

TIME: **CENTRAL EUROPEAN TIME (GMT PLUS ONE HOUR)**

if Western Balkans were 100 people

12 would live in Albania
15 would live in Bosnia & Hercegovina
17 would live in Croatia
8 would live in Kosovo
3 would live in Montenegro
9 would live in North Macedonia
28 would live in Serbia
8 would live in Slovenia

age range
(millions)

7 — 0–24 years
14 — 25–64 years
4 — 65+ years

population per sq km

Western Balkans | Europe | USA

≈ 35 people

History

It's been said that the Balkans have produced more history than they can consume. Indeed, the movement of invaders, settlers and traders back and forth across the region over the centuries has created an intricate and complicated patchwork of cultures, societies, religions, ethnic identifications and conflicts. The region hasn't been controlled by one government since the Roman Empire, and it continues to wrestle with the east–west divide delineated when that superpower split in the 4th century.

Tribes, Colonies & Empires

By around 1000 BC, the Illyrians took centre stage in the area now comprised of Slovenia, Croatia, Serbia, Kosovo, Montenegro and northern and central Albania. It's thought that the modern Albanian language, a linguistic oddity unrelated to any other language, is derived from ancient Illyrian. The often-warring tribes erected hill forts and created distinctive jewellery made from amber and bronze. In time they established a loose federation. The Illyrians had to contend with the Greeks, who established trading colonies on the coast at modern-day Durrës and Butrint in the 7th century BC; Apollonia, Cavtat and Korčula in the 6th century BC; and Budva, Vis and Hvar in the 4th century BC.

Also in the 4th century BC, Celtic tribes began pushing southward, establishing the Noric kingdom, the first 'state' on Slovenian soil. Meanwhile, in ancient Macedonia, the powerful king Philip II (r 359–336 BC) dominated the Greek city-states. Philip's son, Alexander the Great, spread Macedonian might to India. After his death (323 BC), the empire dissolved amid infighting.

In the 3rd century BC, Queen Teuta of the Illyrian Ardiaei tribe committed a fatal tactical error in attacking the Greek colonies. The put-upon Greeks asked the Romans for military support. The Romans pushed their way into the region and by 168 BC they defeated Gentius, the last Illyrian king, and also conquered Macedonia.

The Western Balkans subsequently sat near the heart of the Roman Empire for over 500 years until AD 395, when the unwieldy Empire was split into an eastern, Greek-influenced half ruled from Byzantium (later

Stone implements have been found in Slovenia dating back to 250,000 BC. Neanderthals were established in Slavonia 30,000 years ago and modern humans were living on the Croatian islands at the end of the last ice age, 18,000 years ago. Farming started in the region around 6000 BC.

TIMELINE	1000 BC	7th to 4th century BC	AD 272
	The Illyrian tribes (speaking a forerunner of the Albanian language) come to dominate what is now Slovenia, Croatia, Serbia, Kosovo, Montenegro and parts of Albania.	Greek colonies sprout along the Adriatic coast in present-day Croatia, Montenegro and Albania. The Illyrian tribes found kingdoms and establish themselves as maritime powers.	Roman Emperor Constantine the Great is born in what is today the city of Niš in southern Serbia; he converts to Christianity on his deathbed.

Constantinople, present-day İstanbul) and a western, Latin-influenced half ruled from Rome – the fault line ran right through the centre of the Western Balkans.

The Western Roman Empire was weakened by economic crises, plagues and invaders from the north and west. In the 6th century, the Eastern Roman (Byzantine) Emperor Justinian took control of the previously Rome-ruled parts of the Balkans, pushing out the Ostrogoths who had bowled through the region.

The Coming of the Slavs

In the wake of the collapse of the Western Roman Empire, various Slavic tribes headed south from their original territory north of the Carpathians. Around the same time, the Avars (a nomadic Central Asian people) rampaged brutally through the Balkans and progressed all the way to Constantinople itself, where the Byzantines duly crushed them. Controversy surrounds the role that the Slavs had in the defeat of the Avars. Some claim that the Byzantine Empire called on the Slavs to help in the fight, while others think that they merely filled the void left when the Avars disappeared. Whatever the case, the Slavs spread rapidly through the Balkans, reaching the Adriatic by the early 7th century.

Two closely related Slavic tribal groups eventually came to the fore in the Western Balkans: the Croats and the Serbs. The Croats settled in an area roughly equivalent to present-day Croatia and western Bosnia. Charlemagne's Franks gradually encroached from the west and in AD 800 they seized Dalmatia, baptising the previously pagan Croats en masse. In 925, Tomislav was crowned as the first Croatian king, ruling virtually all of modern Croatia as well as parts of Bosnia and the coast of Montenegro.

In the meantime, a group of Serbian tribes came together near Novi Pazar to found Raška. This principality was short-lived, being snuffed out by Bulgarian Tsar Simeon around 927, but not before Raška recognised the Byzantine emperor as sovereign. The 10th century was marked by wars between the Byzantines and the expansionist Bulgarian state, which had strongholds in today's North Macedonia. Byzantine Emperor Basil II defeated the Bulgarians in 1014 and retook Macedonia.

Another Serbian state, Duklja, sprang up on the site of the Roman town of Doclea (Podgorica) and swiftly expanded its territory to include Dubrovnik and what remained of Raška. By 1040 Duklja was confident enough to rebel against Byzantine control, expand its territory along the Dalmatian coast and establish a capital at Skadar (Shkodra in Albania). Around 1080 Duklja achieved its greatest extent, absorbing present-day Bosnia. Civil wars and various intrigues led to Duklja's downfall and power eventually shifted back to Raška. In the meantime, Croatia came

The word Adriatic (*Jadran* in South Slavic tongues) is thought to be linked to the ancient Etruscan town of Adria, near Venice, but may also be related to the Illyrian word for water.

While most of Dalmatia struggled under Venetian rule, Ragusa (now Dubrovnik) existed as a republic in its own right. A ruling class, abounding in business acumen and diplomatic skill, ensured that this minuscule city-state played a significant role in the region. Napoleon finally swallowed up the republic in 1808.

5th & 6th centuries	c 925	1054	1346–55
Slav tribes (farmers and herders originally from north of the Carpathian mountains) cross south of the Danube River following in the wake of the marauding Avars.	Tomislav, Duke of Croatia, unites his duchy with parts of Pannonia and is recognised by the papacy as the king of the first independent Croatian kingdom.	Christianity faces its first great schism, between the Catholic and Orthodox churches. Slovenes and Croats are on the western (Catholic) side of the divide, while Serbs and Macedonians are on the eastern (Orthodox).	The peak of Serbian Golden Age under Stefan Dušan, the most powerful of the kings from the Nemanjić dynasty, who expands Serbia into one of the largest kingdoms in Europe.

under attack from the Venetians in the south and the Hungarians in the north, who would eventually split the kingdom between them.

In 1190 Stefan Nemanja gained Raška's independence from Byzantium, also claiming present-day Kosovo and North Macedonia for his kingdom. The most powerful of the Serbian kings, Stefan Dušan, was crowned in 1331 (after doing away with his father); he established the Serbian Orthodox Patriarchate at Peć in western Kosovo, introduced a legal code and expanded the Serbian empire. Throughout this period Zeta (as Duklja was now called) remained distinct from Serbia.

The Ottoman Era

The Seljuk Turks swept out of Central Asia into the Byzantine heartland of Anatolia in the 11th century. Their successors, the Ottomans, established a base in Europe in 1354 and steadily increased their European territories over the next century. The Ottoman 'victory' (more of a draw, in fact) over the Serbs at Kosovo Polje in 1389 completed the separation of the southern Slavs; the Slovenes and most of the Croats remained beyond Turkish rule, while the Serbs, Albanians and Macedonians were now under it. The Turks had conquered almost the entire region by 1500. The core of Montenegro remained largely independent under a dynasty of prince-bishops from their mountain stronghold at Cetinje. Suleiman the Magnificent led the Ottoman charge, taking Belgrade in 1521 and pushing on as far as Vienna, which he besieged in 1529.

Over time, many communities (particularly in Bosnia, Albania and Kosovo) converted to Islam. Orthodox Serbs kept the dream of independence alive through romanticising the *hajduci* (bandits) who had taken to the hills to raid Turkish caravans, and through epic poems retelling the betrayals that led to the end of their empire.

Ottoman Decline & Austro-Hungarian Control

By now the Austrian Empire controlled the inland parts of Croatia and – with the fall of Venice in 1797 and the defeat of Napoleon in 1815 – it eventually took control of the coast as well.

The once all-conquering Ottoman Empire started lagging behind the other great European powers from the early 18th century. As Europe industrialised, the Ottomans' Balkan domains instead descended into corrupt agricultural fiefdoms, over which the empire had little direct control but from which it still demanded financial tribute.

After a series of revolts, an independent Serbian kingdom gradually emerged over the course of the 19th century, expanding from its early base around Belgrade. After a brutal Turkish response to Christian revolts

In 1180, Bosnia first emerged as an independent entity under former Byzantine governor Ban Kulin. Bosnia had a patchy golden age between 1180 and 1463, peaking in the late 1370s when Bosnia's King Tvrtko gained Hum (future Hercegovina) and controlled much of Dalmatia.

Beyond the existence of Muslim communities throughout the region, almost five centuries of Ottoman control left their mark, not least architecturally. Turkish tastes infiltrated regional cuisines, with *burek* (heavy pastry stuffed with meat or cheese) and Turkish-style coffee becoming Balkan staples, and various words were adopted into the local languages.

1389	1443–68	1520–66	1815
At the Battle of Kosovo Polje, much of the Serbian nobility is killed by the invading Ottoman Turks. In time, the Ottomans regroup and expand further into the Balkans.	Gjergj Kastrioti Skanderbeg defends Albania against the Ottoman Turks, winning all 25 battles he fought against them; they finally take control of the country in 1479, after Skanderbeg's death.	The Ottoman Empire reaches the height of its power under Suleiman the Magnificent, who takes Belgrade in 1521, Hungary in 1526 and besieges Vienna in 1529.	After the failure of the First Serbian Uprising against the Turks in 1804, Serbia wins de facto independence under Miloš Obrenović through the Second Serbian Uprising.

in Bosnia in 1875 and 1877, Serbia and Montenegro both declared war on Turkey and suddenly the revolts had snowballed into a Balkans-wide tangle of war that was widely known as the Great Eastern Crisis.

The crisis saw Turkey's European forces crushingly defeated, notably through a resurgent Russia and an expanded, newly independent Bulgaria. But the egos of Europe's other big powers had to be stroked. This meant that the eventual carve-up of Turkey's European lands was achieved not on the battlefield but with the 1878 Treaty of Berlin, drawn up with staggering disregard for ethno-linguistic realities. As a counterweight to Russian power in Bulgaria, the Austro-Hungarian Empire was persuaded to take military control of Bosnia in 1878.

The Rise of Yugoslavism & WWI

The bloody decline of Turkish power and the emergence of competing nationalisms gave rise to Yugoslavism – the idea of uniting the southern (*yugo*) Slavs under one flag. Croatian bishop Josip Strossmayer was a strong proponent, founding the Yugoslav Academy of Arts and Sciences in 1867.

Meanwhile, competition between Serbia, Montenegro, Greece and Bulgaria for the remaining Ottoman territories intensified. Ethnic nationalism grew as competing powers manipulated identities and allegiances, particularly in Macedonia, where it resulted in 40 years of rebellion, invasions and reprisals, culminating in the landmark Ilinden uprising of August 1903 and its brutal suppression two weeks later.

The First Balkan War in 1912 pushed the Turks back to Constantinople and forced them to concede Macedonia and Kosovo to Serbia. But the Greeks, Serbs and Bulgarians soon began fighting each other. The conflict spilled into the Second Balkan War of 1913, which drew in Romania and ended unsatisfactorily for all, though it did expand Serbian territory once more. Meanwhile, radical Serbian movements were agitating for the union of Austrian-controlled Bosnia with Serbia and Montenegro.

In this climate, Austrian Archduke Franz Ferdinand was assassinated in Sarajevo on 28 June 1914. Though the assassin was not connected to the Serbian government, this act triggered a domino effect of retaliation throughout Europe, beginning with the Austrian invasion of Serbia. WWI led to unimaginable loss of lives and the downfall of the Austrian and Ottoman Empires and the Kingdom of Montenegro, despite the latter being on the winning side. Out of their ashes arose the Serb-led Kingdom of Serbs, Croats and Slovenes (which also encompassed Bosnia and Montenegro) – a pan-Slavic dream renamed 'Yugoslavia' in 1929. Albania also emerged as an independent state, ruled by the self-proclaimed King Zog.

The Austrian Empire welcomed Serbs fleeing the Ottomans on the condition that they settle within the military frontier, which roughly coincides with the modern border between Bosnia and Croatia. This stark mountainous region became a Serb-majority area within Croatia known as the Krajina, meaning 'borderland'.

1878	1912	1918	1941
Serbia and Montenegro are recognised as fully independent by the Treaty of Berlin. The Austro-Hungarian Empire takes over the administration of Bosnia and Hercegovina; it's officially annexed in 1908.	The First Balkan War begins between the Balkan League and the Ottoman Turks. The Turks are forced to concede present-day North Macedonia and Kosovo to Serbia; Albania declares independence.	The Kingdom of Serbs, Croats and Slovenes is formed after the end of WWI under the Serbian Karađorđević dynasty; it is renamed Yugoslavia in 1929.	Hitler invades Yugoslavia by bombing Belgrade on 6 April; Croatian fascists declare the Independent State of Croatia. Italy occupies Albania, Kosovo, Montenegro, parts of Dalmatia, Istria and southern Slovenia.

WWII

With the outbreak of WWII, Yugoslavia was carved up between Nazi Germany, Mussolini's Italy and the Independent State of Croatia led by the far-right Croatian Ustaše party (installed by the Germans), which included modern Croatia, Bosnia and parts of Serbia and Slovenia. The Ustaše's brutality towards Serbs, in particular, was shocking even by Nazi standards; Ustaše attempts to convert Orthodox Serbs to Catholicism on pain of death and its systematic murder of Serbs, Jews, Roma and communists is said to have given rise to the term 'ethnic cleansing'.

Determined resistance was met with brutal reprisals delivered on civilian populations; at one point the Nazi policy was to murder 100 Serbian civilians for every German killed. Two crucial resistance movements emerged; one was the Serbian royalist Chetniks, led by Draža Mihailović, and the other was the pro-communist Partisans, led by Josip Broz Tito. As well as fighting against the Germans and Ustaše, civil war flared between the Partisans and Chetniks, while the Chetniks committed atrocities against Muslim civilians. Ultimately, the Partisans galvanised the most support throughout the region, eventually winning British and Soviet support. Around 10% of the region's population perished during WWII.

In Albania, the communists under Enver Hoxha led the resistance against the Italians and, after 1943, against the Germans.

DEFINING THE WESTERN BALKANS

The Balkan Peninsula is the name given to the landmass stretching into the Mediterranean east of Italy, terminating in the outspread fingers of Greece. Little about the Balkans is simple, least of all defining exactly what the name actually encompasses.

There's some debate as to where the northern boundary falls, but it's often described as following (from east to west) the Danube, Sava, Vipava and Soča Rivers. Under this definition, it includes all of Bulgaria, North Macedonia, Albania, Montenegro, Kosovo, and Bosnia and Hercegovina; mainland Greece; the European section of Turkey; large chunks of Romania, Serbia, Croatia and Slovenia; and a tiny fragment of Italy. Another definition sees the boundary diverting from the Sava at the Kupa/Kolpa River, hence omitting Slovenia and Italy altogether.

The term 'Western Balkans' is also fraught, given that the EU has started to use it to refer to Albania and only those parts of the former Yugoslavia that have yet to become members. For our part, we use 'Western Balkans' as a handy catch-all for Albania and all of the nations of the former Yugoslavia. Most importantly, we use this grouping as it makes the most sense from a traveller's point of view. Slovenia and Croatia are useful gateways to the region and viewed by the vast majority of travellers as essential stops on a Western Balkans adventure.

1945	1978	1985	1991
After the end of WWII, the leader of the Partisan resistance movement, Josip Broz Tito, forms the new Federal People's Republic of Yugoslavia. Communist leader Enver Hoxha takes power in Albania.	After a gradual worsening of relations, Albania breaks with the People's Republic of China and achieves near-total isolation. The economy is devastated and food shortages become more common.	Albanian dictator Enver Hoxha dies and Ramiz Alia takes over the communist leadership. Restrictions loosen but people no longer bother to work on the collective farms, leading to food shortages in the cities.	Following referendums, Slovenia, Croatia and Macedonia declare independence. War breaks out between the Yugoslav People's Army and Slovenian defence forces, lasting only 10 days, then shifting to Croatia.

Communism & Collectivisation

Yugoslavia and Albania were the only countries in Europe where communists took power without the assistance of the USSR's Red Army. The Yugoslav communist party was quick to collectivise agriculture, but by the late 1940s it faced stagnant growth and dwindling popularity. Fed up with interference from Moscow, Tito broke with Stalin in 1948. The collectivisation of land was reversed in 1953, and within a year most peasants had returned to farming independently. Reforms were successful and the economy was booming in the late 1950s. Albania's leader, Hoxha, looked on Yugoslavia's reforms with utter distaste and kept true to hardline Stalinism. The Albanian communist party controlled every aspect of society – religion was banned during a Chinese-style cultural revolution in the late 1960s and the country became a communist hermit kingdom.

Tito's brand of socialism was different. Almost uniquely, Yugoslavs were able to travel freely to Western countries as well as within the Eastern Bloc. In the 1960s Yugoslavia's self-management principles contributed to a struggle between the republics within it. Richer republics such as Croatia wanted more power devolved to the republics, while Serbia's communist leaders wanted more centralised control. The Albanian majority in Kosovo started to protest against Serbian control in the 1960s, which began the long cycle of riots, violence and repression that lasted until the UN took charge of the territory in 1999.

> After WWII Tito hoped that Albania would become a state of federal Yugoslavia. Stalin had other ideas, wanting Yugoslavia, Bulgaria and Albania to be united into one communist federation. Tito parted ways with the Soviets in 1948. Hoxha remained loyal until 1961, well after Stalin's death.

HISTORY COMMUNISM & COLLECTIVISATION

Things Fall Apart

After Tito's death in 1980 the federal presidency rotated annually among the eight members of the State Presidency. The economy stalled as foreign debt mounted, and rivalries between the constituent republics grew. Serbian communist-party boss, Slobodan Milošević, exploited tensions by playing up disturbances between Serbs and Albanians in Kosovo, allowing him to consolidate his power base. The autonomy Kosovo enjoyed under Yugoslavia's 1974 constitution was suspended by Milošević in 1989, leading to increased unrest.

As the democracy movement swept the Eastern Bloc, tensions grew between the central powers in Belgrade, dominated by Milošević, and pro-democracy, pro-independence forces in the republics. Slovenia declared independence in 1991 and after a 10-day war became the first republic to break free of Yugoslavia. Croatia soon followed, but the Serbs of the Krajina region, with the backing of the Yugoslav People's Army, set up their own state and civil war broke out. Macedonia became independent without much trouble. When Bosnia followed suit, the country fell into a brutal civil war between its three main communities: Bosniaks, Serbs and Croats. The war continued until 1995 and cost 100,000 lives.

1992	1995	1996	1999
Bosnia and Hercegovina holds its own independence referendum and is plunged into a bloody civil war. The communists lose power in Albania and the country descends into a free-market free for all.	The Croatian army overruns separatist Serb territories, ending the war in Croatia. The Dayton Agreement ends the conflict in Bosnia, dividing the country into a Serb republic and a Croat-Muslim federation.	Riots break out after 70% of Albanians lose their savings when private pyramid-investment schemes, believed to have been supported by the government, collapse.	Kosovo becomes a UN protectorate after NATO launches a 78-day bombing campaign on targets in Serbia and Montenegro, aiming to prevent the 'ethnic cleansing' of Kosovar Albanians by Serb forces.

The Dayton Peace Accords divided Bosnia into a loose federation, awarding 49% to the Serbs and 51% to a Croat-Muslim federation. In the same year the Croatian army retook its breakaway Serb regions. Meanwhile, in rump Yugoslavia (Serbia and Montenegro) the worst hyperinflation in history occurred between 1993 and 1995, when prices grew by five quadrillion per cent.

Albania's communist regime was toppled in 1992, and the country descended into anarchy; peasants stole animals and equipment from the old collective farms, people pillaged factories for building materials, and gangsters looted museums and ruled major port towns. It all came to a head in 1997, when the collapse of pyramid banking schemes set off a violent uprising.

Rebel Kosovar Albanians began a guerrilla campaign against Serb forces in 1996, who in turn launched a violent crackdown, driving many Kosovar civilians from their homes. After Serbia refused to desist, NATO unleashed a bombing campaign in 1999. Nearly 850,000 Kosovo Albanians fled to Albania and Macedonia, telling of mass killings and forced expulsions. In June, Milošević agreed to withdraw troops, air strikes ceased, the guerrillas disarmed and the NATO-led KFOR (Kosovo Force; the international force responsible for establishing security in Kosovo) took over.

In 2001 fighting broke out in Macedonia, where around a quarter of the population is ethnic Albanian. Peace was achieved through an accord promising more self-government for Albanian areas.

By 2002 the region was finally mostly peaceful except for lingering fears over the stability of Kosovo and Macedonia. Montenegro declared independence from Serbia in June 2006. Kosovo's declaration of independence in February 2008 has been recognised by 56% of the United Nations states to date, but, crucially, not by Serbia, Bosnia or Russia.

Set during the Bosnian War, Oscar-winning film *No Man's Land* (Ničija Zemlja) sees a Serb and a Bosniak soldier trapped in a trench. More complications occur when the media and UN bumble in. It won the Best Foreign Language Film category in 2001.

Stabilisation & Integration

As armed conflicts ceased, the new states of the Western Balkans began setting their eyes on integration into Europe. However, the Yugoslav wars and the vacuum left by the fall of the Albanian regime had opened the door to organised crime and corruption, which is now rife.

Slovenia joined the EU in 2004 and was followed in 2013 by Croatia (which has haemorrhaged working-age citizens ever since). Since the international community stepped in to lend a hand to Albania, it has made a successful recovery, going from failed state to EU candidate – alongside North Macedonia, Montenegro and Serbia. Bosnia and Hercegovina and Kosovo are listed as 'potential candidates'. Slovenia was welcomed into NATO in 2004, followed by Albania and Croatia in 2009, and Montenegro (despite domestic opposition) in 2017. North Macedonia signed the NATO accession agreement in February 2019.

2006	2008	2017	2019
The state union of Serbia and Montenegro breaks up after a referendum in Montenegro in which 55.5% of voters voted for independence, narrowly passing the 55% threshold.	Kosovo declares independence from Serbia. It's recognised by the US and most of the EU countries, but not by Serbia, Bosnia or Russia. Kosovo Serbs establish their own assembly in Mitrovica.	Montenegro officially joins NATO, despite political discord within the country and allegations of an attempted Serbian- and Russian-backed coup against the government the previous year.	Macedonia changes its name to North Macedonia, resolving a 27-year-long dispute with Greece, and signs the NATO accession agreement.

People & Religion

In this part of the world, questions of ethnicity are so thickly intertwined with history, politics and religion that discussions of identity can be a minefield. Yet to an outsider, the more you travel in the Western Balkans, the more you're struck by the similarities between its various peoples: the warm hospitality, the close family bonds, the social conservatism, the fiery tempers and the passionate approach to life.

People

Throughout the Western Balkans, people tend to identify more by ethnicity than citizenship. This is hardly surprising; a family that has never left its ancestral village may have had children born in Montenegro, parents born in Yugoslavia, grandparents born in the Kingdom of Serbs, Croats and Slovenes, and great-grandparents born in the Ottoman or Austro-Hungarian Empires. Countries may come and go, but self-identity tends to stick around. It's understandable, then, that a person whose family has lived within a present-day country's borders for generations may not identify themselves with that country's dominant nationality.

The region's largest ethnic group are the Serbs (31%) followed by the Albanians (21%), Croats (18%), Bosniaks (8%), Slovenes (7%), Macedonians (5%), Montenegrins (1%) and Hungarians (1%). The remainder includes a myriad of other ethnicities (Roma, Greek, Turkish, Italian, Vlach, Slovak, Bulgarian, Romanian, Ruthenian etc) and a significant portion who would rather not declare an ethnicity at all (for political or other reasons).

In fact, these deeply entrenched 'ethnic' identities have little to do with actual genetic heritage and more to do with linguistic, cultural and religious identification. Despite the multiplicity of ethnicity, around 70% of the population could reasonably be labelled as some flavour of South Slav, with Albanians (21%) and Hungarians (1%) being the largest non-Slavic minorities. Each wave of migration absorbed and colonised the existing people, so it's reasonable to suppose that many people have ancient Illyrian, Macedonian, Greek or Roman roots. Scratch a little further and it's even more complicated, as numerous armies have raped and pillaged their way through these lands over the millennia.

The more people you meet in the Balkans, the more you will be struck by their similarities rather than their differences. You'll have the privilege of meeting opinionated, creative, passionate and slightly eccentric folk in every country of the region, and the one generalisation that can absolutely be made about the lot of them is their shared tradition of warmth and hospitality – although it may not be immediately obvious in your dealings with hospitality staff. A related trait that also transcends ethnic divides is the laid-back approach to time as something to be passed leisurely rather than spent in a hurry. On warm summer evenings, the main street of every major town throughout the region fills up with a parade of well-dressed people of all ages, socialising with their friends, checking each other out and simply enjoying life. In summer, life is lived on the streets.

In 2017, 30 linguists from Bosnia, Croatia, Montenegro and Serbia drafted a declaration (subsequently signed by over 200 linguists, academics and activists) stating that all four official 'languages' are actually variations of the same language.

In the Albanian *kanun* tradition, 'sworn virgins' are women who assume the role (dress, habits, privileges...) of men. From the day they take their oath, they are respected by the family and community as the male patriarch of the family.

Religion

The main factor separating the otherwise virtually indistinguishable Croats, Serbs, Montenegrins and Bosniaks is religion: Croats overwhelmingly adhere to the Roman Catholic faith, Serbs and Montenegrins are just as strongly linked to the Orthodox Church, and Bosniaks are defined by their ancestors' conversion to Islam. Macedonian Slavs are overwhelmingly Orthodox, while Slovenes are predominantly Catholic – as are the Hungarians of Serbia's Vojvodina region.

The only people in the region for whom religion isn't a defining feature of their identity are the Albanians. Albanians are nominally 70% Muslim, 20% Orthodox and 10% Catholic, but more realistic statistics estimate that up to 75% of Albanians are nonreligious. Religion was ruthlessly stamped out in 1967 when Albania officially became the world's first atheist state. While Albania remains a very secular society, Islam does seem to be enjoying a significant comeback among younger people.

The Balkan version of Islam has a reputation for moderation and tolerance. Only a minority of Muslim women choose to wear the veil, and the attitude towards alcohol is fairly loose. Within the region's Islamic communities, the vast majority are Sunni – reflecting their Ottoman heritage. There's also a significant presence of the mystical Sufi dervish order known as the Bektashi, particularly in Bosnia and Albania. Founded in 1501, Bektashism incorporates elements of both Sunni and Shia Islam.

The Serbian Christian tradition of *slava* celebrates family patron saints. During these celebrations, families come together and the family home is open to anyone who wants to visit.

THE OTHER BALKAN RELIGION: SPORT

In 2018, Western Balkans countries filled an extraordinary three of the top 10 slots in the per capita ranking of the Greatest Sporting Nation website, with Croatia at number two, Serbia at five and Slovenia at seven.

Football and basketball are the most popular team sports, and players from the region fill the professional ranks of prestigious international clubs. In 2018, Croatia's men's football team stunned the world by finishing second in the FIFA World Cup, and captain Luka Modrić ended the year ranked as FIFA's Best Men's Player.

Despite not existing for 25 years, Yugoslavia remains the third-highest ranked nation for men's basketball at the Olympics, behind the USA and USSR (Serbia and Croatia are at spots 11 and 14 on the medal tally, respectively). Two-time world champions and three-time European champions, Serbia's men's basketball team currently holds silver medals from the Olympic, World and European Championships.

The region also turns out exceptional tennis players, but none more so than Serbia's Novak Đoković who ended 2018 ranked as the world's top male singles player. As of late 2018, Đoković's extraordinary career included 14 Grand Slam wins. Also in the top 100 singles rankings are his compatriots Dušan Lajović, Aleksandra Krunić, Laslo Đere and Filip Krajinović. Croatia's most famous player was Goran Ivanišević, who won Wimbledon in 2001. Of the current Croatian crop, Marin Čilić and Borna Ćorić ended 2018 ranked at seven and 12 respectively, with Petra Martić and Donna Vekić at numbers 32 and 34 on the women's list. Slovenia's ranked players include Aljaž Bedene, Dalila Jakupović, Tamara Zidanšek and Polona Hercog, while Bosnia has Damir Džumhur and Mirza Bašić.

In water polo, Yugoslavia's men's team took out the Olympics gold three times and silver four times. Serbia, Croatia and Montenegro continue to dominate the men's sport, taking up three of the top four spots at the last two Olympic Games (and at least one place in the four Olympics before that); Serbia and Croatia have one gold apiece.

Skiing is Slovenia's obsession. National heroes include Primož Peterka, ski-jumping World Cup winner in the late 1990s, and extreme skier Davo Karničar, who has skied down the highest mountains in each of the seven continents, including the first uninterrupted descent of Mt Everest on skis in 2000. Tina Maze is the most successful female racer in Slovenian history, winning two golds at the 2014 Winter Olympics. Croatia's Janica Kostelić won three gold medals and a silver in the 2002 Winter Olympics.

The Bektashi moved their world headquarters to Tirana after Sufi orders were banned in secular Turkey by Ataturk in 1925.

The Orthodox-Catholic division has its roots in the split of the Roman Empire at the end of the 4th century. Present-day Croatia and Slovenia found itself on the western side, ruled from Rome, while Serbia and North Macedonia ended up on the Greek-influenced eastern side, ruled from Constantinople (now İstanbul). As time went on, differences developed between western and eastern Christianity, culminating in the Great Schism of 1054, when the churches finally parted ways.

Serbian identity is deeply intertwined with the Serbian Orthodox Church, and several of Serbia's nation-building medieval rulers are venerated as saints. The Macedonian Orthodox Church split from the Serbian church in 1967 and the Montenegrin Orthodox Church followed suit in 1993, claiming to revive the self-governing church of Montenegro's *vladike* (prince-bishops), which was dissolved in 1920. Neither are officially recognised by the other Eastern Orthodox Churches. The Albanian Orthodox Church, however, was declared autocephalous (self-governing) by the Patriarch of Constantinople in 1937.

It would be difficult to overstate the extent to which Catholicism shapes the Croatian national identity. The Croats pledged allegiance to Roman Catholicism as early as the 9th century and were rewarded with the right to conduct Mass and issue religious writings in the local language (as opposed to Latin), using the Glagolitic script. Successive Popes supported the early Croatian kings, who in turn built monasteries and churches to further promote Catholicism. Throughout the long centuries of Croatia's domination by foreign powers, Catholicism was the unifying element in forging a sense of nationhood. Even today, the Church enjoys a respected position in Croatia's cultural and political life, and is the most trusted institution in the country.

The Western Balkans are also home to long-standing Jewish communities, who historically enjoyed the relative protection afforded by both the Venetian Republic and the Ottoman Empire. Dubrovnik is home to the second-oldest still-operating synagogue in the world, while Split's Roman-era palace has ancient Jewish graffiti etched into its basement and a centuries-old synagogue set into its walls. Sarajevo was known as the European Jerusalem for its melting pot of religions, and significant Sephardic and Ashkenazi synagogues are still standing today. Subotica in Serbia is home to a famed art nouveau synagogue.

A large proportion of the Balkans' Jewish population was murdered during WWII, both by the Nazis and by Croatia's Ustaše regime. One inspiring exception was Albania, which started the war with 200 Jews and ended it with 2000 due to the government and local people providing shelter to those who fled there. Today there are around 2000 Jews in Bosnia, 800 in Serbia, upwards of 500 in each of Croatia and Slovenia, 200 in North Macedonia, 40 in Albania and as few as 12 in Montenegro.

Given the national tendency towards tallness, it's little wonder you'll find Montenegrins playing in America's NBA. Current players include Orlando Magic's Nikola Vučević (2.13m), Nikola Mirotić (2.08m) of the New Orleans Pelicans, and Minnesota Timberwolves' Nikola Peković (2.11m). Nikola is clearly a name of great stature.

Sarajevo Rose: A Balkan Jewish Notebook by Stephen Schwartz traces the remnants of a lost Jewish world, which intermingled with the other faiths of the region.

PEOPLE & RELIGION RELIGION

Arts & Architecture

Creative expression has always been integral to defining identity in the Western Balkans. Invading and prevailing cultures played tug-of-war over buildings that even today show the layers of who was here. Similarly, music not only expresses traditions and cultures but has also been used to garner support for political ideology or to rally resistance against it. Visual arts reflect and record history, and artists are generally highly regarded and respected within their home communities.

Visual Arts

Medieval Serbian and Macedonian fresco painting rivals anything produced in the Orthodox world. The frescoes in the churches of Sveti Pantelejmon near Skopje and Sveti Kliment in Ohrid display a skill for expression that predates the Italian Renaissance by 150 years. Albania has a largely unknown tradition of fine Orthodox art, exemplified by the icon painter Onufri, whose colourful, expressive work is contained in a museum in Berat.

An important 20th-century Yugoslav art movement was Zenitism (from the word 'zenith'), which fused French and Russian intellectualism with Balkan passion. Belgrade's Museum of Contemporary Art has a fine collection of Zenitist works. Socialist realist art dedicated to glorifying the worker and the achievements of communism had only a brief heyday in Yugoslavia – artists were allowed to return to their own styles in the early 1950s – but it lasted right up until the early 1990s in Albania. Tirana's National Art Gallery has a salon devoted to socialist realist works.

The region's penchant for quirky statues; look for Rocky Balboa and Bob Marley in Serbia, Bruce Lee in Bosnia and Hercegovina, and Russian singer Vladimir Visotsky in Montenegro.

The region's best-known sculptor is Ivan Meštrović, born into a poor Croatian farming family in 1883. Though he emigrated to the USA, dozens of his works are scattered around the former Yugoslavia, including the Monument to the Unknown Hero on Mt Avala outside Belgrade, the Njegoš Mausoleum in Montenegro and a large collection in his former home in Split.

The conflicts of the 1990s hampered the arts and almost every other sphere of endeavour, but artists of the region survived to re-emerge with much to explore and express. A powerful message was offered by young Bosnian artist Šejla Kamerić, who was growing up in Sarajevo during the time of the siege. In her most recognised and confronting work, *Bosnian Girl,* she has superimposed crude graffiti left in Srebrenica by a Dutch soldier over her photographic portrait.

By far the region's most celebrated contemporary artist is Marina Abramović, known for her thought-provoking performance works in venues such as New York's MoMA and London's Serpentine Gallery. Her return to her native Belgrade for a retrospective exhibition in 2019 marks her first solo show there for 44 years.

Music

Candidates for the oldest living musical traditions in the Balkans are the old Slavonic hymns of the Serbian Orthodox Church and southern Albania's polyphonic singing. Croatia's multi-voice *klapa* music is another unusual a cappella tradition, with its roots in church music. The various Islamic dervish orders have traditions of religious chants on mystical themes.

The beloved traditional music of Bosnia is the melancholy sound of *sevdah,* derived from the Turkish word *'sevda'* (love). Slovenian folk music features accordions and flutes made of wood, clay and reeds, and Central European rhythms such as the polka and waltz are popular. Other folk traditions include Macedonian *gajda* (bagpipe) tunes, accompanied by drums, and Serbian peasant dances led by bagpipes, flutes and fiddles. Kosovar folk music bears the influence of Ottoman military marching songs, with careening flutes over the thudding beat of goatskin drums. One regional curiosity are *trubači,* Serbian trumpet music often played by Roma brass bands at weddings and funerals and at the raucous Guča Festival.

There's a strong tradition of classical music throughout the Balkans, and some of the region's biggest musical exports of recent years have been classical-pop crossover artists such as Croatia's 2Cellos and Montenegrin classical guitarist Miloš Karadaglić. Macedonian baritone Boris Trajanov is an internationally acclaimed opera singer.

However, when it comes to international success, nothing beats the meteoric rise of Kosovar pop stars Rita Ora and Dua Lipa, who have topped the charts around the world. The best-known band from the region would be the veteran Slovenian industrial collective Laibach, whose oddball discography includes an album containing nothing but different versions of the Rolling Stones' *Sympathy for the Devil.*

Another influential character on the international music scene is Goran Bregović. Born in Bosnia to a Serbian mother and a Croatian father, the former rock star is famed for his collaborations with filmmaker Emir Kusturica. Bregović is a strong ambassador for Balkans music, particularly the role of the Roma in the region's musical history. Another advocate of Roma traditions was North Macedonia's Esma Redžepova, known as the 'Queen of the Gypsies' and widely acclaimed for her vocal dexterity.

The instrument most often used in Croatian folk music is the *tamburica,* a three- or five-string long-necked lute that is plucked or strummed. Introduced by the Turks in the 17th century, the instrument rapidly gained a following in eastern Slavonia, Bosnia, Slovenia, Hungary and the Vojvodina region of Serbia.

ARTS & ARCHITECTURE MUSIC

CINEMA

Some exceptional films offer a fascinating window into the Western Balkans. *Lamerica* (1995) by Italian director Gianni Amelio depicts the postcommunist culture of Albania. Bosnian Danis Tanović won an Oscar for *No Man's Land* (Ničija zemlja; 2001), about the relationship between a Serb and a Bosniak trapped in a trench together during the Sarajevo siege. In *Grbavica* (2006) – written and directed by another Bosnian, Jasmila Žbanić – the protagonist learns that her father was not a war hero but that her mother was a victim of a wartime rape. Macedonian director Milcho Manchevski explores ethnic tensions in his Oscar-nominated, cinematically sublime *Before the Rain* (Pred doždot; 1994). Two-time Palme d'Or winner Emir Kusturica playfully and energetically dissects the Balkans in films such as *When Father Was Away on Business* (Otac na službenom putu; 1985) and his famed black comedy *Underground* (Podzemlje; 1995).

Yugoslav-era cinema had some notables successes, particularly the work of director Veljko Bulajić whose debut movie, *Train Without a Timetable* (Vlak bez voznog reda; 1959), was nominated for the Palme d'Or, while *Battle of Neretva* (Bitka na Neretvi; 1969) featuring Yul Brynner and Orson Welles was nominated for an Academy Award. The 'black wave' *(crni talas)* of the 1960s and early '70s is internationally lauded for its creativity, nonconformism and subtle critique of the socialist regime. Notable movies include *Three* (Tri; 1965) and *I Even Met Happy Gypsies* (Skupljači perja, 1967) by Aleksandar Petrović, *Early Works* (Rani radovi; 1969) by Želimir Žilnik and *Mysteries of the Organism* (Misterije organizma; 1971) by Dušan Makavejev.

Enormously popular throughout the region, *turbo-folk* is the lovechild of a dirty affair between folk and pop music. During the Milošević era, *turbo-folk* was appropriated by the regime and heavily impregnated with nationalist messages. Though its nationalist connotations have diminished, *turbo-folk* is the loudest thing left over from the former Yugoslavia; video clips are gloriously reminiscent of the 1980s: female singers with gravity-defying bosom and height-defying hair, flanked by groups of choreographed dancers.

The early 1980s saw the blossoming of a popular New Wave *(novi talas)* scene in Yugoslavia, featuring bands such as Azra, Haustor and Film from Croatia, and Idoli, Električni Orgazam and EKV from Serbia.

The Yugoslav era spawned many bands and solo artists that remain hugely popular. The 2018 death of Croatian singer Oliver Dragojević, a popular figure since the 1960s, saw an outpouring of grief across national boundaries. Yugoslavia's openness to the West meant that the trends that swept London, Dublin and Los Angeles were quickly picked up domestically and delivered in local languages – whether that be 1960s mop-top pop, 1970s guitar heroics or 1980s New Wave jauntiness.

Although audiences have now somewhat fragmented along national lines, there's still a vibrant Balkans music scene comprising everything from electronic dance music to hip-hop and alternative rock – buoyed and influenced by the high-profile international music festivals (especially Exit in Novi Sad and Ultra in Split) that have blossomed over the last two decades.

Literature

Literature in the Balkans began with epic poetry, a tradition which survives in the Dinaric Range from Croatia to Albania and predates Homer. Vast epic poems were memorised and recited to the accompaniment of the violin-like *gusle*, played with a bow. They were passed down through generations like this, recording key historical events, dramatising heroic tales and giving rise to myths.

The 1389 Battle of Kosovo features prominently in Serbian epic poetry. Serbian epic poetry was first written down by the 19th-century writer and linguist Vuk Karadžić, whose works were brought to a wider audience through translations by the likes of Goethe and Walter Scott. Montenegrin literature is dominated by poet and prince-bishop Petar II Petrović Njegoš; his acclaimed work *The Mountain Wreath* (1847) is still highly regarded, despite its genocidal overtones.

Acclaimed poets from the region include Marko Marulić (1450–1524) from Split, Ivan Gundulić (1589–1638) from Ragusa (Dubrovnik), Valentin Vodnik (1758–1819) from Ljubljana, France Prešeren (1800–49) and Oton Župančič (1878–1949) from rural Slovenia, and Tin Ujević (1891–1955) and Vesna Parun (1922–2010) from Dalmatia.

During the 20th century, the region's literature achieved global acclaim. Bosnian-born, Ivo Andrić won the Nobel Prize for Literature in 1961 for classics such as *The Bridge on the Drina* (1945) and *Bosnian Chronicle* (The Day of the Consuls; 1945). Ismail Kadare, Albania's most beloved novelist, was awarded the inaugural Man Booker International Prize in 2005; key titles include *Chronicle in Stone* (1971) and *Broken April* (1978). Other classics include Meša Selimović's *Death and the Dervish* (1966), Miloš Crnjanski's *Migrations* (1929), *The Encyclopaedia of the Dead* (1983) by Danilo Kiš and Miha Mazzini's *Crumbs* (1987).

Comtemporary authors worth seeking out include Ivana Bodrožić, Slavenka Drakulić, Dubravka Ugrešić, David Albahari, Svetislav Basara, Miljenko Jergović, Ismet Prcic, Andrej Nikolaidis and Ognjen Spahić.

Architecture

The region's architecture is a three-dimensional record of previous societies. Buildings have been erected, redesigned, demolished and resurrected throughout history, making for a rich collage of stylistic contrasts.

The Roman amphitheatre at Pula in Croatia is one of the best preserved in the world, while the Euphrasian Basilica at Poreč gained a World Heritage listing for its 6th-century Byzantine mosaics. Romanesque, Gothic, Renaissance and baroque architecture appears mostly in Slovenia and Croatia. The Slovenian, Croatian and Montenegrin coasts are strongly Venetian-influenced, while inland Slovenia's architecture shows links with Austria. Serbia's Vojvodina region has Hungarian-influenced elements, particularly in the art nouveau buildings in Subotica. The Turkish influence in mosques, *madrasas* (colleges for learning the Koran), *hammams* (public baths) and domestic architecture stretches from North Macedonia to Bosnia. Berat in Albania has a particularly fine set of Ottoman-era houses, and Sarajevo and Mostar have an eclectic mix of Ottoman structures, Orthodox churches and Habsburg-era public buildings.

Builders were brought from Turkey to erect authentic structures, so what remains of the Ottoman era is fascinating for the contrast it lends to other styles. The Turkish *konak* is a distinct style of residence throughout the region, generally white with timber framings. The 2nd floor, often balanced on beams, protrudes over the ground floor. These *doksat* (overhanging windowed rooms) would jut over the street so as not to appropriate too much space on it but still afford the people inside a view of its goings-on. Interiors of such residencies were adapted to the lifestyles that played out in them; most of the living rooms were on the 1st floor, often adorned with *peškum* (carved hexagonal coffee tables) and *sećija* (benches along the wall), and draped with *ćilim* (hand-woven carpets). Windows were shuttered so sequestered women inside could enjoy the views without being seen. Many such houses now serve as museums. The classical Ottoman mosque features a large cubed prayer area with a dome on top. Minarets on Ottoman mosques in this region are often taller and slimmer than their Arab counterparts. Inside, the *mihrab* (prayer niche) faces Mecca, and the pulpits are often carved from wood.

Communist architecture has been much maligned for its gloomy greyness, but Yugoslav and Albanian architects produced some eclectic and whimsical buildings which are finding a newfound cache under the moniker socialist modernism. In Yugoslavia, hundreds of WWII monuments *(spomenici)* were built, often on a grand scale; in 2018 they were celebrated in a dedicated show at New York's MoMA. While some have been destroyed or have fallen into ruin, many remain – there are particularly impressive examples in Mostar and Sutjeska National Park in Bosnia. Belgrade has a love-them-or-hate-them crop of envelope-pushing concrete apartment blocks, and there are fantastically angular Yugo-style hotels scattered throughout the region.

Tragically, the Western Balkans' architectural heritage has been caught in the crossfire of its conflicts over the years; hundreds of mosques, churches and monasteries have been vandalised or destroyed. The most recent such spate of attacks occurred in Kosovo and Serbia as a result of Kosovo's independence declaration in 2008; Serbian Orthodox sites in Kosovo continue to be guarded.

On the brighter side, there has been increased effort to rebuild and restore key buildings destroyed or damaged during the wars. In Dubrovnik, for instance, dozens of buildings that were attacked from land and sea have been rebuilt. The most iconic structure in the Balkans to have been resurrected after its destruction during the war is the Stari Most (Old Bridge) in Mostar, which was painstakingly rebuilt in 2004 using 16th-century engineering techniques. The meticulous reconstruction of the 16th-century Ferhadija mosque in Banja Luka, completely destroyed in 1993, was finally finished in 2016.

ARTS & ARCHITECTURE ARCHITECTURE

Serbian post-modernist Milorad Pavić (1929–2009) used nonlinear narrative forms: *Dictionary of the Khazars* (1984) can be read in random order, while *The Inner Side of the Wind* (1998) can be read from the back or the front.

The Cathedral of St Domnius in Split (built as the 3rd century transitioned into the 4th) is the oldest cathedral building in the world, thanks to it inhabiting the original mausoleum of the Roman Emperor Diocletian.

Environment

The Western Balkans is a rich repository of biological diversity. More than a third of Europe's flowering plants, half of its fish species and two-thirds of its birds and mammals can be found in the former Yugoslavia alone. The area around the borders of Albania, Montenegro and Kosovo is one of the least-touched Alpine regions on the continent. However, the shift towards industrial logging and farming is straining the natural environment, and rivers are under threat from proposed hydroelectric projects.

The Land

A wide belt of mountains parallel to the Adriatic coast covers about 60% of the region; this strip is generally made of limestone and has long valleys, dramatic gorges, vast cave systems and oddities such as disappearing rivers and lakes. The Dinaric Range along Croatia's coast has partly sunk into the sea, creating an incredibly convoluted network of islands, peninsulas and bays.

The International Commission for the Protection of the Danube River (www.icpdr.org) offers detailed information about cooperative protection and shared use of the river that flows through 10 countries, including Serbia and Croatia.

A knot of fault lines in the southern part of the region sometimes causes major earthquakes, such as the one in 1963 which demolished North Macedonia's capital, Skopje. The region's highest mountain is Triglav (2864m) in Slovenia's Julian Alps, while the second-highest is Korab (2764m) on the border of Albania and North Macedonia. The Pannonian Plain along the Sava and Danube Rivers in Croatia and northern Serbia was the floor of an ancient sea around 2.5 million years ago.

An interesting cross-border proposal is the Balkans Peace Park project, which aims to create a protected area cutting across Montenegro, Kosovo and Albania. For more on national parks in the region, see individual countries.

Environmental Issues

The standard of environmental protection varies widely across countries in the region, with the most progressive being Slovenia in the north and the most problematic being Albania in the south. However, the compact nature of the land – and, indeed, the interconnectedness of the world – means that issues of water and air quality affect everyone.

Rubbish & Recycling

The temperature of the Adriatic Sea varies greatly: it rises from an average of 7°C (45°F) in December up to a balmy 23°C (73°F) in September.

Slovenia leads the way on the recycling front, but even it only started doing so in 2001. Ljubljana became the first EU capital to adopt a zero-waste strategy, which promotes recycling and aims to reduce the amount of waste sent to landfill sites and incinerators to zero. Other initiatives include promoting composting and encouraging more ecofriendly packaging.

Throughout the rest of the region, recycling is rudimentary or nonexistent. Worse still, waste disposal is inadequate and fly-tipping and littering is rampant. Whole landscapes are scarred by the curse of discarded plastic bags and bottles.

Albania was practically litter-free until the early 1990s, as everything was reused or recycled, but today you'll see rubbish everywhere – even in the remotest parts of the mountains. As much of it is inevitably washed or blown out to sea, beaches along the entire coast – including the most distant Croatian islands – now have a high-tide line almost entirely demarcated by plastic, much of it with Albanian packaging. Beach resorts undertake annual spring clean-ups but chances are you'll still see plastic floating past as you swim. In 2018, Croatia declared an intention to work with Albania on schemes to prevent the waste entering the waterways in the first place.

Air & Water Quality

Between the 1950s and the 1970s, the rate of industrialisation and urbanisation in the Western Balkans was among the highest in the world. Use of energy and raw materials put pressure on natural resources, decreasing forested areas, deteriorating water quality and increasing air pollution. The closure of factories during the chaos of the 1990s gave the environment a temporary reprieve but new issues arose, such as the use of depleted uranium during the NATO air strikes. Unplanned growth in cities coping with an influx of refugees increased demand on already stretched sewage, waste-disposal and water-supply systems.

Air pollution remains a major concern in cities such as Tirana, Belgrade, Pristina and Zenica (home to a major steel plant); in winter, Skopje and Sarajevo have some of the worst air quality in the world.

Sewage outflows in coastal resorts can be a problem when tourist crowds descend in summer, particularly in Durrës (Albania) and the Bay of Kotor (Montenegro). In Serbia, dumping of industrial waste into the Sava River is also a concern.

Overdevelopment

The flurry of construction taking place along the coast and in cities throughout the region is not necessarily planned or controlled with respect to its environmental impact. The struggle to find a balance between commercial desires and conservation imperatives presents a major challenge. In Montenegro, in particular, coastal development continues unabated. With most of the Budva Riviera now given over to hulking resort complexes, attention has shifted to the previously unspoiled Luština Peninsula.

In North Macedonia, Lake Ohrid's growing popularity as a stop-off on the tourist circuit has become cause for concern among conservation groups. Plans were drawn up to create a marina, artificial Mediterranean-style beaches and new apartments by draining an important marshland that acts as a natural filter to the lake. A local initiative called Ohrid SOS was set up in 2015 to help challenge the proposals, and these plans have been shelved. Now Montenegro faces a similar issue (and similar pushback) with a contested development having been announced for the shores of Lake Skadar (see www.skadarlake.org).

Tiny Kosovo is undergoing a huge amount of development, which is causing habitat loss for native species. Genuine wilderness areas big enough to support large mammals are increasingly hard to find.

Hunting, Logging & Fishing

Illegal logging and fishing reached epidemic proportions in Albania during the 1990s, and there are still signs of it today; fishing with dynamite continues along the coast, as does fishing for the endangered koran trout *(Salmo letnica)* in Lake Ohrid; the species is strictly protected on the North Macedonian side of the lake. On the Danube River in Serbia, overfishing of sterlet sturgeon has left the species as one of the most endangered fish species in the world; Ukraine, Romania, Bulgaria and Hungary have already banned the fishing of sterlet.

The Bojana River, on the border of Montenegro and Albania, occasionally performs the unusual trick of flowing upstream. This happens when the swollen winter waters of its Albanian tributary, the Drim, cut across it and the volume of water forces part of the flow back into its source, Lake Skadar.

One of the region's more curious species is the *olm*, a blind salamander that can be found in Montenegro's Biogradska Gora National Park and Slovenia's Postojna Cave, among other places. Its local name *(čovječja/ človeška ribica)* means 'human fish' because of its human-like skin.

ENVIRONMENT ENVIRONMENTAL ISSUES

WILDLIFE

The Balkans is a refuge for many of the larger mammals that were almost eliminated from Western Europe 150 years ago. The rugged forests of the Dinaric Range from Slovenia to Albania shelter wolves, red deer, roe deer, lynx, chamois, wild boar and brown bears. Forests are roughly divided into a conifer zone, beginning between 1500m and 2000m, and including silver fir, spruce and black pine; broad-leafed beech forests, which occur lower down; and a huge variety of oak species below this again.

Birds of prey found in the region include griffon vultures, golden eagles, kestrels and peregrine falcons. The great lakes of Skadar, Ohrid and Prespa in the south are havens for Dalmatian pelicans, herons and spoonbills.

The more populated shores of the Adriatic coast have endangered populations of golden jackals, red foxes and badgers, while bigger predators such as wolves and brown bears have largely been eradicated. Classic Mediterranean species such as junipers, figs and olive trees grow well in the high summer temperatures of this area. The Adriatic shore used to be home to the endangered Mediterranean monk seal, but these are now gone. On a happier note, the population of bottlenose dolphins seems to be growing in Croatia's Kvarner Gulf.

Hunting is a popular pastime in Montenegro and Kosovo, and controls are, at best, loosely enforced. On the Croatian island of Cres, the introduction of wild boars at the behest of the hunting lobby has come at the expense of the semiwild Tramuntana sheep and griffon vulture.

With the tourist boom in Croatia, the demand for fresh fish and shellfish has risen exponentially. The production of farmed sea bass, sea bream and tuna (for export) is rising substantially, resulting in environmental pressure along the coast.

Hydroelectric Projects

While hydro-generated power is by its nature sustainable, the construction of plants requires the building of dams and the flooding of pristine river valleys, forever altering their natural state and the unique habitat they support. In 2018 there were plans to build 2800 new hydroelectric dams in the Balkans. Little North Macedonia alone has 400 dam proposals, including 20 in Mavrovo National Park. As a nominally 'green' energy source, the funding for these projects often comes with government subsidies. Grassroots environmental groups are forming across the region in a battle to save some of Europe's last untouched rivers.

Positive Steps

Slovenia has some of the purest drinking water in the world, and in 2016 its parliament added the right to drinkable water to the country's constitution. In the same year the European Commission awarded Ljubljana the title of European Green Capital in recognition of the pedestrianisation of much of the city centre, the promotion of environmentally friendly transport such as cycling, and the provision of free drinking fountains to discourage people from buying bottled water.

In North Macedonia, millions of trees have been planted each year since the inaugural national tree-planting day in 2008 when 200,000 Macedonians planted more than two million trees (one for every citizen) to heal patches of forest devastated by fires.

In 2014 the Croatian government called for tenders for gas- and oil-exploration licences in the Adriatic, prompting fears of a disaster for both the environment and the country's tourism in the event of a spill. Two years later environmentalists were heralding a victory for people power, after public pressure led to the government declaring a moratorium on exploration.

Reaching up to 95cm in length, the nose-horned viper is the largest and most venomous snake in Europe. It likes rocky habitats and has a zigzag stripe on its body and a distinctive scaly 'horn' on its nose. If you're close enough to spot the horn, you're too close.

Survival Guide

Directory A–Z

Accessible Travel

The region's picturesque cobbled and stepped old-town streets will make travelling difficult for the mobility-impaired. In general, wheelchair-accessible rooms are only available at top-end hotels and are limited in number, so be sure to book in advance. Many museums and sites have disabled access, but many don't.

Slovenia has made the most effort with accessibility. Facilities include public telephones with amplifiers, pedestrian crossings with beepers, Braille on maps at bus stops, ramps in government buildings, and reserved spaces in many car parks. The larger bus and train stations in Croatia are wheelchair-accessible, but the ferries are not. Elsewhere in the region, accessible features are rarer still.

Download Lonely Planet's free Accessible Travel guides from http://lptravel.to/AccessibleTravel.

Accommodation

The coast is extremely popular in summer (June to August) and it pays to book well in advance.

Hotels These range from massive beach resorts to boutique city establishments.

Guesthouses Usually family-run establishments where spare rooms are rented at a bargain price – sometimes with their own bathrooms, sometimes not.

Hostels Mainly in the bigger cities and more popular beach destinations, with dorms and sometimes private rooms too.

Apartments Privately owned holiday units are a staple of the coastal accommodation scene; they're especially good for families.

Campgrounds Tent and caravan sites, often fairly basic.

Booking Services

I Travel Balkans (www.facebook.com/Itravelbalkans) Network of the Western Balkans' best independent hostels.

Autokampi (www.avtokampi.si) Lists campgrounds in Slovenia, Croatia, Bosnia and Hercegovina, Montenegro and Serbia.

World Wide Opportunities on Organic Farms (www.wwoof.net) Information about working on organic farms in exchange for room and board.

Lonely Planet (lonelyplanet.com/balkans/hotels) Recommendations and bookings.

Where to Stay

If you're looking for just one base from which to explore, the pocket where Croatia, Bosnia and Montenegro meet offers the easiest access to the most diverse range of attractions. From Dubrovnik you can take day trips to Mostar, Trebinje, the Bay of Kotor, Budva and various Dalmatian islands. A cheaper alternative is to base yourself in Trebinje; the Bay of Kotor is a happy medium – cheaper than Dubrovnik yet still by the sea.

If it's a beach holiday you're after, Montenegro's tiny stretch of coast is the most crammed, while Albania's is the least; Croatia still offers some quieter escapes on its numerous islands. If it's mountains you're chasing, the obvious choices are Slovenia and Montenegro, but each country has good options. For buzzy city life, head to Belgrade.

Seasons

Rates often plummet outside of high season (typically July and August; on the coast this stretches out from May to September), sometimes by as much as 50%. In places that cater to business travellers, prices are more expensive during the week and cheaper over the weekend.

Camping

Camping is generally your cheapest option but the trade-off may be that you are far away from things you want to see. Before you commit, check out public transport connections and times to and from campsites and towns. Some camping grounds may be geared for motorists, though there's generally also room for tents. Many offer on-site basic cabins, caravans or bungalows that may be cheaper than hostels, though not always. Don't count on these being available during high season.

The standard of camping grounds varies enormously throughout the region; some are extremely basic. Croatia's coast is peppered with clothing-optional camping grounds (signposted with FKK, the German acronym for 'naturist').

➜ Camping grounds may be open from April to October, May to September, or perhaps only June to August, depending on the category of the facility, the location and the demand.

➜ A few private camping grounds may be open all year.

➜ Camping in the wild is usually illegal; ask locals before you pitch your tent on a beach or in an open field.

➜ In some places you may be allowed to build a campfire. Always ask first.

Farmhouses & Ethno Villages

'Village tourism', which means staying at a farmhouse, is highly developed in Slovenia and Serbia. It's like staying in a private room or pension, except the participating farms are in picturesque rural areas. Montenegro's mountains have a good selection of 'ethno' and 'eco' villages: clusters of freestanding rustic cabins.

Guesthouses

Small private guesthouses are common in parts of the Balkans. Typically priced between hotels and private rooms, they usually offer en-suite bathrooms and sometimes basic breakfasts at on-site restaurants. They tend to be smaller and more personal than hotels, which can amount to a bit less privacy.

Homestays & Private Rooms

It used to be common that people would approach travellers arriving at bus and train stations offering private rooms or hostel beds – although this has reduced somewhat in the age of Airbnb and Booking.com. Some carry clipboards and pamphlets; others are little old ladies speaking halting English or German. Taking up these offers can be a good or bad experience; it's impossible to say until you do it. You may be led to a pristine room in the centre of town or to a cupboard in an outer-suburb housing project; don't commit until you're comfortable with the place and clear on the price.

It's usually possible to book private rooms through a tourist office or travel agency, which can offer some level of quality control. Alternatively, look for signs saying *Zimmer* or *Sobe* (respectively, the German and pan-Slavic word for 'rooms').

Staying with friends in the Balkans will be a wonderful experience given the famed hospitality of the region. Bring some small gifts for your hosts – it's a deeply ingrained cultural tradition throughout the region.

Hostels

You don't have to be a 'youth' to be a part of the sociable hostel scene in the Balkans. Hostels vary enormously in character and quality.

➜ Hostel cards are rarely required, though they may give you a small discount.

➜ Hostels give you a bed for the night, plus use of communal facilities. Dorms are the norm, but some offer private rooms with en suites.

➜ Facilities often include small kitchens where you can do your own cooking.

➜ Some hostels require that you have a sleeping sheet; if you don't have one, you may be able to rent one.

➜ Not all hostels are open all year round.

➜ Most hostels accept reservations, but not always during peak periods.

➜ Some hostels in Slovenia, Croatia, Bosnia and Serbia are part of the Youth Hostel Association (YHA), which is affiliated with **Hostelling International** (HI; www.hihostels.com).

Hotels

At the rock-bottom end of the scale, cheap hotels may be no more expensive than private rooms or guesthouses, while at the other end you'll find unimaginable luxury. In both cases, you get what you pay for.

➜ Often you pay for the room and not by the number of people staying in it, so singles may pay the same as a couple.

➜ In some older hotels, cheaper rooms may have washbasins but the toilet and shower may be down the corridor.

➜ Breakfast is often offered, sometimes for a small additional charge; the quality varies enormously.

Rental Apartments

In many cities, and throughout the Croatian and Montenegrin coast, renting an apartment through a

BOOK YOUR STAY ONLINE

For more accommodation reviews by Lonely Planet authors, check out http://lonelyplanet.com/western-balkans/hotels. You'll find independent reviews, as well as recommendations on the best places to stay. Best of all, you can book online.

reputable website or local agency can be an excellent option. Apartments can cost much less than you'd pay for an equivalent stay in a hotel.

➡ The quality of rental accommodation varies considerably.

➡ Cooking facilities are almost always provided, and sometimes laundry facilities as well.

➡ Generally, the longer you stay, the more you can negotiate.

➡ It's usually possible to book apartments through local tourist offices or travel agencies, which can offer some level of quality control.

➡ Increasingly, private apartments are also listed on international booking sites.

University Accommodation

Some universities (notably in Croatia, North Macedonia, Slovenia and Serbia) rent space in student halls during July and August. Accommodation will sometimes be in single rooms, but more commonly in doubles or triples with shared bathrooms. Basic cooking facilities may be available. Ask at the college or university, at student information services or at tourist offices.

Children

Children are fussed over in these parts, so having kids in tow can make for wonderful encounters with locals that you wouldn't have otherwise.

➡ The range of baby food, formulas, disposable nappies and the like is extensive.

➡ Strollers can be problematic in towns and cities with cobblestones or cars parked on the pavements.

➡ If you need children's safety seats for rented cars, book them in advance.

➡ Many restaurants provide high chairs.

➡ Check with your accommodation in advance if you require a cot.

➡ In Albania, praise won't be lavished on your child – nor should you lavish praise on Albanian kids – as there are concerns about the all-observant 'evil eye'.

For inspiration and tips on family travel, pick up a copy of Lonely Planet's *Travel with Children* guide.

Climate

The Balkans can be boiling hot and freezing cold, but neither extreme will prevent travel; this is a fascinating region to visit at any time of year. July and August can be uncomfortably hot, particularly in the cities and Herce-govina, but this is the time when beaches are at their best. From a climatic point of view, May, June and September are the best months in which to visit the region, with nowhere too warm, too cool or too wet.

Customs Regulations

Countries have their own regulations but, as a minimum, duties do not apply if you're bringing in up to:

➡ 200 cigarettes
➡ 1L of liquor.

There are restrictions on food crossing into the EU (ie Croatia and Slovenia) from non-EU countries. Look for Global Blue Tax Free shopping signs in Croatia and Slovenia; you may be able to claim tax back when you leave the EU if you ask for a Tax Free Form when making your purchase (www.globalblue.com).

Electricity

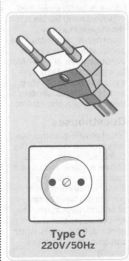

Type C
220V/50Hz

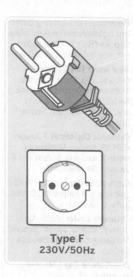

**Type F
230V/50Hz**

Health

The Western Balkans poses no notable health risks to travellers, though as with anywhere else in the world there are basic things you should be aware of.

Before You Go

➡ There are no specific vaccinations required for visiting the Western Balkans. The World Health Organization (WHO) recommends that all travellers be covered for diphtheria, hepatitis B, measles, mumps, pertussis (whooping cough), polio, rubella, tuberculosis, tetanus and varicella (chickenpox), regardless of their destination. You should also consider being vaccinated for hepatitis A. Since most vaccines don't produce immunity until at least two weeks after they're given, visit a physician at least six weeks before departure.

➡ Tick-borne encephalitis is spread by tick bites and is thought to exist in forested areas in the region. It is a serious infection of the brain and vaccination is advised for those in risk areas who

are unable to avoid tick bites (such as campers and hikers).

➡ The US Centers for Disease Control and Prevention recommends a rabies vaccination for long-term travellers, those involved in outdoor activities in remote areas and people working around animals.

➡ EU citizens are generally covered by reciprocal arrangements in Croatia and Slovenia. They should carry their European Health Insurance Card. Other nationals are entitled to emergency medical treatment but must pay for it.

➡ Make sure you take out a comprehensive travel-insurance policy that covers you for the worst possible scenario, such as an accident requiring an ambulance or an emergency flight home. When choosing a policy, check whether the insurance company will make payments directly to providers or reimburse you later for overseas health expenditures.

Availability & Cost of Health Care

Good basic health care is readily available, and pharmacists can give valuable advice and sell over-the-counter medication for minor illnesses. They can also refer you to more specialised help when required. Outside major cities, medical care is not always readily available, but embassies, consulates and five-star hotels can usually recommend doctors or clinics. Health-care costs tend to be less expensive than in Western Europe, but given you may want to go to a private clinic for anything beyond a doctor's consultation, comprehensive health insurance is essential.

Tap Water

Tap water is safe to drink in Bosnia, Croatia, Kosovo, Serbia and Slovenia, and is

also generally safe in Albania, North Macedonia and Montenegro – although it pays to check with locals first as there can sometimes be problems in some areas. For instance, it's advisable not to drink the water in Herceg Novi in May as they close off and clean the pipes from the main reservoir (in Croatia) and revert to a local reservoir. Bottled water is cheap and readily available.

Internet Access

➡ Many cafes, restaurants and bars have free wi-fi; just ask for the password.

➡ Hotels and private guesthouses are almost always equipped with wi-fi.

➡ Free wi-fi access has removed much of the need for internet cafes, but local tourist offices should be able to point you towards those few that remain.

Legal Matters

It may seem obvious, but while you are in the Western Balkans you're covered by local laws, which may differ from those in your home country.

➡ If you're arrested, you have the right to contact your country's embassy or consulate and arresting officers have a responsibility to help you to do so.

➡ Traffic police mount regular speed checks and can impose spot fines. Speed limits are often remarkably low so to avoid trouble, drive with caution. Avoiding a potential fine is the best way to avoid being hit up for a bribe, which is not unheard of.

➡ In most countries you are technically obliged to show some sort of ID on demand, so carry a passport or identity card with you.

➡ If you're caught with drugs, expect severe penalties and possibly a lengthy imprisonment in a local jail.

→ It's unwise and often illegal to take photos of military buildings, vehicles and equipment.

LGBTIQ+ Travellers

Homosexuality has been decriminalised throughout the Western Balkans, and is tolerated but not widely accepted. Public displays of affection between same-sex couples may be met with hostility.

→ Various countries have hosted Pride events, but violent incidents have occurred in the past.

→ There are only a handful of gay venues in the entire region; you'll find them in Ljubljana, Zagreb, Belgrade and Sarajevo.

→ Many towns on the coast have an unofficial gay beach – usually a rocky area at the edge of the nudist section.

→ In other places, LGBTIQ+ life is almost invisible, making the internet the only realistic way to make contact with others. **Grindr** (www.grindr.com) and **Planet Romeo** (www.planetromeo.com) are very popular with local gay and bisexual men.

Money

ATMs are widely available in most towns. Acceptance of credit cards is normally confined to upper-end hotels, restaurants and shops, although it's becoming more widespread.

Currencies

The euro (€) is used in Kosovo, Montenegro and Slovenia. Countries that don't use the euro are Albania (lekë), Bosnia and Hercegovina (convertible mark), Croatia (kuna), North Macedonia (Macedonian denar) and Serbia (Serbian dinar), though some businesses will accept euros.

Tipping

Restaurants Up to 10% in swankier places, but only if you're completely satisfied with the service.

Bars & Cafes Not required but it's normal to round up the bill and possibly add a bit extra.

Taxis Not obligatory but it's normal to round up the fare.

Bargaining

In the states of the former Yugoslavia, some gentle haggling might save you a small amount at a market stall; in all other instances you're expected to pay the stated price. In Albania, it's perfectly acceptable to haggle at markets and at shops selling souvenirs; elsewhere it's not common. For long-distance taxi rides, haggling can be useful.

Opening Hours

Business hours vary across the region, changing by season and arbitrarily at will. As a rough guide:

Banks & Offices 8am–5am Monday to Friday, with an hour or two off over lunch; some open on Saturday mornings

Cafes & Bars 8am–midnight

Restaurants noon–11pm or midnight; often closed Sundays outside peak season

Shops 8am–7pm; siesta can be any time between noon and 4pm

Post

Reliability of postal services varies, but most things usually arrive in the end. In some countries, parcels need to be taken unwrapped to the post office for inspection.

Public Holidays

Religious holidays vary, sometimes within individual countries. The situation within Bosnia and Hercegovina (BiH) is especially complicated with the Muslim-Croat Federation celebrating different holidays to the Republika Srpska (RS). For a detailed list, see individual countries.

New Year's Day 1 January (Albania, BiH, Croatia, Kosovo, Montenegro, North Macedonia, Serbia, Slovenia) and 2 January (BiH, Montenegro, Serbia, Slovenia)

Orthodox Christmas 7 January (BiH RS, Kosovo, Montenegro, North Macedonia, Serbia) and 8 January (Montenegro)

Catholic Easter March or April (Albania, BiH Federation, Croatia, Kosovo, Slovenia)

Orthodox Easter March, April or May (Albania, BiH RS, Kosovo, Montenegro, North Macedonia, Serbia)

May/Labour Day 1 May (all countries)

Ramadan Bajram/Eid al-Fitr June (Albania, BiH Federation, Kosovo)

Kurban Bajram/Eid al-Adha August or September (Albania, BiH Federation, Kosovo)

All Saints' Day 1 November (BiH Federation, Croatia, Slovenia)

Catholic Christmas 25 December (Albania, BiH Federation, Croatia, Kosovo, Slovenia)

Safe Travel

→ Street violence is rare, but you should employ common sense regardless. Be on guard against pickpockets in crowded places.

→ It's not a good idea to travel in Kosovo with Serbian plates on your car: you'll potentially leave yourself open to random attacks or vandalism.

→ Sporadic violence does occur in north Mitrovica and a few other flashpoints where Serbian and Kosovar communities live in close proximity. Check the situation before travelling.

→ The region has two types of venomous vipers but they'll try their best to keep out of your way. If bitten, head immediately to a medical centre for the antivenin.

Landmines

Landmines and unexploded ordnance still affect parts of Croatia, Bosnia and Hercegovina, and Kosovo. The mined areas are generally well signposted with skull-and-crossbones symbols and yellow tape. Don't go wandering off on your own in sensitive regions before checking with a local. Never go poking around an obviously abandoned or ruined house.

Road Safety

Local motorists have no qualms about overtaking on blind corners while talking on their mobile phones. Tooting is a regional pastime but it's best to keep your cool and stick to the speed limit: the traffic police (some of whom have been known to ask for bribes) are everywhere. Albania has a well-enforced zero blood alcohol policy.

Telephone

To call from outside a country, dial your international access code, then the country code, then the local area code (without the initial 0) and the local number. To call from region to region within a country, start with the full area code.

International access code	☏00
Albania	☏355
Bosnia & Hercegovina	☏387
Croatia	☏385
Kosovo	☏383
Montenegro	☏382
North Macedonia	☏389
Serbia	☏381
Slovenia	☏386

Time

The Western Balkans belongs to the Central European Time (GMT + one hour). All countries employ daylight savings, usually from the last Sunday in March until the last Sunday in October. Note that the 24-hour clock is widely used in the Balkans, though not always.

Toilets

➔ Most toilets are of the standard sit-down variety, although you'll sometimes come across squat toilets in some of the older public conveniences.

➔ Public toilets aren't all that common and most charge a small fee.

➔ If you're caught short, head to a cafe-bar – but it's polite to at least buy a drink.

Tourist Information

Albanian Tourist (www.albanian tourist.com)

Bosnia & Hercegovina Tourism (www.bhtourism.ba)

Croatian National Tourist Board (www.croatia.hr)

Macedonia Timeless (www.macedonia-timeless.com)

Montenegro Travel (www.montenegro.travel)

Serbia National Tourism Organisation (www.serbia.travel)

Slovenian Tourist Board (www.slovenia.info)

Visas

➔ Each Western Balkans country has its own regulations, so it pays to check those pertaining to your citizenship on the foreign affairs website of each country you're planning to visit.

➔ Citizens of most European countries, Canada, the USA, Australia, New Zealand and many other nations do not require a visa for stays of up to 90 days.

➔ Make sure you have at least six months left on your passport after your date of arrival.

Volunteering

➔ The Peace Corps has a large presence in Albania but, other than that, there are minimal organised volunteering programs in the country.

➔ In Croatia, consider the **Kuterevo Bear Refuge** (☏053-799 001; www.kuterevo-medvjedi.org; Pod Crikvon 109, Kuterevo; admission by donation; ☺hours vary), the **Sokolarski Centre** (☏091 50 67 610; www.sokolarskicentar.com; Škugori bb, Šibenik; adult/child 50/40KN; ☺9am-7pm Apr-Nov) for the protection of birds of prey, and the **Lošinj Marine Education Centre** (☏051-604 666; www.blue-world.org; Kaštel 24, Lošinj; adult/child 20/15KN; ☺10am-9pm Jul & Aug, to 8pm Jun, 10am-6pm Mon-Fri, to 2pm Sat May & Sep, 10am-2pm Mon-Fri Oct-Apr) ✿. These are small organisations and aren't set up for walk-in volunteers, so be sure to contact them well in advance.

➔ In Serbia, there's **Refugee Aid Serbia** (www.refugeeaidserbia.org), **Mladi Istraživači Srbije** (Young Researchers Serbia; www.mis.org.rs) and **Volonterski Centar Vojvodine** (www.volontiraj.rs).

➔ Slovenian organisations include **Slovene Philanthropy** (www.filantropija.org) and **Voluntariat** (www.zavod-voluntariat.si).

Women Travellers

Other than a passing interest shown by men towards solo women travellers, travelling in the Western Balkans is hassle-free and easy. In Muslim areas, some women wear a headscarf, but most don't.

Transport

GETTING THERE & AWAY

Getting to the Western Balkans is becoming easier year on year, with both budget and full-service airlines flying to various airports. On top of this, buses, trains and ferries also shepherd holidaymakers into the region. Flights, cars and tours can be booked online at lonelyplanet.com/bookings.

Air

There are direct flights to the Western Balkans from a variety of European and Middle Eastern cities year-round, with dozens of seasonal routes and charters added in summer.

For details of the region's international airports and the airlines that serve them, refer to the individual country chapters.

Land

The Western Balkans has land borders (p456) with Italy, Austria, Hungary, Romania, Bulgaria and Greece.

Bus

Direct bus connections link the Western Balkans to all of its neighbours and to as far afield as Norway. In most cases, passports are collected on the bus and handed over at the border; at some borders you're required to disembark and present your passport in person. Useful websites include www.busticket4.me, www.eurolines.com, www.buscroatia.com, www.getbybus.com and www.vollo.net.

Austria To Slovenia, Croatia, Bosnia and Montenegro from Vienna and Graz.

Bulgaria To North Macedonia and Serbia from Sofia.

Germany To Slovenia, Croatia and Bosnia from Berlin, Cologne, Dortmund, Munich and Frankfurt.

Greece To Albania and North Macedonia from Athens and Thessaloniki.

Hungary To Bosnia, Croatia, Serbia and Slovenia from Budapest.

Italy To Slovenia and Croatia from Rome, Milan, Padua, Venice and Trieste.

The Netherlands To Slovenia, Croatia and Bosnia from Amsterdam.

Slovakia To Slovenia from Bratislava.

Switzerland To Slovenia and Croatia from Zürich.

Turkey To North Macedonia, Serbia and Bosnia from İstanbul.

Car & Motorcycle

Outside Albania and Kosovo, most of the roads in the region are good, and driving can give you freedom you wouldn't otherwise have. Keep in mind that some insurance packages won't

---

CLIMATE CHANGE & TRAVEL

Every form of transport that relies on carbon-based fuel generates CO_2, the main cause of human-induced climate change. Modern travel is dependent on aeroplanes, which might use less fuel per kilometre per person than most cars but travel much greater distances. The altitude at which aircraft emit gases (including CO_2) and particles also contributes to their climate change impact. Many websites offer 'carbon calculators' that allow people to estimate the carbon emissions generated by their journey and, for those who wish to do so, to offset the impact of the greenhouse gases emitted with contributions to portfolios of climate-friendly initiatives throughout the world. Lonely Planet offsets the carbon footprint of all staff and author travel.

cover you for all European countries and it's forbidden to take some rental cars into some countries; check specifically for the countries you will be visiting.

Train

There are some epic routes into the Western Balkans from Eastern and Western Europe. In most cases, passports are checked on the train. Useful websites include www.raileurope.com and www.eurail.com. Popular routes include:

Austria Vienna, Villach and Graz to Maribor, Ljubljana, Zagreb and Belgrade; Salzburg to Ljubljana.

Bulgaria Sofia to Belgrade.

Czech Republic Prague to Maribor.

Germany Frankfurt and Munich to Ljubljana and Zagreb.

Hungary Budapest to Belgrade, Zagreb and Ljubljana.

Italy Trieste to Ljubljana, via Postojna, Divača and Sežana.

Switzerland Zürich to Ljubljana and Zagreb.

Sea

There are ferry services from Italy to Albania, Montenegro, Croatia and Slovenia; and from the island of Corfu (Greece) to Albania. Companies include **Jadrolinija** (www.jadrolinija.hr), **Montenegro Lines** (www.montenegrolines.com), **SNAV** (www.snav.com) and **Venezia Lines** (www.venezialines.com). See www.aferry.com and www.ferrysavers.com for discounts.

GETTING AROUND

Air

Major Balkan cities are connected by regular flights to other cities in the region. Only Croatia offers domestic flights, though there is rarely a need to fly internally unless you are in a rush.

Airlines in the Western Balkans

Adria Airways (⏎flight info 04-259 45 82, reservations 01-369 10 10; www.adria.si) Flies from Ljubljana to Podgorica, Pristina, Sarajevo, Skopje and Tirana.

Air Serbia (www.airserbia.com) Flies from Belgrade to Banja Luka, Ljubljana, Podgorica, Sarajevo, Skopje, Tirana, Tivat and Zagreb.

Croatia Airlines (OU; ⏎01-66 76 555; www.croatiaairlines.hr) Flies from Zagreb to Dubrovnik, Mostar, Pula, Sarajevo, Skopje, Split and Zadar; and between Zadar and Pula.

Montenegro Airlines (www.montenegroairlines.com) Flies from Podgorica to Belgrade and Ljubljana; and from Tivat to Belgrade.

Trade Air (TDR; ⏎091 62 65 111; www.trade-air.com) Flights from Osijek to Zagreb, Pula and Rijeka; from Rijeka to Split and Dubrovnik; and from Split to Pula and Dubrovnik.

Bicycle

The cycling experience varies greatly across the region – from Slovenia, where it's a popular way to get around, to Albania, where you can expect lousy road conditions and some abysmal driving from fellow road users. However, the scenery is universally spectacular.

➤ Bike lanes only exist in some of the major cities.

➤ Don't expect drivers to be considerate; wherever possible, try to get off the main roads.

➤ The wearing of helmets is compulsory for children in Croatia and Slovenia.

➤ Much of the terrain is very mountainous; be equipped with sufficiently detailed maps and keep your eye on the contours.

➤ Outside of major cities and tourist towns, bike hire and repair can be hard to find. Specialised parts are hard to come by, so come prepared.

➤ Invest in a sturdy bike lock and use it.

Boat

Croatia has an extensive ferry network, with hubs in Dubrovnik, Split (the main port), Šibenik, Zadar and Rijeka. Water taxis are common in touristy parts of Croatia and Montenegro.

Bus

In general, bus services in the Western Balkans are excellent and relatively inexpensive. In most cases, they're a better option than the trains.

➤ There are often competing companies handling each route, so prices can vary substantially.

➤ Luggage stowed in the baggage compartment under the bus costs extra.

➤ At large stations, bus tickets must be purchased at the office, not from drivers.

➤ Book ahead to be sure of a seat, especially in summer.

➤ Take care not to be left behind at meal or rest stops, which usually occur about every two hours.

➤ Frequency on some routes drops drastically at weekends; some services cease altogether on Sundays.

➤ Useful websites offering schedules and bookings include www.busticket4.me, www.vollo.net and www.getbybus.com.

➤ In Albania, buses compete with privately run minibuses known as *furgon*. They leave when full, and you pay when you're on board. They will stop frequently to let passengers on and off. *Furgons* often have very limited space for luggage.

BORDER CROSSINGS

➡ Expect delays crossing borders heading towards the coast in summer.

➡ Since Kosovo's independence is not recognised by Serbia, if you enter Kosovo via Albania, North Macedonia or Montenegro, officials at the Serbian border will deem that you entered Serbia illegally and you will not be let in. You'll need to exit Kosovo to a third country and then enter Serbia from there. If you entered Kosovo from Serbia, there's no problem returning to Serbia.

Car & Motorcycle

Independent travel by car or motorcycle is an ideal way to discover the region; some of the drives are extraordinary. However, cars can also be a liability in cities that can have baffling one-way systems, incomprehensible parking systems and narrow lanes that may be only fractionally wider than the curvature of your car. Theft from vehicles can also be a problem. Traffic police are everywhere, so stick to speed limits.

In deciding whether you want to drive around the region, remember to factor in the escalated costs not only for petrol but also entry fees, ferry fees, road tolls and taxes, and secured parking at some hotels.

Always have vehicle registration documents and personal identification with you when you drive. Every vehicle crossing an international border should display a sticker showing the country of registration.

Driving Licences

Whatever driving licence you have will likely be recognised in most countries of the region. However, it is wise to obtain an International Driving Permit from your local motoring organisation anyway; it doesn't cost much and minimises the risk of hassle.

Fuel & Spare Parts

Fuel costs vary enormously from country to country. Unleaded petrol (95 or 98 octane) and diesel are widely available. Accessing spare parts generally won't be a problem.

Hire

Car hire in the Western Balkans is as straightforward as anywhere else.

➡ The big international companies offer reliable service and well-maintained vehicles. A key advantage of international companies is that they often allow you to collect a car in one place and return it in another.

➡ Local companies will usually offer lower prices, but ask around so as only to use those with a good reputation – see the local agencies listed for each country or try asking at your hotel.

➡ Pre-booked rates are generally lower than walk-in rates, but don't expect car hire to be cheaper than it is in Western Europe; it can actually cost 20% to 40% more.

➡ Always bear in mind that some companies won't let you take rental cars to some countries; discuss your intended route thoroughly before you take the keys.

➡ It is not recommended to drive rental cars from Serbia into Kosovo or vice versa. In other countries, acts of vandalism based on the plates of wartime adversaries (or football rivals) do occasionally happen but are increasingly rare. If you're worried, Slovenian, Bosnian and Macedonian plates are the least problematic across the region.

Key international hire companies include:

Avis (www.avis.com)

Budget (www.budget.com)

Europcar (www.europcar.com)

Hertz (www.hertz.com)

Sixt (www.sixt.com)

Insurance

Third-party motor insurance is compulsory in EU countries; check requirements for specific non-EU countries with your insurer.

In some countries you will need an International Insurance certificate, known as a Green Card. Get your insurer to issue you with one (which may cost extra). This is a certificate that confirms that your insurance policy meets the legal requirements of the countries in which it is required. Check whether it lists all the countries you plan to drive in. If it doesn't cover everywhere you plan to go, you may need separate third-party cover at the border of the country in question.

Some insurers will need statements of accident. Do not sign an accident statement you cannot understand; insist on a translation and only sign it when you agree with it.

Road Rules & Safety

Make sure you brush up on road rules that apply wherever you are going. For instance, some countries require reflective vests and warning triangles to be in the car at all times, which you must use when parking on a highway or in an emergency. Others require a fire extinguisher and first-aid kit, or spare bulb kits to be on board as well. Lights may be required to be on even during the day. In short, do your research before you start your engine. A recommended place to start is the **Automobile Association** (www.theaa.com/motoring_advice/overseas/country bycountry.html), whose website provides useful country-specific information.

Standard international road rules apply, but you should also keep the following in mind:

➡ Traffic police generally issue fines on the spot. Always ask for a receipt.

➡ Drink-driving is a serious offence; limits vary from 0% (Albania) to 0.05% (Slovenia).

➡ Children under 12 and drunk people aren't allowed in the front seat in most countries.

➡ Driving at night can be particularly hazardous in rural areas where unlit roads can wind into the darkness off a cliff, and where horse-drawn carts and livestock can appear suddenly in front of you.

➡ In the event of an accident, you are supposed to notify the police and file an insurance claim.

➡ If you are bringing in a vehicle that already has significant body damage, point it out to customs on arrival in the country and have it noted down somewhere. Damaged vehicles may only be able to leave with police permission.

➡ Remember that some minor roads may be closed in winter months. Make sure you have necessary equipment for extreme weather conditions, including snow chains.

Road Tolls

There are tolls on some motorways in Bosnia and Hercegovina, Croatia, Montenegro, North Macedonia, Serbia and Slovenia. In most cases, the first set of booths you come across when you enter a motorway dispenses tickets; you need to present this at the booths when you leave the motorway, where it's used to calculate the applicable toll. In Slovenia, however, you must display a *vinjeta* (road-toll sticker) on the windscreen; local rental car companies provide these.

Hitching

Hitching is never entirely safe, and we don't recommend it. Travellers who hitch should understand that they are taking a small but potentially serious risk. That said, hitching isn't uncommon in the states of the former Yugoslavia, but is perhaps more so in Albania.

Local Transport

The region's major cities all have extensive bus networks, which are sometimes joined by trams, trains and trolley-buses.

Train

The mountainous terrain that covers much of the region means the lines that do exist often traverse some of the most scenic parts. However,

the trains are usually a slower, less frequent and more expensive option than the buses. Slovenia's network is the most advanced, and the trains are more comfortable than the buses; that's not the case elsewhere. Trains are generally safe, but some petty crime does occur from time to time.

Baggage Bringing luggage is free on trains; most stations have left-luggage services.

Classes Domestic trains are either 'express' or 'passenger' (local). Prices quoted by Lonely Planet are for unreserved, 2nd-class seating. Express trains have 1st- and 2nd-class cars; they are more expensive than passenger trains and a reservation is advisable.

Direct services include:

➡ Ljubljana to Rijeka and Pula

➡ Ljubljana to Zagreb and Belgrade

➡ Maribor to Zagreb

➡ Belgrade to Podgorica and Bar

➡ Belgrade to Skopje

➡ Pristina to Skopje

Further information about routes, schedules and prices can be found at:

➡ www.zfbh.ba (Bosnia and Hercegovina)

➡ www.hzpp.hr (Croatia)

➡ www.zpcg.me (Montenegro)

➡ www.serbianrailways.com (Serbia)

➡ www.slo-zeleznice.si (Slovenia)

Language

This chapter offers basic vocabulary to help you get around the Western Balkans region. Read our coloured pronunciation guides as if they were English and you'll be understood. The stressed syllables are indicated with italics.

Some phrases in this chapter have both polite and informal forms indicated by the abbreviations 'pol' and 'inf' respectively. The abbreviations 'm' and 'f' indicate masculine and feminine gender respectively.

Linguists commonly refer to the languages spoken in Croatia, Serbia, Montenegro and Bosnia and Hercegovina as members of the macrolanguage Serbo-Croatian, while acknowledging differences between the individual languages. Croats, Serbs, Bosnians and Montenegrins themselves generally maintain that they speak different languages, however – a reflection of their desire to retain separate ethnic identities.

Croatia is perhaps the simplest to classify: the official language is Croatian and the official writing system is the Roman alphabet. Serbia is also fairly straightforward, with Serbian the official language and the Cyrillic alphabet the official writing system (although in reality both Cyrillic and Roman alphabets have equal status and are in common use in government, schools and the media). Things become somewhat complicated in Bosnia and Hercegovina, however, where three languages share official status. Bosnian itself is almost identical to Croatian (with a few lexical variations). It's spoken by the Muslim community (Bosniaks) and is written in the Roman alphabet. Croatian is spoken by the Bosnian Croats; it too is written in the Roman alphabet. Serbian is spoken by the Bosnian Serbs and is written in the Cyrillic alphabet.

Finally, Montenegro's official language is Montenegrin, but Bosnian, Croatian, Serbian (plus Albanian!) are also in official use, and both Roman and Cyrillic alphabets have official status.

ALBANIA

In Albanian – also understood in Kosovo and North Macedonia – ew is pronounced as 'ee' with rounded lips, uh as the 'a' in 'ago', dh as the 'th' in 'that', dz as the 'ds' in 'adds', and zh as the 's' in 'pleasure'. Also, ll and rr are pronounced stronger than when they are written as single letters.

Basics

Hello	Tungjatjeta	toon·dya·tye·ta
Goodbye	Mirupafshim	mee·roo·paf·sheem
Excuse me	Më falni	muh fal·nee
Sorry	Më vjen keq	muh vyen kech
Please	Ju lutem	yoo loo·tem
Thank you	Faleminderit	fa·le·meen·de·reet
Yes	Po	po
No	Jo	yo

What's your name?
Si quheni? — see choo·he·nee

My name is ...
Unë quhem ... — oo·nuh choo·hem ...

Do you speak English?
A flisni anglisht? — a flees·nee ang·leesht

I don't understand.
Unë nuk kuptoj. — oo·nuh nook koop·toy

WANT MORE?

For in-depth language information and handy phrases, check out Lonely Planet's *Eastern Europe Phrasebook*. You'll find it at **shop.lonelyplanet.com**, or you can buy Lonely Planet's iPhone phrasebooks at the Apple App Store.

NUMBERS – ALBANIA

1	një	nyuh
2	dy	dew
3	tre	tre
4	katër	ka·tuhr
5	pesë	pe·suh
6	gjashtë	dyash·tuh
7	shtatë	shta·tuh
8	tetë	te·tuh
9	nëntë	nuhn·tuh
10	dhjetë	dhye·tuh

Eating & Drinking

Is there a vegetarian restaurant near here?
A ka ndonjë restorant vegjetarian këtu afër?
a ka ndo·nyuh res·to·rant ve·dye·ta·ree·an kuh·too a·fuhr

What would you recommend?
Çfarë më rekomandoni?
chfa·ruh muh re·ko·man·do·nee

I'd like the bill/menu, please.
Më sillni faturën/menunë, ju lutem.
muh seell·nee fa·too·ruhn/me·noo·nuh yoo loo·tem

I'll have ...	*Dua ...*	doo·a ...
Cheers!	*Gëzuar!*	guh·zoo·ar

Emergencies

Help!	*Ndihmë!*	ndeeh·muh
Go away!	*Ik!*	eek

Call the doctor/police!
Thirrni doktorin/policinë!
theerr·nee dok·to·reen/po·lee·tsee·nuh

I'm lost.
Kam humbur rrugën.
kam hoom·boor rroo·guhn

I'm ill.
Jam i/e sëmurë. (m/f)
yam ee/e suh·moo·ruh

Shopping & Services

I'm looking for ...
Po kërkoj për ...
po kuhr·koy puhr ...

How much is it?
Sa kushton?
sa koosh·ton

That's too expensive.
Është shumë shtrenjtë.
uhsh·tuh shoo·muh shtreny·tuh

BOSNIA & HERCEGOVINA

The official languages are Bosnian, Croatian and Serbian. The official writing system uses both the Roman and Cyrillic alphabets.

Basics

Hello	Zdravo/Здраво	zdra·vo
Goodbye	Doviđenja/Довиђења	do·vee·dje·nya
Excuse me	Izvinite/Извините	iz·vee·nee·te
Sorry	Žao mi je/Жао ми је	zha·o mi ye
Please	Molim/Молим	mo·lim
Thank you	Hvala/Хвала	hva·la
Yes	Da/Да	da
No	Ne/Не	ne

What's your name?
Kako se zovete/zoveš? (pol/inf)
Како се зовете/зовеш?
ka·ko se zo·ve·te/zo·vesh

My name is ...
Zovem se ...
Зовем се ...
zo·vem se ...

Do you speak English?
Govorite/Govoriš li engleski? (pol/inf)
Говорите/Говориш ли енглески?
go·vo·ri·te/go·vo·rish li en·gle·ski

I don't understand.
Ja ne razumijem.
Ја не разумијем.
ya ne ra·zu·mi·yem

Eating & Drinking

What would you recommend?
Šta biste preporučili?
Шта бисте препоручили?
shta bi·ste pre·po·ru·chi·li

NUMBERS – BOSNIA & HERCEGOVINA

1	jedan/један	ye·dan
2	dva/два	dva
3	tri/три	tri
4	četiri/четири	che·ti·ri
5	pet/пет	pet
6	šest/шест	shest
7	sedam/седам	se·dam
8	osam/осам	o·sam
9	devet/девет	de·vet
10	deset/десет	de·set

Do you have vegetarian food?
Da li imate   da li *i*·ma·te
vegetarijanski obrok? ve·ge·ta·*ri*·yan·ski o·brok

Да ли имате
вегетаријански оброк?

I'd like the bill/menu, please
Mogu li dobiti račun/ mo·gu li *do*·bi·ti ra·chun/
jelovnik, molim?   ye·lov·nik *mo*·lim

Могу ли добити рачун/
јеловник, молим?

I'll have ... *Želim .../*Желим ... zhe·lim ...

Cheers! *Živjeli!/*Живјели! zhi·vye·li

Emergencies

Help! *Upomoć!/* Упомоћ! u·po·moch

Go away! *Idite!/*Идите! *i*·di·te

Call the ...! *Zovite .../!*/Зовите ... ! zo·vi·te ...
  doctor *ljekara/*љекара lye·ka·ra
  police *policiju/*полицију po·*li*·tsi·yu

I'm lost.
Izgubljen/Izgubljena iz·gub·lyen/iz·gub·lyena
sam. (m/f)   sam
Изгубљен/
Изгубљена сам. (m/f)

I'm ill.
Ja sam bolestan/ ya sam bo·le·stan/
bolesna. (m/f)   bo·le·sna
Ја сам болестан/
болесна.

Shopping & Services

I'm looking for ...
Tražim ... tra·zhim
Тражим...

How much is it?
Koliko košta ...? ko·*li*·ko kosh·ta
Колико кошта ...?

That's too expensive.
To je preskupo. to ye pre·sku·po
То је прескупо.

CROATIA

The official language is Croatian and the official writing system is the Roman alphabet. Note that in our pronunciation guides n' is pronounced as the 'ny' in 'canyon', and zh as the 's' in 'pleasure'.

Word stress is also relatively easy in Croatian. In most cases the accent falls on the first vowel in the word – the last syllable of a word is never stressed in Croatian. The stressed syllable is indicated with italics in our pronunciation guides.

NUMBERS – CROATIA

1	*jedan*	*ye*·dan
2	*dva*	dva
3	*tri*	tri
4	*četiri*	*che*·tee·ree
5	*pet*	pet
6	*šest*	shest
7	*sedam*	*se*·dam
8	*osam*	*o*·sam
9	*devet*	*de*·vet
10	*deset*	*de*·set

Basics

Hello	*Bok*	bok
Goodbye	*Zbogom*	*zbo*·gom
Excuse me	*Oprostite*	o·*pro*·sti·te
Sorry	*Žao mi je*	*zha*·o mee ye
Please	*Molim*	*mo*·lim
Thank you	*Hvala*	*hva*·la
Yes	*Da*	da
No	*Ne*	ne

What's your name?
Kako se zovete/ *ka*·ko se zo·ve·te/
zoveš? (pol/inf) zo·vesh

My name is ...
Zovem se ... zo·vem se ...

Do you speak English?
Govorite/Govoriš li go·vo·ree·te/go·vo·reesh
engleski? (pol/inf) li *en*·gle·ski

I (don't) understand.
Ja (ne) razumijem. ya (ne) ra·*zoo*·mee·yem

Eating & Drinking

What would you recommend?
Što biste   shto *bee*·ste
preporučili?   pre·po·*roo*·chee·lee

Do you have vegetarian food?
Da li imate   da li *i*·ma·te
vegetarijanski obrok? ve·ge·ta·*ri*·yan·ski o·brok

Please bring the bill/check.
Molim vas   *mo*·leem vas
donesite račun.   do·*ne*·see·te ra·choon

I'll have ... *Želim ...* zhe·lim ...

Cheers! *Živjeli!* zhi·vye·li

Emergencies

Help!	*Upomoć!*	oo·po·moch
Go away!	*Idite!*	*i*·di·te

WAXING CYRILLICAL

The following list shows the letters of the Macedonian and Serbian/Montenegrin Cyrillic alphabets. The letters are common to all languages unless otherwise specified.

Cyrillic	Sound	Pronunciation
А а	a	short as the 'u' in 'cut'
		long as in 'father'
Б б	b	as in 'but'
В в	v	as in 'van'
Г г	g	as in 'go'
Д д	d	as the 'd' in 'dog'
Ѓ ѓ	j	as in 'judge' (Macedonian only)
Ђ ђ	j	as in 'judge' (Serbian/Montenegrin only)
Е е	e	short as in 'bet'
		long as in 'there'
Ж ж	zh	as the 's' in 'measure'
З з	z	as in 'zoo'
Ѕ ѕ	dz	as the 'ds' in 'suds' (Macedonian only)
И и	i	short as in 'bit'
		long as in 'marine'
Ј ј	y	as in 'young'
К к	k	as in 'kind'
Л л	l	as in 'lamp'

Cyrillic	Sound	Pronunciation
Љ љ	ly	as the 'lli' in 'million'
М м	m	as in 'mat'
Н н	n	as in 'not'
Њ њ	ny	as the 'ny' in 'canyon'
О о	o	short as in 'hot'
		long as in 'for'
П п	p	as in 'pick'
Р р	r	as in 'rub' (but rolled)
С с	s	as in 'sing'
Т т	t	as in 'ten'
Ќ ќ	ch	as in 'check' (Macedonian only)
Ћ ћ	ch	as in 'check' (Serbian/Montenegrin only)
У у	u	as in 'rule'
Ф ф	f	as in 'fan'
Х х	h	as in 'hot'
Ц ц	ts	as in 'tsar'
Ч ч	ch	as in 'check'
Џ џ	j	as the 'j' in 'judge'
Ш ш	sh	as in 'shop'

Call the ...! *Zovite ...!* zo·vee·te ...
doctor *liječnika* lee·yech·nee·ka
police *policiju* po·lee·tsee·yoo

I'm lost.
Izgubio/Izgubila sam se. (m/f) eez·goo·bee·o/eez·goo·bee·la sam se

I'm ill.
Ja sam bolestan/bolesna. (m/f) ya sam bo·le·stan/bo·le·sna

Shopping & Services

I'm just looking.
Ja samo razgledam. ya sa·mo raz·gle·dam

How much is it?
Koliko košta? ko·lee·ko ko·shta

That's too expensive.
To je preskupo. to ye pre·skoo·po

MONTENEGRO

The official language is Montenegrin and the official writing system uses both the Roman and Cyrillic alphabets.

Basics

Hello *Zdravo/*Здраво zdra·vo

Goodbye *Doviđenja/*Довиђења do·vi·dje·nya
Excuse me *Izvinite/*Извините iz·vee·nee·te
Sorry *Žao mi je/*Жао ми је zha·o mee ye
Please *Molim/*Молим mo·leem
Thank you *Hvala/*Хвала hva·la
Yes *Da/*Да da
No *Ne/*Не ne

What's your name?
Kako se zovete/zoveš? (pol/inf) ka·ko se zo·ve·te/zo·vesh
Како се зовете/зовеш?

My name is ...
*Zovem se .../*Зовем се ... zo·vem se ...

Do you speak English?
Govorite/Govoriš li engleski? (pol/inf) go·vo·ree·te/go·vo·reesh lee en·gle·skee
Говорите/Говориш ли енглески?

I (don't) understand.
(Ne) Razumijem. (Ne) ra·zoo·mee·yem
(Не) разумијем.

Eating & Drinking

What would you recommend?
Šta biste preporučili? shta bee·ste pre·po·roo·chee·lee
Шта бисте препоручили?

NUMBERS – MONTENEGRO

1	jedan/један	ye·dan
2	dva/два	dva
3	tri/три	tri
4	četiri/четири	che·tee·ree
5	pet/пет	pet
6	šest/шест	shest
7	sedam/седам	se·dam
8	osam/осам	o·sam
9	devet/девет	de·vet
10	deset/десет	de·set

Do you have vegetarian food?
Da li imate   da lee i·ma·te
vegetarijanski obrok? ve·ge·ta·ree·yan·ski o·brok
Да ли имате
вегетаријански оброк?

I'd like the bill/menu, please.
Mogu li dobiti račun/   mo·gu lee do·bee·tee ra·chun/
jelovnik, molim?   ye·lov·nik mo·leem
Могу ли добити рачун/
јеловник, молим?

I'll have ...	Želim .../Желим ...	zhe·leem ...
Cheers!	Živjeli!/Живјели!	zhi·vye·lee

Emergencies

Help!	Upomoć!/ Упомоћ!	oo·po·moch
Go away!	Idite!/Идите!	i·di·te

Call the ...!	Zovite ...!/Зовите ... !	zo·vee·te ...
doctor	ljekara/љекара	lye·ka·ra
police	policiju/полицију	po·lee·tsee·yoo

I'm lost.
Izgubljen/Izgubljena   iz·gub·lyen/iz·gub·lyena
sam. (m/f)   sam
Изгубљен/
Изгубљена сам. (m/f)

I'm ill.
Ja sam bolestan/   ya sam bo·le·stan/
bolesna. (m/f)   bo·le·sna
Ја сам болестан/
болесна.

Shopping & Services

I'm looking for ...
Tražim ...   tra·zhim
Тражим...

How much is it?
Koliko košta ...?   ko·lee·ko kosh·ta
Колико кошта ...?

That's too expensive.
To je preskupo.   to ye pre·skoo·po
То је прескупо.

NORTH MACEDONIA

Note that dz is pronounced as the 'ds' in 'adds', zh as the 's' in 'pleasure', and r is rolled.

Basics

Hello	Здраво	zdra·vo
Goodbye	До гледање	do gle·da·nye
Excuse me	Извинете	iz·vi·ne·te
Sorry	Простете	pros·te·te
Please	Молам	mo·lam
Thank you	Благодарам	bla·go·da·ram
Yes	Да	da
No	Не	ne

What's your name?
Како се викате/   ka·ko se vi·ka·te/
викаш? (pol/inf)   vi·kash

My name is ...
Jac се викам ...   yas se vi·kam ...

Do you speak English?
Зборувате ли   zbo·ru·va·te li
англиски?   an·glis·ki

I don't understand.
Jac не разбирам.   yas ne raz·bi·ram

Eating & Drinking

What would you recommend?
Што препорачувате   shto pre·po·ra·chu·va·te
вие?   vi·e

Do you have vegetarian food?
Дали имате   da·li i·ma·te
вегетаријанска храна? ve·ge·ta·ri·yan·ska hra·na

NUMBERS – NORTH MACEDONIA

1	еден	e·den
2	два	dva
3	три	tri
4	четири	che·ti·ri
5	пет	pet
6	шест	shest
7	седум	se·dum
8	осум	o·sum
9	девет	de·vet
10	десет	de·set

I'd like the bill/menu, please.

| Ве молам сметката/ мени. | ve mo·lam smet·ka·ta/ me·ni |

I'll have ...

| Jac ќе земам ... | yas kye ze·mam ... |

Cheers!

| На здравје! | na zdrav·ye |

Emergencies

| **Help!** | Помош! | po·mosh |
| **Go away!** | Одете си! | o·de·te si |

Call the doctor/police!

| Викнете лекар/ полиција! | vik·ne·te le·kar/ po·li·tsi·ya |

I'm lost.

| Се загубив. | se za·gu·biv |

I'm ill.

| Jac сум болен/ болна. (m/f) | yas sum bo·len/ bol·na |

Shopping & Services

I'm looking for ...

| Барам ... | ba·ram ... |

How much is it?

| Колку чини тоа? | kol·ku chi·ni to·a |

That's too expensive.

| Тоа е многу скапо. | to·a e mno·gu ska·po |

SERBIA

The official language is Serbian and the official writing system uses both the Roman and Cyrillic alphabets.

Basics

Hello	Zdravo/Здраво	zdra·vo
Goodbye	Doviđenja/Довиђења	do·vee·dje·nya
Excuse me	Izvinite/Извините	iz·vee·nee·te
Sorry	Žao mi je/Жао ми је	zha·o mi ye
Please	Molim/Молим	mo·lim
Thank you	Hvala/Хвала	hva·la
Yes	Da/Да	da
No	Ne/Не	ne

What's your name?

| Kako se zovete/ zoveš? (pol/inf) Како се зовете/ зовеш? | ka·ko se zo·ve·te/ zo·vesh |

My name is ...

| Zovem se ... Зовем се ... | zo·vem se ... |

Do you speak English?

| Govorite/Govoriš li engleski? (pol/inf) | go·vo·ri·te/go·vo·rish li en·gle·ski |

NUMBERS – SERBIA

1	jedan/један	ye·dan
2	dva/два	dva
3	tri/три	tri
4	četiri/четири	che·ti·ri
5	pet/пет	pet
6	šest/шест	shest
7	sedam/седам	se·dam
8	osam/осам	o·sam
9	devet/девет	de·vet
10	deset/десет	de·set

Говорите/Говориш ли енглески?

I don't understand.

| Ja ne razumem. Ја не разумем. | ya ne ra·zu·mem |

Eating & Drinking

What would you recommend?

| Šta biste preporučili? | shta bi·ste pre·po·ru·chi·li |

Шта бисте препоручили?

Do you have vegetarian food?

| Da li imate vegetarijanski obrok? | da li i·ma·te ve·ge·ta·ri·yan·ski o·brok |

Да ли имате вегетаријански оброк?

I'd like the bill/menu, please.

| Mogu li dobiti račun/ jelovnik, molim? | mo·gu li do·bi·ti ra·chun/ ye·lov·nik mo·lim |

Могу ли добити рачун/ јеловник, молим?

| **I'll have ...** | Želim .../Желим ... | zhe·lim ... |
| **Cheers!** | Živeli!/Живели! | zhi·ve·li |

Emergencies

| **Help!** | Upomoć!/Упомоћ! | u·po·moch |
| **Go away!** | Idite!/Идите! | i·di·te |

Call the ...!	Zovite ...!/Зовите ... !	zo·vi·te ...
doctor	lekara/лекара	le·ka·ra
police	policiju/полицију	po·li·tsi·yu

I'm lost.

| Izgubljen/Izgubljena sam. (m/f) | iz·gub·lyen/iz·gub·lyena sam |

Изгубљен/ Изгубљена сам. (m/f)

I'm ill.
Ja sam bolestan/ ya sam *bo·le·stan/*
bolesna. (m/f) *bo·le·sna*

Ja сам болестан/
болесна.

Shopping & Services

I'm looking for ...
Tražim ... *tra·zhim*
Тражим...

How much is it?
Koliko košta ...? *ko·li·ko kosh·ta*
Колико кошта ...?

That's too expensive.
To je preskupo. to ye *pre·sku·po*
То је прескупо.

SLOVENIA

Note that uh is pronounced as the 'a' in 'ago', oh as the 'o' in 'note', ow as in 'how', zh as the 's' in 'pleasure', r is rolled, and the apostrophe (') indicates a slight y sound.

Basics

Hello	Zdravo	zdra·vo
Goodbye	Na svidenje	na svee·den·ye
Excuse me	Dovolite	do·vo·lee·te
Sorry	Oprostite	op·ros·tee·te
Please	Prosim	pro·seem
Thank you	Hvala	hva·la
Yes	Da	da
No	Ne	ne

What's your name?
Kako vam/ti ka·ko vam/tee
je ime? (pol/inf) ye ee·me

My name is ...
Ime mi je ... ee·me mee ye ...

Do you speak English?
Ali govorite a·lee go·vo·ree·te
angleško? ang·lesh·ko

I don't understand.
Ne razumem. ne ra·zoo·mem

Eating & Drinking

What would you recommend?
Kaj priporočate? kai pree·po·ro·cha·te

NUMBERS – SLOVENIA

1	en	en
2	dva	dva
3	trije	tree·ye
4	štirje	shtee·rye
5	pet	pet
6	šest	shest
7	sedem	se·dem
8	osem	o·sem
9	devet	de·vet
10	deset	de·set

Do you have vegetarian food?
Ali imate a·lee ee·ma·te
vegetarijansko hrano? ve·ge·ta·ree·yan·sko hra·no

I'll have ... *Jaz bom ...* yaz bom ...
Cheers! *Na zdravje!* na zdrav·ye

I'd like the ..., *Želim ...,* zhe·leem ...
please. *prosim.* pro·seem
   bill *račun* ra·choon
   menu *jedilni list* ye·deel·nee leest

Emergencies

Help! *Na pomoč!* na po·moch
Go away! *Pojdite stran!* poy·dee·te stran

Call the doctor/police!
Pokličite zdravnika/ pok·lee·chee·te zdrav·nee·ka
policijo! po·lee·tsee·yo

I'm lost.
Izgubil/ eez·goo·beew/
Izgubila sem se. (m/f) eez·goo·bee·la sem se

I'm ill.
Bolan/Bolna sem. (m/f) bo·lan/boh·na sem

Shopping & Services

I'm looking for ...
Iščem ... eesh·chem ...

How much is this?
Koliko stane? ko·lee·ko sta·ne

That's too expensive.
To je predrago. to ye pre·dra·go

Behind the Scenes

SEND US YOUR FEEDBACK

We love to hear from travellers – your comments keep us on our toes and help make our books better. Our well-travelled team reads every word on what you loved or loathed about this book. Although we cannot reply individually to your submissions, we always guarantee that your feedback goes straight to the appropriate authors, in time for the next edition. Each person who sends us information is thanked in the next edition – the most useful submissions are rewarded with a selection of digital PDF chapters.

Visit **lonelyplanet.com/contact** to submit your updates and suggestions or to ask for help. Our award-winning website also features inspirational travel stories, news and discussions.

Note: We may edit, reproduce and incorporate your comments in Lonely Planet products such as guidebooks, websites and digital products, so let us know if you don't want your comments reproduced or your name acknowledged. For a copy of our privacy policy visit **lonelyplanet. com/legal.**

OUR READERS

Many thanks to the travellers who used the last edition and wrote to us with helpful hints, useful advice and interesting anecdotes: Alma Arifhodzic, Ann Kennard, Brian Hortle, Christopher Feierabend, David Kolecki, David Wood, Frank Nowicki, Greg Mason, Ivan Serdarusic, Luca Lietti, Maria Tganoplai, Mark Hebden, Melitta Jalkanen, Mònica Plana Culubret, Moritz Hofmann, Wolfgang Crasemann

WRITER THANKS

Peter Dragicevich

First and foremost, I'd like to say a huge *hvala* to Vojko, Marija, Ivan, Mario and Ivana Dragičević in Split, for the kindness and patience you've shown your distant cousin over the years. Thanks also to Hayley Wright, Slavenko Sucur, and Emma and Ben Hayward for the tips and chats. Special thanks to my destination editors, Anna Tyler and Brana Vladisavljevic, and all of the writers, editors and Lonely Planet staff who contributed to this book.

Mark Baker

Thanks first to folks on the ground in Slovenia, including Najda Đorđević, Yuri Barron, John Bills, Jana Kuhar, Domen Kalajzic and family, Aleksandra Jezeršek Matjašič and Ana Vugrin. My Slovenian friends in Prague: Tjaša Čebulj, Zeljka Sok and Anjuša Belehar for their helpful suggestions. Finally, fellow writers Anthony Ham and Jess Lee, and my destination editor in London, Anna Tyler.

Stuart Butler

The first people I must thank are my wife, Heather, and children, Jake and Grace, for their unending patience while I worked on this project and for being the best travel companions a person could want in Albania. In Kosovo huge thanks to Nol and Virtyt for their help and hiking knowledge. In Albania huge thanks to Amar in Tirana and Altin in Ksamil. Back in Lonely Planet's London office thanks to Brana for all her tips, suggestions and endless Balkan knowledge.

Vesna Maric

I would like to thank Maja Trajkovska, Metodi Chilimanov, Magdalena Lazarevska and Slobodan Đudurović for making my time in Macedonia more special than I could imagine. Big thank yous go to Brana Vladisavljevic for commissioning me and always being such a great and kind editor. Thanks also to Tom Masters for his help.

Brana Vladisavljevic

Hvala puno to James Smart and Jennifer Carey for the support, Kate Morgan for her guidebook authoring advice, co-writer Kevin Raub for excellent work on Belgrade, Novi Sad and Niš updates, Dragiša Mijačić for all his tips on Stara Planina and Kragujevac, and my sister Sandra for keeping me company on the road for a few days.

Anthony Ham

In Croatia, thanks to to Luca, Miriam, Lidija, Marija and all the staff at tourist offices across the country.

BEHIND THE SCENES

In Slovenia, many thanks to Romana Nared, Ana Petrič and Franc Mlakar in the Lož Valley, and to Saša and Jure in Idrija, as well as to all the staff at the tourist offices. At Lonely Planet, I am grateful to my editor Anna Tyler for sending me to such wonderful places, and to my fellow writers Peter, Mark and Jess for their wisdom. To my family – Marina, Jan, Carlota and Valentina: *con todo mi amor.*

Jessica Lee

Big thanks to staff at the tourist information centres for tips, advice and local knowledge across Croatia and Slovenia respectively. In particular the chirpy, friendly folk who went out of their way to help with answering my endless questions at the Slovenian offices (in Celje, Dolenjske Toplice, Murska Sobata and Ptuj). Thank you to the enthusiastic staff at the offices in Croatia (Varaždin, Osijek and Zagreb County) for being founts of knowledge and helpful information. A big thank you to Skanka and Igor, Petra, Daniel and Lea in Slovenia. And in

Croatia, to Anton, Irena, Mila, Tea, Tom and Zvonimir for tips and chats.

Kevin Raub

Thanks to Brana Vladisavljevic and all my fellow partners in crime at Lonely Planet. On the road, Jelena Stanković, Maja Živković, Suna Kažić, Marija Mitrović, Dejan Majić, Tijana Vujasinović, Goran Magdić, Djole Jovanović, Filip Mićić, Luka Pejović and Mihailo Subotić.

ACKNOWLEDGEMENTS

Climate map data adapted from Peel MC, Finlayson BL & McMahon TA (2007) 'Updated World Map of the Köppen-Geiger Climate Classification', *Hydrology and Earth System Sciences*, 11, 1633–44.

Cover photograph: Sveti Naum Monastery (p300), Lake Ohrid, North Macedonia, Lucie Debelkova/4Corners ©

THIS BOOK

This 3rd edition of Lonely Planet's *Western Balkans* guidebook was researched and written by Peter Dragicevich, Mark Baker, Stuart Butler, Vesna Maric, Brana Vladisavljevic, Anthony Ham, Jessica Lee and Kevin Raub. The previous edition was written by Marika McAdam, Jayne D'Arcy, Chris Deliso, Peter Dragicevich, Mark Elliott, Vesna Maric and Anja Mutić.

This guidebook was produced by the following:

Destination Editors Brana Vladisavljevic, Anna Tyler

Senior Product Editor Elizabeth Jones

Product Editor Rachel Rawling

Regional Senior Cartographers Valentina Kremenchutskaya, Anthony Phelan

Book Designer Jessica Rose

Assisting Editors Sarah Bailey, Imogen Bannister, Jacqueline Danam, Samantha Forge, Gabrielle Innes, Alison Morris, Anne Mulvaney, Rosie Nicholson, Kristin Odijk, Charlotte Orr, Monique Perrin, Tamara Sheward, Sarah Stewart, Maja Vatrić

Cover Researcher Brendan Dempsey-Spencer

Thanks to Hannah Cartmel, Vesna Čelebić, Grace Dobell, Shona Gray, Mark Griffiths, Kate Kiely, Kathryn Rowan, Wibowo Rusli

Index

Map Legend

Sights

- Beach
- Bird Sanctuary
- Buddhist
- Castle/Palace
- Christian
- Confucian
- Hindu
- Islamic
- Jain
- Jewish
- Monument
- Museum/Gallery/Historic Building
- Ruin
- Shinto
- Sikh
- Taoist
- Winery/Vineyard
- Zoo/Wildlife Sanctuary
- Other Sight

Activities, Courses & Tours

- Bodysurfing
- Diving
- Canoeing/Kayaking
- Course/Tour
- Sento Hot Baths/Onsen
- Skiing
- Snorkelling
- Surfing
- Swimming/Pool
- Walking
- Windsurfing
- Other Activity

Sleeping

- Sleeping
- Camping
- Hut/Shelter

Eating

- Eating

Drinking & Nightlife

- Drinking & Nightlife
- Cafe

Entertainment

- Entertainment

Shopping

- Shopping

Information

- Bank
- Embassy/Consulate
- Hospital/Medical
- Internet
- Police
- Post Office
- Telephone
- Toilet
- Tourist Information
- Other Information

Geographic

- Beach
- Gate
- Hut/Shelter
- Lighthouse
- Lookout
- Mountain/Volcano
- Oasis
- Park
- Pass
- Picnic Area
- Waterfall

Population

- Capital (National)
- Capital (State/Province)
- City/Large Town
- Town/Village

Transport

- Airport
- Border crossing
- Bus
- Cable car/Funicular
- Cycling
- Ferry
- Metro station
- Monorail
- Parking
- Petrol station
- S-Bahn/Subway station
- Taxi
- T-bane/Tunnelbana station
- Train station/Railway
- Tram
- U-Bahn/Underground station
- Other Transport

Routes

- Tollway
- Freeway
- Primary
- Secondary
- Tertiary
- Lane
- Unsealed road
- Road under construction
- Plaza/Mall
- Steps
- Tunnel
- Pedestrian overpass
- Walking Tour
- Walking Tour detour
- Path/Walking Trail

Boundaries

- International
- State/Province
- Disputed
- Regional/Suburb
- Marine Park
- Cliff
- Wall

Hydrography

- River, Creek
- Intermittent River
- Canal
- Water
- Dry/Salt/Intermittent Lake
- Reef

Areas

- Airport/Runway
- Beach/Desert
- Cemetery (Christian)
- Cemetery (Other)
- Glacier
- Mudflat
- Park/Forest
- Sight (Building)
- Sportsground
- Swamp/Mangrove

Note: Not all symbols displayed above appear on the maps in this book

Brana Vladisavljevic

Serbia Brana grew up in the former Yugoslavia and studied foreign languages and literature in Belgrade. She joined Lonely Planet's Melbourne office in 2004 and has lost count of the phrasebook and guidebook titles she edited over the years. From 2014 to 2019, she was based in the London office as the Destination Editor for Eastern and Southeastern Europe. Brana looked after destinations stretching from the Russian Far East to the Greek islands but has a soft spot for her native Western Balkans region.

Anthony Ham

Croatia, Slovenia Anthony is a freelance writer and photographer who specialises in Spain, East and Southern Africa, the Arctic and the Middle East. When he's not writing for Lonely Planet, Anthony writes about and photographs Spain, Africa and the Middle East for newspapers and magazines in Australia, the UK and the US.

Jessica Lee

Croatia, Slovenia In 2011 Jessica swapped a career as an adventure-tour leader for travel writing and since then her travels for Lonely Planet have taken her across Africa, the Middle East and Asia. She has lived in the Middle East since 2007 and tweets @jessofarabia. Jess has contributed to Lonely Planet's *Egypt, Turkey, Cyprus, Morocco, Marrakesh, Middle East, Europe, Africa, Cambodia* and *Vietnam* guidebooks and her travel writing has appeared in *Wanderlust* magazine, *Daily Telegraph,* the *Independent,* BBC Travel and lonelyplanet.com.

Kevin Raub

Serbia Atlanta native Kevin started his career as a music journalist in New York, working for *Men's Journal* and *Rolling Stone* magazines. He ditched the rock 'n' roll lifestyle for travel writing and has written more than 70 Lonely Planet guides, focused mainly on Brazil, Chile, Colombia, USA, India, the Caribbean and Portugal. Raub also contributes to a variety of travel magazines in both the US and UK. Along the way, the self-confessed hophead is in constant search of wildly high IBUs in local beers. Follow Kevin on Twitter and Instagram (@RaubOnTheRoad).

OUR STORY

A beat-up old car, a few dollars in the pocket and a sense of adventure. In 1972 that's all Tony and Maureen Wheeler needed for the trip of a lifetime – across Europe and Asia overland to Australia. It took several months, and at the end – broke but inspired – they sat at their kitchen table writing and stapling together their first travel guide, *Across Asia on the Cheap*. Within a week they'd sold 1500 copies. Lonely Planet was born.

Today, Lonely Planet has offices in the US, Ireland and China, with a network of over 2000 contributors in every corner of the globe. We share Tony's belief that 'a great guidebook should do three things: inform, educate and amuse'.

OUR WRITERS

Peter Dragicevich

Bosnia & Hercegovina, Croatia, Montenegro After a successful career in niche newspaper and magazine publishing, both in his native New Zealand and in Australia, Peter finally gave in to Kiwi wanderlust, giving up staff jobs to chase his diverse roots around much of Europe. Over the last decade he's written literally dozens of guidebooks for Lonely Planet on an oddly disparate collection of countries, all of which he's come to love. He once again calls Auckland, New Zealand, his home – although his current nomadic existence means he's often elsewhere. Peter also curated the Plan, Understand and Survival Guide sections.

Mark Baker

Slovenia Mark is a freelance travel writer with a penchant for offbeat stories and forgotten places. He's originally from the US, but now makes his home in the Czech capital, Prague. He writes mainly on Eastern and Central Europe for Lonely Planet as well as other leading travel publishers, but finds real satisfaction in digging up stories in places that are too remote or quirky for the guides. Prior to becoming an author, he worked as a journalist for the *Economist, Bloomberg News* and *Radio Free Europe*, among other organisations. Follow him on Instagram and Twitter (@ markbakerprague), and read his blog: www.markbakerprague.com.

Stuart Butler

Albania, Kosovo Stuart has been writing for Lonely Planet for more than a decade and during this time he's come eye to eye with gorillas in the Congolese jungles, met a man with horns on his head who could lie in fire, huffed and puffed over snowbound Himalayan mountain passes, interviewed a king who could turn into a tree, and had his fortune told by a parrot. Oh, and he's met more than his fair share of self-proclaimed gods. When not on the road for Lonely Planet he lives on the beautiful beaches of Southwest France with his wife and two young children. He also works as a photographer and was a finalist in both the 2015 and 2016 Travel Photographer of the Year Awards. In 2015 he walked for six weeks with a Maasai friend across part of Kenya's Maasai lands in order to gather material for a book he is writing (see www.walkingwiththemaasai.com). His website is www.stuartbutlerjournalist.com.

Vesna Maric

North Macedonia Vesna has been a Lonely Planet author for nearly two decades, covering places as far and wide as Bolivia, Algeria, Sicily, Cyprus, Barcelona, London and Croatia, among others. Her latest work has been updating Florida, Greece and North Macedonia.

OVER PAGE MORE WRITERS

Published by Lonely Planet Global Limited
CRN 554153
3rd edition – Oct 2019
ISBN 978 1 78868 277 0
© Lonely Planet 2019   Photographs © as indicated 2019
10 9 8 7 6 5 4
Printed in Singapore